The New Strategic Brand Management

'After reading Kapferer's book, you'll never again think of a brand as just a name. Several exciting new ideas and perspectives on brand building are offered that have been absent from our literature.' **Philip Kotler, Northwestern University**

'A real thought provoker for marketing and business people. *Strategic Brand Management* is an essential tool to develop strong marketing strategy.'
P Desaulles, Vice President, Du Pont de Nemours Europe

'A solid contribution written with depth and insight. I recommend it to all those who desire a further understanding of the various dimensions of brand management.'
David A Aaker, University of California at Berkeley, and author of *Managing Brand Equity*

'The best book on brands yet. It is an invaluable reference for designers, marketing and brand managers.' ***Design Magazine***

'One of the best books on brand management. Kapferer is thought provoking and always able to create new insights on various brand related topics.' **Rik Riezebos, CEO Brand Capital and director of EURIB/European Institute for Brand Management**

'One of the definitive resources on branding for marketing professionals worldwide.'
***The Economic Times*, India**

'Jean Noël Kapferer's hierarchy of brands with six levels of brands is an extraordinary insight.' **Sam Hill and Chris Lederer, authors of *The Infinite Asset*, Harvard Business School Press**

'A fresh perspective on branding that is easy to understand and inspirational.
I believe it to be the finest book on the subject in the marketplace today.'
Marsha Lindsay, President and CEO, Lindsay, Stone and Briggs

'The treatment of brand-product strategies, brand extensions and financial evaluations are also strengths of the book.' ***Journal of Marketing***

'A "think book". It deals with the very essence and culture of branding.'
International Journal of Research in Marketing

'An authoritative analysis about establishing an identity and exploiting it.'
Daily Telegraph

'A full and highly informative text... well written and brought to life through numerous appropriate examples.' ***Journal of the Market Research Society***

FIFTH EDITION

The New Strategic Brand Management
Advanced insights and strategic thinking

Jean-Noël Kapferer

LONDON PHILADELPHIA NEW DELHI

First published in France in hardback in 1992 and in paperback in 1995 by Les Editions d'Organization
Second edition published in Great Britain in 1997 by Kogan Page Limited
Third edition 2004
Reprinted 2005, 2007
Fourth edition 2008
Fifth edition 2012

120 Pentonville Road
London N1 9JN
United Kingdom
www.kogan-page.co.uk

1518 Walnut Street, Suite 1100
Philadelphia PA 19102
USA

4737/23 Ansari Road
Daryaganj
New Delhi 110002
India

ISBN 978 0 7494 6515 5

British Library Cataloguing-in-Publication Data

A CIP record for this book is available from the British Library.

Library of Congress Cataloging-in-Publication Data

Kapferer, Jean-Noël.
The new strategic brand management : advanced insights and strategic thinking / Jean-Noël Kapferer. – 5th ed.
p. cm.
Summary: "Adopted internationally by business schools, MBA programmes and marketing practitioners alike, The New Strategic Brand Management is simply the reference source for senior strategists, positioning professionals and postgraduate students. Over the years it has not only established a reputation as one of the leading works on brand strategy but also has become synonymous with the topic itself. The new edition builds on this impressive reputation and keeps the book at the forefront of strategic brand thinking. Revealing and explaining the latest techniques used by companies worldwide, author Jean-Noël Kapferer covers all the leading issues faced by the brand strategist today, supported by an array of international case studies. With both gravitas and intelligent insight, the book reveals new thinking on topics such as putting culture and content into brands, the impact of private labels, the new dynamics of targeting and the comeback of local brands" – Provided by publisher.
Includes bibliographical references and index.
ISBN 978-0-7494-6515-5 (pbk.)
1. Brand name products–Management. I. Title.
HD69.B7K37 2012
658.8'343–dc23 2011032358

Typeset by Graphicraft Ltd, Hong Kong
Print production managed by Jellyfish
Printed and bound by CPI Group (UK) Ltd, Croydon, CR0 4YY

CONTENTS

LIST OF FIGURES

LIST OF TABLES

PREFACE TO THE FIFTH EDITION

Integrating brand and business

This is a book on strategic brand management. It capitalizes on the success of the former four editions. As far as we understand from our readers worldwide (marketers, advertisers, lawyers, MBA students and so on), this success was based on seven attributes which we have of course maintained:

- **Originality.** *The New Strategic Brand Management* is very different from all the other books on brand management. This is due to its business orientation and its unique balance between advanced theory and cases. It also promotes strong and unique working models and concepts.
- **Relevance.** The cases and illustrations are new, unusual, and not over-exposed. They represent business situations readers will relate to and understand readily. They come from the whole world.
- **Breadth of scope.** We have tried to address most of the key decisions faced by brands.
- **Depth of treatment.** Each facet of brand management receives a deep analysis, hence the size of this edition. This is a book to consult for advice, benchmarks and methodology.
- **Cutting edge,** integrating the latest relevant implications from research such as neurosciences, or culture analysis.
- **Diversity.** Our examples cover the fast-moving consumer goods sector (FMCG) as well as commodities, business-to-business brands, pharmaceutical brands, luxury brands, service brands, e-brands, and distributors' brands.
- **International scope,** with examples from the Americas, Europe and Asia.

This fifth edition is much more than a revision of the previous one. It is a whole new book for understanding today's brands and managing them efficiently in today's markets. Twenty years after the first edition, so much change has happened in the world of brands! This is why this new edition has been thoroughly updated, transformed and enriched. Of course, our proprietary original models and methodologies have not changed in essence, but they have been adapted to reflect current competition and issues.

This edition concentrates on low-cost competition, the main challenge facing brands all over the world.

There are many other significant new features in this edition, which reflect the new competitive environment:

- Because distributors' brands (often described as private labels) are everywhere and often hold a dominant market share, they need their own chapter.
- Significantly, this edition develops its new section on innovation. Curiously, the topic of brands and innovation is almost totally absent from most books on branding. This seems at odds with the fact that innovation and branding has become the number one topic for companies. In fact, as we shall demonstrate, brands grow out of innovation, and innovation is the lifeblood of the brand.
- This new edition is also sensitive to the fact that many modern markets are saturated. How can brands grow in such competitive environments? A full chapter on growth is included, starting with growth from the brand's existing customers.
- The issue of corporate brands and their increasing importance is also tackled, especially in a B2B context.
- We also stress much more than previously the implementation side: how to build interesting brand platforms that are able to stimulate powerful creative advertising that both sells and builds a salient brand; how to activate the brand; how to energize it at

contact points; and how to create more bonding.

- We integrate social medias.

This book also reflects the evolution of the author's thought. Our perspective on brands has changed. We feel that the whole domain of branding is becoming a separate area, perhaps with a risk of being self-centered and narcissistic. A brand is a tool for growing the business profitably. It has been created for that purpose, but business cannot be reduced to brands. The interrelationship between the business strategy and the brand strategy needs to be highlighted, because this is the way companies operate. As a consequence, we move away from the classic partitioning of brand equity into two separate approaches. One of these is customer-based, the other cashflow-based. It is crucial to remember that a brand that produces no additional cashflow is of little value, whatever its image and the public awareness of it. In fact, it is time to think of the brand as a 'great shared idea supported by a viable business model'. In this fifth edition, we try regularly to relate brand decisions to the economic equation of the business.

Today, every organization, country or town wants to have its own brand. We hope this book will help readers significantly, whether they are working in multinationals or in a small dynamic organization, developing a global brand or a local one.

Introduction: Building the brand when the clients are empowered

There are very few strategic assets available to a company that can provide a long-lasting competitive advantage, and even then the time span of the advantage is getting shorter. Brands are one of them, along with R&D, a real consumer orientation, an efficiency culture (cost cutting), employee involvement, and the capacity to change and react rapidly. This is the mantra of Wal-Mart, Starbucks, Apple and Zara.

Managers know that the best kind of loyalty is brand loyalty, not price loyalty or bargain loyalty, even though as a first step it is useful to create behavioural barriers to exit. Finally, A Ehrenberg (1972) has shown through 40 years of panel data analysis that product penetration is correlated with purchase frequency. In other words, big brands have both a high penetration rate and a high purchase frequency per buyer. Growth will necessarily take these two routes, and not only be triggered by customer loyalty.

Beyond brand relevance: more meaningful brands

In our materialistic societies, people want to give meaning to their consumption. Only brands that add value to the product and tell a story about its buyers, or situate their consumption on a ladder of intangible values, can provide this meaning. Hence the cult of luxury brands, or other cultural champions such as Nike or Apple. We stress the need for brands to have brand content, revealing their culture. To resonate with present and future consumers, brands must realize that, apart from market share competition, there is also a values competition.

Extension of the brand concept

Today, every organization wants to have a brand. Beyond the natural brand world of producers and distributors of fast-moving consumer goods, whose brands are competing head to head, branding has become a strategic issue in all sectors: high tech, low tech, commodities, utilities, components, services, business-to-business (B2B), pharmaceutical laboratories, non-governmental organizations (NGOs) and non-profit organizations all see a use for branding.

Amazingly, all types of organizations or even persons now want to be managed like brands: David Beckham, the English soccer star, is an example. Los Angeles Galaxy paid US$250 million to acquire this soccer hero. It expects to recoup this sum through the profits from licensed products using the name, face or signature of David Beckham, which are sold throughout the world. Everything David Beckham does is aimed at reinforcing his image and identity, and thus making sales and profits for the 'Beckham brand'.

Recently, the mayor of Paris decided to define the city as a destination brand and to manage this brand for profit. Many other towns had already done this. Countries also think of themselves in brand terms (Kotler *et al*, 2002). They are right to do so. Whether they want it or not, they act de facto as a brand, a summary of unique values and benefits. Countries, cities, universities and so on compete in a number of markets, just as a conventional brand competes for profitable clients: in the private economic and financial investments market, various raw materials and agricultural markets, the tourism market, the immigration market and so on.

It takes more than branding to build a brand

Although communication is necessary to create a brand, it is far from being sufficient. Certainly a brand encapsulates in its name and its visual symbol all the goodwill created by the positive experiences of clients or prospects with the organization, its products, its channels, its stores, its communication and its people. However, this means that it is necessary to manage these points of contact (from product or service to channel management, to advertising, to Internet site, to word of mouth, the organization's ethics, and so on) in an integrated and focused way. This is the core skill needed. This is why, in this fifth edition of *The New Strategic Brand Management*, while we look in depth at branding decisions as such, we also insist on the 'non-branding' facets of creating a brand. *Paradoxically, it takes more than branding to build a brand.*

Empowered clients

Today, with Web 2.0 and social medias, clients are empowered as never before. They have access to a world of prescription, free advice and secret information on the web. They talk to other clients. It is the end for average brands. Only those that maximize delight will survive, whether they offer extremely low prices or a rewarding experience, service or performance. It is the end of hollow brands, without identity. Retailers are also more powerful than many of the brands they distribute: all brands that do not master their channel are now in a B to B to C situation, and must never forget it.

Building both business and brand

Throughout this fifth edition of *The New Strategic Brand Management*, we relate the brand to the business model, for both are intimately intertwined. We regularly demonstrate how branding decisions are determined by the business model and cannot be understood without this perspective. In fact in a growing number of advanced companies, top managers' salaries are based on three critical criteria: sales, profitability and brand equity. They are determined in part by how fast these managers are building the strategic competitive asset called a brand. The goal of strategy is to build a sustainable advantage over competition, and brands are one of the very few ways of achieving this. The business model is another. This is why tracking brands, product or corporate, is so important.

Looking at brands as strategic assets

For decades the value of a company was measured in terms of its buildings and land, and then its tangible assets (plant and equipment). It is only recently that we have realized that its real value lies outside, in the minds of potential customers. In July 1990, the man who bought the Adidas company summarized his reasons in one sentence: after Coca-Cola and Marlboro, Adidas was the best-known brand in the world.

The truth contained in what many observers took simply to be a clever remark has become increasingly apparent since 1985. In a wave of mergers and acquisitions, market transactions pushed prices way above what could have been expected. For example, Nestlé bought Rowntree for almost three times its stock market value and 26 times its earnings. The Buitoni group was sold for 35 times its earnings. Until then, prices had been on a scale of 8 to 10 times the earnings of the bought-out company.

Paradoxically, what justified these prices and these new standards was invisible, appearing nowhere in the companies' balance sheets. The only assets displayed on corporate balance sheets were fixed, tangible ones, such as machinery and inventory. There was no mention of the brands for which buyers offered sums much greater than the net value of the assets.

By paying very high prices for companies with brands, buyers are actually purchasing positions in the minds of potential consumers. Brand awareness, image, trust and reputation, all painstakingly built up over the years, are the best guarantee of future earnings, thus justifying the prices paid. The value of a brand lies in its capacity to generate such cashflows long term.

It is time to question many of the tools and concepts we have been using so far. The intense competition from international low-cost actors and from private labels requires a more demanding brand management. This is the new strategic brand management.

PART ONE
Why is branding so strategic?

01
Brand equity in question

Brands have become a major player in modern society. In fact they are everywhere. They penetrate all spheres of our life: economic, social, cultural, sporting, even religion. Because of this pervasiveness they have come under growing criticism (Klein, 1999). As a major symbol of our economies and postmodern societies, they can and should be analysed through a number of perspectives: macroeconomics, microeconomics, sociology, psychology, anthropology, history, semiotics, philosophy and so on. Even neurosciences tell us that we do not drive a car but a brand of car, not drink a cola but a Coke or Pepsi.

This book focuses on the managerial perspective: how best to manage brands for profit. Since brands are now recognized as part of a company's capital (hence the concept of brand equity), they should be exploited. Brands are intangible assets, assets that produce added benefits for the business. This is the domain of strategic brand management: how to create value with proper brand management. Before we proceed, we need to clarify the brand concept.

What is a brand?

Curiously, one of the hottest points of disagreement between experts is the definition of a brand. Each expert comes up with his or her own definition, or nuance to the definition. The problem gets more acute when it comes to measurement: how should one measure the strength of a brand? What limited numbers of indicators should one use to evaluate what is commonly called *brand equity*? In addition there is a major schism between two paradigms. One is customer-based and focuses exclusively on the relationship customers have with the brand (from total indifference to attachment, loyalty, and willingness to buy and rebuy based on beliefs of superiority and evoked emotions). The other aims at producing measures in dollars, euros or yen. Both approaches have their own champions. It is the goal of this fifth edition of *The New Strategic Brand Management* to unify these two approaches.

Customer-based definitions

The financial approach measures brand value by isolating the net additional cashflows created by the brand. These additional cashflows are the result of customers' willingness to buy one brand more than its competitors', even when another brand is cheaper. Why then do customers want to pay more? Because of the beliefs and bonds that are created over time in their minds through the marketing of the brand. In brief, customer equity is the preamble of financial equity. Brands have financial value *because* they have created assets in the minds and hearts of customers, distributors, prescribers, opinion leaders. These assets are brand awareness, beliefs of exclusivity and superiority of some valued benefit, and emotional bonding. This is what is expressed in the traditional definition of a brand: 'a brand is a set of mental associations, held by the consumer, which add to the perceived value of a product or service' (Keller, 1998). These associations should be unique (exclusivity), strong (saliency) and positive (desirable).

This definition has two problems. First it focuses on the gain in perceived value brought by the brand.

How do consumers' evaluations of a car change when they know it is a Volkswagen, a Peugeot or a Toyota? In this definition the product itself is left out of the scope of the brand: 'brand' is the set of added perceptions. As a result brand management is seen as mostly a communication task. This is incorrect. Brand management starts with the product and service as the prime vector of perceived value, while communication is there to structure, to orient tangible perceptions and to add intangible ones.

A second point to consider is that Keller's definition is focused on *cognitions*. This is not enough: strong brands have an intense emotional component. Neurosciences prove this.

Brands as conditional asset

Financiers and accountants have realized the value of brands (see Chapter 18). How does the financial perspective help us in defining brands and brand equity?

- First, brands are *intangible assets*, posted eventually in the balance sheet as one of several types of intangible asset (a category that also includes patents, databases and the like).
- Second, brands are *conditional assets*. This is a key point so far overlooked. An asset is an element that is able to produce benefits over a long period of time. Why are brands conditional assets? Because in order to deliver their benefits, their financial value, they need to work in conjunction with other material assets such as production facilities. There are no brands without products or services to carry them. In addition, brands need a profitable business model. For now, this reminds us that some humility is required. Although many people claim that brands are all and everything, brands cannot exist without a support (product or service). This product and service becomes effectively an embodiment of the brand, that by which the brand becomes real. As such it is a main source of brand evaluation. Does it produce high or low satisfaction? Brand management starts with creating products, services and/or places that embody the brand. Interestingly, the legal approach to trademarks and brands also insists on their conditional nature. To be valid, a registered trademark must be used in a real business within five years after its registration.

The legal perspective

An internationally agreed legal definition for brands does exist: 'a sign or set of signs certifying the origin of a product or service and differentiating it from the competition'. Historically, brands were created to defend producers from theft. A cattle brand, a sign burned into the animal's hide, identified the owner and made it apparent if the animal had been stolen. 'Brands' or trademarks also identified the source of the olive oil or wine contained in ancient Greek amphoras, and created value in the eyes of the buyers by building a reputation for the producer or distributor of the oil or wine.

A key point in this legal definition is that trademarks have a 'birthday' – their registration day. From that day they become a property, which needs to be defended against infringements and counterfeiting (see page 215 for defence strategies). Brand rights disappear when they are not well enough defended, or if registration is not renewed. One of the sources of loss of rights is degenerescence. This occurs when a company has let a distinctive brand name become a generic term.

Although the legal approach is most useful for defending the company against copies of its products, it should not become the basis of brand management. Contrary to what the legal definition asserts, a brand is not born but made. It takes time to create a brand, even though we talk about launching brands. In fact this means launching a product or service. Eventually it may become a brand, and it can also cease to be one. What makes a brand recognizable? When do we know if a name has reached the status of a brand? For us, in essence, *a brand is a name that influences buyers,* becoming the purchase criterion.

A brand is a name with the power to influence

This definition captures the essence of a brand. Of course, it is not a question of the choice of the name itself. Certainly a good name helps: that is, one that is easily pronounceable around the world and spontaneously evokes desirable associations. But what really makes a name become a brand is the fact that this name commands trust, respect, passion and even engagement. Today, if a brand cannot create a community, is it a real brand?

We live in an attention economy: there is so much choice and opacity that consumers cannot spend their time comparing before they make a choice. They have no time and even if they did, they cannot be certain of being able to determine the right product or service for them. Brands must convey certitude, trust and emotion. They are a risk reducer. In fact where there is no risk there is no brand. We made this point in an earlier book (Kapferer and Laurent, 1995). The perceived risk could be economic (linked to price), functional (linked to performance), experiential, psychological (linked to our self-concept), or social (linked to our social image). This is why it takes time to build brand saliency (brand awareness), trust (trusted beliefs about the brand's unique benefits) and emotional bonding.

Brand power to influence buyers relies on representations and relationships. A representation is a *system* of mental associations. We stress the word 'system', for these associations are interconnected. They are in a network, so that acting on one impacts some others. These associations (also called brand image) cover the following aspects:

- What is the brand territory (perceived competence, typical products or services, specific know-how)?
- What is its level of quality (low, middle, premium, luxury)?
- What are its qualities?
- What is its most discriminating quality or benefit (also called perceived positioning)?
- What typical buyer does the brand evoke? What is the brand personality and brand imagery?

Beyond mental associations, the pull power of a name is also due to the specific nature of the emotional relationships it develops. A brand, it could be said, is an attitude of non-indifference knitted into consumers' hearts. This attitude goes from emotional resonance to liking, belonging to the evoked set or consideration set, preference, attachment, advocacy, to fanaticism. Finally, designs, patents and rights are of course a key asset: they provide a competitive advantage over a period of time.

In short, *a brand exists when it has acquired power to influence the market.* This acquisition takes time. The time span tends to be short in the case of online brands, fashion brands and brands for teenagers, but longer for, for example, car brands and corporate brands. This power can be lost, if the brand has been mismanaged in comparison with the competition. Even though the brand will still have brand awareness, image and market shares, it might not influence the market any more. People and distributors may buy because of price only, not because they are conscious of any exclusive benefit from the brand.

What makes a name acquire the power of a brand is the product or service, together with the people at points of contact with the market, the price, the places, the communication – all the sources of cumulative brand experience. This is why one should speak of brands as *living systems made up of three poles*: products or services, name and concept. (See Figure 1.1.)

When talking of brands we are sometimes referring to a single aspect such as the name or logo, as do intellectual property lawyers. In brand management, however, we speak of the whole system, relating a concept with inherent value to products and services that are identified by a name and set of proprietary signs (that is, the logo and other symbols). This system reminds us of the conditional nature of the brand asset: it only exists if products and services also exist. Differentiation is summarized by the brand concept, a unique set of attributes (both tangible and intangible) that constitute the remarkable value proposition made by the brand.

To gain market share and leadership, the brand must be:

- able to conjure up a big idea, unique and attractive;
- experienced by people at contact points;
- activated by deeds and behaviours;
- communicated;
- distributed.

One of the best examples of a brand is MINI. This car, worth US$20,000 in functional value, is actually sold for US$30,000. It is one of the very few car brands that gives no rebates and discounts to prospective buyers, who queue to get 'their' MINI. MINI illustrates the role of both intangible and tangible qualities in the success of any brand. Since it is

FIGURE 1.1 The brand system

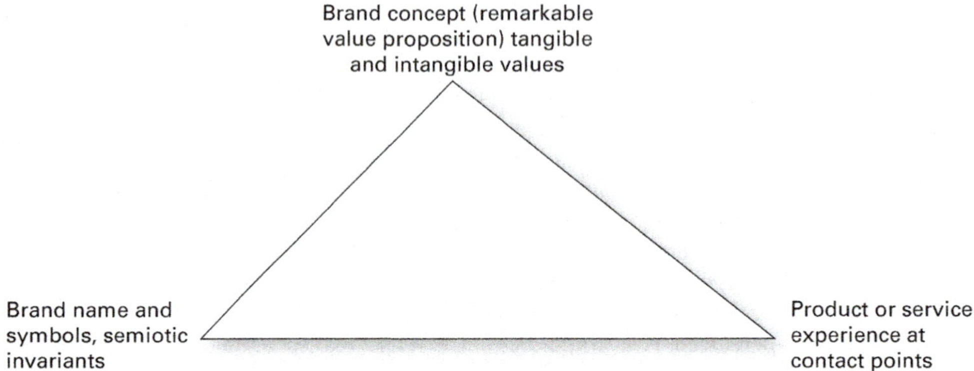

made by BMW, it promises reliability, power and road-holding performance. But the feelings of love towards this brand are created by the powerful memories the brand invokes in buyers of London in the 'Swinging Sixties'. The classic and iconic design is replicated in the new MINI – and each MINI feels like a personal accessory to its owner (each MINI is customized and different).

The brand triangle helps us to structure most of the issues of brand management:

- What concept should one choose, with what balance of tangible and intangible benefits? This is the issue of identity and positioning. Should the brand concept evolve through time? Or across borders (the issue of globalization)?
- How should the brand concept be embodied in its products and services, and its places? How should a product or service of the brand be different, look different? What products can this brand concept encompass? This is the issue of brand extension or brand stretch.
- How should the product and/or services be identified? And where? Should they be identified by the brand name, or by the logo only, as Nike does now? Should organizations create differentiated sets of logos and names as a means of indicating internal differences within their product or service lines? What semiotic invariants?
- What name or signs should one choose to convey the concept internationally?
- How often should the brand symbols be changed, updated or modernized?
- Should the brand name be changed (see Chapter 15)?
- Speaking of internationalization, should one globalize the name (that is, use the same name around the world), or the logo, or the product (a standardized versus customized product), or the concept (aiming at the same global positioning)? Or all three pillars of the brand system, or only two of them?

Since a brand is a name with the power to influence the market, its power increases as more people know it, are convinced by it, trust it and become advocates. Brand management is about gaining power, by making the brand more known, bought and engaging.

In summary, a brand is a shared desirable and exclusive idea embodied in products, services, places and/or experiences. The more this idea is shared by a larger number of people, the more power the brand has. It is because everyone knows 'BMW' and its idea – what it stands for – even those who will never buy a BMW car, that the brand BMW has a great deal of power.

The word 'idea' is important. Do we sell products and services, or values? Of course, the answer is values. For example, 'Volvo' is attached to an idea: cars with the highest possible safety levels. 'Absolut' conjures another idea: the creative vodka. Levi's used to be regarded as the rebel's jeans.

How brand definitions have changed through time

Definitions do change through time. Each definition reflects a vision at a certain moment.

It is interesting to analyse the evolution of the definitions of a brand. They are very indicative of the changing times and of the emergence of new competitors, commanding new managerial thinking.

The early definitions were influenced by the only discipline talking about brands: the law. Brands originated as marks on cattle in the Wild West of the United States to ensure cows were not stolen. Brands guaranteed their origin and differentiated cattle of one ranch from that of another ranch. Then a segmentation of quality appeared to differentiate supply: the brand was not only a proof of origin but a mark to signal the upper quality. Traditional definitions of a brand are a reflection of this origin. For Aaker (1991) 'A brand is a distinguishing name and or/symbol intended to identify the goods or services of one seller from those of competitors' (page 110).

Later on, cognitive psychology became the dominant theory in marketing. Branding was associated with holding a 'share of the mind' (Trout and Ries, 1981). Brand building meant linking a name to a single consumer benefit and mere repetition advertising. Brand theorizing was very much influenced by television commercials. They lasted 30 seconds, and hence one could promote just one single idea: the famous unique selling proposition (USP). P&G at that time was the epitome of branding. Each of its many brands (Tide, Dash, Pampers and so on) was summarized by one single benefit. This is why brand extension created so much surprise and excitement and stimulated so much research among US academics. However, this was largely the result of local ethnocentrism: everywhere else in the world, in Europe and in Asia, brands were covering a vast array of product categories (with Nestlé, the world number 1 food company and brand, as the model, or Samsung, Toshiba, Toyota or even GE). Today Apple ranges from computers to iTunes music services.

Brand theory was then influenced by laundry detergent competition. At that time, one brand meant one product only. Mars was a chocolate bar. That was all. It was hard to disentangle the brand and the product. Traditional definitions of a brand still reflect this implicit vision. Thus for Keller (1998: 4) 'a brand is a product that adds other dimensions to differentiate it in some way from other products designed to satisfy the same need'. This very traditional vision does not disentangle the product and the brand.

Later, brands were conceptualized as a set of mental associations that added to the value of the product itself. Everyone knows that in blind tests Pepsi is preferred to Coke, but that in real life, as soon as people can read the brand, they say they prefer Coke. If brands are not in the product, then they must be in people's minds. Hence there is another classic definition of a brand as a set of mental associations that add value to those already created by the product itself. Although this makes some progress, it has the limitations of the traditional approach promoted by Keller (1998). First, it is too communication driven and tends to put the product out of the scope of the brand. Instead the first thing a brand does is to instil its values into the product. A Toyota car must itself express the brand values, even in blind tests. The first target of this brand is the Toyota engineers. Second, it is purely cognitive. Unlike a network of cognitions, brands are emotional bonds. If they do not drive emotions, they are just the name of a product and not a brand as shown by neurosciences.

In advanced societies, the proliferation of brands within the same category and the rise of trade brands have deeply shaken marketing circles. Even at P&G people are now very defensive. As a result, brand definitions as well as brand equity measures introduced an emphasis on consumer loyalty and repeat purchase. A brand commanding no loyalty is not a strong brand, but there can be forced loyalties, or loyalty through inertia. What brands later wanted was an engaged loyalty, based on emotional ties and consumer commitment. Finally, the latest definitions of a brand underline the role of communities. Web 2.0 obliges. A brand cannot be reduced to a benefit; it has to create a community. No fans, no brand! Today's dominant role of social media is visible here. To exist on the net, a brand must have friends, followers, adepts and proselytes.

It is paradoxical that the more brands are endangered and losing their market share to store brands and private labels (which applies mostly to FMCG brands) the more books are being published emphasizing affect, love, passion and emotions as the central construct of brands ('Love brands', 'emotional branding', 'passion brands', etc). Some authors even urge brands to become 'legendary brands', or 'iconic brands', if they want to survive. It is as if we wished to prevent an unfortunate destiny for many brands in commoditized markets by raising the bar always higher, or by appealing to magic for ultimate help.

But why should all brands survive? Aren't some new ones more fitted to the present competitive environment? Trade brands also are brands (see Chapter 5). They may be more fitted to meet the aspirations of post-modern consumers than our traditional brands. New generations also need new brands. The notion of generation is a new one in history: young people used to be represented as future adults; the son would imitate the father, and the daughter her mother. Generation is a post-war phenomenon and concept, whereby an age group wants to be distinguished by its culture, language and tastes. The younger generation wants to be clearly differentiated from the adults, and so must have its own brands.

The use of such extreme terms as 'passion', 'legend' and 'icon' is a confession that traditional conceptualizations of what a brand is do not work any more. They may have been useful earlier, when competition was different and not as fierce. However, they have not prevented the success of today's non-brands (Uniqlo), trade brands and hard discount products (Aldi, Lidl, etc). The title of former Coca-Cola Chief Marketing Officer Sergio Zyman's book is revealing: *The End of Marketing as We Know It* (1999).

New times call for a new strategic brand management. This is why all organizations should understand the brand as a *name that symbolizes a long-term engagement, crusade or commitment to a unique set of values, embedded into products, services and behaviours, which make the organization, person or product stand apart or stand out.*

The goal of the new strategic brand management is to make this name become the reference (landmark) of the category it competes in.

A brand is strong when it is seen as the champion of values (ie it has authority rather than mere power).

TABLE 1.1 Historical evolution of 'what is a brand?'

- a name and/or sign that guarantees a product's origin and authenticity;
- the name of a different and superior product;
- an identity endowed on a product to make it unique and superior;
- a position strongly held in the consumer's mind;
- a name that means a trusted promise;
- a name that denotes a benefit or a set of values in people's minds;
- a name that adds value beyond the utility of the product it signifies;
- a name with the power to influence markets;
- a name that creates desire and loyalty;
- a name that makes people forget the price;
- the name of a remarkable value proposition;
- a name commanding respect, admiration, love and passion;
- a name that is able to create a community around its values.

Broadening the concept of brand

Another flaw in traditional conceptualizations was that the brand was always perceived as a product. Academic thinking and research remain too focused on FMCG products. Why buy Surf instead of Ariel, Dove instead of Lux? Branding recommendations entailed creating single associations to the product category. Years ago the concept of brand would certainly have evoked an FMCG product such as Tide, Pampers or Gillette, but not any more. Not only do umbrella brands (selling in multiple categories) thrive today in the West and still more in Asia, but it seems that anything can be a brand. Football clubs are brands; David Beckham is a brand worth half a billion euros; museums are no longer places but brands; people talk about towns as brands (Dinnie, 2011) and even of nation brands; London appointed a brand director.

Such change is normal. We live in a global world where most of the things we know are known not through direct experience but through hearsay, images, the internet and so on. They become major emotional symbols, and promote values that create followers or fans.

In addition, after the collapse of communism it was said that politics was dead. It was the 'end of History' (Fukuyama, 2006). But mere consumption is not satisfying enough: it must have meaningfulness. Consumers are looking for it. That is why brands have become cultural champions, and we expect them to add value to our lives.

A final factor has accelerated the trend that everything can be a brand: the growing anthropomorphism of brand theorizing. Brands are said to have a personality (Azoulay and Kapferer, 2003), and are portrayed through celebrities to accentuate this perception. Conversely, if brands are persons, persons may be held as brands, ie a consistent proposition of value, likely to become a business, because it creates desire among a group of people.

When a product or a person is much more than a product or a person it becomes a brand. David Beckham is much more than an excellent soccer player. For world youth he represents a model of new manhood, successful, with virile/feminine ambiguity as a distinctive feature. As a result, people want to possess a representation of their icon, hoping that by magic they too will be blessed, and be endowed with his charisma. David Beckham manages himself as a brand: being a brand means knowing when to say no.

David Beckham chooses the brands he will work with through celebrity endorsement and sponsorship. Instead of accepting all offers and maximizing his gains, he thinks long term and behaves consistently, guided by the values for which he wants to be a symbol. These are the key aspects of brand management: defining one's values; accepting no compromise over these values; thinking long term rather than pursuing short-term profits; and consistency.

Do not call everything a brand

While the brand concept is proving its relevance far beyond FMCG products, its use should be restricted within marketing circles and companies.

Today, there is a dramatic inflation in the usage of the word 'brand'. Some authors cascade the word 'brand' through all levels of the company. They talk of 'corporate brand', 'branch brand', 'division brand', 'subsidiary brand', etc. This is a mistake: there is only one brand; everything else is organization. Another tendency is to cascade the word all through the product line. Here again one should be careful to distinguish the brand from the product. It is not because a product has a name that this name is meant to be a brand. Think of all the names of furniture in an Ikea catalogue: they are not brands. The fewer brands a company carries, the more they have a chance to be powerful and hence justify the definition of 'brand' (a name with the power to influence). After the brand come the range, the product variants, the lines, etc. They will be designated in some way, but a designator is not a brand. Finally, sub-brands should be an exception. A sub-brand is a product that tells a different story from the parent brand. It has a life of its own, eg Ford Mustang or Chevrolet Corvette. There is nothing wrong with being a variant of the parent brand that is targeted to a specific usage and population.

Figure 1.2 illustrates the vocabulary.

Differentiating between brand assets, strength and value

It is time to structure and organize the many terms related to brands and their strength, and to the measurement of brand equity. The official Marketing Science definition of brand equity is 'the set of associations and behavior on the part of a brand's customers, channel members and parent corporation that permits the brand to earn greater volume or greater margins than it could without the brand name' (Leuthesser, 1988).

This definition is very interesting and has been forgotten all too quickly. It is all-encompassing, reminding us that channel members are very important in brand equity. It also specifically ties margins to brand associations and customers' behaviour. Does it mean that unless there is a higher volume or a higher margin as a result of the creation of a brand, there is no brand value? This is not clear, for the word 'margin' seems to refer to gross margin only, whereas brand financial value is measured at the level of earnings before interest and tax (EBIT).

To dispel the existing confusion around the phrase brand equity, created by the abundance of

FIGURE 1.2 Brand vocabulary

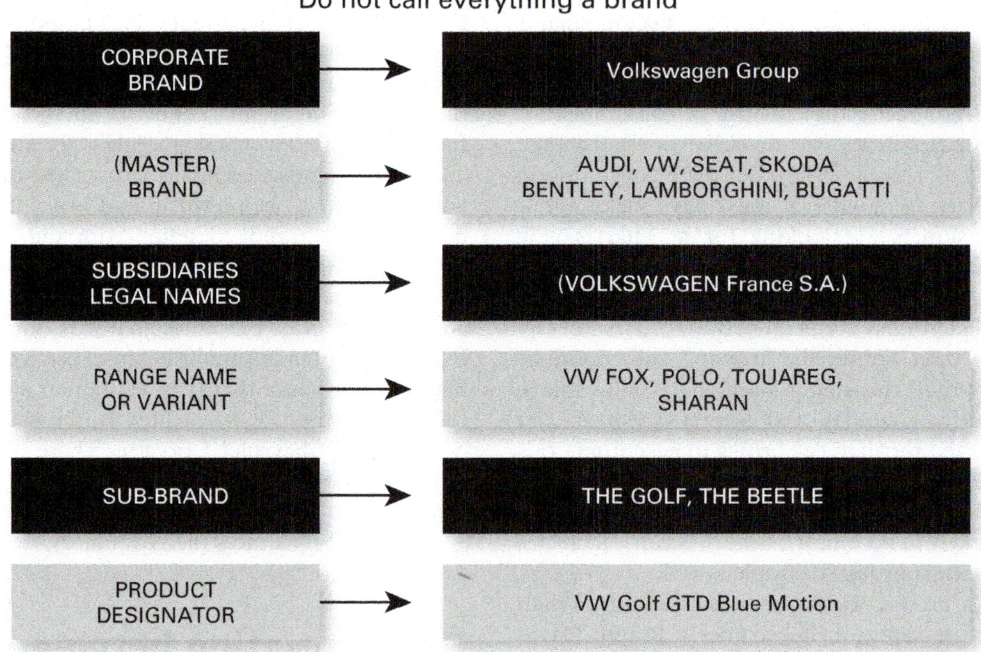

TABLE 1.2 From awareness to financial value

Brand assets →	Brand strength →	Brand value (financial equity)
Brand awareness Brand reputation (attributes, benefits, competence, know-how, etc). Emotion Perceived brand personality Perceived brand values Reflected customer imagery Brand preference or attachment Patents and rights	Market share Market leadership Market penetration Share of requirements Growth rate Loyalty rate Price premium Percentage of products the trade cannot delist	Net discounted cashflow attributable to the brand after paying the cost of capital invested to produce and run the business and the cost of marketing

definitions, concepts, measurement tools and comments by experts, it is important to show how the consumer and financial approaches are connected, and to use clear terms with limited boundaries (see Table 1.2):

- *Brand assets.* These are the sources of influence of the brand (awareness/saliency, emotion, image, strength of relationship with consumers), and patents.
- *Brand strength* at a specific point in time as a result of these assets within a specific market, competitive environment and business model. Brand strength is captured by behavioural competitive indicators: market share, market leadership, loyalty

rates and price premium (if one follows a price premium strategy).

- *Brand value* is the ability of brands to deliver profits. A brand has no financial value unless it can deliver profits. To say that lack of profit is not a brand problem but a business problem is to separate the brand from the business, an intellectual temptation. Certainly brands can be analysed from the standpoint of sociology, psychology, semiotics, anthropology, philosophy and neuroscience, but historically they were created for business purposes and are managed with a view to producing profit.

Only by separating brand assets, strength and value will one end the confusion of the brand equity domain (Feldwick, 1996 takes a similar position). Brand value is the profit potential of the brand assets, mediated by brand market strength.

In Table 1.2, the arrows indicate not a direct but a conditional consequence. The same brand assets may produce different brand strength over time: this is a result of the amount of competitive or distributive pressure. The same assets can also have no value at all by this definition, if no business will ever succeed in making them deliver profits, through establishing a sufficient market share and price premium. For instance if the cost of marketing to sustain this market share and price premium is too high and leaves no residual profit, the brand has no value. Thus the Virgin name proved of little value in the cola business: despite the assets of this brand, the Virgin organization did not succeed in establishing a durable and profitable business through selling Virgin Cola in the many countries where this was tried. The Mini was never profitable until the brand was bought and manufactured by BMW, then relaunched as Mini.

Table 1.2 also shows an underlying time dimension behind these three concepts of assets, strength and value. Brand assets are learnt mental associations and affects. They are acquired through time, from direct or vicarious, material or symbolic interactions with the brand. Brand strength is a measure of the present status of the brand: it is mostly behavioural (market share, leadership, loyalty, price premium). Not all of this brand stature is due to the brand assets. Some brands establish a leading market share without any noticeable brand awareness: their price is the primary driver of preference. There are also brands whose assets are superior to their market strength: that is, they have an image that is far stronger than their position in the market (this is the case with Michelin, for example). The obverse can also be true, for example of many retailer own brands, which are 'push' brands.

Brand value is a projection into the future. Brand financial valuation aims to measure the brand's worth, that is to say, the profits it will create in the future. To have value, brands must produce economic value added (EVA), and part of this EVA must be attributable to the brand itself, and not to other intangibles (such as patents, know-how or databases). This will depend very much on the ability of the business model to face the future. For instance, Nokia lost ground on the Stock Exchange in 2010. The market had judged that the future of the world's number one mobile phone brand was dim. Everywhere in the developed countries, consumers are buying smartphones, but Nokia is lagging. Nokia's present brand stature might be high, but what about its value?

It is time now to move to the topic of tracking brand equity for management purposes. What should managers regularly measure?

Tracking brand equity

What is a brand? A name that influences buyers. What is the source of its influence? A set of mental associations and emotional relationships built up over time among customers or distributors. Brand tracking should aim at measuring these sources of brand power. The role of managers is to build the brand and also the business. This is true of brand managers, but also of local or regional managers. This is why companies now link the level of variable salary not only to increments in sales and profits but also to brand equity. However, such a system presupposes that there is a tracking system for brand equity, so that year after year its progress can be assessed. This system must be valid, reliable, and not too complicated or too costly. What should one measure as a minimum to evaluate brand equity?

An interesting survey carried out by the agency DDB asked marketing directors what they considered to be the characteristics of a strong brand, a significant company asset. The following were the answers in order of importance:

- brand awareness (65 per cent);
- the strength of brand positioning, concept, personality, a precise and distinct image (39 per cent);
- the strength of signs of recognition by the consumer (logo, codes, packaging) (36 per cent);
- brand authority with consumers, brand esteem, perceived status of the brand and consumer loyalty (24 per cent).

Numerous types of survey exist on the measurement of brand value (brand equity). They usually provide a national or international hit parade based just on one component of brand equity: brand awareness (the method may be the first brand brought to mind, aided or unaided depending on the research institute), brand preference, quality image, prestige, first and second buying preferences when the favoured brand is not available, or liking. Certain institutions may combine two of the components: for example, Landor published an indicator of the 'power of the brand' which combined brand-aided awareness and esteem. The advertising agency Young & Rubicam carried out a study called 'Brand Asset Monitor' which positions the brand on two axes: the cognitive axis is a combination of salience and of the degree of perceived difference of the brand among consumers; the emotional axis is the combination of the measures of familiarity and esteem. TNS, in its study Megabrand System, uses five parameters to compare brands: brand awareness, purchase intention, perceived quality, trial, and an item measuring the strength of the brand's imagery.

There is little more consensus among academic researchers. Sattler (1994) analysed 49 American and European studies on brand equity and listed no fewer than 26 different ways of measuring it. These methods vary according to several dimensions:

- Is the measure monetary or not? A large proportion of measures are classified in non-monetary terms (brand awareness, attitude, preference, etc).
- Does the measurement include the time factor – that is, the future of the brand on the market?
- Does the brand measure take the competition into account – that is, the perceived value in relation to other products on the market? Most of them do not.
- Does the measurement include the brand's marketing mix? When you measure brand value, do you only include the value attached to the brand name? Most measures do not include the marketing mix (past advertising expenditure, level of distribution, and so on).
- When estimating brand value do you include the profits that a user or a buyer could obtain due to the synergies that may exist with its own existing brand portfolio (synergies of distribution, production, logistics, etc)? The majority of them do not include this, even though it is a key factor.
- Does the measurement of brand equity include the possibility of brand extensions outside the brand's original market? In general, no.
- Finally, does the measure of brand equity take into account the possibility of geographical extension or globalization? Again, most of the time the answer is no.

We recommend a minimum of four indicators of brand assets (equity):

- *Aided brand awareness.* This measures whether the brand has a minimal resonance.
- *Spontaneous brand awareness.* This is a measure of saliency, of share of mind when cued by the product.
- *Evoked set*, also called *consideration set*. Does the brand belong to the shortlist of two or three brands one would surely consider buying?
- Has the brand been *already consumed* or not?

Some companies add other items like most preferred brand. Empirical research has shown that this item is very much correlated to spontaneous brand awareness, the latter being much more than a mere cognitive measure, but it also captures proximity to the person. Other companies add the item consumed most often. Of course this is typical of fast moving consumer goods; the item is irrelevant for durables. In addition, in empirical research the item is also correlated to evoked set. One should never forget that tracking studies dwell on the customer's memory. This memory is itself very much inferential.

TABLE 1.3
Result of a brand tracking study

	Brand X	
	Japan	Mexico
Aided awareness	99%	97%
Unaided awareness	48%	85%
Evoked set	24%	74%
Consumed	5%	40%

Do people really know what brand they bought last? They infer from their preferences, that logically it should have been brand X or Y.

Table 1.3 gives a typical result of a tracking study for a brand in two different countries.

There are two ways of looking at the brand equity figures in the table. One can compare the countries by line: although it has similar aided awareness levels, this brand has very different status in the two countries. The second mode is vertical, and focuses on the 'transformation ratios'. It is noticeable that in Japan, the evoked set is 50 per cent of unaided brand awareness, whereas it is 87 per cent in Mexico.

Although there is a regular pattern of decreasing figures, from the top line to the bottom line, this is not always the case. For instance in Europe, Pepsi-Cola is not a strong brand: its market share is gained through push marketing and trade offers. As a result, Pepsi-Cola certainly grows its business but not its intrinsic desirability. In tracking studies Pepsi-Cola has a trial rate far higher than the brand's preference rate (evoked set). At the opposite end of the spectrum there are brands that have an equity far superior to their consumption rate. In Europe, Michelin has a clear edge over rival tyre brands as far as image is concerned. However, image does not transform itself into market share if people like the Michelin brand but deem that the use they make of their cars does not justify buying tyres of such a quality and at such a price.

Tracking studies are not simply tools for control. They are tools for diagnosis and action. Transformation ratios tell us where to act.

Comparing brand equity profiles

It is interesting to compare the pull power of different brands across categories. Table 1.4 presents the typical profile of well-known brands (all with assisted brand awareness above 90 per cent). They are ranked by decreasing rate of penetration (percentage trial). The brands are compared on two pillars of their brand equity: awareness and perceived high quality. One expects leading global brands to deliver not only quality, but superior quality. The last two questions are behavioural: the first one measures the past (whether the interviewee has already tried the brand); the second one depicts the future of the brand (whether the consumer intends to buy it in the future). The data, based on a large-scale national sample, have been changed for confidentiality reasons. However, they allow significant comparisons between different types of brands.

The first three brands compete as generalists in the world hi-tech appliance market. Interestingly, in Europe Samsung has become the leading brand in market share in most of its segments (mobile phones, TVs, home equipment, etc). This can be seen in the 'Trial' column: although much more recent than Sony in Europe, Samsung has reached the same level of awareness and trial or purchase. This is the result of systematic innovations in the mobile smartphone business, 3D TVs, high marketing investment, excellent products sold at competitive prices, and excellent trade relationships in the mass market channels. This result in such a short time is remarkable. However, the power of a strong brand is still visible in the case of Sony. All the experts agree that Sony today is not like the Sony of yesterday. The company was at the forefront of innovation in the 1980s. It attracted the cultural elite and creative professions who act as opinion leaders, and its price induced a perception of higher quality. This was a premium brand for excellence, loved for its incredible personal innovations such as the Walkman, the video camera, the Sony PSP, etc. Today the innovations seem to come from other brands – Apple, Samsung, Nintendo, etc – and Sony seems to be absent from the internet revolution.

All this is true, yet the brand has kept an incredible brand capital. The perceived quality of Samsung

TABLE 1.4 Brand capital: how different types of brands bring added value

	Brand awareness	Perceived high quality	Trial	Consider in the future
Samsung	99	75	42	28
Sony	99	86	42	33
LG	93	60	22	16
Nespresso	99	66	18	18
Dior	98	77	14	16
Apple	98	65	12	15
BMW	99	77	5	14

SOURCE Adapted from TNS, France, 2010

products is high, yet still lower than the perceived quality of Sony. Samsung and Sony are equals in terms of former purchases, although this measure favours older brands, longer established in the market. However, Sony still leads in its ability to retain clients and be aspirational for future purchases (33/42 versus 28/42). This demonstrates the value of investing in a brand: although the brand is actually less innovative than it used to be, it retains an inherent desirability. Sony benefits also from its intangible kernel values: the brand is associated with the production of art (via Sony Music, and Sony cameras for cinema). In comparison, Samsung does not carry such aspirational values. This is the result of a communication policy that is exclusively focused on the latest innovations, but this does not create an imprint in the mind: each innovation is pushed out by a newer one. Further, in its advertising no one knows what Samsung really thinks. No vision is presented. It is significant that the product name or sub-brand (like Galaxy) is written in bigger characters than the Samsung brand name itself.

The profile of Nespresso is that of a niche brand. It is well known, but has been tried by only a minority (18 per cent), with the percentage considering trying it in the future not any larger (18 per cent). Its growth will be through selling still more expensive capsules and services to its existing base of clients. Apple has almost the same profile, but its score for future purchases is slightly higher than the penetration rate: this promises growth by acquisition of new clients through brand extensions out of its original core (personal computers) to music, iPads, iPhones, etc, despite the very high price.

The same holds true for Dior, whose revitalization is under way: the future is brighter than the present. Finally, BMW concerns only a minority of people: the happy few who are able or want to pay for its highly priced cars. But notice how the luxury dream is working: three times more people want to buy one in the future!

Goodwill: the convergence of finance and marketing

The corporate vision has changed from one where only tangible assets had value to one where companies now believe that their most important asset is their intangibles, among which brands and patents

TABLE 1.5 Brand financial valuation, 2011

Rank	Brand	Value (US$ billion)
1	Apple	153,285
2	Google	111,498
3	IBM	100,849
4	McDonald's	81,016
5	Microsoft	78,243
6	Coca-Cola	73,752
7	AT&T	69,916
8	Marlboro	67,522
9	China Mobile	57,326
10	GE	50,318
11	ICBC	44,440
12	Vodafone	43,647
13	Verizon	42,828
14	Amazon	37,628
15	Wal-Mart	37,277
16	Wells Fargo	36,876
17	UPS	35,737

SOURCES Brand Z, Millward Brown

come first. This is the equation of success equals a brand backed by innovations, which are intangible (see Tables 1.5 and 18.2). These intangible assets account for 61 per cent of the value of Kellogg's, 57 per cent of Sara Lee and 52 per cent of General Mills. This explains the paradox that even though a company is making a loss it is bought for a very high price because of its well-known brands.

It is important to realize that in accounting and finance, goodwill is in fact the difference between the price paid and the book value of the company. This difference is brought about by the psychological goodwill of consumers, distributors and all the actors in the channels: that is to say, favourable attitudes and predisposition. Thus, a close relationship exists between financial and marketing analyses of brands. Accounting goodwill is the monetary value of the psychological goodwill that the brand has created over time through communication investment and consistent focus on product satisfaction, both of which help build the reputation of the name.

What exactly are the effects of this customer and distributor goodwill?:

- The favourable attitude of distributors that list some products of the brand because of their rotation system. In fact a retailer may lose customers if it does not stock products of a well-known brand that by definition is present everywhere. That is to say, certain customers will go elsewhere to look for the brand. This goodwill ensures the presence of the brand at the point of sale.
- The support of wholesalers and resellers in the market for slow-moving or industrial goods. This is especially true when they are seen as being an exclusive brand with which they are able to associate themselves in the eyes of their customers.
- The desire of consumers or end-users to buy the product. It is their favourable attitude and in certain cases the attachment or even loyalty to the brand that is the key to future sales. Brand loyalty may be reduced to a minimum as the price difference between the brand and its competitors increases but attachment to the brand does not vanish so fast; it resists time.

The brand is a focal point for all the positive and negative impressions created by the buyer over time as he or she comes into contact with the brand's products, distribution channel, personnel and communication. On top of this, by concentrating all its marketing effort on a single name, the latter acquires an aura of exclusivity. The brand continues to be, at least in the short term, a byword for quality even after the patent has expired. The life of the patent is extended thanks to the brand.

Brands are stored in clients' memories, so they exert a lasting influence. Because of this, they are seen as an asset from an accounting point of view: their economic effects extend far beyond the mere consumption of the product. In addition, this asset is not amortized.

In order to understand in what way a strong brand (having acquired distribution, awareness and image) is a generator of growth and profitability it is first necessary to understand the functions that it performs with the consumers themselves, and which are the source of their valuable goodwill.

How brands create value for the customer

Although this book deals primarily with brands and their optimization, it is important to clarify that brands do not necessarily exist in all markets. Even if brands exist in the legal sense they do not always play a role in the buying decision process of consumers. Other factors may be more important. For example, research on 'brand sensitivity' (Kapferer and Laurent, 1988) shows that in several product categories, buyers do not look at the brand when they are making their choice. Who is concerned about the brand when they are buying a writing pad, a rubber, felt-tip pens, markers or photocopy paper? Neither private individuals nor companies. There are no strong brands in such markets as sugar and men's socks. In Germany there is no national brand of flour. Even the beer brands are mostly regional. Location is key with the choice of a bank.

Brand trust

Brands reduce perceived risk, and exist as soon as there is perceived risk. They bring trust. Once the risk perceived by the buyer disappears, the brand no longer has any benefit. It is only a name on a product, and it ceases to be a choice cue, a guide or a source of added value. The perceived risk is greater if the unit price is higher or the repercussions of a bad choice are more severe. Thus the purchase of durable goods is a long-term commitment. On top of this, because humans are social animals, we judge ourselves on certain choices that we make and this explains why a large part of our social identity is built around the logos and the brands that we wear. As far as food is concerned, there is a certain amount of intrinsic risk involved whenever we ingest something and allow it to enter our bodies. The brand's function is to overcome this anxiety, which explains, for example, the importance of brands in the market for spirits such as vodka and gin.

The importance of perceived risk as a generator of the legitimacy of a brand is highlighted by the categories within which distributors' own-brands (and perhaps tomorrow's discount products) dominate: canned vegetables, milk, orange juice, frozen pizzas, bottled water, kitchen roll, toilet paper and petrol. At the same time producers' brands still have a dominant position in the following categories: coffee, tea, cereals, toothpaste, deodorant, cold sauces, fresh pasta, baby food, beauty products, washing powder, etc. For these products the consumer has high involvement and does not want to take any risks, be they physical or psychological.

Nothing is ever acquired permanently, and the degree of perceived risk evolves over time. In certain sectors, as the technology becomes commonplace, all the products comply with standards of quality. Therefore we are moving from a situation where some products 'failed' whereas others 'passed', towards one where all competitors are excellent, but some are 'more excellent' than others. The degree of perceived risk will change depending on the situation. For example, there is less risk involved in buying rum or vodka for a cocktail than for a rum or vodka on the rocks. Lastly, all consumers do not have the same level of involvement. Those who have high involvement are those that worry about small differences between products or who wish to optimize their choice: they will talk for hours about the merits of such and such a computer or of a certain brand of coffee. Those who are less involved are satisfied with a basic product which isn't too expensive, such as a gin or a whisky which may be unknown but seems to be good value for money and is sold in their local shop. The problem for most buyers who feel a certain risk and fear making a mistake is that many products are opaque: we can only discover their inner qualities once we buy the products and consume them. However, many consumers are reluctant to take this step. Therefore it is imperative that the external signs highlight the internal qualities of these opaque products. A reputable brand is the most efficient of these external signals. Examples of other such external indicators are: price, quality marks, the retail outlet where the product is sold and which guarantees it, the style and design of the packaging.

From trust to stimulation

Beyond trust, brands can also bring excitement, joy, empathy and stimulation. This is their second function: they animate the category. They stimulate. Thus they become exciting and unsubstitutable. Soft drinks are a low-involvement, low-risk category, but Coke and Fanta are strong brands, because they went from a no-risk function to a stimulation function. Enjoy!

How brand awareness creates value: the halo effect

Recent marketing research shows that brand awareness is not a mere cognitive measure. It is in fact correlated with many valuable image dimensions. Awareness carries a reassuring message: although it is measured at the individual level, brand awareness is in fact a collective phenomenon. When a brand is known, each individual knows it is known. This leads to spontaneous inferences. As is shown in Table 1.6, awareness is mostly correlated with aspects such as high quality, trust, reliability, closeness to people, a good quality/price ratio, accessibility and traditional styling. However it has a zero correlation with innovativeness, superior class, style, seduction: if aspects such as these are key differentiation facets of the brand, they must be earned on their own merit.

TABLE 1.6 How brand awareness creates value through the halo effect (correlations between awareness and image)

Good quality/price ratio	0.52
Trust	0.46
Reliable	0.44
Quality	0.43
Traditional	0.43
Best	0.40
Down to earth	0.37
Client oriented	0.37
Friendly	0.35
Accessible	0.32
Distinct	0.31
A leader	0.29
Popular	0.29
Fun	0.29
Original	0.27
Energetic	0.25
Friendly	0.25
Performing	0.22
Seductive	0.08
Innovative	0.02

(Base: 9,739 persons, 507 brands)
SOURCE Schuiling and Kapferer, 2004

Transparent and opaque products

At this stage it is interesting to remind ourselves of the classifications drawn up by Nelson (1970) and by Darby and Kami (1973). These authors make the distinction between three types of product characteristics:

- the qualities which are noticed by contact, before buying;
- the qualities which are noticed uniquely by experience, thus after buying;
- credence qualities which cannot be verified even after consumption and which you have to take on trust.

The first type of quality can be seen in the decision to buy a pair of men's socks. The choice is made according to the visible characteristics: the pattern, the style, the material, the feel, the elasticity and the price. There is hardly a need for brands in this market. In fact those that do exist only have a very small market share and target those people who are looking for proof of durability (difficult to tell before buying) or those who wish to be fashionable. This is how Burlington socks work as a hallmark of chic style. Producers' brands do exist but their differential advantage compared to distributors' brands (Marks & Spencer or C&A) is weak, especially if the latter have a good style department and offer a wide variety at a competitive price.

A good example of the second type of quality is the automobile market. Of course, performance, consumption and style can all be assessed before buying, as can the availability of options and the interior space. However, road-holding, the pleasure of driving, reliability and quality cannot be entirely appreciated during a test drive. The response comes from brand image; that is, the collective representation which is shaped over time by the accumulated experiences of oneself, of close relations, by word of mouth and advertising.

Finally, in the market for upmarket cars, the feeling that you have made it, that feeling of fulfilment and personal success through owning a BMW is typically the result of pure faith. It cannot be substantiated by any of the post-purchase driving experiences: it is a collective belief, which is more or less shared by the buyers and the non-buyers. The same logic applies to the feeling of authenticity and inner masculinity which is supposed to result from smoking Marlboro cigarettes.

The role of brands is made clearer by this classification of sought-after qualities. The brand is a sign (therefore external) whose function is to disclose the hidden qualities of the product which are inaccessible to contact (sight, touch, hearing, smell) and possibly those which are accessible through experience but where the consumer does not want to take the risk of trying the product. Lastly, a brand, when it is well known, adds an aura of make-believe when it is consumed, for example the authentic America and rebellious youth of Levi's, the rugged masculinity of Marlboro, the English style of Dunhill, the Californian myth of Apple.

The informational role of the brand varies according to the product or service, the consumption situation and the individual. Thus, a brand is not always useful. On the other hand, a brand becomes necessary once the consumer loses his or her traditional reference points. This is why there is an increase in the demand for branded wine. Consumers were put off by too many small chateaux which were rarely the same and had limited production of varying quality and which sometimes sprung some unpleasant surprises. This paved the way for brands such as Jacob's Creek and Gallo.

A brand provides not only a source of information (thus revealing its values) but performs certain other functions which justify its attractiveness and its monetary return (higher price) when they are valued by buyers. What are these functions? How does a brand create value in the eyes of the consumer? The eight functions of a brand are presented in Table 1.7. The first two are mechanical and concern the essence of the brand; that is, to function as a recognized symbol in order to facilitate choice and to gain time. The following three functions reduce the perceived risk. The last three have a more pleasurable side to them. Ethics show that buyers are expecting, more and more, responsible behaviour from their brands. Many Swedish consumers still refuse Nestlé's products due to the issue of selling Nestlé's baby milk to poor mothers in Africa.

These functions are neither laws nor dues, nor are they automatic; they must be defended at all times. Only a few brands are successful in each market thanks to their supporting investments in quality, R&D, productivity, communication and research in order to better understand foreseeable changes in demand. A priori, nothing confines these functions to producers' brands. Moreover, several producers' brands do not perform these functions. In Great Britain, Marks & Spencer (St Michael) is seen as an important brand and performs these functions, as do Migros in Switzerland, Gap, Zara, Ikea and others.

The usefulness of these functions depends on the product category. There is less need for reference points or risk reducers when the product is transparent (ie its inner qualities are accessible through contact). The price premium is at its lowest and trial costs very little when there is low involvement and the purchase is seen as a chore, eg trying a new, cheaper roll of kitchen paper or aluminium foil. Certain kinds of shops aim primarily at fulfilling certain of these functions, for example hard discounters who have 650 lines with no brands, a product for every need, at the lowest prices and offering excellent quality for the price (thanks to the work on reducing all the costs which do not add value carried out in conjunction with suppliers). This formula offers another alternative to the first five functions: ease of identification on the shelf, practicality, guarantee, optimization at the chosen price level and characterization (refusal to be manipulated by marketing). The absence of other functions is compensated for by the very low price.

Functional analysis of brand role can facilitate the understanding of the rise of distributors' own brands. Whenever brands are just trademarks and operate merely as a recognition signal or as a mere guarantee of quality, distributors' brands can fulfil these functions as well and at a cheaper price.

TABLE 1.7 The functions of the brand for the consumer

Function	Consumer benefit
Identification	To be clearly seen, to quickly identify the sought-after products, to structure the shelf perception.
Practicality	To allow savings of time and energy through identical repurchasing and loyalty.
Guarantee	To be sure of finding the same quality no matter where or when you buy the product or service.
Optimization	To be sure of buying the best product in its category, the best performer for a particular purpose.
Badge	To have confirmation of your self-image or the social image that you present to others.
Continuity	Satisfaction created by a relationship of familiarity and intimacy with the brand that you have been consuming for years.
Hedonistic excitement	Enchantment linked to the attractiveness of the brand, to its logo, to its communication and its experiential rewards.
Ethical	Satisfaction linked to the responsible behaviour of the brand in its relationship with society (sustainable development, CSR, employment, citizenship, advertising which doesn't shock).

Table 1.8 summarizes the relationships between brand role and distributors' own-brands' market share.

How brands create value for the company

Why do financial analysts prefer companies with strong brands? Because they are less risky. Therefore, the brand works in the same way for the financial analyst as for the consumer: the brand removes the risk. The certainty, the guarantee and the removal of the risk are included in the price. By paying a high price for a company with brands the financial analyst is acquiring near certain future cashflows.

If the brand is strong it benefits from a high degree of loyalty and thus from stability of future sales. Ten per cent of the buyers of Volvic mineral water are regular and loyal and represent 50 per cent of the sales. The reputation of the brand is a source of demand and lasting attractiveness, the image of superior quality and added value justifies a premium price. A dominant brand is an entry barrier to competitors because it acts as a reference in its category. If it is prestigious or a trendsetter in terms of style it can generate substantial royalties by granting licences, for example, at its peak, Naf-Naf, a designer brand, earned over £6 million in net royalties. The brand can enter other markets when it is well known, is a symbol of quality and offers a certain promise which is valued by the market. The Palmolive brand name has become symbolic of mildness and has been extended to a number of markets besides that of soap, for example shampoo, shaving cream and washing-up liquid. This is known as brand extension (see Chapter 12) and saves on

TABLE 1.8 Brand functions and the distributor/manufacturer power equilibrium

Main function of brand	Typical product category of brand	Power of manufacturers' brand
Recognition signal	Milk, salt, flour	Very weak
Practicality of choice	Socks	Weak
Guarantee of quality	Food, staples	Weak
Optimization of choice, sign of high-quality performance	Cars, cosmetics, appliances, paint, services	Strong
Personalising one's choice	Perfumes, clothing	Strong
Permanence, bonding, familiarity relationship	Old brands	Strong but challenged
Pleasure and excitement	Polysensual brands, luxury brands	Strong
Ethics and social responsibility	Trust brands, corporate brands	Strong but challenged

the need to create awareness if you had to launch a new product on each of these markets.

In determining the financial value of the brand, the expert must take into account the sources of any additional revenues which are generated by the presence of a strong brand. Additional buyers may be attracted to a product which appears identical to another but which has a brand name with a strong reputation. If such is the company's strategy the brand may command a premium price in addition to providing an added margin due to economies of scale and market domination. Brand extensions into new markets can result in royalties and important leverage effects. To calculate this value, it is necessary to subtract the costs involved in brand management: the costs involved in quality control and in investing in R&D, the costs of a national, indeed international, sales force, advertising costs, the cost of a legal registration, the cost of capital invested, etc. The financial value of the brand is the difference between the extra revenue generated by the brand and the associated costs for the next few years, which are discounted back to today. The number of years is determined by the business plan of the valuer (the potential buyer, the auditors). The discount rate used to weigh these future cashflows is determined by the confidence or the lack of it that the investor has in his or her forecasts. However, a significant fact is that the stronger the brand, the smaller the risk. Thus, future net cashflows are considered more certain when brand strength is high.

Figure 1.3 shows the three generators of profit of the brand: the price premium, more attraction and loyalty, and higher margin. These effects work on the original market for the brand but they can be offered subsequently on other markets and in other product categories, either through direct brand extension (for example, Bic moved from ballpoint pens to lighters to disposable razors and recently to sailboards) or through licensing, from which the manufacturer benefits from royalties (for example all the luxury brands, and Caterpillar).

Once these levers are measured in euros or dollars or any other currency they may serve as a base for evaluating the marginal profit which is attributable to the brand. They only emerge when the company wishes to strategically differentiate its products. This wish can come about through three types of investment:

FIGURE 1.3 The levers of brand profitability

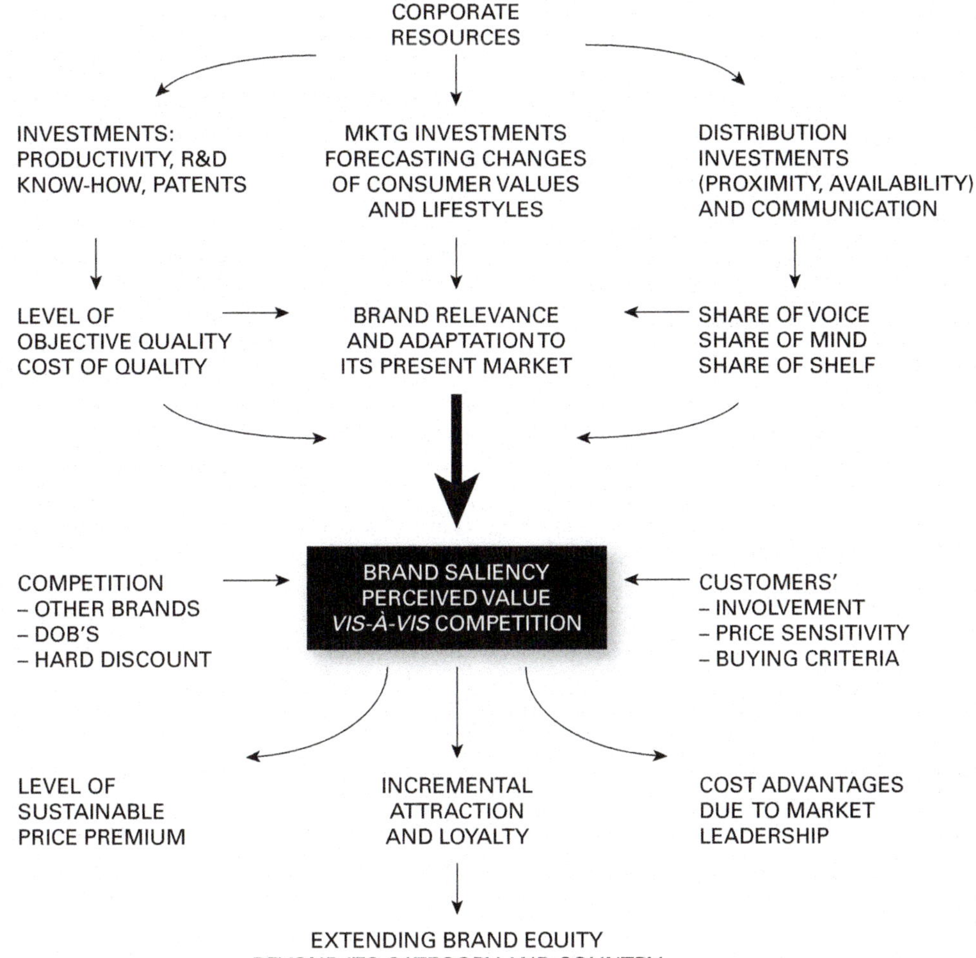

- Investment in production, productivity and R&D. Thanks to these, the company can acquire specific know-how, a knack which cannot be imitated and which in accounting terms is also an intangible asset. Sometimes the company temporarily blocks new entrants by registering a patent. This is the basis of marketing in the pharmaceutical industry (a patent and a brand) but also of companies like Ferrero, whose products are not easily imitated despite their success. Patents are on their own an intangible asset: the activity of the company benefits from them in a lasting manner.
- Investment in research and marketing studies in order to get new insights, to anticipate the changes of consumers' tastes and lifestyles in order to define any important innovations which will match these evolutions. Chrysler's Minivan is an example of a product created in anticipation of the demands of baby boomers with tall children. An understanding of the expectations of distributors is also needed, as they are an essential component of the physical proximity of brands. Nowadays a key element of brand success is understanding and adapting to the logic of distributors, and developing good relations with the channels (even though it is still

necessary when valuing a brand to make a distinction between what part of its sales is due to the power of the company and what part to the brand itself).

- Investment in listing allowances, in the sales force and merchandizing, in trade marketing and, naturally, in communicating to consumers to promote the uniqueness of the brand and to endow it with saliency (awareness), perceived difference and esteem. The hidden intrinsic qualities or intangible values which are associated with consumption would be unknown without brand advertising.

The value of the brand, and thus the legitimacy of implementing a brand policy, depends on the difference between the marginal revenues and the necessary marginal costs associated with brand management.

How brand reputation affects the impact of advertising

Brands are a form of capital that can slowly be built, while in the meantime one is growing business. Of course it is very possible to grow a business without creating such brand capital: a push strategy or a price strategy can deliver high sales and market share without building any brand equity. This is the case for many private labels or own-label brands, for instance. The volume leader in the market for Scotch whisky in France is not Johnnie Walker or Ballantines or Famous Grouse but William Peel, a local brand that aimed all its efforts at the trade (hypermarkets) and sells at a low price. It has almost no saliency (spontaneous brand awareness).

Now managers are being asked to build both business and brand value. Their salary is indexed on these two yardsticks: sales and reputation. One should not see them as separate, leading to a kind of schizophrenia. Chaudhuri's very relevant research (2002) reminds us that advertising and marketing are the key levers of sales. However, their effects on market share and the ability to charge a premium price (two indicators of brand strength) are not direct but are mediated by brand reputation (or esteem). In fact, as shown by the path coefficients of Figure 1.4, brand reputation is created by familiarity (I know it well, I use it a lot) and by brand perceived uniqueness (this brand is unique, is different, there is no substitute). Advertising does play a key role in building sales, but it has no direct impact on gaining both market share and premium price. This is most interesting: in brief, it is only by building a reputational capital that both a higher market share and price premium can be obtained.

Reputation also adds to the impact of advertising on sales. It is well known from evaluations of past campaigns that the more a brand is known, the more its advertisements are noticed and remembered. It is high time to stop treating brands and commerce as opposing forces.

FIGURE 1.4 Branding and sales

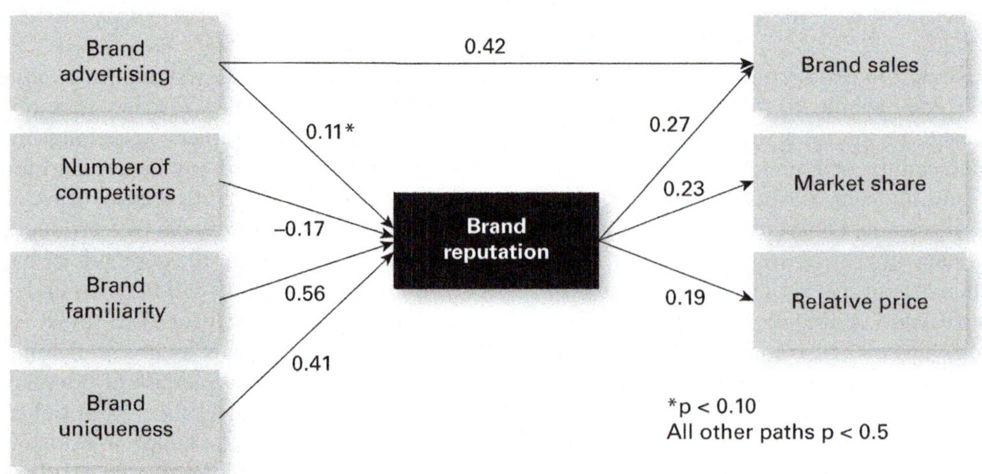

Corporate reputation and the brand

Sony is both a brand and a company. The same holds true for Coca-Cola or Volkswagen. The term 'corporate brand' designates the profile the company wants to promote among its different audiences. The corporation gives depth and humanity to the commercial brand. For new brands, their corporate style and culture are often their best ambassador.

In 2003 Velux, which had become known as the number one brand for roof windows in the world, realized it needed to create a corporate brand. It felt that merely to compete through its product brand was not enough to protect it against the growing number of me-toos all over the world. In addition, its brand equity was stagnating. When any brand reaches a level of 80 per cent of top-of-mind awareness in its category, part of its 'stagnation' is certainly due to a ceiling effect: there is not much room for improvement. However, the company felt that emotional bonding with its brand was not strong enough. Could the product brand alone improve the bond? The diagnosis was that it was high time to reveal 'the brand behind the brand' (Kapferer, 2000) and start building a corporate brand.

In fact many companies that based their success on product brands have now decided to create a corporate brand in order to make company actions, values and missions more salient and to diffuse specific added values. Unilever should soon develop some kind of corporate visibility, as Procter & Gamble does in Asia at this time and will probably do everywhere soon.

There is another reason that corporate brands are a new hot managerial topic: the defence of reputation. Companies have become very sensitive about their reputation. Formerly they used to be sensitive about their image. Why this change? Isn't image (perception) the basis on which global evaluations are formed (and thus reputation)? It is likely that the term 'image' has lost its glamour. It seems to have fallen into disrepute precisely because there was too much publicity about 'image makers', as if image was an artificial construction. Reputation has more depth, is more involving: it is a judgement from the market which needs to be preserved. In any case reputation has become a byword, as witnessed by the annual surveys on the most respected companies that are now made in almost all countries, modelled on Fortune's 'America's most admired companies'. Reputation signals that although the company has many different stakeholders, each one reacting to a specific facet of the company (as employee, as supplier, as financial investor, as client), in fact they are all sensitive to the global ability of the company to meet the expectations of all its stakeholders. Reputation takes the company as a whole. It reunifies all stakeholders and all functions of the corporation.

Because changes in reputation affect all stakeholders, companies monitor and manage their reputation closely. Fombrun has diagnosed that global reputation is based on six factors or 'pillars' (Fombrun, Gardberg and Sever, 2000):

- emotional appeal (trust, admiration and respect);
- products and services (quality, innovativeness, value for money and so on);
- vision and leadership;
- workplace quality (well-managed, appealing workplace; employee talent);
- financial performance;
- social responsibility.

Since companies cannot grow without advocates and the support of their many stakeholders, they need to build a reputational capital among all of them; plus a global reputation, because even specialized stakeholders wish the company to be responsive to all stakeholders. There is a link between reputation and share performance.

As a consequence of this growth of the reputational concept, companies have realized they cannot stay mute, invisible, opaque. They must manage their visibility and that of their actions in order to maximize their reputational capital – in fact their goodwill, to speak like financiers. The corporate brand will be more and more present and visible: through art sponsorship, foundations, charities, advertising. As such it addresses global targets. The corporate brand speaks on behalf of the company, signals the company's presence. Now companies are also developing specialized corporate brands such as 'You' (the recruiting brand of Unilever), or specialized campaigns (such as semi-annual financial roadshows).

Consumers do not see the headquarters or the factories any more. Often delocalized, corporations appear through the press, publicity, PR, advertising, financial reports, trade union reports, all sorts of communications, and of course their products and services. Managing the corporate brand and its communication means managing this profile.

How do corporations relate to product brands? The latter are there to create client goodwill, build growth and profits. In modern mature markets, consumers do not make a complete distinction between the product brand and the corporation: what the corporation does impacts their evaluation of its brands, especially if they share the same name as the corporation or are visibly endorsed by the former. The issue of branding architectures with the four structural types of relationship (independence; umbrella; endorsement; source or branded house) will be covered in Chapter 13. It has strategic implications in terms of the spillover effects (Sullivan, 1988) the organization might or might not want to capitalize on, and in terms of bolstering confidence in the product (Brown and Dacin, 1997), if this is necessary, which is not always the case. For instance LVMH, the world's leading luxury group, remains separate from its 50 brands' communication and marketing: they look independent. GM endorses its brands: it reveals the powerful and respected corporation behind its car marques. GE follows an umbrella strategy: GE Capital Investment, GE Medical Services. A classic strategy, in our world of global communication and synergies, is to use for the corporation the same name as its best brand. This is how BSN became Danone – just as 50 years earlier, Tokyo Tsuhin Kogyo became Sony. As we shall see, there are strong benefits in doing this.

A conceptual issue arises when one speaks, say, of Canon or Nike or Sony or Citibank. Are they corporate brands? Are they commercial brands? Since the company and the brand share the same name it is difficult to say. The answer is that they are both: it depends on the context and objectives and target of communication. Naomi Klein's book *No Logo* (1999) criticized Nike as a company, for all it tries to hide behind the attractive images and sports stars of its commercial brand (for the sweatshops in Asia, the delocalization of manufacturing to developing countries, the lack of reactiveness to critics). To make it clear who speaks, the corporation or the brand, some companies have chosen to differentiate the logo of each source of communication: Nestlé's corporate logo is not that of Nestlé as a commercial brand (which itself is differentiated by product category).

The case is more acute still for service companies: can one differentiate Barclay's Bank or Orange as a brand and as a corporate brand? Since both share the same employees this is more difficult, although looking at the objectives and target of the communication should help. This is why the issue of brand alignment (Ind, 2001) has become so important: the corporation has to align on its brand values. Its whole business should be brand driven.

Reputation focus versus brand focus

In corporate circles, the word 'reputation' was once preferred to that of 'brand'. The latter word was associated with product names and seemed less noble than the corporation itself. CEOs used to talk of reputation as their key concern. This is changing: many CEOs now encourage their managers to promote the company as a brand.

Why this change? Reputation is a defensive concept. Brand is an offensive one. According to academics (Fombrun and Van Riel, 2008), reputation is measured by the sum of all opinions held by all major stakeholders of the company (employees, opinion leaders, journalists, bankers, politicians, and students as prospective employees). Corporate communication directors are typically in charge of this reputation management. No decision is made without first asking: will it hurt our corporate reputation? The consequence is an overly prudent approach to decision making. Reputation managers fear making waves. This was typically the case in the 2009 Toyota product recalls. Instead of immediately reacting and showing that the company was compassionate, it did nothing for fear of losing its quality reputation. By doing so, the Toyota company looked cold, distant and even arrogant.

A brand is a champion of the values it promotes. Brands want to earn the gold medal among all their competitors. Their concern is to become the reference of the category, the one everyone wants to imitate because it sets new standards again and again. This is why instilling the brand mystique within the company aims at making it a champion of a value or a benefit, far beyond being well regarded by everybody. In a race, only the gold medallist is remembered.

Reputation is company focused and introverted. Brand focus is market oriented and value oriented, and takes into account competition. Companies should become brands, that is to say champions with a vision.

From managing the brand to managing *by* the brand

Non-FMCG companies have never taken branding very seriously, but this is changing. Efficiency has been the primary factor of success in managerial circles for 30 years. As a result managerial progress has come from new concepts such as quality circles, *kanban*, globalization of production, optimization of the supply chain, etc.

Now that these important methods and managerial concepts have been diffused all around the world and adopted by companies, what else is there? Companies are faced by two major challenges: 1) mobilizing the workforce or staff; and 2) sustaining demand by recreating desire.

There is a paradox in the corporate world: corporations hope consumers will be loyal to their brands. On the other hand, during the recession, millions of people have lost their jobs. Even in Japan, where people generally would work all their lives for the same employer, companies now act more like Western companies. As a result, cynicism is growing. People realize they are simply part of the workforce and tend to get far less involved in their companies. Today's main challenge is how to mobilize them again.

On the consumer side, once all the production and distribution costs have been reduced and products stripped down, how can one still create desire or create value, knowing that new competition has emerged that is still lower in costs and prices?

Managing *by* the brand addresses the first issue. Inside companies people are cynical about mission statements and other pompous declarations of intent that have proven to be mere words. Everyone should read the Enron mission and values statement.

The brand has the power to mobilize, for it appears as one of the few valuable things that bring pride both inside and outside. As long as the brand keeps its attractiveness, it is motivating to work for it. Everyone needs to keep this attractiveness high to sustain market demand. This is why corporate focus is moving from reputation to brand.

Reputation is the sum of all opinions among all stakeholders about the company. Directors of corporate communication are very anxious about the company reputation. Every single act is now evaluated by one question: will it damage the reputation?

Reputation expresses an enduring concern about what others say or think of the corporation. Brand means leadership. The brand perspective is that of being the champion of something. Competition is like sport: there are winners and losers, ie number 1, number 2, etc.

Sport creates a lot of involvement. In practice this means that companies must become brands. Their own name must become the number 1 criterion of choice in their markets. Just as one chooses Coke, so should one desire GE, IBM, Siemens, Lafarge, etc.

In this process of moving from corporate reputation to corporate brand, corporations need to involve the employees. Brand platforms cannot be decided only by technicians, even if they are marketing experts. Brands do not belong to marketing. In fact brands are made by people. Everyone is concerned by the final output. This is why Toyota spends so much time (more than a week) in talking about the Toyota brand values to all new employees or workers. It is also their concern. One does not work in a company, but for the brand.

Once brand values are understood, people tend to regulate their own behaviour and that of their colleagues around them: is it in line or not with the brand?

This is why taking the brand seriously entails more than speeches, but a whole interactive process of sensitization of the staff. The telephone company Orange has a presence in 220 countries, with 180,000 employees. It undertook a one-year brand sensitization programme with hundreds of interactive small group meetings, organized from top to bottom. The learning of each group was supported and encouraged by somebody from the organizational level just above. This is a strict application of the trickle-down process. At the end, the six Orange core values were clearly understood by the majority. In addition, in each of these meetings or workshops, participants discussed the practical implications at their own level: what they should start doing tomorrow, stop doing or continue doing.

02 Strategic implications of branding

Many companies have forgotten the fundamental purpose of their brands. A great deal of attention is devoted to the marketing activity itself, which involves designers, graphic artists, packaging and advertising agencies. This activity thus becomes an end in itself, receiving most of the attention. In so doing, we forget that it is just a means. Branding is seen as the exclusive prerogative of the marketing and communications staff. This undervalues the role played by the other parts of the company in ensuring a successful branding policy and business growth. Only by mobilizing all of its internal sources of added value can a company set itself apart from its competitors.

What does branding really mean?

Branding means much more than just giving a brand name and signalling to the outside world that such a product or service has been stamped with the mark and imprint of an organization. It requires a corporate long-term involvement, a high level of resources and skills to become the referent.

Branding consists in transforming the product category

Brands are a direct consequence of the strategy of market segmentation and product differentiation. As companies seek to better fulfil the expectations of specific customers, they concentrate on providing the latter, consistently and repeatedly, with the ideal combination of attributes – both tangible and intangible, functional and hedonistic, visible and invisible – under viable economic conditions for their businesses. Companies want to stamp their mark on different sectors and set their imprint on their products. It is no wonder that the word 'brand' also refers to the act of burning a mark into the flesh of an animal as a means to claim ownership of it. The first task in brand analysis is to define precisely all that the brand injects into the product (or service) and how the brand transforms it:

- What attributes materialize?
- What advantages are created?
- What benefits emerge?
- What ideals does it represent?

This deep meaning of the brand concept is often forgotten or wilfully omitted. Branding, though, is not about being on top of something, but within something. The fact that a delabelled item is worth more than a generic product confirms this understanding of branding. In passing, the brand has intrinsically altered it: hence the value of Lacostes without 'Lacoste', Adidases without 'Adidas'. They are worth more than imitations because the brand, though invisible, still prevails. Conversely, the brand on counterfeits, though visible, is in effect absent. This is why counterfeits are sold so cheaply.

Some brands have succeeded in proving with their slogans that they know and understand what their fundamental task is: to transform the product category. A brand not only acts on the market, it organizes the market, driven by a vision, a calling and a clear idea of what the category should become. Too many brands wish only to identify fully with the product category, thereby expecting to control it. In fact they often end up disappearing within it: Polaroid, Xerox, Caddy, Scotch, Kleenex have thus become generic terms.

According to the objective the brand sets itself; transforming the category implies endowing the product with its own separate identity. In concrete terms, that means that the brand is weak when the product is 'transparent'. Talking about 'Greek olive oil, first cold pressing' for example, makes the product transparent, almost entirely defined and epitomized by those sole attributes, yet there are dozens of brands capable of marketing that type of oil. Going from bulk to packaging is also symptomatic of this phenomenon. The weakness of fresh vacuum-packed food brands is partially due to the fact that their packaging, though designed to reassure the buyer – such as with sauerkraut in film-wrapped containers – only recreates transparency. Significantly, Findus and l'Eggs or Hoses do not just show their products, they *show* them *off*. This is the structural cause of Essilor's brand weakness, as perceived by the customers. They do not perceive how Essilor, the world leader in optical glass, transforms the product, nor its input, its added value. To them, glass is just glass to which various options can be added (anti-reflecting, unbreakable, etc). The added value seems to be created solely by the style of the rims (hence the boom in licensing) or the service, both of which are palpable and in the store. What is invisible is not perceived and thus does not exist in their eyes. However, the example of Evian reminds us that it is always possible to make a transparent product become opaque. The major mineral water brands have been able to exist, grow and prosper only because they have made the invisible visible. We can no longer choose our water haphazardly: good health and purity are associated with Evian, fitness with Contrex, vitality with Vittel. These various positionings were justified by the invisible differences in water contents. Generally speaking, anything adding to the complexity of ingredients also contributes to creating distance *vis-à-vis* the product. In this respect, Coca-Cola is doing the right thing by keeping its recipe secret. Antoine Riboud, the former CEO of Danone worldwide, expressed a similar concern when declaring: 'It is not yoghurts that I make, but Danones.'

A brand is a long-term vision

The brand should have its own specific point of view on the product category. Major brands have more than just a specific or dominating position in the market: they hold certain positions within the product category. This position and conception both energize the brand and feed the transformations that are implemented for matching the brand's products with its ideals. It is this conception that justifies the brand's existence, its reason for being on the market, and provides it with a guideline for its life cycle. How many brands are capable today of answering the following crucial question: 'What would the market lack if we did not exist?' The company's ultimate goal is undoubtedly to generate profit and jobs. But brand purpose is something else. Brand strategy is too often mistaken for company strategy. The latter most often results in truisms such as 'increase customer satisfaction'. Specifying brand purpose consists in (re)defining its *raison d'être*, its absolute necessity. The notion of brand purpose is missing in most marketing textbooks. It is a recent idea and conveys the emerging conception of the brand, seen as exerting a creative and powerful influence on a given market. If there is power, there is energy. Naturally, a brand draws its strength from the company's financial and human means, but it derives its energy from its specific niche, vision and ideals. If it does not feel driven by an intense internal necessity, it will not carry the potential for leadership. The analytical notion of brand image does not clearly capture this dynamic dimension, which is demanded by modern brand management.

Thus, many banks put forward the following image of themselves: close to their clients, modern, offering high-performing products and customer service. These features are, of course, useful to market researchers in charge of measuring the perceptions sent back by the market and the level of consumer satisfaction. But from which dynamic programme do they emanate, which vision do they embody?

Certain banks have specified what their purpose is: for some it is 'to change people's relationship to money', while for others it is to remind us that money is just a 'means towards personal development'. Several banks have recently worked at re-defining their singular reason for existence. All of them will have to do so in the future. The Amex vision of money is not that of Visa.

More than most, multi-segment brands need to redetermine their own purpose. Cars are a typical example. A multi-segment brand (also called a generalist brand) wants to cover all market segments. Each model spawns multiple versions, thereby theoretically maximizing the number of potential buyers: diesel, gas, three or five doors, estate, coupé, cabriolet, etc. The problem is that by having to constantly satisfy the key criteria of each segment (bottom range, lower mid-range, upper mid-range and top range), ie to churn out many different versions and to avoid over-typifying a model in order to please everyone, companies tend to create chameleon brands. Apart from the symbol on the car hood or the similarities in the car designs, we no longer perceive an overall plan guiding the creative and productive forces of the company in the conception of these cars. Thus, competitors fight their battles either over the price or the options offered for that price. No longer brands, they become mere names on a hood or on a dealer's office walls. The word has thus lost most of its meaning. What does Opel or Ford mean?

What unifies the products of a brand is not their marque or common external signs, it is their 'religion': what common spirit, vision and ideals are embodied in them.

Major brands can be compared to a pyramid (see Figure 2.1). The top states the brand's vision and purpose – its conception of automobiles, for instance, its idea of the types of cars it wants, and has always wanted, to create, as well as its very own values which either can or cannot be expressed by a slogan. This level leads to the next one down, which shows the general brand style of communication. Indeed, brand personality and style are conveyed

FIGURE 2.1 The brand system

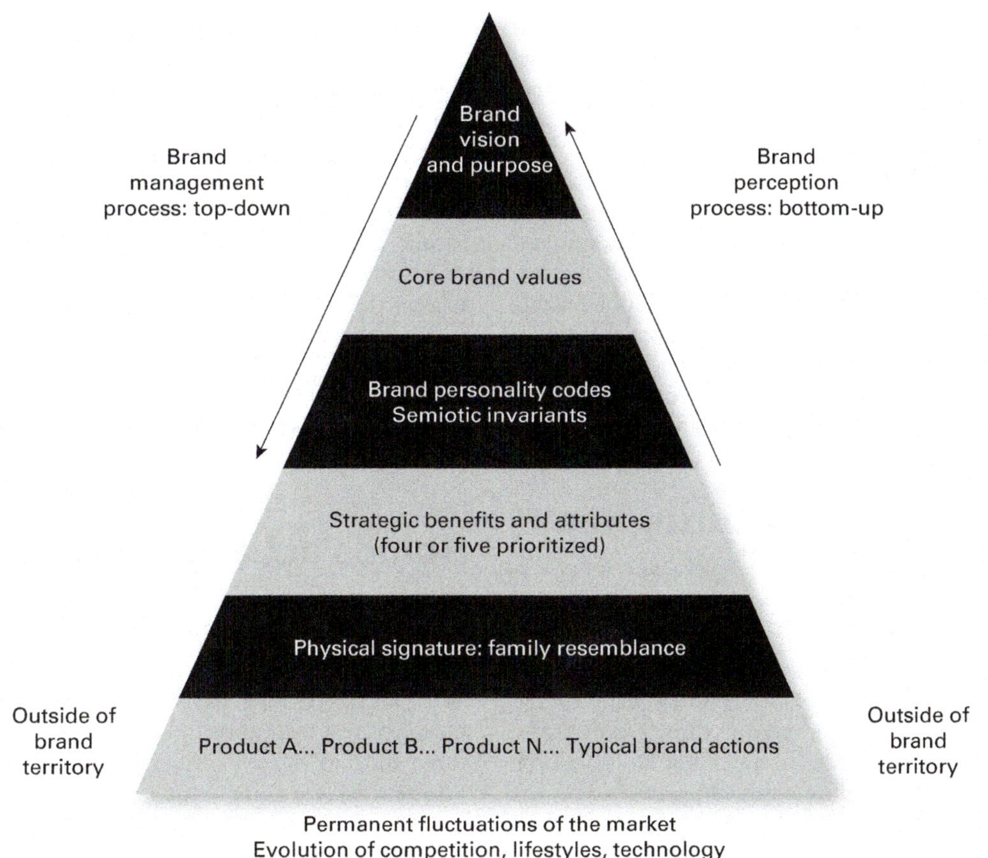

less by words than by a way of being and communicating. These codes should not be exclusively submitted to the fluctuating inspiration of the creative team: they must be defined so as to reflect the brand's unique character. The next level presents the brand's strategic image features: amounting to four or five, they result from the overall vision and materialize in the brand's products, communication and actions. This refers, for example, to the positioning of Volvo as a secure, reliable and robust brand, or of BMW as a dynamic, classy prestigious one. Lastly, the product level, at the bottom of the pyramid, consists of each model's positioning in its respective segment.

The problem is that consumers look at the pyramid from the bottom up. They start with what is real and tangible. The wider the pyramid base is, the more the customers doubt that all these cars do indeed emanate from the same automobile concept, that they carry the same brand essence and bear the stamp of the same automobile project. Brand management consists, for its part, in starting from the top and defining the way the car is conceived by the brand, in order to determine exactly when a car is deserving of the brand name and when it no longer is – in which case, the car should logically no longer bear the brand name, as it then slips out of its brand territory.

Internal hesitation about brand identity is often revealed when searching for slogans. There is no longer a trend toward obvious and meaningless slogans such as 'the automobile spirit', which neither tell us anything about the brand's automobile ideal, nor help to guide engineers, creators, developers or producers in making concrete choices between mutually exclusive features: comfort and road adherence, aerodynamism and feeling of sturdiness, etc.

Permanently nurturing the difference

Our era is one of temporary advantages. It is often argued that certain products of different brands are identical. Some observers thus infer that, under these circumstances, a brand is nothing but a 'bluff', a gimmick used to try to stand out in a market flooded with barely differentiated products.

This view fails to take into account both the time factor and the rules of dynamic competition. Brands draw attention through the new products they create and bring onto the market. Any brand innovation necessarily generates plagiarism. Any progress made quickly becomes a standard to which buyers grow accustomed: competing brands must then adopt it themselves if they do not want to fall short of market expectations. For a while, the innovative brand will thus be able to enjoy a fragile monopoly, which is bound to be quickly challenged unless the innovation is or can be patented. The role of the brand name is precisely to protect the innovation: it acts as a mental patent, by becoming the prototype of the new segment it creates – advantage of being a pioneer.

If it is true that a snapshot of a given market often shows similar products, a dynamic view of it reveals in turn who innovated first, and who has simply followed the leader: brands protect innovators, granting them momentary exclusiveness and rewarding them for their risk-taking attitude. Thus, the accumulation of these momentary differences over time serves to reveal the meaning and purpose of a brand and to justify its economic function, hence its price premium.

Brands cannot, therefore, be reduced to a mere sign on a product, a mere graphic cosmetic touch: they guide a creative process, which yields the new product A today, the new products B and C tomorrow, and so on. McDonald's restaurants keep on adding new benefits and values: safety guaranteed, locally produced meat, 100 per cent powered by renewable electricity, financing homes for parents of very ill children close to the hospital.

As shown in Figure 2.2, brand management alternates between phases of product differentiation and brand image differentiation. The typical example is Sony, whose advertising focuses on innovations when they exist, and on image in between.

Brands act as a genetic programme

A brand does in fact act as a genetic programme. What is done at birth exerts a long-lasting influence on market perceptions. Indeed revitalizing a brand often starts with re-identifying its forgotten genetic programme (see Chapter 16).

Table 2.1 shows how brands are built and exert a long-term influence on customers' memories, which

FIGURE 2.2 The cycle of brand management

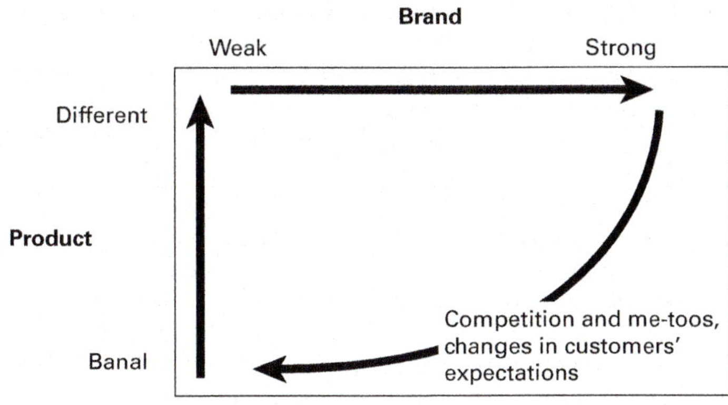

TABLE 2.1 The brand as genetic programme

Early founding acts (past)	Memory (present)	Expectations (future)
First best-selling product First channel of distribution First positioning First advertising campaign First events First CEO Corporate visions and values	Brand prototype Associated benefits Brand image Brand competence and know-how	Legitimate extensions for the future (what other areas of new products)

in turn influence their expectations, attitudes and degree of satisfaction just like a DNA.

In the life of a brand, although they may have been forgotten, the early acts have a very structuring influence. In fact they mould the first and long-lasting meaning of this new name that designates Brand X or Brand Y. Once learnt, this meaning gets reinforced and stored in long-term memory. Then a number of selective processes reinforce the meaning: selective attention, selective perception, selective memory.

This is why brand images are hard to change: they act like fast-setting concrete.

This process has many important managerial consequences. When going international, each country reproduces it. It is of prime importance to define the products to be launched in relationship with the image one wants to create in the long term. Too often they are chosen by local agents just because they will sell very well. They must do both: build the business and build the brand. Brand management introduces long-term effects as criteria for evaluating the relevance of short-term decisions.

New generations discover the brand at different points in time. Some discovered Ford through the Model T, others through the Mustang, others through the Mondeo, others through the Focus. No wonder brand images differ from one generation to another.

The memory factor also partly explains why individual preferences endure: within a given generation, people continue, even 20 years later, to prefer the brands they liked between the ages of 7 and 18 (Guest, 1964; Fry *et al*, 1973; Jacoby and Chestnut, 1978).

It is precisely because a brand is the memory of the products that it can act as a long-lasting and stable reference. Unlike advertising, in which the last message seen is often the only one that truly registers and is best recalled, the first actions and message of a brand are the ones bound to leave the deepest impression, thereby structuring long-term perception. In this respect, brands create a cognitive filter: dissonant and atypical aspects are declared unrepresentative, thus discounted and forgotten. That is why failures in brand extensions on atypical products do not harm the brand in the end even though they do unsettle the investors' trust in the company (Loken and Roedder John, 1993). Bic's failure in perfume is a good example. Making perfumes is not typical of the know-how of Bic as perceived by consumers: sales of ball pens, lighters and razors kept on increasing.

Ridding itself of atypical, dissonant elements, a brand acts as a selective memory, hence endowing people's perceptions with an illusion of permanence and coherence. That is why a brand is less elastic than its products. Once created, like fast-setting concrete it is hard to change. Hence the critical importance of defining the brand platform. What brand meaning does one want to create?

A brand is both the memory and the future of its products. The analogy with the genetic programme is central to understanding how brands function and should be managed. Indeed, the brand memory that develops contains the programme for all future evolution, the characteristics of upcoming models and their common traits, as well as the family resemblances transcending their diverse personalities. By understanding a brand's programme, we can not only trace its legitimate territory but also the area in which it will be able to grow beyond the products that initially gave birth to it. The brand's underlying programme indicates the purpose and meaning of both former and future products. How then can one identify this programme, the brand DNA?

If it exists, this programme can be discovered by analysing the brand's founding acts: products, communication and the most significant actions since its inception. If a guideline or an implicit permanence exists, then it must show through. Research on brand identity has a double purpose: to analyse the brand's most typical production on the one hand and to analyse the reception, ie the image sent back by the market, on the other. The image is indeed a memory in itself, so stable that it is difficult to modify it in the short run. This stability results from the selective perception described above. It also has a function: to create long-lasting references guiding consumers among the abundant supply of consumer goods. That is the reason a company should never turn away from its identity, which alone has managed to attract buyers. Customer loyalty is created by respecting the brand features that initially seduced the buyers. If the products slacken off, weaken or show a lack of investment and thus no longer meet customer expectations, better try to meet them again than to change expectations. In order to build customer loyalty and capitalize on it, brands must stay true to themselves. This is called a return to the future. Back to the DNA.

Questioning the past, trying to detect the brand's underlying programme, does not mean ignoring the future: on the contrary, it is a way of better preparing for it by giving it roots, legitimacy and continuity. The mistake is to embalm the brand and to merely repeat in the present what it produced in the past, like the new VW Beetle and other retro-innovations. In fighting competition, a brand's products must always belong intrinsically to their time, but in their very own way. Rejuvenating Burberrys or Helena Rubinstein means connecting them to modernity, not mummifying them in deference to a past splendour that we might wish to revive.

Respect the brand 'contract': the power to say no!

Brands become credible only through the persistence and repetition of their value proposition. BMW has had the same promise since 1959. Through time they become a quasi contract, unwritten but most effective. This contract binds both parties. The brand must keep its identity, but permanently increase its relevance. It must be loyal to itself, to its mission and to its clients. Each brand is free to choose its values and positioning, but once chosen and advertised, they become the benchmark for customer satisfaction. It is well known that the prime determinant of customer satisfaction is the gap between customers' experiences and their expectations. The brand's positioning sets up these expectations.

As a result, customers are loyal to such a brand.

This mutual commitment explains why brands, whose products have temporarily declined in popularity, do not necessarily disappear. A brand is judged over the long term: a deficiency can always occur. Brand trust gives products a chance to recover. If not, Jaguar would have disappeared long ago: no other brand could have withstood the detrimental effect of the decreasing quality of its cars during the 1970s. That is a good illustration of one of the benefits a brand brings to a company.

The brand contract is economic, not legal. Brands differ in this way from other signs of quality such as quality seals and certification. Quality seals officially and legally testify that a given product meets a set of specific characteristics, previously defined (in conjunction with public authorities, producers/manufacturers and consumers) so as to guarantee a higher level of quality and distinguishing it from similar products. A quality seal is a collective brand controlled by a certification agency which certifies a given product only if it complies with certain specifications. Such certification is thus never definitive and can be withdrawn (like ISO).

Brands do not legally testify that a product meets a set of characteristics. However, through consistent and repeated experience of these characteristics, a brand becomes synonymous with the latter.

A contract implies constraints. The brand contract assumes first of all that the various functions in the organization all converge: R&D, production, methods, logistics, marketing, finance. The same is true of service brands: as the R&D and production aspects are obviously irrelevant in this case, the responsibility for ensuring the brand's continuity and cohesion pass to the management and staff, who play an essential role in clientele relationships.

The brand contract requires internal as well as external marketing. Unlike quality seals, brands set their own ever-increasing standards. Therefore, they must not only meet the latter but also continuously try to improve all their products, even the most basic ones, especially if they represent most of their sales and hence act as the major vehicle of brand image; in so doing, they will be able to satisfy the expectations of clients who will demand that the products keep pace with technological change. They must also communicate and make themselves known to the outside world in order to become the prototype of a segment, a value or a benefit. This is a lonely task for brands, yet they must do it to get the uniqueness and lack of substitutability they need. The brand will have to support its internal and external costs all on its own. These are generated by the brand requirements, which are to:

- Closely forecast the needs and expectations of potential buyers. This is the purpose of market research: both to optimize existing products and to discover needs and expectations that have yet to be fulfilled.
- React to technical and technological progress as soon as it can to create a competitive edge both in terms of cost and performance.
- Provide both product (or service) volume and quality at the same time, since those are the only means of ensuring repeat purchases.
- Control supply quantity and quality.
- Deliver products or services to intermediaries (distributors), both consistently over time and in accordance with their requirements in terms of delivery, packaging and overall conditions.
- Give meaning to the brand and communicate its meaning to the target market, thereby using the brand as both a signal and reference for the product's (or service's) identity and exclusivity. That is what advertising budgets are for.
- Increase the experiential rewards of consumption or interaction.
- Remain ethical and ecology-conscious.

Strong brands thus bring about both internal mobilization and external federation. They create their company's panache and impetus. That is why some companies switch their own name for that of one of their star brands: BSN thus became Danone, CGE became Alcatel. In this respect, the impact of strong brands extends far beyond most corporate strategies. These only last while they are in the making, after which they either vanish or wind up as pompous phrases ('a passion for excellence') posted in hallways. In any case, the corporate brand is the organization's external voice and, as such, it remains both demanding and determined to constantly outdo itself, to aim ever higher.

Becoming aware that the brand is a contract also means taking up many other responsibilities that are all too often ignored. In the fashion market, even if creators wish to change after a while, they cannot entirely forget about their brand contract, which helped them to get known initially, then recognized and eventually praised.

In theory, both the brand's slogan and signature are meant to embody the brand contract. A good slogan is therefore often rejected by managing directors because it means too much commitment for the company and may backfire if the products/services do not match the expectations the brand has created so far. In too many cases brands are seen as mere names: this is very evident in some innovations committee meetings, where new products are reallocated to different brands of the portfolio many times in the same meeting. One brand name or another is perceived as making no difference. Taking the brand seriously, as it is (that is, as a contract) is much more demanding. It provides higher returns. It also requires the authority to say no!

The product and the brand

Since the early theorization on the brand, there has been much discussion on the relationship of brands to products. How do the concepts differ? How are they mutually interrelated? On the one hand, many a CEO repeats to his or her staff that there is no brand without a great product (or service), in order to stimulate their innovativeness and make them think of the product as a prime lever of brand competitiveness. On the other hand, there is ample evidence that market leaders are not the best product in their market. To be the 'best product' in a category means to compete in the premium tier, which is rarely a large segment. Certainly within the laundry detergent category, market leaders such as Tide, Ariel and Skip are those delivering the best performance for heavy-duty laundry, but in other cases it is the brand with the best quality/price ratio that is market leader. Dell is a case in point. Are Dell's computers the best? Surely not. But who really needs a 'best computer'? What would be the criterion for evaluation? 'Best' is a relative concept, depending on the value criteria used to establish comparisons and identify the 'best'. In fact the market is segmented: the largest proportion of the public, and even most of the B2B segment, wants a modern, reliable, cheap computer. Thanks to its build-to-order business model, Dell was able to innovate and become the leader of that segment. Co-branded 'Intel inside', it reassures buyers and surprises them by its astonishing price and one-to-one customization: each person makes his or her own computer. Is Swatch the best watch? Surely not either. But in any case this is not what is asked by Swatch buyers: they buy convenience and style, not long-lasting superior 'performance', whatever this may mean.

It is time to look deeper into the brand–product relationship. Looking at history, most brands are born out of a product or service innovation which outperformed its competitors. A superior product/service was the determining factor of the launch campaign. Later, as the product name evolves into a brand, customers' reasons for purchase may still be the brand's 'superior performance image', although in reality that performance has been matched by new competitors. This has been the basis of Volkswagen's leadership and price premium: a majority of consumers keeps on believing that Volkswagen cars are the most reliable ones. The Golf 7, which is expected in 2012, 40 years after the first Golf, will be 10 per cent more expensive than its two European rivals, the Citroën C4 and the Renault Mégane. This quality reputation is crucial for Golf and for Volkswagen itself: Golf used to represent 28 per cent of its sales and almost half its operating profit.

Figure 2.3 summarizes the product–brand relationship.

Suppose a consumer wants to buy a new car because of the birth of his or her fourth child. This major event creates a new set of expectations, some tangible, some intangible. The consumer wishes to buy a minivan, with two sliding doors, high flexibility within the cabin, and of course a reliable, secure brand, with credentials and some status. By looking at Internet sites, at magazines and visiting dealers, it is possible to identify those models with the requested visible attributes (size, flexibility, sliding doors). Now what about the invisible attributes, like the experiential ones (driving pleasure) or those one has to believe on faith, such as reliability? Obviously, these attributes do or do not belong to the brand's reputational capital. They cannot be observed. This is one of the key roles of brands: to guarantee, to reassure customers about desired benefits which constitute the exclusive strength of the brand, also called its positioning.

Psychologists have also identified the halo effect as a major source of value created by the brand: the fact that knowing the name of the brand does influence consumer's perception of the product advantages beyond what the visible cues had themselves indicated, not to speak of the invisible advantages.

Finally, attached to the brand there are pure intangible associations, which stem from the brand's values, vision, philosophy, its typical buyer, its brand

FIGURE 2.3 The product and the brand

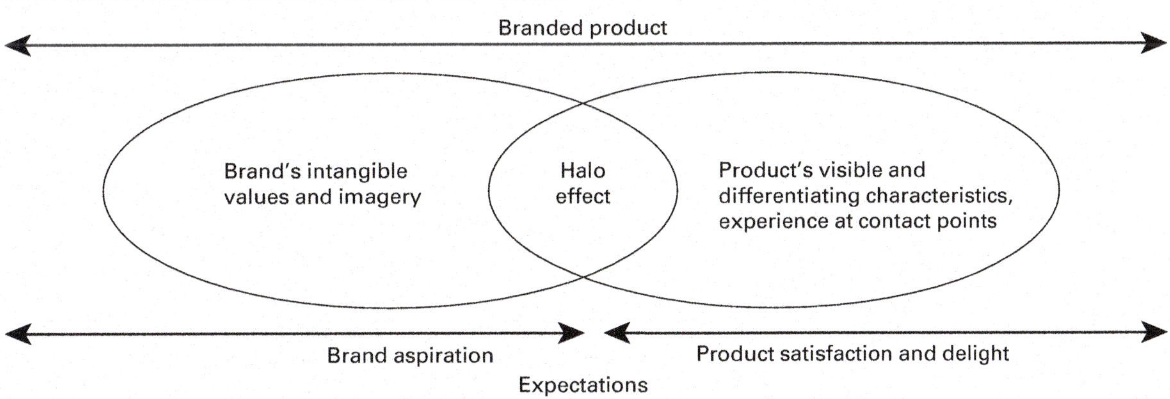

personality and so on. These associations are the source of emotional ties, beyond product satisfaction. In fact, in the car industry, they are the locus of consumers' desire to possess a brand. Some brands sell very good products at fair price but lack thrill or desire: they cannot command a price premium in their segment. Their dealers will have to give more rebates (which undermine brand value and business profitability).

Figure 2.3 reminds us of the double nature of brands. People buy branded products or services, but branding is a not a substitute for marketing. Both are needed. Marketing aims at forecasting the needs of specific consumer segments, and drives the organization to tailor products and services to these needs. This is a skill: some car marques offer minivans with sliding doors, some do not. However, part of the willingness to pay is based on a personal tie with the brand. Uninvolved consumers will bargain a lot. Brand-involved consumers will bargain less. Brand image is directly linked to profitability. In fact, in the Euromonitor car brand tracking study, measuring the image of all automobile brands operating in Europe, it has been said that a positive shift of one unit on the global opinion scale means there is 1 per cent less bargaining by customers.

Halo effect: kernel and peripheral values

A brand is a name with power, the power to influence. How can a name influence? By the evocations and emotions it triggers in consumers' minds. New brands that by definition are unknown can rely only on the spontaneous evocations of the name itself: its sound and its connotations. This is why choosing a good name is so important, as well as adding an evoking symbol, especially for countries where consumers cannot read Western characters. Since the name will be the brand's most durable single identity mark, one should spend as much time as needed to select it (more on names on page 185). However, the main source of these evocations will be consumer learning: through time, the brand will deliver consistent messages and experiences that build a coherent brand image and positioning (what the brand stands for). This image stems from the brand 'prototype' (the product or service line that seems most representative of the brand). In cognitive psychology, the prototype is the instance that summarizes and carries all the meaning of a concept. If one substitutes the word 'brand' for the word 'concept', it is clear that the first best-seller of a brand carries most of the meaning of the brand. This is why single product brands (such as Coke) cannot extend beyond this product after a while.

Evocations triggered by a brand name are not the only sources of influence on the customers (in B2B) or consumers (in B2C). There is the direct product experience brought by vision, touch, smell, hearing, or trial itself and peer-to-peer word of mouth, through the web or directly. Products do send messages to help consumers figure out what to buy and what to expect after usage. These messages are called 'cues', and belong to one of three types:

- *Search cues* are readily accessible to the senses: they are enough to allow selection of an apple in a store just by looking at it, or the choosing of a bottle of wine (all the information is written on the label). Price is a search cue, as it is supposed to be correlated with intrinsic quality.
- *Experience cues* suppose the ability to try the product or service before buying it. Skin care consultants in duty-free zones or department stores enable women to try new make-up and creams. Car dealers suggest a ride or even a trial of the car.
- *Credence cues* are signals that disclose benefits not readily accessible: the reliability of a car and its ability to give information about the driver's personality. Also called 'belief cues', they are based on faith. This is why the first asset of a brand is trust. One earns trust long term by doing what one promises, without compromising. This is why politicians, unlike brands, are not trusted: most of them never achieve what they promised during their election campaign. Since the brands' election campaign is every day, brands have no other choice than to stick to their promises and deliver them through product lines, services, store experience, after-sales service, communication and internet relationships.

Brand evocations influence buyers if they are:

- immediately accessible in buyers' minds (saliency);
- firmly believed (no doubts and no expectations of variance in the brand delivery);
- highly valued (they promise benefits with high utility for the targeted consumers);
- highly differentiated: they are not matched by the competition.

To measure the brand's own 'pull power', or its ability to influence, two types of measures are used. First, there is the so-called 'brand equity monitor' (BEM), which uses simple questions such as: Do you know the brand, even if only by name? Would you consider it in your next choice? Have you already tried or purchased it? There are also variants (see also page 16). Second, there are the brand image studies where consumers are asked to evaluate how much a promise (a physical attribute or a consumer benefit or value) is strongly attributed to a brand and by how much more than to any of its competitors. A brand succeeds when it looks incomparable. Its pull power stems from this ability to stand out in the crowd (be known) and deliver unique benefits as against the competition, through very significant innovations and excellent customer relations and care. Apple is a typical illustration of a loved brand based on these two pillars.

However, one needs to go further for proper brand management. The most relevant theory for brand management is that of social representations. Although the marketing Anglo-Saxon community today is very much influenced by neuroscience advances, holding brand images as a system of nodes and links encoded in human memory, the fact is that brands come before all social constructs. As such the theory of social representations is the most relevant. Its founding father was Solomon Asch (1946), working on the formation of impressions of personality and on the perception of social stereotypes. He identified that a few traits about a person carried the essential weight in impression formation, and that the others were secondary. Since then the theory has been much expanded (Abric, 1994; Flament, 1995; Moliner, 1998; Michel, 1999; Kapferer, 2000).

In brand management the key concept is not brand image or brand associations but brand identity. Identity is an answer to a simple but fundamental question: What makes you you? What makes a BMW a BMW? Image questionnaires do not answer this question: they measure how much an attribute, benefit or value is attributed to a brand, but they do not measure how necessary it is to the brand's own identity.

Following Asch and the German gestalt psychologists' pioneering works, kernel theory makes some radical statements as far as brands are concerned, largely overlooked by the marketing academic community:

- A brand is a system made up of kernel traits and peripheral traits.
- Kernel traits are unconditional; their absence signals that this is not the real brand.
- Peripheral traits are conditional; they may be present or absent depending on the

product within the range or the segment (for a multi-sector umbrella brand). Thus Samsung will have kernel attributes, as well as peripheral attributes, the latter varying depending on whether we are considering Samsung smartphones, Samsung TVs, Samsung PCs, Samsung Galaxy Pads, Samsung refrigerators, Samsung cars, etc.

- Peripheral traits may in the long term become kernel traits. One can say that design, which was once a trait of iMacs only, has now entered the kernel of Apple social representation. Peripheral traits allow an adaptation of the brand to different segments.
- To identify kernel traits one should not use direct questioning or the classical image questionnaires (they measure only attribution, not necessity). Instead one should ask: if the brand does not have X or Y, is it still the brand?

Table 2.2 presents the results of such a study for Toyota in 2009. The left column identifies the percentage of respondents saying that Toyota is not Toyota any longer if it is not safe (88 per cent), solid (87 per cent), etc. Interestingly the results show that there is a 12 per cent gap between the first three items and the fourth one. The former are the kernel items; the following are peripheral items. Recent theory has revealed a sub-segmentation of the peripheral traits (Flament, 1995): primary and secondary peripheral traits.

Now how does this theory relate to the manner in which brands influence choices? Table 2.2 presents consumer evaluations of three concept cars. These concept cars (photographs of the outside and inside of future cars) are positioned in three well-delineated segments: entry (accessibly priced small cars), middle and high-end segments. This is a typical range for a generalist car marque – from low end to high end. Car brands engage in vertical extension to capitalize on consumer loyalty all along the family life cycle and to boost their image.

In this paradigmatic experiment (Tafani, Michel and Rosa, 2009), consumers were asked to rate the concept cars twice, on a scale from 1 to 5: once unbranded, on the 11 items presented in Table 2.2; and three days after, with a clear brand identification – they knew what brand it was.

Table 2.2 presents the difference between consumers' perception when the brand was identified

TABLE 2.2 Toyota halo effect on three unbranded concept cars (difference between the branded and the unbranded perceptions)

		Entry	Middle	High end
Brand core values:				
Safety	88%	+0.56	+0.71	+0.87
Solidity	87%	+1.16	+0.81	+0.56
Reliability	80%	+0.75	+0.90	+0.78
Brand peripheral values:				
Equipment	68%	+0.59	NS	NS
Power	67%	NS	NS	−0.72
Details	66%	NS	+0.63	+0.75
Quality/price	65%	+1.56	NS	NS
Comfort	61%	NS	+0.68	+0.56
Aesthetics	59%	NS	NS	NS
Style	58%	NS	NS	NS
Standing	58%	NS	NS	NS

SOURCE Tafani, Michel and Rosa (2009)

minus when it was not identified. What can be learned?

- Kernel traits exert a 'halo effect' all across the range, from low end to high end. The halo effect is the capacity of the brand name to influence what people perceive, in this case the products (the cars themselves) and what qualities they seem to have. For kernel qualities, all differences of perception are significant and positive. When identified, the Toyota brand makes people rate the product they see higher on the three items identified as kernel.
- Peripheral traits exert a halo effect, but conditionally: it depends on the segment of this vertical line extension. Take the fourth item (the first peripheral item): it exerts a halo effect on the perception of the entry-level concept car only. Power exerts a halo effect on the high-end concept car only; in addition, it is a negative halo effect. Knowing the concept car is a Toyota, consumers have downgraded their perception. Comfort exerts its halo effect in two segments only, but not in the entry one.
- Some peripheral traits of Toyota do not exert any significant effect on perception, for instance aesthetics. This is normal: aesthetics is a search cue. You just judge it by seeing. A car whose design is not liked remains not liked whether its brand is made explicit or not.

The consequences for brand management are clear cut: brand managers must decide what should be the very few kernel values of their brand (also called core values) and exert all their talent and energy to build it consistently through time, products, consumer relationships and care, store and web experience, and pricing. It starts by writing these few kernel values and getting them known inside and outside the company: this is called a brand platform (see Chapter 8). The brand kernel values should not be generic of the category unless one creates this category, in which case the brand itself is the prototype of the category (iPhone for smartphones).

We can now summarize the implications of these findings in Figure 2.4: how brands influence choice:

1. Kernel values are necessarily of two kinds: tangible and intangible. If there is no intangible value, the brand is only a name for a superior product, but it is not likely to create consumer identification, a consumer community and hence emotional loyalty and engagement.
2. Kernel tangible values exert an unconditional 'halo effect' on products' perception across the range, from low end to high end.
3. Kernel intangible values (like fashion, class, coolness, status, manliness, etc) add their own specific utility to the perception of products' utility (once the brand is known) all across the range.
4. Peripheral values also can be either tangible or intangible. They are conditional. It depends on the consumer or product segment.
5. Peripheral values may add their own utility, but conditionally: some do and some don't, depending on the product line (low, middle or high). This utility may be negative, such as the powerfulness of the high-end Toyota range (see Table 2.2).
6. Preferences (versus competition) are the result of the sum of tangible and intangible utilities. Brands thrive by adding intangible utilities (symbolism) to tangible ones (for instance on credence traits such as solidity and reliability).

When assessing the value of a brand name, also called financial brand equity (see Chapter 18), the valuation methods try to measure the 'brand added value': how knowledge of the brand enhances the perception of the products themselves (halo effect) and adds to it the pull power of the symbolism of the brand (what it says about the buyer). Brand value is a differential concept.

Each brand needs a flagship product

A given brand will not be jeopardized by competitors offering similar products, unless there are

FIGURE 2.4 How brands influence choice by adding value and halo effects

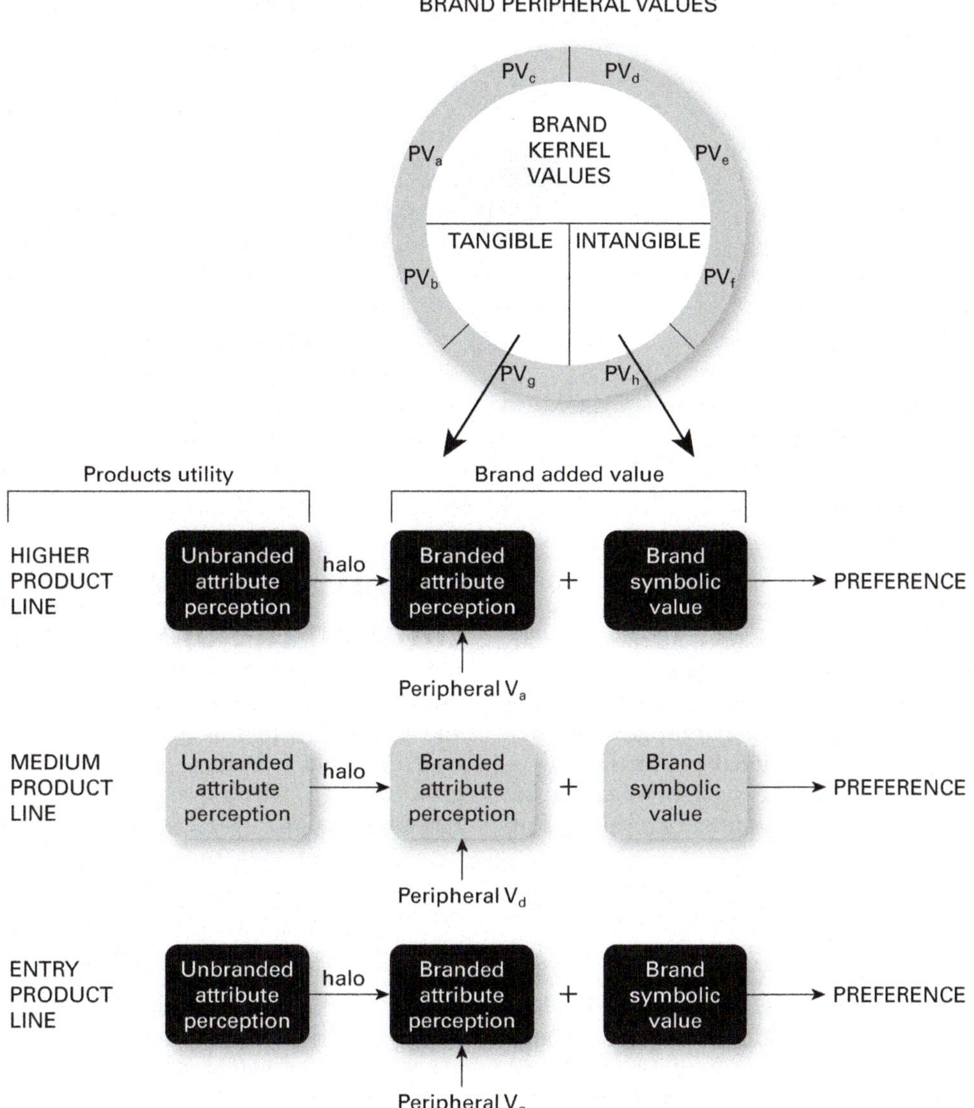

large quantities of the latter. It is indeed inevitable for certain models to be duplicated in the product lines of different brands. Suppose that brand A pursues durability, brand B practicality and brand C innovation: the spirit of each brand will be especially noticeable in certain specific products, those most representative or typical of the brand meaning. They are the brand's 'prototype' products. Each product range thus must contain products demonstrating the brand's guiding value and obsession, flagships for the brand's meaning and purpose. Renault, for instance, is best epitomized by its top minivans, Chanel by No. 5, Lacoste by its shirts, and Apple by the iPhone.

However, there are some products within a given line that do not manage to clearly express the brand's intent and attributes. In the television industry, the cost constraints at the low end of the range are such that trying to manufacture a model radically different from the next-door neighbour's is quite difficult. But, for economic reasons, brands are sometimes forced to take a stake in this very

FIGURE 2.5 Product line overlap among brands

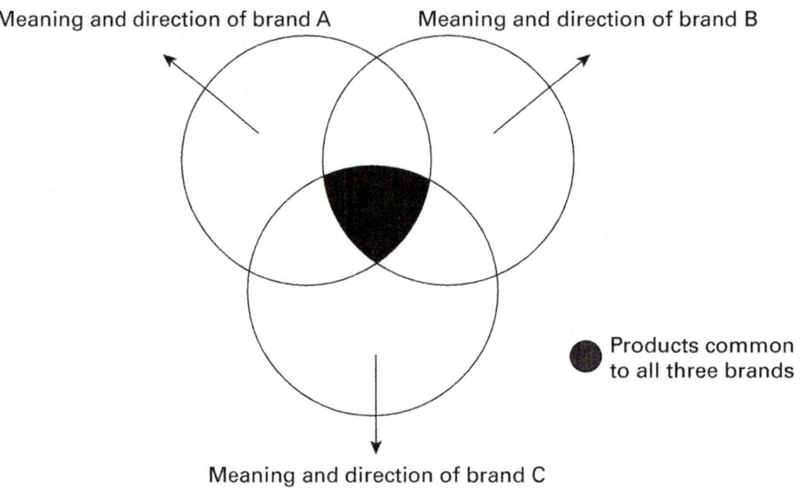

large and overall highly competitive market. Likewise, each bank has had to offer its own savings plan, identical to that of all other banks. All these similar products, though, should only represent a limited aspect of each brand's offer (see Figure 2.5). All in all, each brand stays in focus and progresses in its own direction to make original products. That is why communicating about such products is so important, as they reveal the brand's meaning and purpose.

The problem arises when brands within the same group overlap too much, with one preventing the other from asserting its identity. Using the same motors in Peugeots and Citroëns would harm Peugeot, built on the 'dynamic car' image. It is when several brands sell the same product that a brand can become a caricature of itself. In order to compete against Renault's Espace and Chrysler's Voyager, neither Peugeot or Citroën, Fiat or Lancia could take the economic risk of building a manufacturing plant on their own; neither could Ford or Volkswagen. A single minivan was made for the first four brands. Similarly, a Ford–Volkswagen plant in Portugal was set to produce a common car. The outcome, however, is that in producing a common vehicle, the brand becomes reduced to a mere external gadget. The identity message was simply relegated to the shell. So each brand has had to exaggerate its outward appearance in order to be easily recognized.

Advertising products through the brand prism

Products are mute: the brand gives them meaning and purpose, telling us how a product should be read. A brand is both a prism and a magnifying glass through which products can be decoded. BMW invites us to perceive its models as 'cars for man's pleasure'. On the one hand, brands guide our perception of products. On the other hand, products send back a signal that brands use to underwrite and build their identity. The automobile industry is a case in point, as most technical innovations quickly spread among all brands. Thus the ABS system is offered by Volvo as well as by BMW, yet it cannot be said that they share the same identity. Is this a case of brand inconsistency? Not at all: ABS has simply become a must for all.

However, brands can only develop through long-term consistency, which is both the source and reflection of its identity. Hence the same ABS will not bear the same meaning for two different carmakers. For Volvo, which epitomizes total safety, ABS is an utter necessity serving the brand's values and obsessions: it encapsulates the brand's essence. BMW, which symbolizes high-performance, cannot speak of ABS in these terms: it would amount to denying the BMW ideology and value system which has inspired the whole organization and helped

FIGURE 2.6 Brands give innovations meaning and purpose

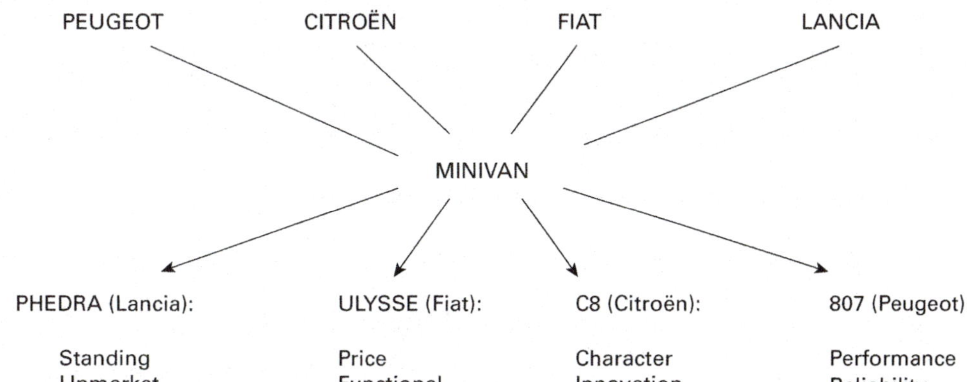

generate the famous models of the Munich brand. BMW introduced ABS as a way to go faster. Likewise, how did the safety-conscious brand, Volvo, justify its participation in the European leisure car championships? By saying 'We *really* test our products so that they last longer.'

The minivans of Peugeot, Citroën, Fiat and Lancia are built on a common platform. What role is left for the respective brands to play? Their role is to shape their own model with the intrinsic values of the brand – imagination and flair for Citroën, quality driving and reliability for Peugeot, high class and flair for Lancia, and practicality for Fiat. (See Figure 2.6.)

Thus brand identity never results from a detail, yet a detail can, once interpreted, serve to express a broader strategy. Details can only have an impact on a brand's identity if they are in synergy with it, echoing and amplifying the brand's values. That is why weak brands do not succeed in capitalizing on their innovations: they do not manage either to enhance the brand's meaning or create that all-important resonance.

A brand is thus a prism helping us to decipher products. It defines what and how much to expect from the products bearing its name. An innovation which would be considered very original for a Fiat, for instance, will be considered commonplace for a Ford. However, though insufficient engine power may scarcely have been an issue for many car-makers, for Peugeot it is a major problem. It disavows Peugeot's deeply-rooted identity and frustrates the expectations that have been raised. It would be at odds with what should be called Peugeot's 'brand obligations'.

In fact, consumers rarely evaluate innovations in an isolated way, but in relation to a specific brand. Once a brand has chosen a specific positioning or meaning, it has to assume all of its implications and fulfil its promises. Brands should respect the contract that made them successful by attracting customers. They owe it to them.

Brands versus other signs of quality

In many sectors, brands coexist with other quality signs. The food industry, for instance, is also filled with quality seals, certificates of norm compliance and controlled origin and guarantees. The proliferation of these other signs results from a double objective: to promote and to protect.

Certifications of origin (eg real Scotch whisky) are intended to protect a branch of agriculture and products whose quality is deeply rooted in a specific location and know-how. The controlled origin guarantee capitalizes on a subjective and cultural conception of quality, coupled with a touch of mystery and of the area's unique character. It segments the market by refusing the certification of origin to any goods that have not been produced within a certain area or raised in the traditional way. Thus in Europe since 2003, Feta cheese has been a name tied to a controlled Greek origin. Even if Danish or French cheese-makers were to produce a 'feta' cheese elsewhere that buyers were unable to tell apart from the feta cheese made in Greece in the traditional way, their products can no longer lay claim to the name 'feta'.

Quality seals are promotional tools. They convey a different concept of quality, which is both more industrial and scientific. In this respect, a given type of cheese, for example, involves objective know-how, using a certain kind of milk mixed with selected bacteria, etc. Quality seals create a vertical segmentation, consisting of different levels of objective quality. The issue here is not so much to present typical characteristics as to satisfy a stringent set of objective criteria.

The legal guarantee of typicality brought by a 'certified origin' seal means more than a simple designation of origin, a mere label indicating where a product comes from, in that the latter implies no natural or social specificity – although it may mislead the buyer into thinking that there is one. Moreover, several modern cheese-makers deliberately mix up what is genuine and what is not, inventing foreign names for their new products that are reminiscent of places or villages in an effort to build their own rustic, parochial imagery.

From the corporate point of view, choosing between brand policy and collective signs is a matter of strategy and of available resource allocation.

Often, quality certificates reduce perceived difference. Unknown small brands can also receive them. Brands define their own standards: legally, they guarantee nothing, but empirically they convey clusters of attributes and values. In doing so, they seek to become a reference in themselves, if not the one and only reference (as is the case with Bacardi, the epitome of rum). Thus, in essence, brands differentiate and share very little. Brands distinguish their products. Strong brands are those that diffuse values and manage to segment the market with their own means.

In handling the 'mad cow' crisis, McDonald's wondered whether they should rely on their own brand only or also on the collective signs and certificates of origin.

On an operational level, let us once again underline the fact that brands do not boil down to a mere act of advertising. They contain recommendations regarding the long-term specificities of the products bearing their name, such as attractive prices, efficient distribution and merchandizing, as well as identity building through advertising. It is easier for a small company to earn a quality seal for one of its products through strict efforts on quality, than it is to undertake the gruelling task of creating a brand, which requires so many financial, human, technical and commercial resources. Even without a brand, the small company's product can thus step out of the ordinary, thanks in part to the legal indicators of quality.

Obstacles to the implementation of branding

Within the same company, brand policy often conflicts with other policies. As these are unwritten and implicit, they may seem innocuous, when in fact they are a hindrance to a true brand policy.

Current corporate accounting, as such, is unfavourable towards brands. Accounting is ruled by the prudence principle: consequently, any outlay for which payback is uncertain is counted as an expense rather than valued as an asset. This is the case of investments made in communications in order to inform the general public about the brand's identity. Because it is impossible to measure exactly what share of the annual communications budget generates returns immediately, or within a specified number of years, the whole sum is taken as an operating expense which is subtracted from the financial year's profits. Yet advertising, like investments in machinery, talented staff and R&D, also helps build brand capital. Accounting thus creates a bias that handicaps brand companies because it projects an undervalued image of them. Take the case of company A, which invests heavily to develop the awareness and renown of its brand name. Having to write off this investment as an expense results in low annual profits and a small asset value on the balance sheet. This usually occurs during a critical period in the company's growth, when it could actually use some help from outside investors and bankers. Now compare A to company B, which invests the same amounts in machines and production and nothing whatsoever in either name, image or renown. As it is allowed to value these tangible investments as fixed assets and to depreciate them gradually over several years, B can announce higher profits and its balance sheet, displaying bigger assets, will project a more flattering image. B will thus look better in terms of accounting, when, in fact, A is in a better position to differentiate its products.

The principle of annual accounting also hinders brand policy. Every product manager is judged on his yearly results and on the net contribution generated by his product. This leads to 'short-termism' in decision making: those decisions which produce fast, measurable results are favoured over those that build up brand capital, slowly no doubt, but more reliably in the long term. Moreover, product-based accounting discourages product managers from putting out any additional advertising effort that would serve essentially to bolster the brand as a whole, when the latter serves as an umbrella and sign for other products. Managers thus only focus on one thing: any new expenditure in the general interest will be charged to their own account statement. For example, Palmolive is a brand covering several products: liquid detergent, shampoo, shaving cream, etc. The brand could decide to communicate only one of these products singled out as a prominent image leader, capitalizing on image spillover reciprocal effects (Balachander, 2003). But the investment made would certainly be higher than could be justified solely by the sales forecast of that product. This new expenditure will in fact always be on the given product, even though its ultimate purpose is to collectively benefit all products under the umbrella brand.

In order to react against the short-term bias caused by accounting practices and the underestimation of (corporate) value as shown in the balance sheets, some British companies have begun to list their own brands as assets on their balance sheets. This has triggered a discussion on the fundamental validity of accounting practices that emerged in the 'age of commodities', when the essential part of capital consisted of real estate and equipment. Today, on the contrary, intangible assets (know-how, patents, reputation) are what make the difference in the long run. Beyond the need for an open debate in Europe and the United States on how to capitalize brands, it has become just as important to find a way for companies to account for the long-term pros and cons of short-term brand decisions in their books. It is all the more compelling as brand decision-makers themselves rotate often, perhaps too often.

Even the way in which the various types of communication agencies are organized fails to comply with the requirements of sound brand policy. Even if an advertising agency has its own network of partner companies – in charge of proximity marketing, CRM, e-business and so on – and can thus promote itself as an integrated communications group, it remains the crux of the network. Furthermore, advertising agencies think only in terms of campaigns, operating in a short, one-year time frame. Brand policy is different: it develops over a long period and requires that all means be considered at once, in a fully integrated way.

It is clear that a company rarely finds contacts inside so-called communications groups who are actually in charge of strategic thinking and of providing overall recommendations rather than merely focusing on advertising or on the necessity to sell campaigns. Moreover, advertising agencies are not in a position to address strategic issues, such as what should be the optimal number of brands in a portfolio. As these affect the survival of the brands that are under their advertising responsibility, the agencies find themselves in the awkward position of being judge and jury. That is why a new profession has been created: strategic brand management consulting. The time had indeed come for companies to meet professionals with a mid-term vision who are capable of providing consistent, integrated guidelines for the development of brand portfolios without focusing on one single technique.

A high personnel turnover disrupts the continuity a brand needs. Yet companies today actually plan for their personnel to rotate on different brands! Thus, brands are often entrusted to young graduates with impressive degrees but little experience and the promotion they expect often consists of being assigned to yet another brand! Thus, product managers must achieve visible results in the short term. This helps to explain why there are so many changes in advertising strategy and implementation as well as in decisions on brand extension, promotion or discounts. These are in fact caused by changes in personnel.

It is significant that brands that have maintained a continuous and homogeneous image belong to companies with stable brand decision makers. This is the case for luxury brands: the long-lasting presence of the creator or founder allows for sound, long-term management. The same is true of major retailers where senior managers often handle the communication themselves or at least make the final decisions. As a means to alleviate the effects of excessive brand manager rotation, companies aim not only at incorporating brand value into their accounts, but also at creating a long-term brand image charter. The latter represents both a vital safeguard and an instrument of continuity.

Another syndrome pertains to the relationship between production and sales. In the Electrolux group, for instance, production units are specialized according to product. Both mono-product and multi-market, they sell their product to the sales units who are, on the contrary, mono-market and multi-product (grouped under an umbrella brand). The problem is that these autonomous sales divisions, who each have their own brand, all want to benefit from the latest product innovation so as to maximize their division's turnover. What is missing is a structure for managing and allocating innovations in accordance with a consistent and global vision of the brand portfolio. As we will see later, there is no point in entrusting a strong innovation to a weak brand. Moreover, this undermines the very basis of the brand concept: differentiation.

Lastly, if words mean anything at all, communications managers should have the power to prevent actions that go against the brand's interest. Thus, Philips never succeeded in fully taking advantage of its former brand baseline: 'Philips, tomorrow is already here'. In order to do so, they would have needed to ban all advertising on batteries or electric light bulbs that either trivialized the assertion, contradicted it, or reduced it to mere advertising hype. It would also have been possible to communicate only about future bulb types rather than about the best current sales. Unfortunately, nobody in the organization had the power (or the desire) to impose these kinds of constraints. When the Whirlpool brand appeared, however, the managers from Philips actually created the organization they needed for implementing a real brand policy: as it was directly linked to general management, the communications department was able to ensure the optimal circumstances for launching the Whirlpool brand, by banning over a three-year period any communication about a commonplace product or even a best-selling product.

Failing to manage innovations has a very negative impact on brand equity. Even though salespeople go up in arms when they are not given the responsibility of a strong innovation, it is a mistake to assign the latter to a weak brand, especially in multi-brand groups. When dealing with a weak brand, attractive pricing must indeed be offered to distributors as an incentive to include the latter in their reference listing. But since the brand's consumers do not expect this innovation (each brand defines its type and level of consumer expectations), the product turnover is insufficient. As for the non-buyers, such a brand is not reassuring. If the innovation is launched a few weeks later under a leading brand name, distributors will refuse to pay for the price premium due to a leader because they purchased it at a lower price just a while back from the same company. Thus, even with the strong brand, the sales price eventually has to be cut.

Breeding many strong brands, l'Oréal allocates its inventions to its various businesses according to brand potency. Innovation is thus first entrusted to prestigious brands sold in selective channels as the products' high prices will help cancel out the high research cost incurred. Thus, liposomes were first commercialized by Lancôme, the new sun filter Mexoryl SX by Vichy. Innovation is then diffused to the other channels and eventually to the large retailers. By then, the selective channel brands are already likely to have launched another differentiating novelty.

However, this process is affected by the fact that innovation is not exclusively owned by any one company; it quickly spreads to competitors, which calls for immediate reaction.

Along the same lines, when a producer supplies a distributor's brand with the same product it sells under its own brand, it will eventually erode its brand equity and, more generally, the very respectability of the concept of a brand. This simply means that what customers pay more for in a brand is the name and nothing else. When the brand is dissociated from the product it enhances and represents, it becomes merely superficial and artificial, devoid of any rational legitimacy. Ultimately, companies pay a price for this as sales decrease and distributors seize the opportunity to declare in their advertising that national brands alienate consumers, but that consumers can resist by purchasing distributors' own-brands. This also justifies the sluggishness of public authorities regarding the increasing amount of counterfeit products among distributors' own-brands. Finally, such practices foster a false collective understanding of what brands are, even among opinion leaders, which contributes to the rumour that nowadays all products are just the same!

Asia's branding culture

There is an Asian paradox about brands. Asia has become the factory of the world, and now Asian brands invade the world. Despite their success measured in terms of market share and often market dominance, these brands still lack dream power and intrinsic desirability. Do consumers dream of having a Samsung Galaxy S as much as others dream of an Apple iPhone?

Another paradox is that Asians have a love affair with brands, but mostly with Western ones (at least for fashion and luxury).

We should not look at Asia with the eyes of the West, but must be sensitive to its culture and economic environment. It is important that those teaching executive seminars in China, Korea, Japan and India avoid caricatures in analysing the situation. Can one lump these four remarkable countries into one global concept called Asia? With regard at least to Japan and Korea, their strengths are well known:

- a fantastic belief in the future, which is a reflection of the young demography;
- through education and a remarkable ability to copy, reaching the level of the 'master' and later bypassing the master;
- a speed to action once decisions are made;
- collective decision-making processes, ensuring adhesion.

A typical facet of Asian brands however is that they tend to be corporate or at least umbrella brands. In Asia, corporate size is a factor of respect, and is tied to the oligopolistic nature of the economy, itself inherited from the political structure. As a result, companies tend to use their name in the many sectors they address, as diversified conglomerates. Japanese and Korean countries are also obsessed by quality and the cult of detail. Because they are too often used as low-cost factories for cost reduction purposes by Western brands, Chinese companies have not yet developed a focus on high quality, with the exception of craftsmanship for the luxury and art industry.

Now strengths can also be weaknesses. Copying the master, when held as a cardinal virtue since primary school, does not encourage managerial creativity, and differentiation. However, it has led to the successful launch of Lexus, certainly helped by the advance of hybrid engines. In Korea it has made a local brand, Bean Pole, the main competitor of Ralph Lauren. Fear of losing one's face in public certainly promotes conformism both inside the company and outside (which is why there are so many Louis Vuitton bags in Tokyo). The importance given to consensus impedes fast decision making and also proper brand management. Since brand management means having the power to say no, all cultures that try to avoid conflict will be reluctant to sometimes say no (when the decision is in conflict with the brand values, for instance).

Finally, we have found that the brand platforms of Asian brands are often not sharp enough, but are wrapped in global consensual terms. The brand platform is the cornerstone of brand management (see page 173): a single-page statement of what the brand wants to stand for. Most often this document is written with great care and attention paid to formal inner coherence, but nothing is really inspiring. Grandiloquent 'brand essences' are proposed that surely boost self-pride inside the companies but just look like overused words from outside (such as the 'relentless passion to inspire lives' or the 'utmost quality for life').

Now to avoid oversimplification, we should remember that, despite these so-called deficiencies, Asian companies have produced many powerful brands: Nikon, Canon, Ricoh, Sony, Yamaha, Lexus, Toyota, Toshiba, Samsung, LG, Shiseido, Sue Uemura, Sulwhasoo, La Neige, SK2, Wills, Mittal, etc. New car brands, such as Kia and Hyundai, are emerging, and using their main asset: quality and value for money.

A good case to analyse is Samsung, a remarkable brand turnaround. This brand, which few people wanted to buy some 20 years ago, had become number one or two in most product categories of consumer electronics in Europe in 2010. It is not a low-cost brand, but gained its broad appeal by its value for money and technological innovations. Samsung provides the latest technologies at an interesting price, and hence its success in integrated distribution. Its trade relations are excellent too.

But still one does not dream of Samsung. Why?

- First its commercial success has happened fast: brand building needs more time. Samsung aimed at a market share success, with now a desire to trade up. But the brand is a popular one. Instead Canon and Nikon started by selling to the elite and only later traded down to increase their volume.

- Samsung, like most Asian companies, is highly centralized, and exclusively Korean in its management despite being aimed at the world. There are no Westerners on its board or in important strategic positions, in which it differs from Sony. It creates distance: its products are felt to come from far away, exported by a company with no face.
- Local subsidiaries are distribution companies. Their job is to receive the innovations of the year and to promote them in the channels of distribution and through media advertising. However, since this year's innovation replaces that of last year, there is no capitalization.
- The focus is not on the brand but on the products, which themselves change from one year to another. It is very significant that, in the campaign to promote the Samsung Galaxy against Apple's iPhone, 'Galaxy' was written in big characters and 'Samsung' in small ones. This is just the reverse of what Apple did.
- Samsung innovations are not disruptive. Galaxy looks very much like another iPhone.
- Communication is centralized in Seoul. That is why, locally, Samsung communication does not create much emotion. There is no local freedom or budget, at the country level, to build emotional intangibles.

What about the future? We know some advanced Asian companies are already very conscious of the above-mentioned problems. Some of them have even decided to develop creativity sessions – the Western way (see Osborne, 1963). Since organisms can survive only by adapting to the environment, one can predict that, once the limits of a model are reached, some Asian companies will change faster than others. China for instance has a fantastic asset: its demographic size and educational system. Some companies there have ten times more PhDs than L'Oréal. In R&D, size matters, and the chances of making breakthrough innovations are increased. China's low-cost structure also makes it very suitable to market at the bottom of the pyramid. There is a huge growth opportunity there. Now it is well known that brands at the base of the pyramid do not create as many dreams as those at the top. So what?

Other companies have reacted by creating a new position in the organization, so far managed as a group of independent silos: a brand VP. Up until 2001, there was no management of the Toshiba brand. The company organization was based on a branched structure, and thus no one was responsible for the cross-company resource that was the brand. The medical branch had one view of Toshiba, while the PC branch had another, and so on. There was no coordination or global brand platform, or an insignificant one with global catch-all terminology. The name of the game was to sell as many imported products as possible, not to build the brand. It was perhaps hypothesized that the brand would grow as a side benefit of a high market share. Regional managers' remuneration packages were calculated on sales, not on brand equity progression.

The final question is: should Asian brands look like Western ones? It is often said that high-equity brands must be global, but most of the US so-called high-equity brands were local for decades. McDonald's was invented by and for Americans. The same holds true for Wal-Mart. These brands had no stores outside the United States and yet, because of the size of the US domestic market, were already world number one in size. They just rolled out their US marketing mix later, internationally.

The same happens to Asian brands, quite unknown by Westerners, but held as local heroes or icons.

A second question is that of expansion: should Asian brands try to sell to the West or should they aim first at their neighbours with close cultural ties? The Korean skin care brand Sulwhasoo, promoting Korean medicine, is closer to China than to the United States.

Finally, much of traditional brand theorizing has been moulded by product-brand examples, like detergent brands Tide, Ariel, Persil and Dash (one brand for one product). This early theorizing made the brand a synonym of a single-minded proposition, promise or benefit. In line with their culture, Asian brands seem to promote more values than mental associations with the product class. This is also true of Western brands with a wide scope, such as Nestlé, Heinz or Nivea.

03 Brand and business models

How do companies grow both the brand and business? What does it take to build a brand? What are the necessary steps and phases? In this chapter we address these questions with a particular emphasis on integration of efforts. Brand building is not done apart, it is the result of a clear strategy and of excellence in implementation at the product, price, place, people and communication levels. There are prerequisites before a brand can be built, and they need to be understood.

Are brands for all companies? Yes

The brand is not an end in itself. It needs to be managed for what it is – an instrument for company growth and profitability, a business tool. Does branding affect all companies? Yes. Are all companies aware of this? No. For many industrial companies or commodity sellers, the concept of the brand applies only to mass markets, high-consumption products and the fast-moving consumer goods (FMCG) sector. This is a misconception. A brand is a name that influences buyers and prescribers alike. Industrial brands have their own markets: Air Liquide sells to industry, Somfy sells its tubular motors to window-blind installers and fitters, Saint Gobain Gypsum and Lafarge sell to companies and craftspeople in the construction and public works sectors, and Senoble is famous among retailers for the quality of its trade relationships (it produces only for retail brands).

The benefits of being a brand: magazines as brands

Why be a brand? Everyone and everything now want to be seen as brands: towns, countries, celebrities, universities, sports clubs, museums, etc. The meaning of a brand has certainly changed: it used to mean Persil or Tide, Mars or Activia, that is to say product brands. Today it means a name with personality, the power of influence, being driven by values, and a source of innovations that give birth to a community. Thus corporations are brands in many ways beyond their own market; they become models in corporate social responsibility (CSR) or aspirations for young graduates who wish to be hired by them, the pathway to their professional success and accomplishment.

The best way to illustrate the benefits of being a brand is to consider an example. Magazines can be brands. Not all of them are, of course. Some magazines are only products. They exploit a formula. For instance, there are many magazines showing the times of television programmes. One of them may show the programmes for a two-week period. It may sell very well and have high loyalty rates. However, that does not make it a brand: it is a unique and well-differentiated product, but it creates no specific emotional ties with its public.

When is a magazine a brand? It is a brand when it is much more than a magazine. *Vogue* is the world authority on fashion: young women wear T-shirts branded *Vogue*. The same holds true for *Elle*, symbolizing the Parisian woman's magazine, with magazine editions all around the world and a large number of licences for accessories. In Asia there is *Elle* Baby, *Elle* Petite, *Elle* for Man, *Elle* Active Wear, *Elle* Sport, *Elle* Home, *Elle* Decoration and *Elle* à Table (cuisine and restaurants) plus a premium licence *Elle* Paris. *Elle* manages 250 licensees, and earns annually 20 million euros in royalties (for an equivalent of 400 million euros in sales at wholesale level).

GEO is known as a magazine. It is also a real brand. The magazine is a global brand, with local publications in many countries. The first *GEO* was published in 1976 by Prisma Press. It promotes self-discovery through travel, and emphasizes the discovery of other people too, more than the landscapes. Hence it is not just a magazine with postcard views. Its content is as important as its pictures. Little by little, year after year, *GEO* has gained brand awareness, respect and authority even among the people who do not read it, and has become a moral reference. It is much more than a good product; it is a view on the world (not of the world).

In all countries, *GEO* is called *GEO* and is written as such, even in Russia. The marque is also green everywhere, and the layout is the same. The brand physical identity is consistent across the world and through time. *GEO* has set a number of strict guidelines for its copywriters, photographers and authors, who embody the magazine's specific values.

For a magazine, what are the benefits of being a brand? First, it enhances the perception of exclusivity. Readers feel this is an unsubstitutable product. Second, it is a springboard for diversification (line extensions and brand extensions), business that is often more profitable than the core business.

As a result, *GEO* is valuable and uses its reputation to extend its range. What are the line extensions of this brand?

- *GEO* travel guides;
- *GEO* illustrated books;
- *GEO* history;
- *GEO* with a regional focus;
- *GEO* teenagers (licensing).

GEO now licenses its name to fostering discovery travel, stationery, calendars and diaries. In co-branding, sponsorship is a full-time activity there. Seen as much more than a magazine, the brand is asked to endorse events and films. This raises it well above the mass of other titles of photography and travel magazines. It also has a feedback effect that reinforces its special ethical status.

In the same sector, *National Geographic* acts as a luxury brand (Kapferer and Bastien, 2009). It is a rare product, with a 120-year heritage, representing exploration without limits. It is read by an elite, happy few (although it is not expensive), it fully controls its articles (80 per cent are produced in-house), and its photographs become icons of art. It now extends to a cruise boat, the *National Geographic Explorer*, which offers visits to less-known parts of the world. A greatly respected brand, the *National Geographic* is highly sought after for co-branding purposes.

Differentiating a commodity by the brand

Brands are an economic concept that was produced by the industrial revolution. Most markets were commodity markets. In fact economic theory talks only about commodities, optimal pricing to reach equilibrium conditions, and the difficulty of long-term differentiation between suppliers. Branding is the only strategy to get out of commodity markets. This is why economic theory does not like brands.

As a rule people tend to say that a commodity market is one where differentiation is impossible. The market is driven by price alone and maybe corporate reputation to secure the buyers. The brutal truth is that a commodity market is one where no one has invested enough in differentiation. It is a lazy market. Now we do not mean that no one has advertised, as is too often believed, but that no one has thought of a new 'value curve' for a specific target. A 'value curve' is a specific set of utilities delivered by the brand to a chosen and well-delineated target. One does not differentiate a market all at once, but little by little. Major worldwide brands are brands that first decommoditized their market:

- Coca-Cola is nothing but a syrup with carbonates added to water. As such the physical product is a commodity. Although the formula is said to be secret, it can be copied and even bypassed. In blind tastings Pepsi-Cola got better ratings to the point of leading the Coca-Cola Company to make the marketing blunder of the century (launching a 'new Coke'). How did Coke differentiate the commodity? By the brand and distribution. Both were needed. One was not enough. The business model of Coke, too often overlooked, is to control consumer behaviour by having a local monopoly. In most bars in the world you find Coke, not Pepsi. This is typical of B2B marketing. The trade (bars, restaurants, etc) do not want to offer choice to their consumers but to simplify their task. The Coca-Cola Company or its local bottlers provide the whole range of soft drinks they need, thus creating a barrier to entry to competition even if it has a 'better' product. Thus, having secured volume, the local bottlers, acting exclusively for the Coca-Cola Company, could invest in massive consumer communication to make the brand top of mind and well liked. The brand promise is non-tangible: 'enjoy happiness together'.

- Evian water, the world's number one premium water, started as a modest company in a world dominated by tap water. Water was water. Evian capitalized by means of a major deep insight: mothers fear for the health of their newborn babies. As a result, they fear tap water, which has a taste (because of the special mechanical and chemical treatments to purify it). They do not want a medical thermal water (with an imbalance of mineral ingredients): the differentiating factor of Evian is precisely that it has no internal differentiation. Its minerals are balanced, with no specific effect promised (unlike Contrex water, which promises slimness, or Hepar for liver problems). Evian capitalized on fear of the non-purity of water, but instead of just selling purified water, as in the United States or the UK, Evian added that 'minerals' were good for babies. It capitalized on two highly symbolic ingredients:
  - the Alps as the magic purifier of water, acting throughout centuries;
  - the minerals (like symbolic bricks) to build the body of the newborn.

  Because the mineral profile of Evian was bland, mothers had nothing to fear. This is how Evian started: the only water for babies. Then later, they had the wisdom not to stay in this niche, but to follow the growth of the child, up to the adult. Evian is today positioned as a source of youth, capitalizing on its early identity.
- Services are a classic way to differentiate commodities in B2B. To fight against low-cost suppliers that suppress all services in order to reach the lowest cost and offer a price-killing proposition, there is no other solution than to invest in intangibles: services plus image reputation. Business credit cards fight by proposing to be more than cards but rather partners in cost control, accounting, funds and flow management, etc. Air Liquide, like Linde or Air Products, makes 80 per cent of its profits on 20 per cent of its volume. Eighty per cent of the volume is a commodity (bottled oxygen for hospitals, for instance), but the company develops tailor-made speciality gases for niches identified as mainstream segments. These niches are price insensitive: the fresh food industry seeks a special gas to sustain the crispiness of packaged salad leaves for more than a week, as does the retailer.

A final example is public utilities: electricity, for instance. Everyone is now thinking low-cost, and new entrants fight on the lowest cost possible. However, in Germany Yello thought and acted differently, to avoid price competition. It is a very good example of what an experiential brand should be: it does not talk about values, but enacts them and makes its customers live them too.

Decommoditizing by an experiential brand: Yello

What colour is electricity? Yellow, says Yello. This German company and brand now has 1.3 million clients. Is it a low-cost operator? No. A green operator then? No.

Yello, a subsidiary of EnBW, the regional electricity company of Baden-Württemberg, is one of the few success stories of decommoditization. Electricity is typically what one would call a commodity. After the era of national or regional monopolies came the low-cost operators, offering the lowest costs.

Instead the Yello Strom company decided to capitalize on consumers' experience, backed up by the technology of Microsoft and by a brand, Yello. It has made Yello the prototype of the experiential brand, that is to say a brand that creates at all contact points feelings of delight and satisfaction that add up to build a coherent whole and make people forget price somehow.

The strategic insight was simple: consumers receive their bill four times a year and each time spend on average ten minutes reading it, after having looked at the price they have to pay at the bottom of the bill. It meant Yello had four times ten minutes per year to make a break. This was the moment of truth, the apex of consumer experience with the new brand.

Instead of fighting on price against low-cost operators, Yello created value, and delivered a pleasant experience while reading the bill. First, Yello had to be yellow. All buildings, offices, cars, bills, letters, etc are yellow. The virtual hostess on the website, called Eve, is dressed in yellow. Now you do not convince more than a million German consumers to switch to Yello just because of the colour. Yello worked with Microsoft to be the first to install intelligent meters, clearly visible in the basement of buildings because of their colour. Most importantly, these meters allow an online permanent check of consumption, room by room, with access to time series of consumption by period. The bills themselves present in a readable and pleasant way historical back data that enable money to be saved next time by working on those usages or plugs that are heaviest in electricity use as indicated by the intelligent bills received. In brief, Yello is not very cheap, but it gives consumers all the information to save by better controlling their consumption, room per room, quarter after quarter. As indicated in Figure 3.1, Yello does not differentiate the product itself (electricity), but the services and consumer experience (the intelligent bill, the call centre, the communication, the vans, the pleasantness of staff, the colour, etc).

We live in an experience society. The success of Starbucks is due to the customer experience: it is made every day by the two persons working in each Starbucks. They deliver the unique experience. This is why Starbucks never advertises: advertising money goes into staff training instead. Staff members are not naturally good at creating the Starbucks experience. That is why a lot of training is needed, not advertising. How to create consumer

FIGURE 3.1 How to build an electricity brand: Yello

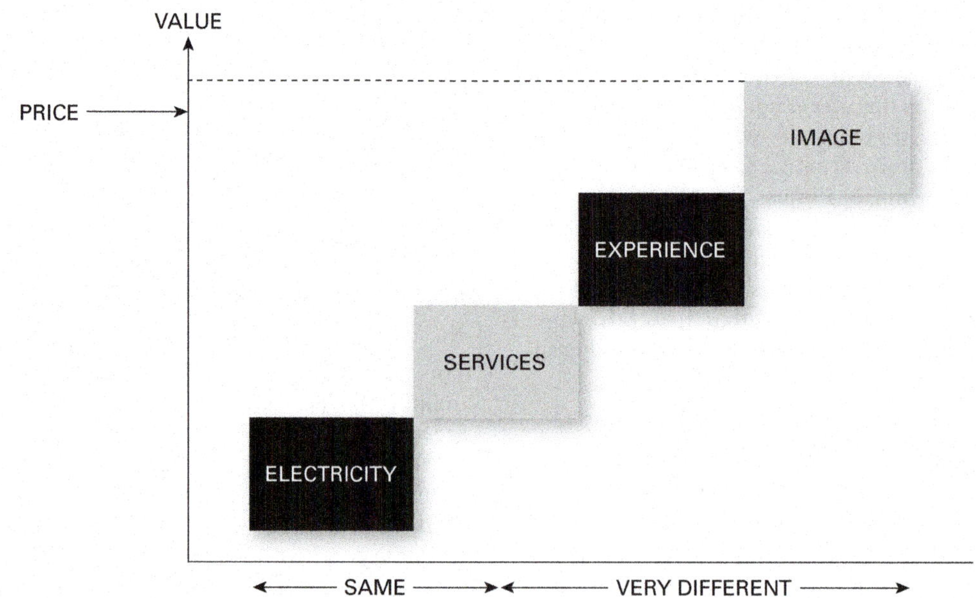

delight? This is not so much a problem of cream or coffee as a question of attitude vis-à-vis the client. As Howard Schultz, Starbucks CEO, once said, 'I am not in the business of coffee, serving people. I am in the business of people, serving coffee.'

Building a market leader without advertising: Jacob's Creek wine

What does it take to build a brand? Brand definitions are innumerable (see the discussion on page 12), and almost every author in the field has his or her own. Although they can be useful, definitions tell us very little about how to build a brand. Definitions are static: they take the brand for granted. Building the brand is dynamic.

In general, in our executive seminars, when we ask attendees how to build a market-leading brand, typical answers include advertise, create an image, and develop awareness. They are mostly answers that focus on communication.

Instead of answering that question frontally, we shall look at an interesting case: how did an unknown Australian company, Orlando Wyndham, build the UK's leading bottled wine brand, Jacob's Creek? This brand is now the leader in volume and the leader in spontaneous brand awareness, with a very strong image. All that was achieved without mass-market advertising before 2000. It is most interesting also to note that between 1984 and 2000, the UK wine market doubled in size. What then was needed to create a successful wine brand in the UK mass market?:

- The first condition is to have enough volume. Addressing the mass market means being able to fulfil trade expectations. Multiple retailers hate to deal with companies that cannot provide sufficient supply if a product is a success. For a wine maker this means being able to rely on a very large supply source.
- The second condition is to secure a stable quality. The first role of any brand is to reduce perceived risk: the consumer experience must be the same whenever and wherever the product is bought. (This is why branding services is tougher than branding tangible products: human variability works against this stability.) For a wine maker, it means mastering the art of blending, to make sure consumer expectations are not betrayed. Once consumers discover they like a specific wine taste, their repurchase indicates a willingness to reduce risk and re-find the same taste, the same pleasure.
- For a mass-market brand, price is key: it must be mainstream. Everything must be done, at the back office level, to ensure higher productivity, and hence a lower production cost, while not altering the quality and taste.
- It is essential to be end-user driven, and find the right taste for the particular market. Many UK consumers are not long-practised wine drinkers. Their tastes have been shaped by cold soft drinks and beer. This means that they prefer wines with a specific taste and in-mouth profile. In addition, if an organization hits the right local expectations it can expect to obtain good publicity, medals and press coverage, thus reinforcing the trade support.
- One should also create barriers to entry. Success stimulates copying. Barriers are achieved in two ways:
  - a 'blue ocean strategy', choosing a bundle of benefits that French wines could not imitate (here an adaptation for the local taste of new drinkers);
  - moving fast to become the reference name of the sub-category one creates (here New World wines).
- Another requirement is a national sales force. Wine is mostly chosen at the point of purchase. On-shelf visibility and point-of-purchase advertising are success factors. It is important to draw up national agreements with the major multiple retailers (in this case Sainsbury, Asda, Tesco and a few others) to achieve this, but even when these are in place a day-to-day check needs to be carried out, store by store, to make sure everything is in place. Only a national sales force can achieve this. In addition, an intensive wet trial phase

is needed, to encourage customers to pause in wandering up and down the store aisles and taste the product. This too requires a national sales force.

These six steps to build a brand in the market may seem straightforward and easy to follow. Actually they are not. French wines could not meet the conditions, while New World wines, and Australian wines in particular, could. Let us examine why, for each condition.

Old World wines are based on one principle. The quality of the wine is totally dependent on natural factors: the specific type of soil, the sun, the climate, the air. As a consequence, hundreds of wines have been created, differentiated by the wine-growing area, or even specific vineyard, from which they come, and its unique characteristics. Each vineyard claims its soil is better than that of competitors, for example. As a consequence, the product is fragmented. For example, behind each of the 5,000 marques of Bordeaux wine there is a different grower, usually rather small. This prevents suppliers from responding to the first condition for building a brand: enough volume.

Old World wines have tried to secure their market leadership by transforming their wine-producing practices into laws. Producing a Burgundy or a Bordeaux wine means obeying these laws. What was intended as a quality control system has become a major block against innovating to address the competition from emerging growing areas.

If a wine is to be called a Pauillac, a Graves or whatever (these are subregions within Bordeaux), its producers are not permitted to mix the grapes from this region with grapes grown anywhere else, or only at a very small level. If one season is dry they cannot irrigate; nor can they add chemicals to moderate the differences in quality caused by differences in climate from year to year. Because they respect these laws, Old World wines have an inherent variability: they are the true produce of nature, more than the produce of man. There is much more variety of soils and variance in climate from year to year in Europe than in Australia, California or Argentina, and this too leads to differences between one Old World wine and another.

Branding means suppressing this variability: to secure the same taste from year to year, one must master the art of blending grapes coming from very different soils – and regions, if one of them is underproducing. Australia, as a relatively newly settled country without a long wine-growing tradition, had few laws governing wine producing; it could do it. It was not so for wine makers from Bordeaux or Burgundy.

The same holds true for getting the right quality at low production costs. French wine makers are not allowed to use mechanized harvesting: they are required to harvest by hand. They cannot irrigate, and so radically increase the productivity of their soils; they cannot make use of chemical additives. In France too, wine is stored in barrels as a rule. In Australia wine is kept in huge aluminium tanks, and wood cuttings are put in the wine: there is more wood surface in contact with the wine, which accelerates the process of giving the wine the right 'woody' taste. Time being money, this reduces production costs.

Point four concerns getting the right taste to appeal to the target market. New World wines have no tradition to respect: they started from the customer. They adapted their product to the taste of customers in emerging markets, used to drinking soft drinks and beer. Their wine had to be fruit-driven, very soft, very smooth, easy to drink for all occasions. Some varietals (types of grape) such as Chardonnay and Semillon Chardonnay could deliver such a taste. These were not the varieties that made the reputation of Bordeaux or Burgundy wines.

One other dimension of being client-driven is language. Marketing research showed that the English were still broadly an 'island race': many of them are not well versed in European languages and the cultural traditions of Continental Europe. Unlike the maze of thousands of hard-to-pronounce wine names from Europe, Jacob's Creek is an English name, and the wording on the wine labels is written in English. Until recently French wines rarely provided any labelling information in English. Furthermore, Australia is part of the Commonwealth, and some English people identify more closely with it than with France.

In addition, each New World country has become associated with a small number of grape varieties. This means that consumers find it easier to forecast the taste of an Australian wine than of a French wine. The country of origin adds its own risk-reducing role to the brand.

Last but not least, the industry's organization in the Old World is too fragmented. Individual growers cannot afford a dedicated sales force even in their homeland. Even when the wine is produced by cooperatives of growers, the coops tend to want to remain independent and refuse to join larger organizations, the only viable path to reaching the critical size to create a brand.

As a result, in the 16 years to 2001, Australian wines, led by Jacob's Creek, went from zero to a 16.9 per cent share by volume and a 20.1 per cent share by value of the British market. Meanwhile the market doubled in size. Interestingly, as is shown by the value share being higher than the volume share, price is not the main reason consumers choose Australian wines. The New World growers have succeeded in persuading customers to trade up, by offering higher quality brand extensions designed to appeal to former novice wine drinkers who are now willing to explore more complex wines.

Can Old World wines come back and stop their sharp decline? As long as they do not suppress their internally based regulations, their production laws, and do not encourage supplier concentration, they will not be able to fulfil the five conditions for building brands. Bordeaux and Burgundy cannot do it. However, the Languedoc wine-growing region is the biggest in the world. As such it fulfils the first condition. In this region, which historically produced lower-status wine than Bordeaux and Burgundy, there are very few production rules to obey. The future is in the hands of Languedoc's growers if they can concentrate and meet customers' requirements, not only in the UK but also in Japan, Korea and other countries with a growing market for wine. They might also export their know-how and build brands where the future market is: China. This is why so many players are signing joint ventures with Chinese companies and authorities, to grow grapes in China and develop brands that have none of the Old World wine industry's self-imposed limitations.

What lessons can be drawn and generalized? New World wine brands have succeeded because they innovated, breaking with the competition's conventions for consumer profit. They have not stopped innovating and disrupting conventions. In Australia, Jacob's Creek recently introduced screw cap closures on its Riesling varieties, abandoning a sacred cow: cork closure. Riesling is more likely than wines from some other grape varieties to be affected by problems of cork quality, and half-bottles are especially vulnerable. Both consumers and the trade reacted favourably to this small but revolutionary innovation.

A second lesson is that a part of Jacob's Creek appeal was based on one enduring weakness of competition: it was not an elitist brand, and it had no snob value. It was approachable for everybody. It created a blue ocean!

The product's quality–price ratio was excellent, attracting praise from experts and taste makers. This is an endless race: each year the brand continues to improve the quality, thus winning continuous publicity. Since it was the first of the major Australian wine exporters, Jacob's Creek benefited from the 'pioneer advantage', and became the symbol of Australian wine. Interestingly, Orlando Wyndham, the company that owns the brand, is far smaller than some of its Australian competitors such as Hardy's, but all its energy and efforts were focused on this one single brand.

Many brands have developed by contact and retail without advertising: Google, Zara, Amazon. This is not the only brand-building model. Yellow Tail became the number one wine brand in the United States thanks to a huge advertising campaign, a fun personality and a price which strongly motivated its main distributor. In addition it was aimed at the wide field of non-experts in wine.

Brand building: from product to values, and vice versa

It takes time to build a really strong brand. There are two routes, two models for doing so: from product advantage to intangible values, or from values to product. However, with time, this two-way movement becomes the essence of brand management: brands have two legs.

Most brands did not start as such: their founders just wanted to create a business, based on a very specific product or service: an innovation, a good idea to start their business and open the distributors' closed doors. Through time, their name or the name of the product became a brand: well known and endowed with market power (the ability to influence buyers). It did not simply designate a product or a person, but little by little came to be associated with imagery, with intangible benefits,

FIGURE 3.2 The two routes for building the brand ladder through time

Intangible values

Mission, vision
Brand heritage
Brand culture
Brand territory
Brand personality
Customer's image
...
Unique benefit
Unique promise
Unique attributes
...
Unique ingredients

Tangible values

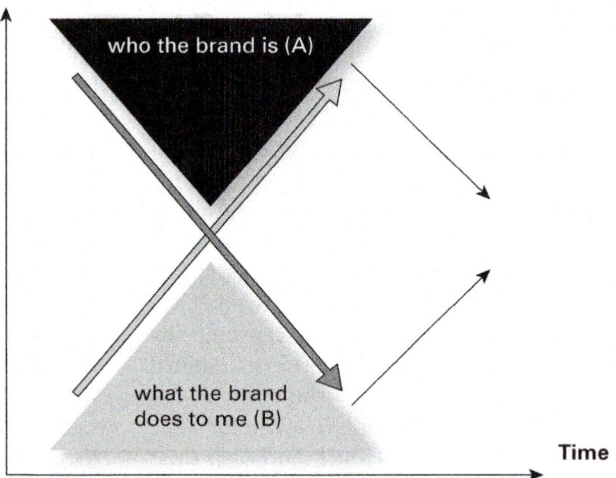

with brand personality and so on. Perception had moved upwards from objects to benefits, from tangible to intangible values.

As is shown by the upward-pointing arrow (A) in Figure 3.2, most brands start not as brands but as a name on an innovative product or service. Nike started out as a meaningless name on a pair of innovative running shoes: if they had not been innovative no distributor would have paid attention to Phil Knight in the first place. With time, that name acquired awareness, status and trust, if not respect or liking. This is the result of all the communication and stars which accompanied the business building. Little by little an inversion takes place in the process: instead of the product building the brand awareness and reputation (the bottom-up arrow of influence), it is the brand that differentiates and endows the product/service with its unique values (the top-down dotted arrow). In fact at this time the brand determines which new products match its desired image. Nike is now in the phase of brand extensions: the brand has stretched from running shoes to sports apparel and now golf clubs.

Through time, brand associations typically move up a ladder (the vertical axis of Figure 3.2), from ingredient (Dove with hydrating cream) to attribute (softening), to benefit (protection), to brand personality, brand values and even mission (Apple or Virgin have a mission), at the very top intangible end.

Now this does not mean that, with time, brand management should not be concerned with material issues and differentiation any more. Brands are two-legged. Even luxury brands, bought for the sake of show, must give their buyers the feeling that they have bought a great product and that the price difference is legitimate. But material differentiation is a never-ending race: competitors copy your best ideas. Attaching the brand to an intangible value adds value and prevents substitutability. The Mercedes price premium is permanently explained by product-based advertising copy, but also by PR operations that accentuate the unique status of the brand.

This first brand-building model concerns brands that started as a product. There exists a second model of brand building: many brands start as concepts or ideas. This is true of all licensed brands (Paloma Picasso perfume, Harry Potter products and so on) and of many fashion brands, spirits or cigarette brands. The Axe/Lynx men's hygiene line started from an insight as well: teenagers feel insecure about their sex appeal.

This second model (B) also provides a reminder that even when launching a product brand (that is, a brand based on a product advantage) it is important to incorporate from the start the higher levels of meaning that are intended to attach to the brand in the longer term. The brand should not simply acquire them, by accumulation or sedimentation;

they should be planned from the start and incorporated at birth. Incorporating this perspective from the start accelerates the process by which products become brands. This is why product launch and brand launch are not the same.

This is also why brand names should never be descriptive of the product. The first reason is that what is descriptive soon becomes generic, when competitors come into the market with the same product. Second, clients will soon learn what the business is about. Names should better aim at telling an intangible story. Amazon speaks of newness, force and abundance (like the River Amazon), and Orange says 'definitely non-technical', just as Apple Computers did 35 years earlier.

Finally, as is illustrated by the arrows of the graph, brand management consists of a permanent coming and going between tangible and intangible values. Brands are two-legged value producing systems. This means that having an excellent product is not enough in modern competition. However, neither luxury nor image brands can afford to forget the functional realities of products.

Are leading brands the best products or the best value curve?

To create a brand is much more than simply marking a product or service, the necessary first step of brand differentiation. It is about owning a remarkable value proposition.

It is often held to be a paradox that the number one brands are not the best products. Was the original IBM PC the best PC available at the time? No. Is Pentium the best chip? Who knows? Are Dell computers the best computers? No.

The paradox stems from the word 'best': best for whom, and at what? Let's take the analogy of a school class. Academic gradings are determined according to well-understood criteria: students who do well display qualities such as excellent memory, the ability to solve problems fast, to work accurately and to present their work well. These are the values of the schoolroom; and similarly, each market has values. To become number one in any market it is necessary to understand what the market values are. Of course, one cannot succeed without a good product or service. Those who try the product must like it enough to make repeat purchases, to refer others to it; the product must build brand loyalty. In the truck tyre market, Michelin is certainly the number one: it holds 66 per cent of the original tyre market (that is, the tyres the manufacturer supplies with the truck). But in the replacement market, the so-called 'aftermarket', although Michelin is still the market leader, its share falls to 29 per cent. It looks as if Michelin is not as well oriented to the values of the buyers in this aftermarket, fleet owners and those who maintain their trucks.

In the spirits market, Bacardi is world number one; is it the best spirit? One could certainly argue that it is nothing of the kind: it has no taste, and in all blind testings it fares very poorly. So why does it sell in such volume? The source of its business is not experts deliberating over its taste, but casual drinkers and partygoers. They generally want a spirit that will blend well in a cocktail, and an ideal mixer should have a very neutral taste. This is exactly what Carta Blanca delivers; it provides 90 per cent of Bacardi's sales. It also evokes tropical parties.

Branding starts from the customer, and asks, what does he or she value? Bacardi is certainly not the 'better', but it could be called the 'batter'. One of its key intangible added values is its personality, epitomized by its symbol: a bat. The first Bacardi factory in Cuba was full of bats. This became the brand's symbol, adding an enduring halo of mystery to it.

Another example can be found in the educational market. The Master's degree in Business Administration (MBA) is a passport to success. It was first introduced in US universities. To get their MBA, students at US universities need two years of intense work: one year to learn the fundamentals, and one year to specialize in a major field.

Insead is now a respected brand in the MBA market, and Europe's best-known MBA.

However, the *Financial Times* has rated HEC Paris as best European MBA since 2008. Very few people know that Insead's MBA course lasts less than a year. HEC Paris's MBA course lasts two years, like US MBAs such as that from Harvard. That is the power of branding: in this case, a strong brand awareness is enough to capture the demand of candidates and employers who are unaware of product differences. Because it created the MBA category in Europe, Insead soon benefited from the pioneer advantage: its name effectively became the local standard, because of the lack of competition.

Understanding the value curve of the target

Insead became Europe's best-known MBA by understanding the value curve of European human resources directors who hire young executives. In delivering an MBA based on the US model, super-premium business schools such as HEC did not understand the local value curve. In Europe, recruiters do not really care how much time students have spent on campus: the extra salary one gets after having spent two years at Harvard, Stanford or HEC Paris instead of less than a year at Insead is very small. One thing recruiters do value, however, is an intensive immersion in a truly international programme, in which students learn to work with different nationalities.

MBA used to be the designator of a typical product. Now it is a 'collective brand' acting as magic passport, hiding a huge variance in products. The name of the game is brand!

Since not all clients are alike, different brands can coexist in the same sector, because they address the value curve of different segments. This is why groups build brand portfolios. GM has a portfolio of car marques, as does the Volkswagen Group. LVMH has a portfolio of brands.

Breaking the rule and acting fast

The MBA example also illustrates another issue: to build a brand one must quickly reach the critical size to create barriers to entry (such as top-of-mind awareness). By breaking the two-year convention, Insead was able to produce twice as many graduates as a US school of the same size, and so to reach the critical volume of alumni who act as its referees within companies in half the time. Recently it made a strategic move by doubling the number of graduates produced per year, thus accentuating its market share and increasing its productivity (the number of students per professor). It also decided to capitalize on its now well-known brand to open a branch in Asia, and produce still more graduates.

Many lessons should be drawn from the above examples:

- The first is that all brands start by being non-brands, with zero awareness and image. However, they were based on an innovation that succeeded. Starting a brand means finding a disrupting innovation.
- Second, creating a market is the best way to lead it. This is the well-known pioneer advantage. However, to be able to create a market, one must break free from the conventions and codes that create herdism in the marketplace.
- Third, time is an essential ingredient of success. The winners start first and move fast so as to rapidly create a gap from the incoming competition.
- Fourth, it is important to reach the critical size rapidly, to reinforce that gap from the competition. This creates more resources for advertising, communication and word-of-mouth activation.
- Fifth, a brand is not a producer's brand or a retailer's, as is often heard in marketing circles: it is the customer's brand. A brand epitomizes values, but as we know, value lies in the eyes of the beholder, the customer. It is essential to be market focused and ask, what is the value curve of the target? Then comes the question how to address this value curve better than the existing competition. The best way is to create a disruption (Dru, 2002), to break the conventions of the market.

Backing the brand by a business model

Competition between brands is often competition between business models: easyJet versus British Airways, Dell versus HP, or Amazon versus Barnes & Noble.

What is a soft drink? In a material sense it consists of water, flavourings, a sweetening agent

TABLE 3.1 Consumer price (in euros/litre) of various orange-flavour drinks in Europe

Brand	Price
Hard discount	0.25
Carrefour Standard Orange juice	0.70
National brand	0.84
Sunny Delight	1.08
Tropicana	2.45
Tesco Finest	2.50

and carbonate. In the fruit juice market, brands are having a hard time: in Germany, hard-discount labels hold more than 50 per cent of the market. The same process is taking place in the UK and all over Europe, where unlike in the United States, distribution is very concentrated and discount labels do not mean poor-quality products. The problem faced by brands is how to differentiate a product like orange juice that seems generic. In addition, the raw cost of orange juice is high: this creates pressure on the margins, and as a consequence on the level of advertising budget affordable, when selling prices are under pressure from retailer own-labels and unbranded generic products.

In the fruit juice market, there are not many ways of finding a favourable economic equation. Tropicana follows a premium price strategy, based on permanent product innovations (freshly collected oranges for instance) and a premium image. These are trading-up innovations, increasing the price paid by consumers per litre. It is the premium market leader, and a global brand, but in each country it is a small player in volume.

As always, Procter & Gamble followed a high-tech approach to differentiate its product. It introduced Sunny Delight as a competitor in the fruit juice market although it has almost totally artificial ingredients (there is only 5 per cent orange in it, for legal reasons). These created a taste and texture that beat all the competitors using natural fruit juice. It also added vitamins to appeal to mothers. Thanks to its name, its colour (orange, and variants for the different flavours) and logo (a round sun), Procter & Gamble created an innovative product, which was reminiscent of orange juice and was certainly thought by some consumers to be orange-based. Its artificial chemical formula is patentable, which creates a barrier to entry and prevents it from being directly copied. Most important, it is priced high, whereas its raw material cost is far lower than that of natural orange juice.

Coca-Cola is an opaque product: almost black, mysterious, with a secret formula, it created from the start the conditions, both real and psychological, of a product that is not fully substitutable. In the cola market, Coke is much more than a brand: it is a remarkable business model. Throughout more than a century the Coca-Cola brand has pursued one single objective, now on a worldwide scale: to continue to grow the cola category. It was in competition first with sodas in America, then with other soft drinks, and now with virtually all other types of drink, including water in Europe or tea in Asia.

In making its brand the number one drink in the world, Coke benefited from being made from a syrup that is easy to transport at low cost, with high efficiency (that is, it can be highly concentrated, so many litres of Coca-Cola are produced from a single litre of concentrate) and remarkably high resistance to temperature and time (it can be stored for a long time, anywhere, unlike most fruit-based soft drinks). It is definitively a great physical product. In addition, the tuning of its acidity/sweetness ratio is optimal so customers can drink many glasses or cans in a row without being satiated. The cola syrup itself is very cheap to produce, thus allowing high margins and as a consequence high marketing budgets to reinforce its top-of-mind position (a key competitive advantage in this low-involvement category, where the buying decision is based on impulse). It is resold to bottlers at five times its production price, so profit can be located at the company level and pressure can be exerted on bottlers/distributors to pursue a high-volume strategy if they want to be profitable.

To grow the business through the expansion of the category, the strategy rests on three facets, which are always the same: availability, accessibility, attractiveness, in that order. Most people focus on communication, but the key of Coke's domination is in these three levers:

- Availability, the distributive lever, comes first. 'Put Coke at arms' reach'. The aim is for people to find Coke everywhere: bars, fast-food restaurants, canteens, retailers, vending machines in streets and public places, refrigerators in offices, classrooms soon.... An essential point to appreciate is that building both the business and the brand image is tied to the active presence on premises. On-premise presence gives status to a drink, and creates consumption habits. In addition, unlike multiple retailers (Wal-Mart, Asda, Ikea, Carrefour, Aldi and the like), which do not sell one brand exclusively, but their clients have the choice, on-premise customers do give exclusive rights, thereby granting a local monopoly to the brand. This is why Coke makes global alliances with McDonald's and other synergistic organizations. One condition of this type of exclusive deal is that the supplier provides, and the outlet agrees to stock, its full portfolio of soft drink brands. The goal is to create a barrier to entry to any soft drink competitor.

  As part of competing on availability, one should not forget access to the bottlers: in many countries there are few good bottlers, and eventually one only. Controlling this bottler is a sure way to prevent competition entering the country. Conversely, it is a way to push competition out, as when the Venezuelan bottler that had formerly handled Pepsi decided to work for Coke. Within a day, Pepsi operations in Venezuela were closed.
- Accessibility is the price factor: 'In China, in India, sell Coke at the price of tea'. This is made possible by the low cost of syrup production, its easy transportability, and also the volume-based strategy. Economies of scale create another pressure on the competition, if not a total barrier to entry. Having located the profit at the company level (exactly as Disney Corporation does through licensing royalties, while some of its foreign entertainment parks are not profitable), the Coca-Cola Corporation can afford to have its local companies lose money for the sake of rapidly growing a high per capita consumption rate. In addition, to push competition out of the market (whether it is defined as cola drinks or more widely), the company exerts a high-price pressure on the whole market. For instance, it seems that specific prices on Coke are granted to trade distributors if they give preference to the company's other brands, such as Fanta, Minute Maid and Aquarius. This is why the Coca-Cola Company is now being sued by the European authorities on charges of anti-competitive manoeuvres.
- Attractiveness is the third factor: it is the communication issue. Although Coke's advertising is conspicuous, non-media communication (relationship, proximity, music and sports sponsorship, and on-premise communications) represents the main part of the budget. Share-of-mind domination is made possible, let us remind, by the low production cost. Last but not least, Coke's image is not that of a product but of a bond: it delivers both tangible promises (refreshment) and intangible ones (modernity, dynamism, energy, American-ness, feeling part of the world) which make it so special, much more now than its secret formula.

Coca-Cola's main challenger worldwide, Pepsi-Cola, is following exactly the same brand and business model. Its differentiation is based on the fact that it was introduced more recently than Coke, and did not create the category. As a challenger, its brand image and market grip are lower. It challenges the leader on three facets: price, product and image:

- Price: it is a dime cheaper than Coke, at consumer level, but this creates a higher pressure profitability.
- Product: since it is not the referent, Pepsi is more daring and permanently works on the product to beat Coke on palatability and taste (the 'Pepsi challenge'). Its formula is actually preferred to Coke in most blind tests. It pushed Coca-Cola Corporation to make the 'marketing blunder of the century' launching New Coke in 1985 to replace the classic Coke, the water of the United States.

More innovating by necessity, it practised line extensions such as Diet Pepsi well before Coke.

- Image: Pepsi is younger than Coke. Capitalizing on the only durable weakness of Coke, its advertising positioning makes Pepsi the choice of the new generation. Pepsi's essence is 'the soft drink for today's taste and experiences'.

To secure a presence for Pepsi-Cola on premises and circumvent the barriers to entry created by Coke, the Pepsico Company had to diversify into restaurants and fast-food chains.

Other rivals to Coke have had an even harder time. In February 2000, Richard Branson of Virgin admitted defeat in its war against Coca-Cola and Pepsi in the United States, less than two years after he rode into New York's Times Square in a tank to launch his challenge. On reviewing the brand and business model that is common to both Coke and Pepsi, it is easy to understand why Virgin Cola failed everywhere but in the UK, its domestic base. Even there it won less than 5 per cent of the market. Brand is not enough.

Virgin Cola bought the Canadian company Cott's, which was able to make a very good syrup: it makes the cola sold under Loblaw's President's Choice private label. It proposed a cheaper price than Coke or Pepsi. But Virgin Cola never got the distribution, it never accessed the consumer. Branson's whole idea was to save on advertising and thus make a cheaper price possible by taking advantage of the Virgin umbrella brand. Unlike the two world-leading carbonated soft drink companies, which both follow a product brand policy (one brand per type of flavour), Virgin's only brand asset is its core brand, which has been extended to all types of category (see Chapter 12), and in the process gained extensive worldwide awareness. As well as a low volume of advertising and selling a large volume on promotion, Virgin had a small sales force, a sure handicap for trade marketing and store-by-store direct relationships. Finally, Virgin Cola was not able to work in the market without a full portfolio of soft drinks to support it. This is necessary to access the on-premise consumption sector, and is also the only way to make a true national sales force economically possible.

As a rule, extension failures are immediately attributed to some image-based reason that it is impossible for the brand to extend to the new category. The brand and business perspective shows us that this explanation is superficial. It was not the Virgin brand that was the source of the failure, but the fact that Virgin could not compete on the same business model as its two Goliath competitors. Fairy tales are one thing, but most of the time David gets killed.

Virgin Cola failed to get enough distribution: in Europe, for instance, it never entered the main multiple retailers. It was not sold sufficiently in the fashionable bars and restaurants. To do better in distribution terms it would have needed a real sales force and a real portfolio of brands and products. Arguably it should have looked for alliances with soft drink manufacturers looking for a branded cola.

Without advertising, the cola was mostly sold on a promotional basis. It is questionable whether that creates the basis for a long-term preference. Also, Virgin wanted to be perceived as the anti-Coke cola. However, throughout the worldwide market this role already belonged to Pepsi. Finally, is the Virgin brand image that strong among the young generation outside the UK?

What other brand and business model could exist in this sector? At this time, two alternative models are surviving: ethnic colas and colas dedicated to trade. In its edition of Sunday 12 January 2003, the *New York Times* published an article, 'Ire at America helps create the Anti-Coke'. This announced the creation of Mecca Cola by a young Tunisian-born entrepreneur. He targeted it at the Muslims of France and soon of other countries. This brand had two strengths. The first was immediate goodwill in the Muslim community: its identity is based on a real feeling of community and resentment against what is felt as an imperialist drink and brand. The second was an immediate presence in the specific channel of distribution held by this community, innumerable small convenience stores that open long hours.

It is too early to judge its success, since this will only be evidenced by long-term durability. However, sales are skyrocketing. Interestingly, other colas have burgeoned, based on the same approach: they capitalize on religious, ethnic or geographical feelings of community and identity. For instance there are Corsica Cola and Breiz'h Cola (sold in Brittany), aimed at two regions with strong identity and even independentist movements. This model can be reproduced elsewhere: Irish cola? Scottish cola?

In the era of globalization, regional identities are revived to resist what is perceived as a loss of essence, soul, and quality of life. Such attempts access local distribution or the local stores of national multiple retailers. No store owner or manager wants to take the risk of hurting the local feelings of the community living around its store.

Monarch Beverage Company has created an interesting alternative brand and business model. It is totally trade oriented, thereby securing access to modern distribution, worldwide. However it is not simply providing cola for retailers' own labels. This is a true branding approach.

The problem for multiple retailers is to get free from the grip of Coke and Pepsi. Unfortunately, with some exceptions (Sainsbury's Cola in the UK, President's Choice Cola in Canada), market shares of own labels remain very small. This is probably because compared with the real thing, private labels look like faked cola. Parents who buy own-label colas to save money risk being criticized by their children. Private labels have no image in a category that has been decommoditized by brand image. Coke's identity encapsulates the American dream, authenticity and pleasure. Pepsi has the same associations, although to a lesser extent, and also means youth. Own-labels create no such value in the eyes of the young heavy consumers. They create bad will.

The Monarch Beverage Company was created in Atlanta, USA, by two former Coca-Cola marketing VPs. With the help of a former Coca-Cola chemist, it knew how to produce a good cola syrup. Most important, instead of focusing on the end-consumer (the mistake of Virgin) and running the risk of having no access to mass distribution, it focused on the customer problem: to increase the share of its own label with profit. Even if they were given away free, own-label colas would not be consumed: they lack authenticity, a reassurance on quality and taste, and fail to deliver the right intangible values. Monarch has created a portfolio of brands, all looking American (like 'American Cola'), and coming from a true American company based in the Mecca of colas, Atlanta, close to Coca-Cola's own headquarters. These brands, owned by Monarch, are granted under licence to multiple retailers. Each mass multiple retailer therefore has its own brand, different from its competitors', for its operations worldwide. Carrefour for instance has American Cola. The syrup is made by Monarch to match each retailer's specifications. The company provides the brand and the product; it leaves its customers totally free to manage their own bottlers, prices and promotion. No national sales force is needed: negotiations are carried out at the corporate level, with the category global manager.

This in-depth comparison of alternative brand and business models has illustrated the benefits of enlarging the perspective on competitive strategies, beyond communication and brand image. Brand leadership is gained through the synergy of multiple levers within a viable economic equation. Thus is the true condition of brand equity.

04 Brand diversity: how specific are different sectors?

What becomes of these brand principles in specific markets? It is worth asking the question, given the disparities between markets as varied as industry, business-to-business (B2B) and medical prescription on one side, and the world of service and luxury on the other. Are internet brands controlled using the same levers? What should we think of the emergence of the brand in sectors such as fresh produce, previously the domain of generic products or a variety resulting from nature and regional tendencies? Finally, we should examine these new extensions of the brand domain: countries, towns, educational establishments, and also television programmes and sporting heroes.

These questions on the adaptation of brand principles to specific sectors are raised by sector managers themselves, since they all recognize the trans-sectoral validity of brand logic, its points of application, and the brand activation modes, which are bound to differ according to the different markets. This chapter is dedicated to these differences.

How a brand can save lives: the Red Cross

Although the word 'brand' itself is forbidden in the organization, everybody at the Red Cross is well aware of the value of its name and symbol. If they could not get the support of the local people, the ambulance drivers would not be able to reach the war zones to bring help to whoever is wounded, regardless of camp, religion, etc. It becomes a question of life and death. Today, 66 per cent of all activities of the Red Cross take place in Muslim countries. However, in two adjacent valleys of Pakistan or Afghanistan, the responses evoked by the Red Cross may vary: in one case the ambulance might be allowed to drive freely; in the other it could be blocked. Some people there call them *Salibee*, which means 'crusaders'. When the symbol is put on a hospital it means the hospital is protected: its aura makes it respected even during wartime.

It does not matter whether organizations use the word 'brand'. This is corporate culture. All organizations define what they consider as normal or not. In our interaction with the International Olympic Committee (IOC), the word 'brand' was not used either. In fact the Olympic rings are not a brand: they have the status of an international flag, and as such are protected by the Nairobi Agreement, not by intellectual property rights.

The Red Cross has the morphology and content of a brand:

- It has a symbol, remarkable by its simplicity, visibility and meaningfulness.
- It is based on a great idea, a founding belief or conviction: even your enemy needs to be helped!
- It is enacted, or transformed into acts (local, national and global): all agents live the Red Cross values and put them into action.

- These actions are driven by fundamental values: neutrality, impartiality and humanity.
- The organization is managed according to specific working principles.
- The Red Cross's brand equity is high: the symbol has 98 per cent recognition. There is strong support for the idea behind the Red Cross, although not always for the services, depending on the country. The attributes of the brand Red Cross are: medical, emergency, trustworthy.

This is a very special brand to work for: the communication director does not own the brand. It is owned by the thousands of local Red Cross agencies. They build its reputation locally, and they can also destroy it long term. The symbol is protected by international laws.

Unlike the IOC, whose leader is visible, or the United Nations, the Red Cross is a faceless organization, which does not portray its leaders. When there is a problem it is always the local leader who appears. The Red Cross shows those close to the action. People tend to form their image from indirect or virtual experience (media or social media) much more than from direct experience.

As with all brands, the Red Cross's challenge is to differentiate itself from the competition. It competes for the same stakeholders. Who is the competition? Not only other NGOs, but states and armies that dispute the right of the Red Cross to intervene in the war zones. The Red Cross needs both financing and support or acceptance.

There is also a need to differentiate the Red Cross from the humanitarian sector, whose image is becoming negative, owing to the lack of clarity of the goals of some of its well-known examples. It is important that the local Red Cross agents always feel protected by their emblem. The Red Cross must also take care not to be perceived as a one-sided partial actor (as the United Nations is now perceived in the emerging countries).

Luxury brands are specific

Recently there has been a surge of interest in luxury brands. It is true that they are the polar opposite of low cost: here, the company has complete freedom to fix its prices – as high as possible. How much does a bottle of Royal Salute cost in a Shanghai disco? The answer is €1,000. This is why financial groups have been set up to relaunch luxury brands – the world number one, LVMH, was born from the talent of its founder, B Arnault, who acquired a fading star, Dior, at a low price. Then he got his hands on Vuitton, now the world's leading luxury brand in terms of financial value.

But what is luxury? How is it different from premium brands, such as Coach, Victoria's Secret lingerie, Callaway golf clubs, Belvedere vodka or Nespresso coffee? These brands are typical of trading up, as consumers move up the range. Admittedly there is a little of luxury's ingredients in these brands (better quality, selective distribution, emotive value), but luxury is elsewhere. Let us return to its etymology. The word 'luxury' derives from the Latin *luxatio*, meaning distance: luxury is an enormous distance. There is a discontinuity between premium and luxury.

Luxury is not more of premium

Many authors use the word 'luxury' as an all-encompassing word to describe a situation where an item is priced well above what the utility of its physical attributes would command. Unfortunately this definition is valid also for fashion goods and for premium goods. A pair of Levi's jeans is sold at a price that exceeds 10 times the manufacturing cost. An Audi is sold at a higher price than its twin product signed Volkswagen, itself sold at a higher price than its twin product at Skoda, etc. Most people use the words 'premium' and 'luxury' interchangeably. As a result of this confusion the mass crystal jeweller Swarovski is said to be luxury, as well as the fashion premium leather brands Coach and Longchamp. It is a mistake: luxury is special. That is its role. It is not by asking consumers that one identifies the difference between these concepts, but by understanding the function of luxury in society.

Inherited from ranks and titles of nobility in aristocratic times, today luxury brands are to civilians the equivalent of what medals are for military officers. They are a personal reward, a deep pleasure and a message about where the person stands in the social hierarchy. Even former classless societies re-create hierarchies and use subtle signals to position

FIGURE 4.1 Differentiating luxury, fashion and premium

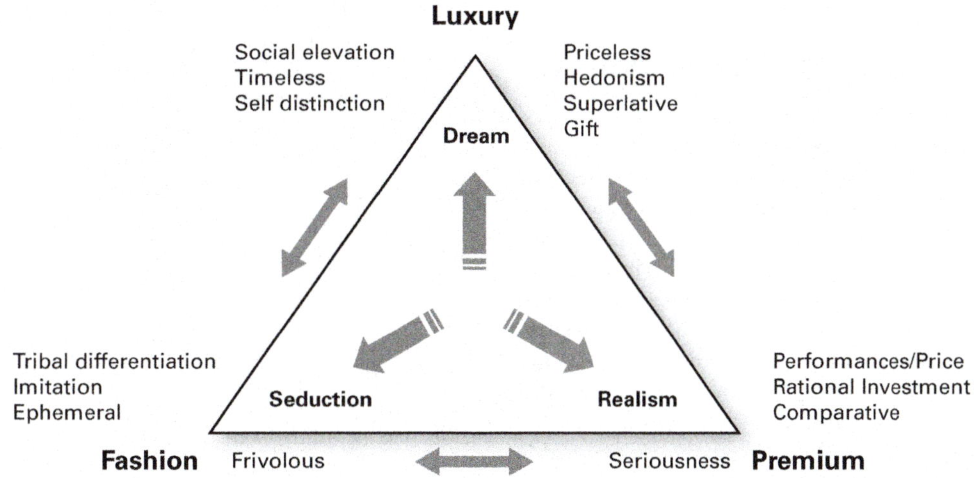

people (prestigious university names, for instance, or golf clubs, or areas of residence). In China the luxury sector thrives because today nobody wants to be perceived to be at the bottom of the pyramid. In emerging countries, social mobility is active: the vertical elevator is marked by possession of goods as long as they are culturally coded: not just a necklace of diamonds but from Tiffany or Cartier. Buying a luxury bag makes people feel elevated. Luxury is about elevation (Kapferer and Bastien, 2009). Through conspicuous logos, consumers indulge in magic behaviours. They hope the aura of the charismatic creator of the luxury brand is extending to themselves, and making them stand apart, above others. They symbolically are part of the creator's community.

From the triangle in Figure 4.1 it is clear that a luxury strategy aims at producing the highest level of intangible added value, based on products that themselves are of an exceptional quality. Premium products are also of very high quality, but are lacking the magic of luxury. This magic is created:

- through creators with charismatic authority;
- through networking with transgressive artists;
- through rituals (yearly defilés);
- through theatralization of retail seen as a point of aura transmission from creator to consumer;
- through worshipping heritage and history;
- through production of excess;
- through sumptuous communication that builds an extraordinary world.

Luxury is creator driven, not consumer oriented. It is not managed at all like normal brands. Classical marketing kills it. Premium products are more traditionally managed, and follow classic marketing principles.

The fashion system is very different from that of luxury. Fashion is obsessed with being out of fashion. As soon as this happens, prices must be cut by 50 per cent, and profitability disappears. As a result, fashion does not produce high-quality products: it is not worth it. Clothes are not supposed to last after the season. Fashion is ephemeral; luxury is enduring: Porsche 911, Chanel No. 5. Finally, to reduce costs all products are made in China, whereas a true luxury strategy never delocalizes (Kapferer and Bastien, 2009).

A luxury strategy is driven by an obsession: never be comparable. This is why luxury brands never compare themselves to anyone. Conversely, a premium or even super-premium strategy loves comparisons, eg 'Grey Goose, the world's best-tasting vodka'. In South Korea Lexus automobile ads emphasize their differences from Mercedes E Class cars. A premium car has to demonstrate why its price is normal. Luxury sets price above normality:

the prices have to mark the gap. Luxury is another world – an inaccessible one, yet accessible.

Why luxury? Status and hedonism

To return to the essence of luxury, it is customers' desire to mark their difference. The first luxury manager was King Louis XIV of France. Aristocracy is now dead, but it has been replaced by the power of money. Everywhere in China, in Russia, in the United States and in Dubai, recent fortunes grant more than unlimited purchasing power: they grant power, pure and simple. This is the heart of luxury: giving men and women of power the privileges that accompany it. For power must be shown off in our democratic societies. Once upon a time, the mere name of the noble marked the unbridgeable distance between him or her and an ordinary person. Nowadays, the frontier still exists and it must be marked.

Russian oligarchs, Chinese billionaires and Wall Street's golden boys do not buy Coach bags or Ralph Lauren for their partners. They want Dior, Louis Vuitton or Cartier.

The luxury business model aims to outgrow this niche in order to exploit the fundamental mechanism described by R Girard: desire born of imitating a model, but as a means of self-elevation. Luxury brands know how to create more accessible product lines for those who wish to introduce a little luxury into their lives, to enliven their daily grind from time to time. These are luxury's 'day trippers'. This created the luxury business.

The four types of luxury

Luxury can vary as widely as East from West. Everyone can see where it is, but it is constantly on the move. Luxury is relative. For a modest individual, luxury is eating in a good restaurant once a year. For one of the City's golden boys, it is buying a Ferrari with their annual bonus. For Bill Gates, it is playing tennis with the world number one or buying a Picasso.

Our own research has delved more deeply into the notion of luxury among consumers. There are profound differences between people questioned on their concept of luxury. Analysis of the traits that – in their minds – define luxury reveals four concepts of luxury, each with its most representative brand(s) (that is, those that are judged the best example of the type of luxury by interviewees) (Kapferer, 1998) (see Table 4.1).

The first type of luxury, according to an international sample of affluent young executives with high purchasing power, is the closest to the general hierarchy, the average emerging from our study. It gives prominence to the beauty of the object and the excellence and uniqueness of the product, more so than all the other types. The brand most representative of this type of luxury is Rolls-Royce, but Cartier and Hermès also show these characteristics. The second concept of luxury in the world exalts creativity, the sensuality of the products. Its luxury 'prototypes' are Gucci, Boss and J-P Gaultier. The third vision of luxury values timelessness and international reputation more than any other facets. Its symbols are Porsche, with its immutable design, Vuitton and Dunhill. Finally, the fourth type values the feeling of being among only a few to possess the brand. In their eyes, the prototype of the brand purchased by the select few is Chivas Royal Salute.

We also find Mercedes in this category: this might seem curious, given the recent diffusion of Mercedes – now more than 1,300,000 vehicles sold worldwide each year. However, our research dates from 1998, when Mercedes produced only 700,000 cars per year, and its dynamism and product attractiveness were called into question. This is what led to the revolution we all know about (multiplication of models, introduction of aesthetics, the A class, the M class and so on). Its presence as a symbol of this fourth type of luxury testifies to the brand's problems. Only a few years ago, its only potential market was among those looking for the luxury, not of a sensory pleasure, but of status, the badge of belonging in a class with money and a desire to flaunt it. We should add, however, that in China, India, Brazil and Russia, it is the very expensive and status-loaded Mercedes S Class that sells. These are *de facto* inaccessible cars.

Luxury business models

The only real success is commercial, yet there are many roads to this destination. An examination of 'new luxury' brands such as Ralph Lauren, Calvin Klein and Coach proves that it is possible to become an overnight success in the middle class market without the long pedigree of a Christian Dior,

TABLE 4.1 The four types of luxury

Consumer group	Type 1 Bespoke, authentic	Type 2 Modern, creative	Type 3 Conformist, recognition seeking	Type 4 Flashy, standing out
What defines luxury (percentage giving each answer):				
Beauty of an object	97	63	86	44
Excellence of the products	88	3	9	38
Magic	76	50	88	75
Uniqueness	59	10	3	6
Tradition and savoir faire	26	40	40	38
Creativity	35	100	38	6
Sensuality of the products	26	83	21	6
Feeling of exceptionality	23	23	31	31
Never out of fashion	21	27	78	19
International reputation	15	27	78	19
Produced by a craftsperson	12	30	9	3
Long history	6	7	16	13
Likeable creator	6	7	10	13
Belonging to a minority	6	3	2	63
Very few purchasers	0	3	2	69
At the cutting edge of fashion	0	17	36	31
Typical luxury brands of this type according to interviewees:	Rolls-Royce Cartier Hermès	Gucci Boss Gaultier	Vuitton Porsche Dunhill	Chivas Mercedes

SOURCE Kapferer (1998b)

Chanel or Givenchy. True, these newer brands have not yet demonstrated their ability to price up and survive beyond the death of their founders, but their commercial success is evidence of their attractiveness to middle-class customers the world over. We need to distinguish between two different business models for brands. The first includes brands with a 'history' behind them, while the second covers brands that, lacking such a history of their own, have invented a 'story' for themselves. It comes as no surprise that these companies are US-based: this young, modern country is a past master in the art of weaving dreams from stories. After all, both Hollywood and Disneyland are American inventions.

Furthermore, the European luxury brands – rooted as they are in a craftsperson-based tradition predicated upon rare, unique pieces of work – place considerable emphasis on the actual product as a factor in their success, while the US brands concentrate much more on merchandizing, and the atmosphere and image created by the outlets dedicated to their brand, in the realm of customer contact and distribution. What we see is the creation of a dichotomy between heritage, skilled work and the product on the one hand, and 'stories' and distribution on the other. Let us examine and compare these two brand and business models in more detail.

The first brand and business model may be represented by the luxury pyramid (see Figure 4.2). At the top of the pyramid, there is the *griffe* – the creator's signature engraved on a unique work. This explains what it fears most: copies. Brands, on the other hand, particularly fear fakes or counterfeits.

FIGURE 4.2 The pyramid brand and business model in the luxury market

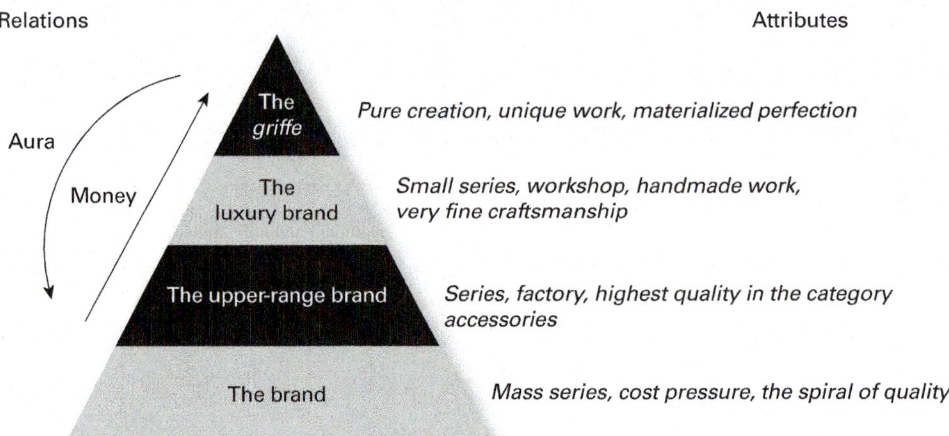

The second level is that of luxury brands produced in small series within a workshop: a 'manufacture' in its etymological sense, which is seen as the sole warrant of a 'good-facture'. Examples include Hermès, Rolls-Royce and Cartier. The third level is that of streamlined mass production: here we find Dior and Yves Saint Laurent cosmetics, and YSL Diffusion clothes. At this level of industrialization, the brand's fame generates an aura of intangible added values for expensive and prime quality products, which nonetheless gradually tend to look more and more like the rest of the market. Hence its name equals mass prestige.

In this model, luxury management is based on the interactions between the three levels. The perpetuation of *griffes* depends on their integration in financial groups that are able to provide the necessary resources for the first level, and on their licensing to industrial groups able to create, launch and distribute worldwide products at the third level (such as P&G, Unilever and l'Oréal). Profit accrues at this level, and is the only means to make the huge investments on the *griffe* pay off. These investments are necessary to recreate the dream around the brand. Reality consumes dreams: the more we buy a luxury brand, the less we dream of it. Hence, somewhat paradoxically, the more a luxury brand gets purchased, the more its aura needs to be permanently recreated.

This is exactly how the LVMH group operates. The model is best explained in the actual words of Bernard Arnault, the CEO of LVMH, the world's leading luxury group, which owns 50 luxury brands. What are the key factors in the success of its brands? Arnault (2000: p 65) lists them in the following order:

- product quality;
- creativity;
- image;
- company spirit;
- a drive to reinvent oneself and to be the best.

As we can see, in this pyramid model, with its base which expands to feed the brand's overall cashflow (through licensing, extensions and a less elective distribution system), there must be a constant regeneration of value at the tip. This is where creativity, signature and creator come in, supplying the brand with its artistic inventiveness. Here we are in the realm of art, not mere styling. Each show is a pure artistic event. Unlike the second brand and business model (as we shall see), it is not a question of presenting clothing which will be worn in a year's time. As Arnault puts it, 'One does not invite a thousand guests to watch a procession of dresses which could be seen on a coat hanger or in a show room' (p 70); 'most competitors prefer to show off mass-produced clothing on their catwalks, or indulge in American-style marketing. We are not interested in working this way' (p 73); and 'Marc Jacobs, John

FIGURE 4.3 The constellation model of luxury brands

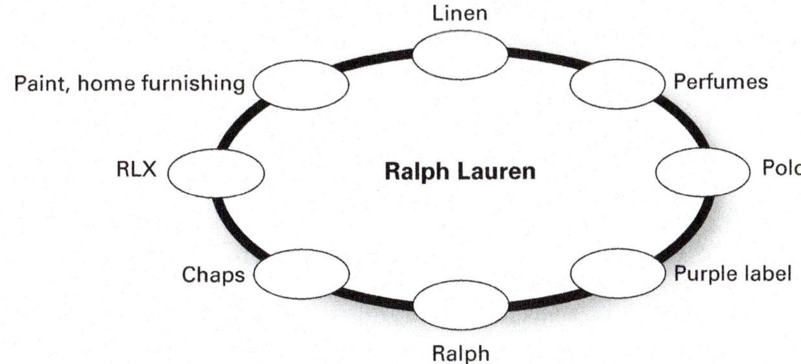

Galliano and Alexander McQueen are innovators; fashion inventors; artists who create' (p 75).

The creativity of the signature label, at the tip of the pyramid, is at the heart of the business model: within a few years of the arrival of the charismatic John Galliano at Dior, sales had increased four fold. Never before had Dior been talked about so much worldwide. Dior was back at the centre of world artistic creation for women.

The disadvantage of this model – and after all, every model has a disadvantage – is that the more accessible secondary lines are entrusted to other designers, and the further away you move from the tip of the pyramid, the less creativity there is. In this model, there is a strong danger that brand extensions will show little of the creativity of the brand itself: they will merely exploit its name.

The second brand and business model originated in the United States, but we should also include the likes of Armani and Boss in this category. At the centre is the brand ideal, while all manifestations of the brand (its extensions, licence and so on) are around the edge, at a more or less equal distance from the centre. Consequently, these extensions are all treated with equal care, since each of them brings its own individual expression of this ideal to its target market. Each portrays the brand in an equally important way, and plays its own part in shaping it. For example, Ralph Lauren's home textile extension (bed sheets, blankets, tablecloths, bath towels and so on) is a complete expression of the patrician East Coast ideal and its values: indeed, the tactic of merchandizing the range in the corners of department stores aims to create an idealized reconstruction of a room in a house.

This second model can include brand 'places' such as The House of Ralph Lauren – superstores which not only stock the entire brand range and its various collections and extensions, but are also specifically designed to give flesh, structure and meaning to the brand ideal. Ralph Lifshitz, Ralph Lauren's founder, built his brand on his own ideal: that of looking like American aristocracy, symbolized by Boston high society. Ralph Lauren's flagship stores are three-dimensional recreations of this fanciful illusion (Figure 4.3).

To compensate for the risk of massification of the brand, Ralph Lauren engages in trading up and licensing: Richemont/Cartier produces the $10,000 Ralph Lauren watch. Ralph Lauren's recent Purple Collection features Italian-made outfits produced from quality materials, and a price tag to match: €3,000 per outfit.

This brand extension policy makes matters easier for distributors, who have come to understand that the rate of return on investment increases as the store sales area expands. Each store can now offer a rich assortment of products which are no longer mere accessories, but extensions in their own right – and in so doing, can increase the value of the average shopping trip.

It should be noted that 'pyramid-based' brands face a rather perverse problem. If they create too many accessible extensions, they reduce the profitability of the sales outlets. In a Chanel boutique, it makes more sense to spend 10 minutes selling a customer a Chanel bag – given the margin it offers – rather than a perfume or a product from the Chanel Precision range. Clearly, the extension policy is inseparable from the distribution policy.

Service brands

There is no legal difference between product, trade or service brands. These are economic distinctions, not legal ones. By focusing only on branding *per se*, ie on signs only, the law does not help us much to understand either how brands and the branding process work or what the specific characteristics among the various players are.

Service brands do exist: Europcar, Hertz, Ecco, Manpower, Visa, Club Med, Marriott's, Méridien, HEC, Harvard, BT, etc. Each one represents a specific cluster of attributes embodied in a quite concrete, though intangible, type of service: car rental, temporary work, computer services, leisure activities, hotel business or higher education. However, some service sectors seem to be just entering the brand age. They either do not consider themselves as being a part of it yet or have just started becoming aware that they are. This evolution is fascinating to watch, as it highlights all that the brand approach involves and reveals the specificities of branding an intangible service.

The banking industry is a fine example. If bank customers were asked what bank brands they knew, they probably would not know or understand what to answer. They know the names of banks, but not bank brands. This is significant: for the public, these names are not brands, identifying a specific service, but corporate names or business signs linked to a specific place.

Until recently, bank names designated either the owner of the corporation entrusted with the customers' funds (Morgan, Rothschild) or a specific place (Citibank) or a particular customer group. Name contraction often signals that a brand concept is in formation. Thus, for example, Banque Nationale de Paris has become BNP. Some observers consider this as just a desire to simplify the name, as per the advertising principle 'what's easy to say is easy to remember', as short signatures make it easier to identify the signer. Such abbreviations have definitely had an impact; however, they seem to reduce the whole branding concept to a mere part of the writing and printing process solely within the realm of communication.

As they are contracted, these bank names come to represent some kind of contract instead of a mere person or place. In order to become visible, this contract may take the form of specific 'bank products' (or standard policies in the insurance industry). But these visible and easy-to-imitate products are not the explanation and justification for why they have decided to build a true brand. They are merely the brand's external manifestation. Banks and insurance companies have understood the key to what makes them different: the relationships that develop between a customer and a banker under the auspices of the brand.

Finally, one aspect of service brands that contrasts with product brands is that service is invisible (Levitt, 1981; Eiglier and Langeard, 1990). What does a bank have to show, except customers or consultants? Structurally, service brands are handicapped in that they cannot be easily illustrated. That is why service brands use slogans. No wonder: slogans are indeed vocal, they are the brand's *vocatio*, ie the brand's vocation or calling. Slogans are a commandment for both internal and external relations. Through a slogan, the brand defines its behavioural guidelines, and these guidelines give the customer the right to be dissatisfied if they are transgressed. Claiming to be the bank with a smile or the bank who cares is not enough. These attributes must be fully internalized by the people who offer and deliver the service. The fact that humans are intrinsically and unavoidably variable is definitely a challenge for the brand approach in service industries.

This is why brand alignment has become so important if the whole organization is to 'live the brand' (Ind, 2001). Brand alignment is the process by which organizations think of themselves as brands. The brand experience in the service sector is totally driven by what happens at points of contact, where customers meet the company's staff, salespeople and so on. This is true of Starbucks as well as of Citibank or HSBC. It is also crucial at Dell. This company is actually not a computer manufacturer but a service company, identifying each client's need and assembling the product to fit it. There is hardly any R&D investment at Dell. All the efforts are concentrated on the customers and organizing the company by customer segment to better listen and react. People are essential in this process, not machines.

How service brands create value

A service brand, like all brands, must be able to provide consistency of service delivery through time

FIGURE 4.4 How service brands create value

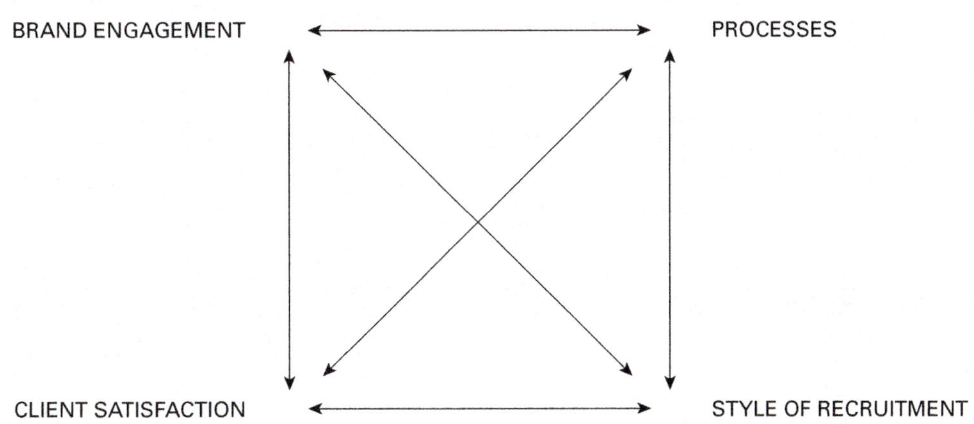

and space. Since each place (restaurant, office, aeroplane, etc) is a decentralized *servuction* centre (this word purposely mixing 'service' and 'production') (Eiglier and Langeard, 1990), common processes are needed to ensure this consistency and hence the clients' satisfaction. These processes are sometimes based on machines (like those in a McDonald's restaurant) or may be purely intangible (like the procedures that differentiate consulting agencies, or auditing and accounting agencies). When the same processes cannot be applied or should not be applied (through lack of relevance to the client segment), there should be another brand name. This is why Deloitte has created the sub-brand In Extenso to deliver accounting services to the 'Soho' (small office, home office) market. In reality the processes of client treatment do differ. The service brand is enacted by human beings. As a result, its recruitment style is part of the creation of value.

Branding in the service sector entails a double recognition. Within the company, people must recognize the brand values as their own. The internalization process is crucial. It means explaining and justifying these values to each cell within the company. It also means stimulating the self-discovery of how these values might modify everyday behaviour. At the client level it also means that clients recognize these values as those to which they are attracted.

One point must not be overlooked. Brand management in the service sector means not only delivering a differentiated experience but ensuring that the resulting satisfaction will be attributed to the right brand. This is why the design and branding of all contact points are so important. Places of business, call centres, websites and the like must all convey the brand. Just posting one's logo on the front door is not enough.

The human component of the service brand

In services, there is no difference between the internal and the external. In other words, it is what is behind the brand that makes the brand. Thus, on a return flight from Tokyo to Paris, customers of the airline are in contact with its staff for 14 hours at a time. It is the attentive personnel who carry the brand, not a few seconds of stealth advertising. This is what makes passengers forget the frustration of the delays that build up from the beginning, disrupting executives' best-laid plans. What has built Starbucks' worldwide reputation, if not the politeness of its employees? For products it is quite the opposite: Evian is visible in bottles, in shops and in advertising. We never see the factory or the workers.

The first consequence of this is that the service brand is constructed internally. Orange is built up through hours and hours of training all staff how to behave in an Orange way, according to Orange's codes and values. This concerns all points of contact with the customer, in the store, from the call centre or over the internet. The second consequence is that employees cannot be expected to treat customers well if they are not happy themselves. In order to create the relaxed, warm atmosphere that characterizes Starbucks, its founder Howard Schultz innovated by responding to the worries of many part-time staff: with good health insurance cover, for example.

Another essential distinction between services and products is that the 'factory' is in the store. The location for the service production is also the place of its consumption: post office, hospital or restaurant. This is why it is so important to take care of the little details, since they lead to expectations and feelings. The rise of architectural and interior design expresses the desire for greater control over the impressions produced by the immediate environment on what is known as the customer experience, and therefore customer satisfaction.

Since service is carried out by people, their variability is a risk for the brand. The brand promises regular and dependable quality – hence the importance of defining strong behavioural norms, supported by plenty of training (McDonald's and Disney are models of this type). The alternative is to keep the personalized connection between customers and the agents themselves, who found a lasting relationship, based on mutual recognition. However, this second approach conflicts with the need to move staff around.

Service, process and recruitment brands

In the services sector, in order to carry out the primary function of any major brand (guaranteeing the same quality of service), the brand is necessarily linked to the setting up of internal and customer-facing processes. To take the example of accounting and audit consultancies, to be 'Mazars' is to differentiate oneself from the big international agencies, the famous 'big four' who are all Anglo-Saxon, and therefore offer a different culture. However, it is still necessary to homogenize the internal processes, to provide more regularity and the client experience. The brand is not only a common seal linking profoundly independent agencies in order to give an impression of size, but the sharing of the same concept of the profession. In services, it is important to make the intangible tangible – hence the importance of common processes (Figure 4.4).

Naturally, this has an impact on what is commonly known as the employer brand, since the raw material of service is the personality and competence of the people. For the employer brand, the task is to develop its reputation among executives or students of the top universities, based not on better salaries, but on shared values.

The branding of nature

Many mass-consumption food product brands were born through the disappearance of fresh produce in bulk. Sweetcorn, peas and gherkins were all canned, giving birth to Green Giant, Bonduelle and so on. Findus was the first brand to freeze vegetables. The big brands were therefore born through providing progress and practicality, precisely connected to the removal of the vagaries of fresh produce and the drawback of its perishable nature.

Innovation in fresh produce

The times are changing, with the emergence of fresh produce brands. Fresh produce has an intrinsic variability derived from the vagaries of nature: some customers prefer more regularity and certainty. Here we find the essence of the brand, the suppression of perceived risk – here the qualitative risk of variations of pleasure and taste.

This is what the Saveol tomato brand, the Philibon melon brand from Guadeloupe and the Gillardeau oyster brand, to mention but a few of the best known, have done: it is the sign of a true brand policy. It would be wrong to assume that these brands are products of communication: as always, everything began through product-related innovation. They are based on flavour, and the shape that makes a food item either more practical or more interesting.

The Saveol brand is the banner under which dozens of tomato producers have joined together, united by a single desire to create a superior and different product, to respect the same innovative production processes while eliminating insecticides (replaced by ladybirds), and to invent a true range of flavourful products, in previously unseen forms suitable for different types of consumption (cherry tomatoes, olive tomatoes, etc). This policy of innovation is accompanied by mass-media communication: Saveol's objective is for its name to be the tomato brand spontaneously cited by half the population by 2010.

Philibon, the melon from Guadeloupe, guarantees exceptional flavour all year round.

Mr Gillardeau is the creator of an eponymous brand that has become omnipresent in restaurants in just a few years. The brand guarantee relates to the qualitative aspect of Gillardeau oysters, with guaranteed taste and flesh all year round, everywhere in the world. Gillardeau has built its brand through the restaurant trade, which has then rebounded into a reputation among the general oyster-eating public. The market insight on which the brand is based comes from an understanding of the problems faced by restaurateurs, who wish to ensure a strong, risk-free experience for their customers. Top-of-the-range restaurants made Gillardeau a success, since these restaurants want to avoid any possible problem or disappointment with their oysters: they are committed to the pursuit of perfection. However, its market also contains the small quality brasserie, which by only offering Gillardeau oysters can reassure customers, who habitually mistrust the provenance of the oyster basket.

Furthermore, Gillardeau was able to implement a selective and controlled distribution policy, ensuring exclusivities at the wholesaler level, so that it knows exactly where it is sold and where it is not. Control over its own distribution is the first condition of the premium brand.

Building a wine brand

Wine may also be considered as the application of a brand to a living product. The majority of new wine consumers in France, and more particularly in other countries, justifiably expect no surprises from wine: they expect to find the same pleasurable taste each time, as with Coca-Cola. The major American successes of Yellow Tail, and also Two Bucks Chuck (wine priced at US$2, as its name suggests) and the Australian Jacob's Creek, are a specific response to this expectation.

These wines have brushed aside the old-world wines, since they were designed entirely on the basis of the expectations of the modern (generally Anglo-Saxon) customer and of the distributor. They are the answer to the B to B to C world in which we are now living. The key components of their success are these:

- the ability to supply mass distribution in quantity (therefore reaching critical mass in production terms: an end to the patchwork of small independent cooperatives, and the emergence of big capitalist groups);
- a fruity, easy to drink flavour, designed to please consumers who generally drink beer or soft drinks, with priority given to white wine served chilled;
- maintaining the taste of the wine from year to year, thanks to the blending of different sources;
- the lowest production costs, thanks to legitimate innovations in productivity, which make it possible to reap higher margins, capable of largely financing their distributors;
- investment in the brand, rather than the region, so as not to be limited in quantity, and above all to generate loyalty to a single name: the brand's own;
- logical grape variety: remember that modern customers are not brought up on wine;
- the capacity to create a national sales force to visit all points of purchase and carry out promotions at point of purchase (brand visibility means the product will be picked up);
- investment in communication to cause the brand to emerge in spontaneous awareness, and therefore set itself apart from the thousands of small wine brands;
- the capacity for regular innovation, in order to make waves in the press and achieve good scores from juries, or in wine magazine categories;
- labels written in English, since the wines hail from California, or Australia or New Zealand, or even from South Africa.

There is nothing to say that we will never see international brands for French wine, other than the classic grands crus. The first condition for an international table wine brand is the existence of production capacity able to meet the expectations of mass distribution: from this point of view Languedoc-Roussillon, the world's largest vineyard, offers genuine opportunities and the necessary flexibility for adapting supply to demand, rather than the other way around.

Pharmaceutical brands

Some might be surprised to hear talk of pharmaceutical brands, since the role of a drug's constituents, and therefore of the intimate link of the active ingredients with the success of the drug, seems to defy any other element. Nevertheless, doctors do not prescribe products, but brands, where the generic product is not available. Science comes to us not in the form of the international scientific denomination of the chemical compound, but in the form of its brand name: Zantac, Tagamet, Clamoxyl, Prozac, Viagra and so on, not to mention medicines sold without prescription, which fall under classic marketing (Malox, Aspro, Doliprane and so on).

The medical environment is characterized by several factors that outline how and why 'brand building' is specific to it:

- All prescribers are known, put on file and stored on a database, some even visited directly several times a year (if they represent large volumes). In each country, there are a limited number of doctors, specialists and so on. It is therefore a closed environment. Each laboratory has one or more sales forces, known as medical delegates, who personally meet with all the doctors in order to inform them of the progress of the medicines they are tasked with promoting.
- The available information is almost complete. Through doctors' panels and pharmacists it is possible to know which doctor is prescribing what, and in what quantities, for what conditions, together with which other drugs, and so on.
- In this market, it is possible to model demand in an econometric fashion, due to the completeness of the information. Each laboratory is aware of the pressure it exerts on each doctor (measured by the number of visits, the time of the visit, the number of calls, time spent on the internet, etc). Since they also know the effect on sales through medical prescription, it is possible to establish a mathematical function linking inputs with outputs, causes with effects.
- The subject is highly scientific. Even if 'business to consumer' communication is now sometimes permitted under certain stringent conditions, the end client has little say in the final prescription decision, although this does not mean no say at all. In fact, a general public medical culture has grown up in our ageing, over-informed societies: all mass-media magazines regularly talk about advances in the treatment of this or that ailment. Without citing the drug prescribed by name, they talk of active ingredients. The internet has also considerably increased the general public's level of awareness – nowadays, although people respect their doctor, they also have their own opinion. Furthermore, general practitioners wish to generate loyalty in their clientele: they listen to their clients.
- Prescription is increasingly influenced by the final payer: this is particularly true of generic drugs. Aware of the enormous and growing black hole of health spending, public authorities have exerted pressure for a compulsory switch to generic drugs, where possible. The pharmacist has even been given the right of substitution: if a generic exists, the pharmacist has authority to substitute it for the brand-name drug indicated by the doctor. If the patient refuses, he or she will receive a smaller reimbursement from their mutual fund.
- It is a market where, given the short lifespan of patents – 20 years – the day and year of the generic drug's launch can be predicted. Brand-name drugs attempt to delay this date, the signal for their programmed decline, which may be slower or faster depending on the country:
  - for example, through patenting of original medicinal forms;
  - or through continual modifications to the product, in order to extend the patent's duration of protection;
  - or through hyper-segmentation of the range and the dosages, in order to make the generic drug less profitable;

  - or through a lowering of prices at the end of the product's life cycle to make the switch less attractive.

Public authorities, however, tend to oppose these manoeuvres, because the pressure on public health finances demands drastic savings.

We should also note that certain countries, such as Thailand in February 2007, have decided to bypass intellectual property rights by authorizing the manufacturing and storing of generic forms of two famous anti-AIDS drugs, while they are still under patent protection. The Thai government invokes the argument of protecting its population: these two drugs are too expensive and therefore not accessible. AIDS is causing devastation in Thailand. Note that France did the same when it was a question of building stocks to protect the French population against the risk of anthrax, in the case of a chemical terrorist attack.

- It is an increasingly regulated market. Given its low margins, if too many generic producers offer the same product, they will struggle to turn a profit. Thus, in some countries, the state gives one leading generic producer leave to market even before the expiry of the patent, or to enjoy a temporary monopoly.
- It is a market where counterfeits now flourish. In fact, the active ingredients of drugs can be bought at very low prices in India or China. It is therefore easy to manufacture counterfeits. To date they have been sold via the internet, at the internet user's own risk. However, they are now finding their way into pharmaceutical channels.

How brand personality affects medical prescription

Very few sectors demonstrate the value of branding as much as the pharmaceutical sector. This sector is dominated by the ideology of progress through science. Those prescribing drugs are rational and make what they perceive as the best choice for the patient. Normally this should imply a product-driven market, in which brands are a forbidden word.

Our recent research has shown however that medicines have a personality, as do all brands. By 'personality' we mean that both generalist doctors and specialists find it possible to attribute human personality traits to medicines. Not only did they not refuse to answer questions about brand personality, but statistical data analysis showed that some of the personality traits they ascribed to drugs were correlated with prescription levels (Kapferer, 1998).

When looking at Table 4.2, you will see that the anti-ulcer medicines that are most prescribed are described as more 'dynamic' and 'close' than other forms of medication. A product, an active ingredient cannot be dynamic or close; a brand can. Thus brands of drugs do have a mental existence and influence in the minds of the prescribers.

How brands create preference

Interestingly too, Table 4.3 shows that although they recognized the products themselves as being totally identical and saw two brands as fully similar in the functional benefits they delivered, respondents prescribed one three times more frequently than the other. However, the chosen one was endowed with significantly more 'status' than the less chosen one. Status is an intangible dimension created by impressions of leadership, of presence, of proximity to the doctors, of intensity of communication. It is created by marketing once the drug has been developed. Once created, this serves as competitive edge against 'me-too' products, at least before a new drug replaces the existing one as market leader.

This example illustrates the fact that even in the high-tech sector, brands are a psychological reality, which operate even in the context of rational decision makers who are disposed to make optimal rational decisions. Choice is always a risk: products increase the range of choice, and thus of perceived risk. Brands make choice easier by reducing the number of alternatives.

Medical prescription therefore typically follows a 'two-steps flow of influence' model. Communication with leaders creates status and reputation, which then makes it necessary for people to be informed about this brand that everyone is talking about: familiarity with the product follows this desire created by its reputation (Figure 4.5).

Tomorrow, for certain chronic illnesses, it will be even easier to carry out direct to consumer (DTC) information advertising, mentioning the laboratory

TABLE 4.2 Brand personality is related to prescription levels

	Personality score (1 to 3) of highly prescribed vs less prescribed medical brands					
	Anti-hypertension		Antibiotics		Anti-ulcer	
	Low P	High P	Low P	High P	Low P	High P
Dynamic	2.01	2.20+++	2.17	2.37+++	2.10	2.46+++
Creative	1.87	1.92	1.81	1.93+	2.03	2.22+++
Optimistic	2.02	2.21+++	2.00	2.23+++	2.22	2.31
Prudent	2.13	2.11	2.08	1.98	2.08+++	1.90
Hard	1.58+++	1.39	1.70+++	1.45	1.56+++	1.31
Cold	1.67+++	1.45	1.72+++	1.40	1.60+++	1.33
Caring	2.04	2.11	2.01	2.09	2.03	2.09
Rational	2.28	2.23	2.38	2.27	2.23	2.15
Generous	1.85	1.95	1.87	2.02+++	1.93	2.02
Empathetic	1.88	2.09+++	1.90	2.02++	1.99	2.01
Close	2.06	2.09	2.16	2.25	2.08	2.13
Elegant	1.97	1.97	1.99	2.04	1.92	2.03
Class	2.01	2.04	1.87	1.94	1.93	2.20+++
Serene	2.10	2.12	2.12	2.25+	2.20	2.11
Calm	2.15	2.07	2.16+	2.04	2.12+++	1.90

SOURCE Kapferer (1998)
(+++ level of statistical significance)

and the active ingredients of the drug, but not the brand.

Today, the role of the internet in the dissemination of information to patients, who know more on the subject than their general practitioners do, and interrogate them about the new brands and compounds, is being measured. When updating this research, the patient's own point of view should be included as a new lever in medical prescription. Thanks to the internet, patients arrive at their doctor's office already well informed: they have heard about this treatment or that drug on a blog, a forum, a website, in a women's magazine and so on. Doctors need to generate loyalty among their clientele and

TABLE 4.3 The brand influence in medical prescription

	Category: anti-ulcer	
	Brand A	Me-too
Product image		
Efficient	2.9	2.9
Rapid	2.7	2.7
Prevents recurrence	2.7	2.7
No side-effects	2.7	2.6
No anti-acid	2.6	2.6
Low cost	1.4	1.4
Brand status		
It is a reference product	3.7+++++	3.1-----
High reputation	3.8+++++	3.3-----
Superior quality	3.3	3.1
Major product	3.7+	3.6–
Prescription	6.7+++++	3.3-----

SOURCE Kapferer (1998)

FIGURE 4.5 How brands impact on medical prescription: two-steps flow of influence

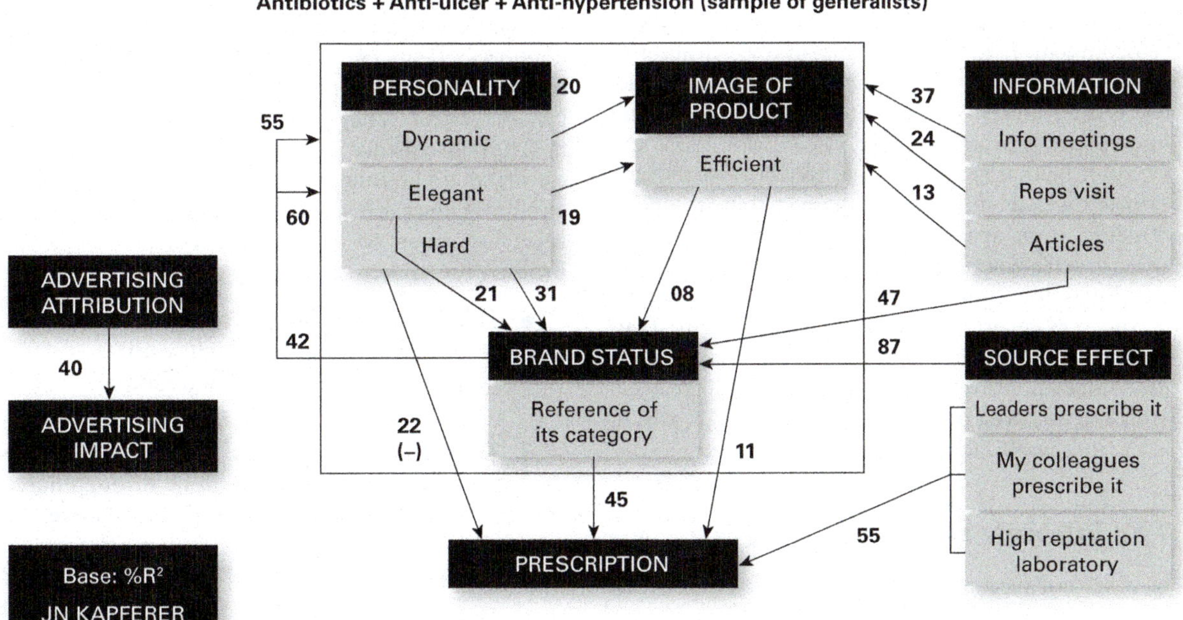

SOURCE Kapferer (1998)
Figures are squared correlation coefficients

are reluctant to act against the patient's wishes, even if they can. For chronic illnesses, the patient's feelings on the unpleasantness of the treatment also play a part. Price should also be integrated as a new lever: in fact, the preoccupation with reducing health expenditure is now shared by doctors themselves.

In another of our studies, we showed how certain facets of the laboratory's image can directly influence medical prescription. This is why, in today's global drug marketing, it is first necessary to establish the laboratory's credibility, one country at a time. In this way it can then enjoy the source effect.

Becoming aware of the intangible

The research outlined above shows that the intangible factor is also present in medical brands, and in this they are brands in the fullest sense. Big brands inspire confidence, and have an attractive personality. However, big brands sometimes possess an intangible dimension that escapes the laboratory, in both senses of the word: due to its rationalist culture, it is not aware of it, and also it does not control it.

Prozac is a major brand. Its reputation has in many ways transcended the context of a medical environment. In fact, more than simply a drug, it is a cultural revolution. By launching Prozac, Lilly did more than launch a new anti-depressant: without knowing it, it overturned Judeo-Christian ideology. Could it be that man was no longer born to suffer? Prozac owes its diffusion to the fact that it is now possible, even apart from genuine depression, to smooth over emotional traumas (divorce, relationship breakdown and so on). It now seems that forces in the service of this ideology have chosen it as a target. Those sects that exploit the fragility of individuals in distress to recruit members have even attacked this drug by any means possible. Clearly, it is the intangible factor that drives the emotion.

The laboratory brand influence

In a second piece of research, we investigated the importance of the laboratory's own image in medical prescription. Of course the characteristics of the brand-name drug outweigh everything else, as they should, but the image traits of the laboratory appear in fifth place, in particular the laboratory's perceived competence in the field, and its ability to hear and respond to information from doctors (highly reactive services and call centres, consultation, the type of medical delegates, and so on) is also significant. They wish to know 'the brand behind the brand'. This means that in the worldwide launch of a new drug, it is first necessary to establish confidence in the laboratory itself among opinion leaders and prescribers, country by country.

Defending against generics

Today, medical brand power is threatened. As soon as the patent that protects the brand expires, a generic is launched, and strong forces accelerate radically the decline of the sales of the brand. It is not so much a decay of the brand's attractiveness or a faltering demand from physicians, or even end users, as requests from those who pay: insurance companies and social security systems. In countries where the population is getting older, the costs of health are skyrocketing. To keep them under control, proactive policies favouring generics are enforced everywhere. In many countries, pharmacies have now gained what is called 'a substitution right'. They can propose substituting the generic version for the brand indicated in the prescription. In some countries clients cannot refuse; in others they can, but they are reimbursed only for the price of the generic version. They pay the difference themselves.

The consequence is that brands must be defended during their lifetime, not when their patents have expired. Figure 4.6 shows that there are three strategies for doing so, which all revolve around the product life cycle:

- The first strategy means accelerating the rate of penetration at launch, with supplementary sales staff and more promotion.
- The second strategy aims at heightening the peak of sales. This can be done through line extensions, new applications of the active ingredient, or even a switch to non-prescription (and then increasing the price).
- The third is a classic defensive strategy largely using the law to extend the duration of patents or make the copying of the brand more difficult in the short term.

FIGURE 4.6 How laboratories fight generics in the prescription market

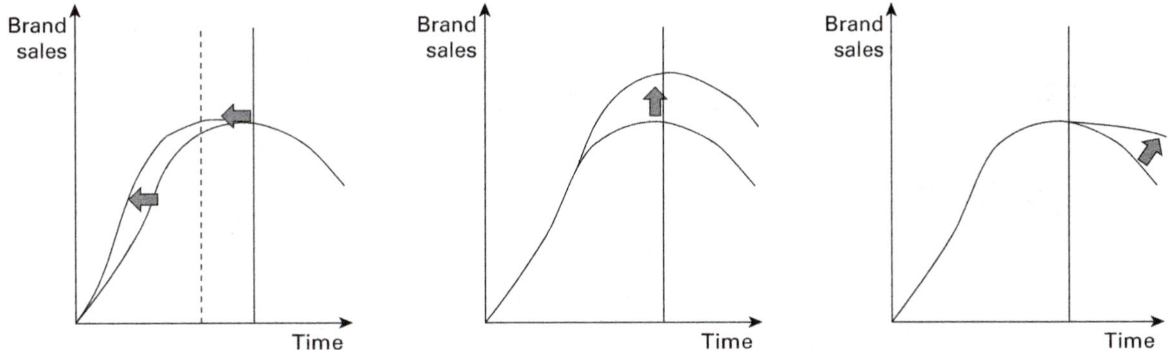

Business-to-business brands

Managers working in the B2B domain regularly complain of the lack of theorization on B2B brands. They are rarely found in academic works on brands, where most examples are drawn from mass-consumption brands, generally food products with low involvement (yoghurts, soft drinks and the like). This is why, in this book, we have purposely used different examples and introduced a genuine variety of sectors, in order to establish the relevance of the models proposed as a tool for decision making.

The company behind the brand

One key dimension of B2B is that buyers engage in relationships, not simply transactions. Most B2B purchases are risky: they concern ingredients of a product or service. Their cost will determine the end price of that product or service, but their reliability will affect the reputation of the brand end clients are in contact with.

This is why in B2B the corporate brand plays a much greater role than in consumer goods. Before deciding to use a strategic ingredient A or B, or part C or D for a car, the purchasing agent must be sure that the company selling these ingredients or parts will still be in business in five years. In B2B one does not buy products, but trust. The corporate brand is the source of trust. The product brand is there to claim its uniqueness in delivering delight.

Figure 4.7 delineates the specific territories of each type of brand, with its targets and promises.

Is B2B different?

One thing is certain: there are indeed B2B brands. If we define the brand as a name with power, a name considered by industrial players as an indispensable reference in conjunction with a particular need, there are plenty of examples: Cisco, IBM, Atos, etc.

First, the B2B world has its product brands: for example, the building trade buys Giproc or Pregipan plasterboards, Sikkens or Levi's paint, Agilia cement, Daikin air-conditioning, Legrand or Hager electrical equipment, Technal or Wicona aluminium and so on. The automobile sector, although under constant pressure on prices, is conscious of equipment brands such as Sekurit for windscreens and Gefco for logistics requirements: the transport upstream and downstream of supply chains of industrial production. Note that these product brands are often names of former companies that, once acquired by a group, cease to be companies and become brand ranges in a catalogue. This is the case for Giproc – now owned by Saint Gobain – and Merlin Gerin at Schneider Electric. Of course these names alone do not ensure sales and loyalty generation, but they contribute strongly to it.

B2B studies also show the influence of corporate reputation. This is composed of awareness and the image of power, commercial dynamism, innovation and ethics. It influences the selection of a company in weighty decisions – weighty because of both their

FIGURE 4.7 Scope of the corporate brand and of product brands

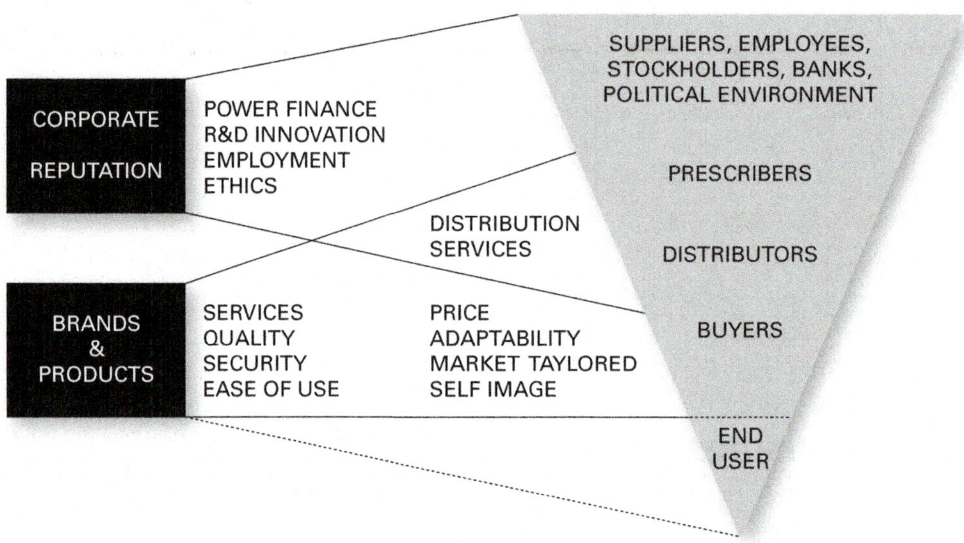

financial total and the length of the commitment. There is a high degree of correlation between the recognition and image of a company and the readiness to 'strongly consider this company for any future tenders', or even to refuse to do so. Of course this does not mean that it is the only factor affecting the choice: in fact, in an industrial environment, consideration does not equal selection, and the tangible components of the tender and the price will of course weigh heavily. It does prove, however, that the name of these companies has acquired the power of a brand as a result of the specific reputation they have built through their expertise and their skill in communicating it. To be considered on the mental, or even the official, 'shortlist' is one of the major benefits of a brand – that is, the reputation that is attached to it. When the brand no longer possesses this power, entire sectors fall to the principle of the lowest bidder, where only the price per kilo or per tonne counts. The function of a brand policy is precisely to avoid this.

Is there no difference, then, between B2B brands and B to B to C brands? In our view there is one essential difference: pressure on costs. B2B purchasing generally forms part of the cost price of another product. A truck or a set of tyres for an articulated lorry is part of the price of transport, which will consequently affect the sale price of products transported by road. In fact, freighters are demanding ever lower prices from transporters, who increasingly view their truck or tyre purchases from an accounting, even a financial, perspective. This leads to a constant B2B pressure towards commoditization. This difference has a major effect on three facets of the brand: the brand function, the brand weight, and the brand's point of application.

Functions of the industrial brand

In our research on sensitivity to brands, with Professor G Laurent (Kapferer and Laurent, 1995), the brand's role as a reducer of risk quickly became apparent. This is not enough in many mass consumption markets: consumers no longer see any risk there. In B2B, very often the products and services play a part in the composition of the products sold, making them components of customer satisfaction and therefore reputation. The Lafarge signature is important for concrete, just as the word Siemens is important for turbines. Of course, concrete could be considered a commodity, where suppliers have shifted the competitive playing field towards services. In the choice of concrete, however, engineering consultancies issuing invitations to tender are sensitive to the risks linked to failures in building infrastructure. This may not be a question of an individual suburban dwelling in Calcutta in India, but of a new council housing office, or a planned new skyscraper in Berlin.

In B2B, every ingredient forms an integral part of the offer that the purchasing company makes to its own clients. Its reputation depends on them. This is why car manufacturers, with their mechanical background, buy Bosch, the specialist in electrical equipment. They know that the weak link in today's cars is not the mechanics, but the electronics. The company 'covers itself' by buying from the top name in the sector for its clients downstream. Furthermore, nowadays it is the equipment makers that provide the innovations. Automobile brands are designers and builders. This is why in B2B it is so important for a brand to worry about the clients of its clients. This is where the big brand's function as a guarantor of quality comes in.

This is its first, even its predominant function in B2B, as the level of perceived risk rises. However, this is not its only function: the B2B brand is also an instrument of pride. It can add an intangible dimension that also increases the brand's potential to attract and earn loyalty. For example, the American company ITW (Illinois Tool Works) has so far spurned umbrella, multi-sector brands. It sells equipment and tools to carpenters, electricians and plumbers, taking care to offer them a brand for each trade. Thus Spit is dedicated to carpenters alone. This differentiation makes it possible to capitalize on each profession's conviction that it is different, and its desire to mark that difference: tool brands either help or hinder this.

One of the problems causing the fall in sales of Black & Decker – a multi-market umbrella brand – is that it sells both to the general public, through major stores, and also to professionals, forgetting the brand's intangible function as an instrument of self-expression for professionals. It reacted, but too late, by launching a new brand dedicated to professionals alone, De Walt.

When the IBM PC was the best-selling PC, everyone was in agreement that the product was average, or in any case far from being the best. However, in 1981 it was reassuring to company IT directors who were uncomfortable with this new market (of personal computing), since it came from their supplier of larger systems: the giant IBM. For users, the IBM seal offered them the satisfaction of saying to themselves (mentalization) or communicating to others (self-reflection) that they must be serious executives, since they had an IBM. The recent transfer of IBM to Le Novo (a Chinese company) reflects how much the PC market has been commoditized. The perceived risk in the purchase has shifted from the assembler of the PC to the components themselves (Intel, AMD), which now become parameters of choice, and the operating system (Windows Vista). Hence the struggle for component manufacturers to build themselves up as brands: that is, as major choice criteria. They do this through co-branding and major financial involvement in the communications budgets of their partner assembly brands.

The real weight of the industrial brand

An enduring suspicion regarding the real weight of the brand in industry decisions relates to the questioning methods used in the sector – surveys with direct questions are used. Thus, during a study on the factors involved in the choice of a maritime transporter for major shippers (such as the industrialists Saint Gobain for glass, and Michelin for tyres), the five main criteria given by logistics directors were price, dates and times, reliability, capacity for last-minute delivery, and the availability of information throughout the journey. The brand is the last criterion named. In contrast, when an indirect questioning method is used, of identifying choice factors – by varying the parameters of maritime companies' offers and examining the impact on the shippers' choices – we see that reputation (or in other words, the brand) becomes a key factor, if not the principal factor.

There is nothing irrational in this, as too many people in the industrial sector experience it or say it. How, in fact, can one know in advance whether everything will go well before and during maritime transport? None of us are soothsayers. We must therefore make hypotheses: a well-known brand is not well known by accident. It carries in itself the quasi-certainty – subjective but based on experience – that everything will go well, or better than it otherwise would.

It would be wrong to suggest that reputation (and therefore the power of the brand) is the number one criterion in all B2B selling. Office Depot, the office furnishings distributor, delivering direct to companies, owes its profitability to its product policy. Office Depot sells first and foremost its remarkable service to companies. Products come second, with Office Depot attempting as far as possible to substitute its own products for branded products: in fact, the latter are now in a minority. It retains only a few Scotch products, for example, and not all of them: it offers adhesive tape under its own NiceDay brand. Of course, it is sometimes still obliged to offer Stabilo Boss, Bic Crystal and Post-Its, and the Dymo label printer, but that is all. And yet all the brands deleted from its catalogue are well known. Today, however, this is not enough. The end users – secretaries, managers or employees – do not even notice that the product they find on their desks is not the true Post-It, but a cheaper distributor's brand copy. A strong brand is a brand with indispensable products or with strong intangible added value (reassurance or pride).

This shows us that among industrial distributors, and now in B2B, there is an obsession with substituting brands, as Carrefour has done since 1967 in the mass market. A study among wholesalers of electric heating indicated that they had in stock three electric water heaters: the first because 'everyone asks for it', the second because 'people ask for it', and the third for its price. Saying that 'people ask for it' clearly reveals that in the industrial sector, the brand is a prescription. All of the brand's B2B marketing should focus on the distributor's clients, or the professional buyer's clients within the company. If this prescription is not created, for example through a dedicated sales force, then the brand enters into a downward spiral through the distributor and the buyer, who only thinks about the price. Legrand's great strength is that it has understood this: Legrand has made its brand such a 'must' for electricians that to Legrand, wholesalers are merely stockists. It needs them only for this stock function.

Corporate and brand equilibrium

One of the characteristic traits of the B2B brand is that it has a double nature. It may be the company itself, or the products and ranges, or a combination of the two. However, the level of risk is such that the reputation of the source and of the company is most often called into play.

At Air Liquide, the brand is the corporate name for the sale of commodities with little differentiation: the prestige attached to this leading company cannot overcome a price handicap, but where prices are the same, it will add its guarantee of seriousness and regularity of provision. It may even be enough to justify a small price difference. In order to move away from the 'commoditized' market, Air Liquide has developed and co-created specialized lines, together with its clients, such as for example the gas brand Aligal, intended for the preservation of fresh produce in plastic packaging. These innovations carry a name that refers back to the corporate name through its prefix (Al) and specifies the destination market. At Gaz de France, the range of prices and associated services has been promoted under the Provalis name, in order to de-commoditize it.

Industrial B2B companies often believe that they can manage without the corporate brand reputation, and that only the product reputation matters. This is an error that passes unnoticed until the day that financial analysts signal undervaluing on the stock exchange arising specifically from the absence of a brand. This is the case with Sage. Sage is rather like Europe: an economic giant, but a political dwarf. Sage is one of the giants of management software for companies, but it is not recognized as such. It is true that the company has grown through external growth, buying companies that became product names within its product portfolio (of management software). With a turnover of €2 billion, Sage is an expert in marketing products and remarkably successful at selling them. Its competitors in this market are SAP, which turns over €10 billion, Oracle, which turns over €6 billion, and Microsoft, which turns over only €1 billion but has the highest growth rate in the software market for SMEs. These figures suggest to the stock market that a consolidation is on the cards: it awaits a takeover bid for Sage, which appears to show a lack of dynamism, due to its low recognition as the key actor in the sector. The stock market wants Sage to demonstrate that it has the capacity for organic growth.

Divided by market, Sage allows its divisions to run their own autonomous communications: the largest divisions therefore communicate the most. These are the ones that are active on the historically best-known major markets (accounting, pay and human resources). They therefore drag Sage's image down, to the detriment of the new markets, which show promise for future organic growth, but where sales are still small. The failure to take into account the reputation needs of the parent brand itself, Sage, makes it a weak brand. It is a portfolio of products and clients, but not a brand. For any development of legislation or regulations relating to the SME, governments consult Microsoft or SAP, not Sage: Sage is not perceived as a genuine actor in its sector.

Its reputation is less than that of its products. Significantly, there are only 200 links leading to its website, whereas it has more than 300 licensed distributors – a sign that to them, Sage is not a necessary reference.

It appears that, having neglected to organize themselves and to invest in order to create a reputed and recognized crossover brand, companies suffer the consequences at a given point in their growth. Organization by product and by market creates sales, but also silos: worried about the figures in their annual evaluations, nobody works on the collective reputation, which costs money without bringing short-term benefit.

The activation points of the B2B brand are different

The B2B brand is a relational brand. Other than in commodities markets, people do not buy a product, but rather a supplier, with a view to durable joint development. Wholesalers themselves do not just stock a brand – they represent it, and are thus committed to it. They therefore expect it to behave like a brand, with a guarantee, innovation, services with added value, development of markets through communication, and activation of networks. The carriers of the brand are both products and the consultation of commercial delegates, their reactions and the quality of their follow-up and service.

Facom's reputation was built on a fleet of trucks that visited garages, not to sell, but to explain the products and listen to the garage mechanics, their comments and requests, from 7 am when the workshop opened. This is how the spread of lowest-bidder tenders, where the only things that matter are the price and the regularity of provision, can be avoided.

The B2B brand is a prescription

Lastly, the B2B brand focuses on prescribers. The decision to buy within a company always involves not one, but several people. The brand is therefore built up through identifying the key prescribers: the architect, the research offices, the consultancies, the technical departments and so on, all the way to the final client. Thus Legrand does without wholesalers, except for logistics, since it carries out permanent promotional campaigns among electricians and the general public, to let them know about innovations so that they can demand them from their electrician. All the success of Lycra, the brand that de-commoditized generic elastane fibre, consisted of working first of all with those who acted as guides and opinion leaders for the entire textile sector: the luxury and premium brands. When they developed common applications, the innovations made were noticed by the entire sector. In the meantime, Lycra had acquired a precious aura to justify a price much higher than generic fibres. Tactel followed the same approach to constructing its brand, through co-creation and the decision to target leaders with strong prescriptive power.

Multi-brand groups specialize their brands according to their business model, which is linked to prescription. The Norwegian Norsk Hydro group, a leader in aluminium applications, has three brands in Europe for aluminium profiles intended for construction: Wicona, Technal and Domal. The first is aimed at large projects, and therefore capitalizes on the prescriptions of architects, design offices and engineering consultants. Technal uses the final customer as the lever of prescription on the installers themselves. Domal aims at small companies directly.

Moving away from a commoditized market

The risk of commoditization is the sword of Damocles for B2B. Of course there are niches where the level of perceived risk ensures positional income, as with companies specializing in the analysis of aviation fuel quality, but these are exceptions. For the world leader in industrial paints, Akzo Nobel, the brands have a single objective: to bring value to the client in order to move away from competition on price. Therefore it pursues a policy of global brands, each dedicated to a target, according to a global segmentation built on painters' expectations.

A market is commoditized when the actors have not worked hard enough on it. The brand is not a miraculous answer, but the name that takes a genuine marketing approach of creating value for a dedicated target. It is therefore necessary first of all to analyse the clients, to understand them – to go beyond the machine-gun volleys of surveys that show the client only cares about price. All markets are segmented, even the low-cost markets. Everything depends on what is offered alongside the price.

Thus any chemical company will claim that the silicones market is a purely commoditized market. In reality, as with many other industrial markets, there are four segments:

- those clients who want innovation in order to be able to innovate themselves for their clients;
- those clients who want to improve their efficiency and productivity;
- those clients who want to reduce the total production cost;
- those clients who want the lowest possible price.

Three segments here are sensitive to price, and would probably put this criterion in first place in an opinion poll with direct questions. However, a more in-depth investigation might show the client's problem with its own client, downstream: this is where we find fertile soil for the added value that must be created. If we consider the fourth segment lost, it is necessary to concentrate on segments two and three.

This is what Dow does: it has created a business known as Xiameter, separate from Dow's core business, aimed at the cost-oriented segment. Then began the work on the value curve of the Xiameter offer. It is necessary in fact to stop talking about the product, but to envisage the delivery of silicones as the creation of value for the client. If you wish to offer a low price, but also value alongside it, it is important to analyse the facets that the client is likely to neglect (and therefore reduce them to zero) in order to maximize those of which the client expects most. This innovation, known as 'value innovation' since it redefines an attractive value curve previously unseen in the sector, makes it possible to innovate in the price segment (see Chapter 9 on value innovation). Of course, in the case of Xiameter, everything was carried out via the internet, which made it possible to set prices according to stock levels, rather like yield management of prices in air and TGV travel.

The internet brand

How do internet brands function, the purely online brands such as Facebook, Google, eBay and Amazon? What are the specific mechanisms of their growth, seemingly so rapid while it is taking place? We now have the benefit of distance to guide our analysis.

In brief, internet brands have the following major characteristics:

- They do not have clients, but users, known one by one.
- They promise a price advantage.
- They prove by experience.
- They are permanently adapting and updating.
- They are easy to globalize.

The internet brand is both experiential and relational. It is experiential, because each person forms their own idea by visiting personally, by living the experience. One only has to visit Google to be impressed by what a simple click can obtain, time after time. It is a typical process of loyalty generation through the systematic distribution of gratifying experiences to the user.

It is relational, because the great strength of the internet is its ability to learn from each individual, one to one, and to demonstrate what it has learnt to that same individual. Amazon is the model here: the user only has to go online to see that he or she is recognized, and welcomed with good, personalized news (new books chosen for him or her, based on recent purchases). Amazon is more congenial to deal with than many bookshops.

To this is added the positive effect of 'network externalities'. eBay has benefited from these, as has Facebook: the more visitors there are to an auction site, the greater the chance that the sellers will find a better buyer able to offer a better price, and likewise the greater the chance that the visitors will find a seller with the product they have always wanted, but had despaired of ever finding. It is a giant virtual car boot sale, like the Paris flea market or the Portobello market in London, except that it is transparent: the user can tell immediately who is offering what. Visitors to eBay have all the more reason to revisit the site, since it continues to grow – not to mention the fact that by returning to the same site, users have no need to relearn how to use it. They already have their bearings, even when they are not recognized, spotted and greeted like a dear friend. These are all factors that create, if not a barrier to leaving or to visiting rival sites, at least a mechanical propensity to revisit. Of course the service is high quality, and is always improving, to adapt to clients that are becoming more sophisticated and whose demands are growing. Like any brand, the internet brand must continually create value for each fragment of its clientele, almost one to one.

The internet is also a mass medium of affinity: users can immediately communicate with their friends and community how satisfied they are with a particular site, and what they have just found or experienced there. Electronic word of mouth, or 'word of mouse', finds an accelerator out of all proportion to usual word of mouth, hence the recent notion of the 'viral rumour'.

Virtual closeness and psychological closeness

What is a brand? Fundamentally it is a name (and its associated symbols) that has a lasting influence on purchasing behaviour. What is a big brand? A name that is also linked with emotion by a very large number of potential purchasers. A big brand has no effect without an emotive relationship. It is this attachment, or commitment, that generates the desire to pursue the relationship, from the purchaser's point of view, which translates to loyalty to the brand. The value of a brand is measured by its capacity to create a personal tie of loyalty with the consumer, at a particular price level.

Are the pure internet brands brands like any other? Studies show that closeness is still lacking for many brands. This might appear paradoxical at a time when the internet is presented as the alpha and omega of personalization. However, those are the facts. When asked, consumers are hesitant to say of dot.coms, 'This is a brand I feel close to', as if the relationship of repeat visits had not yet been translated into a genuine intimacy and complicity. Do we visit Price Minister, a price search engine, because we prefer Price Minister? Or simply because this is the only name that immediately springs to mind, so that we click on it, and then click on it again, using the economy of effort represented by a favourites list?

For some analysts, this lack of closeness is structural: the pure dot.com brands will always lack the sensory, physical and palpable dimension without which there can be no genuine closeness. What is left of these brands once the screen is switched off?

Brands such as eBay took four years of silent work to progressively refine their concept and their services: they made little use of advertising, but much more of word of mouth of satisfied pioneers, then early adopters and finally customer-ambassadors. Their reputation was built through interactions with enthusiastic surfers, who had the feeling of being listened to, which in addition to their recommendation also had the effect of lending these brands an emotive dimension and closeness.

The closeness and complicity are those of shared values and emotions – hence the phenomenal success of a site such as Facebook or YouTube, both bought by Google for a king's ransom for that reason. Amazon, for example, is a genuine brand in the sense that it carries values that extend beyond the product. It has moved beyond the marketplace by offering on its site a new way of interacting with other people on the subject of books, and now many other products as well. It symbolizes more than the new economy – it prefigures a new society and a new era.

One question remains: are they creating long-term loyalty? Are Twitter and Facebook used because the product is remarkable but could be abandoned tomorrow if another innovation came along? Who is still using AltaVista or Yahoo!?

Country brands

Among the most spectacular extensions of the notion of a brand, we find countries. There is no shortage of symbols: in New Delhi, more than 100 people work full-time on 'Brand India' and on the implementation of a global communications programme 'Incredible India', with the goal of modifying behaviour towards this infinitely varied country by working on people's perception of it and even giving it a positioning. Books such as *Rebuilding Brand America* (Martin, 2007) or *The Marketing of Nations* (Kotler, 1997) mark how countries have become symbols, words charged with emotion, and sources of influence over the actions of people who, for the most part, have never visited them. In fact, countries are associated with snippets of history, recent or more distant, imaginary elements, the personality traits of their inhabitants, key competences and accomplishments. The reputation of certain countries is based more on their history; for others it is based more on their accomplishments. This is why companies and their commercial brands shape the country brand itself through their success, and sketch out the international stereotype of their key competence. The reputation of its universities also creates the country brand.

The country's evocative power

Countries are therefore names with brand power: they have the power to influence through the spontaneous associations they evoke, for good or ill, and through the emotions that they stir up. This brand power (influence) is nevertheless linked to specific products: Italy is the great cultural brand, a sign of quality and creativity in the fashion market, for example. The United States has a wider effect: we voluntarily 'consume' the US brand and its affective evocations when we buy Coca-Cola (the water of America), jeans (the clothing of America), American cinema from Hollywood, American hamburgers, when we smoke Marlboro cigarettes, the metaphor inhaled from American Westerns, and when the whole world accepts the dollar as the base of international exchanges despite the huge US debt. However, we no longer buy their cars, ill suited to the era of expensive and soon to be scarce petrol.

As with all strong global brands, the country brand encapsulates a myth, a stereotype that boosts its own attractiveness through an emotive resonance. The United States, a country built by immigrants, encapsulates worldwide the mythology of liberty (hence the famous statue of that name) and the self-made man, the accomplishment of success through hard work and effort. In fact, in the DNA of American identity, we find immigrants fleeing their miserable living conditions in their home countries in Asia and Europe, who have rebuilt their life in this new promised land.

The country brand combines information at all levels: from political to social to cultural to economic to tourist, from the past to the present, real and imaginary, in complete syncretism. Managing the country brand entails working specifically on the salience of these different facets, burying some (by saying nothing) and making others more visible.

The 'Made in...' stereotype

We have known for a long time how much the words 'Made in Germany' create value in the automobile industry and industrial equipment worldwide. In just 10 years, 'Made in Australia' has become a symbol of value in the current wine market, through daily and relaxed usages. The words 'Made in Korea' have moved from a devaluating status (second-rate copies) to a symbol of respected quality between 2000 and 2012. The biggest question for the Western world today hinges on whether 'Made in China' has the ability to follow the same positive trajectory in the same short time frame.

Marketing research itself has set up 'country of origin' as a specific, rich and prolific field, demonstrating how much countries are associated with attributes, competences, real or imaginary representations that combine to create relevant value (or not). This research teaches us that the 'country of origin effect' is not uniform. It varies:

- according to the sector (France for perfumes, Germany for machine tools);
- according to the consumer (national stereotypes have more influence for novices and laypersons: professional buyers and experts rightly move beyond them to seek partners and new suppliers for their own company);
- according to the level of perceived risk attaching to the decision, its individual or collective nature (the need to prove to others that the choice is a reasoned one).

To recapitulate the paradigm of research into persuasion (Kapferer, 1990), the words 'made in country X' act as a sign of specific qualities and faults, but also like any source of communication. If it is a credible source, it relieves the receiver of the need to look too deeply into it, and lowers his or her resistance to persuasion. If it is not credible, it will lead directly to rejection.

Why look at countries as brands?

A good country image helps business. One can and should estimate the financial value of a nation brand. Bastien, Dubourdeau and Leclère (2011) extended the classical brand valuation methods (see Chapter 18) to the measurement of France as a brand. Brand valuation methods entail two steps: the first one is the identification of the added value brought by the name, in each economic sector; the second is the application of a discount rate to calculate the present value of the flow of added profits brought by the brand in the forthcoming years.

The added value brought by a country name in an economic sector refers first to exports: what is the pull power of the 'Made in...' label (country of origin, COO) or the 'Designed in...' label (country of design, COD) on foreign consumers? Countries also create value by attracting merely through their name a flow of migrant workers, tourists, corporate headquarters, business conferences or symposia, students, researchers, financial investments, factories, and expatriates asking for political asylum.

The COO or COD added value varies considerably by sector and country (Steenkamp *et al*, 1999). Nobody in the United States knows that Bic is a French company. Lacoste does not explicitly insist on its French nationality. Total, the oil giant, sees itself as a European company with French roots. In all these instances France adds nothing in terms of brand preferences.

The same holds true for Samsung, or LG or Hyundai: they are certainly perceived as Korean brands, but Korea has no image. It is likely that the image of South Korea will in fact be built by the image of its multinationals succeeding abroad. Indeed the communication agenda of South Korea is fully controlled by its closest enemy, North Korea. When the hunger of its people necessitates aid from the developed countries, North Korea stages war-like provocations immediately followed by secret negotiations to release the pressure in exchange for food.

Why else is it very useful to look at countries as brands?

Looking at countries as brands acts as a counterweight to the myopia of domestic views. This is a typical problem among politicians, who put their country at the centre of the world. The brand-as-country perspective asks another disturbing question: does the country name play a role in influencing foreign audiences' choices of products or services? Politicians are proud to praise local industry for employment reasons, but it is not at all certain that foreign markets perceive it.

For example, in the UK everyone used to talk about Concorde, the only civil aeroplane that could fly at Mach 2, as a British product. Well, it was actually a co-creation of the UK and France. The same holds true for Airbus: because its final assembly takes place in Toulouse, in south-west France, most politicians take it for French. In fact it is a product of the cooperation between many European states and not at all a national output.

Looking at a country in terms of the concepts of branding also casts a new light on the situation.

FIGURE 4.8 'France brand' architecture

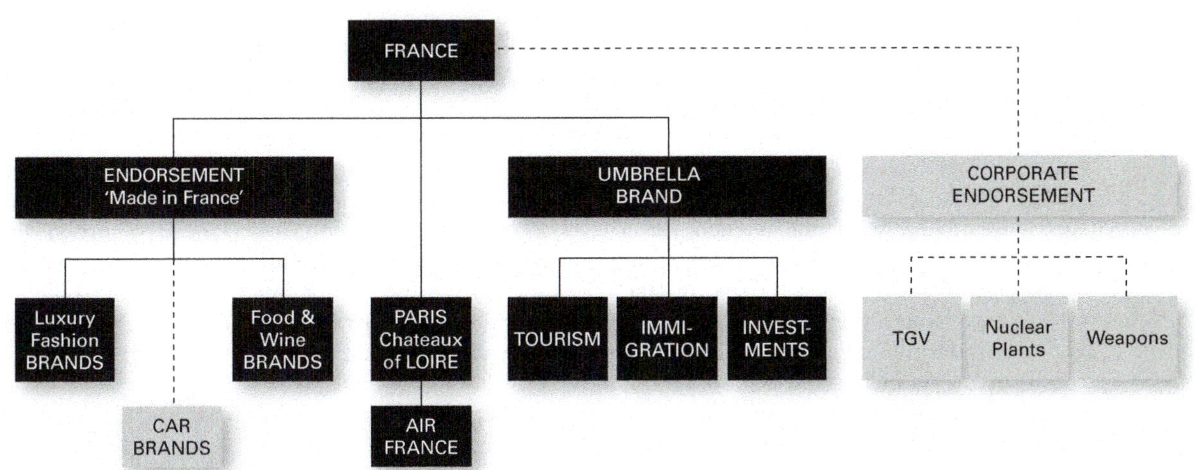

Brand architecture depicts the ways the brand meets the consumers, either directly or through sub-brands. In the latter case, the parent brand may have either an endorsing role or a source role (see Chapter 13).

Interestingly brand France uses a number of architectures, depending on the sector of activity:

- It acts as a single brand, attracting people into the country because of the quality of life, the infrastructure, the educational system and social security. This umbrella brand has a direct impact on tourism, business exhibitions, corporate headquarters localization, workforce immigration and foreign investment. The prototype of France, its 'star product', is Paris. Air France is a typical ambassador of the global hedonistic lifestyle promise. Major national strikes also communicate the will of the French people to keep their hedonistic lifestyle at all costs. The collapse of the French soccer team at the World Cup in South Africa does not create either an image of willpower and resistance to effort.
- It acts as endorsing brand for the luxury industry through COO labels on Vuitton or Chanel brands, on foie gras or on bottles of champagne and cognac.
- It acts as shadow endorser to many brands that do not make clear use of their country of origin. All German car marques play on their nationality. Volkswagen's worldwide slogan is 'das Auto' and is not translated from German. However, Renault, Peugeot and Citroën do not explicitly make use of their nationality.
- It acts as corporate endorsing brand behind major exports such as TGV fast trains, nuclear plants and public utilities (eg water supply treatment, waste management for towns and cities). We underline the notion of 'corporate', for it is the state that in fact sells to other states. The choice is driven not by market preferences, but by political counterparts. As such, these exports do not build a public image (the brand), but only a private image (B2B) among a small circle of insiders.
- It acts finally as non-endorser of many companies that hide their nationality or at least do not communicate it.

The result is a vicious circle. The tip of the iceberg (brand France), the only visible part, is strongly hedonistic and experiential: it makes France the number one tourist destination in the world. It is formed from luxury brands that by definition use their roots and history as sources of added value. It is also formed from Paris, the capital city and also France's most symbolic product. Paris is known as a romantic city, which is a very different image from that of London (multicultural), Berlin or New York. This image is contradictory with another historical part of French exports (infrastructure, high-tech fast trains, nuclear plants, military jets and weapons), whose brands or companies are not known to the public. France's image does not help either the equipment industry or the car industry.

Thinking of towns as brands

Today, all municipalities will perforce have to turn to brand concepts in order to manage their town more efficiently and contribute to its growth. Two structural factors lead them towards this. The first is the growth in the number of large transnational actors with large sums of money designated for site regeneration. These are the actors that the town must convince – for example the World Bank, the European Union or regional development funds. Second comes the movement towards decentralization and delegation of power at the local level. It is no longer a question of the municipality lobbying Paris, but rather of it fending for itself with its own budget.

Mayors know that they are in competition with other towns on various markets: they must therefore know how to sell themselves. By creating a good reputation for their town they give themselves a voice. Like brands, towns need to grow: they therefore need to attract new resources (people, workers, companies, finances and so on). Like any brand, they must also be able to define where their unique attractiveness lies, or what is known as positioning.

A town, on the other hand, is first and foremost a human, local and immovable reality (which is not to say that it is unchangeable), anchored in history, culture and its ecosystem. It can and should be altered to adapt to evolution, to the economic and social needs of the present day. However, the brand cannot be built without it. It must be reckoned with. The construction of the brand should first of all involve a consensus among the town's key actors.

How does the town choose its positioning, this long-term, mobilizing, attractive differentiation strategy? By digging deep into its own DNA, its identity. A town is a living and complex social body, which has its own genes. There is everything to be gained, not by reproducing the past and what the town once was, but by reinventing it on the basis of the values, competences and ideals that have moved it throughout its history. This is why it is necessary to dig into the town's soil, identify its genes, beyond the vicissitudes of recent history, in order to define its identity kernel. This retrospective study is the necessary prelude to selecting the positioning that will project the brand into its future. Then the 'products' that will carry the brand and be its best exemplars have to be activated (football teams, museums, headquarters, sites, etc).

TABLE 4.4 The top 10 European business schools

1	HEC Paris (France)
2	London Business School (UK)
3	Insead (France)
4	IMD (Switzerland)
5	IE (Spain)
6	RSM Erasmus University (Netherlands)
7	ESCP-EAP (France/Germany/Spain/Italy)
8	Esade (Spain)
9	Iese (Spain)
10	EMLyon (France)

SOURCE *Financial Times*, 2010

Universities and business schools are brands

Nowadays, the dynamism of a country is judged not by its history, its monuments or its cuisine, but by its brands, in particular those that spell attraction, modernity and intellectual power.

Higher education institutions are now also engaged in a brand war. Revealingly, there are now global rankings of the quality of universities and business schools – a sign that the market is now global. The same is true for wine. In Europe, the *Financial Times* draws up the ranking of 55 European business schools. Its 2010 ranking is shown in Table 4.4.

The challenge that European universities must meet is considerable. Their resources are so small that they do not even appear in worldwide evaluations. Like Oxford, the Sorbonne is a true brand, whose reputation has been built over centuries and diffused worldwide. Its excellence in literary studies is well known, carried by the excellence of its professors. However, an objective analysis of the service that each student receives illustrates that in terms of teaching, as with any brand, the intangible components are not enough. Major financial resources are required to bring today's teaching up to the standards of global excellence in education. This will be the great challenge for Europe brand: to give its universities the financial resources to shine internationally. If the state cannot do it, then companies must, and therefore it is necessary to change the relationships between companies and the university. This is why the big business schools everywhere have already acquired the status of global brands.

Every country has its star brands: the United States has Harvard and MIT for example, the United Kingdom has Oxford and Cambridge, and China has Tsing Hua; in France, HEC and Insead are brands. Of course the United States also has other excellent business schools, as global comparative rankings continue to demonstrate. However, only some of these have additional emotive value, strongly linked to intangible components, the vague feeling of entering into more than simply a university or school, but into a very exclusive and global club.

It is striking to see how globalization poses new problems for educational institutions, which were previously sheltered from it. Like it or not, they must now think like global brands, and give themselves the resources to do so. What is a brand, if not a name with strong influence and power to attract – since their market at least is global? Reputation is the inevitable attraction vector: an aura attached to a name able to bring the world's students and major executives to Europe to round off their education at great expense.

It is therefore necessary to know how to export our qualifications, if Europe wishes to remain in the hunt as a great country. However, globalization requires a complete revision of our certainties, practices and habits. It is now necessary to think globally in order to remain number one.

This global market is now revealed by global judges, who have drawn up their evaluations as objective rankings. In the international evaluation by the *Financial Times*, considered the reference on business schools the world over (as summarized in Table 4.4), HEC Paris occupies the top European spot, just above the London Business School, Insead and IMD in Switzerland and the three Spanish business schools. In worldwide terms, HEC is now 18th, even ahead of the Kellogg Business School (Northwestern University). This evaluation by the *Financial Times* is based on a multi-criteria analysis objectifying the performance parameters of each business school, its ability to deliver added value to its students on all programmes, and to executives who go there to improve their competencies.

These new evaluating authorities define the objective criteria for their judgements: they measure the true added value for each business school. In so doing, they impact the products and the processes.

The discreet but systematic rise of HEC Paris on the world stage was slower than many executives would have liked. The university or school brand is built through its products: it does not flood the media with big promotional campaigns. On the contrary, its ambassadors are the quality and success of its students, hence the importance of selection and the critical mass of the number of former students, and publications by professors in the best scientific management journals, as a way of durably impacting managerial thinking. Professor Philip Kotler has made Northwestern known as a global marketing Mecca, and Michael Porter has strengthened the status of Harvard Business School. Another contribution comes from the reputation of international pedagogical engineering missions by the biggest groups, and the ongoing training of executives worldwide.

Thinking of celebrities as brands

It is common to talk about brands as we talk about people. We will see, furthermore, that one of the facets that make up the singularity and the identity of a brand is its personality, its character. This derives from an increasingly anthropomorphic conception of the brand. This is one of the consequences of the need to pursue so-called relational marketing: that is, worrying less about the imminent sale than about establishing an enduring relationship between the customers and the brand. We form relationships with people, not products – hence the notion of brand personality, as if we were describing the profile of a friend. To communicate this, the brand may sometimes associate itself with a genuine personality, someone who brings their own attractiveness and incarnates the brand's values. Michael Jordan and Tiger Woods are the prototypes of this practice: where would Nike be without them? L'Oréal Paris, whose personality is glamour, is represented by what they call the 'dream team', a team of Hollywood stars and global top models who appear in all its advertising.

Conversely, some celebrities became genuine brands and were managed as such. By brand, we mean a name capable of generating enthusiasm, fans and customers. Think for example of James Bond or Harry Potter, virtual celebrities whose spin-off products create genuine, profitable and durable business. The failing perfume house Coty rebounded by developing a new business model: creating perfumes for stars (Alain Delon, Celine Dion), just as others, upon leaving HEC, hit on the brilliant idea of offering to create a perfume for Salvador Dali (to their great surprise, he accepted, and it is one of the best-selling perfumes in Japan).

Picasso is not only the name of a famous painter, but also a brand. The company set up by his heirs, with its headquarters on the Place Vendôme in Paris, works constantly to prevent the name falling into the public domain. In order to prevent this, it must be in proven and meaningful commercial use. This is why, 10 years ago, the company went around the car manufacturers and offered them the licence to the Picasso name. Citroën accepted: the name increased the perception of novelty and creativity of its new model, which would go on to successfully challenge the Renault Scenic in the segment it created.

The newest development is that sports stars, for example, are becoming brands. Not all of them – far from it – but some of them. Neither George Best, nor Roger Federer, despite being the world number one in tennis became brands. In contrast, the lyrical poet-footballer Eric Cantona could have become one, as his too-rare excursions into cinema show.

Among the great footballers, perhaps David Beckham, previously of Manchester United and Real Madrid, best represents the notion of a celebrity becoming a brand (Milligan, 2004). It is well known in football that celebrities make a profit for their clubs. If Manchester United has 17 million fans in Asia, imagine the number of spin-off products that could be sold to them as objects of their cult.

What is the difference between David Beckham, Zinedine Zidane and Michel Platini? All three have been very talented professionals in the world's most popular sport, soccer.

Are they brands? To ask this question means 'Can they become brands?', which – as we now understand – means 'Can their names have power beyond that of being great footballers? Can they create a lasting consumer engagement, even when they stop playing football? Can they create a community of fans, willing to buy all the products touched by their icons, hoping that, by the magic of contagion, the aura of their idols will take hold of them?'

When asking the brand question, we do not talk here of sponsorship, for example Gillette hiring Thierry Henry, Roger Federer and Tiger Woods, or Rolex also hiring Federer. These co-brandings are expected: prestige brands like to hire the fame of the present idols when there is a good fit between their values (Rolex is a paragon of regularity and precision, just as Federer is, and both are Swiss). Since Gillette wants to stand for 'the best a man can get', it gets the best men to say it worldwide.

Why does Nadal not yet have his own fragrance? Or Roger Federer? The world's number one fragrance company, Franco-American Coty, has invented the business model of celebrity fragrances. Transforming a person into a fragrance is the ultimate test of the capacity of a celebrity to become a product. The fragrance captures the spirit of the person, the essence. The question Coty is asking is that of the brand potential, and then of the channel of distribution. Celine Dion has her own fragrance, sold in all supermarkets. Jennifer Aniston, although she is a great TV star, does not have her own fragrance. A precise diagnosis must be made before making such decisions: failure is costly.

Our most recent research (Denier and Kapferer, 2012) identified five factors predicting the ability of a sports celebrity to become a profitable brand: product potential, brand awareness and image, brand depth, brand resistance, and size of business (see Table 4.5).

These factors explain why Nadal is not a good brand, however remarkable a tennis player he is. Nadal has damaged his image by not knowing when to say no. He has accepted all kinds of sponsorships, with no coherence, just for the money: Peruvian cookies, Cola Cao chocolate, a bank, Seat automobiles, Lanvin clothing, etc. Federer also does not have good brand potential: being the nicest guy does not create enough intangible qualities and personality traits to transform into a world fragrance.

Now let's come back to our former question about Beckham, Platini and Zidane. Would they pass the grid? They would, but we need to introduce here a fundamental conceptual distinction, which will have a bearing on the weights attributed to the factors of the grid:

- David Beckham is a commercial brand, which could legitimately sell physical appearance items (fragrance, suits for men, fashion accessories, etc). His taste is original and defines the new manhood, with a little ambiguity.
- Michel Platini is a corporate brand, a B2B brand: his impression is very strong inside the limits of the football profession. Known for his seriousness and integrity, he is now at the head of FIFA.
- Zinedine Zidane is an institutional brand: he stands for values. He sells reputation. This is why Danone Corporation has hired him as company and brand international ambassador and sponsor of the Danone Nations Cup for young people.

TABLE 4.5 Can a sports celebrity become a brand? The decision grid

	0	1	2
Product potential			
Is X handsome or with an interesting uniqueness?			
Is X brilliant in his/her own sports?			
Has X an interesting and rich personality?			
Brand awareness & image			
Is X already a «people» or a media icon?			
Is X's sport highly mediatized?			
Brand depth			
Does X represent strong human collective values?			
Brand resistance			
Is X well advised? (clubs, coaches, sport agents)			
Are the sponsors of X well known and powerful?			
Does X know to say No?			
Does X protect his/her image?			
Can X survive a scandal or when he/she retires from sport?			
Size of business			
Has X fans beyond the frontiers of his/her sport?			
Is X durable or just the present «hype»?			

SOURCE Denier and Kapferer (2012)

In managerial terms, knowing that they are a brand leads such people to managing themselves as such, or even taking on an agent who will be better placed to do so. The essential requirement is to preserve the brand value, doing nothing that would destroy even a little of its attraction. The goal is for the brand to outlive the sportsperson – since all champions have to retire in the end. Thus, far from accepting all commercial contracts, however lucrative, it is important to know how to say no to some of them. What products should they create under their name: perfume, clothing or...?

05 Managing retail brands

Today, 50 per cent of all fast-moving consumer products sold on the shelves of supermarkets in Europe are retail brands or even no-brands. Gone is the time when brand management meant only big brands such as Ariel, Pampers, Gillette, Mars, etc. The new strategic brand management must extend its scope to this 50 per cent. In addition retail brands now include consumer durables, banking and travel services, telephone, utilities, petrol, pharmaceuticals and even B2B.

Restricted for a long time to the mass consumption sector, distributors' brands are part of the competitive environment in the mass prestige store Sephora, automobile equipment (the Norauto tyre retail brand is the biggest seller in France), agricultural cooperatives, pharmacy groups and so on. Until recently, merely the cheapest products, they have now become innovators which are quick to offer consumers products that keep pace with the latest trends in society (organic farming, fair trade, exoticism, gourmet dishes and so on). In many cases, these have become inseparable from the store: thus Picard frozen food stores sell only their distributor's brand. The Body Shop, now part of the l'Oréal family, sells only its own distributor's brand. Gap began life as an exclusive retailer of Levi Strauss, stocking jeans in all sizes, but changed its strategy when discount arrived in the United States. Now Gap only sells... Gap. Other examples include Ikea, Habitat, Roche and Bobois, Crate & Barrel and William Sonoma. Marks & Spencer's has done the same since its inception.

In the B2B sector, distributors' brands and low-cost products are also present: Asian companies are competing to supply them. Thus a Facom key for a mechanic costs €10, but only €3 if made in Taiwan. In the office furnishings market, Office Depot has based its success on distributors' brands: apart from the so-called obligatory products (certain Pentel products, Stabilo Boss, Post-It, Staedtler, Dymo, Bic) it sells only the products of its own brand. And is there not something paradoxical about the way that the same big companies that complain about the rise of distributors' brands then buy the Niceday brand from Office Depot instead of buying major branded products? In short, they are criticizing consumers for doing what they are themselves doing: managing their spending.

Evolution of the distributor's brand

Academic studies have until recently failed to pay sufficient attention to distributors' brands. With the producer's brand being considered as the only point of reference, distributors' brands were thought of as 'non-brands', attracting price-sensitive customers. Moreover, the distributor's brand is less extensive in the United States than in Europe. In fact, in the United States, with the exception of Wal-Mart, no distributor dominates: distribution is regional, and the national brands still have power in the distribution channel. This is why distributors' brands have long been perceived in the United States as low-cost, low-quality alternatives, an assessment that failed to take the full measure of the phenomenon.

It is revealing that the recent book published in the United States about distributors' brands (Kumar

FIGURE 5.1 Ending the confusion: stores, store brands and brands

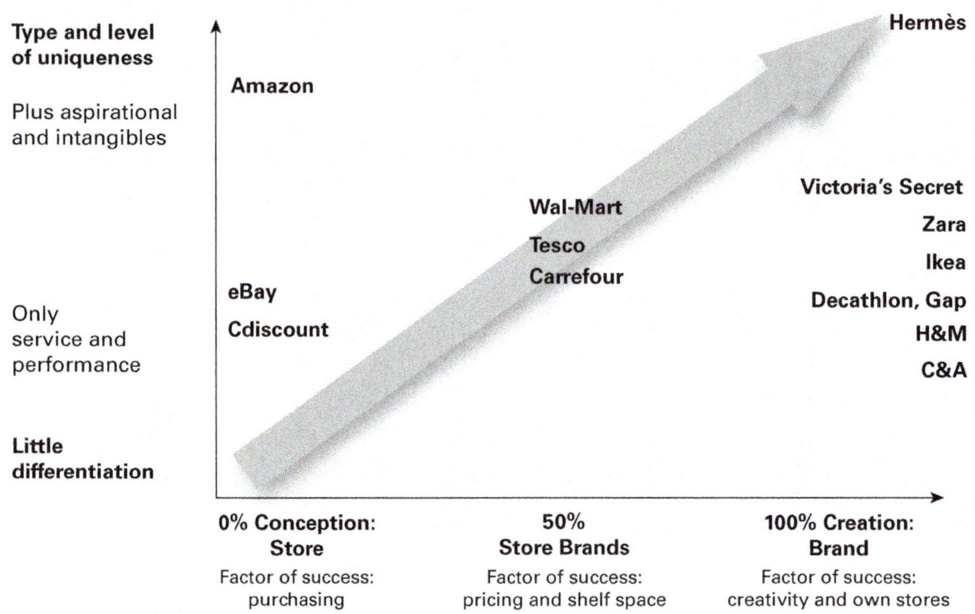

and Steenkamp, 2007) chose 'private label' and not 'trade brands' as its title: the notion of 'private label' categorizes the distributor's brand as a thing apart, and not using the word 'brand' therefore fails to account for the true reach of distributors' brands. They are indeed brands in the eyes of consumers, who are now loyal to them, even if, as will appear, they are not brands like the others.

At Tesco, the number one distributor in Britain, a survey of the fruit juice aisle is revealing: far from being a product, the distributor's brand is in reality a segmented range, from the lowest possible price (Tesco Value), priced at £0.33 per litre, to £1.84 for the top of the range, under the label 'Tesco Finest'. Tropicana's product, by the way, is sold at £1.62 per litre.

In fact, distributors are well schooled in distributors' brands. They:

- allocate the majority of their shelf space to them, eliminating all weaker brands;
- have segmented their portfolio of distributors' brands in order to meet the different expectations of their clients (a far cry from the 'Soviet' own brand, signalling the absence of choice) without forcing them to identify with the shop name (Wal-Mart named its men's clothing range George);
- segment their range in order to cover not only different price levels, from the cheapest to the highest price on the entire shelf, but also the emerging needs known as 'trends' (such as Tesco Fair Trade, Tesco Organic and Tesco Healthy Eating).

The distributor's brand, managed with strength and ambition, is strategic. Not only does it wish to increase the profitability of the shelf, but its fundamental goal is to differentiate the store.

Throughout the world, the distributor's brand is becoming the only true competitor to the producer's brand, when it is not the shelf leader in volume. Too many brand managers have not yet accepted this reality: their brands are in a minority. Their enemy is not the other 'big' brand, but the distributor's much cheaper products, with an increasingly comparable quality level. To make things worse, on hypermarket and supermarket shelves we find the producer's brand, the distributor's brand and now the lowest-price products, 60 per cent cheaper. This further heightens the urgency to act (Quelch and Harding, 1996) and position the major producer's brand firmly and squarely on its pillars of

FIGURE 5.2 Relative positioning of the different distributors' brands

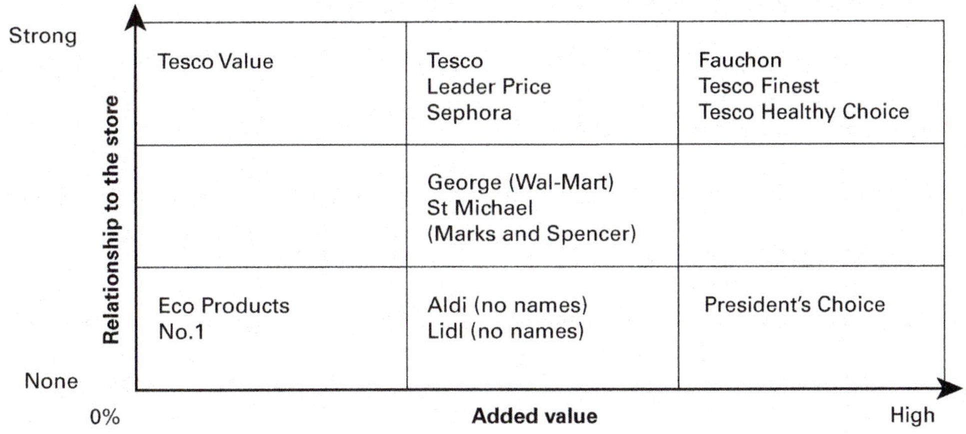

Relationship to the store (Strong → None) / Added value (0% → High)			
Strong	Tesco Value	Tesco Leader Price Sephora	Fauchon Tesco Finest Tesco Healthy Choice
		George (Wal-Mart) St Michael (Marks and Spencer)	
None	Eco Products No.1	Aldi (no names) Lidl (no names)	President's Choice
	0%	Added value	High

differentiation: innovation and quality on the one side, and emotional added value on the other.

The distributor's brand is not a phenomenon linked to low income. In Switzerland – which has one of the highest per capita incomes in the world – the leading food brand is Migros, well ahead of Nestlé. This is hardly surprising, as Migros is a dominant distributor: every village has its own Migros store. Migros – without exception – sells only Migros products. The citizens of Germany, Europe's most powerful country, enjoy their luxury cars, but they buy most of their food from the Aldi and Lidl hard discounters, which also – almost without exception – sell only no-name products. It is hard to imagine that the Germans would buy poor-quality goods. Loblaw's, a Canadian chain, has built its reputation on its President's Choice brand. The story is the same at Carrefour, Albert Heijn in Holland and Ika in Scandinavia.

Distributors now manage their brand portfolios as part of an overall vision for the category and for the store. They have to choose their 'brand mix' for each category segment, and make a decision with regard to the type of brand to offer: producer's or distributor's brand? The latter may offer either ranges of economical products, a value-for-money line (often in the distributor's own name) or own brands (private labels) offering more flexibility in terms of positioning – perhaps even genuinely premium positioning.

It is true that within the meaning of the catch-all term 'distributor's brand' there are distinctions to be made between very different realities. Two axes give structure to all the distributor's products or brands: the level of value added, and the relation to the store (see Figure 5.2).

In terms of added value, at the bottom of the scale are the low-cost products, hastily designed by mass-distribution multiple retailers to counter the breakthrough of the so-called 'hard-discount' German stores (Aldi and Lidl). These products are the result of a minimalist conception of quality: low-cost sardines have the legal right to be called sardines, but make no pretence at anything more. Their low price is obtained through the purchase of the cheapest sardine lots in fish auctions the world over. Low-price gingerbread contains not one gram of honey. This should not be confused with the low cost business model of the hard discounters such as Aldi and Lidl, which established precise quality specifications with industrialists, aiming to obtain decent quality despite the rock-bottom prices, via economies of scale pushed to the extreme: the manufacturer recruited will produce only one reference, in astronomical quantities. At the other extreme of added value, we find products such as Tesco Finest, for example fresh fruit juices made less than three days earlier and with a limited shelf life (without preservatives) and Fauchon, which offers luxury products. In the United States and Canada, the President's Choice line from Loblaw's aims high in terms of quality, as its name suggests.

In terms of nominal relationship to the store, a distributor's brand may either carry the name of the store or its own name: one or the other. Thus, at Carrefour, there are 'Carrefour products', Tex (for textiles) and BlueSky (for televisions). Of course, intermediate situations do exist, where the store endorses its own products: all Marks and Spencer products are called St Michael.

We thus arrive at the bottom line of Figure 5.2. The store does not impose its name directly:

- when its insufficient reputation is a handicap for product sales;
- when the brand name fulfils a badge function (for example wine or clothes);
- when the level of added value of the products is too low and could reflect negatively on the store name: for example, at Carrefour low-cost products are labelled No. 1 or Eco, without any mention of Carrefour.

Other terms are used to denote the forms of distributors' brands:

- The **own brand** or **private label** is a distributor's brand that has its own name and does not generally refer to the company's name (for example Miss Helen for cosmetics at Monoprix, or Jodhpur for textiles at Galeries Lafayette).
- The **counter brand**: this word designates a distributor's brand, generally a private label, created to divert clientele from a particular big brand, by slavishly imitating its packaging in order to play on client confusion and the psychological principle according to which everything that looks very much alike is in fact very similar.
- The **positioning brand**: these are ranges that, far from being content with offering the best quality/price ratio, position themselves on trends or in the premium segment. Take for example Tesco Healthy Choice.

Certain stores use their name in all segments. The highly respected British retailer uses its name Tesco both for low-cost products (Tesco Value) and for the top of the range (Finest) and niches and trends (Tesco Healthy Eating). Capitalizing on a single name makes the customer's job easier, and profits the store, but of course means that high standards must be achieved in all segments, even at low prices. Other retailers prefer not to run the risk to their reputation, and do not use their name on the cheapest products.

Are they brands like the others?

The big brands have long regarded distributors' brands with condescension, and would deny their new type of products the sacred title of 'brands'. That would call their historic hegemony into question, a kind of *lèse-majesté*: until now, the big brands have led the field and dominated it. For them, stores were distributors, a revealing term, since it refers more to logistics and transport than to a talent for composing an overall offer or for managing the shelves. This is why stores insist on being called retailers. The rise of the distributor's own brand (DOB) is all the harder to accept since it signifies the end of a particular type of marketing.

Is the distributor's brand managed like a manufacturer's brand?

From a managerial point of view, distributors' brands are, broadly speaking, brands like any other. They have all the features of a brand (thinking of a particular target, selecting a principal competitor whose clients they will attempt to divert, defining an offer and a price, setting themselves up with packaging and communication) but in addition they have to respond to two different constraints simultaneously. They have to find their place in the distributor's marketing mix, in which they now represent a key component of identity, differentiation and loyalty generation (although the effect on customers' loyalty to the store has not yet been proven: see Corstjens and Lal, 2000). And they generally use price as the driving force behind their own marketing mix, even when, exceptionally, they are positioned in a premium segment.

For this reason, management of these brands does not have the same autonomy as a producer's brand. Their image positioning is based on that of the company. As for their price positioning, it is generally relative, set between the two client benchmarks of the big brand prices and hard-discount product prices.

In formal terms, the distributor's brand often takes on the form of the umbrella brand: Carrefour products or Tesco products. Admittedly, there are also private labels that make no reference to the store but present themselves as isolated, thematic brands. The hypermarket chain Intermarché has its own boats and factories: it sells seafood under the Captain Cook brand, and its processed meats under the name Monique Ranoux. Carrefour sells a range of over 100 regional products under the brand *Reflets de France* (Reflections of France).

To concentrate on the store brand, also known as the banner brand, since it capitalizes on the reputation of the store's name, it typically covers a large number of products, or even shelves: through its extension, it brings a service of practicality to the customer, who can find it by passing from shelf to shelf. It functions like a common factor, a decisional marker across the store horizontally.

The manufacturer's brand, on the other hand, signifies competence: its extension is therefore necessarily more limited (see Chapter 13). Fleury Michon, the French specialist in processed meat and fresh delicatessen products, would not dream of selling jam. The brand has a vertical expertise and a *savoir-faire* that underpin its progress, materialized through innovations.

This does not mean that a distributor's brand may serve as an umbrella for anything and everything. Bringing everything together under the umbrella of a name is not an end in itself: the brand is there not to save money, but to create value for customers. From this point of view, it is revealing that the big supermarkets develop a portfolio of umbrella brands, in order to cover the whole scope of their offer while also seeking the level and type of client involvement (Kapferer and Laurent, 1988). At Monoprix Miss Helen is the feminine beauty and hygiene brand, just as at Wal-Mart George is the male clothing brand. In contrast, Monoprix aims to associate its name with emerging consumer trends: organic, sustainable development, gourmet, openness to the world, healthy eating, etc in the form of 'line brands', as does Tesco (healthy choice, organic, sustainable development, etc).

How retail brands innovate

It is impossible to talk about brands without touching on the question of innovation. In fact, the function of the national brand, the big brand, is to supply progress through innovation, change, fashion, design and so on. This requires marketing expertise – long-term thinking on the expressed, or latent and unconscious, expectations of future clients. They also have the expertise of the major industrialists. Thus in 2006, Fleury Michon, in accordance with its brand charter, launched hams without preservatives, since these are the future, even if today's customer is not aware of it. To be a brand is to be a leader, to look far into the client's future. Eliminating the chemical preservatives implies replacing them with natural preservatives: it took three years of R&D to find bouillons to carry out the same preservative function. Some years previously, during the mad cow crisis, Fleury Michon was able to innovate in offering ham steaks. It is also the brand of turkey ham, and other unusual products.

Can the distributor's brand also innovate? Its business model assumes light marketing – in order to reduce the costs linked to the dozens of product managers – and the fact that it follows quickly in the wake of what is already working, that is the innovations of the successful manufacturers, by copying them to within a few details. In fact, the product specifications of subcontractors tasked with manufacturing a distributor's brand product are up to 80 per cent defined by the characteristics of the successful product to be imitated. If Henkel invents tablets to replace washing powder, the DOB must then manufacture identical tablets. According to the stores, the remaining 20 per cent of the specifications will be a way of providing differentiation linked to the store's own values. However, in order to be able to appear quickly on the shelves with an identical offer at a 30 per cent lower price, it is necessary to economize on marketing and R&D: the distributor's brand business model is that of copying, of imitation taken to the maximum.

A common riposte is that distributors' brands were the first to introduce such and such an innovation in terms of packaging: for example, turning shampoo bottles upside down, in accordance with their actual position in the bathroom. However, the distribution brand, by the very construction of its economic model, does not seek to innovate: its price is obtained through turning the efforts and investments of the manufacturer's brand to its advantage, profiting from its strong position in the relationship, which means that the manufacturer needs the store far more than the store needs the manufacturer. Upon the launch of new food, hygiene and maintenance products, the mass distribution stores today request immediate access to the same innovation for their own brand.

The examples most often given to prove that distributors' brands can innovate are *Reflets de France* and *Escapades Gourmandes* (Gourmet Escapades). We know that this revolutionary concept consists of revitalizing the production of 100 regional recipes, having them produced by SMEs in these regions, and bringing them together under the same brand, sold in all the Carrefour Group's stores. Private labels excel in incremental innovations. As a consequence, own label products account for 62 per cent of the 4,600 new product launches of the British food and drinks market.

When the distributor behaves like a true brand, it opts for own brands, and becomes the store of the brand and not the brand of the store. For example, Gap, which was the exclusive seller of Levi's, began to introduce its DOB, and progressively ceased to sell anything but its own store brand products. However, it was then necessary to clearly define a brand concept, the store becoming the place where the brand was expressed and experienced. Gap defined the concept as anti-fashion. Decathlon does the same. It is symptomatic that in order to accentuate its status as a designer/manufacturer with its own stores, Decathlon gave up its store brand (there are no longer any Decathlon products) in order to organize everything under what it called 'passion' brands: that is, a portfolio of private labels. We present below this interesting case of a distributor becoming a creator (Figure 5.1).

Consumer relationships with distributors' brands

Let us now look at the question (are distributors' brands truly brands?) from the angle of the consumers themselves. For consumers in mature countries, distributors' brands are perceived as genuine brands, with their attributes of awareness and image always combined with an attractive price.

When asked the classic awareness question ('What are the yoghurt or bicycle brands that you know, even if only by name?'), consumers name Asda or Decathlon. When asked if they intend to buy them (general client opinion) or buy them again (behavioural loyalty), the scores are just as high. It is no accident that on the majority of mass-consumption shelves, lowest-price products and distributors' brands hold the dominant market share. Over time, some distributors' brands are able to achieve the typical brand effect, as shown by Table 5.1, which looks at the United Kingdom, for many years a leader in this field. According to the Brandz study, the consumer's proximity to the brand moves from a feeling of presence (awareness, recognition) to a feeling of relevance (it's for me) to the perception of performance and a clear advantage, and ultimately to a genuine affective attachment. It is interesting to note that two distributors' brands have made it into the top 10 of British brands studied by Brandz: Marks & Spencer and Boots.

TABLE 5.1 Brand attachment: the 10 winning brands in the UK

Rank	Brand	Score	Rank	Brand	Score
1	Gillette	57	**7**	Nescafé	39
2	BT	56	**8**	Heinz	39
3	Pampers	53	**9**	Kellogg's	39
4	Marks & Spencer	42	**10**	Boots	37
5	McDonald's	42	**11**	Colgate	32
6	BBC	40	**12**	Royal Mail	32

SOURCE Brandz (UK)

C Terrasse (Terrasse and Kapferer, 2006) worked on four product categories, in order to compare engagement with the Carrefour brand with that for the big brand in the same category. Engagement with the brand means more than repeat purchase.

Engagement – personal involvement with the brand – measures a strong relationship with the brand, meaning that if the brand were not there, the client would prefer to wait than buy an alternative. For the consumer, there is no substitutability. The reverse is indifference, or sensitivity to the slightest rise in price. This engagement comes from two sources. The first is a strong perception of proximity (the customer feels a closeness with the brand), and the second, satisfaction linked to a perception of difference in product performance.

As Table 5.2 demonstrates, engagement with the store brand is driven by feelings of proximity. It is relational. On the contrary, for the manufacturer's brand, 'fans' are fans because of a strong experience of the product's superiority.

C Terrasse also examines the consequences of engagement with the brand. In theory, the more people are engaged with the producer's or distributor's brand, the less they will seek variety when

TABLE 5.2 How attachment to distributors' and producers' brands differs

	Carrefour brand	Big brand
Satisfaction linked to perceived product superiority	0.161	**0.539**
Perceived proximity with the brand or store	**0.601**	0.236

SOURCE C Terrasse/J-N Kapferer, 2006 (correlation coefficients with the attachment score)

shopping in this aisle, and the less sensitive they will be to the price. This is exactly what happens with the big brand: repeat purchase results directly from the client's engagement with the brand and its reductive effect on two key factors of disloyalty (enjoying variety and being sensitive to price). For the store brand, engagement with Carrefour certainly influences the repeat purchase, and certainly diminishes the appeal of variety, but does not make the client insensitive to the price. This means that the repeat purchase of the distributor's brand is always contingent on the price: it is highly conditional. These shelves are now seeing the advent of lowest-price products. The customer buying the trade brand always keeps an eye on price differences on the shelf. It is not an absolute brand.

This is why distributors' brands have difficulty creating loyalty to the store, as is often observed in studies: admittedly they create repeat purchasers within the store, but they do not appear to offer discriminating reasons, or even overriding reasons for visiting one store over another. The distributor's brand therefore plays less of a role in differentiating itself from the competition than the manufacturer's brand, which works only for itself. These results have been shown again in very recent analyses (Szymanowski, 2007).

This does not mean that all distributors' brands are perceived to be equal: the image of the store (quality, cleanliness, popular or elitist character, and so on) reflects on everything that bears its name, therefore firstly on the distributor's brand.

Why sell distributors' brands?

In 2010, at the world's number one distributor Wal-Mart, out of a turnover of US$400 billion, 40 per cent was made from the distributor's brand. This percentage is 60 per cent at Tesco, the fourth-largest distributor in the world, 35 per cent at Metro, but 90 per cent at Aldi, the king of the hard discounters. In the field of sports products, it is 51 per cent at Decathlon. Why do distributors come to set up their own brands, to the point that – like Gap or Ikea – they eventually sell nothing else?

For an answer to this question, we should not look to the consumer, who is only too happy to have finally found a cheaper product. In reality, the true economic motor of the unstoppable growth of distributors' brands lies with the industry: the distributors and producers themselves.

In the mass consumption sector, the early distributors' brands are almost always born of a conflict between the distributor and the producer. Dissatisfied with the poor treatment it receives, the distributor has its goods produced elsewhere, in order to plug a gap, and sells them either under its own name or under a private label. The atmosphere of conflict persists, particularly since – in Europe for example – brands now typically depend on a very small number of distributor clients (four) for 60 per cent of their sales. Procter & Gamble makes 16 per cent of its worldwide turnover (US$80 billion) from a single client: Wal-Mart. Decathlon accounts for more than 10 per cent of Nike's sales in Europe. Furthermore, these distributors' brands help the worldwide development of distributors, leading them to match the expectations of quality products at lower prices that are prevalent in emerging countries (Brazil, Eastern Europe, Russia, India and so on).

Consumers are selective. They decide in which categories they are the most tempted to buy distributors' brands: those in which they have a low degree of involvement (Kapferer and Laurent, 1995). Remember that brands exist wherever customers perceive a high risk in purchasing. Conversely, where they see no risk, they are tempted by the distributor's brand, particularly if they consider that distributor to have a good reputation and an image of quality. For example, the butter category is now dominated by distributors' brands. Three-quarters of all the processed meat sold in self-service stores in France is low-cost or distributors' brand products, but the same is not true of new food products, such as low-fat butters and unsalted hams, which suggests product development is a source of concern, and consumers need the reassurance of a well-known brand name. In all cases where the consumer expects superior performance (cosmetics, for example), the producer's brand leads. The same is true wherever the product has assumed the status of a symbol or 'badge': again, the distributor's brand fails to make an impression, except where it has become itself a declaration of self (the Gap is the anti-fashion).

Now, emboldened by satisfactory past experiences, consumers are taking the plunge: there are distributors' brands for PCs, €120 bicycles, hi-fis and domestic appliances. Consumers may want a Sony or Samsung television for their living room, but in the kitchen or in a child's bedroom they are less involved: they may be tempted by a BlueSky (Carrefour's low-cost hi-fi brand). The same is true for home computing. Dell is a product assembler, and sells under its distributor's brand. However, its products are guaranteed 'Intel inside'.

In reality, the distributor's brand is based on supply, not demand. Whenever distribution is concentrated, and the size of the domestic market makes it economically possible, there is no other way for the retailer of increasing his return on investment (ROI).

Bear in mind that growth in distribution is achieved over time, through the elimination of competing channels or other forms of commerce, followed by the competitors themselves. In this way, in Europe, small traders have vanished altogether in many categories, having been swamped by the supermarkets and the hard discounters; this was how the distributors first started to grow. Having reached the end of this path, distributors have turned to the international market and cost reductions: hence the fashion for cost-cutting techniques such as efficient consumer response (ECR) mode and trade marketing. The final stage is the distributor's brand as a means of improving ROI.

Finally, we should not forget what the major distributors sometimes call upstream marketing. The distributor's brand makes it possible for large stores to present themselves as objective allies of local and regional SMEs against the multinationals, since it is the SMEs that manufacture the distributors' brands.

Everyone knows that mass distribution does not always have a good image. The crushing of small businesses has contributed in large measure to the desertion of town centres, and of complete suburban zones: society as a whole is paying a steep price for this. In their eagerness to position themselves as the cheapest, the major players in distribution and their massive bulk buying have launched themselves on the world like hunting dogs, driven by a single idea: to always find it cheaper and import it as quickly as possible. This quest – with the approval of consumers only too happy to save money in the short term – has led to the downfall of companies, entire sectors and towns, leaving thousands of local workers unemployed. This social cost has passed largely unnoticed. The salaries in mass distribution are among the lowest in the country: the store owners are rich, but the prospects for salary increases for a cashier over 10 years are minimal, a situation dictated by the price war.

What has society gained from this frenetic competition between the major distributors? Conscious of the collateral damage for society, mass distributors make use of two levers to give themselves a clear conscience. Either, like Carrefour, they flatter national pride, since the company has exported itself worldwide (although this does not create more jobs in France), or like Leclerc, they present themselves as the defender of SMEs, the majority suppliers of distributors' brand products. Having been crushed by the multinationals, SMEs will be saved by mass distribution. We know that this is provisional, since this preference for SMEs derives from the refusal of the major industrial groups to produce DOBs. Where they do so, there are no SMEs. Now the question for all boards of directors of the major industrial groups is: why leave this market to the SMEs?

Should manufacturers produce goods for DOBs?

One of the questions all company managers ask concerns the opportunity to work for distributors' brands. This question is even more urgent today, since with the shrinking of the shelf space allocated to branded industrialists, their economic model is under threat. How can they maintain the volumes that create profitability?

Those industrialists in favour of producing DOB goods advance the following arguments:

- It relieves the burden of fixed costs.
- It allows them to benefit from economies of scale.
- It may be intrinsically profitable, since there is no need for marketing, communication, or sales force.
- If they do not do it, their competitors will.

In contrast, those who oppose it are right to argue that it will undermine the long-term legitimacy of the company's own brands, since the industrialist will not be capable of producing a bad product. For a while the product Olympia manufactured for Carrefour was superior to the comparable product of the brand itself. An examination of the figures in the cheese sector also shows that the most profitable cheese maker is Bel, which sells only branded products (Laughing Cow, Mini Babybel, Leerdammer, etc).

Rather than drawing up a pointless balance sheet for and against, it is worth turning to research in this case. HEC has carried out several specific studies on this important theme for companies in all sectors, under the direction of M Santi (Santi, 1996). The selected criterion is operational profitability compared with turnover, and the sample comprised 167 cases drawn from numerous mass-consumption sectors. What does this research have to teach us?

- The profitability level is maximal when the policy is the result of a voluntary strategy (9 per cent) and not an opportunistic reaction to a short-term demand (5.19 per cent) or a survival strategy (6.53 per cent).
- The profitability level also depends on the underlying motivations: it is at its highest when the company is seeking to create a genuine partnership with distributors, in order to defend its own strong brands (7.90 per cent). If the brands are weak and the DOB manufacturing approach is an attempt to save them, the profitability in the sample is less (3.50 per cent).
- The profitability is maximal if this is the dominant or even exclusive activity of the industrialist (7.51 per cent).
- The profitability is maximal if the market is not a commodity market (7.64 per cent).
- The profitability is weakened by the fact that the industrialist does not make a distinction between its brand and the distributor's brand it is producing: this is an important point, since many industrialists distinguish between the two only through the packaging, in order to make the most of the economies of scale and long production runs.
- The profitability is better when the manufacturer works with distributors that promote quality.

What can we draw from this HEC research data? Whether or not to manufacture distributors' brand products is a strategic choice, and should be analysed as such.

Should they do it? Refusal to do so is clearly the result of a long-term vision: Procter & Gamble, Gillette and l'Oréal all invest too much in research to wish to share the benefits they reap from it. They reserve the first fruits for their own brands, within a structured portfolio.

Which companies should do it? There is no correlation between any classic company description and profitability in DOB production: rather, profitability is linked to the manner in which it is implemented.

In which segments should they operate? The least commoditized possible, those where there is still innovation.

Which distributors should they work with? Here, too, selectivity in the choice of distributors proves to be rewarding in terms of profitability over turnover.

The financial equation of the distributor's brand

In a competitive market, the distributor's brand is a logical stage in the growth of the distributor. It satisfies the need to maintain ROI once all other approaches have been exhausted. Alternatively, it may have been the key differentiating component from the outset (as in the case of Ikea, Starbucks, Body Shop and so on).

Let us look again at the principle of ROI, in order to understand why the distributor's brand is an advisable step at a certain stage in a distributor's growth.

Net margin = Gross margin – Costs

Stock rotation = Sales per square metre/ Investment per square metre

ROI = Net margin × Stock rotation

What does a distributor do when it wants to increase ROI from 20 per cent to 22 per cent (an increase of 10 per cent of the current ROI)? Suppose that this is a major distributor with a net margin of 2 per cent and a stock rotation of 10 per cent. Two possible options are available: either to increase sales by 10 per cent per square metre (giving a rotation of 11), or to increase net margin from 2 per cent to 2.2 per cent through selling private labels and demanding even more price concessions from brand producers, or a share of the profits from their advertising/promotional campaigns (which ultimately amounts to the same thing).

This second option – increasing the net margin – is a much easier way of increasing ROI: everyone knows how hard it is in a mature market to increase turnover per square metre. This is why all distributors are choosing, or will choose, the distributor's brand if they wish to make optimal profits. In fact, the first lever for improving ROI arises from the fact that the margin on DOBs is better than that on national brands (Ailawadi and Harlam, 2004).

The second reason for introducing a distributor's brand relates to the increase in negotiating power with the manufacturer. Not only does the distributor improve its margins on the DOB, it also receives better margins from makers of national brands, who wish to persuade it not to go further.

A third effect on distributor profitability induced by the introduction of DOBs relates to the increase in the number of innovations launched by the manufacturer. Distributors receive listing fees on these products. Moreover, they are rarely low-price innovations (Pauwels and Srinivasan, 2004).

Finally, distributors hope that their distributors' brands will contribute to increasing loyalty to the store itself. In theory, these are products that can only be found there. Research carried out at HEC Paris demonstrates that this effect has not yet been proven. Among the reasons for loyalty to a store, the distributor's brand is almost never cited, except for stores that have developed distributors' brands with strong added value (Monoprix, Tesco) and have acquired a reputation of their own.

The three stages of the distributors' brand

History shows that there are three stages in the business growth of distributors' brands: oblative, imitative and identity.

The first stage is known as reactive or oblative: historically, it results from the refusal of sale by the major industrialists. This is how many own-brand products are born. However, it is also strengthened through identifying gaps in the ranges of the major producers. A category management approach quickly identifies those segments where something should be offered to the client, but where the major brands have nothing to offer, since it is not their strategy. These gaps need to be filled.

The second stage is imitative: here, the distributor examines its competitors' distributor's brand ranges, and sets about imitating them, producing the same products typically supplied by its other competition. By means of this emulative method, the distributor's brand core offer is constructed, created from all the references common to all the distributors' brands. We should add that this is also typically a phase during which the distributor, for lack of investment in its own distributor's brand identity, chooses to imitate, trait for trait, the packaging of the brand products that it is targeting (generally the category leader). The objective of this copycat approach is clear: a deliberate intent to take market share from the big brands by allocating more space to one's own distributor's brand, a similar copy, and to increase the average price of the big brands in order to attract clients to the distributor's brand (Pauwels and Srinivasan, 2002).

This imitative or 'copycat' approach borders on trademark infringement, and sometimes gives rise to court cases by the outraged and wronged producers, complaining of either an infringement of their brand rights, or unfair competition (see

TABLE 5.3 How copycat resemblance influences consumers' perceptions

	They are made by the same manufacturer (%)			I trust the private label (%)
Rank of packaging resemblance	**Definitely**	**Probably**	**Total**	**Yes**
1 Panzani/Padori (pastas)	39	41	80	78
2 Martini/Fortini (spirits)	30	31	61	56
3 Amora/Mama (ketchup)	21	46	67	62
4 Ricore/Incore (coffee)	16	17	33	38

SOURCE Kapferer (1995a)

page 215), or economic parasitism. A visit to the aisles of mass distribution is enough to note the striking similarity between the copy and the brand packaging. In most cases, however, disputes – arising from the overzealousness of the designers – are resolved amicably. Furthermore, the distributor takes refuge in the fact that the issue is not brand codes, but rather category codes. The real aim of this approach (the imitation of the essential attributes of branded product packaging), which dominates mass distribution, is to cause confusion, profiting from the average attention span of the shopper in the aisle. Through lack of attention, the consumer may take the distributor's brand instead of the major brand product.

The InVivo company has actually calculated that, for mass consumption products, in hypermarkets, consumers spend 7 seconds on each purchase: speed matters to them. When there is intentionally strong resemblance between the packaging, a hurried buyer with an average attention span can be confused.

Our research into the imitation of brand packaging (trade dress) by distributor's brands (Kapferer, 1997; Kapferer and Thoenig, 1992) has shown that the unconscious recognition factors in the aisle were, in decreasing order of importance:

1 Colour.

2 Packaging shape.

3 Key designs.

4 Name, typography and so on.

This is exactly what distributors' brand products copy: Ricoré's (Nestlé) packaging is yellow, and so Calicoré's (Auchan's product).

As our results (shown in Table 5.3) demonstrate, where the private label copy/original product pairs are placed in decreasing order of resemblance, the stronger the perceived resemblance in trade dress, the more the consumer infers that the producer of the two products is one and the same – and the more confidence the copy inspires.

Another study has shown that the discovery of a quality distributor's brand created a less positive attitude towards the leading brand. J Zaichowsky and R Simpson (1996) conducted consumer trials with Lora Cola, a distributor's brand imitating the appearance of Coca-Cola cans. The taste of the product was manipulated in such a way that one section of consumers would find it very good, while others would find it bad. Among the latter group, the Coca-Cola evaluation, measured twice (before and after trying Lora Cola) did not change (5.41 versus 5.71). However, it did fall significantly in the case where the consumers liked the taste of the copy (falling from 5.67 to 5.22, or a drop of –0.45).

The third stage is the identity stage: the distributor's brand is used to capture market share from competitors. It becomes a genuine instrument of strategic differentiation, expressing the identity, values and positioning of the store itself. It should generate loyalty not just to itself (through its effect on the share of requirements), but also – more challengingly – to the store.

During this stage, the distributor's brand management is no longer in the hands of the purchaser alone. A purchaser strives for an optimal mix of purchase and resale conditions. Making the brand into an instrument for shaping identity and positioning presupposes genuine marketing strategy, and also the construction of a range that reflects the brand's ability to communicate the distributor's own values and identity. Here, the goal is to effect a shift from purchase driven by confusion to one driven by preference.

In this situation, the distributor's brand holds key positioning importance, since its content and products express the values of the (distributor's) store. To this end, it offers one or more components of added value, based on the ingredients, packaging, traceability, concept and so on.

This is generally the point at which trade brands appear for which the main sales argument is no longer price, but a real concept. It is true that often they have no equivalent among the branded producers, for a simple reason: these producers are specialized by category, product or trade. For example, what producer could construct an umbrella brand around the concept of 'Pleasures of yesterday', bringing together more than a hundred of the best products from every region of the country, along with rediscovered recipes and method of manufacture? Nestlé would be incapable of doing this, as it does not produce oils, jams, biscuits and the like. The same is true of Unilever, Philip Morris and Danone. Carrefour, however, can: all it needs to do is promote the concept among small regional companies in each country where it operates.

The case of Decathlon

Few stores reveal as much about modern distribution as Decathlon and the key role that its own brands play in its growth. In a recent article, Anglo-Saxon academic research notes that the share of shelf space given over to distributors' brands among US distributors is less than among European distributors (Corstjens *et al*, 2006). The US distributors allocate shelf space according to a simple short-term profit equation. It is true that in the United States distributors' brands have a poor reputation. They do not allow for positioning of the store or the loyalty generation through attachment to the store. The situation is different in Europe and Canada, where, very early in their brand history, distributors' brands had a combative vocation: fighting not to launch a price war, but to offer the consumer genuine value. Just think of Migros, the dominant chain in Switzerland, which does not sell products by Nestlé, the world's leading food company with its headquarters in Switzerland, but rather Migros products. In this case, the long-term strategic dimension takes precedence in decisions on shelf space allocation: this is the best way to get consumers to try the product, and therefore to begin a cycle of loyalty generation.

In our view, the main difference between the approaches of the distributors themselves in the United States and in Europe is that, in the United States, it is a question of selling the store's brand alongside the big brands, whereas in Europe it is a question of making it the store of the brand, with a few other brands alongside it. Decathlon has now become a designer of brands that controls its own distribution. This is what differentiates it from the sports section of Wal-Mart or Sports Unlimited. Even its lowest-price products are labelled as 'best-price technical' products, to remind us that the ethics of sport forbid sacrificing everything for money: there is a threshold below which a football is no longer a genuine football in terms of quality and security. Others might sell it anyway, in order to maintain the image of always having the lowest price, but not Decathlon.

This process, which transformed the store into a brand, may also be illustrated by Gap (Figure 5.1). The Decathlon ideal is the same as Gap's – to reduce its main manufacturer brand (in this case, Nike) to 10 per cent of sales in the running department. This is already the case in the camping department: all the rucksacks, sleeping bags and tents are private label products. In order to succeed, Decathlon needs to do much more than buy and sell: it needs to innovate, design, establish its own production plans, and choose its own partners. This is why Decathlon is now the world's fifth largest producer of sports goods. Its business model is the integration of design/production/distribution.

Decathlon is a €5.5 billion sports retailer, half of it being international. It began life in 1976 as a simple discount store. It sold all branded products, and only branded products, in all sports. Today, more than 55 per cent of its turnover is made on store brands, although, in accordance with its company culture, Decathlon never speaks of store brands, only of 'passion brands'. The word 'passion' here is not a slogan, but a true understanding of the brand in sport. The sports brand is built first internally; it is a true culture. Then it is carried outward by those who are passionate about it.

Moreover, few stores take their own brands as seriously as Decathlon does. Decathlon shows how the organization must be able to adapt to the brand, rather than the reverse. Finally, Decathlon enacts its brand policy worldwide, which is all the more challenging since Decathlon dominates its original market, France, by some distance, but is only just making its debut in China, where its products are produced, and has pulled out of the United States. It has 340 stores.

Decathlon's vocation is to give as many people as possible access to the pleasure of sport. The key values are vitality, truth, fraternity and responsibility. It is a low-cost operator, but one that has always favoured product quality over selling at the lowest possible price. Loyalty is not generated through prices, but through client satisfaction. At the same time, it is the best way of defending the chain against the entry of discounters from the food sector, such as Wal-Mart Sport. This policy is a success: in the bicycle sector, for example, not only is Decathlon the brand that first comes to mind for French consumers, but in addition it is also the one that is necessarily taken into account when making the next purchase, with a consideration score double that of the first producer's brand (Raleigh or Peugeot Cycles).

The store, founded in 1976 by Michel Leclerq, quickly took the distributor's brand option, capitalizing on the strong name awareness of the Decathlon company, and its dominant distribution. Decathlon seeks the development of the largest possible number of its clients through sport. The store is positioned on the hedonistic side of sport, and designs very comfortable products, aimed at well-being, with emphasis on safety. It is a diffuser of pleasure.

The components of its success in France were like those of any store: the quality of its store sites, the range (that is, the choice of goods for 60 sports under the same roof), unprecedented low prices, remarkable computerized logistics that avoid stock breakdowns by supplying stores once or twice daily, young, helpful and competent salespeople, and finally the freedom to choose, with aisles so well constructed that customers could easily dispense with the salesperson. The defeat suffered in the United States also hinged on the fact that the majority of these success factors could not be implemented in the discount chain acquired, first among them being the site quality. Secondly, the US discount store was renamed Decathlon before the stores could be 'Decathlonized'. It is not easy in the United States, a country with low unemployment, to find passionate and motivated young people, genuinely attached to their store.

In 1999 in France, after 23 years of uninterrupted growth, for the first time in its history its turnover per square metre fell. The diagnosis was simple: the policy of a single brand, Decathlon, strongly emphasized in all its stores, together with its dominance of the national market, created a monopolistic situation and a 'Soviet-like' brand. Whether on the beach, on the ski lift, while hiking in the forest, everyone wore Decathlon-branded products. Customers increasingly got the impression of a lack of choice.

The strength of distributors, often family-type businesses, is their ability to take decisions quickly, and to enact radical changes in order to produce tangible, measurable results. This is what Decathlon did:

- It abandoned nearly 25 years of one single store brand policy, in France and abroad, to move towards a portfolio of brands segmented by sport. In order to create these brands, it began with the observation that there were 60 sports under Decathlon's roof. For each brand to reach critical mass and justify its overheads, a shortlist of 17 was drawn up, combined into seven finally. Then it was decided to increase this number, since modern sports are 'tribes' that cannot easily be brought under the same tent in the name of 'critical mass'. Thus Domyos was separated into roller sports and running. Tennis and golf were also separated, having previously been united under the common brand Inesis.
- These brands are autonomous, decentralized business units, with dedicated teams. Their goal is for each to become recognized leaders in its sport. Now three-quarters of the operational budgets are spent on the brands, with one quarter remaining for transverse

tasks. Decathlon abandoned its historical central organization at Villeneuve d'Ascq in order to turn these brands not into labels on products, but forces for creative proposals at the best prices, based on passionate men and women. At Decathlon, semantics are crucial: these brands are named passion brands, not as a slogan or an advertising gimmick but as a profound reality, first internally, and then externally.

- These brands need to be located close to where the sports are practised, so that the internal teams can live them out, and local opinion leaders can play a role in their creation: Tribord by the sea, Quechua in the mountains. They communicate independently of one another. For example, *Chulanka* is Quechua's magazine, distributed in stores: it circulates 2 million copies. This is the highest circulation of any of the mountain magazines.
- These brands are named passion brands because they are each entrusted to a passionate manager, who creates and carries them, with a dedicated team, on autonomous sites, with a genuine business plan and a high degree of autonomy. In the stores, the salespeople are also passionate. In time, the goods may be distributed beyond the flagship Decathlon store. In December 2006, Decathlon announced a historic agreement with independent ski equipment hire stores in the mountains. This very lucrative market had previously been locked up by the manufacturer brands. This will make it possible for skiers and snowboarders to try Quechua products in the stations themselves. The internet will be the medium for hiring: clients can reserve in advance and at low prices.
- In order to build these passion brands, with imaginary qualities that are weaker than those of the major brands, the only thing that matters is product innovation and quality levels. This is why the Decathlon Group also invests in ingredient brands that lend credibility to the offer, becoming technological labels themselves. It is a question of prying open the vicelike grip on costs exerted by the technological brands such as Lycra, Goretex and Coolmax. For this reason, the ingredient brands of the Decathlon group are also autonomous business units, seeking to increase their opportunities outside the Group.

Decathlon's challenge is international. Decathlon is currently the 10th largest sports distributor in the world: the margin of progression is still strong. The brand policy described above is global. Decathlon's strength was built in France, progressively (over 30 years) using a different model – that of the single brand (Decathlon) which was also the name of the store. This contributed to creating enormous communication synergies.

The country manager's situation, for example in China, Hungary or the United States, will be very different. The start-up will be implemented with the passion brands: in China they represent 70 per cent of the range. However, the store is not known there, and will not have 20 years to build recognition. Therefore the pricing policy must be more discount-based. The name Decathlon, however, should no longer in theory be visible on the products, since they all now stem from one of the passion brands. The principle of the passion brand, as with any brand, is in fact autonomy. Only the back office cuts across all brands. This consideration, a pragmatic one at the international level, explains the maintenance of a 'Decathlon creation' brand inside the product, in order to establish the link between the store and its brands.

Factors in the success of distributors' brands

As always, the rise of a new brand is also the result of the actions (or lack of action) taken by the competition. For example, distributors' brands have strong market share in the cosmetics sector in Germany. The reverse is true in France, and yet both are among the more highly developed countries. Setting aside any possible differences between the two countries' relative conceptions of beauty, one explanation lies in an analysis of the competition. In France, l'Oréal has dragged all other brands into a war fought on scientifically proven performance, supported by colossal advertising budgets. In Germany the leading national brand is Nivea, which relies much more on empathy, softness and a close relationship than on the rational approach of proven results. We believe this explains why distributors' brands have found it easier to make inroads there: consumers have not perceived them to be all that different from Nivea.

Hoch and Banerji (1993) have analysed the factors behind distributors' brands' market share.

These are:

- the size of the potential market: the distributor opts for long production runs;
- the high margin in the sector;
- the low advertising expenditure;
- the ability to achieve quality (few or no patents);
- consumers' price sensitivity.

However, these authors also maintain that market fragmentation does not appear to constitute a barrier to the growth of distributors' brands.

Conversely, it is known that a factor that does affect the penetration of distributors' brands is the rate of innovation in a sector (measured by the share of new products in companies' turnover): it forces product ranges to be continually renewed, and is associated with a large amount of advertising. In fact, it is also the most natural reaction by producers confronted with distributors' brands: to increase their rate of innovation.

As has been observed, most of the factors mentioned above are linked to management deficits among the producers: insufficient rate of innovation, high margins, low advertising. When the brand is treated as a 'cash cow', the door is opened to distributors' brands. Moreover, many brand companies are willing to manufacture distributors' branded products. For example, the tyres at Norauto (a chain of stores selling spare parts and services to motorists) are manufactured by the Michelin Group; it is inconceivable that they should be low-quality products.

In this way, the success of distributors' brands is linked to a supply effect (by strong promotion on distributors' shelves and the creation of 'me-toos' that ape big-brand products) but also by a lack of competitiveness from high-profile brands, which are too used to high margins, and do not innovate.

Lastly, this penetration depends on the specific range and category. It is strong in basic products, but no longer unique to them. Kapferer and Laurent (1995) linked the attractiveness of distributors' brands to consumers' degree of involvement, either in an enduring sense (interest in the product) or as a temporary feeling at the moment of purchase (Is the purchase a risky one? Does it have badge value? Will it give me pleasure?). It is therefore hardly surprising to find that the categories listed in Table 5.4 are those in which DOBs have the highest penetration.

Note that studies on distributors' brand customers have shown that their penetration has now reached all segments of the population. Nevertheless, there is a core target of people with reduced financial resources who have a low sensitivity to quality. In C Lewi's thesis at HEC (Lewi and Kapferer, 1996), even though they were given a biscuit that was objectively poor (in the light of results in blind tests), 18 per cent of these people decided to buy it anyway because it was cheap. Furthermore, these are the people who least noticed the difference in flavour.

Garretson's (2002) and Ajawadi's (2001) works provide an interesting new path for study: according to these authors, customers who resist distributors' brands are those who link price with quality. For these people, the price is the measure of the quality. It should be added here that hard discount itself finds its most frequent shoppers, and those whose average basket is fullest, among families with several teenagers still living at home.

Launching a store brand: eight steps

One after the other, retailers think of creating their own brand. This is just the logical answer to profitable growth issues. Where do you grow once you have acquired or defeated most of your direct competitors? Retailers have to take sales and margins from their own suppliers, not only through better trade conditions, but by selling the products under their own store brand. Some retail formats entail 100 per cent private labels because of the business model: hard discounters (Aldi, Lidl, etc) achieve their targeted 60 per cent price discount versus main brands only through full control of the value chain.

Historically the origin of private labels has been conflictual: because suppliers refused to sell, or to

TABLE 5.4 Ten years of evolution of store-brand/private labels (market share in value, Europe)

	2000	2010	
Plastic bags	54.7	68.0	+13.3
All-purpose paper	50.8	62.1	+11.3
Canned vegetables	49.0	57.0	+8.0
Frozen food	38.0	55.5	+17.5
Prepared fish	29.8	54.5	+24.7
Ham, pork	40.7	51.0	+10.3
Fruit drinks (natural)	44.5	46.2	+1.7
Canned fruits	30.8	43.0	+12.2
Chicken	25.9	40.1	+14.2
Yoghurts	22.1	32.2	+10.1
Biscuits	19.4	30.6	+11.2
Pet food	20.0	25.1	+5.1
Sparkling wines	17.0	18.7	+1.7
Detergents	6.7	11.9	+5.2
Carbonated soft drinks	8.0	7.4	−0.6
Skin care, make-up	4.5	6.8	+2.3
Shampoo	4.9	5.8	+0.9
Baby food	0.6	5.1	+4.5
Total (42 families)	21.2	29.7	+8.5

reduce prices, retailers decided to create their own lines. This is why the private label issues are inherently emotional. The purpose of this section is to make it a rational one. Introducing private labels is a cultural and managerial revolution for a retailer, moving from distribution to creation, production control and marketing of one's own products. The classical culture of retailers is buying and selling;

now it becomes designer and manufacturer (even if production is subcontracted), which means recruiting new people for the new activity directly from the main FMCG companies. The private label or store brand will be a major ambassador for the specific positioning of the retailer. Launching one's own brand is a decision that cannot be taken haphazardly. Once the decision is made, eight specific steps should be followed to ensure success:

1 The first step is to specify the reasons why the retailer needs a private label now. What is expected from it? What are its objectives and ambitions? This is a strategic move that will involve the whole organization, each category manager, the supply chain, communication, etc. In addition, we recommend that, every year, retailers should audit why they have private labels.

2 The second question is that of the scope: what products should be covered? A private label policy certainly grows in scope through time and experience, but retailers must set out from the start its level of ambition. Hypermarket chains must decide whether they want to cover food and non-food. Each chain may find a different answer based on its own positioning: the imitation of other competing retailers is not a good clue. What is relevant for one retailer may not be relevant for another. The question of adding non-food categories to the private label offer entails that the retailer first specifies what the non-food overall strategy is, as well as the role of non-food in the general profit and sales results of the stores. Only once this strategy is understood can one define the criteria to be used to select and accept private labels in each of the non-food categories. As a rule, the store brand (using the retailer's own name) wants to be compared to the best big brands. Consequently the store brand needs first to enter categories where such big brands exist, in order to communicate its positioning. There surely are exceptions, such as wine, where there are no strong brands (luxury excepted) and consumers are willing to be helped by the retailers' advice. In France, the number one wine brand in terms of sales is a private label. In food categories, width of offer is the barrier. One cannot build a credible private brand offer in coffee, for instance, without a vast choice of aromas, origins, types, etc. In non-food categories, the unavailability of supply can be the major barrier. Advanced high-tech innovators like Samsung, Sony or Philips have no idle manufacturing capacity nor desire to share their latest know-how and products with anyone. This is another story in low-tech activities such as paint and DIY tools. Black & Decker does not want to manufacture power or garden tools for retailers' own brands, but there are a lot of Chinese companies able to supply look-alikes at incredible prices. The same holds true for ironing tables; however, since there are no real brands there, it may not be a prime necessity to be present in the initial launch line.

3 How many price lines should there be? Hypermarkets and many retailers are facing two kinds of competition: the big brands and now the low-cost retailers. This is why an important question is that of the number of price lines. Manutan, Europe's leading e-retailer for non-strategic supplies, introduced private labels in 2008. In its domain, there are few real brands. It decided to launch two price lines simultaneously: minus 25 per cent and minus 45 per cent. Not only are some clients now asking for the lowest-priced items (eg staples), but also, as the company had a low-cost line, could one say that the other line was a qualitative one, since it was not the cheapest? The lowest cost acted as ladder of quality perception for the other.

4 How many brands should there be? Tesco used its own name over all segments within a given product class: from the lowest-priced orange juices to the highest-priced freshly squeezed, even above Tropicana. It also calls by its name its thematic lines (biological agriculture, sustainable trade, gourmet, etc). Some retailers would segment: a store brand for the core offer, and private labels (looking like small brands) for each segment. Thus Galeries Lafayette have Galfa as store brand

and a vast number of couture private labels positioned by age and style. Sephora, the number one upscale skin care and make-up world retailer, uses its own name on basic products but small names on speciality products. These decisions may change through time and growth. Decathlon, the multi-sport world retailer, started with one brand, Decathlon, across all the 25 sport families. In the late 1990s, because of its success, the brand name was overly visible. It moved to more than 10 private labels, one for each sport family (running, water sports, riding, golf, glide sports, hiking, etc). Decathlon remains as the store name only.

5 How far should retailers go in the specifications? So far, life has been easy to retailers: they bought and sold. Now they themselves have to write the specifications. This is essential to make people understand that the retailer wants a quality product. Since the retailer brand is positioned against the market leader, this task of specification must specify the point of superiority one wants to build, generally in terms of ease of use or packaging. Some retailers, such as Decathlon, specify the exact nature, size and quantities of each ingredient to be used in manufacturing each single item and the exact production process, minute by minute. For food the creation of these specifications is fast. In non-food it may take many months: first, the product of the leading brand has to be sent to a laboratory to be analysed and identified.

6 Check what proposals should really be launched. It is important to set up a committee to fulfil this task, check all the proposals and recommend whether or not to launch. Certain factors need to be taken into account:

- What is the market size?
- What are the intensity of competition and the sales forecast?
- Does the actual product meet the quality target?
- Does it meet the price and high margin target (higher than on a big brand)?
- Can one ensure regular delivery from the supplier?
- Should one launch if there is a single supplier only?
- Is there a risk of being sued for counterfeiting (it can even be in the resemblance of the instruction notice for a television set or the packaging itself)?
- What are the overall costs and margins taking into account marketing costs (even if they are incurred inside the store, these promotional and merchandizing costs should be estimated)?

7 Validate the choice of supplier. At this point it must be ensured that the supplier is able to produce the given quantities at the established price, respecting the quality specifications. The supplier must accept quality controls and produce enough stock of all spare parts to ensure after-sales service. There should be penalties for late delivery. To prevent the supplier selling the same product to others, one should take precautions. For instance, the brand name could be engraved in the mould of a non-food item. Retailers should remember that they are now themselves responsible in terms of the consumer and the law. Solid and reliable suppliers should be looked for, with a capacity to make proposals for innovations and to offer added features.

8 Launch inside and outside. Enthusiasm and pride are the key words. It is important to sell the private label policy inside first. Generally a special task force backed by the executive committee is set up for the whole private label project, from conception to strategy and launch of the first lines. Then it becomes the shared project of each of the category managers, who need to balance their actions between the two major actors now: the big brands and the store brand/ private labels. The launch should also be made at consumer level through all the means of merchandizing and customer relationship management.

Note: The author thanks Patrick Rebuffié for his input to this section.

Optimizing the store brand marketing mix

The notion of a distributor's brand is therefore heterogeneous, offering the store a range of possibilities for getting its overall offer across. Research has analysed how each type of distributor's brand was able to increase its market share to the detriment of the leading brands of the segment, and also to reduce the price differential between the two, thereby boosting profitability (Levy and Kapferer, 1998). More than 500 mothers, in a simulated store, were presented with a choice between the leader in chocolate biscuits (Pepito by Lu/Danone group) and a distributor's brand. This choice varied from one customer to the next according to four criteria:

- presence or absence of the store name itself in the brand name (DOB or private label);
- whether there was a 'copycat' of the Pepito packaging, or a clearly differentiated packaging;
- objective quality of the distributor biscuit (established through blind tests): identical or markedly inferior to Pepito;
- level of price difference with Pepito: index 50, 65 and 80.

The combination of these variables makes it possible to reproduce any form of distributor's brand currently active on this market. The key findings of this research were:

- The quality of the distributor product has a strong and positive impact on the intention to purchase the distributor product. It increases from 16 per cent when the product tasted is inferior to Pepito, to 34 per cent when it is equal.
- The store's reputation also has a bearing on the intention to purchase. When the store name is masked (private label strategy), the average intention to purchase is only 20 per cent. It increases to 30 per cent once the name is known.

It is the interactions, however, that prove most interesting in practice, as Table 5.5 demonstrates. Each line refers to a different form of distributor's brand:

- The first line concerns a DOB that carries the store name, therefore bringing its reputation into play, and packaging that is not a copy of Pepito's. It is acting like a true brand (reputation and differentiation and quality). What do we observe? This is where the demand for the distributor product is strongest (38 per cent). Furthermore, it is the strongest even though the price difference is less (20 per cent cheaper): therefore the profitability is maximal. Interestingly, the demand does not increase when the price is lowered (35 per cent

TABLE 5.5 Price elasticity of different retail brands

Brand and packaging type	Price gap from segment leader		
	–20%	–35%	–50%
Store brand (not copycat)	**38**	**38**	28
Store brand (copycat)	17	28	38
Private label (copycat)	26	31	27
Private label (not copycat)	21	24	31

NOTE Percentages of consumers who intend to buy the retail brand cheaper); on the contrary, it decreases to 28 per cent when the price is lowered still further (50 per cent cheaper), probably as a result of the anxiety that this price arouses in mothers (this is a product for children, after all). The moral is that the DOB is most dangerous to national brands, and also most profitable, when it behaves most like a true brand.

- The second line shows a store brand copy: this is the most common form of a distributor's brand in the food departments of superstores. Here the demand only increases if the price decreases. Although it also reaches 38 per cent of pure demand, this time it is only at a rock-bottom price (50 per cent cheaper): profitability is therefore not as good as with the previous line.
- The third line is what is known as a 'counterbrand': the store name is absent, and the product is marked by an unknown brand (that is, a private label). Furthermore, its only option is to slavishly copy the packaging of the leader, in order to create confusion and allow clients to think that there is a similarity between the products, since the packaging is so alike. Demand follows an inverted U-shaped curve, with the best intention to purchase scores for the distributor product (31 per cent of intentions) at the intermediate price level (35 per cent cheaper).
- In the fourth line the store is unknown but the packaging is different from the leader's. Here the distributor's brand resembles a small, unknown brand, and the client has no point of reference for evaluating it. It is therefore not surprising that price is the only motivator: demand grows as the price falls. This is typically the case for lowest-price products, created to counter the products on the hard-discount circuit.

What can we draw from this analysis? When the distributor's brand behaves like a true big brand, it reaps the benefits (market share and profitability): however, it must have the will and the means to do so. Not everyone can be Decathlon or Tesco.

How trade brands become real brands

Trade brands compete on price with big brands. To do so they first follow a pure me-too strategy, at the limits of imitation and counterfeiting (see page 105), copying the best-selling product of national brands as closely as possible. They feel protected by their power and believe the national brands that need them as distributors will not go to court to defend their intellectual property rights. This is a short-term strategy, as research has shown: behaving like a real brand, not as a copy, pays off more, even for store brands.

How do you move to a real-brand strategy? With what kind of differences? How can trade brands innovate?

Some retailers have moved from the status of pure retailer (buy and sell) to that of creator, inventor, supervisor of production, and distributor. This is the case of the now fully international Decathlon, which has 100 product managers inventing new sport, camping and hiking items for its portfolio of 13 'passion brands'.

What about more traditional retailers such as Tesco or Carrefour or Pao de Azucar in Brazil? Innovation will be focused not on the technology of the products themselves (this is the real know-how of global brands) but on side benefits: for instance, a lot can be done to make shampoo bottles more practical (opening system, storage, handling, waste management) or more ecological, with a lower CO_2 imprint, etc.

Multinationals' strength is economies of scale: this is why L'Oréal tends to use exactly the same formats of packaging for all its brands. This creates barriers to change, an opportunity for trade brands.

Trade brands exploit other areas where multinationals are slow movers. Global brands are not reactive enough when new trends emerge. Global brands make no decision unless the new product can be global, sold to the world. Thus retailers have been the first to launch new private labels offering, among other things:

- eco-friendly lines;
- equitable trade lines;
- local production lines;
- organic food lines;
- gourmet lines.

Another strategy is to boost the perceived value of the trade brand through co-branding. In Spain, to beat Pampers (P&G's leading nappy brand), Carrefour uses Disney characters on Carrefour nappies. Indeed Carrefour is Disney's number one client for licences.

More difficult is how to compete against Gillette. Retailers should use a blue ocean strategy to capture part of the gold mine of Gillette, the blades. Here one cannot compete without changing the rules themselves. The business model of Gillette is based on patenting the system that attaches the blades to the handle of each new razor version. Thus the retailers cannot invent substitutable blades, as that would infringe the patents of the system. Gillette is de facto in a monopoly situation: only its blades can be used. As a result the prices of blades provide very high margins.

How then does one change the rules? Knowing that there are now Asian high-technology companies able to manufacture blades practically as good as those of Gillette, the good solution for a retail brand of razor would be to give the razor handle free of charge and to provide blades with this at half the price of Gillette's blades. The risk is nil for consumers willing to try to escape Gillette prices: if not satisfied by the quality of the shave, they will not have lost much, for the razor handle was free and the blades cost half the price.

In the high-tech markets it is much more difficult for trade brands to compete: they just cannot access the latest innovations. Samsung, Sony and Philips do not want to share them with retailers. That is why, for white or brown goods, private labels are price fighters, aiming at the late majority, those people who do not want the latest hi-tech products.

Finally to become real brands trade brands use communication:

- Decathlon promotes the innovations of its trade brands on television (such as a tent that can be put up in eight seconds).
- Tesco advertises the unique qualities of its food products.
- Children-oriented trade brands create their own community on the internet and have a Facebook page.
- Thematic private labels also create their own brand content (on natural foods, ethical trade, etc) diffused on the Web.
- Trade brands are strongly promoted in the leaflets distributed in mail boxes.

When are more retail brands too much?

Today in Europe, 50 per cent of all FMCG products on the shelves of supermarkets and hypermarkets are retail brands, whether store brands (Carrefour, Tesco, etc), thematic private labels or even no-names, as for the hard discounters (HD).

Table 5.6 shows the market share in value in six major countries.

The rate of store brands at a given retailer is strategic. Different retailers may differ about this. Some want to go beyond 50 per cent; others wish to differentiate by having far less than this. But the trend in FMCG is to go upwards: this is the result of retailer concentration. When you are big and have acquired all the smaller retailers, how do you grow? Is the sky the limit?

TABLE 5.6 Retail brands' overall market share in Europe

	France	Spain	Netherlands	UK	Germany	Italy
Market share of store brands within hypermarkets/supermarkets	30	39	28	45	33	16
Market share of hard discounters	14	16	18	5	38	15
Total share of price brands	40	49	41	48	60	29

SOURCE SymphonyIRI

FIGURE 5.3 Retail brands: supply share creates demand share (in volume)

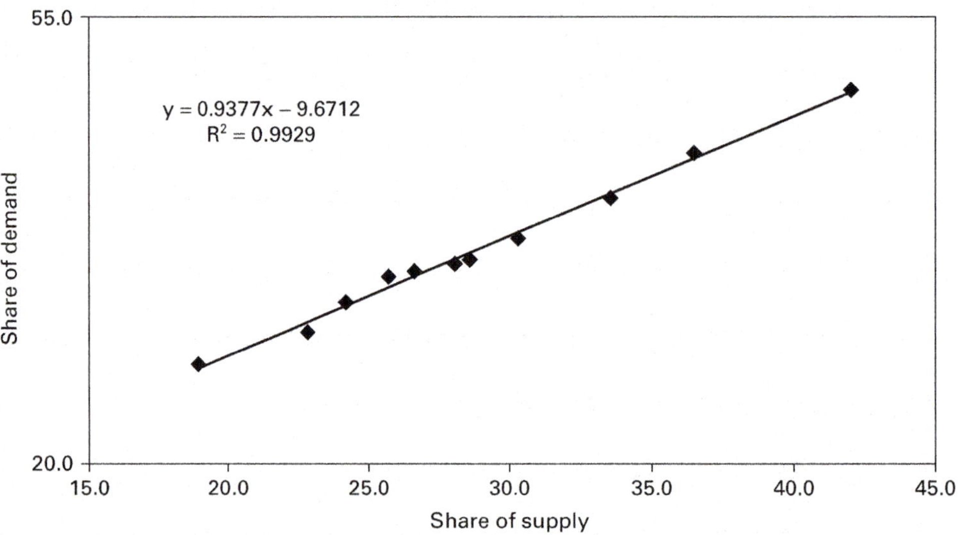

SOURCE SymphonyIRI

When Decathlon was created in 1976, it had no private labels, only producers' brands in each of its 25 sports categories. Now private labels represent more than 55 per cent of all the sales. Carrefour has declared that it wants to push that figure still higher. On the contrary, Lidl, the German hard discounter, has decided to introduce a breach in its traditional zero brand policy: it now carries some specific SKUs of big brands (Mars bar, Kinder surprise egg, the family format of the Laughing Cow, etc). This is to increase the rate of purchase per consumer and to fight against Aldi's better profitability based on higher volumes, hence economies of scale.

Since private labels do compete against the best products of the retailer's main supplier, this is a source of friction between them both. Retailers tend to see no limit to the growth of their private labels. They should. Certainly supply created demand: there is a strict correlation between the amount of supply (number of SKUs of private labels) and their market share. Retail brands use a push strategy.

However, there is a point where increasing the share of supply of private label SKUs on the shelves of the store actually changes the store's positioning and creates frustration among consumers, who may move to another retailer, at first from time to time and later more frequently. If hypermarkets are born to maximize choice, when are there too many private labels? When are there not enough brands? When are there not enough niche brands?

Recent European data from SymphonyIRI demonstrate this risk of going too far for the retailer's own interest. Figure 5.3 shows that the growth of the private labels is a supply-driven phenomenon. In the yoghurt sector (2.5 per cent of all sales of a hypermarket) there is a strict correlation between the share of supply (measured by SKUs) and the share of demand in volume.

Interestingly however, from one year to another category managers of retailers tend to push the number of SKUs of their own label, but this may prove counterproductive in terms of profitability. Figure 5.4 shows that increasing the presence of retailer brands is most often not followed by any increase in sales of the private labels.

This marginal analysis should be made category by category by the retailer. One example of counterproductive excess of retailer own brands is shown in the arabica coffee case (Figure 5.5).

Fewer private labels does not mean more big brands

It is important to understand that the above results do not imply that big brands should take the shelf

FIGURE 5.4 Retailer brands' increased presence does not always create more sales

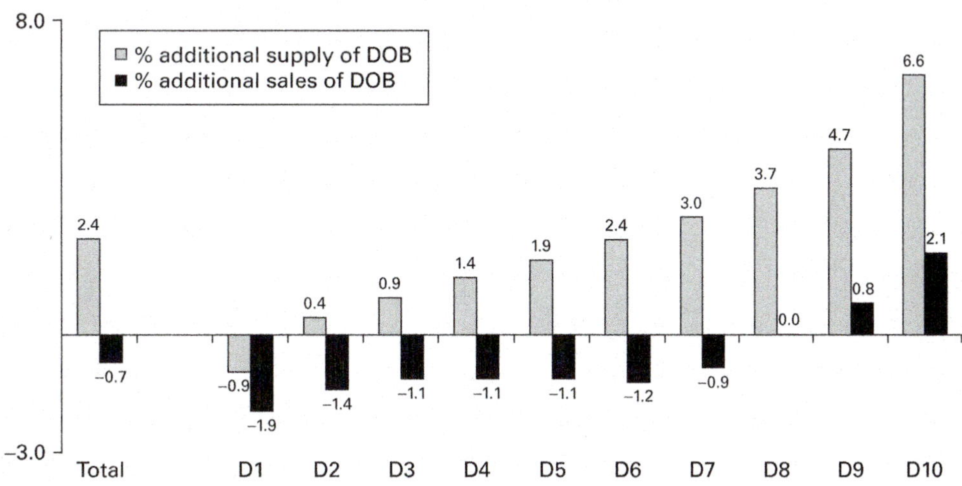

SOURCE SymphonyIRI, De Vera

FIGURE 5.5 Retailer own-brand mismanagement in a food category

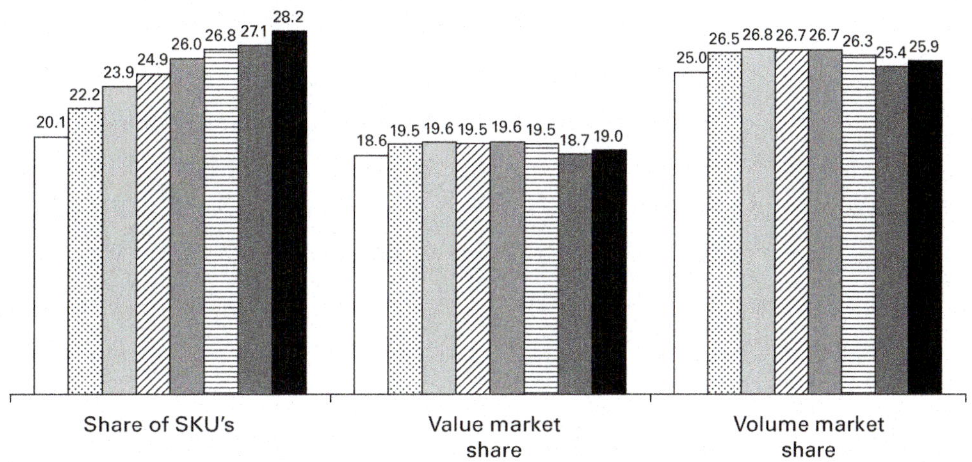

SOURCE Symphonyiri, De Vera

space left by retailers' own brands. Retailers might as well introduce more brands, but niche or regional ones. In our fast-changing economic world, new trends emerge. Retailers have to detect them and send signals to consumers that they are being reactive fast enough.

It is a fact that many signs of 'alterconsumption' are visible. More and more people are looking for an alternative to the present system without being anti-capitalist. They look for organic foods, if possible bought directly from farmers, or from equitable trade, etc. Big brands are not likely to embrace these weak signals, precisely because they are weak. The door is open: either to niche brands that will bring the trend addicts back into the stores (these trends have created their own speciality channels); or to private labels, which will then act as innovators, with no competition from big brands. The benefit is that these private labels can charge more: they do not have to be priced 25 per cent less than the market leader.

PART TWO
The challenges of modern markets

06 The new brand management

Since the 1990s companies have been aware that brands are an asset, and that consequently they should always be reinforced and nurtured by tangible innovations and intangible added values.

The 10 key principles of strategic brand management are known:

- Capitalize on very few strategic brands, which all convey a big idea, a vision, and are driven by the desire to change the customer's life. No brand should be without a strong intangible component.
- Nest all variants and sub-brands under these mega-brands, to nurture them.
- Act as a leader and be passionate about increasing the standards of the category.
- Sustain the brands by a constant flow of innovations (product, service, etc) in line with their positioning.
- Create direct ties with your end customers to deepen the link and the attachment, especially in markets where the trade pushes its trade brands. In fact the main competitor of many a so-called strong brand is now the trade brand.
- Deliver personalized services.
- Reward customers' involvement to make them become active promoters of your brand, not simply loyalists. Word of mouth is indeed the real sign of success: customers become active ambassadors because they feel passionate about the brand – as a result of what it did to them and the community of values. Reichheld (2006) has shown that the rate of promoters among the customer base is directly correlated to the growth rate of the company or the brand.
- Encourage communities that share your values, on the internet or elsewhere.
- Quickly globalize the brand and its products.
- Be responsible: big is not beautiful any more, and consumers have become cynical about size. Do not adopt only the perspective of individual benefits, also take into account collective benefits (recyclable products, organic ingredients, ethical and sustainable trade, helping the poor, etc).

If the brand principles given above have remained constant, their implementation has been challenged.

Brand building runs into four stumbling blocks today:

- Are there durable, meaningful differences between products these days?
- Is there still a large amount of shelf space available for brands in the big superstores or with wholesalers, which are now pushing their own brands?
- Are there still mass media, taking into account the fractioning of the audience and the appeal of the internet?
- Are there still loyalists? The rise in the rate of promotions makes customers more sensitive to price, less faithful, more opportunistic.

The limits of a certain type of marketing

This was forged by P&G, the inventors of marketing for mass-consumption products. Since I began my career in this company, I have experienced it. Traditionally, at P&G the brand is a superior product. Everything begins with the product and hinges upon it. It must prove its worth all alone: brutally, this company only launches mass-consumption products if they can speak up for themselves and 'make the difference' in use. Hence the importance of 'blind tests' in this sector. In these tests clients must judge the product without seeing the brand, so that they are not biased in their perception by recognition of it. With Pampers, the baby must be drier; Always must absorb better; Ariel must wash better, and the difference must be visible to the naked eye; Sunny Delight, an orange-flavoured drink but without real oranges, must taste infinitely better on the tongue, and so on. Note that in its luxury products division (licensed Boss and Lacoste perfumes, etc) P&G uses the same rules: sniff tests decide if a fragrance is launched or not.

In and of itself, the principle that a brand begins with a great product remains a pillar of the great brand. Laughing Cow has an organoleptic quality superior to other soft cheeses. In business to business, Facom mechanic's keys are the benchmarks in the market. IPhone is superior to all others.

But the model begins to seize up when it continues ad infinitum: then we reach the zone of diminishing returns. The cost of marginal improvement becomes increasingly high. Making a Michelin tyre safer than it already is involves considerable investments in research and development, which must be absorbed either over very large product runs (hence the notion of a global product) or over smaller, more expensive runs.

This one-dimensional strategy reaches its limits: there comes to be an imbalance between the additional cost of marginal progress, and the customer's perceived needs.

This product development model still seems to work for certain brands: Gillette is a typical example. After the single-blade close-shave razor came the two-blade razor for an even closer shave, then three blades, then the roller, then vibrating razors. Gillette is a past master in the art of planned obsolescence in its products.

It is no accident that P&G took over Gillette in 2004. These two companies share basically the same product culture, and the same mode of innovation: always more. To achieve this, P&G is now prepared to look beyond its own walls for the innovations of tomorrow: in university laboratories, in start-ups and so on. For the majority of companies, however, the model no longer functions.

In fact the incremental improvements are no longer perceptible or meaningful; on the other hand, the increase in price is. Consumers can thus make

FIGURE 6.1 Limits of traditional marketing

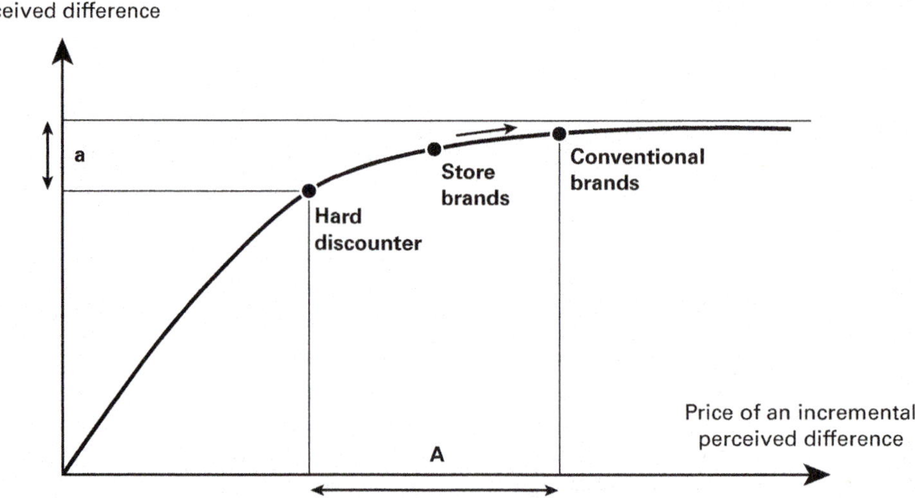

considerable savings (typically 35 per cent) by buying distributor brand products with an equivalent degree of functional satisfaction. The loss in terms of function is minimal compared with the economy achieved.

This reasoning is also true for truck tyres. This is why, although the market share of Michelin Trucks at first tyre mounting is 65 per cent in Europe and the West, it falls by 50 per cent in the second-mounting market, when it comes to replacing the tyres (although Michelin remains the leader).

The reasoning is the same in food: what does an even better albacore tuna at Saupiquet mean? Tesco Finest sells indistinguishable albacore tuna. What does an even crustier gherkin from Amora mean? A cul-de-sac has been reached.

With experience, consumers see no difference, except for the price. Hence the systematic rise in all European studies of the opinion that 'distributor brands are a better price/quality choice than major brands'. Agreement with this opinion is at 59 per cent in France, 57 per cent in Germany, 55 per cent in Britain, 54 per cent in Italy and so on (2011). This is made easier by the fact that nowadays the majority of large groups supply distributor brands. Some do so openly: the strategy of the Lactalis Group is to dominate the camembert market in two ways; via the President brand itself, and via distributor brand products.

The weakness of the idea of 'best product' is that it is often defined without taking the customer's point of view – that is, without considering the use to which it will be put. This is its greatest shortcoming. Take the example of DIY: given that an electric drill will, on average, be used for a few seconds per year in a normal household, what point is there in buying a Bosch-branded one? In functional terms it makes no sense. On the other hand, if the consumer picks a cheaper alternative, the intangible satisfaction of owning 'a Bosch' will be frustrated: this is a key aspect of the strong brand. Bosch enjoys the values associated with its country of origin (Germany), which make the buyer proud.

The end of brands as we knew them

Are our traditional definitions of a brand still working? They started as a distinguishing name or symbol, proof of the authentic origin of products, which differentiated them from those of different suppliers (Aaker, 1991: p 110). This definition is that of lawyers and intellectual rights consultants: as a sign the brand must be registered and protected. Its value depends on the trust people can have when they see it. In many countries trust has disappeared, as there are too many counterfeited products.

Later – under the influence of academic consumer research – brands were conceptualized as 'associations that add value to those already evoked by the product itself' (Keller, 1998: p 4). The problem with this traditional conceptualization, as we said before, is that, in practice, it implies that a brand is meant to add a halo of perception to a product with little utility itself. This conceptualization is based on consumer studies demonstrating that branded products have a higher perceived value than the same product but unbranded (see also pages 541 and 45).

This definition of a brand has fostered a negative practice and vision of brands: they are thought of as a badge adding value that is *not* in the product. Hence there is an often heard criticism that brands 'are just a name'. Now it is a fact that brands exert a halo effect, the consequence of the power of this name, but, for managerial practice, sound brand management entails endowing the unbranded product itself with added values. An unbranded Lacoste polo shirt must have the 25 kilometres of Pima cotton thread that has made it the best polo shirt in the world since 1933. Things go awry when a famous name is badged on an average product, exploiting the gullibility of the masses. This has created the moral criticism of licensing, as an easy way to make financial profits by mass prestige brands.

The emphasis on added value has encouraged brand management to become communication management. It has been said that 'perception is reality': because the halo effect creates a desirable perception, many consumers may have been badly treated. This practice will not survive the internet, the source of renewed consumer power. Web 2.0 tells the truth about products by means of experts, bloggers, objective comparisons between products, and peer-to-peer advice. The internet has created a breach in the halo effect: are Volkswagens really as reliable as their image says? Aren't Hyundai cars as reliable in fact although the brand has not yet gained credentials? The many product recalls of Toyota cars demonstrate that brand image is built by former experiences and is never up to date: Toyota quality is no longer what its image says it is. Becoming world number one car manufacturer, held as the cardinal corporate mission statement of the Toyota Company just to beat the US GM company and somehow symbolize the revenge of Japan, has led to the brand mission and quality engagement being forgotten.

What will tomorrow's world be?

In what kind of world will consumers live tomorrow? What economic, political and social parameters will have a bearing on their lives?

The world consumers will experience from now on will be new and problematic as it never was before, at least in peaceful times. It will be a world of disequilibriums. Let us list them:

- **Economic disequilibrium.** After the Second World War, there was an equilibrium: the USSR versus the free world, symbolized and protected by the United States; communism versus capitalism; the planned economy versus free entrepreneurship. Things were clear. The equilibrium of terror secured peace, even during the Cuban crisis. The collapse of the Berlin Wall has meant that capitalism no longer has an enemy. Even modern China has adopted capitalism, while remaining a politically communist country. Is it the end of history, as Fukuyama (2006) put it? No. When capitalism no longer has an enemy, like a champion without a challenger, it seems lost. Its values are diluted. Its excesses soon appeared in the 2009 financial recession. There will be others, for nothing controls capitalism any more. That is why alternatives to capitalism are stemming from outside the economic sphere: one from religion (it is called religious integrism, and is a way of refusing the advances of Western consumer society) and the other from ecology (it is called zero growth or negative growth).
- **Political disequilibrium.** The United States has been said to be the first and only hyperpower in humankind's history. It is a problem for it not to have challengers, because, at the time of the USSR, the United States seemed to be guided by a clear ideal: to defend freedom against communist gulags. Today, US policy is guided by self-interest, as many countries have realized. The world is becoming more complex, with groups of countries emerging as alternative powers (in South America, Europe, Asia and soon Africa).
- **Financial disequilibrium.** China is now the United States' banker. It holds most of the public and private debt created by the US economy's dynamism, ie US households spend more than they earn (hence the sub-primes crisis). The same holds true for the US federal states, eg California too is going bankrupt. If the gold standard had not been abandoned by the US government (no one can ask the US government to guarantee the dollar value by a reserve stock of gold), the United States would have gone bankrupt too, as Greece did. How long will it last? As long as China wants. The United States has now become dependent on China.
- **Ecological disequilibrium.** So far, earth has been more or less able to provide the resources for the four Fs (food, feed, fuel and forest). If one party wanted more of something (wheat, corn, water or whatever), it just had to pay more. The rules of efficient markets meant that demand always met supply: it was a matter of price. What is new today? There won't be enough resources for everybody. The world is no longer infinite. That is why China is so forcefully engaged in a foreign policy of resources versus infrastructure. The Chinese prime minister spends a lot of his time visiting all the strategic emerging countries (in Africa, Asia and South America) to secure Chinese factories – since China has become the factory of the world – with fuel, gas, ore, copper, aluminium, lithium, etc. In exchange Chinese engineers and workers build highways, airports, buildings and soccer stadiums. Remember, we have now entered the world of lack of resources. Another dimension of the ecological disequilibrium is that the notion of country or nation disappears when one thinks about the planet. Even if the United States has refused to sign the Kyoto agreement, the fact is that there is

global warming, created by humans. Each of our acts has a modest impact on it. Billions of modest impacts create the disequilibrium. Biodiversity is everyone's concern.

- **Demographic disequilibrium.** We shall soon reach 9 billion human beings. However, most of them will be at the bottom of the pyramid, and hence the excitement when looking at these poor people as an economic opportunity. Whether one looks at this cynically as a source of business or humanistically as a necessity to provide support and help, the fact is that a third of the world's population are not even consumers. They wish to be so: today they are survivors. Individual actions, like that of Muhammad Yunus, 2006 Nobel Prize winner, founder of the Grameen Bank and inventor of micro-credit, paved the way. Instead of pouring in money to help, it is better to create the conditions for a real economy to develop there (Prahalad, 2009). Danone is also a forerunner: it knows that its future growth will come from the emerging countries. Their populations are growing fast and need good food. This is why all companies will have to develop new business models to market profitably products adapted to the needs, resources and channels of distribution of these countries. One cannot just cut and paste what worked in Europe. A brand needs a business model. Emerging countries will have their own brands and business models.

The co-existence of four mentalities

What are the effects on consumer and corporate behaviour? The difficulty is that the question is too big and cannot have one answer only. Let us take two opposite examples. In China and India, 3 billion people want access to the consumption society symbolized by the Western lifestyles they have watched on television for decades (cars, home comforts, televisions, Big Macs, etc). In Europe, some countries are engaged in demographic suicide: they are no longer producing many babies (eg Germany and Spain). Others are (eg France), but the countries' populations are getting older, and the baby boomers are now retiring.

This is the paradox of today. Our world has never been so global (through cheap-transport airlines, television channels, the internet, social media, etc): we know in a second what happens in Cairo, Tripoli, Sao Paulo or Riyadh and are affected by it. In the meantime, the world is divided into separate socio-economic continents that do not converge.

Unlike traditional consumer segmentation, which tends to allocate people to clusters within a typology (thus one is 100 per cent part of a given type), modern sociology recognizes that mentalities do not change but are added to. As we still have a reptilian brain beneath the cortex, mentalities do not disappear but are contained (within some restricted areas, moments and situations). Four mentalities have been identified, each one with its value hierarchy, mode of conduct, behaviours and type of relationships (Bonnal, 2008) (see Figure 6.2):

FIGURE 6.2 The four social mentalities

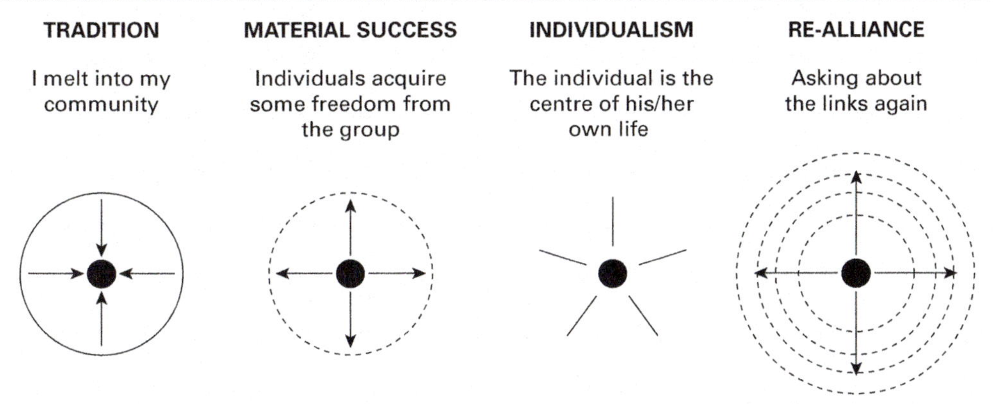

SOURCE Bonnal (2008)

FIGURE 6.3 How mentalities add to each other but do not disappear

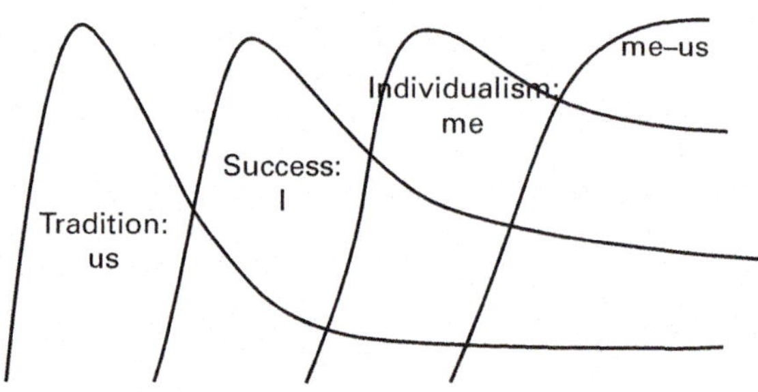

SOURCE Bonnal (2008)

- The first mentality has been dominant for thousands of years. It is the traditional one. You are what your parents are. The notion of self does not exist. People inherit their religion, their tastes, their way of being dressed, their profession and their visions of the world. Sometimes they do not even choose their own wife or husband. Interestingly, although it was thought that this mentality was declining, the return of integrism, that is to say the purity of the sources, puts this model back at the forefront in many countries.
- The second mentality is the one dominating China today. It praises material success. Becoming a person is the number one goal. Millions of Chinese who could not think of themselves under the cultural revolution are now discovering the pleasure of consumption as a means of existing as a person. Since political expression is under control, freedom to be oneself is achieved through choices of clothing brands, furniture, consumer electronics, etc. Shopping is the primary leisure occupation in Seoul or Shanghai, the 'malling' of Asia being a response to this demand. 'I buy therefore I am', to paraphrase philosopher René Descartes.
- The third mentality has been that of the West till now: a hymn to individualism and the reification of the person, leading to egoism at the extreme and a self-centred vision of human relationships.
- It seems that some of us have entered a fourth era, which should be called 'me–us', that is to say a deeper me, but in connection with the collectivity (us). Of course, this is a mirror of Web 2.0, the social networks, but it means also that no individual benefit can be fully experienced if it does not deliver collective benefits too. The me and the us are one again in alliance.

Now the problem is that these mentalities are superposed on one another at a specific time and place (see Figure 6.3). No one adheres to just one of them. *Playboy* as a magazine worships mentalities two and three, *Forbes* the first and second.

What are tomorrow's brands?

In practice, for managerial purposes, it is important that CEOs realize the new role of brands in this disenchanted world: a brand will be a name that symbolizes a long-term engagement, crusade or commitment to a unique set of values, embedded into products, services and behaviours, which make the organization more than stand apart, but stand above!

Internally everybody in a brand-driven organization must be driven by one ideal: to make the name the unique purchase criterion of the targets. Why is Coke the number one brand in the Interbrand Financial Evaluation Hit Parade, with US$72 billion in 2010? Former Coke CEO Roberto Goizueta said: 'Because everywhere in the world billions of consumers ask for a Coke, never for a cola.' Brand management pursues an ideal: to make the name become the reference (landmark) of a category or territory it has itself created. Then people will put the brand as number one choice criterion: Apple!

The best predictors of the brands of tomorrow are young consumers. When they are interviewed about the brands they are passionate about they quote specific characteristics:

- being known, a normal prerequisite, and very active in communication;
- symbolizing a unique and strong 'value proposition';
- moved by deep, authentic and long-term values;
- being flawlessly incarnated into products or services that change consumers' lives;
- being brands one can meet, interact with and experience through people and places and by

whatever mode (digital or bricks and mortar); and finally

- being very ethical.

This is what some brands have already achieved. Apple was created in 1976; now people are queuing, freezing, for a whole night on Fifth Avenue to be the first to buy the latest innovation when the Apple Store opens its doors. Is this a miracle? No. What makes Apple so loved is:

- 35 years of unchanged, meaningful high goals;
- consistency in delivery;
- disruptive innovations, which create new categories and change lives;
- optimism and peacefulness;
- holding values and never compromising with them, even when under pressure;
- charisma, with Steve Jobs acting as the John Galliano of high technology made pleasurable, epitomizing the company spirit and seeming to have the magic touch. By contagion, the products are magic.

It is noticeable that Steve Jobs has never uttered corporate goals such as 'We want to become number one in the market.' Has Louis Vuitton ever said it wanted to be the world's number one luxury brand? Lexus boasts it is the number one imported luxury car in the United States, thus demonstrating that quantity is more important than quality. Being number one is a classic of journalistic headlines, or stock market short cuts to seduce prospective investors who are risk averse. Size is not a consumer problem: 'What's in it for me and now for us all, to incorporate concern for the planet?'

It is also interesting to reveal that Apple has ethical principles. iPhone is known for its many applications. Apple does not want to repeat the historical strategic mistake it made when there were many more developers working on PCs than on Macs. However, Apple forbids all applications with sexual connotations. This created a problem with the Playboy corporation, but values are values. What is a value if compromises are made as soon as maximization of revenue is concerned?

In brief, Apple defines the profile of the postmodern brand: a brand creates passion when it is perceived to be the champion of values that have changed the lives of many for the better (it pursues authority rather than mere power).

Note that price is never mentioned when talking about the factors of success for Apple. In fact Apple prices are those of a luxury brand (see Kapferer and Bastien, 2009).

Brands and price

Brands are here to make people forget price. This is true of Apple, Louis Vuitton, Nespresso, Krups and Audi, as well as Zara, Bic, easyJet and Wal-Mart.

Does one ask the price of an Audi? Audi is worth it. This is the only goal of Audi's brand management. Audi represents 'progress through technique'; as such it is deeply German and does not hide it. Buying an Audi, one buys the good parts of progress (eg aluminium and therefore ultra-light, sophisticated diesel engines, which are less polluting than hybrid engines). Audi is more than a car: it is a vision on progress. All premium brands succeed because they deserve their price. They make the price irrelevant. Certainly, not everybody can afford one (this is called market segmentation), but very few people question the price of Audis. That is the power of the brand.

Very few people feel much fear when they enter an easyJet, RyanAir or Southwest Airlines aeroplane. They might with Asian Air, a new low-cost airline, which launched a €300 return trip to Kuala Lumpur in Malaysia. But Asian Air is not yet a brand. It is a name on an aeroplane and on a website. EasyJet and RyanAir are brands: they come to mind immediately, and evoke trust and empathy. Why trust? There used to be charter flights selling cheap flights years ago, but there were no brands. Travellers were packed like sardines into inferior aeroplanes of unknown companies. EasyJet, because of its business model, buys the latest and best aeroplanes in the world from Airbus. Consumers feel totally secure. In addition, these aeroplanes are more kerosene efficient. EasyJet and RyanAir have opened the dream society to all of us. Today there are no longer travel destinations just for the rich. Hotels maybe, but saving on travel allows most of us to afford a good hotel or perhaps a very good one just for the experience. This is how the luxury market has benefited from low-cost airlines. Interestingly, this is a typical re-alliance mentality (see Figure 6.2). EasyJet and RyanAir are not just egoistic cheap fares; they provide a collective benefit. Finally, their obsession with top-of-mind brand awareness is linked to internet sales: which will be clicked first?

Individual and collective benefits

Being a brand means being in advance. From now on, the brand promises will need to bring collective benefits too. Brands cannot simply bring individualistic pleasure. This explains the success of the hybrid engine, which, although it is more polluting than an advanced diesel engine with particle filter, seems to symbolize the re-alliance of progress with clean air and collective necessities. The same holds true for Tesla, the US luxury electric car. We have entered the era of conspicuous altruism. Ikea is already a re-alliance brand. Superficially it sells an economy of price or a personal benefit. In fact its remarkable value proposition is 'Tomorrow your home will be really nice, even at a low cost.' This is about personal pride for all. In addition the company has values that make it stand apart or stand above (humanistic, ethical, attentive, caring, listening, passionate).

The market will have to separate the wheat from the chaff. Many brands, well advised, have already engaged in a greenwashing campaign. Take McDonald's, whose logo is now green, to look clean. Anyone who has seen the movie *Super Size Me* knows how much McDonald's carries a moral responsibility in the growth of obesity. The world will have to eat less meat for ecological reasons. McDonald's does not talk about this at all.

Brands of the future will need to be authentically responsible. It means the ethical dimension of their activity will be part of their global attractiveness and desirability. In any case, with internet watchdogs, Wikileaks and its many siblings, all is known sooner or later. From a financial standpoint, big is good because of the economies of scale. However, from a brand appeal standpoint, big is responsible too, if possible proactively, not just reactively or to follow the bandwagon.

Brands of the future will also need to be optimistic. Facing the complexity of the world and its many disequilibriums, if not threats, consumers have two possibilities. One is to forget and escape through distractions: this what Jensen (1999) called the *dream society*. Consumers will like brands that create an air of happiness (Disney, etc) or that nourish social ties: modern electronics are experiential, connect us to the world and allow interactivity. The second possibility is to work harder. Yes, there are difficulties, but it is better to confront them than to negate them. Nike's 'Just do it' resonates favourably again, as does Johnnie Walker's 'Keep walking'. These slogans are hymns to solo willpower. Sport is like life.

The new key words of strategic brand management

Words are more than words: they are visions of the world. Management concepts are deeply influenced by the nature of the competitive situation and the tools to market. The 30-second TV commercial led brands to be obsessed with the unique selling proposition (USP), a single-minded reduction of a brand to one word or phrase. Tide 'washes better'! Today there is the internet; that is to say, the consumer is in power. The trade is in power too, with its retail brands that hold growing market shares in many product categories. Can the same old concepts of brand as a difference or a relevance still work? Isn't the least you can expect from a product to be relevant to the need it purports to fill? But what about brands? How should they react to the changing times and world, as depicted above?

Beyond the brand essence: brand engagement

The mantra of traditional brand management is the DNA and genes of the brand: the brand essence. Tons of money is poured into in-depth research, to unveil it at last and worship it as the Holy Grail. But brand essences are static. If brands are to lead markets, create passionate communities and have followers, they must adopt dynamic concepts and forget the static ones. Brand essence is a static concept. The problem today both inside and outside companies is engagement. People are less passionate and feel less concerned. One does not engage consumers if the brand is not engaged itself.

A brand has no difficulty commanding a higher price if it seems moved by something other than selling products. Why is the Innocent smoothies brand growing faster and priced higher than its main competitor? Because, as an activist brand, it set up a fundamental debate between bad food and good food, between industry practices for the sake of reducing costs and what is good for consumers. This is why it called its brand Innocent, ie not guilty.

Interestingly, Innocent did not create this market, but came second. A brand called Pete & Johnny's was the first mover in 1994. Innocent came in 1998. However, Pete & Johnny's (PJ's) was just a marketing brand, trying to emulate the success of Ben & Jerry's. It was just a brand targeted at youth with all the tool kit: a brand essence (natural), a promise (health) and a brand personality (fun). It had no authenticity, no real brand content, no true story and no capacity to execute the promise without compromise at any cost – only a lot of money, as it was backed by Pepsi. The result was straightforward: Innocent was growing by 91 per cent, PJ's by 10 per cent, and private labels by 24 per cent (Simmons, 2008).

The notion of engagement is important, for it suggests that some people may rally to our cause and support it. Such people are crusaders for the brand: for Apple they were the creative elite of the US west coast. As such they are a very small group but they have enormous viral power at the beginning.

'Why does the brand exist?' is the most important question

Something is going wrong with classic brand models. In current thinking, branding means associating a promise or benefit with a name through repetition of customer direct experience and communication. The key analytical concepts stem from consumer choice theory: to make consumers choose your brand, tell them how good your products are and how they will get benefits by using the products.

The key concepts of 'positioning' and 'battle of the mind' (Trout and Ries, 1970) ask that we focus on one single benefit, like the old advertising USP. But the USP was a consequence of the 30-second TV commercial format: just say one thing; make it simple. Jack Trout and Al Ries themselves came from advertising agencies.

Are brands just a benefit associated with a name? Can Ikea, Nike, Apple, Google, Volvo and Dior be summarized in this way? Can passion be built up from a single benefit or a name be able to evoke strong emotions and engagement from a core target in just this way?

We have to move away from cognitive static models of branding (brands as a network of mental associations – Keller, 1998) to energizing and social models of branding. Brands should be conceived of and managed as social crusade. People love champions. As in sport, to be a champion you need a fight, a cause and a competitor. Competition builds champions. Brand USA used to be the champion of freedom versus the USSR (Anholt and Hildreth, 2005). With the fall of communism, this brand has lost much of its inner attractiveness. It is now the champion of what? Of what cause?

To fight private labels and hard-discount products, FMCG brands need a strong reason for being, an inner turbo-engine, creating passion inside before they drive it outside (see also Edwards and Day, 2005).

Creating a community, or fans or followers, necessitates much more than a positioning statement or 'reason to believe it'. The brand must rally people more than simply convince them. The single most important question of the brand platform is 'Why does the brand exist?' and not 'Why should one choose this product as against the products of competitors?'

Before your differences, focus on your high goals: stand apart or rise above?

Old concepts remain pervasive in current brand thinking as if the situation had not changed. We used to say that a brand needs difference and relevance. These have not prevented the demise of FMCG brands in numerous markets: in Europe many of P&G's iconic brands are now losing ground, confronted by advanced private labels or thematic ones (private labels that foster a cause).

There is an implicit danger in these two commonsense notions: difference and relevance. First, obsession with difference leads to the famous 'better mousetrap syndrome'. Finding a difference at any price has led to consumer indifference.

There is a lot to learn from big brands: they never forget the big picture. Their promise extends beyond the category. Danone does not say 'We have better yoghurts.' It does not define itself as a yoghurt maker, but as enhancer of food for humanity with special application to dairies.

Moreover, big brands like Nike, Danone and Toyota do not focus on their differences but on their high goals. Danone wants to 'bring health through food to the many': this is why it is so engaged in its global operations with Muhammad Yunus's microcredit bank and the bottom-of-the-pyramid activities in Bangladesh for instance. Nike is a hymn to sport as a metaphor for life (Cameron and Holt, 2010). Toyota wants to create a cleaner planet now.

Finally, big brands target the many. They have high goals, but unlike luxury brands that restrict their privileges to a few they aim at distributing them to the many. This is why they are loved brands.

Big brands are more than a product or a single category, but they still pursue the same obsession across all categories. They are a whole, a vision, a set of values, stories or services, an experience, a taste, etc. Big brands take their values seriously: this is why they are loved. Since Virgin's creation, Richard Branson has never compromised on the Virgin values: fun, value for money, quality, innovation, competitive challenge and brilliant customer service. Virgin just hates fake competition, like the competition that has been going on between Coca-Cola and Pepsi since 1930, which divides the market between these two old brands, with entrance forbidden to any newcomer.

Beyond brand relevance: think meaningfulness

In mature countries needs are fulfilled on the whole. In our high-consumption societies, a demand grows for meaningfulness, not just relevance. Meaningfulness situates the problem of consumers at a higher level in Maslow's hierarchy. Relevance is a need-based concept. It applies to a product. Does the product match the need?

In our future world of disequilibriums, threats, lack of resources, and questions about the meaning of economic growth, big brands will need to be much more than relevant. They will need to propose a new meaning for consumption, which answers profoundly the demands raised by the evolution of society. People are looking for meaning in their life. They know that 'Buy more and be happy' does not work (Chinese consumers who are discovering a new prosperity and purchasing power still believe in it, but will soon learn that having two Louis Vuitton bags does not make you twice as happy).

One of the driving forces behind private labels is that they propose another kind of meaningfulness. They say: why spend more? Keep your money for yourself! Enjoy it. Reducing private labels to a low-cost offer relevant to the needs of the price-sensitive segment is a caricature. Reducing Ikea to a 'do-it-yourself offer' relevant to a specific life cycle segment (couples in their first flat together or with growing children) means reducing consumers to cost optimizers.

Innocent smoothies create meaningfulness: it is not just 'tastes better because our fruit is better'. They say: control your health; do not believe what the industry tells you. Nike says fight; it is a hymn to solo willpower and as such matches the ideals of changing US society, one that is discovering post-communist complexity.

Targeting for the new strategic brand management

The new strategic brand management recognizes three different targets (see Figure 6.4) for what must be called influencer marketing.

FIGURE 6.4
The new strategic brand targeting

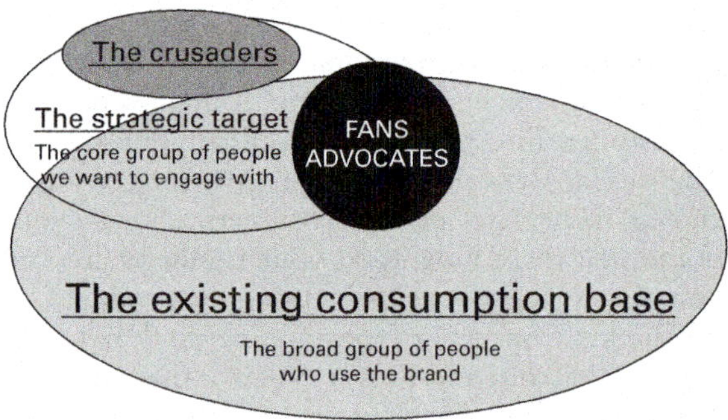

- The crusaders are those people who naturally identify with the cause or crusade of the brand (this supposes of course that the brand has one). The brand ideals create an immediate resonance among them. For Nike it has been the youth sub-culture living in the ghettos. For them life is harder: recession adds to their normal difficulties. To succeed they can only count on their own will, energy and art. Sport is a way out and a metaphor for life. Nike epitomizes this in the slogan 'Just do it' and its intimate relationships with sub-groups from the ghetto culture, as well as with their sport heroes. Crusaders are those aspirational individuals who stand for the deep human insight of the brand. Absolut Vodka used the New York art gay community as crusaders when it was first launched in the United States in 1979. Brands choose their crusaders. Now George Clooney is not a crusader for Nespresso. Everyone knows he is paid to be the advertising voice of Nespresso. Typical crusaders for Nespresso were the cultural elite, for whom pleasure is a culture.

- Fans are proselyte consumers. They are totally engaged in the brand, which is their one and only choice. They are also heavy buyers: this is not a platonic relationship. Advocates, also called evangelists, are less exclusive in their choice. Both fans and advocates are the 'promoters' identified by the net promoter score (NPS) (Reichheld, 2005). This score rests on the 'ultimate question': would you recommend the brand to a friend? To do so one must be not just satisfied, but enthusiastic. This question taps both rational sources of satisfaction (quality) and emotional ones. All brands can and should measure the number of their fans and advocates. It is a major predictor of sustainable success. In addition, through customer relationship marketing (CRM) they can be identified and treated separately, as a community (Figure 6.5).
- The consumption target is made up of heavy, medium and low users. From a marketing standpoint it is common to segment consumers of a brand behaviourally, separating buyers from non-buyers, and then isolating heavy or frequent buyers from low-volume or occasional buyers. This segmentation is useful for organic growth. Why are some people infrequent users? What is the way to increase their rate of usage or of click? The customer equity perspective addresses this issue: how to make existing clients buy more? This has built the success of the Coca-Cola Corporation. On average each US citizen drinks 412 eight-ounce drinks of Coke per year. It was only 275 in 1988. By segmenting the range (diet, low-carb, low-caffeine, zero, etc) Coke has suppressed the barriers to consuming more. It has also

FIGURE 6.5 Identifying brand proselytes and fans: strategic segmentation

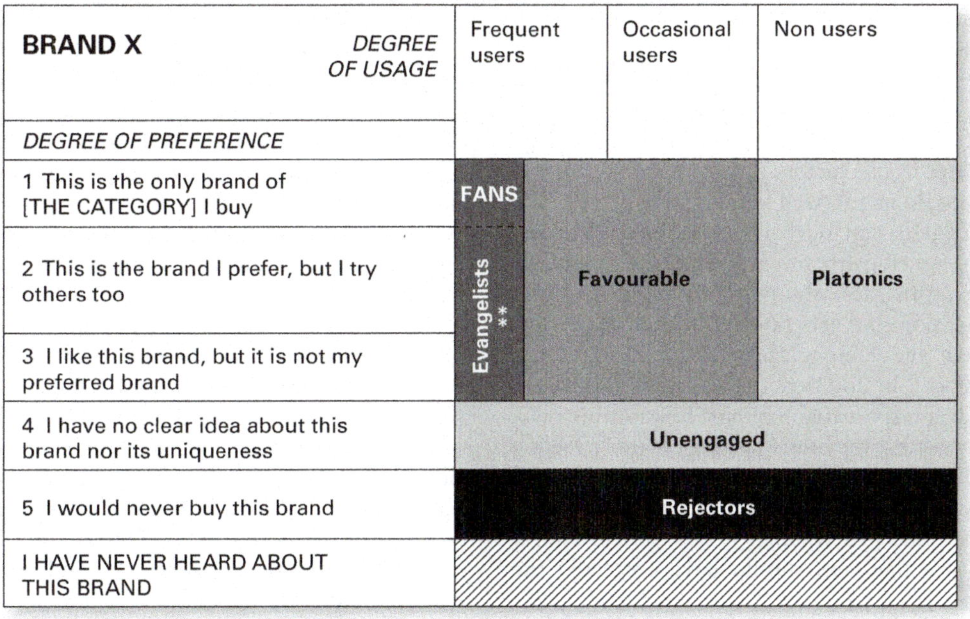

BRAND X *DEGREE OF USAGE*	Frequent users	Occasional users	Non users
DEGREE OF PREFERENCE			
1 This is the only brand of [THE CATEGORY] I buy	FANS	Favourable	Platonics
2 This is the brand I prefer, but I try others too	Evangelists **		
3 I like this brand, but it is not my preferred brand			
4 I have no clear idea about this brand nor its uniqueness	Unengaged		
5 I would never buy this brand	Rejectors		
I HAVE NEVER HEARD ABOUT THIS BRAND			

extended Coke's distribution to put it at arm's reach.

From brand activation to brand activism

Brands are not promises. Promises are words. They should be experienced. That is why modern brand management talks first about brand activation. Values do not exist unless they are activated and today, one would add, unless they are experienced by the clients themselves, fully, at each point of contact, now renamed point of equity building.

Many brands still have significant progress to make here, at the contact points. People have become cynical about brands because they have had so many negative experiences, at odds with what they see in advertising. Most brand promises are not kept.

Burger King deserves its name: the Whopper is the best burger in the world. However, even downtown New York Burger King restaurants can kill the pleasure. It is true that the business logic of master franchises, used by Burger King, explains why from one restaurant to another there is so much variability in quality, cleanliness, smiles, welcome and so on. Some restaurants can be compared to stables, and hardly meet the basic standards of any fast food in a modern capital.

On a recent visit to Burberry's store in New York, the author noticed that the buttons on a US$2,500 coat on display were falling off, because they were not properly sewn on. The Burberry sales assistant, instead of taking the coat to have the sewing improved, explained why the buttons were sewn on inadequately: the coat came from a factory (in an emerging country) that did not do its job well enough.

This suggests that Burberry is not controlling its operations either upstream or downstream. It invests in increasing the desirability of the brand through communication, but lets poorly finished expensive coats leave the factory (probably manufactured under licence). In addition the store sales assistant does not feel responsible for that. It is not his task. This indicates that the brand has not created a feeling of belongingness among the people working for it. Normally the person setting up the coat on display should have checked whether it was perfect and, if that was not the case, should have corrected the situation.

A final example comes from Visa. In its trading-up policy Visa urges some of its clients to switch to Visa Premier, the top of the range. With this card come benefits and services, the least one would expect if denoted as a VIP or premier person. One of the key features of Visa Premier is its insurance policy. Cardholders are encouraged to pay as many times as possible with the card: if there is a theft or cancellation (of a trip) the cardholder is reimbursed. The problem starts when the insurance is put into practice. In fact Visa Premier delegates its insurance to an insurance company, so while clients are in despair, hoping to get some consideration from Visa Premier, they are told to send their claims to a company they have never heard about before. Then the nightmare starts. This insurance company, fully independent, does not act as an ambassador of Visa's Premier service, but simply as an insurance company, that is to say a company that suspects all claims may be fraudulent.

To act as a brand is to exert quality and experience control all along the value chain.

As shown in Figure 6.6, once this is achieved, brands will need to be perceived as key actors in their category: innovation does this. Only innovation creates value by raising the standards and providing progress. Innovation makes people forget the price. Everyone is pleased: the end user, the retailer and the brand. We shall address the issue of innovation in Chapter 9.

Finally, some brands are more than actors; they are activists: they act as stimulants of the whole category and beyond. They raise debates and stimulate issues. As such they are more than suppliers; they demonstrate energy and concern for the future of the category and the well-being of the end users. This kind of brand is able to raise a community and have followers. Today, fostered by the internet revolution, which made salient the forgotten major role of social influence, brands are community builders.

What is a community? It is much more than a group or a segment: it is a set of people interacting together, physically or virtually, connected by the pursuit of common goals or common ideals and likings. In a community some people are passionate; others are engaged; some are followers. To create passionate people the brand itself needs to be passionate (Derek *et al*, 2005). This is why the words and concepts used by traditional brand management do not match the challenges of today.

FIGURE 6.6 From activation to activism

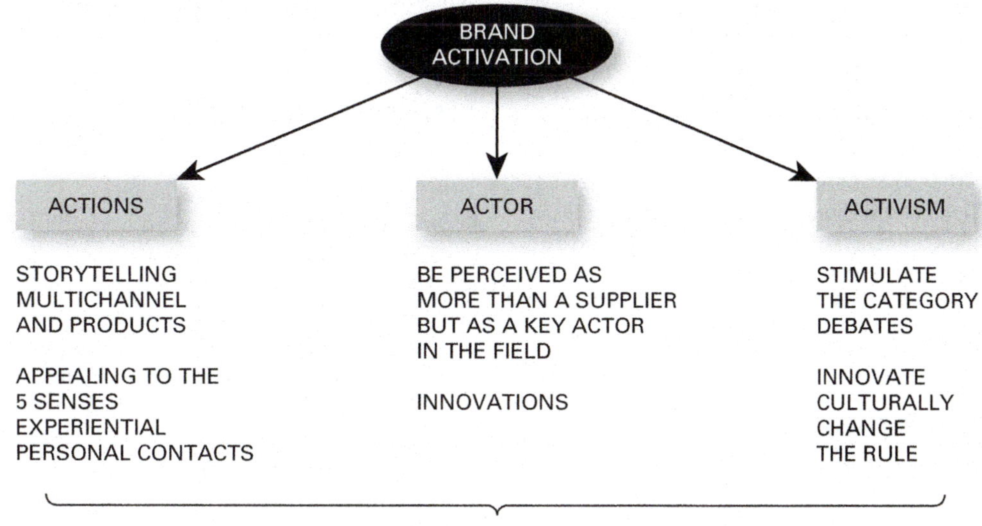

Adapting to new market realities

The new brand management is the fruit of the adaptation of companies to their new environment. What are the facets of this environment?

The rise of the shopper

A revolution is taking hold of lifestyles in our modern societies: what we call 'shopping' has become one of the three favourite pastimes at a time when television consumption is systematically decreasing, as is reading. Everywhere, in Western cities as in Asia, we like to visit shopping centres; we like to wander through arcades, malls, brand shops, factory shops. Asian tourists visiting France expect only one thing after the obligatory visits to the Eiffel Tower and the Louvre: a visit to the shops. Airports have become more than 'air malls': they are 'air fashion malls'.

Marketing shows little interest in the shopper, but talks only of consumers. The two are very different, like two faces of the same coin. It is always consumers who are consulted in telephone surveys and on the internet. It is consumers who are scrutinized in focus group meetings, where everyone is collectively liberated, the comfortable chairs and canapés helping this process. The *consumer* writes the list of products and brands to buy. It is the *shopper* who decides on the spot whether to take this or that. It is the shopper who has now become so eclectic, and who passes from a large, gleaming store to a discounter or a bazaar in the same afternoon. As a result, shopping has become exciting, surprising, full of emotions, the key being the possibility of doing business, enjoying oneself at the same time by wandering through places designed for the pleasure of – the shopper.

There is a tendency to confuse the concepts of the consumer and the shopper. In the B2B sector, they are two separate entities: the user and the purchaser. Each has different criteria and objectives, hence they also have conflicts of interest. The rise of the shopper is general: shopping is therefore no longer a race, a chore, but a way to exercise one's talent and to gain money by spending less of it. People also shop on the internet, which explains the rise of e-commerce.

Shops, like internet sites, in fact become complete destinations for an afternoon full of what is called 'retail-tainment', that is, the fusion of 'retail' and 'entertainment'. In mass consumption, the internet, the proliferation of shopping centres, factory shops and brand centres convey a single fact: shopping is not necessarily a chore, but a leisure activity. People can simultaneously find pleasure, excitement, and an opportunity to go out as a group and to do business. Shopping takes on the air of a safari, where people seek deals, and good deals. Through their internet search behaviour, or in the aisles, clients now set their own price; they are not subjected to a price offering. They can decide whether to pay the higher price on the ticket, and be certain that they have found the latest thing, and in the right size, or wait for the sales, but take the risk of not finding the desired product, or finding it only in the wrong size.

Markets are fragmenting, and volumes too

Traditional marketing also stumbles on the pitfall of market fragmentation. The mass market is dead, even though we continue to speak of 'mass-consumption products'. It is enough to look at the figures: even for a product as global as Diet Coke, in this country 8 per cent of purchasers represent 40 per cent of its volume and more than half of its profits. What product can boast a penetration rate higher than 20 per cent?

Nowadays we no longer talk about segments, but rather fragments. The segment remains a valid notion at a macroeconomic level: in the car trade, there are the segments B1, B2, M1, M2 and so on. These are divisions of the car market according to the range level. The car makers create a platform corresponding to each segment, on the basis of which they will in reality build different models, themselves divided into highly differentiated versions, each aimed at a specific fragment. You might think this is nothing new: haven't car makers always broken down their basic model into multiple peripheral versions (coupe, cabriolet, estate)? What is new is that there is no longer a basic model. Peugeot initiated this strategic approach and uses it for each launch. Thus the 207 is launched in seven versions, all highly specialized according to the lifestyle fragment they are aimed at; but there is no more talk of a basic version.

Ralph Lauren has created more than 10 sub-brands or daughter brands targeted according to the time of day and week – more or less casual or elegant – and according to sex and age. Nevertheless, this does not fragment the brand, since it has a highly compact central kernel, a very clear identity, symbolized by Mr Lauren himself and created in any Ralph Lauren shop (see page 163).

Media fragmentation

Every day a typical American has a choice between 7,000 hours of television. The 32 per cent of households equipped with a TiVo can not only watch their chosen television programmes 'a la carte', pre-recorded and available exactly when they choose, but also cut out all the commercial breaks. As for young people, they spend hours every day on the internet.

In short, normal advertising communications now face a real problem in reaching their targets. People channel-hop, they get up during commercial breaks, they are online or on the phone or on their PlayStation. This is why television channels are trying to remain faithful to their etymology. What is a television channel? It is simply a link. Television has to re-demonstrate its ability to be an audience aggregator. This involves the production of successful series, of talk shows that mirror today's society, where everybody is telling their life story to somebody, like a case study to be discussed collectively among households.

Sport is an ideal means for reuniting the exploded audience around an intense emotional ceremony. We may also see a return to soap operas: the name dates back to the 1930s, when soap brands financed programmes themselves, precisely in order to attract the audience and justify their advertising.

With the internet, the consumer has seized power

Technology is the consumers' friend: this is why they have adopted it. In fact, it has modified their relationship to manufacturers, to controlled or official information, and therefore to political cant. This revolution has an impact on brand management, which must also integrate this freedom technology.

Some key figures are useful to depict the new world that brands inhabit:

- More mobile phones are sold worldwide than televisions.
- The premier digital camera brand is not Canon or Fuji but Nokia.

- 80 per cent of Koreans have a mobile phone with a digital camera.
- Nearly 20 per cent of internet users give their opinions on internet sites dedicated to the evaluation of products and services by the clients themselves.
- Three months after the appearance of a consumer comment on the bikeforum.com site from someone who was amused at having been able to open a lock with a Bic ballpoint, and the circulation through the blogosphere of an amateur film proving this could be done, the Kryptonite company, which had spent 30 years building its reputation in the United States on safety, incurred a loss of US$10 million recalling all the vulnerable locks on the market. The same was true for Apple following the creation of the site Appledirtysecret.com, revealing the shortcomings of the iPod battery. Blogs start conversations, and the traditional media pick up on them.

All traditional marketing was founded on the asymmetry of power in the manufacturer's favour. Customers found it hard to become well informed, and therefore based their buying decisions on the familiarity of the brands, small distributors were grateful to the major brands for letting them deliver their goods, and competition was waged by every means except on price. This is over: the consumer has never had so much power.

This is also true of B2B clients:

- They are rare, and know it. They like to be seduced by brands.
- They are informed: today everything is known. They can search online to find out what is thought about such and such a product by looking on e-pinion sites, consulting their sector community on social medias. They can easily find the best vendor sites where the product is sold for less. The frontiers of the company and the brand are now porous. This is why IBM prefers to authorize certain key people in the company to create their own blogs, which open it up to the flow of questions, and at the same time make it possible to gain familiarity with what is being said.
- They can form blocs, and exert pressure on the company through collective internet action, their virtual community and e-lobbying. The impact of iPoddirty secret.com, which alerted all fans to the battery problems of the first iPod, is well known.
- They have acquired a communicative, participative, interactive culture. This leads to new opportunities for brands, which will cease to work as before – 'for customers but without them'. Nowadays involvement is at stake: the more customers or prospective customers are involved, the more they nurture a genuine engagement with the brand.

The goal of any brand is to make each customer a member, part of a virtual club of which he or she is not the centre, but where the customers' preoccupations, and their interests, are at the club's core. It is necessary to go beyond the notion of technical, relational marketing, which is admittedly useful, but which, like any technique, bypasses the essential. The more customers feel listened to, involved, required not to purchase but to act as advisors, the more a genuine link, a genuine community will be created around and with the brand.

Web 2.0 has set the seal on client or consumer power. The internet is no longer visionary or prophetic: it is easy, practical, social, abounding in services and information or games. Blogs have become the truth of the market, the true consumer magazine, while the brand websites, and in particular consumer magazines on glossy paper, are the 'official' truth.

The power of communities

Nowadays it is no longer consumers who build brands, but communities. It was New York's gay community that made Absolut a success, whereas that of Los Angeles made a success of Bombay Sapphire. It was the community of designers and creative people who supported Apple in its lowest periods.

Today in the United States the talk is all of 'community marketing'. Marketing plans are highly differentiated according to whether they are addressed at African-Americans, Chinese-Americans, or Americans of Hispanic or Puerto Rican origin.

What does the notion of community add to the notion of segment? Why not simply talk about the Chinese or Puerto Rican segment? A segment is a marketing abstraction designating people with the same profile or the same expectations. In contrast, a community is a living group, daily weaving new links through communication, exchange and participation. A community exists, lives, grows and has an identity. A segment is defined and measured: it agglomerates. The community expresses, and brings together. It lives through social medias.

The power of communities is admittedly not new: the cases of Absolut and Bombay Sapphire prove it. However, the internet has given a new perspective; communities are beehives of communication. The internet is their medium, as are mobile phones. The power of communities therefore ceases to be a sociological abstraction, or a recuperation technique: it becomes a true lever, if the brand knows how to put itself at the community's disposal. For example:

- Converse has 13 million fans on Facebook, Victoria's Secret 12, Zara 8, H&M 6 and Lacoste 5.
- Danone, via the 'Danone and you' website, puts itself genuinely at the service of mothers of young families.
- The aluminium extrusion brand Technal has created a new profession, that of the aluminium worker, and places itself at its service.
- The La Roche Posay brand stakes the centre of its communication activity on the effective involvement of the dermatological community.
- Quiksilver, Oxbow and Billabong strongly involve and become involved in the world of true surfers.
- Nike has created true niche marketing by becoming involved in the streets, with rappers or with the different tribes within each sport.

We have entered B to B to C marketing

The first edition of Philip Kotler's seminal book *Marketing Management* in 1971 dwelt on the revolution of B to C: the marketing share of the end client. Thirty years later, new realities have arrived and this notion must be amended. In many sectors, we have passed from B to C (business to consumer) marketing to B to B to C. We need to integrate the whole chain into the discussion, and ask ourselves what added value we bring to it.

The brand that does not have the luxury of independent distribution of its own must first of all consider the manner in which it will help the distributor/retailer to reach its own objectives. It is the distributor that must be convinced first of all. What is the use of a 'major brand' if it does not appear on the shelf, like all the other brands that have disappeared, not because clients no longer like them, but because they are no longer strategic for the distributors or retailers?

In a rolling market, for low-cost products such as toilet paper, or paper for other uses, an examination of a supermarket shelf might lead us to ask where the 'major brands' (Lotus, Kleenex, Charmin, Trèfle) have gone. They have all been replaced by Carrefour, Tesco, Sainsbury and other distributor brands. There remains only one manufacturer brand, Okay, positioned on its price/quality ratio. The Portuguese brand Renova, however, managed to retain this market. This SME first conquered its domestic market, then Spain, and now European mass distribution. Its entry into mass distribution was based on a double diagnosis of the distribution: 1) This shelf does not earn money: it is necessary to give it value through innovation. 2) This shelf is typically threatened by hard discounters. Renova therefore did not arrive as a product but as a new partner for each distributor/retailer, primed with a double offer. At the top of the range it offered hydrated paper and soft paper, and at the bottom of the range, the ability to maximize offers (12 for 8, 24 for 18). This promotional range was presented pre-packaged on wheeled stands.

In *The Devil Wears Prada*, Meryl Streep asks where her Jarlsberg is. This is the name of a famous Norwegian cheese, not dissimilar to Emmental. Its market share in the United States, where it has been sold for at least 40 years, is considerable. What was the key to its success? The fact that its roundels only weigh 10 kg, whereas the Swiss ones weigh 30 kg, so it is easier and more economical for stockists. It is through understanding the trade's expectations that Jarlsberg has made allies.

Everyone has heard of the phenomenal success of Yellow Tail, the Australian wine, in the United States. Nobody doubts that it is a good product, suited to the market, at a good price. Still, this was a wholly unexpected success. The Australian maker,

Casela, however, had had two good ideas, typical of a good B to B to C understanding of the market. First, it gave shares to the US distributor, which motivated it to promote the product everywhere in the US specialized distribution sector, and second, it fixed the price at a level that allowed it to pay these same distributors even more than the competition.

The indisputable fact that brands that no longer have their own distribution circuits are in fact engaged in B to B to C marketing is not given enough recognition. It is time that the distributor ceased to be considered as a 'distributor'. This word stems from the vocabulary of logistics, like stockist, dispatcher or wholesaler. A distributor is above all a retailer with its own differentiation strategy, and therefore its own brands. It is necessary to envisage it as a partner, and to start from its key problems, which are the same as those of the brand: the differentiation of its name, creating loyalty to its name, and profitability. It is concerned with the profitability of its own company, not of Danone or l'Oréal.

The power of business models

Yellow Tail offered more than a new brand, however: in the United States, it provided a new business model based on distribution. This was the number one problem to be resolved in the United States, bearing in mind that there are three levels of distribution there, as opposed to only two in Britain. The revolution was the business model. In Britain, where Yellow Tail arrived years after Jacob's Creek, its strategy did not work. It was Jacob's Creek that enjoyed the pioneer effect with *its* new business model.

EasyJet and Ryanair are more than just new and reassuring brands at low prices. They offer a radically different business model, that the regular airlines are unable to copy, since it is so widely opposed to their own model. This is why British Airways failed with its subsidiary, Buzz (it was perceived as a subsidiary however independent it actually was). In contrast, British Airways exploits to the fullest the structural advantages of the 'hub' business model, which offers great flexibility to international travellers.

The fundamental lesson to be learnt here is that the brand is not a self-sufficient asset. By itself, it can do nothing: it is therefore conditional. It only produces its effects in interaction with the business model that supports it. This is the case for all successful new entrants: Dell, eBay, Google, Zara and so on.

Take textiles as an example. Everyone emphasizes the extraordinary rise of the Zara brand worldwide, providing high fashion at low prices. To make this possible, however, it was in the mode of management that Zara really innovated. It managed to destabilize all those low-price competitors, such as Promod and Kiabi, that ran on different business models and therefore were not able to adapt. Zara is based on the fast turnover of small stocks of each item. The shortage of each garment is organized as a system of desirability promoting regular customer return to the shop. It treats the shop as a theatre stage, does no advertising, and has a remarkable system for eliciting qualitative information on the latest customer expectations. On the other hand, unlike its competitors Zara does not manufacture its clothing in China, in which case it could expect only two deliveries per year. It needs greater flexibility, which can only be obtained through a swarm of dedicated SMEs producing goods close by.

In mass consumption goods, it is notable that German-style hard discounters offer a better quality/price ratio than cheap products launched by the supermarkets in an attempt to resist them. This is due to their low cost business model: the Germans launched on the basis of long-term agreements with reputable manufacturers, who could then invest in the production of a very restricted number of products. This therefore reduces the cost price, but the products remain of good quality. The supermarkets for their part are resistant to anything that ties them to a single supplier in the long term; their business model is based on being able to permanently exert pressure on their sources, and change them at the first opportunity. There is a fundamental difference between buying merchandise at the lowest price, wherever it may come from, and creating an industrial and logistical system to produce a product of acceptable quality at half the price, from reliable suppliers.

In order to create a shampoo brand today, it is best to begin from a hairdressing label and create a complete range under licence in this name, sold in major shops: this business model was created by J Dessanges for l'Oréal. It has since been taken up by J C Biguine, J F David and others. At l'Oréal, every brand in fact has a different business model.

Building the brand at contact points

If managers think of the brand in a 'top down' manner, beginning with its essence and its values, then moving towards the tangible, its concrete activation, consumers proceed in the opposite manner. They begin with the tangible and the perceived. Everything begins with the concrete experience: I only believe what I see and feel.

My colleague at Columbia University, B Schmitt, brought the attention of the marketing community to the experiential dimension of the brand (Schmitt and Zhang, 2001; Schmitt, 2003). The brand is lived, felt, touched or heard: this goes without saying in the airline industry. Our impression of Air France or Singapore Airlines is built during the 12 hours of the flight from Paris to Tokyo or Singapore, through contact with the onboard staff: they are the brand during those hours. The Air France brand, however, is also tied up in the treatment of customers in telephone contacts with reservations, by ground hostesses, when things go well, and when they go badly and there are delays. Understanding the perceptible dimension of the brand makes us forget the product alone, in order to take into account the sum total of the client experiences on contact with the brand (see also page 54).

Brands that are only products must add an experiential dimension that will involve the client. Involvement is the prerequisite for engagement with the brand: that is, a true affective loyalty and not a repeated purchase for the sake of gaining miles or points. How can this experiential dimension be created?

- Putting on l'Oréal make-up is a true ritual, using little tubs and pots which are beautifully thought-out and decorated.
- Danone gives personalized health advice on its 'Danone and you' website.
- Car makers are now highly attentive to the experiential elements (door noises, softness of the leather, position of the armrests and so on).
- Complaint handling is increasingly practised in advance. Scripts are prepared so that the response reduces the negative effect, or even leaves customers satisfied, and so surprised by their good experience that they become ambassadors for the brand.
- Champagne makers offer visits to their cellars where the mystery of creation can be felt.
- Société Roquefort constructs its cellars as 3D shows in stone in order to accentuate the perceptible visitor experience.
- The fabulous ascension of the Pernod Ricard group stems from its progress into experiential territory. The core of brand investment goes on organizing events in bars, cafes, hotels and discos, based around the brand's values, its history and its imagined qualities.
- The Fedex brand has identified that the delivery person who comes to pick up the sealed envelopes or delivers them is the key personality in the Fedex experience for companies. To this is added the ergonomy of the website for tracking letters and parcels, the call centres and so on.
- Sponsorship is also a perceptible experience: visually associating the brand with an event, a sporting team or the like.
- Donations to good causes can demonstrate the brand is not insensitive to the world around it.

Finally, everyone will have noticed the tendency of brands to create a brand universe for themselves in increasingly large flagship stores, designed as experiential places, where the client feels the brand 120 per cent. Louis Vuitton opened its two biggest shops in the world in Tokyo on 31 August 2006, and in Shanghai in 2005. On 19 May 2006, a riot took place on Fifth Avenue in New York at the opening of the Apple Megastore, beneath a giant glass cube, opposite Central Park. Open day and night, clients can find all their iPhone accessories here, and enter into discussion, not with salespeople, but with Apple experts, all of them very young, and able to answer all technical problems.

Every Ralph Lauren shop could be Ralph Lauren's own house, with mahogany furniture, carpets, sofas, armchairs, pictures and photos, all aimed at creating a fake 'true' history. Remarkably, this perceptible Ralph Lauren ambience is also reproduced in the simple corners of the brand in department stores.

Tomorrow, just as there is a first division and a second division in football, these new brand cathedrals will sort the major brands from the small brands.

Retail as experience

All the exemplary cases of recent success, those that are praised to the skies worldwide in management seminars and symposia, are brands that have integrated distribution into their value offer. This is the case with Starbucks, Zara, Amazon, Dell, l'Occitane, Sephora and so on: they are all equally brands and distributors. We go to Zara in order to buy Zara.

It is interesting to note that Starbucks, Zara, Amazon and Google, to mention but a few, did not bother with advertising. On the contrary, they invested in training, men, women, architecture, the sensory contact, ergonomy, touch and the like.

It is revealing that all the stars of modern management, presented in all the management seminars, are brands whose shops are a source of enjoyment for the shopper: through the environment, choice, atmosphere and so on.

The enlarged scope of brand management

Brand management itself is much influenced by the revolution that has shaken marketing theory and practice: a shift from a mere transactional perspective to a relational perspective. This has led theorists to ask new questions, and propose new working methods, new modes of thinking, new tools, which often claim to be substitutes for the former 'old' ones.

From transaction to relationships

Traditionally marketing focused on consumer behaviour: it aimed at influencing choice. Its focus was on understanding purchase, and the choice criteria that prompted it, whether they were tangible or intangible, product-based or image-based. Its tool for influencing demand was the marketing mix, with its sacred four Ps: product, price, place and publicity. Marketing research aimed at identifying the attributes that predict purchase, and its typical statistical tool was a multi-attribute model. Segmentation is another key concept of transactional marketing: recognizing that transactions are facilitated when expectations are higher, and the mass market has been segmented into groups, or types with similar expectations. Then brands could be profiled and created to meet each set of expectations.

Because competition is fierce, imitation rapid, and consumers sometimes seemed overwhelmed by these very tightly tailored proposals and brands, the focus of marketing has moved from conquering clients to keeping them, from brand capital to customer capital. The new buzz words of good efficient brand management are share of requirements, shared loyalty and CRM. The focus is on building lasting relationships through time, and on post-purchase activities, all of which is subsumed under the term 'relationship marketing'. The focus of research has moved from predicting choice to classifying the different types of relationships consumers have with brands (Fournier, 1998), or the different types of interactions companies engage in with their clients, beyond selling a product or service (Rapp and Collins, 1994; Peppers and Rogers, 1993).

It should be noted that relationship marketing is a financially driven concept. Customers are still segmented, but the distinctions are behavioural. In traditional marketing, segmentation is aimed at maximizing the value created by the brand or company for its customers. In relationship marketing, segmentation is based on the value a customer brings to the company: only profitable customers should receive repeated attention. Hence the concept of lifelong customer value. Internet technology has created the means to meet this demand for more and more efficiency in tracking, analysing, servicing and selling to each one of these important customers.

Of course, these two approaches are complementary. The best loyalties are not based on mere calculus and loyalty cards: they are internalized as voluntary loyalty, as brand commitment. On the other hand, weak brands need to start somewhere. Behavioural loyalty programmes create the conditions for deepening the customer–brand relationship, and create emotional connections between consumers and the brand.

From purchase to satisfaction and experiential delight

Another consequence of this shift towards post-purchase phenomena is the focus on product/service satisfaction. How does what the product/service delivers match the expectations of the consumer? How can this satisfaction be raised, improved relentlessly? In this process the conditions of the consumption situation need to be taken into consideration. A product is always consumed in a context. The nature of this context affects the degree of satisfaction that the customer reports, through the notion of a 'rewarding experience'. In fact all marketers have known for a long time that food served in a pleasant atmosphere is judged to taste better than food eaten in unpleasant surroundings. Philip Kotler (1973) has coined the term 'atmospherics' to point out this facet of consumption, the experiential facet. Today, stores such as Niketown and the House of Ralph Lauren are typical applications of this experiential concept (Kozinets, 2002). As early as 1982, a pioneering paper by Holbrook and Hirschmann insisted on the necessity of providing modern consumers with fantasies, feelings and fun in their experiential consumption. Schmitt (1999) has coined the term 'experiential marketing' to refer to 'how to get customers to sense, feel, think, act and relate to your company and brands'.

Bonding through aspirational values

Beyond functional and experiential rewards, brands must now also be aspirational. It is through their intangible values that they help consumers to forge their identities, at a time when inherited identities are weaker. The famous and elusive 'customer bonding' is based on product satisfaction, on a rewarding consumption experience (which includes the tailoring of proactive services even for products). It cannot exist if the brand values do not fit the consumers' values. All brands have to be somehow aspirational. Beyond materialistic and hedonistic satisfactions, they say, 'We understand each other, we share the same values, the same spirit.' This is why it is so important to specify these non-product-based values. Visions and missions are the typical source of these values.

It is therefore possible to plot the extension of the scope of brand management on a two-dimensional matrix (Figure 6.7). The horizontal axis refers to the time perspective of the relationship sought (from

FIGURE 6.7 The extension of brand management

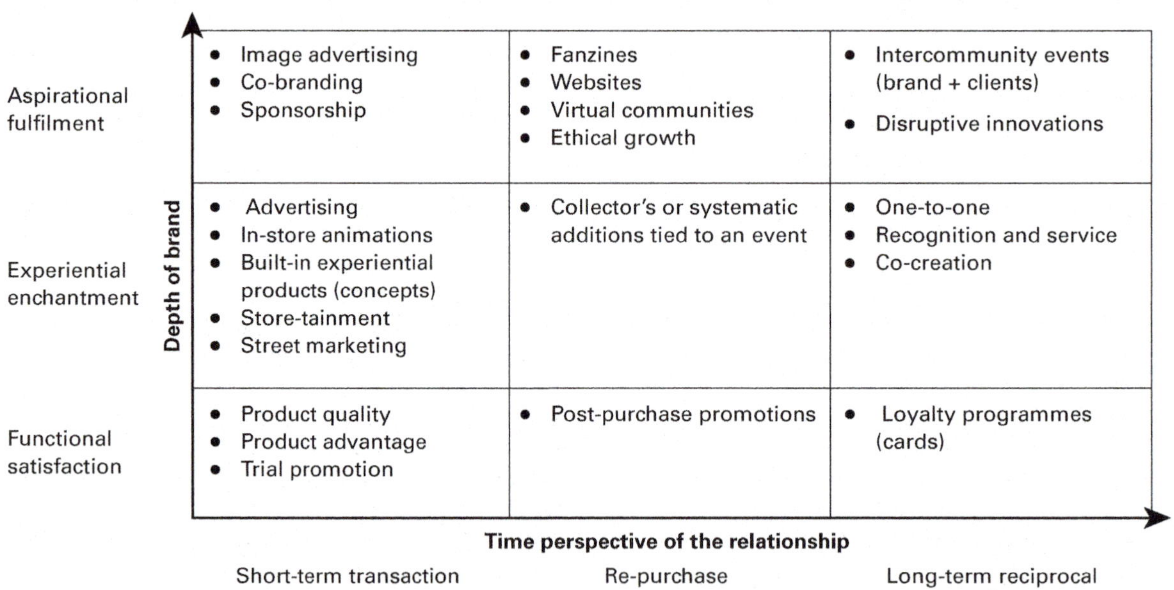

immediate transaction to repeat purchase to long-term commitment), while the vertical axis refers to the depth of customer bonding. It has three tiers: product satisfaction, experiential enchantment and aspirational intimacy, or the sharing of deep values. At the intercept, it is possible to position the new tools and behaviours of modern brand management.

Brand communities

How many fans does the Manchester United football team have all around the world? Five million in the UK and 50 million elsewhere in the world? Most of these will never see the team play in the flesh, but they watch real-time television showings or connect to webcasts of the team's matches on the internet. They consume merchandise such as T-shirts. In the Old Trafford stadium, UK fans drink only Manchester United Cola. This is a real community; thanks to it, the team can hire the most expensive players, such as Wayne Rooney. The income from the merchandise sold by association with the most famous players virtually covers their enormous wages and transfer fees.

Traditionally, in consumer research consumers were seen as individuals, who were eventually aggregated into market segments. Most multi-attribute models aiming at predicting purchase made that implicit assumption, for they were based on individual responses. One could argue that consumers are not isolated individuals: they belong to groups, tribes or communities, either stable or transient, durable or situational. In fact, the brand acquires meaning not through a summation of individual evaluations, but after a collective screening made of conversations within the reference groups, the community, where opinion leaders can play a determining role.

Along with advertising, new forms of behaviour have emerged through which brands are *enacted*, that is, they eventually 'live' their values with consumer communities in a non-commercial environment. Classical examples of this are the Michelin-sponsored races around the world, or the Harley-Davidson rally where management and bikers meet once a year. The modern brand also animates communities created around itself or a topic (parenthood for Pampers, rock music for Jack Daniel's). Internet sites, 'fanzines', hotlines, brand clubs and events, are the classic tools to implement this new attitude and share the brand values through servicing or animations. The brand becomes 'mediactive', it helps its customers get in touch with each other, on the net or in reality through specific events. Building *brand communities* is now part of the scope of brand management (Hagel, 1999). For consumers, getting together and sharing experiences is another form of reward. Feather (2000) has identified four drivers of e-communities: they can be interest-based, transaction-based, relationship-based or fantasy-based. Each one determines a specific type of site, of content, of interaction between the brand and this very involved public; it goes beyond mere purchasing and looks for interactions with the brand and other customers. The customers are driven by the rewards of community interaction and transaction.

Brands need brand content

Who does not know Michelin, the world-leading company in the tyre business? It is present in 170 countries, with 120,000 employees, and 68 plants in 19 countries. Global sales turnover is €15 billion, of which 90 per cent is tyres.

In 1900, a small booklet was produced and given free to the 2,400 clients who had a car at that time. This was how the *Michelin Guide* started: clients exploring the French countryside with their quite unreliable cars had to know where a flat tyre could be fixed. In addition, they were informed about the town where this garage could be found: what hotel and what restaurant they could choose, just in case they had to wait there. Since then, the *Michelin Guide* has become the premier judge of high cuisine worldwide. Its awards are the universal marque of excellence, sought after by chefs from all countries. If they want to be recognized by their peers and clientele, they must earn one, two or three Michelin stars!

In the 20th century, 30 million guides were sold. There are 26 editions in 23 countries. The latest are Tokyo, Shanghai and Hong Kong, following New York, London, etc. This is a small part of group sales, but probably more than half of all its publicity (no figures exist owing to the group confidentiality rules). Michelin has invented many remarkable tyres (the radial, etc). It also invented 'brand content', one of the most important new concepts for modern strategic brand management.

Brand content should not be confused with 'branded content' or with 'storytelling'. Branded content is close to sponsorship. The brand is just endorsing and often financing a show on television. Storytelling is a technique, a narcissistic tactic of inventing anecdotes or legends (authors). 'Brand content' is a new paradigm (Bo and Guevel, 2009). Brand content aims at creating an editorial strong experience. Examples are Benetton *Colors* magazine and Louis Vuitton travel guides and books. Brand content engages consumers to relate to the brand, because it does not talk about its products, but about a domain of mutual interest between the brand and its public.

Why has brand content emerged only recently as a fundamental concept? Because of Web 2.0.

Brands have to exist on the net. In this regard, one should forget websites, which are like a store. Web 2.0 is about peer-to-peer interaction, socializing, prescription, entertainment, etc. What does the brand have to say when it is not talking about its products? Brands without 'brand content' will be absent as the main source of information of consumers. Consumers do not visit sites to be exposed to a sales pitch. To lead, brands will have to deliver content on the web. As a result they will need to think of themselves as media, as curators, as publishers and as a television channel. Brand content gives content to brands, as well as depth and emotion. This content has to drive attention and become viral. Apart from viral techniques (there are now agencies that promise to make messages viral based on some proven techniques), the question is: what is the brand about when it is not products or services? Brand content emphasizes the cultural dimension of all brands, and their intangibles. Brand content is the link between the brand and citizens or netizens (people cannot be reduced to the single role of consumers).

Yesterday, in traditional marketing, brands talked to consumers through advertising. They bought space. This was intrusive marketing (Godin, 1998). Public relations were there to penetrate the magazine's own content: this is how magazine pages showing products are made up. With Web 2.0, intrusion is dead, except for banners. Consumers just go where they want (generally not to a brand website): they want to talk to others, or are looking for interesting content about what they like in life. Brand content is now necessary to get in contact with them.

Some have long realized that they needed content, well before the web. Look at Ralph Lauren: the company has published books on Ralph Lauren's life, his car collection, his ranch, his wife's famous recipes, and her taste in home decorating. One can guess that the recent book, available only on Kindle, comparing the lives of Ralph Lauren and Coco Chanel was planned by the Ralph Lauren company. The books can be bought in all the Ralph Lauren mega-stores. Artful documentaries on Calvin Klein, Marc Jacobs and Karl Lagerfeld, probably initiated at the behest of their companies, are visible everywhere, even in aeroplane movie programmes and now on the web.

The web has given a new scale to brand content: a worldwide scale. Ralph Lauren books were available to a few: their price segmented the readership. They were lovely presents or gifts, and thus reinforced the status of the brand. The web makes brand content available to anyone in the world. Of course, unlike posters in the street, visible to all even if they are not potential buyers, web content is selected by its audience. It cannot impose itself as advertising used to. Web content follows the same paths of diffusion as rumours (Kapferer, 1990).

The main question for all major brands today is: what brand content should I create, for what purpose and for whom? A lot of care, energy, time and money have to be invested by brands to produce both interesting and entertaining content. The media of the encounter will be the social networks. This is where people meet now, not in a lonely crowd, but in chosen communities.

This is why a brand that is not able to create its own community is weak. Is it even a brand? Brands are a bit like religions demanding faith and loyalty: they do start small but soon have apostles and an active community.

There are three types of brand content: entertaining, practical/useful and informative/discovery:

- BMW has posted on the net a series of small movies, made by famous directors (Martin Scorsese, Quentin Tarantino), casting famous Hollywood stars (Clyve Donner) or singers (Madonna). These small movies would never have been aired on TV: they are much too long (five minutes) and thus too costly. They became hot on the net and benefited from viral retransmissions. Catwalk presentation by Louis Vuitton on Facebook allowed all LV fans to see the spectacle even better than those happy few invited there. With special cameras and augmented reality the result is breathtaking.

FIGURE 6.8 The brand in the digital context

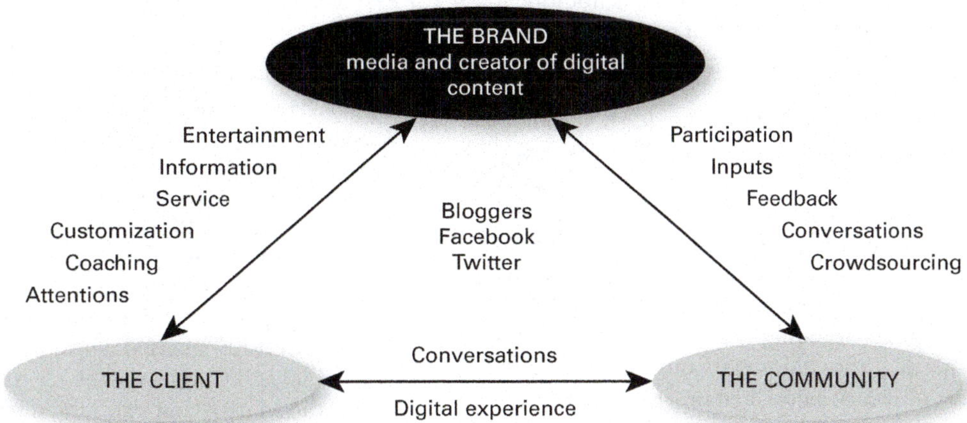

- Practical information can take the form of iPhone applications: in China, Lancôme recruited a young Chinese blogger to be a make-up artist and give lessons on a video on the internet.
- Informative/discovery content includes invitations to meet JC Elena, the 'nose' of Hermès fragrances. All brands could edit the 'making of' their own advertising, to involve the clients.

Brand content is not a one-shot action. It has to be produced continually, just like innovations. This way one attracts people again and again. Brand content also demonstrates your leadership, not in market share but in driving or shaping the category. In B2B this has a major implication: you have to forget the policy of secrecy. All studies should be put online as soon as they are no longer strategic. In any case, competitors have probably commissioned exactly the same study (prospective trends, market share, segmentation, etc).

B2C studies are read in a month and then put in a drawer and forgotten. Put them on the net. The result is that you build your status as a reference.

Brand content sells. It gives density to the brand. It can animate a community. It creates social acquiescence. The brand acts as taste maker and think tank, leading competition.

Although we have focused mainly on the internet, brand content should be accessible through multi-channels, online or not.

How co-branding grows the business

Products that have two creators, and advertise the fact through double branding, are on the increase: for example Inneov by Nestlé and l'Oréal, the first nutritional pill to prevent hair loss, launched in pharmacies in November 2006. We are already familiar with Danao, by Danone and Minute Maid. Philips created a revolution with its Coolskin razor with a moisturizing cream, entrusted to Nivea worldwide – a fact that appears on all the razor's packaging, and in advertising. Everyone knows the 'Intel Inside' signature that appears on all computers that use Intel, and in their advertising.

The rise of co-branding is symptomatic of our era, with its culture of networking and partnerships. It is also the result of a desire to remain within the company's key competences, to the point of looking elsewhere for those competences that are missing. It therefore merits an in-depth discussion.

Why this rise in co-branding?

Co-branding is fundamentally a response to the need for continual growth. However, whereas yesterday companies would have sought at any price to acquire the new competences that were missing and restricting their ability to innovate, today they seek to find a partner with which to co-create. This is the era of alliances, partnerships and the networked economy, where each party retains its specialization and its key competence, and utilizes those of others to the fullest extent. In the pursuit of growth, it is not long before we encounter the difficulty in reconciling this with maintaining the brand's specificity and the company's expertise.

In the West, the brand is the name for a specific expertise or state of mind (in Asia, the brand is far less specialized). When trying to grow, the brand can reach the limits of its own identity and its specificity: it therefore has need of an ally to fill the gaps where it is not competent or legitimate. When this ally is competent but not legitimate, the partnership does not give rise to co-branding. For example, Weight Watchers needed the industrial and distribution competences of Fleury Michon in order to develop a genuinely qualitative range of vacuum-packed ready meals. However, this was not mentioned anywhere on the packaging. In fact, not only is the Weight Watchers brand sufficient for diet disciples, its 'marriage' with Fleury Michon, the epicure's brand, suggestive of French-style good living, is unclear and even contradictory.

In contrast, when the two images complement one another, both brands strongly endorse it. Thus, in order to please the youth of today, increasingly seduced by computer games and consoles, Lego decided to add an electronics line to its products. However Lego not only has no industrial competence in this field (which can always be subcontracted), crucially its brand image would not lend credibility to the new products. The signature of a brand with a strong reputation in electronics among young people would remove this obstacle. Mattel had already worked with Compaq to create a line of interactive, high-tech toys.

We can see therefore that several strategic questions arise on the subject of co-branding:

- Will the visible alliance of two brands create a favourable impression among clients?
- Is there a high degree of complementarity between the two brand images that will create value?
- Is there a good 'fit' between these two brands, given the perceived status of each? As with any successful marriage, of course there must be complementarity, but also a common vision and shared values.
- Will the innovation be attributed to both partners, or only to one of them?

Typical situations that lead to co-branding

- Co-branding is necessary to increase the chances of success for a brand's extension beyond its original market. Thus, as a strongly child-centred brand, Kellogg's explicitly marked its new range of cereals for health-conscious adults with the Healthy Choice brand, already well-known in this segment. Danone and Motta pooled their competences and their images to launch Yolka, a yoghurt ice cream. This was also the case for a refrigerated fruit juice from Minute Maid/Danone, and as mentioned above, the Mattel-Compaq interactive toy.
- Co-branding is also necessary when the brand's image makes it difficult to communicate with a particular target. In that case, it needs an intermediary, someone to open doors for it, another brand that has the ear of this target and can therefore act as a relay. When Orangina, primarily thought of as a child's drink, wanted to boost its sales by targeting adolescents, the biggest consumers of soft drinks, its childish image was a handicap. It created a partnership with NRJ, the most popular radio station among young people, and a jeans brand, Lee Cooper. Orangina cans were co-branded NRJ and Orangina.
- Co-branding makes it possible to develop a product line that is often sold in a separate distribution channel. The goal, in addition to selling to a previously reluctant clientele, is to nurture certain traits of the brand's identity kernel. Thus, in order to create a relationship with 'creative' young women, Tefal developed a range of specific products internationally with the young, unconventional, up-and-coming and very media-friendly British chef, Jamie Oliver. This line is sold worldwide. The partnership between Jamie Oliver and Tefal is that of two – admittedly different – actors who nevertheless share the same vision: a taste for simplicity, pleasure and conviviality. The marketing positioning of this product line will be just below the top of the range: it will only be found in selective channels.

- Co-branding makes it possible to move up a level. In food products, it is difficult for a known brand to move up a level, and therefore up in price, to become a mass-market brand. It needs a credibility link. This is why all pre-cooked meals, even distributors' brands, have created lines that are co-endorsed by a famous chef: Ducasse, Troisgros, Robuchon and so on.
- Ingredient brands are also a way to send the client a message about the product's superior quality, and to lift it above the more ordinary copies, thereby justifying its higher price. Diam's, by Dim, displays the Lycra logo. The same goes for Goretex, Woolmark, Tactel, and for Nutrasweet in the food sector. In B2B, the practice is also on the increase: the 'Intel Inside' brand is exhibited by all computer assemblers that use Intel chips and agree to say so in their communications, in return for which Intel pays half of its clients' advertising expenses.

  For the distributor Decathlon, which creates its own brands, co-brands are strategically valuable since they boost the perceived technicality of the products of its passion brands, which are still relatively unknown to the end customer. All of Damart's structure and profitability is based on an ingredient brand, Thermolactyl. This brand, which is owned by Damart, designates a generic fibre that retains heat (rhovilon): this gives Damart the appearance of exclusivity. While many other distributors offer warm underwear, only Damart has Thermolactyl!
- Co-branding is also a response to the fragmentation of the market and the emergence of communities. Take, for example, the telephone and internet brand Orange. How can it grow? It can sell wholesale to virtual operators, the mobile virtual network operations (MVNOs), which will act as discounters (for example Carrefour, Darty and so on). In this first phase, the Orange brand name disappears: customers believe they are buying their internet services from Carrefour. It may also propose an association with those brands that already have a captive audience, and offer specific value-added content aimed at this audience. For example, loyal customers of Fnac (a rival of Virgin Megastores) can buy Fnac telephone packages: these clearly show the Orange logo. They offer more than just a price – that is, services and contents aimed solely at Fnac customers. Orange reassures them, and manages the whole business.

  Orange does likewise with football clubs, creating subscriptions in the club's name, associated with Orange's: fans benefit from ad hoc content, with a strong football focus. When their club wins, they also win promotions, the opportunity to send free SMSs, or to 'chat' with the star players. Orange has also negotiated exclusive mobile phone retransmission rights for certain major competitions. In this way, Orange has succeeded in adapting to market fragmentation.

  On the internet, co-branding also has a role to play. This is normal: online brands reference one another, in order to mark a community of values, interests and audiences.
- Co-branding, in the form of licences, was one way to boost sales for car models at the end of their life cycle, when the product itself no longer has the value of technical novelty. New value was added by customizing the car in the style of a famous designer or couturier. Prominent examples include the Peugeot 205 Lacoste and the Citroen Bic. This approach is now used at the beginning of the life cycle, in order to put a sociocultural stamp on the vehicle and emphasize its positioning: Twingo Kenzo illustrated the car's central proposition, that 'It's up to you to invent the life that goes with it', and strengthened its creative aspect. The Citroën Picasso was also a response to the desire to strengthen Citroën's positioning as an innovator, competing against the Renault Espace. For the Picasso family themselves, this maintains the brand status of their surname, and prevents it from falling into the public domain through lack of commercial use.
- Co-branding sometimes aims to provide a buzz around the brand among opinion leaders, to create an image. This is the case with the specially designed products Mark

Newson has created for Tefal. In the same way, to give itself a fashionable, stylish touch, Adidas has entrusted designer Stella McCartney with the task of developing a co-branded product line. The brand is effectively seeking to have a presence on the style market and not only the technical market. This approach of co-branding with a creator is prevalent in the sportswear sector: Puma has done likewise. H&M caused a riot by launching a limited series by Karl Lagerfeld: customers were queuing up outside from midnight.

- Finally, co-branding is the visible – confidence-inspiring – sign of a brand union. Skyteam is the airline alliance formed around Air France and KLM, in order to standardize their loyalty programmes and enable travellers to increase their air miles still further – an additional defence against the low-cost airlines.

Co-branding, alliances and partnerships

The modern world is a world of alliances and partnerships between groups, companies, brands and so on. Co-branding is the symbol of an alliance that neither party is seeking to hide (unlike subcontracting, for example).

An analysis of company strategies since 1990 saw certain forms of behaviour, such as alliances, undergo considerable growth, and even saw new, hybrid forms emerge – hence the creation of new concepts and terms to capture them. One of these is 'coopetition' – an alliance with a competitor.

Before we proceed, let us give some definitions. An alliance is indeed a strategic decision, with long-term implications, aiming to bring together complementary competences in order to develop innovative processes and products/services, and finally new markets. It is therefore distinct from a simple partnership, which is limited both in time and in the scope of the cooperation. As for the neologism 'coopetition', it refers to alliances involving two mutually competitive companies. Thus it is coopetition when PSA and Toyota create a common manufacturing unit together in Slovenia, to produce the same small car model. It is a partnership when PSA carries out various cooperation and exchange projects with Ford on diesel engines. It is also a partnership when, in order to exist in this gigantic country, Evian entrusts its US distribution to Coca-Cola. It is apparent that this agreement may be called into question at any time. It is also a partnership when Nestlé entrusts Krups with the European development of a coffee maker that uses Nespresso, the famous and vastly expensive top-of-the-range coffee capsules. Tomorrow, or in another part of the world, Krups could be replaced by another famous brand.

Alliances are nothing new. Think back to Ariane, Airbus and Concorde – all projects on such a scale that even at the planning stage nationalism, competition and sensitivities had to be forgotten in order to fuse cutting-edge competences in a meta project that no single company, or even single country, could achieve alone.

In strategic terms, an alliance is an alternative to acquisition and fusion. This latter is a common type of company growth, buying out key competences or market shares through the sacrosanct critical mass. All of the following companies are the result of fusions or acquisitions: Novartis, Aventis, Vinci, Vivendi, Aviva, Arcelor-Mittal and Sony-Ericsson. An analysis of the components of the success or – as it is admitted nowadays – lack of success of fusions and acquisitions between companies is not relevant to this section. As for the alliance, it preserves the cultures, identities and legal forms of the companies that come together in a common, large-scale project.

In terms of visibility, the members of alliances are not always clearly identified. This is the case when a new name and often a new collectively managed structure are created for the project in question: Airbus Industries, Eurocopter, Thalys, Eurostar or Arianespace. However, it is sometimes the case that the parents are clearly identified by their names and logos. In fact, many products are clearly endorsed by both creators: Philips Alessi, Samsung B&O and so on.

TABLE 6.1 Strategic uses of co-branding

How	Sources of growth Increasing frequency per customer	Enhancing proximity to a target	Enhancing perceived quality	Creating a new market
Same product	Co-branded loyalty cards – Air France AMEX – Smiles	Image strategy – Orangina Lee Cooper cans – Orangina Kookaï	Component co-branding – Collective (Intel/Lycra) – Proprietary (Damart)	
Line extension/ variant		Limited series – Peugeot 205 Lacoste – Renault Clio Kenzo	Endorsement – Weight Watchers by Fleury Michon – Max Havelaar and coffee brands	
New full line		Co-creation – Tefal line designed by/for Jamie Oliver – Philips–Alessi – Hilfiger–Thierry Henry		
Value innovation/ disruption				Co-creation – Danoe (Minute Maid–Danone) – Nespresso–Krups – Lacoste-Citroën

07 Brand identity and positioning

A brand is not the name of a product. It is the vision that drives the creation of products and services under that name. That vision, the key belief of the brands and its core values is called identity. It drives vibrant brands able to create advocates, a real cult and loyalty.

Modern competition calls for two essential tools of brand management: 'brand identity', specifying the facets of brands' uniqueness and value, and 'brand positioning', the main difference creating preference in a specific market at a specific time for its products.

For existing brands, identity is the source of brand positioning. Brand positioning specifies the angle used by the products of that brand to attack a market in order to grow their market share at the expense of competition.

Defining what a brand is made of helps answer many questions that are asked every day, such as: Can the brand sponsor such and such event or sport? Does the advertising campaign suit the brand? Is the opportunity for launching a new product inside the brand's boundaries or outside? How can the brand change its communication style, yet remain true to itself? How can decision making in communications be decentralized regionally or internationally, without jeopardizing brand congruence? All such decisions pose the problem of brand identity.

Brand identity: a necessary concept

The concept of brand identity is recent. It started in Europe (Kapferer, 1986). The perception of its paramount importance has slowly gained worldwide recognition; in the first American book on brand equity (Aaker, 1991), the word 'identity' is in fact totally absent, as is the concept. Keller (1998) mentions it on only two pages within his textbook.

Today, most advanced marketing companies have specified the identity of their brand through proprietary models such as 'brand key' (Unilever), 'footprint' (Johnson & Johnson), 'bulls' eyes' and 'brand stewardship', which organize in a specific form a list of concepts related to brand identity. However, they are rather checklists. Is identity a sheer linguistic novelty, or is it essential to understanding what brands are?

What is identity?

To appreciate the meaning of this significant concept in brand management, we shall begin by considering the many ways in which the word is used today.

For example, we speak of 'identity cards' – a personal, non-transferable document that tells in a few words who we are, what our name is and what distinguishable features we have that can be instantly recognized. We also hear of 'identity of opinion' between several people, meaning that they have an identical point of view. In terms of communication, this second interpretation of the word suggests brand identity is the common element sending a single message amid the wide variety of its products, actions and communications. This is important since the more the brand expands and diversifies, the more customers are inclined to feel that they are, in fact, dealing with several different brands rather than a single one. If products and communication go their separate ways, how can customers possibly perceive these different routes as converging towards a common vision and brand?

Speaking of identical points of view also raises the question of permanence and continuity. As civil status and physical appearance change, identity cards get updated, yet the fingerprint of their holders always remains the same. The identity concept questions how time will affect the unique and permanent quality of the sender, the brand or the retailer. In this respect, psychologists speak of the 'identity crisis' which adolescents often go through. When their identity structure is still weak, teenagers tend to move from one role model to another. These constant shifts create a gap and force the basic question: 'What is the real me?'

Finally, in studies on social groups or minorities, we often speak of 'cultural identity'. In seeking an identity, they are in fact seeking a pivotal basis on which to hinge not only their inherent difference but also their membership of a specific cultural entity.

Brand identity may be a recent notion, but many researchers have already delved into the organizational identity of companies (Schwebig, 1988; Moingeon and Soenen, 2003). There, the simplest verbal expression of identity often consists in saying: 'Oh, yes, I see, but it's not the same in our company!' In other words, corporate identity is what helps an organization, or a part of it, feel that it truly exists and that it is a coherent and unique being, with a history and a place of its own, different from others.

From these various meanings, we can infer that having an identity means being your true self, driven by a personal goal that is both different from others' and resistant to change. Thus, brand identity will be clearly defined once the following questions are answered:

- What is the brand's particular vision and aim?
- What makes it different?
- What need is the brand fulfilling?
- What is its permanent crusade?
- What are its value or values?
- What is its field of competence? Of legitimacy?
- What are the signs which make the brand recognizable?

These questions could indeed constitute the brand's platform. This type of official document would help better brand management in the medium term, both in terms of form and content, and so better address future communication and extension issues. Communication tools such as the copy strategy are essentially linked to advertising campaigns, and so are only committed to the short term. There must be specific guidelines to ensure that there is indeed only one brand forming a solid and coherent entity.

Brand identity and graphic identity charters

Many readers will make the point that their firms already make use of graphic identity 'bibles', either for corporate or specific brand purposes. We do indeed find many graphic identity charters, books of standards and visual identity guides. Urged on by graphic identity agencies, companies have rightly sought to harmonize the messages conveyed by their brands. Such charters therefore define the norms for visual recognition of the brand, ie the brand's colours, graphic design and type of print.

Although this may be a necessary first step, it isn't the be all and end all. Moreover, it puts the cart before the horse. What really matters is the key message that we want to communicate. Formal aspects, outward appearance and overall looks result from the brand's core substance and intrinsic identity. Choosing symbols requires a clear definition of what the brand means. However, while graphic manuals are quite easy to find nowadays, explicit definitions of brand identity *per se* are still very rare. Yet, the essential questions above (ie the nature of the identity to be conveyed) must be properly answered before we begin discussing and defining what the communication means and what the codes of outward recognition should be. The brand's deepest values must be reflected in the external signs of recognition, and these must be apparent at first glance. The family resemblance between the various models of BMW conveys a strong identity, yet it is not *the* identity. This brand's identity and essence can actually be defined by addressing the issue of its difference, its permanence, its value and its personal view on automobiles.

Many firms have unnecessarily constrained their brand because they formulated a graphic charter before defining their identity. Not knowing who they really are, they merely perpetuate purely formal codes by, for example, using a certain photographic style that may not be the most suitable.

Knowing brand identity paradoxically gives extra freedom of expression, since it emphasizes the pre-eminence of substance over strictly formal features. Brand identity defines what must stay and what is free to change. Brands are living systems. They must have degrees of freedom to match modern market diversity.

Identity: a contemporary concept

That a new concept – identity – has emerged in the field of management, already well versed in brand image and positioning, is really no great surprise. Today's problems are more complex than those of 10 or 20 years ago and so there is now a need for more refined concepts that allow a closer connection with reality.

First of all, we cannot overemphasize the fact that we are currently living in a society saturated in communications. Everybody wants to communicate these days.

The second problem is consumer-centricity. In traditional marketing everything should start from the consumer. By using the same marketing studies on the same consumers, brands end up looking like each other, because they lack identity. They neglect their DNA or their roots.

The third factor explaining the urgent need to understand brand identity is the pressure constantly put on brands. We have now entered an age of marketing similarities. When a brand innovates, it creates a new standard. The other brands must then catch up if they want to stay in the race, hence the increasing number of 'me-too' products with similar attributes, not to mention the copies produced by distributors. Regulations also cause similarities to spread. Bank operations, for example, have become so much alike that banks are now unable to fully express their individuality and identity. Market research also generates herdism within a given sector. As all companies base themselves on the same life-style studies, the conclusions they reach are bound to be similar as are the products and advertising campaigns they launch, in which sometimes even the same words are used.

Finally, technology is responsible for growing similarity. Why do cars increasingly look alike, in spite of their different makes? Because car makers are all equally concerned about fluidity, inner car space constraints, motorization and economy, and these problems cannot be solved in all that many different ways. Moreover, when the models of four car brands (Audi, Volkswagen, Seat and Skoda) share many identical parts (eg chassis, engine, gearbox), for either productivity or competitiveness purposes, it is mainly brand identity, along with, to a lesser extent, what's left unique of each car, which will distinguish the makes from one another.

Why speak of identity rather than image?

What does the notion of identity have to offer that the image of a brand or a company or a retailer doesn't have? After all, firms spend large amounts of money measuring image.

Brand image is on the receiver's side. Image research focuses on the way in which certain groups perceive a product, a brand, a politician, a company or a country. The image refers to the way in which these groups decode all of the signals emanating from the products, services and communication covered by the brand.

Identity is on the sender's side. The purpose, in this case, is to specify the brand's meaning, aim and self-image. Image is both the result and interpretation thereof. In terms of brand management, identity precedes image. Before projecting an image to the public, we must know exactly what we want to project. Before it is received, we must know what to send and how to send it. As shown in Figure 7.1, an image is a synthesis made by the public of all the various brand messages, eg brand name, visual symbols, products, advertisements, sponsoring, patronage, articles. An image results from decoding a message, extracting meaning, interpreting signs.

Where do all these signs come from? There are two possible sources: brand identity of course, but also extraneous factors. What are these extraneous factors?

First, there are companies that choose to imitate competitors, as they have no clear idea of what their own brand identity is. They focus on their competitors and imitate their marketing communication and products.

Second, there are companies that are obsessed with the willingness to build an appealing image that will be favourably perceived by all. So they focus on meeting every one of the public's expectations. That is how the brand gets caught in the game

FIGURE 7.1 Identity and image

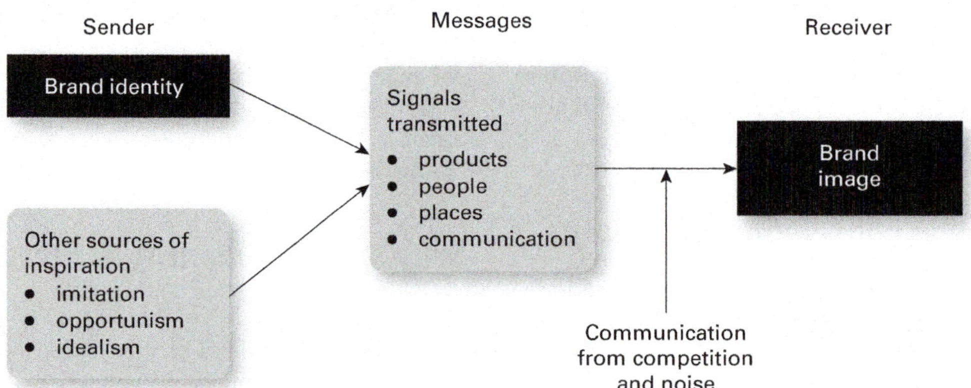

of always having to please the consumer and ends up surfing on the changing waves of social and cultural fads. Yesterday, brands were into glamour, today, they are into 'cocooning'; so what's next? The brand can appear opportunistic and popularity seeking, and thus devoid of any meaningful substance. It becomes a mere façade, a meaningless cosmetic camouflage.

The third source is fantasized identity: the brand as one would ideally like to see it, but not as it actually is. As a result, we notice, albeit too late, that the advertisements do not help people remember the brand because they are either too remotely connected to it or so radically disconnected from it that they cause perplexity or rejection.

Since brand identity has now been recognized as the prevailing concept, these three potential communication glitches can be prevented.

The identity concept thus serves to emphasize the fact that, with time, brands do eventually gain their independence and their own meaning, even though they may start out as mere product names. As living memory of past products and advertisements, identity does not fade away: it acts as a DNA agent.

Obviously, brands should not curl up in a shell and cut themselves off from the public and from market evolutions.

Identity and positioning

It is also common to distinguish brands according to their positioning. Positioning a brand means emphasizing the distinctive characteristics that make it different from its competitors and appealing to the public. It results from an analytical process based on the four following questions:

- A brand for what benefit? This refers to the brand promise and consumer benefit aspect: Orangina has real orange pulp, The Body Shop is ethical and friendly, Twix gets rid of hunger, Volkswagen is reliable.
- A brand for whom? This refers to the target aspect. For a long time, Schweppes was the drink of the refined, Snapple the soft drink for adults, Pepsi the drink for teenagers.
- Reason? This refers to the elements, factual or subjective, that support the claimed benefit. Innocent has zero chemicals.
- A brand against whom? In today's competitive context, this question defines the main competitor(s), ie those whose clientele we think we can partly capture. Tuborg and other expensive imported beers thus also compete against whisky, gin and vodka.

Positioning is a crucial concept (Figure 7.2). It reminds us that all consumer choices are made on the basis of comparison. Thus, a product will only be considered if it is clearly part of a selection process. Hence the four questions that help position the new product or brand and make its contribution immediately obvious to the customer. Positioning is a two-stage process:

FIGURE 7.2 Positioning a brand

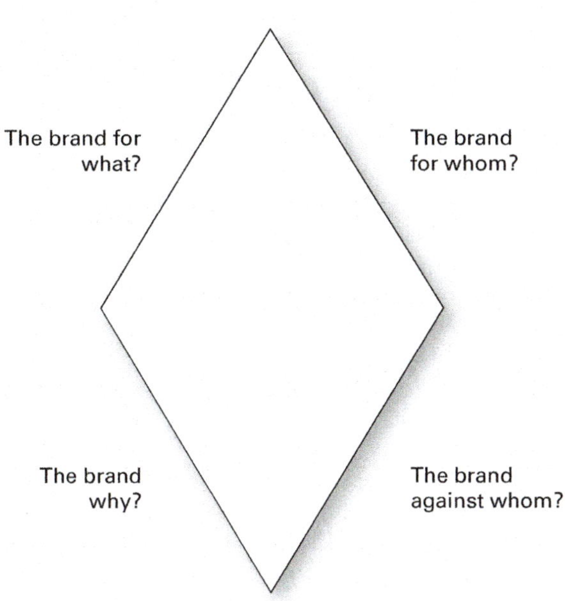

- First, indicate to what 'competitive set' the brand should be associated and compared.
- Second, indicate what the brand's essential difference and *raison d'être* is in comparison to the other products and brands of that set.

Choosing the competitive set is essential. While this may be quite easy to do for a new toothpaste, it is not so for very original and unique products. The Gaines burger launched by the Gaines company, for instance, was a new dog food, a semi-dehydrated product presented as red ground meat in a round shape like a hamburger. Unlike normal canned pet foods, moreover, it did not need to be refrigerated, nor did it exude that normal open-can smell.

Given these characteristics, the product could be positioned in several different ways, for example by:

- Attacking the canned pet food market by appealing to well-to-do dog owners. The gist of the message would then be 'the can without the can', in other words, the benefits of meat without its inconveniences (smell, freshness constraints, etc).
- Attacking the dehydrated pet food segment (dried pellets) by offering a product that would help the owner not to feel guilty for not giving meat to the dog on the basis that it is just not practical. The fresh-ground, round look could justify this positioning.
- Targeting owners who feed leftovers to their dogs by presenting Gaines as a complete, nutritious supplement (and no longer as a main meal as in the two former strategies).
- Targeting all dog owners by presenting this product as a nutritious treat, a kind of doggy Mars bar.

The choice between these alternative strategies was made by assessing each one against certain measurable criteria (Table 7.1).

The firm ended up choosing the first positioning and launched this product as the 'Gaines burger'.

TABLE 7.1 Criteria to evaluate and choose a brand positioning

- Are the product's current looks and ingredients compatible with this positioning?
- How strong is the assumed consumer motivation behind this positioning? (what insight?)
- What size of market is involved by such a positioning?
- Is this positioning credible?
- Does it capitalize on a competitor's actual or latent durable weakness?
- What financial means are required by such a positioning?
- Is this positioning specific and distinctive?
- Is this a sustainable positioning which cannot be imitated by competitors?
- Does this positioning leave any possibility for an alternative solution in case of failure?
- Does this positioning justify a price premium?
- Is there a growth potential under this positioning?

What does the identity concept add to that of positioning? Why do we even need another concept?

In the first place, because positioning focuses more on the product itself. What then does positioning mean in the case of a multi-product brand? How can these four questions on positioning be answered if we are not focusing on one particular product category? We know how to position the various Scotch-brite scrubbing pads as well as the Scotch adhesives, but what does the positioning concept mean for the Scotch brand as a whole, not to mention the 3M corporate brand? This is precisely where the concept of brand identity comes in handy.

Second, positioning does not reveal all the brand's richness of meaning nor reflect all of its potential. The brand is restricted once reduced to four questions. Positioning does not help fully differentiate Coca-Cola from Pepsi-Cola. The four positioning questions thus fail to encapsulate such nuances. They do not allow us to fully explore the identity and singularity of the brand.

Worse still, positioning allows communication to be entirely dictated by creative whims and current fads. Positioning does not say a word about communication style, form or spirit. This is a major deficiency since brands have the gift of speech: they state both the objective and subjective qualities of a given product. The speech they deliver – in these days of digital supremacy – is made of words, of course, but even more of pictures, sounds, colours, movement and style. Positioning controls the words only, leaving the rest up to the unpredictable outcome of creative hunches and pretests. Yet brand language should never result from creativity only. It expresses the brand's personality and values.

Creative hunches are only useful if they are consistent with the brand's legitimate territory. Furthermore, though pretest evaluations are needed to verify that the brand's message is well received, the public should not be allowed to dictate brand language: its style needs to be found within itself. Brand uniqueness often tends to get eroded by consumer expectations and thus starts regressing to a level at which it risks losing its identity.

A brand's message is the outward expression of the brand's inner substance. Thus we can no longer dissociate brand substance from brand style, ie from its verbal, visual and musical attributes. Brand identity provides the framework for overall brand coherence. It is a concept that serves to offset the limitations of positioning and to monitor the means of expression, the unity and durability of a brand.

Why brands need identity and positioning

A brand's positioning is a key concept in its management. It is based on one fundamental principle: all choices are comparative. Remember that identity expresses the brand's tangible and intangible characteristics – everything that makes the brand what it is, and without which it would be something different. Identity draws upon the brand's roots and heritage – everything that gives it its unique authority and legitimacy within a realm of precise values and benefits. Positioning is competitive: when it comes to brands, customers make a choice, but with products, they make a comparison. This raises two questions. First, what do they compare it with? For this, we need to look at the field of competition: what area do we want to be considered as part of? Second, what are we offering the customer as a key decision-making factor?

A brand that does not position itself leaves these two questions unanswered. It is a mistake to suppose that customers will find answers themselves: there are too many choices available today for customers to make the effort to work out what makes a particular brand specific. Communicating this information is the responsibility of the brand. Remember, products increase customer choice; brands simplify it. This is why a brand that does not want to stand for something stands for nothing.

The aim of positioning is to identify, and take possession of, a strong purchasing rationale that gives us a real or perceived advantage. It implies a desire to take up a long-term position and defend it. Positioning is competition-oriented: it specifies the best way to attack competitors' market share. It may change through time: one grows by expanding the field of competition. Identity is more stable and long-lasting, for it is tied to the brand roots and fixed parameters. Thus Coke's positioning was 'the original' as long as it competed against other colas. To grow the business, it now competes against all soft drinks: its positioning is 'the most refreshing bond between people of the world', whereas its identity remains 'the symbol of America, the essence of the American way of life'.

How is positioning achieved? The standard positioning formula is as follows:

For ... (definition of targeted consumers)
Brand X is ... (definition of competitive set and subjective category)
Which gives the most ... (promise or consumer benefit)
Because of ... (reason to believe).

Let us look at these points in detail.

The target specifies the nature and psychological or sociological profile of the individuals to be influenced, that is, buyers or potential consumers.

The frame of reference is the subjective definition of the category, which will specify the nature of the competition. What other brands or products effectively serve the same purpose? This is a strategic decision: it marks out the 'field of battle'. It must not under any circumstances be confused with the objective description of the product or category. For example, there is no real rum market in the UK, yet Bacardi is very popular. This is because it is perfectly possible to drink Bacardi without realizing that it *is* a rum: it is the party mixer *par excellence*.

Another example illustrates the strategic importance of defining the frame of reference. Objectively speaking, Perrier is fizzy mineral water. Subjectively, however, it is also a drink for adults. Seen in the light of this field of reference, it acquires its strongest competitive advantage: a slight natural quirkiness. As we can see, the choice of the field of competition should be informed by the strategic value of that field: how big, how fast growing, how profitable? But it also lends the brand a competitive advantage through its identity and potential. Perceived as water for the table, Perrier has no significant competitive advantage over other fizzy mineral waters, even though this market is a very large one. However, when viewed in relation to a field of competition defined as 'drinks for adults', Perrier becomes competitive again: it has strong differentiating advantages. What are its competitors? They include alcoholic drinks, Diet Coke, Schweppes and tomato juice.

The third point specifies the aspect of difference which creates the preference and the choice of a decisive competitive advantage: it may be expressed in terms of a promise (for instance, Volvo is the strongest of all cars) or a benefit (such as, Volvo is the 'safety' brand).

The fourth point reinforces the promise or benefit, and is known as the 'reason to believe'. For example, in the case of the Dove brand, which promises to be the most moisturizing, the reason is that all of its products contain 25 per cent of moisturizing cream.

Positioning is a necessary concept, first because all choices are comparative, and so it makes sense to start off by stating the area in which we are strongest; and second because in marketing, perception is reality. Positioning is a concept which starts with customers, by putting ourselves in their place: faced with a plethora of brands, are consumers able to identify the strong point of each, the factor that distinguishes it from the rest? This is why, ideally, a customer should be capable of paraphrasing a brand's positioning: 'Only Brand X will do this for me, because it has, or it is...'

No instrument is neutral. The above positioning formula was created by companies such as Kraft–General Foods, Procter & Gamble, and Unilever. It is designed for businesses that base competitive advantage on their products, and works perfectly for the l'Oréal Group which, with its 2,500 researchers worldwide, only ever launches new products if they are of demonstrably superior performance. This fact is then promoted through advertising.

There are cases where the brand makes no promise, or where the benefit it brings could sound trivial. For example, how would you define the positioning of a perfume such as Obsession by Calvin Klein in a way that clearly represented its true nature and originality? It would be wrong to claim that Obsession makes any specific promise to its customers, or that they will obtain any particular benefit from the product apart from feeling good (a property which is common to all perfumes). In reality, Obsession's attractiveness stems from its imagery, the imaginary world of subversive androgyny which it embodies. In the same way, Angel appeals to young people through its inherently neo-futuristic world, and Chanel stands for timeless elegance.

What actually sells these perfumes is the satisfaction derived from participating in the symbolic world of the brand. The same is true of alcohol and spirits: Jack Daniel's is selling a symbolic participation in an eternal, authentic untamed America. To say that Jack Daniel's is selling the satisfaction of being the finest choice would be a mere commonplace, like the tired old cliché that customers are satisfied at having made a choice that set them apart from the masses (a classic benefit stated by small brands attempting to emphasize their advantage over large ones).

Faced with this conceptual dilemma, there are three possible approaches. The first of these is to define positioning as the sum of every point that differentiates the brand. This has been Unilever's approach: the 60-page mini-opus known as the Brand Key, which explains how to define a brand across the entire world, starts with the phrase: 'Brand Key builds on and replaces the brand positioning statement...'. There are eight headings to Brand Key:

1. The competitive environment.
2. The target.
3. The consumer insight on which the brand is based.
4. The benefits brought by the brand.
5. Brand values and personality.
6. The reasons to believe.
7. The discriminator (single most compelling reason to choose).
8. The brand essence.

Fundamentally, therefore, this collection forms the positioning of a brand. However, the concept that most closely resembles positioning in the strict sense of the word is referred to here as the 'discriminator'. McDonald's also adopts a similar reasoning (see Figure 7.3). Larry Light defends the idea that positioning is defined when this chain of means–ends is completed (this is a parallel concept to the 'ladder' – moving from the tangible to the intangible).

FIGURE 7.3
The McDonald's positioning ladder

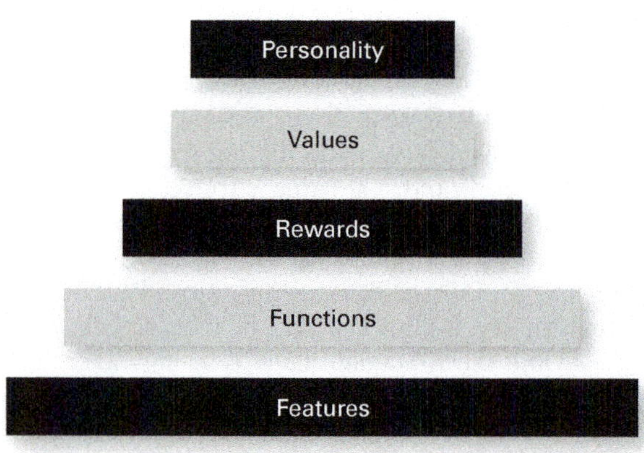

SOURCE L Light

Our position is that two tools are needed to manage the brand. One defines the brand's identity, while the other is competitive and specifies the competitive proposition made at any given time in any given market. This is the brand's most compelling value proposition. Thus the tool called 'brand platform' will comprise, first, the 'brand identity', that is to say, brand uniqueness and singularity throughout the world and whatever the product. Brand identity has six facets, and is therefore larger than the mere positioning. It is represented by the identity prism. At its centre one finds the brand essence, the central value it symbolizes.

Second, the brand platform comprises 'brand positioning': choosing a market means choosing a specific angle to attack it. Brand positioning must be based on a customer insight relevant to this market. Brand positioning exploits one of the brand identity facets. Positioning can be summed up in four key questions: for whom, why, when and against whom? It is summarized in one brand platform.

In positioning, the brand/product makes a remarkable value proposition. The proposition may additionally be supported by a 'reason to believe', but this is not essential. Marlboro presents its smoker as a man – a real man, symbolized by the untamed cowboy of the Wild West. No support is offered for this proposition; no proof is necessary. It is true because the brand says so. And the more often it is repeated, the more credible it becomes.

In this way the brand's proposition, which forms the basis of the chosen positioning at a given moment in a particular market, may be fuelled by various 'edges' contained within the brand's identity:

- a differentiating attribute (25 per cent moisturizing cream in Dove, the smoothness and bite of Mars bars, the bubbles of Perrier);
- an objective benefit: an iPad is user-friendly, Dell offers unbeatable value for money;
- a subjective benefit: you feel secure with IBM;
- an aspect of the brand's personality: the mystery of the Bacardi bat, Jack Daniel's is macho, Axe/Lynx is cool;
- the realm of the imaginary, of imagery and meaning (the American Wild West for Marlboro, Old New England for Ralph Lauren);

- a reflection of a consumer type: successful people for Amex;
- 'deep' values (Nike's sports mentality, Nestlé's maternal love), or even a mission (The Body Shop, Virgin and so on).

A few introductory remarks should be made at this juncture.

What is the connection between identity and positioning? It is the degree of freedom between identity and positioning that enables a brand to change over time while still remaining itself. Thus, over time (40 years), Evian has changed its slogan and baseline on several occasions, symbolizing a change in its angle of market attack: for indeed, the market itself has changed. It has become increasingly saturated with competing brands, the original consumers have aged, and low-cost brands have carved out a significant share. On each occasion, these changes have led to a re-examination of the most compelling value proposition, the angle of market attack. There has thus been a shift from 'water for babies' to the purest of waters, water from the Alps, well-balanced water, and now the water of youth (this time round, the campaign is worldwide). However, each positioning has remained true to the essence of the Evian brand, which is more than any other water distinguished by its origins, its composition, its first campaign (babies) and so on. Evian is about life itself.

What is the connection between the positioning of the brand and the positioning of its products? It is true that today's brands are increasingly based on multiple products: Dove was born as a soap in the United States, but now encompasses shampoos, shower gels, moisturizing cream, deodorants and so on. The essence of Dove is 'Femininity restored'. But Dove is being launched in a market via one or more products that have to fight for their own space amid a host of competitors: hence when Dove soap was launched, its positioning was: 'Dove is a premium beauty bar for the mature women, worried about their skin, which won't dry your skin like soap because it contains one quarter moisturizing cream.'

This example is a good illustration of how the product's positioning promotes a consumer attribute or benefit, while the parent brand specifies the value proposition that this attribute and benefit enables the consumer to reach. When a brand consists of multiple products, care should be taken to ensure that their respective positioning converges on attaining the same core value (that of the parent brand). If this is not the case, either the product requires repositioning, or the question should be asked whether it is part of the right brand at all.

Table 7.2 illustrates the link between the essence of the l'Oréal Paris parent brand and the positioning of its products such as Elsève and Studio Line.

TABLE 7.2 How the master brand positioning is relayed by sub-brands

	Elsève	Revitalift	Studio Line	l'Oréal Paris (brand)
Target market	Women with dry and brittle hair	Women aged over 45	Men and women under 35	All adults, men and women
Market segment	Shampoo	Skin care products	Hair styling products	Beauty and hygiene products
Positioning	Nourishes and repairs damaged hair (consequence)	Reduces wrinkles and firms the skin (consequence)	Enables you to create the hairstyle of your choice (consequence)	Enhances consumers' self image ('because you're worth it')

The six facets of brand identity

In order to become 'passion brands', engaging brands must not be hollow, but have a deep inner inspiration. They must also have character, their own beliefs, and as a result help consumers in their life, and also in discovering their own identity.

What is brand identity made of? Many ad hoc lists have been proposed in the brand literature, with varying items. One of the sources of this diversity is their lack of theoretical basis. By being too analytical, some of these tools get their users into a muddle.

In fact, leaving the classical stimulus–response paradigm, modern brand communication theory reminds us that when one communicates, one builds representations of who speaks (source re-presentation), of who is the addressee (recipient re-presentation), and what specific relationship the communication builds between them. This is the constructivist school of theorizing about communications. Since brands speak about the product, and are perceived as sources of products, services and satisfactions, communication theory is directly relevant. As such it reminds us that brand identity has six facets. We call this the 'brand identity prism'.

The identity prism

Brand identity should be represented by a hexagonal prism (see Figure 7.4):

1. A brand, first of all, has physical specificities and qualities – its 'physique'. It is made of a combination of either salient objective features (which immediately come to mind when the brand is quoted in a survey) or emerging ones.

   Physique is both the brand's backbone and its tangible added value. If the brand is a flower, its physique is the stem. Without the stem, the flower dies: it is the flower's objective and tangible basis. This is how branding traditionally works: focusing on know-how and classic positioning, relying on certain key product and brand attributes and benefits. Physical appearance is important but it is not all. Nevertheless, the first step in developing a brand is to define its physical aspect: What is it concretely? What does it do? What does it look like? The physical facet also comprises the brand's 'prototype': the flagship product that is representative of the brand's qualities, its best exemplar.

   That is why the small round bottle is so important each time Orangina is launched in

FIGURE 7.4 Brand identity prism

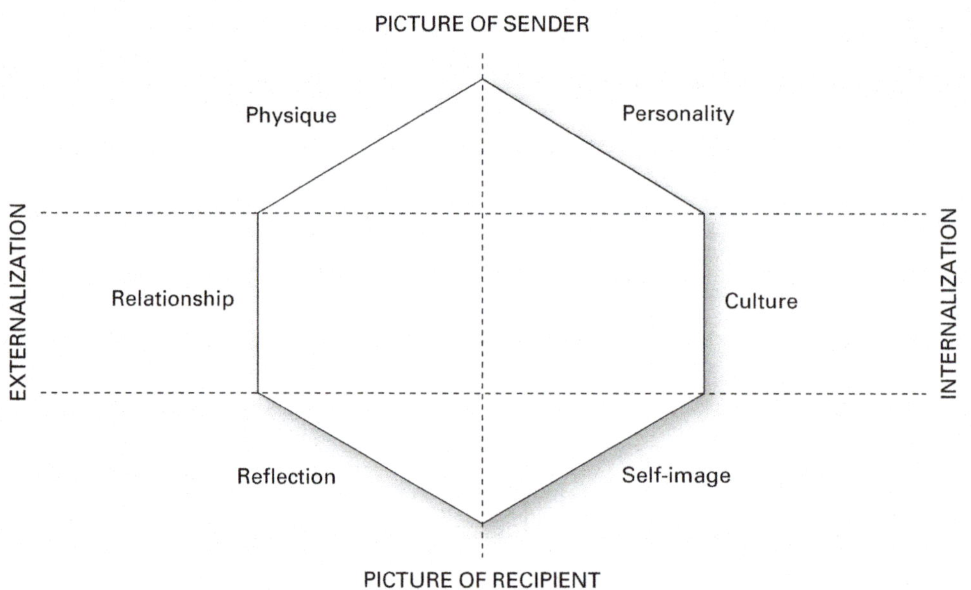

a new country. The bottle used today is the same as it has always been. From the beginning, it has served to position Orangina, thanks to its unique shape and to the orange pulp that we can actually see. Only later was it marketed in standard family-size PET bottles and in cans. In this respect, it is also quite significant that there used to be a picture of the famous Coca-Cola bottle on all Coke cans. It is true that modern packaging tends to standardize brands, making them all clones of one another. Thus, in using the image of its traditional bottle, Coca-Cola aims to remind us of its roots.

There are several delicate issues regarding Coke's physical facet. For example, is the dark colour part of its identity? It is certainly a key contributor to the mystery of the brand. If it belongs to the brand's kernel, key identity traits, then there could never be any such thing as colourless Crystal Coke, even though there is such a thing as Crystal Pepsi. Likewise, would grapefruit Orangina in the classic round bottle be possible?

Many brands have problems with their physical facet because their functional added value is weak. Even an image-based brand must deliver material benefits. Brands are two-legged value-adding systems.

2 A brand has a personality. By communicating, it gradually builds up character. The way in which it speaks of its products or services shows what kind of person it would be if it were human.

'Brand personality' has been the main focus of brand advertising since 1970. Numerous advertising agencies have made it a prerequisite for any type of communication. This explains why the idea of having a famous character represent the brand has become so widespread. The easiest way of creating instant personality is to give the brand a spokesperson or a figurehead, whether real or symbolic. Pepsi-Cola often uses this method, as do all perfume or ready-to-wear brands.

In the identity prism, brand identity is the personality facet of the source. It should not be confused with the customer reflected image, which is a portrayal of the ideal receiver.

Thus, brand personality is described and measured by those human personality traits that are relevant for brands (see page 78 for an application). Since 1996, academic research has focused on brand personality, after J Aaker's (1995) creation of a so-called 'brand personality scale'. However, despite its wide diffusion among scholars, this scale does not measure brand personality, but various dimensions that are more or less related to it, and that correspond in fact to other facets of a brand's identity (Azoulay and Kapferer, 2003). Recent empirical research (Romaniuk and Ehrenberg, 2003) has corroborated this. For instance, computers or electronic equipment were the categories most associated with the 'up to date' trait, as ice creams were associated with the 'sensuous' trait, and energizer drinks with 'energizing'. These data demonstrate that this scale is not measuring personality: a lot of its traits instead measure a physical facet of the brand, while some others relate to the cultural facet of the identity prism, thus creating conceptual confusion in the field. This is because J Aaker's conceptualization of brand personality is inherited from the old habit of advertising agencies of describing as 'brand personality' in their creative briefing and copy strategy everything that was not related to the product's tangible benefits.

Brand personality fulfils a psychological function. It allows consumers either to identify with it or to project themselves into it. Brand personality is also the main source of tone and style of advertising.

3 A brand is a culture. Strong brands are a vision of the world. They are much more than product benefits or a personality; they are an ideology too. The cultural facet of the brand makes this explicit. It is the most important facet of brand identity. Major brands are not only driven by a culture but convey their culture. The cultural facet is key to understanding the difference between Nike, Adidas and Reebok. They are engaged in cultural competition.

Every brand wants to become a cult brand, at least for some group. Apple enjoyed this position soon after it was created. There is a direct link between 'culture' and 'cult'.

So-called cult brands have become cult because of their ideological underpinnings, becoming answers to a social crisis felt by a social sub-group. One does not create a community just on the basis of product attributes, however clever they may be. People tend to gather around causes, ideas, ideals and values. This is what the cultural facet of the brand is about. It is the ideological glue that ties everything together long term.

Although present since 1991 in our brand identity prism, this cultural dimension of brands has only quite recently been recognized by academics and practitioners (Cova, 2000; Bo and Guevel, 2010; Holt and Cameron, 2011).

What is Nike about? Superficially it is a brand of fashion sneakers with a sports halo, celebrated by a few semi-gods called Tiger Woods, Michael Jordan, etc. What is Innocent about? Is it just a brand of natural smoothies, with no artificial ingredients added? What is American Express about? Is it simply a premium card for financial services? What is Johnnie Walker about? The most famous international premium whisky brand?

These may be facts, but the 'brand essences' are only the tip of the iceberg, a good summary of the brand's physical facet. Surely brands must first define themselves, and tell what they are, if they want to stand for something. This is why brand platforms love to encapsulate it in a few words (see our discussion on brand platforms, page 173). However, building emotional ties today needs another kind of self-definition, a much deeper one, which energizes the brand and its followers.

Traditional branding theory still talks about 'brand relevance' (Aaker, 2011). The new strategic brand management acknowledges the need for meaningfulness. In Maslow's pyramid of needs, the advanced countries now stand at the top, but the end of ideologies (communism and socialism), the crisis of capitalism and of liberalism, and the 11 September attack have created disarray and doubts, if not disappointment and, some would say, disenchantment. In the advanced countries, hyper-consumption creates emptiness: we know that the accumulation of goods does not create happiness.

That is why brands must be cultural champions: they must foster an ideal. Brands must address this new demand for meaningfulness. Opportunities appear everywhere. This is why brands will need to identify deeper insights than the ones brought by focus groups or questionnaires. Sociology is more fruitful than psychology for this purpose. Society is changing, with new social fractures and new social conditions. This creates opportunities for new, meaningful brands, which beyond their products are an answer to a deeper demand for meaning (brand as an ideology that resonates deeply among the core target of the brand).

Nike is the champion of 'solo willpower' with a dose of optimism ('Just do it!') (Holt and Cameron, 2011). Nike addresses a major sociological insight: millions of people in the world today know that they can count only on themselves. Johnnie Walker addresses the masses of young entrepreneurs who aspire to climb the ladder and reap the benefits of social mobility. Nobody is going to help them either: just their own energy ('Keep walking!'). American Express sells the American dream to the world: its logo is the dollar. But one has to fight to get it. Innocent is not called Innocent by chance. It means that it is not guilty. Innocent is a critique of the whole food industry.

The cultural facet of brands' identity underlines that brands are engaged in an ideological competition. Top managers must realize it.

The cultural facet of banks' identity refers to the specific vision of money that drives them. All banks borrow and lend money, but ideologies differ widely from bank to bank. That is why they do not address the same consumers: some banks consider money as a goal, or as a personal yardstick of success, or as simply a tool. These ideas will resonate in the hearts of some consumers but repel many others.

Working with Asian brands in the electronics market often leads to frustration. They all tend to define themselves in generic terms and focus on product attributes or empty and overworn words such as 'technology', 'quality', 'customer-centric', etc. (We analysed the reasons on page 49.) Sony is an exception: it has always acted as a cultural champion. This is why, despite a lack of innovation today, it still enjoys considerable brand capital (see page 18).

The brand cultural crusade leads to a new approach towards targets. A brand like Johnnie Walker has millions of consumers throughout the world, male and female, of all ages, in all classes, each group driven by different motivations. The usual segmentations isolate heavy users, users and non-users, etc. We will now have to identify the group of people for whom the brand ideology resonates most, those who are themselves already champions of the ideology. They will be the brand crusaders, even if they do not consume it (see page 130).

4 A brand is a relationship. Indeed, brands are often at the crux of transactions and exchanges between people. This is particularly true of brands in the service sector and also of retailers, as we shall see later. The Yves Saint Laurent brand functions with charm: the underlying idea of a love affair permeates both its products and its advertising (even when no man is shown). Dior's symbolizes another type of relationship: one that is grandiose and ostentatious (not in the negative sense), flaunting the desire to shine like gold.

Nike bears a Greek name that relates it to specific cultural values, to the Olympic Games and to the glorification of human effort. IBM symbolizes orderliness, whereas Apple conveys friendliness. Moulinex defines itself as 'the friend of women'. The Laughing Cow is at the heart of a mother–child

TABLE 7.3 How Victoria's Secret defines its customer reflection

Customer reflection	Brand core values	First segment to dominate
Good taste	Feminine	Bras
Intelligent		
Loves fashion		
Enjoys shopping	Glamorous (romantic, ornate, natural)	
In her 20s		
Travels the world		
Career minded	Innovative	
Enjoys wearing beautiful lingerie		
Stays fit and healthy		
Cares about how she looks	Modern (comfort and wearability, high-tech fabric and prudent design)	

relationship. The relationship aspect is crucial for banks, banking brands and services in general. Service is by definition a relationship. This facet defines the mode of conduct that most identifies the brand. This has a number of implications for the way the brand acts, delivers services, relates to its customers.

5 A brand is a customer reflection. When asked for their views on certain car brands, people immediately answer in terms of the brand's perceived client type: that's a brand for young people! for fathers! for show-offs! for old folks! Because its communication and its most striking products build up over time, a brand will always tend to build a reflection or an image of the buyer or user which it seems to be addressing.

Reflection and target often get mixed up. The target describes the brand's potential purchasers or users. Reflecting the customer is not describing the target; rather, the customer should be reflected as he/she wishes to be seen as a result of using a brand. It provides a model with which to identify. Coca-Cola, for instance, has a much wider clientele than suggested by the narrow segment it reflects (15- to 18-year-olds). How can such a paradox be explained? For the younger segment (8- to 13-year-olds), the Coca-Cola protagonists embody their dream, what they want to become and do later on when they get older (and thus freed from the strong parental relationship), ie an independent life full of fun, sports and friends will then become true. Youth identifies with those heroes. As for adults, they perceive them as representatives of a certain way of life and of certain values rather than of a narrowly defined age group. Thus, the brand also succeeds in bringing 30- or 40-year-old consumers to identify with this special way of life. Many dairy brands positioned on lightness or fitness and based on low fat products project a sporty young female customer reflection: yet they are actually purchased in the main by older people.

The confusion between reflection and target is quite frequent and causes problems. So many managers continue to require advertising to show the targeted buyers as they really are, ignoring the fact that they do not want to be portrayed as such, but rather as they wish to be – as a result of purchasing a given brand (or shopping at a given retailer's). Consumers indeed use brands to build their own identity. In the ready-to-wear industry, the obsession to look younger should concern the brands' reflection, not necessarily their target. This is how brands create value (see Table 7.3).

6 Finally, a brand speaks to our self-image. If reflection is the target's outward mirror (they are ...), self-image is the target's own internal mirror (I feel, I am ...). Through our attitude towards certain brands, we indeed develop a certain type of inner relationship with ourselves.

In buying a Porsche, for example, many Porsche owners simply want to prove to themselves that they have the ability to buy such a car. In fact, this purchase might be premature in terms of career prospects and to some extent a gamble on their materialization. In this sense, Porsche is constantly forcing to push beyond one's limits (hence its slogan: 'Try racing against yourself, it's the only race that will never have an end'). As we can see, Porsche's reflection is different from its consumers' self-image: having let the brand develop such a negative reflection is a major problem.

Even if they do not practise any sports, Lacoste clients inwardly picture themselves (so the studies show) as members of a chic sports club – an open club with no race, sex or age discrimination, but which endows its members with distinction. This works because sport is universal. One of the characteristics of people who eat Gayelord Hauser health and diet products is that they picture themselves not just as consumers, but as proselytes. When two Gayelord Hauser fans meet, they can strike up a conversation immediately as if they were of the same religious obedience. In promoting a brand, one pledges allegiance, demonstrating both a community of thought and of self-image, which facilitates or even stimulates communication.

These are the six facets which define the identity of a brand as well as the boundaries within which it is free to change or to develop. The brand identity prism demonstrates that these facets are all interrelated and form a well-structured entity. The content of one facet echoes that of another. The identity prism derives from one basic concept – that brands have the gift of speech. Brands can only exist if they communicate. As a matter of fact, they grow obsolete if they remain silent or unused for too long. Since a brand is a speech in itself (as it speaks of the products it creates and endorses the products which epitomize it), it can thus be analysed like any other speech or form of communication.

Semiologists have taught us that behind any type of communication there is a sender, either real or made up. Even when dealing with products or retailers, communication builds an image of its speaker or sender and conveys it to us. It is truly a building process in the sense that brands have no real, concrete senders (unlike corporate communication). Nevertheless, customers, when asked through projective techniques, do not hesitate to describe the brand's sender, ie the person bearing the brand name. Both the physique and personality help define the sender thus built for that purpose.

Every form of communication also builds a recipient: when we speak, everything seems as if we were addressing a certain type of person or audience. Both the reflection and self-image facets help define this recipient, who, thus built, also belongs to the brand's identity. The last two facets, relationship and culture, bridge the gap between sender and recipient.

The brand identity prism also includes a vertical division (see Figure 7.4). The facets to the left – physique, relationship and reflection – are the social facets which give the brand its outward expression. All three are visible facets. The facets to the right – personality, culture and self-image – are those incorporated within the brand itself, within its spirit.

FIGURE 7.5 Sample brand identity prisms

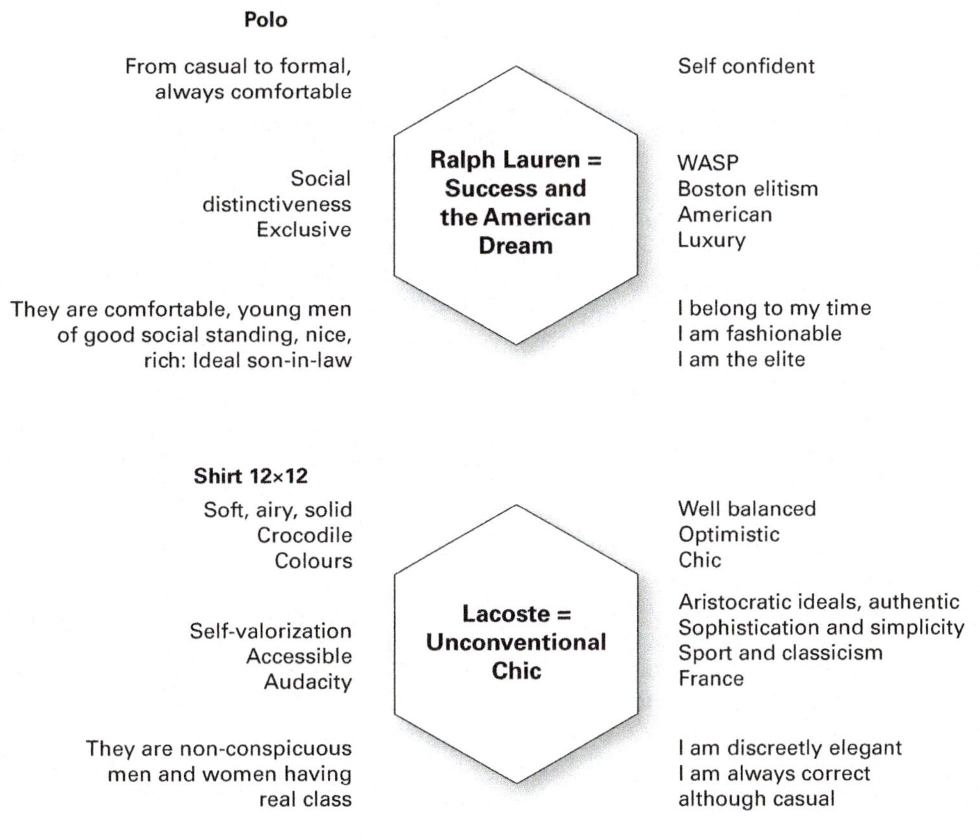

This prism helps us to understand the essence of both brand and retailer identities (Tesco, Asda, Aldi, etc).

Clues for strong identity prisms

Identity reflects the different facets of brand long-term singularity and attractiveness. As such it must be concise, sharp and interesting. Let us remember that brand charters are management tools: they are necessary for decentralized decision making. They must help all the people working on the brand to understand how the brand is special, in all its dimensions. They must also stimulate creative ideas: they are a springboard for brand activation. Finally, they must help us to decide when an action falls within the brand territory and when it does not.

As a consequence, a good identity prism is recognizable by the following formal characteristics:

- There are few words to each facet.
- The words are not the same on different facets.
- All words have strength and are not lukewarm: identity is what makes a brand stand out.

Too often, in our consulting activity, we notice just the opposite:

- Facets are filled up with image traits that derive from the last usage and attitude study. Let us remember that identity is not the same as image. The question is, which of these very many image items does the brand want to identify with?
- There is a lot of redundancy between facets, the same words being used many times. This should not be possible. Although related, each facet addresses a different dimension of brand uniqueness.
- Most of the words are looking for consensus, instead of looking for sharpness. Consumers do not see the strategies, nor do they see the brand platforms. They do experience the brand by its creations, or at contact, or in its places. To produce ideas, creative people need flesh: an identity with soul, body, forms, a real profile, not an average excellent profile, where nothing really stands out.

Sources of identity: brand DNA

How can we define a brand's identity? Brand image research does not provide any satisfactory answer. Neither do the purchasers when asked to say what they expect from the brand. Generally, they haven't a clue. At best, they answer in terms of the brand's current positioning.

Consumers and prospects are often asked what their ideal brand would be and what attributes it would need in order to get universally approved. This approach fails to segment properly the expectations and thus to produce any definition other than the average brand ideal. It is typical for consumers to expect banks to provide expertise and attention, availability and competence, proximity and know-how. These expectations are also ideal in the sense that they are often incompatible. In pursuing them, such brands may lose their identity and regress to the average level. In seeking at all costs to resemble the ideal brand described by the consumers (or industrial buyers), brands thus often begin to downplay their differences and look average.

The mistake is to pursue this market 'ideal': it's up to each brand to pursue an ideal of its own. Commercial pressure naturally requires a firm to stay attuned to the market. Of course no brand envies the destiny of Van Gogh, who lived a life of misery and became famous only after he died. Nonetheless, present brand management policy must be reappraised, because unfortunately it still assumes that consumers are the masters of brand identity and strategy. Consumers are actually quite incapable of carrying out such functions. Firms should, therefore, begin to focus more on the sending side of brand marketing and less on the receiving side.

Identity is to be inferred from the marks left by the brand, ie the products it has chosen to endorse and the symbols by which it is represented through time. That is why identity research must start from the typical products (or services) endorsed by the brand as well as on the brand name itself, the brand symbol if there is one, the logo, the country of origin, the advertisements and the packaging. The purpose of all this is to semiologically analyse the sending process by trying to discover the original plan underlying the brand's objectives, products and symbols. Generally, this plan is simply unconscious, neither written anywhere, nor explicitly described. It is simply enacted in daily decisions. Even creators of famous brand names (Christian Lacroix, Yves Saint Laurent, Calvin Klein or Liz Claiborne) are not conscious of it: when asked about the general plan, they are indeed unable to explain it clearly, yet they can easily say what their brand encompasses and what it does not. Brand and creator merge. We have shown (Kapferer and Bastien, 2009) that, paradoxically, a luxury brand does not really begin to exist until its creator dies. It then shifts from body and instinct to plan and programme.

In conducting research on brand identity, it may well be that we discover several underlying plans. The history of a brand indeed reflects a certain discontinuity in the decisions made by different brand managers over time. Thus Citroën changed when it was purchased by Michelin, and later by Peugeot. A lot of its cars have left no print, although they reached a high level of sales. Rather than attempt the impossible task of making sense of all its products, brand managers must choose the sense that will best serve the brand in its targeted market and focus only on that one. Finally, when dealing with a weak brand, we might not discover any consistent plan at all: in this case, the brand is more like a name stuck on a product than a real player in the field. This situation is very similar to the initial stage of brand creation: the brand has great latitude and almost infinite possibilities, even though it has already planted the seeds of its potential identity in the memory of the market.

The brand's most typical products

The product is the first source of brand identity. A brand indeed reveals its plan and its uniqueness through the products (or services) it chooses to endorse. A genuine brand does not usually remain a mere name printed on a product, ie a mere graphic accessory added on at the end of a production or distribution process. The brand actually injects its values in the production and distribution process as well as in the corollary services offered at the point of sale. The brand's values must therefore be embodied in the brand's most highly symbolic products. This last sentence calls for some attention. Cognitive psychology (Kleiber, 1990; Rosch, 1978; Lakoff, 1987) has taught us that it is easier to define certain categories by simply showing their most typical members than by specifying what product features are required to be considered a member of those categories. As stated in this example, it is difficult to define the 'game' concept, ie to specify the characteristics which could help us identify when we are in a game situation and when we are not. For abstract categories, made of heterogeneous products, the difficulty is even greater. In this case, brands can serve as examples only if they are not exclusively attached to one specific product. What is Danone? When does a product deserve to be named Danone and when does it not? The same holds true for Philips or Whirlpool.

Consumers can easily answer this question: they are indeed able to group products in terms of their capacity to typically represent and perfectly exemplify a large spectrum brand. The most representative product is called the 'brand prototype', not in the sense of an airplane or car prototype, but rather in that of the best exemplar of the brand's meaning. The cognitive psychologists around Rosch (1978) claim that prototypes actually transfer some of their features to the product category (Kleiber, 1990). In other words, if there were no definition of Danone, the public would probably be able to come up with one anyway, by taking a close look at the features of Danone's most representative products. This is what we call prototype semantics. It is true that each brand spontaneously brings to mind certain products – some more than others – and actions as well as a certain style of communication. These prototype products are representative of the various facets of brand identity. According to some cognitive psychologists, such products may convey brand identity, but above all they generate it. That is why, to change a brand image, one must create a new prototype.

Historically, it is quite significant that Danone became famous with its plain yoghurt, a product which had previously been sold in pharmacies as natural medication. That is where Danone's health identity originated. And it is now revived by the creation of the Danone Foundation. But the duality of its prototypes has also contributed to soften Danone's image: Danette cream dessert signifies hedonism, pleasure and opulence. Danone's brand identity is thus dual: both health and pleasure. As such it captures the largest share of the market. It leaves the smallest shares to brands that do not provide this balance to consumers: they offer either diet brands or sweet confectionery brands like Cadbury's.

If this theory holds, another question comes to mind: just what is it, in a typical product, that conveys meaning? A brand's values only convey meaning if they are at the core of the product. Brand intangible and tangible realities go hand in hand: values drive reality, and reality manifests these values.

For example, the essence of Benetton's brand identity is tolerance and friendship. Colour is more than an advertising theme. It is both the symbolic and industrial basis of the brand. Using a technical innovation, dyeing sweaters at the last minute, Benetton could stay ahead of its competitors through its capacity to meet the latest fashion requirements, ie the new colours of the season. Saying it is not enough though: the toughest part is doing it, and they did. Unlike their competitors, Benetton innovated by dyeing pullovers after they were made and not before, which helped save lots of precious time. By delaying their decision on the final colours, they were indeed better prepared for the whims of fashion and last-minute changes. If summer turned out to be magenta, Benetton could immediately react and fulfil expectations. However, although it is an essential physical facet of Benetton's brand identity, colour is not just a question of physique (in the identity prism): the colour element also impacts on the other facets of the prism, especially the cultural (which has sometimes made brands look like religions), a key facet when a brand markets to youth.

Colour does not merely serve to position the brand (the colourful brand); it is the outward sign of an ideology, a set of values and a brand culture. In its very slogan 'United Colours of Benetton', as in its posters showing a blond and a black baby, the brand expresses its inspiration and its idealistic vision of a united world in which all colours and races live together in harmony. Colour then ceases to be a mere feature distinguishing the manufacturer. It is a banner, a sign of allegiance. Colour is celebrated by the youth who wears it. Brotherhood and cultural tolerance are the brand's values. That is why the provocative style of Benetton's recent advertising was so disturbing: it was at odds with the brand's past identity. It is incredible to see how much Benetton today has forgotten its role of cultural champion.

In Nivea's case, the prototype is Nivea cream and its characteristic blue box – the means via which the brand gains entry to each country, and thus the brand's underpinning factor. More than a mere product, Nivea cream in its round box constitutes one of the first acts of love and protection that a mother performs for a baby. After all, doesn't everyone remember the typical scent, feel, softness and sensuality of this white cream, reinforced by the Nivea blue? The blue box is thus the brand's true foundation in all senses:

- It is the first Nivea product people encounter in their life, from the age of four.
- It bears the Nivea values.
- It constitutes the first sales of Nivea in every country where the brand is established.

So what is the significance of this blue colour and this flagship moisturizing cream, the cornerstones of the whole edifice?

Remember that blue is the favourite colour of more than half the population of the Western world, including the United States and Canada. It is the colour of dreams (the sky), calm (the night), faithful, pure love (the Virgin Mary has been depicted in blue since the 12th century), peace (UN peacekeepers) and the simple, universal appeal of blue jeans (Pastoureau, 1992). The cream's whiteness is the white of purity, health, discretion, simplicity and peace (a white flag). As for the moisturizing cream itself, it adds water to the skin, an essential injection of a human aspect to one's natural environment.

This reveals the values of the brand. Nivea's philosophy penetrates to its very core: a view of life founded on human coexistence, and containing strong moral values such as confidence, generosity, responsibility, honesty, harmony and love. In terms of competence, it stands for safety, nature, softness and innovation. Lastly, it sells itself as timeless, simple and accessible, at a fair price. And this is the way in which the Nivea brand itself is identified worldwide. Even if at any given moment, within a particular group, segment or country, these values are not perceived, they remain the values that form the basic identity of the brand. What does Nivea sell in essence? Pure love and care.

The Lacoste shirt now only represents 30 per cent of the company's world sales. It is nonetheless a core product, since it conveys the brand's original values. This shirt was indeed designed at a time when tennis was still being played in long trousers and shirts with rolled-up sleeves. In 1926 (Kapferer and Gaston Breton, 2002), René Lacoste asked his friend André Gilliet to make a 'false' shirt: something that would look like a shirt (so as not to shock the Queen at Wimbledon), yet would be more practical, ie airy (hence the cotton knit), sturdy and with straight sleeves. Thus right from the beginning, and by accident, René Lacoste's audacious innovation came to embody the individualistic and aristocratic ideal of living both courageously and elegantly. Whatever the occasion, a Lacoste is always elegant: perfectly suited to the person who, overall, cares to respect proper dress codes, but not in very minute detail. Lacoste is neither trendy nor stuffy: it is simply always chic.

All major brands thus have a core product in charge of conveying the brand's meaning. Chanel has its gold chain, Chaumet its pearls and Van Cleef a patented technique of setting stones in invisible slots. These features do not merely characterize the products, they actually embody the brands' values. Dupont, on the other hand, does not seem to have much at stake: it certainly endorses superb lighters, but beyond them is there any dynamic brand concept in evidence? In terms of ready-to-wear clothing, 501 jeans are at the heart of the Levi's brand and of the carefree and unconventional ideology it represents. (On this point, it is significant that the product most frequently worn with a Lacoste shirt is a pair of jeans.) Conversely, brands such as Newman suffer from never having created a real core product, one exclusive to the brand which conveys its very identity.

These examples serve to illustrate a key principle for brand credibility and durability: all facets of brand identity must be closely linked. Moreover, the brand's intangible facets must necessarily be reflected in its products' physique. This 'laddering' process is illustrated by the Benetton case (Table 7.4). Likewise, Lacoste's identity prism can neither be dissociated from the story behind its famous shirt nor from the values of its emblematic sport, tennis.

TABLE 7.4 Brand laddering process: the Benetton case

- Physical attribute: colour and price.
- Objective advantage: the latest fashion.
- Subjective advantage: the brand for young people who want to be 'in'.
- Value: tolerance and brotherhood.

The power of brand names

The brand's name is often revealing of the brand's intentions. This is obviously the case for brand names which, from the start, are specifically chosen to convey certain objective or subjective characteristics of the brand (Steelcase or Pampers). But it is also true of other brand names which were chosen for subjective reasons rather than for any apparent objective or rational ones: they too have the capacity to mark the brand's legitimate territory. Why did Steve Jobs and Steve Wozniak choose Apple as their brand name? Surely, this name neither popped out of any creative research nor of any computer software for brand name creation. It is simply the name that seemed plainly obvious to the two creative geniuses. In one word, the Apple brand name conveyed the exact same values as those which had driven them to revolutionize computer science.

What must be explained is why they did not go for the leading name style of that period, ie International Computers, Micro Computers Corporation or even Iris. The majority of entrepreneurs would have chosen this type of name. In deciding to call it Apple, Jobs and Wozniak wanted to emphasize the unconventional nature of this new brand: in using the name of a fruit (and the visual symbol of a munched apple), they thought different. With this choice, the brand demonstrated its values: in refusing to idolize computer science, Apple was in fact preparing to completely overturn the traditional human/machine relationship. The machine had, indeed, to become something to enjoy rather than to revere or to fear. Clearly, the brand name had in itself all the necessary ingredients to produce a major breakthrough and establish a new norm (which all seems so obvious to us now). What worked for Apple also worked for Orange. This name reflected the founders' values, which materialized into user-friendly mobile phone services. Similarly Amazon conveys strength, power, richness and permanent flow.

The brand name is thus one of the most powerful sources of identity. When a brand questions its identity, the best answer is therefore to thoroughly examine its name and so try to understand the reasoning behind its creation. In so doing, we can discover the brand's intentions and programme. As the Latin saying goes: *nomen est omen* – a name is an omen. Examining the brand name thus amounts to decoding this omen, ie the brand's programme, its area of legitimacy and know-how as well as its scope of competence.

Many brands make every effort to acquire qualities which their brand name fails to reflect or simply excludes altogether. 'Apple' sounds fun, not serious.

Other brands simply proceed by ignoring their name. The temptation for a brand to just forget about its name is caused by a rash interpretation of the principle of brand autonomy. Experience indeed shows that brands become autonomous as they start to give words specific meanings other than those in the dictionary. Thus when hearing of 'Birds Eye', no one thinks of a bird. The same is true of Nike. Mercedes is a Spanish Christian name, yet the brand has made it a symbol of Germany. This ability is not only characteristic of brands but also of proper nouns: we do not think of roofing when talking of Mrs Thatcher. Thus, strong brands force their own lexical definitions into the glossaries: they give words another meaning. There is no doubt that this process takes place, but the time it requires varies according to its complexity.

A name – like an identity – has to be managed. Certain names may have a double meaning. The purpose of communication then is to select one and drop the other. Thus, Shell naturally chose to emphasize the sea-shell meaning (as represented in its logo) rather than the bomb-shell one! Likewise, the international temporary employment agency, Ecco, has never chosen to exploit the potential link with economy suggested in its name. On the other hand, it does use its name as a natural means to reinforce its positioning in the segment of high quality service: its advertising cleverly plays upon the theme of duplication – those stepping in from Ecco will of course perfectly duplicate and echo those stepping out of the company.

Generally speaking, it is best to follow the brand's overall direction as well as its underlying identity, whenever possible. All Hugo Boss is entirely contained in that one short, yet international, name – Boss: it conveys aggressive success, professional achievement, conformity and city life. Rexona is a harsh name all over the world because of its abrupt R and its sharp X: thus it implicitly promises efficiency.

Brand characters

Just as brands are a company's capital, emblems are a brand's capital equity. An emblem serves to symbolize brand identity through a visual figure other than the brand name. It has many functions such as:

- To help identify and recognize the brand. Emblems must identify something before they signify anything. They are particularly useful when marketing to children, since the latter favour pictures over text, or when marketing worldwide (every whisky has its own emblem).
- To guarantee the brand.
- To give the brand durability – since emblems are permanent signs – thereby enabling the company to capitalize on it. Thus Hermès' legendary horse is the common emblem of 'Equipage', 'Amazone' and 'Calèche'.
- To help differentiate and personalize: an emblem transfers its personality to the brand. In doing so, it enhances brand value. But it also facilitates the identification process in which consumers are involved.

Animal emblems are often used to perform this last function. Animals symbolize the brand's personality. It is quite significant, in this respect, that both the Chinese and Western horoscopes represent human characters by animals. The Greek veneration of animals reflected their conception of a certain spiritual mystery. The animal is not only allegorical of the brand's personality but also of the psychological characteristics of the targeted public. Wild Turkey symbolizes the independent mind and free spirit of the drinker of this particular bourbon. The red grouse, symbol of Scotland and a rare bird, has been chosen as the emblem of Famous Grouse whisky in order to reflect the aesthetic ideal of its consumers. Lacoste is a crocodile.

Emblems epitomize more than one facet of brand identity; that is why they play such a crucial role in building identity capital. The world of whisky is filled with wild, rare, untameable animals that symbolize the natural, pure and authentic character of this alcohol. The associated risk perceived by the customer is thus reduced. They also demonstrate, as we saw above, the brand's personality: the red grouse is known for its noble gait and carriage; the wild turkey is a stubborn and clever bird symbolizing independence in the US. These animals also represent the brand's value and culture facet, either because they are geographical symbols (the grouse for Scotland, the wild turkey for the USA) or because they refer to the brand's essence itself.

Many other brands have chosen to be represented by a character. A character can, for example, be either the brand's creator and endorser (Richard Branson for Virgin) or an endorser other than the creator (Tiger Woods for Nike). It can also be a direct symbol of the brand's qualities (Nestlé's bunny rabbit, Mr Clean, the Michelin bibendum). Some characters serve to build a certain relationship and an emotional, prescriptive link between the brand and its public (Smack's frog, Esso's tiger). Others, finally, serve as brand ambassadors: though Italian, Isabella Rossellini embodied the type of French beauty that Lancôme promises to all women.

Such characters say a lot about brand identity. They were indeed chosen as brand portraits, ie as the brand's traits, in the etymological sense. They do not make the brand, yet they define the way in which the brand brings to reality its traits and features.

Visual symbols and logotypes

Everybody knows Mercedes' emblem, Renault's diamond, Nike's swoosh, Adidas' three stripes, Nestlé's nest and Yoplait's little flower. These symbols help us to understand the brand's culture and personality. They are actually chosen as such: the corporate specifications handed over to graphic identity and design agencies mainly pertain to the brand's personality traits and values.

What is important about these symbols and logos is not so much that they help identify the brand but that the brand identifies with them. When companies change logos, it usually means that either they or their brands are about to be transformed: as soon as they no longer identify with their past style, they want to start modifying it. Some companies proceed otherwise: to revitalize their brands and recover their identity, they milk their forlorn brand emblems for the energy and aggressiveness they need in order to be able to change. Just as human personality can be reflected in a signature, brand essence and self-image can be reflected in symbols.

Geographical and historical roots

Identity is born out of the early founding acts of a brand. Among these one finds products, channels, communications and also places.

The identity of Patek Philippe is intimately associated with that of Switzerland. The same is true of Air France abroad or of Barclay's Bank. Outside of the United States, the Ford brand represents the cars of the New World. Certain brands naturally convey the identity of their country of origin. Others are totally international (Ford, Opel, Mars, Nuts). Others still have made every possible effort to hide their national identity: Canon never refers to Japan, while Technics has adopted an Anglo-Saxon identity though the company is Japanese.

Some brands draw their identity and uniqueness from their geographical roots. It is a deliberate choice on their part. What advantage did Finlandia expect to gain, for example, by launching a premium vodka? As its name suggests, Finland is the country where the earth ends – a cold, austere, unspoilt, remote land, where the sun scrapes the ground. This spontaneous vision both feeds and supports the creation of an extremely pure water and vodka.

Brands can benefit from the values of their native soil. Apple has thus adopted the Californian values of both social and technological progress and innovation. There is a touch of alternative culture in this Californian brand (which is not true of all Silicon valley brands, such as Atari). IBM epitomizes East coast order, power and conservatism. Evian's symbolism is linked to the Alps, or rather to the image of the Alps, as projected by the company. Roots are crucial for alcoholic drinks too: Glenfiddich means Deer Valley, Grouse is the fetish bird of Scotland. The Malibu drink, on the contrary, had not defined its origin: only recently has its advertising specified that its home was the Caribbean.

The brand's creator: early visions

Brand identity cannot be dissociated from the creator's identity. There is still a lot of Richard Branson in Virgin's brand identity. Inspired by its creator, Yves Saint Laurent's brand identity is that of a feminine, self-assured and strong-minded 30-year-old woman. The YSL brand celebrates the beauty of body, of charm, of surrender to romance, and is flavoured with a hint of ostentatious indecency. The relationship between a brand and its creator can last far beyond the death of the creator. Chanel is a good example of this: charismatic Karl Lagerfeld does not try to imitate the Chanel style, but to interpret it in a modern way. The world is changing: the brand's values must be respected, yet adapted to modern times. The same holds true for John Galliano and Dior, or Elbaz for Lanvin.

When its creator passes away, the brand becomes autonomous. The brand is the creator's name woven into a set of values and a pattern of inspiration. Thus, it cannot be used by another member of the creator's family. This was confirmed in court in 1984 when Olivier Lapidus, son of the founder of the Ted Lapidus ready-to-wear brand, was refused the right to use the word 'Lapidus'. Even blood kinship thus does not entitle one to use brand name equity in the same sector.

Advertising: content and form

Let us not forget that it is advertising which writes the history of a brand, retailer or company. Volkswagen can no longer be dissociated from the advertising saga that helped it develop. The same is true of Budweiser and Nike. This is only logical: brands have the gift of speech and they can only exist by communicating. Since they are responsible for announcing their products or services, they need to speak up at all times.

When communicating, we always end up saying a lot more than we think we do. Any type of communication implicitly says something about the sender, the source (who is speaking?), about the recipient we are apparently addressing and the relationship we are trying to build between the two. The brand identity prism is based on this hard fact.

How is this implicit message slipped between the lines and conveyed to us? Simply through style. In these times of audio-visual media, a 30-second TV ad says just as much about the style of the brand sending the message and of the recipient apparently being targeted as about the benefits of the product being announced. Whether or not they are managed, planned or wanted, all brands acquire a history, a culture, a personality and a reflection through their cumulative communications. To manage a brand is to proactively channel this gradual accumulation of attributes towards a given objective rather than just to sit and wait to inherit a given brand image.

Yet what is inherited can also be a boon. Volkswagen tightly controls its marketing, but entirely delegates its communications to its agency. Thus all Volkswagen cars are launched under the same name, no matter what the country. However, the Volkswagen style is definitely a legacy of the advertising genius, Bill Bernbach: indeed, he succeeded in making the entire DDB network follow the stylistic guidelines which he had defined. It is thus through the memorable VW Beetle campaigns that both the brand's specific style and scope of communication began to take shape.

Both in its advertising films and spots, the VW brand has always freely played with the motifs of both the cars and the logo. The brand's style of expression is one of humour and humour only, as shown in its attitude of self-derision, false modesty and impertinence towards competitors as well as in the use of paradox. Volkswagen's advertisements have thus built a powerfully intimate relationship with the public. They appeal to consumers' intelligence, reflecting the image of the pragmatic people who prefer functional features to fancy ones.

The paradox of Volkswagen is that it has always managed to speak of a quite prosaic product in an almost elitist, yet friendly and humorous style. This has enabled Volkswagen to introduce minor modifications as major developments. The selling points put across in the adverts are based on facts and on certain values, which the brand has always conveyed, such as product quality, durability, weather-resistance, reliability, reasonable prices and good trade-in value.

But this advertising style, though created outside the Volkswagen company, was not just artificially added to the brand. Who could possibly have created such a monstrous car with an insect name (the Beetle), which so completely defied the trends in the US automobile world at the time? It could only have been an extremely genuine, honest creator, with a long-term vision. To encourage its own customers to buy, the brand had not only to flatter their ego and intelligence but also to acknowledge them for breaking away – if only this one time – from the stylistic clichés of North American cars. In a tongue-in-cheek style, the brand manages to convey its values and its culture. The Volkswagen style *is* Volkswagen, even though it was created by Bernbach.

Building an inspiring brand platform

Brand platforms are the cornerstone of brand management. Each brand should have its explicit, concise

FIGURE 7.6 A typical brand platform: Jack Daniel's

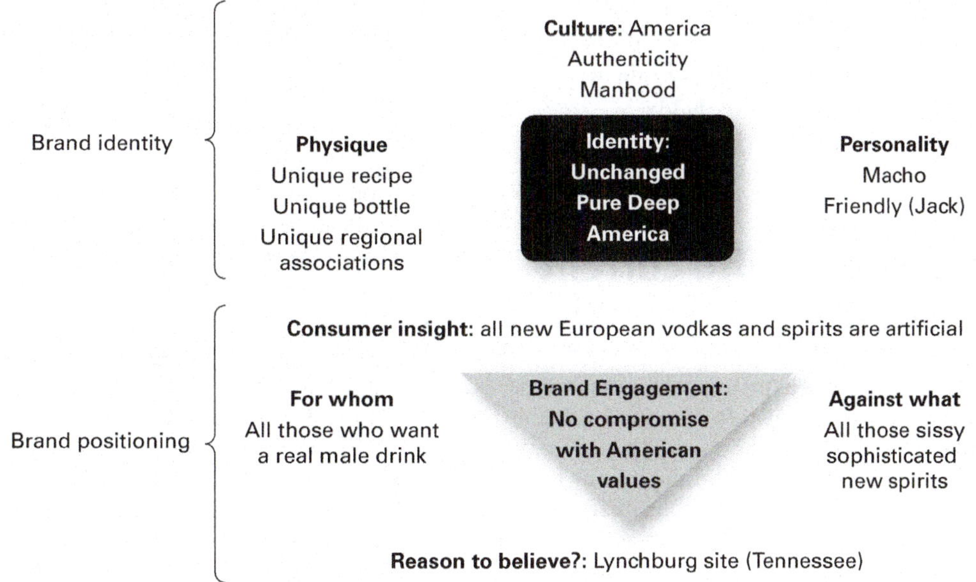

SOURCE J-N Kapferer

and sharp written brand platform, making clear what it wants to stand for. The brand platform is the normative blueprint of the brand the company wants to build, summarizing the two key pillars of brand management: brand identity and brand positioning.

Strategy will specify the path to follow in order to bridge the gap between the current brand image and the desired image outlined in the brand platform. The wider the gap, the lengthier and more difficult it may be. Audi took 25 years to reach it with a few landmark new models to shape the desired image of Audi. Burberry took six years (see page 397).

Since 1990 many formats of brand platforms have been promoted in the marketing community. Each major company has religiously built its own, diffusing it among its managers: sharing the same brand planning tool worldwide is a necessary first step of global branding. These formats are very diverse in shape but hold the same content, with minor variants. They define the facets of a brand, from the highest intangible values and brand personality down to products' differentiating attributes and reasons for the alleged promises. Typical brand platforms contain such items as 'brand essence', 'brand pillars or distinctive values' (also called the 'brand equities'), 'brand personality', etc.

The most known brand platforms are:

- The simple 'positioning statement', a short sentence specifying what single benefit needs to be attached long term to the brand name, in what product category or sub-category, for what target and with what reason to believe (Trout and Ries, 1978). It is inherited from the classic USP.
- The 'footprint' (used by Johnson & Johnson), which asks questions about essence, values, personality, capsule and positioning.
- The 'bull's-eye' (starting from the brand essence in the middle and then moving to brand personality, brand values, brand benefits and product attributes).
- The brand key (Unilever), with a lot of information designed as a keyhole (brand values, benefits, personality, reason to believe, discriminator and brand roots). At Unilever there is a brand key written not only for the masterbrand but for each of the sub-brands too.
- The brand pyramid, promoted by the academic researcher K L Keller and many consulting companies, asking brand

managers to specify in detail from top to bottom such information as brand resonance, consumer judgements and feelings, brand performance, brand imagery and so on, right down to brand salience.

- The Mars key, McDonald's ladder, etc. In 2010 most of these companies expressed frustrations with their tool.

What is wrong with current brand platforms?

Why are most companies expressing discontent with their brand platforms? They just do not work! The proof is that, everywhere in the world, the forces of commoditization are growing, and the brands have to recede. Even the largest mass consumer goods companies, such as P&G, once the Mecca of FMCG marketing, are now hurt by the growth of private labels or hard-discount products (see Chapter 10). P&G's main concern, as evidenced by the many internal seminars it now runs worldwide, is how to fight against private labels through premiumization. These forces extend to all sectors of the economy: services (low-cost airlines), pharmaceuticals (generics) and B2B (there are also private labels).

Companies realize they spend an awful lot of time answering all the questions of the brand platforms, but at the end of the year market shares are often once again declining when facing private labels, for instance, or low-cost competition. As we are regularly consulted on these issues, what is our diagnosis?

Brand platforms have become a merely formal exercise

There is something pathetic about the increased sophistication of brand platforms developed by brand consulting companies. They seem like an illustration of Jared Diamond's remarkable book on the fall of civilizations (2008). This author noticed that Easter Island's famous statues were made bigger and bigger as the economic situation got worse on the island because of growing deforestation that ruined the soil. Instead of taking the correct rational move, the Easter Island inhabitants looked more and more for mercy from their gods to solve their human-created problems.

Why are most brand platforms leading companies astray in practice?

- Their authors become enamoured of their own sophistication. Sophistication is a value in the academic or research world. It becomes a limit to action in the real world.
- Most companies are now global: the sophistication of concepts means a higher level of misunderstanding from managers all around the world whose culture is not Western and whose first language is not English.
- The establishment of a new brand platform is very time consuming, and requires consultants from costly strategic consulting companies to help the brand managers answer the many questions or even understand the concepts themselves. Then endless discussions revolve around understanding the ill-defined concepts: the difference between personality and value seems clear at first sight. Now take 'honesty' as an example: is it a value or a personality statement? Aren't the values you hold part of your personality?
- The more sophisticated they are the more they give a false feeling of robustness to management. Their inner structure seems logical, with no gaps and holes in the reasoning. This is often due to brand platforms actually being completed once the advertising claim has been found. It is easy then retroactively to fill each single compartment of the platform. Certainly, the resulting global picture looks very coherent, but this is an artefact. These models hold inner consistency as their primary quality. A superb brand platform is one where from top to bottom the means–ends chain flows naturally.
- The more questions there are, the more redundancy there is between the questions. Managers feel some dismay when using the same words from one question to another. This redundancy stems from the fact that managers move from one company to another and export the brand equity model they are used to working with. Now if the company they join has another model, what happens is a trend to mix both and add

complexity. For instance, at P&G people talk about PODs (points of difference) and POPs (points of parity). A baby food brand at P&G would have such PODs as:

- highest safety level;
- all nutrition for my baby;
- interactive, professional advice.

Now another company would say that its brand has three 'values': safety, nutrition and interactivity. Another one still would talk about 'distinctive consumer benefits': 'I feel safe and not anxious.' In the end, one finds brand platforms that embody layers coming from many sources (with PODs, POPs, values, benefits, etc). This looks like a maze, with too much redundancy from too many new product developers and communication agencies.

- They lead the brand to get entangled in a net of complexity. Brand platform models miss their primary goal: to be a springboard for action. They deter action. Marketing uses a lot of external agencies to activate the brand: when the brand platform is presented to them, their first question is about simplification. In a pyramid full of words, which are the ones that really are the most important to drive action?
- Brand platforms are often static in their concepts and wording. They are not tools of mobilization. What is more static than the concept of 'brand essence'? Huge amounts of money are spent to unveil this brand essence, once and for all. Now when you say that Woolite's brand essence is 'trusted care for everything you wear', how does this mobilize internally and externally?
- When a baby food brand writes 'mothers' partner for growing healthy babies', isn't that the essence of most competing brands in this market? In fact many brands in the same category pursue the same goals and try to provide the same core category benefits: both Nestlé and Danone want to bring health through food. The difference is in the path to achieving the same promise. For instance, all skin care brands propose the same consumer benefits (eternal youth, seduction, self-assurance): however, Caudalie is dedicated to vine leaves as the source of all benefits, Amore Pacific believes only in the virtues of green tea, and Biotherm trusts in thermal water. The 'reason why' is actually the source of the crusade of the brand, or what it is fully dedicated to.
- Most of all, these models of brand platforms are based on conceptual models unable to meet the new demands of the markets and of the new competitive situation. Brands now have to create communities. Today one does not create fans, proselytes and consumer engagement without a good cause. But a good cause is not the old 'reason to believe' of a consumer benefit or a product promise. The good cause is a call to mobilization, whereas a 'reason to believe' is just a persuasion device (like the sponsorship by the US Dental Association for Crest).
- Brand platform models are implicitly driven by microtheoretical notions stemming from consumer psychology and now the neurosciences, which have made inroads into marketing academia. However, for a brand to get social resonance, to create proselytes and use its social impact, individual psychology or individual consumer choice models are irrelevant. We need to turn much more towards understanding not consumers but the society as a whole: more sociology and more cultural anthropology are needed (see also Holt and Cameron, 2011).

What should one expect from a brand platform?

Companies are now looking for better brand platforms, able to energize the whole value chain and mobilize internally and then externally. A lot of our own present consulting is about this. We recommend not using ready-made platforms hired from another company. Each brand should build its own one as long as it fulfils six major conditions and goals:

- Energize: set a high level of ambition for the brand.
- Inspire: what deep consumer insight or what societal tension does it address?

- Passion: what is the big ideal or crusade for the brand?
- Consistency: we need a common creative activation all across the range.
- Deliver: products matching real needs, with passion and edge.
- Facilitate: for global understanding and adhesion, only a few words are suitable.

Forget brand essence: be inspirational

Brand platforms are often called 'brand equity platforms' within companies when they are used to detail what the brand wants to stand for across all its products or product lines, and to demonstrate the means–ends internal coherence, from high-end values to down-to-earth product differentiators. Such platforms remind people what the equities of the brand should be ('What distinctive benefits do we want to associate with our brand?'). Then market research companies yearly measure the progression of these associations in the target's mind. This is why the brand equities, also called pillars of equity or PODs, look like typical items one finds in an agree/disagree questionnaire.

At a time of growing lack of involvement with brands, hence the growing market share of low-cost alternatives, private labels, etc, what brands need to do is re-create consumer engagement. The problem is that 'brand essences' are too static. As concise summaries of what the brand stands for they are fine, but they are unsatisfactory where consumer engagement is concerned.

Let us take a typical brand essence, that of Bombay Sapphire, the famous gin. It reads: 'Naturally elegant, worldly, intriguing and creative'. Another one, typical of hi-tech Asian companies selling hi-fis, televisions, home equipment and telephones, would be 'passionate to enrich the life of consumers'. What then? How is a brand community created from this brand essence?

Brands stand for something in people's hearts only through a great collective benefit, uncompromising execution, obsession with detail, and a clear creative territory. Do current brand platforms express the brand engagement, the reason to commit oneself to the brand? Do they inspire action and creative execution? Not really. Brand platforms should be springboards for product development and creativity, a tool to inspire great campaigns that have an impact on consumers, not a maze of redundant words with no clear priority between them, or a generic sentence true for all actors of the product category. Brand essence is a static concept, not an engaging one. Trying to summarize the whole brand in a few words is considered an achievement by the brand team. They would be better asking: What is the brand's engagement? How does this brand want to change the world? But this kind of questioning rarely comes out of consulting organizations. Building emotional brands is not in their genes. Building coherent wholes is.

Because they are obsessed with conformity, Asian brands have quite bland brand platforms (see also page 49). As a result their communications are merely product focused and not remembered unless they can afford huge budgets. The typical communication of LG or Samsung or Haier focuses on one innovation after another, year after year, but leaves no mark. All hi-tech brands can say that they are relentlessly pursuing excellence, or passionately trying to give great experiences to their consumers, but these are words. Where is the brand crusade? How can great campaigns be inspired by these generic brand essence statements? They cannot. And this is not to mention the brand values, most often category generic ones (innovation, design and consumer concern).

The internet has become the main mode of communication between the brand and its public and among consumers themselves. This is why brands need *brand content*. Brand content is a radical new managerial concept stemming from the digital revolution. When intrusive media advertising held sway, people came across it, but did not look for it. Hence creativity was important to attract the attention of consumers while they watched their television series or browsed through their favourite magazine. They watched television or read the press for its own content and were exposed to commercial ads haphazardly.

The internet has introduced a major revolution. On the web people look directly for content, most often peer to peer. If brands now want to reach consumers, the only way is to provide their own interesting content. This does not mean advertising or just banners. Now how do you create content out of a brand platform? Let us take Beechnut, the US baby food brand. Its brand platform says: good taste, nutritious and safe. What brand content derives from this? Remember that people do not go on the web to be taught about your product qualities. They want to escape marketing and sales pitches.

Brand content asks brands to be more than single benefits attached to a name. They must have depth and content if they want to edit content on the web.

What do you talk about when you do not just talk about your products? Beyond talking, how do you become useful to your target, or entertaining, or both? This is the challenge of brand content.

'Why the brand exists' is the most important item

People are looking for authenticity. They give their sympathy according to it. As regards the Innocent brand, what made three young people making a lot of money in consulting or advertising companies engage together in the adventure of producing and selling smoothies? What was the compelling force? It was certainly not just a strategic market analysis looking for a gap in the market, a 'blue ocean' or a hidden gold mine. No: they just wanted to change the industry practices that they felt were poisoning people's health. Nothing less. In fact, early buyers loved this more than the product itself. You cannot build a community just by selling a natural smoothie. You have to be a pure natural smoothie plus a cause to defend at all costs.

Table 7.5 summarizes the 10 questions to ask in order to build the platform.

TABLE 7.5 Ten steps towards the brand platform

1.	Why must this brand exist? *What would customers be missing if the brand did not exist?*
2.	Vision. *What is the brand's long-term vision of the product category?*
3.	Ambition. *What does the brand want to change in people's lives?*
4.	What are our values? *What will the brand never compromise on?*
5.	Know-how. *What is the brand's specific know-how? Its unique capabilities?*
6.	Heritage. *What are our brand truths?*
7.	Territory. *Where can the brand legitimately provide its benefit, in which product categories?*
8.	Typical products or actions. *Which products and actions best embody, best exemplify the brand's values and vision?*
9.	Style and language. *What are the brand's stylistic idiosyncrasies? Its semiotic invariants?*
10.	Reflection. *Who are we addressing? What image do we want to render of the clients themselves?*

What should the brand platform be if the brand covers multiple categories?

With time and in order to grow, brands come to cover a wide array of markets and product categories. Nivea is make-up and skin care, but also shower gels, shampoos, baby care, male toiletries, etc. Hero is jam, baby food, cereals, etc. Should one build a platform for the overarching brand, or many platforms, one for each category? In fact both. If the brand has been extended to a number of categories it is because its identity and crusade – its values – are very meaningful in each of these categories. They should be stated, along with the major consumer insight or vision that justifies them. If the brand is the key, what is the lock?

For instance, Dove as an overarching brand rests on a major societal insight: most skin care brands foster an image of women that is in fact made by men (women are here to seduce and be nice). Take L'Oréal Paris, for instance, with its dream team of glamorous movie stars acting as brand ambassadors and saying to each consumer at the end of all commercials 'Because you're worth it'. Dove wants to address another concern, another image of women, which is made by women. In essence, it sells the self-worth of women.

The masterbrand platform should specify the level of ambition of the brand, and its role in the group portfolio, so that all managers become conscious of the stakes. The common executional activation across categories must also be clearly stated.

Finally, in order to guide the judgements of advertising execution and tone of voice, it is necessary to specify what is called 'brand personality' (see Azoulay *et al*, 2000). Thus Woolite is 'sensual but not sexual'.

Since brands exist only through product lines, it is also necessary to build a platform for each line. Naturally each line will repeat the masterbrand values, but the product line platform will also contain specific items:

- Why is it a business opportunity?
- What is the product or category insight (very useful for explaining how one of the brand values got incarnated in a specific product feature)?
- How does this product line contribute to building the masterbrand equity (what dimension of it in particular)?

From brand platform to product lines

Brands are experienced bottom up. People do not buy a brand; they buy products or services from a brand, in a store or on the web, and consult communications, attend events, try promotions, engage in discussions on the net, etc. The key numbers of brand experience are: 360° and 24/24.

It is important that most of the range tells the same story. We shall analyse in depth (Chapter 13) the relationships between the brand and its product lines: this issue is called 'brand architecture'. Let us say here that building brands should avoid sub-brands as long as the brand does not mean something clear in people's minds. Brands need variants: Apple has only variants. iPhone is the variant in the smartphone market; iPod is the variant in the MP3 market; iMac is the variant in the computer market, etc. Managers have a tendency to secessionism. While the brand is still being built in people's minds, those inside the company may be too much in love with sub-brands, that is to say in practice other brands, somehow distant from the parent brand. It is not possible to build a family spirit if all the offspring go their own way.

As a result we recommend that brand engagement be activated through the same creative idea all across the line. The brand platform should specify for each of the product lines (Figure 7.7):

1. Why is there a business opportunity?
2. What is its specific target?
3. What insight drives the creation of the product itself? How can the masterbrand values translate into specific features here?
4. How does the product line contribute to building the masterbrand itself? What kernel values are emphasized most by this product line?
5. What peripheral values are added by this product line (see also page 41)? What specific values need to be added? For instance, if the masterbrand Hero means naturalness, Hero Baby may need a boost of science to increase its credibility among anxious mothers.
6. What specific activation may be needed in terms of communication to the target?

FIGURE 7.7 After the brand: product platforms

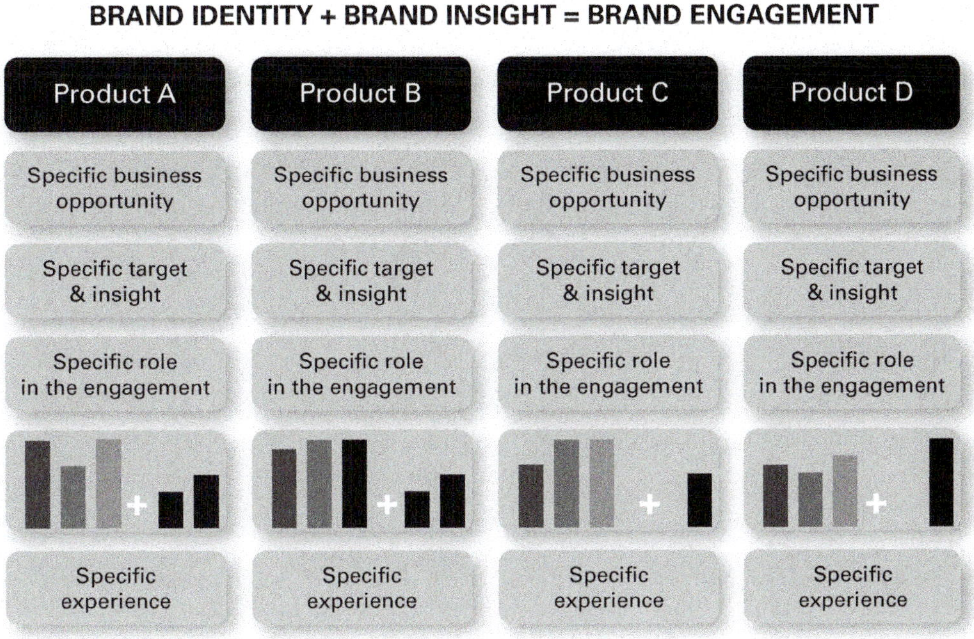

BRAND IDENTITY + BRAND INSIGHT = BRAND ENGAGEMENT

Product A	Product B	Product C	Product D
Specific business opportunity	Specific business opportunity	Specific business opportunity	Specific business opportunity
Specific target & insight	Specific target & insight	Specific target & insight	Specific target & insight
Specific role in the engagement	Specific role in the engagement	Specific role in the engagement	Specific role in the engagement
+	+	+	+
Specific experience	Specific experience	Specific experience	Specific experience

PART THREE
Creating and sustaining brand equity

08 Launching the brand

When they came into being, all the major brands examined so far – Nike, Lacoste, Amazon, Orange, l'Oréal, Nivea, Ariel – were of course also new brands. Over the years, and often by intuition, chance or accident, they became major brands, leading brands, powerful brands.

Since at one point they were all necessarily new, we might ask ourselves what the established brands have or have done that the others don't have or have not done.

Launching a brand and launching a product are not the same

Marketing books devote chapters to the definition of new products, but none to the launching of new brands, except for an occasional word or two on how to choose the name of a new product. This confusion between product and brand is an enduring problem. Most famous brands, rich in meaning and values, started out as the ordinary names of innovative products or services, different from those of competitors. These names were generally randomly chosen, without any prior study or analysis: Coca-Cola reflected the contents of the new product; Mercedes was the name of Mr Daimler's daughter; Citroën was a family name; Adidas is a spin-off of Adolphe Dassler; likewise Lip of Lippman and Harpic of Harry Picman. The new product had to be given a new name so that it could be advertised. Advertising was then put in charge of presenting the advantages of the new product as well as the benefits which consumers could expect from it.

After some time, new products usually get copied by competitors. They then get replaced by new, higher quality products, which often benefit from the fame of the existing product name. However, although products change, brands stay. In the beginning then, advertisements will boast the merits of the new, initial product, say X. But, since all products naturally become obsolete over time, X will soon come to announce that it's about to update and upgrade itself by lending its name to a higher quality product. And that's how a new brand comes to life. From then on, it is no longer advertising that will sell the products, but the brand itself.

Over time, the brand will gain greater autonomy and part with its original meaning (often the name of the company founder or of a specific feature of the product) by developing its own way of communicating (about the products), of addressing the public and of behaving. Few British people think of 'clean' when saying 'Kleenex' and few French think of the lotus leaf when saying 'Lotus'. The product name has become a proper noun, meaningless in itself, yet loaded with associations that have built up through experience (of the products and services), word-of-mouth and advertising. Advertising gives us hints of who the X who is now communicating really is: what is its core activity, its project, its cultural reference, its set of values, its personality, and whom is it addressing? Over time, the meaning of X has changed: it is no longer the mere name of a product, it is the very meaning of all products X, present and yet to come. The famous brand, X, is now the purveyor of values, from which its own endorsed products can benefit (as soon as they enter production).

In terms of brand creation, there is only one simple lesson to be learnt from this: if the new brand does not convey its values from the very start, ie as soon as it is created and launched, it is quite unlikely that it will manage to become a major brand.

On an operational level, this means that in launching a new brand, knowing its intangible values is just as important as deciding on the product advantage.

A successful launch requires that the new brand be treated as a full brand, right from the very start – not as a mere product name presented in advertising. Launching a new brand means acting before the product name becomes a brand symbol, with a much broader and deeper meaning than previously. Modern management must show results a lot sooner. From the very beginning, the new brand must be considered in full, ie endowing it with both functional and non-functional values. Creating a brand means acting straightaway as if it is a well-established brand, rich in meaning. This entails a few fundamental principles.

Defining the brand's platform

Unlike the product launch, the brand launch is, from the very start, a long-term project. Such launch will modify the existing order, values and market shares of the category. It aims at establishing a new order and different values and at impacting on the market for a long period of time. This can only be achieved if people are convinced of the brand's absolute necessity and are ready to give it all they have. In order to keep staff, management, bankers, clients, opinion leaders and salespeople mobilized for the long term, the company must be driven by a real brand project and a true vision. The latter will indeed serve to justify, internally and externally, why the brand is being launched and what its essential purpose is.

Creating a brand implies first drafting the brand's programme, which underlies the brand identity and positioning. Presenting the brand in a programmatic format is fruitful. It indicates where the brand stems from, where it draws its energy, what big project lies behind the brand. This is useful as a step in the brand thinking process itself, before the brand identity prism and brand positioning are defined.

The economics of brand positioning

Brand platforms engage the future. A brand does not immediately find the right positioning. Instead we recommend you always build different scenarios and evaluate them financially before choosing one and writing the final brand platform. There are five phases to this process: understanding, exploring, testing, strategic evaluation and selection, and implementing or activating the brand:

1. *The understanding phase* is about identifying all potential added values for the brand, based on its identity, roots, heritage and prototypes, as well as its current image. This is a self-centred approach: a brand's truth lies within itself. However, in order to detect which area of potential is most likely to be profitable for the business, an analysis of customers and competition is required. Markets are also analysed for this reason, as well as developments among consumers looking for 'insights' – consumers' aspirations or dissatisfactions on whom the brand can build. Lastly, the aim of analysing the competition is to identify opportunities, gaps, exploitables and areas of interest. The tool for this is perceptual mapping, for in marketing the fight is over perceptions. Perceptual maps do produce a remarkably synthetic model of the mind of the consumer – the psychological battlefield.
2. *The exploration phase* is about suggesting scenarios for the brand. Finding the brand platform is not something that can be done in one fell swoop: it takes an iterative approach, using repeated eliminations and adjustments. For example, what would the possible scenarios be for a brand such as Havana Club? This is the only rum produced in Cuba, an island famous for the quality of its sugar cane (and thus its rum), and seeks to promote this quality on a worldwide scale. Going back to our four questions – against whom? why? for when? for whom? – we can identify four major scenarios, each of which uses its own approach to express the full richness of the imagery evoked by Cuba and its capital Havana, which have remained authentic and intact over time (see Table 8.1). Note that these four scenarios do not each rely on the same product. As is the case with many brands, preferences can differ from one country to another. For example, in the case

TABLE 8.1 Comparing positioning scenarios: typical positioning scenarios for a new Cuban rum brand

	White mixer		Dark straight	
	A	B	C	D
	Better-tasting mixer than the leader	Experience Cubania	The 'absolute' rum	An original spirit
Against whom?	The leader	All mixers	Premium rums	Whiskies, cognac
Why?	'Taste'	'The Cuban drink'	'The best rum'	'Be different'
When?	Cocktail/mixed	Night/mixed	Home/bars/straight	Home/after dinner
To whom?	25/40 Spain, UK, Canada, Germany Bacardi drinkers	16/30 Urban/B in Europe and Canada, non-rum drinkers	25/40 Urban/heavy rum drinkers in Canada, Spain, Italy, UK	30/45 Urban heavy spirit drinkers in Europe, Canada, Asia
Flagship product	White	White/3 yrs	Anejo (dark)	7 yrs (dark)
Pricing	–10% vs leader	Par with leader	Premium	Par with whiskies
Communication – Target size – Business potential – Financial potential	Mass media	2-step marketing	2-step marketing	2-step marketing

of rum, some countries consume only white rum, while others consume only dark rum. Evidently not all of these countries could be penetrated using the same product. This has a strong impact on positioning, as the competition faced by a white alcohol will not be the same as that facing a dark rum. In one case, Havana Club will try to take market share away from gin and vodka, while in the other it will be up against whiskies, malts and brandies. Within the white alcohols sector, the question concerning the competition needs to be asked again: are we targeting the leader or not?

It all depends on the subjective category and the targeted competitors: to define oneself as rum is already to have specified the nature of the competition. In the UK, however, there is no rum market – despite the fact that Bacardi sells very well there. But to drink Bacardi, do you necessarily have to be aware that it is a rum? It is – thanks to Cuba – perhaps the very epitome of the party cocktail drink.

The angle of attack will differ depending on whether the target is Bacardi (the world leader), mixers and quality rums, or dark spirits in general (whiskies, brandies and so on).

3 *The test phase* is the time when scenarios are either refined or eliminated. It requires consumer studies to evaluate the credibility and emotive resonance of each scenario. What are being tested at this stage are ideas and formulations, but certainly not whole campaigns.

4 *The strategic evaluation* takes the form of a comparison of scenarios based on criteria, followed by the economic evaluation of potential sales and profits. The latter is conducted in 'bottom-up' fashion, through the summation of sales and contribution of forecasts from each country in question and so on (Table 8.1).

Let us look again at some of the 11 criteria for evaluating positioning (see page 153). The second of these raises the question of the strength of the 'consumer insight' on which it is based. Is there a genuine business opportunity here? The fifth is a reminder that all positioning has to target a weakness in the competition – and indeed, a long-term weakness. Positioning itself is a durable decision. So you might ask the question, how do you find your competitor's long-term weakness? Paradoxically, through its very strength (Neyrinck, 2000). For example, what is the long-term weakness of the world leader, Bacardi? It is the very fact that it is the world leader. To sell in such quantities, you have to sell at low prices, and thus produce everything locally. Bacardi may have been born in Cuba; but its rum no longer comes from Cuba, for a variety of commercial and economic reasons.

To evaluate a positioning, one must always take the trade into account. For example, in the world of shampoo, would a positioning of the 'for men' type constitute good positioning? The answer would seem to be 'yes' when judged by certain strategic evaluation criteria. It achieves differentiation and it represents a 'customer insight' (a genuine purchasing motive). But adopting the philosophy of the retailer leads us to a different conclusion. Retailers such as Wal-Mart, Carrefour and Asda tend to have a special men's section for hygiene and cosmetics products. This would immediately attract those arguing for this positioning. But it tends to be women who buy for men, and these women tend to choose for their men a shampoo from their own section. Thus, in terms of sales potential, it makes more sense to leave the product in the normal shampoo section. If it were put in the men's section, sales would fall by 50 per cent. Furthermore, let us suppose that the brand was in the men's section, at which point the 'for men' positioning stops being a source of differentiation, since that section contains nothing but products and brands for men only!

5 The fifth phase is that of *implementation and activation* once the platform has been chosen and drawn up. This new term clearly expresses the fact that today, a brand's values must be made palpable and tangible; and the brand must therefore transform them into acts at 360°.

This is all about defining the brand's marketing strategy, functional objectives and campaign plan. Will it be mainly mass-media advertising, or mainly proximity marketing? How will the brand be activated? Here again, choices will be determined by the competitive environment. Consider the example of Dolmio – the European leader in Italian sauces – whose marketing strategy cannot be the same for both the UK and Ireland. In the UK, Dolmio controls a mere 20 per cent of the market, while in the latter it is the comfortable leader with 50 per cent. Furthermore, far more proximity marketing can be carried out in a country with a small population than in a very large country. Activation is the phase during which strategy becomes behaviour and tangible actions, thus transcending mere advertising and promotion. (See Figure 8.1.)

Implementing the strategy: what flagship product?

A brand is built by its flagship product, also called its 'prototype'. In launching a new brand, companies have to be extremely careful in choosing which product or service to present in their first campaign and how to speak about it. This 'star product' should be the one that best represents the brand's intentions, ie the one that best conveys the brand's potential to bring about change in the market.

FIGURE 8.1 From brand platform to activation

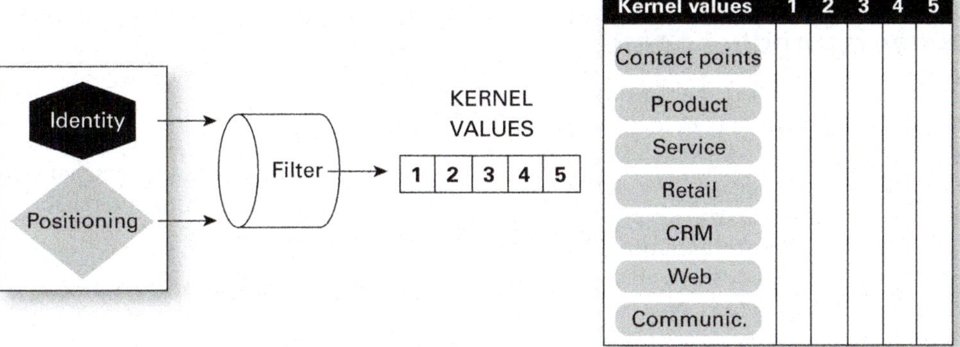

Not all products of a brand equally represent it. Only those which truly epitomize the brand's identity should be used as support in a launch campaign. Ideally, this identity must be visible. The major car manufacturers are well aware of this. Car design must be the outward expression of the brand's long-term design. The choice of the brand's best exemplar may conflict with short-term business objectives. The product that would sell the best might not be representative of the brand identity to be fostered. In this situation the long term should determine the short term, since it is evident that without business there is no brand.

Choosing a name for a strong brand

Manufacturers make products; consumers buy brands. Pharmaceutical laboratories produce chemical compounds, but doctors prescribe brands. In an economic system where demand and prescription focus on brands, brand names naturally take on a pre-eminent role. For if the brand concept encompasses all of the brand's distinctive signs (name, logo, symbol, colours, endorsing characteristics and even its slogan), it is the brand name that is talked about, asked for or prescribed. It is therefore natural that we should devote particular attention to this facet of the brand creation process: choosing a name for the brand.

What is the best name to choose to build a strong brand? Is there anywhere a particular type of name that can thus guarantee brand success? Looking at some so-called strong brands will help us answer these usual questions: Coca-Cola, IBM, Marlboro, Perrier, Dim, Kodak, Schweppes... What do these brand names have in common? Coca-Cola referred to the product's ingredients when it was first created; the original meaning of IBM (International Business Machines) has disappeared; Schweppes is hard to pronounce; Marlboro is a place; Kodak, an onomatopoeia. The conclusion of this quick overview is reassuring: to make a strong brand, any name can be used (or almost any), provided that there is a consistent effort over time to give meaning to this name, ie to give the brand a meaning of its own.

Does this mean that there is no need to give much thought to the brand name, apart from the mere problem of ensuring that the brand can be registered? Not at all, because following some basic selection rules and trying to choose the right name will save you time, perhaps several years, when it comes to making the baby brand a big brand. The question of time is crucial: the brand has to conquer a territory of its own. From the very start, therefore, it must anticipate all of its potential changes. The brand name must be chosen with a view to the brand's future and destiny, not in relation to the specific market and product situation at the time of its birth. As companies generally function the other way around, it seems more than appropriate to provide some immediate information on the usual pitfalls to avoid when choosing a brand name, and also to give a reminder of certain principles.

Brand name or product name?

Choosing a name depends on the destiny that is assigned to the brand. One must therefore distinguish the type of research related to creating a full-fledged brand name – destined to expand internationally, to cover a large product line, to expand to other categories, and to last – from the opposite related to creating a product name with a more limited scope in space and time. Emphasis, process time and financial investments will certainly be different in both cases.

The danger of descriptive names

Ninety per cent of the time, manufacturers want the brand name to describe the product which the brand is going to endorse. They like the name to describe what the product does (an aspirin that would be called Headache) or is (a biscuit brand that would be called Biscuito; a direct banking service called Bank Direct). This preference for denotative names shows that companies do not understand what brands are all about and what their purpose really is. Remember: brands do not describe products – brands distinguish products.

Choosing a descriptive name also amounts to missing out on all the potential of global communication. The product's characteristics and qualities will be presented to the target audience thanks to the advertisements, the sales people, direct marketing, articles in specialized periodicals and the comparative studies done by consumer associations. It would thus be a waste to have the brand name merely repeat the same message that all these communication means will convey in a much more efficient and complete way. The name, on the contrary, must serve to add extra meaning, to convey the spirit of the brand. For products do not live forever: their life cycle is indeed limited. The meaning of the brand name should not get mixed up with the product characteristics that a brand presents when it is first created. The founders of Apple were well aware of this: within a few weeks the market would know that Apple made microcomputers. It was therefore unnecessary to fall into the trap of names such as Micro-Computers International or Computer Research Systems. In calling themselves Apple, on the contrary, they could straightaway convey the brand's durable uniqueness (and not just the characteristics of the temporary Apple-1): this uniqueness has to do more with the other facets of brand identity than with its physique (ie its culture, its relationship, its personality, etc).

The brand is not the product. The brand name therefore should not describe what the product does but reveal or suggest a difference.

Taking the copy phenomenon into account

Any strong brand has its copy or even its counterfeit. There is no way out of this. First of all, manufacturing patents end up being public one day. So what is left to preserve the firm's competitive advantage and provide legitimate recompense for investing in research and development and innovating? Well, the brand name. The pharmaceutical industry is the perfect example: today, as soon as patents become public, all laboratories can produce the given compound at no R&D cost and generic products start flooding the market. A brand name that simply describes the product and the product's function will be unable to differentiate the brand from copies and generic products entering the market. Choosing a descriptive name boils down to making the brand a generic product in the long run. That is exactly how the first antibiotics got trapped: they were given names indicating that they were made from penicillin – Vibramycine, Terramycine, etc.

Today, however, the pharmaceutical industry has become aware that the name is in itself a patent which protects the brand from copies. This name must therefore be different from that of the generic product: in becoming distinctive and unique, it also becomes inimitable. The Glaxo-Roche laboratory, for instance, discovered an anti-ulcer agent which it called 'ranitidine'. Yet the brand name is 'Zantac'. Their competitor, Smith, Kline and French, also identified an anti-ulcer agent called 'cimetidine', but sold it under the Tagamet brand name. This naming policy is a good hedge against copies and counterfeits. Doctors are under the impression that Vibramycine and Terramycine are the same thing. Tagamet, though, seems unique, as does Zantac. The inevitable generic products that will eventually take advantage of the cimetidine or ranitidine patents will not use the Tagamet or Zantac names.

An original name can protect the brand since it reinforces the latter's defence against all imitations, whether they be fraudulent or not. The perfume name Kerius, for example, was considered as a counterfeit of Kouros: in litigation, legal experts do not judge counterfeit in terms of nominal or perfect similarity but in terms of overall resemblance. Thus Kerius became Xerius, while another cosmetics company had to pull out the products it had just launched under the name, Mieva because of Nivea. Descriptive names fail to act as patents. A brand called Biscuito would be very little protected: only the 'o' could be protected so as to prevent someone from naming a product 'Biscuita'! Even Coca-Cola was unable to prevent the Pepsi-Cola name! Quick-burger, Love Burger and Burger King have similar names, whereas McDonald's name is inimitable.

Distributors' own brands have greatly taken advantage of descriptive brands' scarce protection. Planning to win over some of the leading brands' customers, distributors have chosen names for their own brands that are very similar to those of the strong brands to which they refer: this way, consumers are likely to easily mistake one for the other. Ricoré by Nestlé has thus been copied by Incoré, l'Oréal's Studio Line by Microline, etc. Because the packages look alike (Incoré is in a yellow can like Ricoré's, with a picture of a cup and table setting also like Ricoré's...), consumers get all the more confused as they only rely on visual signs to find their way through the store aisles. As a matter of fact, recent research has shown that confusion rates are often above 40 per cent (Kapferer, 1995).

Preventing generism

The way in which the pharmaceutical industry has been handling the copy problem is extremely promising in terms of the long-term survival of all brands. By creating at the same time a product name (that of a specific compound) and a brand name, they have avoided the Walkman, Xerox or Scotch syndrome. These proper nouns now tend to become common names, merely used to designate the product. In order to overcome such risk of 'generism', companies must create an adjective-brand (the Walkman pocket music-player), not a noun-brand (a walkman). When creating a brand name, it might therefore also be necessary to coin a new name for the product itself (in this case, the pocket music-player).

Taking time into account

Many names end up preventing the brand from developing naturally over time because they are too restrictive:

- 'Europ Assistance' hinders the geographical extension of this brand and has also facilitated the creation of Mondial Assistance.
- Calor etymologically (meaning 'heat' in Latin) refers to heating appliance technology (irons, hair-dryers), and thus excludes refrigerators. The Radiola brand never managed to impose itself in the field of household appliances: its brand name was much too reminiscent of one specific sector.
- As time goes by, Sport 2000, the sporting goods distributor, seems less and less modern and futuristic.
- The non-fat yoghurt name, Silhouette, was too restrictive in terms of consumer benefit: slimness for the sake of slimness does not necessarily prevail anymore. This is why Yoplait decided to change the name to Yoplait fat-free, after having invested over 20 million dollars since 1975 in advertising the first brand name.

Thinking internationally

Any brand must be given the potential to become international in case it should want to become so one day. Yet many brands still discover quite late that, if such is their desire, they are limited by their name: Suze, the bitter French aperitif wine, almost literally means sweet in German. Nike cannot be registered in certain Arab countries. The Computer Research Services brand name causes problems in France, as does Toyota's MR2. In the United States, the almighty CGE name cannot be protected against the famous GE (General Electric) brand name. Prior to internationalizing a brand, one must ensure that the name is easy to pronounce, that it has no adverse connotations and that it can be registered without problems. These new requirements explain why there is so much interest in the 1,300 words which all seven major languages of the European Union have in common. It also explains the current tendency to choose abstract names which, having no previous meaning, can thus create their own.

Building brand awareness

The first step of brand building is brand awareness. The precondition of brand power is that it exists in people's minds. This is the first goal of any new brand's launch. The name must first stand for a specific new offer: What are you about? What are you selling? What market are you in?

Internet brands in particular must specify what they are about, because they have nothing to show. A car brand simply shows a car to tell people what it sells. But what is Meetic about? Or e-Bazar? Meetic allows men and women to find their ideal counterpart. e-Bazar was a kind of eBay: allowing people to sell whatever they wanted to other people.

But what type of brand awareness should one pursue?

- Top of mind ('What brand of [the competitive class] comes to your mind first?').
- Spontaneous ('What are all the brands of [the competitive class] that come to your mind?').
- Aided or prompted ('Here is a list of brands of [the competitive class]. Which ones do you know, even if only by name?').

The answer depends on the budget and the sector. It has been demonstrated by research (Laurent, Roussel and Kapferer, 1995) that spontaneous awareness worked as a restricted entrance club. There is an interesting empirical regularity: people tend to quote three brands on average, across sectors. Although they know dozens, spontaneously there seems to be what we have called 'a memory blockage'. This means that, to get into the club of those three brands, one of the brands has to be pushed out.

This is a hard task. However, is spontaneous (also called unaided) awareness a worthwhile communication objective? Yes, it is, for soft drinks, spirits or beers, because the person in a bar has five seconds to answer when asked 'What will you have?' What about other sectors? Brand managers must make their own diagnosis.

Spontaneous (unaided) brand awareness is critical for B2C as well as B2B brands:

- Fedex suffers by being number four in brand awareness in the UK. The name Fedex does not come first to the mind of someone who has to send an express item to New York immediately. That is why Fedex decided to invest in the European Rugby Cup for five years.
- Ricoh suffers too from insufficient brand awareness. Being number one in market share in Europe, thanks to excellent products and an impressive sales force, the Ricoh Corporation does not invest much in media communication to build its brand outside Japan. Subsidiaries are in fact sales organizations. This causes losses in the countries. The Ricoh salespeople are very good at diagnosing unmet needs within companies. Once they submit their proposal to the companies, the purchasing director often feels uncomfortable with a brand that does not come to mind spontaneously, and then invites bids or tenders. Competitors like Xerox or Canon win the bid. They may have come last but, being more known, they look reassuring in a way that Ricoh does not.
- The Belron Group is the world's number one group for repairing car windscreens. The group acquires local leaders if they lead in brand awareness in their home country: in Europe Carglass, in the United States Safelite, etc. When the windscreen breaks, there is a need for an immediate solution. The first name to mind counts.
- EasyJet and RyanAir compete on spontaneous brand awareness. Since they sell only through the internet, the first to be clicked has a competitive advantage.

Brand building through sponsorship

Sponsorship has become a classic way of brand awareness building. Many small companies realizing the costs of media advertising are tempted by sport sponsorship. There are no end of sailors willing to compete in around-the-globe sailing races and desperately looking for a sponsor to finance their boat.

This is a casino-type decision. Sponsorship is useful as long as it provides press results and TV coverage. However, because the investment is accessible, it may be tempting as long as it is not a one-shot decision, but a desire to invest in brand building during many years that way. It should be managed in the same way as all investments:

- Define the goals and the target people one wants to sell to.
- Evaluate the potential sponsorships accordingly.
- Evaluate the fit with the company values.
- Evaluate the size of the investment and its duration.
- Measure regularly the growth of brand awareness, and try to assess the correlation with sponsorship exposure.

Sport sponsorship is helpful for young companies that want to build their brand:

- It creates an internal source of mobilization (brands are made by people).
- It creates a good image in the immediate environment (social, political, economic).
- It boosts its image of social responsibility.
- It gives an occasion to talk about something else with the trade or the intermediaries.
- It provides a source of PR invitations for VIPs.
- It can eventually hit the jackpot if the sponsored person wins.

Now big brands too are tempted by sponsorship for just the same reasons when they go global. Why are Formula 1 circuits closing in Europe and opening in Dubai, Singapore, etc? Because Formula 1 is a medium, whose business model is based on broadcasting rights and sponsors. Today big brands look for growth in the BRIC countries (Brazil, Russia, India and China) and soon in the CIVETS countries (Colombia, Indonesia, Vietnam, Egypt, Turkey and South Africa). This is why brands seek sports that will attract the audiences of these countries and also that have a good fit with their values. The goal is first to create brand awareness and recognition and if possible to generate positive goodwill.

Fedex sponsored the European Rugby Cup because its unaided awareness (a key success factor in the express mail business) lagged behind UPS and DHL in the UK. People do not like to watch television adverts on express mail. In addition, it is a B2B activity; how could the decision makers who work during the day be reached? Broadcasting commercials in primetime would be a waste. Fedex decided to sponsor rugby because it is a typically English sport. Second, it rests on the values of team spirit, cooperation and coordination, so that the ball gets into the player's hands just in time, just like express mail. In other words, there is a fit between this sport and the business of Fedex. By 'fit' is meant a correspondence of values and working principles: it just makes sense both ways.

Sometimes the relationship between the sponsor and the sport does not make sense both ways. There is asymmetry. McDonald's is a global sponsor of all Olympic events and programmes, just like Coca-Cola, Samsung, Visa, Omega or GE. The Olympic Movement is a collaborative organization: it provides high goals, a fantastic brand (the rings) and an unsubstitutable experience by its own staff. One clearly sees how McDonald's benefits from sponsoring the Olympic games. Through this sponsorship McDonald's aims at creating goodwill for its own brand, permanently under attack for having contributed to the dramatically high obesity rates in its home country, the United States, and now exporting it worldwide. But what deep correspondence is there between McDonald's and the Olympic Movement? McDonald's is a very powerful medium itself in the world, and a key value of the Olympic movement is universality.

Recent research has explored the concept of congruity between the sport and the sponsor. However, one needs to separate meaningfulness and expectedness. Meaningfulness is when one can say that it makes sense. One really sees what the brand can gain by sponsoring, why it is relevant (value fit) and so on. Expectedness relates to the predictable nature of the choice of sport by the sponsor.

A lot of sponsorships are just opportunistic ways to reaching elusive targets in countries where mass media do not exist. Why would a bank sponsor Formula 1, if not to be visible on all local television screens? Figure 8.2 demonstrates how lack of fit and unexpectedness do not produce any increase in attitude towards the brand. However, it is striking that the most beneficial sponsorship is sponsorship that has meaningfulness or fit but that is quite unexpected. Nothing is more expected than Red Bull sponsoring an F1 sports team. An example of unexpected sponsorship would be for chess or deep sea diving.

FIGURE 8.2 How the unexpected sponsorship builds the brand

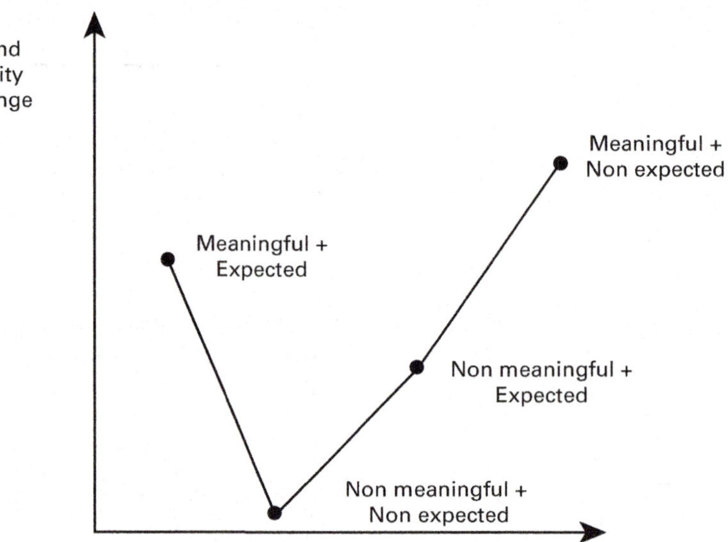

Brand campaign or product campaign?

Volkswagen has never produced communications about anything other than its products. Since the beginning, its ads have consistently reflected a deliberate choice of graphic style – that of purity: hence, the motif of a car on a white background. So, even if the brand treats the rational arguments aloofly, humorously, impertinently or paradoxically, the car remains the 'hero' of the ad. Sony occasionally launches so-called 'brand campaigns', which aim to emphasize the brand's slogan. Whenever a brand is created, there are two alternative strategies: to communicate the brand's meaning either directly, or by focusing on a particular product. Which path is followed depends on the company's ability to select one product which will fully convey the brand's meaning. It is no wonder that Volkswagen took the second option. The Beetle plainly demonstrated the genius of an original artist, an outsider, and obviously represented a different car culture.

In launching its brand in Europe, Whirlpool, the white goods world leader, decided to forbid any product ad for three years. It wanted to create a thrill around its name that no product campaign would have created, through a very imaginative and symbolic campaign.

The reason banks prefer brand campaigns is quite logical. As service companies, they have nothing tangible to show the potential customer. They can only symbolize their values and their identity. They also encapsulate the essence of their identity in slogans, in this way hoping to make up for their lack of visible products. Apple runs only product campaigns. They are not at all creative, as the products themselves are very creative.

Brand language and territory of communication

Today's vocabulary is no longer just verbal, it may even be said to be predominantly visual. In this multimedia era, in which only a few split-seconds' attention are spent on advertisements in magazines, pictures are far more important than words.

A territory of communication does not appear from nowhere, nor can it be arbitrarily assigned to the brand. Brand language allows brands to freely express their ideology. Not knowing which language to speak, we merely repeat the same groups of words or pictures over and over again, so that the whole brand message eventually becomes clogged. There is such a great urge to create unity, resemblance and a common spirit among the different campaigns that in the end they all seem merely to repeat one another. Each specific campaign message thus gets obliterated by an excessive concern to find the missing code!

The code is always rather artificial whereas language is natural: it conveys the personality, culture and values of the sender, helping the latter either to announce products and services or to charm customers.

Brand language finally serves as a means of decentralizing decisions. Thanks to the use of a common glossary of terms, different subsidiaries worldwide can adapt the theme of their messages to local market and product requirements and yet preserve the brand's overall unity and indivisible nature. Brand identity must reconcile freedom with coherence, a task which expression guides (also called brand charters) are meant to facilitate. These should not merely address issues such as the position of the brand name on the page and so on. They must also specify the following:

- dominant features of style;
- the audio-visual characteristics such as a gesture, a close-up of a customer's face, a jingle;
- the graphic layout or narrative structure codes, and the brand's colour codes;
- the principles determining if and how the brand – and its signature, if it has one – can be used in some circumstances.

Such cases must indeed be anticipated and defined in the expression guide.

Making creative 360° communications work for the brand at all contact points

In the world of mature countries, advertising is a challenge: it is costly, and its results are not always measurable. They are, however, measurable at the time of the brand's launch, at which time it quickly becomes apparent whether the public's demand and attitudes – as well as those of the trade – have changed.

The cost factor raises questions as to the appropriateness of advertising. There are sectors where launches are unthinkable without advertising: the FMCG sector, for example. But even in this case, it all depends on the precise category. The UK's current number one wine, Jacob's Creek (an Australian brand) was launched in the country in 1984, and its first large advertising campaign was in 2000. The brand has since stopped advertising, and now sponsors successful television programmes. The brand's success was built on an excellent, multiple-award-winning product, trade support, public relations, plenty of in-store promotions, and encouraging consumers to try it at the point of sale, to say nothing of on-site promotions. It also develops product placement, a real lever to create and maintain the 'cool factor' of a brand.

Top-of-the-range brands also work on winning the long-term support of opinion leaders, capitalizing on word of mouth. In the world of the internet, ebay – the only start-up company to have been profitable from the start, making it the internet's real success story – operates only through online referral and public relations.

When advertising is needed to give a boost to sales and business, the familiar old maxim springs to mind, 'Half of my advertising budget is wasted – but I don't know which half.' Actually, we believe that this half can easily be identified. Wasted advertising is advertising that:

- is not sufficiently creative, and so will not be seen;
- misses its target, so will not be seen by the right people;
- will be seen in places with no stores, where there is no distribution system in place.

These three points are the true causes of the waste; and the first of them is the most important. The question it raises is not so much the quality of the advertising agency as that of the client/advertiser. An advertiser can make a major contribution to the creativity of its agency – and thus to the quality of the campaign – in two ways: through the quality of its brief, and by the ability to take creative risks.

To achieve a leap of creative genius, a great creative idea, the brand proposition must be incisive, not bland. What can a creative person do with a brand value proposition coming from a typical McKinsey-style consultancy output, such as 'Brand X is the ultimate (whisky for instance)'. There is a real problem with the tools and consulting companies that excel in analytics but produce no ideas. Because of the reduction in the demand for strategic consulting, most of the big consulting companies have reoriented their staff. They want now to accompany the client all through the executional process. However, analytical people, recruited for data processing skills, produce thick and exhaustive reports and a mass of matrices, but a dearth of actionable ideas.

The mistake is to think one can rely on the agency to transform as if by a miracle the bland proposition into a great creative concept. It just does not happen this way.

The second condition for a creative leap is to realize that the advertising target must be radicalized. It cannot be a simple description of those who will buy, but should provide their reflection. If advertising is to break out of the clutter, it must not present plain people. Think of the Budweiser advertising saga 'Wazzup': by choosing quite radical characters in the commercials, the brand showed strong signs of modernity, of reinvention and of reinvolvement of the public. This was a challenge for this mainstream popular brand, which all Americans have known almost since they were born.

Building brand authority through opinion leaders and communities

Unless one wants to position the brand in a niche at the very high end, high market shares and sales will come from a mass market positioning. However, paradoxically in order to influence the mass of the market, the people less involved with the brand, the 'switchers', a brand must be carried by a smaller group of opinion leaders. Consumer behaviour relies too much on an individual approach to consumer choice, using the paradigm of a person deciding in a social vacuum. But everyone belongs to a network, a group, a tribe. Building a brand means getting closer to these groups, which are mediators of influence.

Proximity to opinion leaders

In all groups there are influencers, also called opinion leaders. The concept of opinion leadership is not new, but its significance has been hidden by an over-reliance on advertising. In fact, to build a brand one of the first questions to ask is, what group(s) will carry the brand? Here we do not speak of the market segment, but of the group(s) who will influence the market segment. A brand alone cannot convince. It needs relayers, committed relayers. Modern taste makers belong to tribes: micro-ethnic, cultural and geographical groups. These groups need proper identification and a programme of continuous direct relationship. They must experience the brand, its values, and eventually interact with it. The brand must understand them, and present itself as being on their sides, sharing the same values.

Who are these influencers? Who are the opinion leaders? The two concepts need to be distinguished. Recent research (Valette Florence, 2004) suggests that opinion leaders combine three necessary traits. They are perceived as experts, are endowed with charisma and have a desire to be different from others, and have a high social visibility. Not all experts are opinion leaders: they are influencers, as are salespeople or prescriptors.

Influencers can be professionals. Canson would not have succeeded without the close ties that it is permanently weaving with the teacher community. Pedigree (pet food) relies on professionals too. L'Oréal relies on hairdressers, Head & Shoulders on dermatologists.

They can be hobbyists. T-fal, positioned as tools for the successful cuisine, develops ties with cookery schools and with all the professionals engaged in developing a high level of skill in cuisine.

They can be the persons most involved in the category: all consumers are not equal. Some are more involved, more interested in all that concerns, not the product itself, but the need. They read more, use the internet much more, participate in chats and forums. For instance, mothers with more children play an influencing role.

Opinion leaders are to be found in specific community groups. We stress the word 'groups' because one should now speak of trend-setting tribes. As a result, the goal is to interact not with a sum of individuals, but with pre-organized groups, be they formal or informal. These groups can be met at specific places. Groups are organized, so it is easier to organize events with them. Salomon is obsessed with increasing the level of interaction with surfer groups all around the world, for they are trendsetters. Absolut Vodka succeeded because it came to be available at all the parties of the New York gay community. Bombay Sapphire gin did the same in Los Angeles.

To reach these groups, direct contact is needed and virtual intimacy on the net is necessary. One does not create strong ties at a distance. The goal is to show that the brand is becoming part of their world, by means of participating in occasions that show the brand and group share the same values, in some way or another. Eventually the brand should be creating these occasions.

Creating a hard core of ambassadors

As soon as the brand is launched the reflex must be of creating a hard core of supporters, involved in the brand. Clarins, a very small cosmetic company when it started in 1954, facing giants such as Estée Lauder and l'Oréal, was extremely innovative in that respect, but it went unnoticed up to the point when market research showed to its competitors that the small brand was getting bigger, and that it experienced a high rate of loyal and even fanatical clients: with each product there was an invitation to write to the company and to Mr Courtin, its founder. One-to-one and CRM were already there, far before these became 'musts' for management.

There are many frameworks that have shown how consumers can be segmented on a dimension of closeness of the relationship to the brand. Typical segments range from hell to paradise, with a mix of behavioural and emotional dimensions:

1. Those consumers who dislike the brand, even hate it. It is really not part of their world.
2. Those who are not consumers because they consider the brand is underperforming on a sought attribute.
3. Those who simply are not consumers, without a specific reason (simply the brand has nothing salient to their eyes to induce trial).
4. Those who would like to buy but cannot (no availability, no accessibility, price problem).
5. Those who buy from time to time, switching between brands.
6. Those who buy more often.
7. Those buyers who are involved, engaged with the brand, its ambassadors.

As soon as the brand is launched everything must be done to create and identify consumers in segments 6 and 7, the heavy buyers and the involved consumers.

Asking for identification is a sure way to build the precious database that will enable the organization to give VIP treatment to these forerunners: specific tips, a specific code number on the website, specific invitations, specific offers, PR events and online sales.

There is another way of creating a hard core of supporters. It can be summed up in one key phrase formulated 50 years ago by Paul Ricard: *faites-vous un ami par jour* (make a friend every day). Of course, this is easy to say if you happen to be – as Ricard was – the man who created what is now the world's second-largest spirits group. But the phrase deserves closer examination:. He did not say 'make a customer every day', but 'a friend'. Service, free gifts, responsiveness, personalized relationships, attentiveness and the sharing of enthusiasm at small and large gatherings alike are the rungs on this upward ladder.

Word of mouth should not however be seen as an alternative to advertising. Advertising is surely not dead. Brands have two feet: shared emotions and renewed products.

Advertising remains a fantastic tool to shape these common, shared imageries, or to create instant knowledge of an innovation.

How can one create the buzz, this modern, fashionable word for word of mouth, or positive rumours (Kapferer, 1991, 2004)?

The first approach is to make plenty of time for the press and media. Naturally, it is a good idea to recruit a specialist agent, but journalists will be flattered to be welcomed by managers themselves. This is where the work of making friends should begin: it is crucially important to know how to assist a journalist (for whom, as we all know, time is in short supply). We should also remember that everyone deserves attention, from the big-name television reporter to the freelancer from the small trade journal. The high-powered editor of the future is sure to be lurking among the dozens of freelancers you meet.

The second approach – which should become a discipline – is to do nothing without considering the press fallout. As the adage goes, every dollar you spend on public relations requires another to promote the fact. A buzz has to be activated and energized: it does not always start on its own.

The third approach is always to look for the difference and disruption in everything (Dru, 2002). It is said that in the world of PR, it has all been done before. This means that your job is to surprise, because surprise is what gets people talking.

This is why brands create their own events, engage in street marketing, tie up with celebrities, invest in sport or music sponsorship and so on.

09 Growing the brand

Brand growth is about extending the penetration of the brand in its target market, building both the brand equity and the business. It involves all facets of the marketing mix: line extensions at the product level, price differentiation, retail or channel extension, communication, and creating relations rather than transactions only. It aims at making previous buyers repeat their purchases and remain loyal: servicing, CRM and internet relationships will play a great role.

It is necessary to distinguish between bottom-of-the-pyramid (BOP) brands and brands for mature countries. In the first case the challenge is that of the business model: can one profitably develop a sustainable business after the momentum of the launch has faded away? It involves mostly creativity in production, in the supply chain, in financing independent salespeople, etc.

Brand management is another challenge in mature markets. How to build the business where consumers have their needs amply fulfilled, face considerable choïce, become price-sensitive and find allies in multiple retailers who want a larger share of the added value created by brands?

Drawing from multiple cases and models, we look at the main strategies that can be followed to find growth in no-growth markets.

The first, short-term strategy is to build on existing clients. Customer relationship management (CRM), database management and relationship marketing have not emerged so forcefully in the panoply of modern brand management without a compelling reason. It is necessary to get still closer to the consumer, one's own consumers, who may be faced with too much choice. Seducing new customers seems too costly (Reichheld, 1996).

The second one is to carry out more research. What needs, or lacks of satisfaction or untapped uses can be better met? For instance, packaging and design innovations, although not spectacular, are able to provide incremental sources of share, especially if they are differentiated according to the distribution channel.

However, for the long term, the two main options are to explore foreign markets and to innovate. We turn to these strategies now.

Growth through existing customers

The first source of growth is to be found among the existing customers of the brand. There are growth opportunities to be searched, evaluated and exploited. This is too often overlooked by managers who wish to move quickly to consumers' conversion.

Building volume per capita

Brand management over time is the permanent pursuit of growth. One way of achieving this is to move from a pattern of low-volume use to a pattern of potentially higher-volume use. For example, Bailey's Irish Cream – a worldwide spirits brand created in 1974 – suffered from a serious restriction to its growth. Its consumption was highly seasonalized, and sales mostly took the form of Christmas and New Year presents. It was consumed mainly by little old ladies, partaking on their own as a sort of sugary treat. It was taken neat in small measures, on account of its sweet taste. If it was to grow in volume, things had to change. The brand's future also depended on its ability to compete outside its category (narrowly defined as Irish cream liqueur). A major campaign was thus launched around the concept of Bailey's on ice. The creative idea was to communicate how the sensuousness of Bailey's allowed you to connect to your friends and family. The intention was to encourage groups of people to drink Bailey's on the rocks (which in fact increases the desire for another glass). A creative media campaign backed this new positioning, exploring how to link the brand to the key sensual moments in the media. For example, Bailey's sponsored *Sex and the City*.

But most important were the on-premise implications of the campaign. Drinking Bailey's on ice required a normal-sized glass, not a liqueur glass as before. The marketers had to persuade the trade to take the campaign seriously. They designed a new Bailey's glass for bar chains, 6,000 ice consumer kits, 4,000 large-measure POS kits, and 16,000 optics to deliver a suitable measure of Bailey's for drinking over ice. As a result on-trade sales grew from a low 46,000 cases in December/January 1989 to 107,000 in December/January 1996. It had become more hype, young and trendy to drink Bailey's on ice.

In the United States Jack Daniel's – suffering from its stereotypically 'macho' image – attempted to increase its per capita volume. To do this, the brand needed to create an association with parties (a consumption situation which has a galvanising effect on volume). The brand created a micro-marketing plan specifically for this purpose, 'The Jack Daniel's occasion'. The exemplar for this was the barbecue people enjoy around the back of their car after arriving at a sports event a few hours early. The brand developed specific paraphernalia and specific advertising designed to promote use in this context, which was placed in sports magazines.

Coca-Cola is a best practice exemplar in terms of increasing consumption per capita. Its goal is to bring consumers around the world closer to the consumption rate of American consumers, who drink 118 litres per person per year. Its first key strategic lever is not to use a cost-plus price fixing method, but to target the price of the most popular drink in each country: the price of tea in China, for instance. Because this put a strain on the profitability of local bottlers, the aim is to achieve a quick hike in sales. Profitability is guaranteed to the Coca-Cola Company itself, because it receives the difference between the cost of production of the cola syrup and its resale price (five times as high) to the bottler.

The second key lever is to gain local monopolies. 'Local' in this context means as close as possible to a thirsty person's impulse to drink. Ideally the product should be at an arm's reach, via automatic machines or small refrigerators, everywhere: in hotels, universities, hospitals, and also in bars and cafeterias, for on-premise consumption.

The third lever is to adapt pricing to the consumption situations, so that an identical litre of Coke is sold at very different prices according to when and where it is bought.

Last but not least, specific marketing plans are devoted to specific situations such as lunch and dinner, breakfast and evenings. In many countries consumers drink tap water, bottled water or mineral water. They do this by habit and also for health reasons: consuming too many sugary drinks leads to obesity and other health problems, which are being faced by many Americans at present. Coca-Cola's plan is to modify local customs, starting with children and young people whose habits are yet to be formed. Hence the global alliance with McDonald's, a key social change agent and a chain of which young people are heavy users. Similarly, Coke has another alliance with Bacardi, the world's leading spirit drink. It is significant that advertisements for Bacardi Carta Blanca show a 'Cuba Libre' cocktail, which is made up of rum and Coke.

Building volume by addressing the barriers to consumption

Branding is too obsessed by image, and not obsessed enough by usage. Even though Coca-Cola is held up as the paragon of good brand management, if we are honest we have to acknowledge that it took almost a century for its managers to address perhaps the most important reason for its non-consumption: it is perceived as an unhealthy drink containing too much sugar.

Certainly the Coca-Cola Company has realized the growth of fitness and health as purchase motivations, in a country where baby boomers were ageing. It launched Tab in 1963, just after Diet Royal Crown Cola and just before Diet Pepsi. However, Diet Coke was launched as late as 1983. It soon became the leader in its category, and what the company calls 'the world's second soft drink'. Later would come caffeine-free Coke, caffeine-free Diet Coke, Cherry Coke, Vanilla Coke, Coke and Lemon, Coke Zero and Coke Low Carb. Each of these products was an answer to a consumer problem. Some consumers wanted to drink as much Coke as possible but were prevented from doing so by Coke itself. Some could not have any more sugar, while others could not take caffeine.

Thus, there were huge opportunities for increased consumption per capita among Coke's own clients. They were probably heard, but never listened to. Identifying the barriers of consumption and relieving them was a service not only to clients but also to profitability: aspartame (the sweetening ingredient in Diet Coke) is less costly than sugar.

In the Coke example, the reasons for consumer's limited consumption were known, but the company was deaf. It confused the brand with the product. By claiming 'Coke is it', it had made Coke symbolize one product and only one, period.

In the task of growing volume through higher consumption per capita, identification of what blocks consumption is not always obvious. Research is needed. One way to do it is to segment the clientele according to the strategic matrix shown in Figure 9.1.

This matrix segments customers according to two dimensions, both related to behaviour. The first is the household's share of requirements (among 100 occasions to purchase, how many times is the specific brand bought?), and the second is the household's level of consumption (is it a small, medium or heavy buyer?).

This creates eight cells (not nine because one of them is theoretically possible but empirically empty), and each household can be allocated to one of these cells. Of course this matrix can be used for any type of purchase, or purchaser, including companies in B to B markets. Each cell represents a percentage of the total number of households, and a percentage of the total volume sold of the category and of the brand. These figures are important in themselves. The key segment is the bottom right of the matrix, which represents high-consumption households that allocate the highest part of their requirements to the brand. For instance, in Europe households in this cell consume 70 per cent by volume of Coke Light, but only 48 per cent by volume of Coke. These two figures highlight how a single innovative product can release the barriers that prevent people from consuming more.

The brand manager's task is to move as many people as possible progressively in the direction of this bottom-right cell. This can be done, starting from other cells and going vertically or horizontally. But it is first necessary to understand the very specific circumstances and motivations of consumers in each cell. To increase a specific type of behaviour requires behavioural segmentation, then an in-depth understanding of those in each of these behavioural segments. Who are they? Why don't they consume more? Is it a taste problem, a satiety problem, a price problem, a format problem, a packaging problem, an insufficient variety of line extensions, a distribution problem? It is very rarely an image problem, because

FIGURE 9.1 Increasing volume per capita: strategic matrix

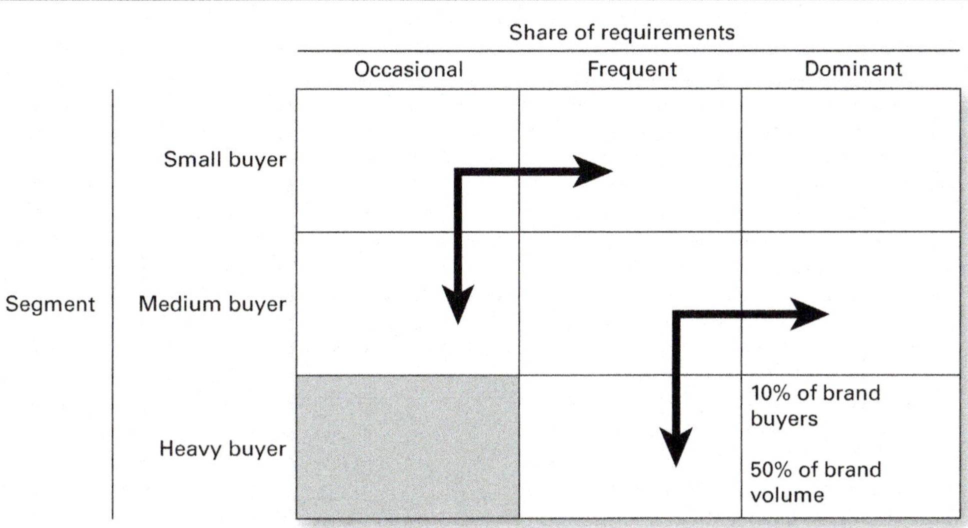

those being considered here are already clients. In modern markets we know from panel data that even for loyal customers, the brand's share of requirements is never 100 per cent. It is sometimes no more than 40 per cent. However, managers lack information on why these consumers choose other brands 60 per cent of the time.

The result is a new marketing mix, often involving specific product improvement, higher experiential benefits, range extensions (formats, taste and so on), designed to target each behavioural segment.

Growth through new uses and situations

Like it or not, every product is consumed within a particular situation. This is one of the four aspects of the positioning diamond (see page 153). Customers are looking for solutions to problems related to highly specific situations. For example, different things are expected of a car depending on whether it is intended primarily for town use, town use plus other short trips, or fairly long trips. The growth of a brand is thus often a matter of tackling new situations of use, knowing that these situations may well include the same customers, as it is possible for one person to consume the same product in several different situations. For many companies, the situation of use is now the one real criterion for segmentation, rather than the characteristics of the users themselves. A product is always consumed in a particular situation – and it is this situation that defines the brand's competitive set. The situation is the brand's true battleground. Each situation is associated not only with a different subset of competitors, but also with expectations, needs, volumes, and growth and profitability rates (Figure 9.2).

It is understandable that brands should seek to grow by breaking into high-growth-rate consumption situations in which their attributes give them a high degree of relevance. Such a movement often requires the launch of a new product or line extension.

This is why Mars launched the mini-Mars bar, a new product designed for consumers of the brand aged over 35 who were reducing their consumption of chocolate bars. This new product also changes Mars' positioning: in terms of its physical size, it is a 'sweet'. The situation into which it now fits is that of 'indulgence', rather than a meal substitute or re-energizer.

In the United States, Captain Morgan is a rum brand with a masculine personality: it is the rum of 'fun and adventure'. To achieve growth, the market was segmented according to the situations of use. Seeking to gain a foothold in the so-called 'partying' segment – a large group of friends indulging in noisy

FIGURE 9.2 Segmenting by situation

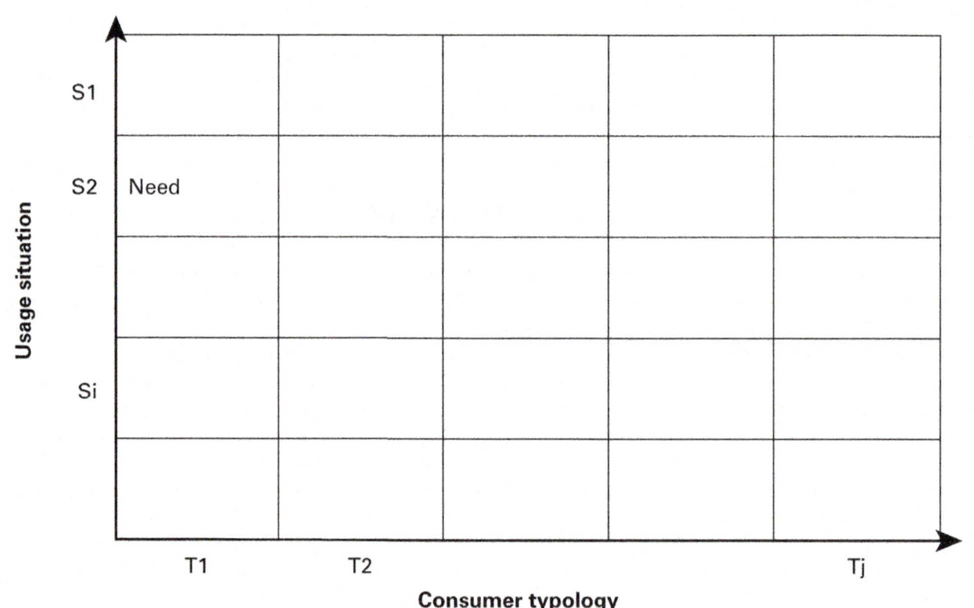

partying, dancing and drinking – the company launched Captain Morgan Spice. It then targeted the so-called 'lively socializing' segment – a smaller group of friends getting together for a cocktail – but the first attempt was a failure. Captain Morgan Coconut Rum suffered too much from the Captain Morgan umbrella name and its highly characteristic values. In the latter use situation, the key is to address a more feminine, elegant, romantic set of values, rather than some sort of macho ritual. This is why the second test product to be launched was Parrot Bay, a product merely endorsed by Captain Morgan.

Growth through trading up

A classic growth strategy is trading up. Customers may wish to receive an upgraded service or product from the brand. Gift packs and 'special series' capitalize on collectors' motivations. Larger formats have a built-in attractiveness too.

Extending the range can also be a way to increase profitability. Thus if it costs €3 to produce a litre of three-star cognac (that is, cognac aged for 3 years), €4.5 for a VSOP (4 to 5 years), €15 for an XO (30–35 years) and €21 for a litre of *Extra Vieux*, the customer trade-up is very profitable, as consumer prices are around the €15, €30, €60 and €150 mark respectively, according to the type of cognac.

Line extensions: necessity and limits

Today, most new product launches are range or line extensions. Shelves are replete with line extensions. As the examples we have given have demonstrated, extending the range is a necessary step in the evolution of a brand through time. Just as living species only survive if they adapt through evolution to their environment and seek to extend their ecological realm, the brand, which historically is designated by a single product (like Coca-Cola or McCain French fries) breaks up into sub-species. The extension of the line or range (we will address the difference between the two concepts later) typically takes on the following shapes:

- Multiplication of formats and sizes (typical in cars but also in soft drinks).
- Multiplication of the variety of tastes and flavours.
- Multiplication of the type of ingredients (for example Coca-Cola with or without sugar, with or without caffeine, types of motors in the Ford Escort).
- Multiplication of generic forms for medicine.
- Multiplication of physical forms such as Ariel in powder, liquid or micro formula.
- Multiplication of product add-ons under the same name, corresponding to a same consumer need in what is called line extension. Thus, Basic Homme by Vichy comprises a line of toiletries including shaving foam, soothing and energizing balm, deodorant, and shower gel.
- Multiplication of versions having a specific application. For example, the Johnson company transformed its successful spray polish, Pliz, which was a mono-product brand for a long time, into a range called Pliz 'Classic', which offered products specialized for the type of surface. In doing so it also seized the opportunity to reduce its brand portfolio. Favor, a weak brand, became Pliz with beeswax especially for wood. Shampoo brands multiply endlessly, with varieties suited to different types of hair and scalp condition.

Line or range extension must be distinguished from brand extension, which is a real diversification towards different product categories and different clients. It is a highly sensitive and strategic choice that will be addressed in a separate chapter. Why does Yamaha brand both motorcycles and pianos? Line and range extensions represent 85 per cent of new product launches in consumer goods. It is the most common form of innovation in these markets.

Range extension naturally follows the logic of marketing and of even finer segmentation to better adapt the offer to the specific needs of consumers, needs that never stop evolving. At its beginning, we may recall, each brand was a unique product, in both meanings of the word: it is different and there is only one form of it. This was, for example, the case with the famous Ford: everyone could have it in the colour of their choice, as long as it was black. It was the same with the Coca-Cola and the Orangina bottle. With time, the brand becomes less narrow-minded, and acknowledging differentiated expectations, decides to respond to them. As the

American advertising for Burger King, the competitor of McDonald's, says, 'Have it your way' (whatever way you like it, with or without sauce, onions, etc). Again, taking the example of Coca-Cola, while retaining its identity (the dark colour, cola taste, and other physical and symbolic attributes of the brand), the company was able to extend the power of attraction of its brand by allowing people who up until then were reluctant to try the product to indulge in Coke. The multiplication of versions (with or without sugar, with or without caffeine) increased the number of potential consumers. We therefore see that range extension can reinforce the brand by widening its market and its customer base. A variety of formats has the same effect. In the world of soft drinks, the launch of a new format may be considered the same as launching a new soft drink. Indeed, each new format allows the brand to enter a new usage mode.

In so doing, the brand proves itself to be full of energy and sensitivity. It recognizes the different expectations of the public and responds to them. It follows the evolution of consumers and changes with them. Club Med was thus able to widen its offer beyond the simple Robinson Crusoe lodge to keep or attract families, then people in their forties seeking more comfort, and finally older people, children of the baby boom. The range extension is a token of the brand's attentive and caring character. Extending the brand range thus makes the brand interesting and friendly and maintains through these successive mini-launchings a strong visibility. From this point of view, instead of trying to force New Coke on Americans and make them give up the original flavour, the Coca-Cola Company would have done better to have launched the New Coke as an extension alongside the classic Coke!

Range extension is a way of revitalizing many failing brands, by making sure they move closely to meet the expectations of today's customers. What saved Campari was the launching onto the market of a 'flanker' product: Campari Soda. Martini would have fallen by the wayside if it had not been for the launching of Martini Bianco, more in touch with the new modes of alcohol consumption. Smirnoff made a step towards customers who were not used to the strong taste of vodka by launching Smirnoff Mule and Smirnoff Ice in small individual bottles.

These motives may be worthy of praise, but the current proliferation of range extensions to be observed in all consumer goods markets results from frantic competition and from the new psychology of organizations.

In these markets there is a strong relationship between market share and the number of facings, ie the share of shelf space taken up. This is not surprising: the customer involvement in these products is average if not low and the number of impulse buyers (when the choice of brand is done on-site) never stops growing. It is, therefore, in the brand manager's interest to take up the most shelf space possible because it will attract even more attention from the customer, especially if a shelf is not extendible and competitors get pushed out. In many markets, demand is no longer growing and DOBs also occupy a share of the shelf, so the brand manager tries to position his product as 'captain of the category' by presenting a unique offer and so dominating the shelf reserved for national brands.

Distributors have an ambivalent attitude towards range extensions. On the one hand they oppose what is now considered hypersegmentation, the proliferation of range extension. But as each brand tends to offer the same extensions, this creates bottlenecks because of the obsession each brand has to gain access to maximum distribution. This fight for ever-reducing shelf space strengthens the power of distributors and puts them in a position to ask for increasing amounts of money as a listing fee (Chinardet, 1994).

The problem is that the turnover of extensions, because of their novelty and their price premium, is often lower than that of the original product. When the distributor realizes this (if he ever does), he withdraws the extension and awaits the offer of other brands, along with any kind of listing fee that might come with it.

Criticized by, but at the same time popular with distributors, range extensions are appreciated by product and brand managers. First of all, the amount of time needed for development is shorter than that needed for the launching of a new brand. The costs are less than those for the launching of a new brand (they are estimated to be one-fifth), and sales forecasts are more reliable. In the short term at least, it seems an almost automatic way of gaining market share and thus creating observable results that can be attributed to the actions of the manager in a relatively short time span. This counts for quick promotion within the company, or on another brand in another country. Few managers are willing to take the risk of launching a new brand, but would rather extend the range.

The proliferation of product extensions produces insidious negative effects that are not immediately measurable or measured. First of all, because of small production runs and the increased complexity of production, logistics and management, extensions are more expensive to produce, the cost of which puts up the higher wholesale and retail price. According to Quelch and Kenny (1994), compared to an index of 100 for the cost of production of a mono-product, the corresponding production cost index of differentiated products in a range is, for example, 145 in the car industry, 135 for hosiery and 132 in the food industry. Moreover, in companies which do not take into account direct costs (eg raw materials, advertising), many costs are considered as common to the entire range and are allocated to different products within it according to sales. The best-sellers therefore attract more of the costs than range extensions, which makes the profitability of the latter rather illusory.

Second, non-controlled extension weakens the range logic. The first to find problems with this are the salespeople: the salesforce of Ariel or Dash, used to promoting the brand against Skip, had to undertake within a few months a complete cultural revolution. They had to promote Ariel in powder, in liquid and in micro formula formats all together and without ever explaining that one was superior to the other, or what advantages one format has in comparison to the others. The more extensions multiply, the more the specific positioning of each extension becomes subtle. This is accentuated by the fact that extensions are added without withdrawing the existing versions. Organizations always have a good reason for not cancelling this or that version. The thought of losing the odd customer here and there rules the notion out. This thinking overlooks the fact that product withdrawals should also be managed to gently propel customers towards newer, better versions.

The range logic is also lost on the shelf: indeed, the distributor is reluctant to take on the whole range. He will shop around and take only part of a range, which undermines the consistency of the range on the shelf.

Finally, brand loyalty might be undermined by a proliferation of extensions. The hyper-segmentation of shampoos according to new hair needs, leads the customer to take into account more needs in his/her choosing process. The brand is but a feature in an ever longer list of criteria. This result was verified empirically by Rubinson (1992).

In reaction to the proliferation of extensions, Procter & Gamble eliminated within 18 months 15 to 25 per cent of the product extensions that were not achieving a sufficient turnover. In the sector for cleaning products, the growth of new multi-usage products (all-in-one) is on the same principle of simplification. Economies of scale apply all the more since the product is designed for the worldwide market. The extreme strategy of counter-segmentation is applied by hard-discounters: there is absolutely no choice and products are generally only available in a single version with no variety. Thus, there will only be one type of diaper, whatever the weight or the gender of the baby, in contrast to Phases (boy or girl) by Pampers. On the other hand, because of this it will be 40 per cent cheaper than, say, Pampers.

Quelch and Kenny (1994) recommend four immediate actions for better management of range extensions:

- Improve the cost accounting system to be able to catch the additional costs incurred by a new variety all along the value chain. This enables the real profitability of each one to be assessed.
- Allocate resources more to high-margin products than to extensions that only appeal to occasional buyers.
- Make sure that each salesperson can sum up in a few words the role of each product within the range.
- Implement a new philosophy where product withdrawals are not only accepted but encouraged. Some companies only launch an extension after having cancelled another with a low turnover. This withdrawal does not have to be brutal, but can be done gradually so that clients turn to other products within the range.

Growth through innovation

When Moulinex was asked why its results were bad, executives answered that the company had only offered 10 per cent innovation when the average in the industry was 26 per cent.

Innovation, source of growth and competitiveness, does not come easy. Here too, there are no miracles.

The firms that innovate most, such as KAO, l'Oréal and Ajinomoto, devote on average 3.4 per cent of their sales to research and development. Is there a lesson here for the food companies competing against DOBs and price leaders? The giants in the food industry spend much less in comparison on R&D: Unilever devotes 2.1 per cent of its sales to R&D, Nestlé 1.7 per cent, and Procter & Gamble 2.5 per cent.

Companies innovate at both ends of the price spectrum: trading up in mature markets where private labels dominate, trading down in emerging countries through reverse engineering, and what is called Bottom of Pyramid innovation (Indovation, chinovation).

Incremental innovations

Innovation does not have to mean a technological breakthrough. Gillette is an extreme case: the Sensor required 10 years in research and led to 22 patents, the Sensor Excel 5 years and 29 patents, Sensor Plus Pour Elle 5 years and 25 patents. Many innovations can be linked to the service brought by the brand, in its packaging for example.

The head start that Evian took over Contrex and Vittel lies mostly in the micro-services which it was able to provide the customer with first. This service, although not spectacular or linked to advertising, allowed a gain of 0.5 per cent in market share, which, given the volumes involved, is gigantic. Evian was thus the first to withdraw the metal capsule which sealed the bottle, which the consumer ripped off more often than not. That year, its sales jumped by 12 per cent when the market only grew by 7 per cent. The brand was also the first to introduce the handle which made the six-bottle pack carryable, the compactable bottle and so on.

On low-involvement products, incremental innovations are much appreciated by the consumer, the distributors amplifying the move if competitors do not react quickly – distributors prefer novelty.

In order to de-commoditize milk and to curb the surge of hard discounters, the milk brand Candia multiplied its innovations, giving each its own specific name to accentuate the differentiation and allow for strong advertising support: Viva (milk with vitamins), Grand Milk (enriched milk), Grand Life Growing (for children), Future Mother (ie for pregnant women). These 'daughter brands' of Candia stemmed the advance of hard-discount products and enabled distributors to work with high-margin and high-turnover products. These were not major technological innovations, but were add-ons of vitamins, minerals and so on to respond to the expectations of demanding customers. In doing so, Candia made the whole category advance forward. Actually, nowadays Viva is rarely bought for its vitamins but for the brand and for what it stands for (a dynamic lifestyle, full of life, of youth). This product, which at first was advanced or premium, becomes the basis of milk, the reference. Candia was thus instrumental in enhancing the reference level for milk. The premium becomes a standard.

What are the factors of success for innovations today?

Innovations are brand oxygen. They re-create leadership, focus the market on value not on price, and give a goal to the organization, reminding it that brands are about progress once they are on the market. Where would Apple be without the iPod, iTunes, the iPhone and the iPad? Today innovations are more than ever necessary: the brand needs them, the consumer wants them and the trade requires them. A brand's engagement is only proven by its actions, first and foremost the relentless flow of innovations and their capacity to delight the consumer, or the customer in B2B. Since clients are supposed to be the focus of brands, it could not be otherwise. In a world where change is the norm, new consumer insights emerge regularly: there is ample room for innovation. Most of them are incremental, but this attention to details, if judged significant, is a proof of an authentic consumer concern.

Consumers are shoppers too. When they visit a store – online or bricks and mortar – they take the opportunity to see what is on promotion and to try new products if they see any. Visiting a store can also bring fun, if not pleasure: as a result, in saturated shelves that cannot be extended, store managers want variation, liveliness and profitability. They are prone to substitute a new item for an old one with ailing sales trends or not delivering enough profit. Innovations bring life to the shelf, as well as added margins (as part of launch trade support, even if sales are low). Since today in modern and well-managed hypermarkets one SKU replaces another, it is essential to understand the conditions of success for innovations. Both the trade and the brands need innovations to build the growth of their categories. Sales promotion does not do it: it is a quick fix. Often consumers try an innovation in addition to their regular product.

A major factor should now be taken into account: the after-effects of the recession. Consumers have reduced their impulse purchases; stock-up promotions ('Buy four: it's cheaper') work less well, for consumers feel they do not need so many products. Consumers also use purchasing lists more, and go straight to the shelf for the product they are looking for. Since the store is the first source of information about innovations, if browsing diminishes this constitutes a major challenge for future innovations. Most people will not see them.

Are innovations visible enough?

Recent wide-scale European research (SymphonyIRI, 2011) reports that 73 per cent of consumers say they did not see innovations on a shelf after they had visited it. This should certainly lead to heightened merchandizing attention. This worrying figure may also be due to the nature of the innovation itself. For consumers, any new SKU is not an innovation, meaning 'a meaningful innovation'. It is true that the first result of benchmarking is imitation or a search for parity: brands launch new SKUs just to match a competitor's idea. This is no news for the consumers. Interestingly, because they do not communicate on television or elsewhere, private labels tend to launch down-to-earth innovations very much based on simple consumer insights, like a more practical shampoo packaging based on at-home observations (people put their shampoo bottle upside down in the shower).

Learning from innovation champions

Since in modern hypermarkets introducing a new SKU means deleting one, a key performance indicator of any new product is its sales performance versus that of the previous product or, to make it easier, versus the average sales of the SKUs on the shelf. What are the characteristics of the champions, those new SKUs with the highest performance ratio?

SymphonyIRI's European study reveals interesting insights:

- Champions are champions from the start. Indeed the fate of most new launches is predictable from the start. This may be a chicken-and-egg effect for the weaker ones, the trade being quick to stop them in any case, once their results are known. Today weak innovations have no second chance in hypermarkets.
- Interestingly the champions are also the most expensive ones. Success is measured by the ratio of the innovation sales to the category's average sales. Taking as index the ratio of the price of the new SKU versus the average price of the category, it is striking that champions are above 130, whereas failures are around 110 (see Table 9.1). This could look like a contradiction to consumers' price sensitivity, especially after the recession, but it is not. Why are some innovations priced high? Because they are sure that they create value to the consumers. Pricing an innovation at a low price is an implicit statement that it is not really a meaningful innovation. The consumers agree with this by not buying.
- The champions invest significantly more in shelf visibility (new packaging, out-of-shelf promotional material). Delocalization out of the regular shelf is also a major lever of visibility.
- Finally, on-pack information about the benefits are fundamental to overcome the

TABLE 9.1 Price index of successful FMCG innovations

Superstars	133
Stars	124
Just pass	118
Fail	110

SOURCE Adapted from SymphonyIRI (2011)

fear of buying an unnecessary product if there are no longer in-store trials.

New lines and old lines: the virtuous circle

There is a virtuous circle between new lines and old lines. Innovations bring new blood (new consumers, new relevance, new peripheral values, etc) to the brand. This sustains its long-term relevance. Old product lines bring profits and finance new product launches. However, they must be realigned with the new brand positioning, which directly feeds R&D and the exploration of potential innovations. For instance, Danone means 'active health'. Former product lines talked about the cereals or calcium they contained. As to the new products, they are all advanced innovations that are good for health (Activia for digestive comfort, Actimel with probiotics, Essensis for the skin and Danacol for cholesterol).

Beyond the halo of modernity effect, some extensions can also directly affect the sales of old products. Smirnoff Ice boosted the sales of the standard bottle of Smirnoff. iPod and iPhone brought new consumers to the Apple stores and made that brand more known, understood and desirable to many PC addicts: this created a positive spillover feedback effect on iMacs.

This virtuous circle is depicted in Figure 9.3.

What finances innovation: old lines. What gives a halo of modernity to old lines: innovations. This is why it is a mistake to allocate advertising budgets according to the sales weight of each one. Some lines should receive no advertising at all (if they aim at price-sensitive people). Some lines should receive strong advertising support, for they build the brand credentials in a new technology or area.

A typical example is Gillette, now with Procter & Gamble. The disposable razor is no longer backed by media advertising, only by point-of-purchase promotion (POP). In any case, 50 per cent of its volume comes from the twin-blade model, whereas the latest Gillette innovation has five blades. Disposable clients focus on the replacement costs. They just want a low-cost solution: two blades are enough. That is why launching a disposable Mach 3 was not a good decision.

The virtuous cycle of innovation

What managerial conclusions can be drawn from the above points? The brand can be managed in two ways.

FIGURE 9.3 Managing brand sustainability: the virtuous circle

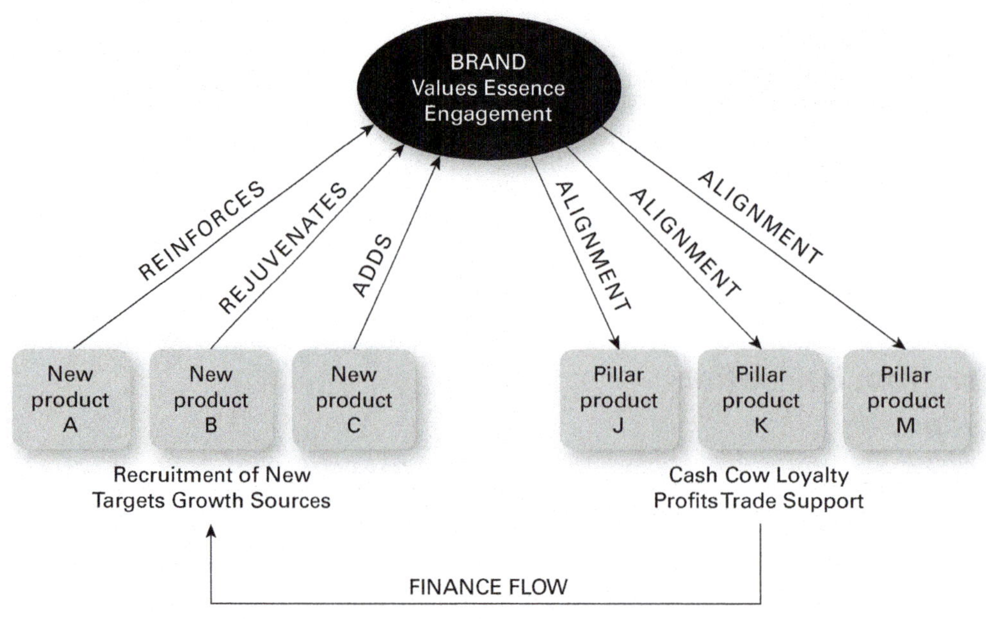

Brand management is thus a balance between preservation, renewal, extension and growth of the prototype on the one hand, and on the other the creation of new products and services to capture new circumstances of use and new customers, and to open new segments. The first part maintains, feeds and consolidates the brand base, while the second opens bridgeheads into the future, carrying what will tomorrow become the brand's new prototype.

The effect of innovation on sales

Innovation does not merely work for itself: it benefits the brand in terms of both image and sales. It is what is known as the spillover effect, that is, the effect that advertising for one product has on the sales of another product in the brand. This effect, which is well known to companies, has been confirmed by marketing research (Balachander and Ghose, 2003). Examining the sales of Dannon in the United States, the authors observed that advertising for a new Dannon product also had an effect on the sales of the prototype flagship product – the existing product most commonly identified with Dannon (which they wrongly name the 'parent brand' – strictly speaking, this term should refer only to Dannon itself, and not its products). Most importantly, this effect is three times greater than the effect that the prototype's own advertising has on its own sales (a 14.4 per cent rise in the probability of choosing the flagship product following advertising for the new product, compared with a mere 5.7 per cent following its own advertising).

There are several possible explanations for this phenomenon. The first – advanced by the authors themselves – is derived by reasoning. Since the prototype/flagship is strongly associated with the brand in consumers' memories, the stimulation of the brand name through the promotion of a new product produces a feedback effect which activates a path leading to the cornerstone product, the prototype. We believe there is another explanation. Every new product draws in new consumers distinct from those already consuming the established products. In so doing, they re-evaluate their overall perception of the brand, and are thus more tempted to explore its other hitherto ignored or undervalued products, and the brand's flagship best-seller in particular. Innovation reframes the brand's image and feeds it with the new tangible and intangible attributes brought by this innovation.

Disrupting markets through value innovation: blue ocean

It is well known that markets grow by the reduction of unit prices: this is how the computer became a household necessity, mobile phone sales skyrocketed, and so on. In mature markets, the goal is no longer to increase the market in volume, but to increase it in value. There are obvious limits to usage for most products: nobody wants to shampoo their hair four times a day. The main question is really how to make the consumer willing to pay more. This added value will then be shared between the distributor and the producer.

The goal of all brands is to look for value innovations, an unprecedented bundle of attributes that shifts the preference function of consumers (Chan and Mauborne, 2000). 'Value innovation' consists in sacrificing some attributes (by suppressing them) in order to raise valued attributes to an unprecedented level. The best example is the Accor Formule 1 hotel chain created in 1985. This became the fastest-growing hotel chain in Europe. How did Accor, Europe's leading hotel group, achieve this?

The first point was in the identification of an 'oilfield', a source of growth nobody had thought of before, or that previously could not have been served profitably. Many people never go to a hotel, because they cannot afford it. This is true of students, young couples, families, workers – a huge potential market. When they travel they tend to stay with friends or family. This matches their price expectations (it is free for them) but creates a number of disutilities (lack of privacy, obligation to eat and spend time with their hosts, lack of freedom and so on). An analysis of the value curve of this very competition (staying at friends or parents) reveals what bundle of attributes will move consumer preferences. The solution is still to be very accessible pricewise but to offer all the guarantees of a clean, safe, quiet, practical hotel.

How to do that profitably? How to base the brand on a valid economic equation? Only by sacrificing an attribute. The disruptive nature of the Formule 1 innovation was in suppressing some of the features that all previous players in the hotel market had held to be essential, such as ensuite bathrooms. In Formule 1 there were no baths or toilets in the individual rooms, but collective ones at the end of each hall, auto-washed and disinfected after each usage.

Formule 1 succeeded in tapping a hidden need, and also adopted a successful development strategy. This strategy consisted in quickly reaching the critical size (250 units) to be able to cover the country (that is, initially, France). Customer approval was transformed into loyal behaviour (which was only possible if they found a Formule 1 hotel wherever they went), and it was also possible for the brand to access television advertising, hence reaching the status of top-of-mind brand leader for the whole hotel category.

This brand did not meet the same success in all countries. In the UK for instance, land costs and the difficulty of finding good hotel locations prevented the fast development of the chain, and hence access to the critical size, essential in the brand and business-building model.

The breakthrough brought about by Virgin Atlantic did not reside in its price or in the logo, but in the ability to create a different in-flight experience through a number of innovations that have now been widely copied. In addition Virgin offered business-class travellers a full service before and after the flight itself, adding new benefits to the Virgin experience. They could be picked up at their offices by chauffeurs in Volvo cars and driven to the airport. In addition they were offered access to a shower room after landing, to get ready for their business day. This not only attracted new clients but stimulated a higher frequency rate among all clients.

Another case illustrates the concept of value innovation: ballpoint pens. What made the success of Bic, which launched the ballpoint pen on a commercial scale in 1950? Mastering quality at a low price. The prototype is the Cristal model, the all-time best-seller. It encapsulated the values of the brand: reliability, an excellent quality/price ratio and durability. Competition certainly came from lower-priced pens, with a lower quality, sold by discount chains or as distributors' brands. However the real challenge for Bic came from Pilot and Sanford, which introduced a lot of value innovations (ink gel, ink points, ink balls, more colours, better grip, new more sensual materials) at around five times the price of a Bic. When they encountered these products, which delivered experiential added values, closing the gap with classical ink pens, and provided a permanent thrill by frequently introducing new collections – as did Swatch, Gap and Zara in different fields – consumers were seduced. To survive, Bic had to change part of its business model, introducing variety to match what now emerged as very fragmented needs, thanks to an outsourcing policy, which had until then been forbidden within the Bic Group. Innovations now represent 25 per cent of each year's sales.

Do blue ocean innovations really work?

One of the recent real breakthrough concepts in management is that of blue ocean. Instead of trying to invent a product superior to the competition, innovators should aim at creating new markets

FIGURE 9.4 A disruptive value curve: Formule 1 hotels

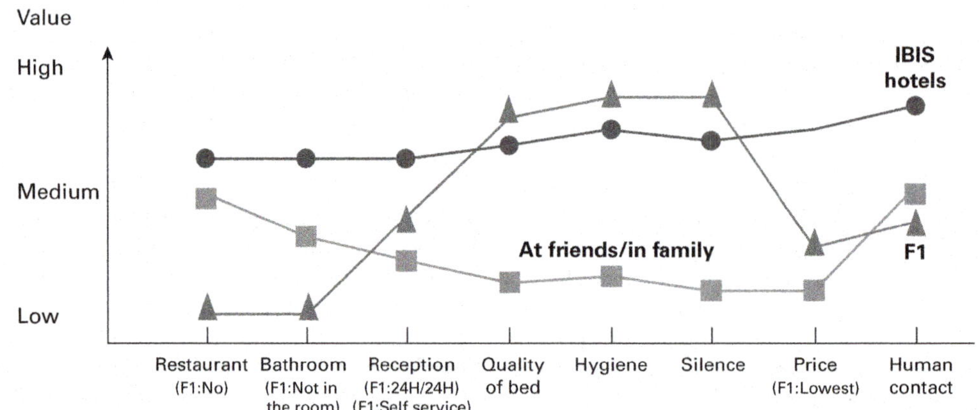

where there is no competition. For the authors of this concept (Kim and Mauborgne, 1998), most innovations are driven by the desire to do better than the competition, a process that leads to a red ocean, a bloody and fierce endless competition. Disruption is another concept of our times (Dru, 19XX), which also fosters the need to think differently. Indeed blue ocean innovations are disruptive innovations. They are also called value innovations, for they rely on a very different set of values from those of the vast majority of existing competitors within a market. They are not just providing more from the same range of values; they change the set of values.

Blue ocean has become a methodology to follow in order to think differently from the majority of one's competitors and invent 'value innovations'. The first step is to list all the common beliefs held by the profession within a market and to be able to challenge all of them. Another key tool is that of looking at products and services as a 'value curve' and boldly deciding to suppress one of these values in order to provide a breakthrough on another value. The underlying idea is that so far, in a red ocean, the value curves of all the competitors are parallel: some are above (providing overall more utility to clients), and others are below. The guiding principle of a blue ocean methodology is to break this parallel pattern and come out, say, with a Himalayan shape for the value curve, with deep valleys (suppressing a value), in order to create incredible peaks on other values.

The typical examples are well known:

- EasyJet is an airline that suppressed the consumer services typically offered by airline companies either on board or on the ground in order to offer incredible prices and create a low-cost air travel market in Europe.
- James Dyson questioned a taboo of the industry: the bag in the vacuum cleaner. He offered his innovations to all the leading brands (Hoover, Philips, etc) and was rejected, so he decided to launch his innovation under his own name: Dyson. Without bags that get full of dirt, vacuum cleaners have a constant and more efficient power.
- Nespresso turned its back on the cut-throat price competition (against private labels) and decided instead to offer the most expensive espresso on earth with an automatic espresso machine and a service for supplying the valuable capsules.
- Cirque du Soleil does not show animals, but stands halfway between typical Broadway musical comedies and circus (with acrobats, etc).

Like all theories that rely on *ex post facto* well-selected examples, blue ocean strategy seems to be a compelling argument, a sure promise of success and wealth, but what about the blue ocean innovations that failed? The authors do not talk about them. In addition, it is a false idea that incremental innovation is bad. Not only is it necessary to defend the pillars of brand sales by sustaining their value (the pillars are those 20 per cent of products that make up 70 per cent of the brand's business), but incremental innovation can indeed help create new brands. Lexus, the premium brand of the Toyota Group, was created by benchmarking the Mercedes E Class and taking as its simple objective the provision of better performance than the E Class on each of its attributes. Thus Lexus was launched as a value-for-money follower that, 'for less money, gives you more than a Mercedes E Class'. Lexus is the opposite of a value innovation: it used benchmarking to do better. However, through lack of a prestige image and by strategy, Toyota decided to price the Lexus new line just below the Mercedes E Class to accelerate its diffusion in the US market.

Like all *ex post facto* theories, blue ocean is an incomplete theory, based on the selection of successful cases. However, innovation history is full of blue ocean innovations that failed.

A good example is easyJet. Bolstered by his success, Stelios Haji-Ioannou decided to expand his winning low-cost business model to a vast number of categories, thus disrupting the market and traditional competition. All these extensions failed. For instance, a natural extension was car rental. On paper it seemed fine, but in reality, unlike the pilot and steward who are paid to clean up the cabin in 10 minutes, car renters are less disciplined and leave cars needing more washing and cleaning, thus reducing the ability of a single car to be immediately rented again.

Another example is Bic. Very few companies have thrived almost exclusively through breakthrough innovations. Bic is one of them. Bic, known for its ballpoint pens, subsequently became number one for disposable lighters. Then it decided to commit a sacrilege, and attacked Gillette with a value innovation, the first disposable razor. It would no longer be necessary to buy blades. They would come with the razor. Bic created the disposable razor market when Gillette did not, aiming at youth. Later Bic decided to commit another sacrilege, and launched a fragrance with no glamour or prestige image, just a great, natural, highest-quality product. The target was again youth. The whole industry held that, to succeed, a fragrance needed a very nice bottle and a glamour image. Bic boldly questioned this assumption, just as the blue ocean methodology suggests. Would a significant part of the youth market think and act differently to their parents? By suppressing the traditional costly bottle and glamorous marketing launch, Bic was able to have a very high-quality fragrance, with costly, fully natural ingredients, and to price this fragrance at a very competitive price, far less than competitors' prices. This fragrance was inserted in a pack that looked like the disposable lighter. Unfortunately it was a failure: sales did not match the break-even objectives. This showed that for purchases of fragrances, unlike other product categories, young people are quite conservative and act like their parents.

Recently Bic launched another value innovation: a mobile phone. Whereas mobiles in general keep on adding applications and features, the Bic phone was a reverse innovation: simplifying the product as much as possible to only two functions (voice and SMS), with no internet and no camera. The mobile was not costly. The target was tourists temporarily needing a local phone, people aged over 35 who lacked money and hence wanted to pay as little as possible, very young children who needed to be in constant contact with their parents, and elderly people needing the utmost simplicity. This was not a success either, despite the strength of Orange, the licensed company for creation, production, distribution, and sales of the prepaid cards.

What lessons can be drawn from these blue ocean failures?

First, value innovation is not the only way to create new brands. The success of the Samsung Galaxy is not based on value innovation. It will soon be the world's number one mobile phone brand, ahead of Nokia and way ahead of Apple. Lexus is a success based on a typical Asian strategy: imitate the master as closely as possible and then bypass it.

The second lesson is that value innovation, suppressing a major attribute held as a must-have by all competitors, is no guarantee of success if there is not sufficient demand for this innovation, or at least not a profitable one.

In short, value innovation can lead to no ocean at all.

Increasing experiential benefits

Anyone who has visited a Nike Town cannot forget this experience. The same holds true for the House of Ralph Lauren, for Ikea and for Virgin Megastores. These places embody all the brand values in 3D, and in addition they deliver a memorable sensual experience. In developed countries, people have met their needs, and are now looking for exciting experiences. This creates a new source of growth: increasing experiential benefits.

The concept of experiential marketing has not emerged by chance over the past few years (Schmitt, 1999; Hirschmann and Holbrook, 1982; Firat and Dholakia, 1998). Consumers in developed countries and mature markets try to build thrills into their existence. This is why, for instance, they love to patronize thematic restaurants and amusement parks, and want to discover New World wines. Through these consumptions, their minds and senses are stimulated. They live differently through the product.

Swatch has based its success on the delivery of repeated experiential benefits to each of its clients, through collections, design and a general sense of fun. Garnier, one of the mass-market global brands of the l'Oréal Group, has defined itself as a full experiential brand: this is apparent in everything from the touch and colour of the packagings to the internet site and the importance of street marketing in its brand building (with the creation of Garnier-owned buses, travelling around the country in Germany as well as in Shanghai). This also means that everything needs to change faster, to maintain the thrill: product lines, advertising, promotions, the contents of internet sites and so on.

In this respect, service acquires more and more importance, even for product brands. This can take the form of making the brand 'mediactive', a mode which favours communications among members of a virtual community through consumer magazines, forums and chatlines, FAQs and other communication devices. It can also be achieved simply through levels of service, such as the call centres created by Pampers and by Nestlé Infant Food to answer specific questions about babies.

Managing fragmented markets

Customization is also a response to the slackening of desire among those who have become blasé. In the Maslow chain, individualization comes high in the ladder. Everything that creates an ability to tie the brand and its products to the singularity of each client is to be looked for, within an economically favourable equation, of course. One quarter of the revenues of Harley-Davidson comes from accessories. They enhance the experience of both bike riders and non-riders, and meet these needs for individualization.

Customization has its limits in terms of cost and profitability. Segmentation can circumvent them. It is very interesting to analyse the Ralph Lauren range, which takes seriously the issue of market fragmentation (Table 9.2). Actually there are no fewer than 10 ranges within the Ralph Lauren empire, from the very expensive Purple Collection (with jackets price ranging from US $2,000) to the more inexpensive Polo Jeans and RLX. Each label provides a full range of products and line extensions. This policy has a number of advantages:

- It creates a built-in coherence that distributors might not match without guidance.
- It allows the distributor to allocate specific labels to specific stores and locations.
- It matches the inclination of consumers to feel different in the morning, afternoon and evening, while continuing to wear Ralph Lauren clothes.
- It increases the perception of rarity, of exclusivity, a feat for a brand that in fact is more and more diffused.

The car industry has also discovered the virtues of range fragmentation. It is not certain that consumers

TABLE 9.2 Addressing market fragmentation

Ralph Lauren's situation brands, 'portraying core lifestyle themes'				
Ralph Lauren Collection (Purple Label, etc)				
Polo Ralph Lauren	Polo Sport Ralph Lauren	Rlx Polo Sport	Polo Golf Ralph Lauren	Polo Jeans Ralph Lauren
Ralph Lauren	Ralph Lauren Collection	Ralph Lauren Sport		
Ralph, Ralph Lauren				
Lauren, Ralph Lauren				
Chaps, Ralph Lauren				
Ralph Lauren, Children's Wear				
Ralph Lauren, Home				

would want a fully personalized car. The number of alternatives available would make the choice a chore. However, they do expect to be able to choose between prepackaged variations on the same model. This is why modern car-makers increase the level of involvement of consumers with their cars by planning in advance the line extensions that target specific highly conspicuous targets, or valued lifestyles. The sales of a new model are in fact made by the addition of segmented offers.

Mercedes decided to address the fragmentation of needs. It sold 700,000 cars in 1995, and has now reached 1,250,000 a year. Meanwhile the number of models has made a leap, reaching 23 in 2005.

Nike's success can be explained the same way (Bedbury, 2002). It offers an increasingly broad array of niche products (a sign of mass customization), thereby creating relationships with subsets of the market, with fragments. Being more involved with a product tailored to them, customers are ready to pay more. Nike now produces a number of collections even for a single sport. Also to maintain the thrill, product life cycles have been shortened from one year to three months.

As a whole, all these examples demonstrate the need for greater innovation in all aspects of the marketing mix, from product, channel and store to communication to match the fragmentation of demand.

From technological to cultural innovations

Two main factors drive the world: technology and social change. One tends to think only in terms of technology, but to become meaningful brands must capture the deep social changes that affect the ideals and aspirations of consumers, or rather people. Traditional marketing theory talks only about consumers and now shoppers. People do not exist in the classical marketing language, nor persons.

However, 'consumer' is a myopic word. People exist before they consume. This is what Nike understood so well. The brand is known to be one of the most innovative in its field, but is this the key of its success? As Cameron and Holt (2011) summarized, Nike was a cultural innovator. It captured the ideals and anxieties of the post-Vietnam War US social crisis. Nike addressed the US people and said: now energize yourself; don't get defeated in your mind and body (hence the slogan 'Just do it!'). This is also why Nike partners so much with the ghetto subculture: those who are left behind by capitalism.

Why are social networks so popular? Because of the evolution of society, communitarianism, the increasing difficulty of talking to strangers on the street, the loss of social ties, etc. Consumer psychology reduces people to machines, making trade-offs between costs and benefits. Brands should get a sociological acumen and analyse the deep social changes that structure people's aspirations. All brands should now evaluate the social impact of the 2011 Japan earthquake, tsunami and nuclear disaster.

Brands should be technologically up to date but also cultural champions.

Growth through cross-selling between brands

Is the brand perspective sometimes detrimental to growth? This provocative question has been raised by Accor Hotels, the number one European hotelier. Even though it had built a portfolio of strong brands, it wondered if, for growth purposes, it was not time to adopt a consumer orientation. With its complete portfolio of zero to four-star brands (Formule 1, Motel 6, Etap, Ibis, Novotel, Mercure, Sofitel and Suit'hotel), it realized that single-chain loyalty cards were causing its clients to defect to the competition.

This is because a businessperson travelling during the week does so at the company's expense, and his or her family cannot afford to stay in the same hotel at weekends. Although they were all Accor hotels, a loyalty card for Novotel (the three-star brand) conferred no benefits at Etap (one-star) or Formule 1 hotels. Seeing things from the client's point of view led to the planning not of product brands, but of a horizontal brand – Accor Hotels itself – as a loyalty vehicle. This allowed the client to be kept within the whole portfolio of the group's brands.

Seeing that Nivea enjoyed high levels of loyalty because of its umbrella branding architecture (all is Nivea), l'Oréal Paris decided to become a truly horizontal brand with a greater importance than that of its daughter brands (such as Elsève, Plénitude and Elnett). The aim of this mother brand was to increase cross-loyalty between the daughter brands.

Analysing its client database, Unilever calculated that 78 per cent of the most valuable consumers (MVCs) of Skip were also MVCs for Unilever products in general. This was also true of 76 per cent of MVCs for Sun, 69 per cent for Dove, 66 per cent for Lipton Ice Tea, and 63 per cent for Signal. Ultimately, this posed the question of a horizontal Unilever brand – a tricky issue in an organization founded on a variety of unrelated product brands, in a 'house of brands' architecture.

However, in the short term there was an opportunity to be exploited: for example, to tell Skip's MVCs about the group's other products. Hence the creation of group CRM, not only for this reason, but also as a way of shouldering fixed costs collectively.

The key questions with regard to CRM are those concerning the single-brand or multi-brand approach. Consumer magazines such as *Danoe* and *Living Magazine* (Unilever), and their Procter & Gamble equivalents, illustrate the multi-brand approach and customize each mailshot to a great extent, deciding what coupons and new products will be offered to which customers. These magazines place a strong emphasis on cross-selling. This does not stop each brand from conducting its own relationship-based programme, for example, by organizing conferences on issues relevant to customers, either face-to-face or through forums on the brand's website. Other channels also exist to enable such contact: for example, call centres providing real consumer services.

Growth through internationalization

If domestic markets are mature, brands should look for better markets. This is why all brands look eastward, towards the Eastern European countries and Russia, and towards India and China. The two-digit growth markets of tomorrow are there. We address these issues in our chapter on globalization. Brazil and Argentina should also qualify as growth markets once the Argentinian financial crisis is over. Finally, brands meeting sophisticated needs can find in North America the wanted source of growth.

For instance, Evian water has since 1991 faced an unprecedented challenge in its home country: the emergence of low-cost bottled water, sold at a third of Evian's price. These waters are not 'mineral water', with a guaranteed proportion of mineral ingredients in them, but 'spring water'. (Another category is 'purified water', such as Coke's now famous Dasani, Dannon water and Nestlé Aquarel. These brands are mostly sold in North America and in emerging countries, and hardly at all in Europe.) While Evian is still the leader in value share, the volume-share leader is a low-cost brand, Cristaline.

It is easy to see how difficult it is to have to suddenly justify a major price gap. In 1972, four brands represented 80 per cent of the 2 billion litre bottled water market, and Evian was the leader with 653 million litres. Since then 17 major competitors have entered the market, and in 2010 the four main brands represented only 40 per cent of what had grown to be a 7 billion litre market. Evian's annual sales volume is now 793 million litres. The brand succeeded in growing its sales in value through three strategic actions:

- Permanent innovations in the format, packaging and handling of the packs. All these apparently tiny improvements gain significance when one has to shop for water.
- Systematic repositionings of the brand, from generic health and nature to equilibrium and now to the concept of eternal youth, while remaining within the brand's identity.
- Extending the brand. As early as 1962, Evian was a pioneer in brand extension. In response to hospital requests it introduced a spray to vaporize water on the faces of patients and babies. In 2001 Evian Affinity, another brand of facial spray, was launched in alliance with Johnson and Johnson. Two years after its launch it had become the number five brand by sales in the sector of mass market facial cosmetics. It now plans to launch in other countries such as Japan and Korea. This extension is consistent with the repositioning of Evian less as a water than as a source of health and beauty.

To make the business of Evian far more profitable, a simple calculus shows that a litre of water can be sold at a double price in developed countries such as the UK, Germany, the United States, Canada and Japan: there is a growing demand for healthy bottled drinks that is in reaction to the over-consumption of soft drinks, and the obesity syndrome attached to it. The real *un-cola* is not Sprite or Seven Up: it is Evian. Despite transportation costs, selling Evian in the United States delivers a high margin. The main problem is to access consumers and to justify the price premium in a market where Nestlé and Coca-Cola Corporation have established cheaper brands of purified water. This is why an alliance was needed with Coca-Cola to distribute Evian in North America in every outlet and vending machine.

Today, export represents 50 per cent of Evian sales. In each country the brand's role is to create the market for mineral water (not simply purified water), in order to build the business and become its referent, the brand with a fashionable, premium positioning.

10
Sustaining a brand long term

Many apparently modern and up-to-date brands have actually been with us for a long time: Coca-Cola was born on 29 May 1887, American Express in 1850, the Michelin bibendum appeared in 1898, Whirlpool in 1911, Camel in 1913, Danone in 1919, Alka-Seltzer in 1931, Marlboro in 1937 and Calvin Klein in 1968, to name a few. These are the brands that have survived – others have disappeared from the market even if their names do ring a bell.

The perennial appeal of some brands reminds us that, although products are mortal and governed by a more or less long life cycle which can be delayed but not avoided, brands can escape the effects of time.

Many great and well-known brands have disappeared, others are struggling. Why do some brands last throughout time and seem forever young, whereas others do not?

Time is but a proxy variable, a convenient indicator of the changes that affect society as well as markets, subjecting the brand to the risk of obsolescence on a double front – technological and cultural. With time, technological advances become more widely available and new cheaper entrants arrive that destabilize the balance of added value of established brands, forcing them into a never-ending cycle of constant improvement. With the passing of time, consumers either become more sophisticated and expect customized offers, or become blasé and prefer a simplified and cheaper offer. Time also marks the cultural evolution of values, mores and consumer habits. As time goes by, current clients grow older and a new generation emerges which has to be won over from scratch all over again. Generation Z differs from Generation Y, itself different from Generation X.

Changes in the retail sector have far-reaching consequences. Take, for example, the rise of hard-discount in Europe, originating in Germany – where it has already become the leading form of retail, and is now getting close to a 20 per cent market share in Europe. In response to this, to pre-empt the risk that clients will desert them, hypermarkets have created low-price product ranges and – in order to avoid harming their store brand – have widened the price gap with the big brands. Stronger and stronger brands are needed to support this price differential, which has grown suddenly. In Japan, too, the retail sector is changing: in the wines and spirits market, bars have seen their market share fall from 32 per cent to 30 per cent, small independent stores have slipped from 14 per cent to 10 per cent and liquor stores are down from 34 per cent to 28 per cent. They have all lost share to the supermarkets, which have grown from 20 per cent to 32 per cent. Unlike the three first-named outlets, which offered little choice but could provide recommendations, supermarkets present a wide range – but in self-service style, with no recommendations. This change has come as a blow to all wines that formerly relied on a push strategy via in-store recommendation: it gives an advantage to Australian and US wines, which rely entirely on the brand's high profile.

Brands associated with a particular distribution channel are thus subject to the vagaries of the channel with which they are so closely linked. In terms of hygiene and beauty, the chemist's store channel is constantly losing ground to the hypermarkets and supermarkets. Indeed, the supermarket and hypermarket brands are improving their performance: Pond's, Olay, Bioré, l'Oréal Paris, Nivea and so on. This makes the channel more and more attractive, and increases the pressure on other distribution channels. There are two possible responses to this, the first of which is to strengthen brands in the threatened channel and thus increase their attractiveness. This is the approach taken by the likes of Eucerin (Nivea), La Roche Posay and Vichy. The other approach is that of the twin channel, taking advantage of the reputation acquired in the chemist's store to sell the product in the supermarket. This is the Neutrogena option, tempting from the point of view of sales growth, but potentially threatening to brand equity. After all, sales may increase, but what will happen to the brand's reputation?

Is there a common feature of the seemingly everlasting nature of some brands? The following sentence epitomizing the problem is attributed to Antoine Riboud (former CEO of Danone worldwide): 'I do not believe in the overpowering might of brands, but I believe in work.' A brand is not a once-and-for-all construction, but the aim of a constant effort to reconstruct the added value. The current product has to be continuously adapted to meet changing demand while at the same time the new concepts of the future have to be invented that will sustain the growth of the brand.

An analysis of the numerous brands that have survived the crises and lasted down the years may point to the key success factors of this virtuous spiral and is the purpose of the present chapter.

Is there a brand life cycle?

Curiously, the concept of brand life cycle is absent from most books on branding, as a review of their indexes shows. Does that mean that, unlike products, brands do not have a life cycle? In practice however, the question whether brands have a life cycle is pervasive in a number of legal disputes. For instance, in 2002 LVMH, the world leading group for luxury brands and goods, sued the famous consulting group Morgan Stanley for having expressed the opinion that the Louis Vuitton brand (born in 1854) was now a 'mature brand', a judgement that carried implicit and explicit consequences for financial analysts and their clients, stock investors. Maturity is a typical phase of the product life cycle, the third after launch and growth, and just before decline. To describe a brand as in its maturity does indeed imply it is not far from decline, and so could hurt its reputation and the LVMH stock valuation.

The product life cycle does exist. Historical evidence proves it. All products (by which we mean the bundle of physical attributes) have an end. The problem is that the concept of product life cycle was mostly developed in hindsight. It is easy to reconstruct now the product life cycle of nylon, of transistors, of mainframe computers, of minicomputers, of word processing machines and so on. These products were replaced by more efficient solutions. Microsoft killed Wang: word processing software was a better solution than dedicated hardware. Looking at aggregate sales figures of the whole nylon industry, one finds the typical pattern: a birth and launch phase, a growth phase, a maturity phase and a decline. Maturity is signalled by a plateau, a levelling of sales.

As an after-the-fact concept, the product life cycle model is always correct. But as Popper showed us in the philosophy of science, concepts and theories that cannot be falsified are not thereby right. In practice, managers are never at their ease as to where they stand in the product life cycle. Should they interpret any stabilization of sales as an evidence that the maturity phase has been reached, and make appropriate marketing decisions. Instead, they might argue that the decline was only due to weakened marketing, and that more work to identify and correct the causes of this stabilization would make sales grow again. The routes to product growth recovery are multiple:

- through line extensions to capture the short-term new tendencies of the market and increase brand visibility;
- through distribution extensions to make the brand more available wherever customers are;
- through a reduction in the price differential from cheaper potential substitutes;
- through permanent 'facelifts' or innovations to deliver more value to customers and recreate perceived differentiation;
- through repositioning, and renewed advertising or communication in order to adapt the value proposition to the present competitive conditions.

A brand is not a product. Certainly it is based on a product or service: Nike started as a pair of sneakers, Lacoste as a shirt, l'Oréal as a hair dye. But as these examples imply, brands start from one product then continue to grow from multiple products. Louis Vuitton started as a luggage maker for the aristocracy: since then, it has become a full luxury brand covering many product categories. Recently the creative designer Marc Jacobs was hired to create the first Louis Vuitton clothing line. There should be perfumes soon. The brand keeps on surfing new products and their intrinsic growth. As such, has this process an end? Do brands managed in this way reach a levelling-off stage much later if ever?

One thing is sure. Brands that are not managed in this way, but remain attached to a single product, or even a single version of a product, are subject to the product life cycle. We all know of brands that in fact designate a very specific product: Marmite (that peculiarly English savoury spread), Xerox (photocopiers), Polaroid (instant cameras), Wonderbra and so on.

Certainly, brands such as Ariel or Skip are not growing any more in the heavy-duty low-suds detergent market. Their market share hovers around 11 to 12 per cent in Europe. They do try to create disruptions through regular innovations, but these are soon imitated, so this has become a yard-by-yard 'trench war'. Their growth will come from two sources. The first is geographical: the Russian market and all the former communist countries remain to be conquered, as does Asia (although this will be done by Tide, the equivalent of Ariel in the United States). The second is brand extensions. Why should Ariel be satisfied by just being the co-leader of the detergent market? Shouldn't it redefine its scope, its mission, as fabric care as a whole?

In any case the emerging overriding rule of accounting for brand value (see Chapter 18) has given a clear answer to the question of the practical existence of a brand life cycle. Brand values should not be amortized for the single simple reason that no sure forecast can be made about their span of life. To amortize over 5, 10 or 40 years one needs such forecasts. The accounting standards and norms that are coming to be accepted worldwide dispel the notion of a brand life cycle as an operating concept (rather than a historical explanation).

Resisting the low-cost revolution

The new strategic brand management is the answer to the most important brand threat: the low-cost revolution. We devote a full section to the major hypercompetition of the low-cost revolution, focusing first on retailer brands and then on low-cost business models.

Competing against distributors' brands

We are frequently asked, how is it best to compete with distributors' brands, which are – as their market share attests – the number one competitor of the big brands? There are different levels of response to the question above, some tactical, others involving a revision, not of the brand, but of the business model.

A precondition: do not tolerate brand imitations

In developed countries, brands fall victim to unfair competition on the part of distributors' brand products, in the form of imitations of their distinctive symbols. This imitation is anything but accidental, as the design and packaging agencies recruited for the purpose well know. The national brand product is used as a brief, not for what to avoid – according to good brand principles – but what the rival should most resemble. This is where competitors increase their 'me-too' product's chances of success, by closely imitating – albeit with a few differences – the characteristics of the targeted brand product, as well as its distinctive marks. To be considered as an unfair threat, the imitation must be likely to cause confusion in a consumer of average attentiveness.

Actual legal proceedings against the distributor are rare. Big companies, many of whose products are stocked by the distributor, fear a Pyrrhic victory and prefer to build up a dossier with the aim of avoiding legal action and resolving disputes amicably. The dossier consists of a form of proof that could be produced as legal evidence if required, for it is in fact possible to devise a scientific approach to prove illegal imitation. Two methods exist.

The first works on the legal definition: the imitation is illegal if it is likely to create confusion in a consumer of average attentiveness. There are two techniques capable of demonstrating such a risk of confusion, without actually asking customers directly whether they would be confused by the copycat (an invalid method). The first is the use of a tachistoscope, which 'flashes' a picture of the copy at consumers, first at high speed, then at slower speeds. They are then simply asked to describe or name what they have seen (Kapferer, 1995b), and the number of times the copy is mistaken for the original is measured. The second method is to start with a computer-degraded image of the copy, and to build it up, step by step, using computer software. Consumers indicate what they think they can see on the computer screen (Kapferer, 1995a). These two techniques produce a working imitation of consumers of average attentiveness, either by limiting the length of their exposure to the product, and then increasing it (the tachistoscope) or by presenting low-resolution pictures (computer method) and steadily increasing the resolution. Using the first method, we have found confusion scores of 40 per cent.

The second approach ignores the legal concept of confusion. Indeed, although they pay lip service to it in their rulings, judges do not truly use the concept of confusion. Rather, they concentrate on excessive manifest resemblance. They pay more attention to resemblances and less to differences (as advanced by the imitator's lawyer). Objective proof of an excessive resemblance can be obtained by asking one group of consumers to describe the original, and then asking an identical group of consumers to describe the copy. An analysis is made of which aspects were mentioned first, second, third and so on, for each of the two products, and the level of agreement between the aspects stated first by each group.

Once these results on the reality of the prejudice have been obtained, contact with the distributor must be made at a high managerial level in order to emphasize the seriousness of the matter. Furthermore, this is the level at which long-term interests are best appreciated. The distributor needs big brands, a dynamic aspect to its store shelves, the value innovations the brands bring to the category and the margins they give the distributor. The manufacturer needs the distributor to gain access to the customer. At lower managerial levels, the producer–distributor relationship is more antagonistic. The outcome of such contact is the modification of the trade dress or packaging of the distributor's disputed products.

In general terms, brand management must plan for these phenomena and put the brand in a position to be able to defend itself strongly. Thus, in order for a brand colour to be defensible, the brand itself must also defend it internally. For example, the brand's product lines are very often segmented: this leads to the use of different colours to identify each segment. In this way, the ability to claim that the brand is characterized by a particular colour is reduced. Thus, if a Coke label is red, and a Diet Coke label is silver, red is no longer the colour of the Coca-Cola brand: after all, when producing their own colas, distributors always start by producing red packaging.

In general terms, the brand must become a moving target through innovation and regular modifications to its packaging and its characteristic components. However, it must always be remembered that the aim of these modifications is to bring more value to the consumer. The difficulty that this permanent movement creates for copies is a secondary effect.

On the design front, the brand must accentuate and radicalize the signs of its own individuality, in order to be able to defend them better, and at the same time make them recognizable to consumers of average attentiveness. It is significant that the often-imitated Bailey's goes as far as to print the word 'Original' twice on its front label: 'Original Irish Cream' and 'Bailey's the original'.

Nurturing the perceived difference

Brands should always be 'good news'. A brand is the name that progress takes to gain access to the market. The progress marked by the inclusion of enzymes in detergents is called Ariel or Skip or Tide. The progress in convenience coffee is called Nescafé. But progress does not stop. The latest level of quality or performance is quickly integrated by the market and becomes a standard. Before long it can be found in DOBs. Continuous, but from now on selective, innovation is the brand's fate. This also applies to products with a strong intangible added value: the cologne brand Eau Jeune (literally Young Water) can only survive if it launches new versions capable on each occasion of moving with the times. This applies just as much to stylish brands and to fashion designers as to luxury brands that have to renew constantly not their art but their products. Luxury must move with the times lest it become embalmed.

The exceptional longevity and leadership of Nescafé on the market can only thus be explained. Created in 1945, the brand has never stopped innovating, either by little imperceptible touches which when put together have produced an instant coffee whose taste is ever improving, or by major technological breakthroughs which helped recapture some of the 900 aromas that build a 'coffee taste'. The product has never stopped developing either in taste or in convenience (glass packaging replaced iron in 1962), or in its ecological considerations (the introduction of refills), or by its look. To signal the technical breakthrough and the progress made by lyophilization, Nescafé took on the aspect of small grains under the name 'Special Filter'. In 1981, more aromas were recaptured, which was signalled by the creation of a real product range (Alta Rica, Cap Colombie), and new advertising focusing on South America. Later, a new manufacturing process called 'full aroma' was able to capture even better the aroma of freshly roasted coffee. Innovation and advertising are the two pillars of the long-lasting success of this brand. This incremental process never ends.

The leadership of Gillette follows the same pattern. Thirty-seven per cent of the sales of this multinational are accounted for by products that have been launched in the five previous years. In launching new products when the previous ones are barely established, Gillette keeps ahead of the pack, justifying a comfortable price premium and putting DOBs on short allowance (18 per cent volume on the disposables segment alone). Figure 10.1 demonstrates this well: there is a strict linear relationship between the innovation rate in a product category and the penetration of DOBs. When brands get lazy, cheaper copies can take a share of the market. It is significant that each year in the Lego catalogue out of 250 product references, 80 are new. In many sectors, the minute the innovation rate of a company goes down, it starts losing ground.

With their massive presence in distribution and daily presence on the table or in commercials, brands have become familiar, friendly and close, a source of empathy, even of loyalty and attachment. To maintain the strength of brands, it is vital to nourish the two pillars which make the relationship with the brand: one cognitive, the other emotional. Innovation serves precisely this purpose. It enables the brand to differentiate itself objectively and to draw once again the market's attention.

With time, it is noticeable that perceived differences erode faster than the emotional relationship. The liking persists even though we can see that the brand no longer has a monopoly over performance. A study conducted by the American agency, Young & Rubicam, is a reminder of this psychological fact. The survey, called Brand Asset Monitor and conducted on 2,000 brands worldwide, situates them against two facets of their relationship: cognitive and emotional (bearing in mind the fact that during the growth of the brand, the first facet precedes the second). The customer learns through communication

FIGURE 10.1 Innovation: the key to competitiveness

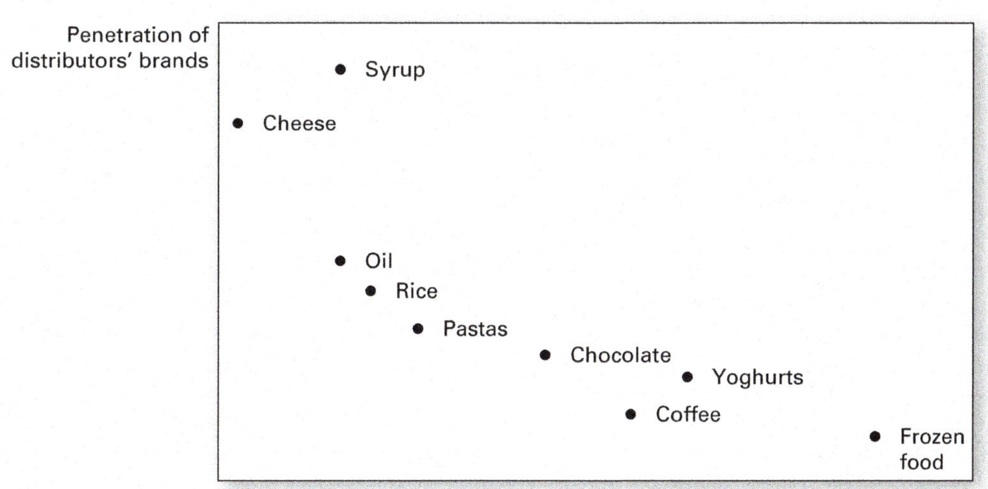

SOURCE McKinsey, UK

FIGURE 10.2 Paths of brand growth and decline

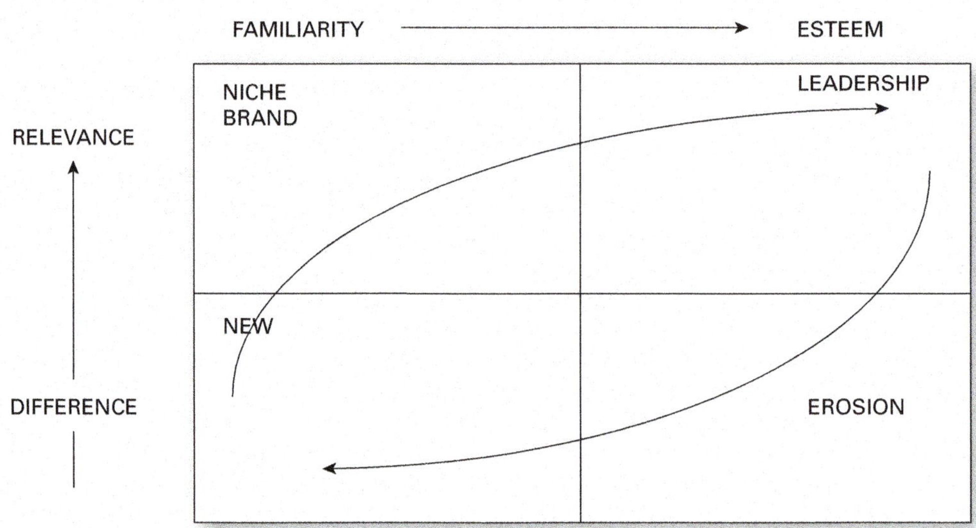

SOURCE Brand Asset Monitor (Y&R)

and distribution the existence of a brand before grasping its difference, which then leads to its pertinence. In the meantime, the seeds of familiarity and esteem have been sown, reminding us that prompted brand awareness precedes spontaneous awareness and that the latter is correlated with the emotional evaluation. The brands that come to mind spontaneously, as they belong to this group, also happen to be our favourite brands.

As shown by Figure 10.2, the decline of a brand, however, begins with a slide in the level of perceived difference between it and the competition and, in particular, with the opinion leaders of the product category. The esteem and the emotional ties are still alive and well, but the consumer realizes that the quality gap has been bridged between the brand and its competition. He still likes it but may now become disloyal!

The benefit of this study is to underscore that the drop in differentiation signals the beginning of the decline, however strong the liking score may be. Unfortunately, many leaders are no longer considered as the qualitative reference of their branch. We like Lotus, Kleenex, brands that we have known since childhood, but we no longer think that they are the sign of superior product quality. They will have to refocus on the product to regain their leadership. The Coke vs Pepsi duel in the United States is a good example of this. One often reduces the struggle between the two giants to a battle of advertising budget size. Actually, Coca-Cola's philosophy lies in the so-called 3A principle: Availability, Affordability and Awareness. Coca-Cola must be within reach everywhere, cheap and on one's mind. Another phrase sums up Coca-Cola's ambitions: 'To be the best, cheapest soft drink in the world' (Pendergrast, 1993). What is exactly the strategy deployed by Pepsi-Cola? As it could not compete in the communication, sponsoring, animation and promotion race it focused on product and price. Pepsi-Cola has always tried to improve its taste to fit as best it could the evolution in the taste of the American public. This is what founded the very aggressive advertising campaigns from 1975 onwards, such as the 'Take the Pepsi challenge', where surprised customers found they preferred the taste of Pepsi in a blind test. Moreover, Pepsi has always sought to be a couple of cents cheaper than Coca-Cola. The strategy proved effective: we know it forced Coca-Cola to change its formula in 1985 so as not to take the risk of being surpassed in taste. This was the famous episode concerning New Coke.

How do you preserve the superior image of a brand, this capital of perceived difference?

- One way is to renew the product regularly, to upgrade it to the current level of expectation. This is why Volkswagen introduced the Golf, then Golf 2, 3, 4, 5, 6 and 7. Detergent manufacturers make minor adjustments every two years or so, and make major changes in their formula every five years. This is how Ariel and Skip maintain their qualitative leadership, making them both the two most expensive brands and the leaders on the market. Moreover, for want of financial means, DOBs cannot keep up in the R&D race, a race which can become an obsession.

- A second way is to integrate new and emerging needs while holding onto the same positioning. In doing so, any car brand, even if it is not specifically positioned on safety as is Volvo, must from now on show that it is equally concerned with security and even the environment.
- A third way is to constantly confirm one's superiority by extending the line. A brand of shampoo treating hair loss should rapidly propose line extensions covering the different needs of people suffering from this problem – creams, lotions and so on. These extensions demonstrate the concern of the brand to address as best it can the different aspects of the problem on which it focuses and to affirm its leadership by becoming the reference linked to the need.
- The fourth way lies in adapting to one's own customers who themselves change and become more experienced. Line extensions should propose new products adapted to their more sophisticated needs, to prevent them from trying the competition.

Jacob's Creek is a good example of this. Over 20 years, from 1984 to 2004, the UK became a wine-drinking country. Consumption per capita was raised from a low 7 litres per person per year to more than 21 litres. This was the result, as ever, of three converging forces:

- Multiple grocers realized that this new category was very attractive. They wished to make it a 'destination category'.
- Consumers travelling in Europe or Australia tried wine and wished to pursue the experience back home.
- New players understood the UK consumer better than existing competition did, and the New World wine makers understood them best of all. Jacob's Creek introduced its first two varieties in 1986 (a dry red and a dry white): it is now the UK's number one bottled wine brand.

New drinkers are fast learners. Thanks to the magic of wine, they want to flex their newly acquired wine appreciation muscles and explore the category. Soon they wanted to discard their former simplistic brands in search of new experiences. This consumer maturity was soon perceived as a potential threat by Jacob's Creek, which it met by introducing gradual line extensions. A permanently renewed top range of special limited series was designed to keep up with opinion leaders' expectations (Parker's wine guide, wine buffs, restaurants), and a number of sub-brands based on more complex grape varietals were designed to keep customers and at the same time demonstrate the competence of the brand, as a true leader should. Jacob's Creek extended its line upwards: prices in 2010 ranged from a basic £4.59 to £6.99 for sparkling wine and even £8.99 for a rare reserve Shiraz.

In the banking sector, credit cards are constantly launching extensions to satisfy a customer base which, over time, is becoming more affluent and expects increasingly high-performance service and insurance products. After Visa came Visa Premier, followed by Visa Infinite. With their very low cost but high perceived value, innovations generate revenue for the entire chain, starting with the broker and continuing to the bank which promotes the product to certain segments of its clientèle, thus increasing the profitability of each customer. In addition, it produces a feeling of exclusivity among carriers of the most expensive cards, a feeling which is destroyed by the spread of so-called 'standard' cards. This is the typical American Express strategy.

Investing in media communication

After the 2008 economic recession, P&G decided to reinvest strongly in its main brands. Lacking media support, they had receded against retail brands. In 2002, the Danone group undertook a significant move. It decided to increase significantly (by over 20 per cent) the media budget of its strongest brands. Since then, their share of voice and market

FIGURE 10.3 Penetration of distributors' brands and advertising intensity

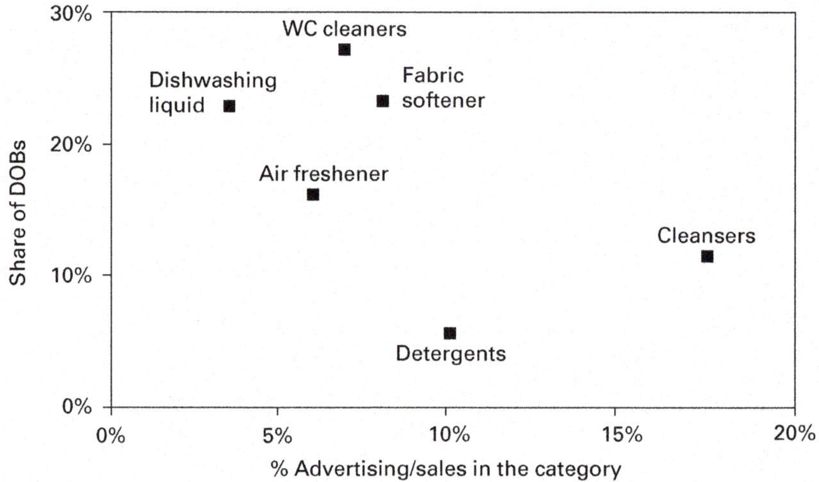

SOURCE McKinsey, UK

leadership have increased. Similarly the whole l'Oréal success story is based on two pillars: research and advertising.

Communication is the brand's weapon. It alone can unveil what is invisible, reveal the basic differences hidden by the packaging which often looks the same among competitors, especially when this similarity is precisely the impression sought by DOBs to create confusion. It alone can sustain the attachment to the brand, by promoting intangible values, even if this loyalty is eroded by many in-store promotions. Advertising is a result of the rise of self-service distribution and reductions in the numbers of salespeople. It is the necessary consequence of investments in R&D that have to pay off ever faster and therefore need an ever bigger public. That this has to be repeated over and over is the proof that there is a confusion in people's minds about the legitimacy of advertising, even within marketing teams, and is why we will use numbers to back our statements.

As Figure 10.3 demonstrates, there is a linear relationship between the penetration of DOBs and the extent of advertising expenditure in a market, measured in percentage of sales spent on advertising. Advertising is a barrier to entry. However, upon examining the product categories, it becomes clear that the categories with a high investment in advertising are also those that invest in innovations and renovations, which are perfect opportunities for re-establishing the saliency of the brand in the public consciousness. It is the conjunction of these two factors (innovation and advertising) that produces added value.

The role of advertising in defending and sustaining the brand capital is shown by Table 10.1. With the exception of jam, where there is much consumption by children and the idealized reference to home-made jam favours small brands, advertising is quite efficient. Once more, we may notice that the categories that invest heavily in advertising are also those that regularly innovate and strongly differentiate their products.

Re-communicating on the risks

Asian imports, DOBs and discount products enter first into the categories with low perceived risk. A first reaction is to remind people of the risks, to regenerate involvement in the category. For example, in 2005 one book became the talk of France, despite its size and its forbidding cover, which showed two nutritionists (Cohen and Serog, 2006). The whole press talked about it, and television devoted time to it. In fact, this book revealed a truth that big distribution would much prefer to keep hidden: the lowest-price products are not good for your health. The drastic reduction in price is made by forcing through awkward compromises, where client health and pleasure hardly enter into the equation. All

TABLE 10.1 Advertising pressure and trade brands' penetration

	Advertising sales ratio %	Trade brand market share %
Cereals	10	15
Detergents	8	11
Coffee	8	13
Jam	7	47
Butter	5	6
Soft drinks	5	20
Tea	5	26
Yoghurts	2	39
Cider	2	36
Fish	0.7	26
Wine	0.5	61

SOURCE McKinsey, UK

that matters is the price. This is where we learnt that low-cost gingerbread contains no honey, and so on.

Bic did something similar in 2006 among tobacconists. The brand is known as the leader in disposable cigarette lighters, disposable razors, ballpoint pens and so on. It practises a single umbrella brand policy: everything is sold under the same name, Bic. It is essentially a company based on its sales force. In Europe, the disposable lighters division, strengthened by its market share, lived on its reputation and spent nothing on advertising. This prudent budgeting, however, had a drawback: for years, there had been nothing to communicate to customers why they should prefer a Bic lighter. In fact, until then, in service stations and tobacconists, there had been nothing but Bic. In 2004 Chinese products arrived, under the PROF brand, which retailers bought 50 per cent cheaper than Bic and sold for the same price as a Bic lighter. The increased margin for the retailers was such that they now sold nothing but PROF. Moreover, Chinese products were more fun and their decorations changed three times a year. The end consumers made no complaint – they were happy to find something new on the shelves, with more entertaining products.

The decision was made to boost the perceived risk. Chinese lighters are in fact dangerous: for example, they can explode if left on the rear shelf of a car. This does not happen with Bic lighters, which are products of remarkable quality. The problem is that in marketing, perception is reality. By not communicating the advantages of the product, Bic had admittedly made savings, but it had weakened the brand and paved the way for Chinese imports, chosen by the trade, which was unconscious of the considerably higher safety of a Bic and the danger of Chinese lighters. Bic created a magazine for its distributors in order to put the word out, and remind them of their legal responsibility if a Chinese lighter sold by one of them were to cause physical harm to a client. At the same time, it took action to raise the level of the criteria for approval for sale on European territory.

Reducing the price gap

Facing competitors with look-alike products sold from 30 to 60 per cent more cheaply, brands must justify the huge price gaps. It is tempting to reduce the price in order to restore the lost balance of perceived value and price.

This approach is logical, but carries several drawbacks. There is nothing easier than lowering prices. What will they do when an even cheaper Asian competitor appears? Lower them again – taking the money from which budget? Should it not be a question of recreating value by increasing quality and price? Also in many stores, the consumers do not even walk past the big brands: for them, the brand is too expensive by definition! They would not even notice the reduced price. The anticipated effect on sales would misfire. The price, and therefore the margins, would be decreased without benefiting from superior volumes.

An interesting study (Pauwels and Srinivasan, 2004) showed that the premium brands should not fear DOBs, since the market is segmented. On the contrary: statistical analysis showed that, after the introduction of DOBs, their sales became less price-dependent, and their turnover increased. The intermediate brands, on the other hand, saw their price sensitivity increase and their sales fall.

Several conclusions emerge at this stage. First, the era of systematic price increases upon the launch of new products is over. It is necessary to place price at the heart of the innovation, and move on to a value analysis.

The non-premium big brands should take care to create a ladder enabling them to increase penetration through a product at an accessible price, and then practise trading up, once the client is aware of the quality of the brand's products. The difficulty, it must be admitted, is the reaction of distributors, since these mini or economy-priced products compete directly with their DOBs, whose strategic role in their margins has already been discussed.

Thus, having bought all Colgate Palmolive's washing powders, Procter & Gamble decided to use Gama as a 'fighting brand'. In the second quarter of 2006, the price of Gama was reduced by 25 per cent, from €6.65 to €4.95 per 27-measure tub (Ariel is priced at €10). Gama became an 'everyday low price' brand, at a price lower than some DOBs. The goal was to bring hard-discount purchasers back into the superstores, since studies showed that they were particularly attracted by the cheapest washing powders. Sales increased by 54 per cent in four months, increasing market share from 3 per cent to 5.4 per cent.

The effect of price reductions on leader brands cannot be guaranteed: thus, in order to combat the products of the hard-discounter Aldi, Always (Procter & Gamble's feminine hygiene brand) lowered its prices in Germany, moving from an index of 240 to 197, with Aldi's index at 100. Aldi's market share remained stable at around 45 per cent. Always' market share moved from 21.7 per cent to only 24.7 per cent. It was a failure. The same tactic was successful, however, for Pampers: by moving from index 131 to 116, the market share jumped from 31.1 per cent to 42.2 per cent, and Aldi's product fell from 53.9 per cent to 45.9 per cent. A significant difference between these two cases is the far smaller difference in price for Pampers than for Always. Is it really worthwhile for premium brands to lower their prices? Interestingly, Pampers has now created three lines:

- Simply Dry, a low-cost version, which is 20 per cent more expensive than private labels;
- the core range, which is 20 per cent more expensive than Simply Dry;
- the super-premium range, which is 20 per cent more expensive than the core range.

The company now communicates much more on television on innovations in the super-premium range. This strategy is a success.

Facing hard-discount competition

It would be hard to underestimate the rise of hard-discount and lowest-price ranges as a fundamental phenomenon in mature societies. Offering a reduced range or a pared-back service at an unbeatable price, hard discount is more than just a price – it is a business model. It also represents a new attitude towards consumption, and heralds a crisis for added value. It throws marketing itself into question, and thus brands too. This is why no organizations should consider themselves safe from this phenomenon.

Even in the country that invented the hypermarket, and where this form of commerce is now dominant, hard discount has succeeded in capturing nearly 12 per cent of market share (in value) over 15 years. Given that in food products, the price gap between discounters and the leading brands varies between 30 per cent and 50 per cent, it can be seen that this represents between 18 per cent and 24 per cent by volume. And of course – depending on the category – these figures may be even higher. For example, in the pre-packed cold meats (ham) market, the hard discounters' market share by value is of the order of 16.5 per cent.

Hard discount is more than just a price. It is a new way of doing business, with its own specific retailers: German (Lidl and Aldi) or French (Ed, Leader Price). At present, the most recent European panel figures suggest that 62 per cent of households shop at a hard-discount food store. The phenomenon will reach a limit, however, reflecting the segmentation of the market: in food products, a threshold of 20 per cent in value market share should be expected. In the DIY sector, the major retailers have created separate hard-discount-style retail brands. The phenomenon now also extends to textiles: the classic discount stores were well known, but now new hard-discount retailers are emerging.

All these figures show that hard discount cannot simply be turned into a phenomenon that targets only lower-income groups. Hard discount is a necessity for the poorest in society, but also an opportunity for the better-off. It offers an alternative way of living: consumers can do the daily shop close to their home, in 10 minutes, thanks to the simplification offered by a reduced range of goods, freeing buyers from the torments of too much choice. Hard discount does not represent a return to asceticism, but to reason. Among consumers who could afford to buy elsewhere, it attests to a desire to simplify, to un-complicate, and to retake control. It will exert strong pressure on brands with low added value, the average brands, which do not possess a strong enough dream value. Hard discount advocates a form of intangible value: the return to a kind of simplicity for people who are not limited to it through a lack of resources. Hard discount is a search for purification of one's life, de-pollution, and liberation from imposed constraints.

This is a genuine challenge for the major brands, as this growing form of distribution excludes them in favour of the discounters' own products. For the major brands, this further erosion of their accessibility on store shelves compounds the problem created by the amount of space already set aside for distributors' brands in the hypermarkets and supermarkets. Indeed, even retailers' brands are coming under threat from this increasingly cut-price competition, which attracts clients to another store. This is why they have been strengthened, which will make them even more of a danger to the major brands as well. In fact, in 2011, the distributor's brand is now typically 35 per cent cheaper than the national brand. As it increases in quality, however, its competitiveness also increases.

The hard-discount phenomenon is set to spread. Everyone will look for a way to increase their purchasing power in an ultimately painless way, by making shrewder purchasing decisions in respect of a portion of their consumption. This will affect telephone communications, the internet, transport, petrol, clothing and other areas. No company is immune to this phenomenon, because the competition has changed: consumers have become highly versatile, situation-driven and pragmatic. They are quite capable of shopping both at a hard-discount store and at Harrods on the same day. They learn where the best prices are from the internet.

It would be a mistake to believe that hard discount will become the norm. In France, Cristalline spring water, sold at a price three times cheaper than Evian, does not control 100 per cent of the market, and Evian is still the leader by value. However, it will grow, until it reaches its threshold – and in so doing it may lead to a re-evaluation of attitudes and behaviour. As is always the case in our modern societies, contradictory tendencies appear, coexist and learn to live together – but what they cannot do any longer is ignore each other.

An examination of the specific strategies of companies and brands to combat hard discount reveals the following themes, all of which capitalize on the enduring weakness of hard-discount.

What link is there between Ryanair, Virgin Express, and Asda or Aldi? They are all so-called low-cost companies. How have the traditional competitors responded? Through the introduction of a new, lowest-price product offer to its existing range. The brand must create a stepped price range, with accessible products that make it possible to experiment with and to discover the brand. Furthermore, this contradicts the discounters' arguments, since they wish to stereotype all manufacturer brands as 'expensive'.

In air travel, for example, Air France has shown that the famous bait-and-switch prices of the low-cost companies (€20 flights from Paris to London) applied only to a few seats and time slots. Conversely, Air France's promotion of its lowest prices, and of reduced prices in the case of reservation long in advance, has also demonstrated that its price range is much wider than the low-cost companies had claimed. The SNCF (French national rail) created e-TGV to reduce prices. Thanks to yield management and process optimization, Air France and British Airways can also offer a quota of seats at very low prices. These may be obtained by booking far in advance, reserving over the internet, and so on. In this way, the SNCF's e-TGV puts Marseilles only a €20 journey away from Paris.

The superstores have offered products even cheaper than the hard discounters, but under specific brands (the No. 1 brand at Carrefour, for example). This reduces the temptation to look elsewhere by capitalizing on the hypermarket's traditional strength, 'one-stop shopping'. The difference in terminology is revealing: 'low-cost' is a business model; 'even cheaper product' was the result of an emergency action.

For 50 years Aldi and Lidl have been designing an efficient business model in order to provide a quality product at the lowest price, based on the elimination of all unnecessary costs, and on a new vision: long-term agreements with suppliers, dedicated factories with a common design, not to mention a store concept without flourishes, with a greatly reduced range of goods. If Aldi's fruit juice is still the market leader in Germany, it is because it is good: its quality/price ratio is unbeatable.

Conversely, the lowest price products at Carrefour, sold under a brand that (significantly) makes no reference to Carrefour, were created in haste to block the client drain, and obtained through increased pressure on suppliers, and therefore on the quality of constituents. Thus the fruit juice at this price will only have perhaps the legal minimum required amount of fruit juice. This is why hard discount, unlike the hypermarket's lowest price range, satisfies its clients.

Suppressing unnecessary costs

Retailers' brands are already occupying a share of shelf, but a new factor affects brands' survival: the arrival of the hard discounters (Aldi, Lidl, etc). To retain their clients, retailers have allocated a share of their shelf to low-cost products (less than 70 per cent). Hence not only do big brands look really expensive, but their shelf space is further reduced.

Even if innovation and advertising do increase added value, loyalty at all costs does not exist. Customers can be both sensitive to the brand but disloyal to it, estimating that the price of the brand goes beyond the price span that they are willing to pay for the product category, and beyond the brand premium that seems reasonable to them given the added satisfaction which is expected. Distributors also have the same attitude.

During years of economic growth, the biggest brands were tempted to regularly increase their prices to maximize the overall profit accruing from a strong price premium and a large batch of loyal clients. For financial directors concerned about showing ever-increasing profits, what does a price increase of a few pence or cents per unit represent? For the market, however, it now has the utmost importance. In April 1993, one of the most famous brands, Marlboro, noting a slump in sales, was the first to put into reverse this inclination by unilaterally lowering its prices in the United States. Wall Street reacted badly, thinking the bell was tolling for brands: on that day the stocks of all consumer goods companies dropped significantly. More than a year later, in August 1994, Marlboro's market share reached unprecedented heights (29.1 per cent), seven points more than in March of 1993 just before the famous 'Marlboro Friday'. In France 10 years ago, Philip Morris decided to bring down the price of Chesterfields from 11.60F to 10F at at time when competitors were preparing to pass on to customers the 15 per cent tax increase imposed by the government. Within two months the sales of Chesterfields jumped by 300 per cent. The market share of the brand went from less than 1 per cent to 12.2 per cent in two years. It became, in a year, the favourite cigarette for young people (71 per cent of buyers were under 25).

One may recall that Procter & Gamble significantly reduced the price of its brands in the United States in accordance with its brand-boosting programme, thanks to the allocation of part of the savings accruing from an impressive programme to increase industrial productivity, marketing and sales. These price reductions were part of the EDLP (Every Day Low Price) policy which put an end to the myriad of micro-promotions. These price reductions show that the brand has to stay within the core of the market if it wants to continue.

FIGURE 10.4 Sources of price difference between brands and hard-discount products

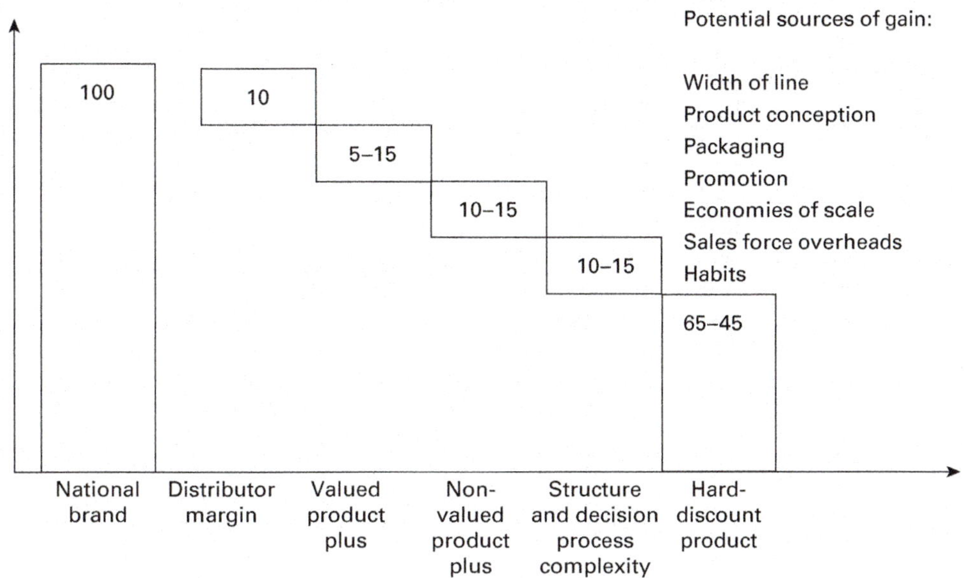

SOURCE OC&C

To preserve their margins, big brands must compete on volume again and thus reduce their unnecessary costs. Niche strategies destroy economies of scale and should be limited to super-premium brands. As is shown in Figure 10.4, the latent savings unexploited by industrialists could represent up to 30 per cent of costs. It is true that part of the benefits linked to the product are sometimes not valued by customers or that the upgrade in production costs is not worth it in the customers' eyes. There is more to be gained by suppressing these costs and finding a new price competitiveness again. Besides, trade-off analyses demonstrate that the logic of 'bigger and better' can be counterproductive if it entails an increase in price. Beyond a certain performance threshold, utility slumps.

Fighting value destruction through education and innovation

Price reduction may apply to FMCG brands now priced too high, but is it a long-term answer to the problem of brand value? The case of white goods is an interesting one.

Consumers of white goods do not have a clear idea of prices. Theory (Monroe, 1973; Blattberg, 1995) tells us that consumers have an internal reference price (IRP) acting as anchor point. The theory may hold true for frequently purchased items. For durable products bought every five years, the notion of internal reference price developed for FMCG markets is less accurate.

According to market studies, when consumers go into a store looking for a good modern dishwasher, they believe they should pay €500. However, the trade and discount e-commerce sites emphasize low-cost products. As a result everyone tries to sell products around €250. The sector is engaged in a process of value destruction. Because products are sold under the internal reference price, consumers receive a gift they did not ask for. In addition they are destabilized, having lost their landmarks about the value of things.

There is a real crisis of value. The task of manufacturers will be to teach the value of products again. In any supermarket coffee pots that are made in China can be found at €9. Brands such as Philips, Krups and Rowenta will have to teach consumers that a real coffee pot is worth more than €9. This needs explanation and time, which is why only the channels that provide advice to consumers see their sales go up.

This is confirmed by sales statistics for small appliances, comparing store and internet sales: in stores the average price of purchased items is €52; on the internet it is €68 (€137 for two products). For large appliances, the results are the same: €430 versus €554.

In stores one can hardly find a salesperson any more, especially during peak times, and this salesperson does not really know how to sell the expensive items. Salespeople immediately push the lower-priced items, which are easier to sell. On the internet there is much more choice, and consumers buy more items. Finally, you get better information by buying on the net.

This is why brands should really get a hold on the internet: this is their new play and education field. Private labels have nothing to talk about there apart from their low price and the length of their guarantee period. The internet is the prescription. Whoever holds the internet holds the prescription.

Is this then the end of salespeople? Can a salesperson know 100 products? By definition, no. The internet can. However, a salesperson can understand the real needs of clients better and orient them accordingly, unless the salesperson's task is to drive consumers to the latest innovations, creating value.

Only innovations avoid deflation tendencies and drive markets up. Soon smartphone sales of the iPhone, Samsung Galaxy and BlackBerry will overtake regular phone sales. The SEB Actifry fryer is the iPhone of small appliances: it is the most sold product of the whole market. The second is the Philips Senseo coffee machine. However, the SEB Actifry is three times more expensive than the average price of the market. Unlike the function of low-cost producers, the role of a brand is to sell as high as it can the progress it brings to the market.

Only innovation drives markets up. However, innovations reach consumers through brands and the trade.

A market's economic future is determined by the behaviour of the leading distributor and that of the leading brand. Apple launched its iPhone worldwide in each country through an exclusive distribution agreement with the local referent operator: Orange, Vodaphone, etc. Later it was forced to trade with other operators, but still in a position of force. Apple held its prices and conditions.

Taking the case of small appliances, where the referent distributor is Carrefour and the referent manufacturers are SEB or Philips, there is no downgrading of value. The market creates value and encourages innovation. In Germany, the referent trade is Saturn, but there is no referent manufacturer. As a consequence, price cuts dominate managerial practices, and innovations are blocked.

Creating entry barriers

By focusing exclusively on the consumer's psychology, brand academic research has overlooked the crucial role of the management of the offer itself, which can make it impossible for competitors to enter on the market. The impenetrability of the market is the best warranty for the latter, and the example of Black & Decker is quite revealing.

Why are there hardly any DOBs in the drilling machine market? Because Black & Decker makes it economically impossible for them to enter the market. DOBs sprout up when one or more of the following conditions are fulfilled:

- there is a high volume in the market;
- there is little product innovation;
- brands are expensive;
- customers perceive little risk;
- customers make their choice essentially according to the visible characteristics of the product;
- technology is accessible at low cost.

Much to the contrary, the market for drills is small, and moreover is cut up into many segments. Black & Decker drives the market and makes it develop at a fast technological pace. In addition, Black & Decker has globalized its production: each plant produces one single product for the worldwide market. The production cost level thus becomes unbeatable, and as Black & Decker is not overkeen to increase its retail price, it does not leave much room for copycats to manoeuvre. Lastly, the customer feels safe when buying such a well-known and ubiquitous brand.

What are the main sources of entry barriers?

- The cost of the factors of production is the most important, which leads to a long-lasting competitive advantage. This is the strategy of

Dell, and also of Decathlon, the world's fifth largest sports goods retailer and eleventh largest producer. Decathlon may become for some sports the European number one manufacturer far ahead of any others because of the economies of scale accruing from its products developed at a European level.

- Mastering technology and quality is a key success factor for Procter & Gamble, Gillette, l'Oréal and 3M. Turning down any offer to yield an iota of their know-how to DOBs, these companies keep for themselves their main added-value leverage. This is what enables them to constantly innovate and to remain the reference of the market in terms of quality. Kellogg's even goes to the extent of indicating on its boxes that it does not supply DOBs.
- Domination through distribution and communication is Coca-Cola's mainstay, although it does not hinder a K-Mart or a Sainsbury brand cola from borrowing as much as possible the distinctive signs of Coke and selling at a lower price. In hard times, sensitivity to price is exacerbated. But as a worldwide brand, Coca-Cola had access to the sponsoring of the Olympic Games in Atlanta and was able to pass on the benefits to bottlers worldwide. This is also the weapon of Nike, Reebok and Adidas. Coca-Cola as a company has also created a barrier to entry on trade. It offers a portfolio of brands (Coke, Fanta, etc). An outlet does not need anything else.
- Controlling the relationship with opinion leaders is one of the key success factors for a brand looking to the future. Canson, a school-supplies brand which is part of the Arjomari-Wiggins group, provides an illustration. What is more natural than a sheet of tracing paper or drawing paper for a schoolchild? However, despite the share of supermarket shelf space given to DOBs' drawing and tracing paper, only that of Canson sells. For more than 20 years the brand has developed a close relationship with teachers, for instance organizing drawing competitions between classes on a national level. The long-lasting presence of Canson on a child's shopping list for school supplies is due to the excellence of what is now called relationship marketing. The main asset of Canson is its loyal teachers within the public education system.

How HP defends its business

In Europe in 2008, 7 million inkjet printers were sold. The leader was HP with a 44 per cent market share, followed by Canon with 22 per cent, Epson with 20 per cent, Lexmark with 6 per cent, and Brother also with 6 per cent.

A printer needs on average six to eight cartridges per year. The price of a printer has incredibly gone down: it is now €100. But the price of consumables is ever increasing: €22 for a black HP338, €39 for a colour HP344. Despite this high price, the retail margin on cartridges is low: 25 to 30 per cent, all included.

Why this pricing strategy? Manufacturers simply buy market share by offering extremely low prices for advanced printers, distributed everywhere, with the reassurance of a strong brand. Then they use the Gillette or Nespresso business model: the margin is in the consumables. It has been remarked that, at $22 per quarter-ounce, an HP colour inkjet cartridge is more expensive than imported Russian caviar. A British consumer magazine pointed out that a colour HP cartridge was seven times more expensive than a vintage Dom Pérignon: £1.70 per millilitre versus £0.23! As a result, in 2008, on US$29 billion revenues from HP's Imaging and Printing Division, consumables represented $18.3 billion (63 per cent).

If the margin on printers is very low, the margin on consumables is very high (70–80 per cent). The Imaging and Printing Division has a contribution of 14.6 per cent (against 10.5 per cent for the whole HP Group).

Such margins are prone to attract competition. There are either compatible brands (such as Armor, Pelikan, NewCote, etc) or private labels (Office Depot, etc).

To fight, and defend their huge margins, manufacturers create barriers to entry:

- by creating a new model of cartridge each time a new printer is launched;
- by a lot of patents on each cartridge to block the compatibles;

TABLE 10.2 Economics of competition against compatible brands and private labels (all prices in euros)

	OEM	Compatibles	Private labels
Retail public price (euros)	23.50	16.50	15.30
Retail public price (wthout VAT)	19.65	13.80	12.80
Retail margin	4.91	5.52	6.40
Retail margin percentage	25%	40%	50%
Purchasing price	14.74	8.28	6.40
Rear margin	1.96	0.69	0.64
Rear margin percentage	10%	5%	5%
Total trade margin	6.87	6.21	7.04
Total trade margin percentage	35%	45%	55%
Net selling price	12.78	7.59	5.96
Manufacturer margin	8.95	3.41	2.38
Manufacturer margin percentage	70%	45%	40%
Cost of production	3.83	4.18	3.58

- by adding chips so that the printer recognizes if it is an OEM cartridge and works only with these ones;
- by using fear appeals to consumers: 'You are going to lose your guarantee';
- by incentivizing the trade: loyalty financial rewards, exclusivities, rear margins at the end of the year;
- by imposing a public price at retail: no retailer can take the risk of losing HP by refusing (a shelf cannot exist without the market leader);
- by recuperating the empty cartridges themselves to prevent compatible manufacturers from doing so.

There are two types of compatibles: those refilled, for HP and Lexmark (with an integrated printer head), and the new compatibles for Canon, Epson and Brother. Why these two compatible types? Because of manufacturers' patents, refilling is less risky (for cartridges with printer heads like HP or Lexmark). However, recuperation costs are high, so manufacturing new ones in China is more economical for cartridges without a printer head.

Compatibles have a major argument beyond price, being less expensive by 30–50 per cent: they are more ecological (the cartridges are recycled and refilled), there is no waste of plastic and chips, and the trade makes more money (the trade margin is 50 per cent).

Today compatible brands suffer. They are stuck in the middle, between big brands and private labels (see Table 10.2).

How to succeed in trading up

To survive, trading up has become an obligation for most brands, now facing very competitive private labels and the low-cost suppliers. How do you compete against Zara, H&M, Mango, C&A, etc? As a jeans brand, how do you compete against jeans sold at €5 at Carrefour, the world's number two retailer? Gone is the time when private labels meant lowest quality. This was perhaps the case when low price was the result of using poor ingredients to manufacture the products, using low wages, non-qualified workers, no controls, etc. The low prices today are based on productivity gains and high efficiency: German hard discounters such as Lidl and Aldi are masters in Taylorization of production and supply chain, leading to incredibly low prices, not low quality. The same holds true for Ikea, which invented new production processes to meet the targeted extremely low price. Southwest Airlines invented the low-cost airline, followed by easyJet and RyanAir.

Competing on value

As a result, most brands have no other choice than to compete on value. Naturally they must also eliminate all non-productive sources of costs (in overhead costs for instance, staffing, and general expenses). Competing on value means adding new values and becoming less comparable. The consequence also is an increase in price premium.

Looking at the denim jeans industry over 15 years, one sees how much Diesel has been following a trading-up strategy. In 1985 the jeans market was driven by brands with a casual image, playing on Western authenticity, Levi's being the icon. But this market became a fashion market, with luxury brands creating a new segment (above €300). At the bottom, low-cost jeans were also produced. Levi's remained more or less at the same price positioning, but Diesel moved from €60 to €150. It is not a luxury brand, but aims at the super-premium market. From Table 10.3 it can be seen that the lowest-cost offers exert a vertical push on all the actors.

Now one cannot increase the prices of a brand if no added value is attached to this change. Only such

TABLE 10.3 Trading up in the denim market

	1985	2010
€300–500		Gucci, Dolce & Gabbana
€130–300		Diesel
€100–130		CK, Emporio Armani, Pepe Jeans, Replay
€80–100	Moschino, Emporio Armani	
€70–90		Levi's, Lee
€60–70		Wrangler
€50–60	Diesel, Levi's	
€35–40	Wrangler	Zara
€30		Private labels at Carrefour
€5		Unbranded at Carrefour

brands as Chanel, Louis Vuitton or Hermès, true luxury brands, increased their prices by 15 per cent during the 2009 recession to offset the drop in consumer demand. Their profits boomed during this period, as well as their exclusive image. As a rule, trading up is carried out over years with a systematic upgrading of all facets of the marketing mix, including line extension towards higher-value-delivering products.

Giving time to time

It takes time to trade up, the time to create added value.

Audi, the German car maker, was given 20 years to succeed by F Piech, the visionary CEO of the Volkswagen Group. Audi's long-term objective was to compete against BMW and Mercedes. Now at the time Audi was created, this was a brand with no big history, no special roots, made up by the fusion of three former brands (Auto Union, DKW and NSU Prinz). The first cars were conservative and not very appealing, with no future. To make the brand turn around, Audi built a stairway made of technology, sportiness and design milestones: the Audi Quattro, the Audi 100, the aluminium engine, etc, plus systematic significant price increases when one model was being replaced by another. The result was that former clients could not follow the brand. They were welcomed by Volkswagen.

Jameson, the leading Irish whiskey, was going nowhere in the United States. Mainly drunk as a mixer with the famous Irish coffee in Irish bars, it had no real spontaneous brand awareness and was thus positioned as an exotic whiskey (coming from Ireland). But in 2000 consumers started abandoning whisky to move to white spirits (vodka, gin, tequila, etc). As a result, sales of such icons as Johnnie Walker Red and Canadian whisky faltered. Paradoxically this downward movement did not affect the premium brands: Jack Daniel's, Maker's Mark, etc. It was then decided to double the sales of Jameson long term by positioning it against these premium brands, thus abandoning the reference to the price of Johnnie Walker Red and moving the price up to that of Johnnie Walker Black, 20 per cent above Jameson's current price.

To achieve this trading up, 10 years were needed in order to:

- start building spontaneous awareness through advertising investments;
- find the right brand positioning (what engagement? what value proposition?);
- slightly change the packaging to deliver more status;
- penetrate new states and distribution (on trade and off trade) far beyond Irish bars;
- organize thousands of trade parties and events in these new outlets to convey the brand values to the new target of 'young social aspirationals'.

Segment your distribution

Trading up means creating new products delivering more value, as well as inventing new services and new experiences. This is why many airlines have revitalized their once deceased first class.

When brands trade up, they want to attract new consumers who value some selectivity, a key intangible value. This is why trading up often means adding new channels of distribution, where the traded-up line only is sold. You do not sell the Amex Black Centurion as you sell the Amex Gold and a fortiori the green card.

Even if the former distribution of the brand asks for the new expensive lines, one should refuse. Channels are messages. Building more intangible values necessitates a new channel able to build these intangible values, or at least a separate area. The example of Dom Pérignon is enlightening. The number one client of the paragon of champagne excellence is Costco – not a glamorous trade. However, to carry this brand Costco agreed to create in its stores a separate corner with a few other elite spirits.

Ralph Lauren is a typical brand trading up: it created two new lines, Black Label and Purple Label, with clothes 'made in Italy'. These new lines, much more expensive, are sold in some of Ralph Lauren's mega-stores only, in a few towns, and have a separate zone.

Beware of sub-brands

Armani has remarkably succeeded in both trading up and trading down thanks to a well-segmented distribution, plus a remarkable branding architecture.

Trading up is achieved through the new sub-brand called Armani Privé, the equivalent of French haute couture, a very selective, expensive and creative line of clothes and cosmetics. Trading down is achieved through Emporio Armani (against Burberry Prorsum) and Armani Jeans (against Diesel). Between these extremes one finds the sub-brands Giorgio Armani and Armani Collezione. One never finds the whole collection at the same place. Privé has its exclusive outlets; Giorgio Armani is not only a sub-brand but a specific store; the same holds true for Emporio Armani; the other sub-brands are sold in their own corners within department stores.

Now one remarkable thing about the Armani brand architecture is that it kept the Armani spine central. The same holds true for Ralph Lauren: Black Label and Purple Label high-priced clothes are explicitly Ralph Lauren.

Absolut vodka did not follow this strategy and thus failed in launching Level in 2004. Entry into the super-premium segment was symbolized by Grey Goose. Absolut was threatened with becoming mainstream by the dual effect of both its sales volume (being the world's fourth spirit) and the arrival of Grey Goose, which was 20 per cent more expensive. Grey Goose was fashionable in Tribeca (New York), and de-positioned Absolut in image. To react, Absolut launched Level, but Level did not make a strong explicit reference to Absolut:

- Nothing in the Level bottle remind one of the Absolut iconic bottle (can you imagine Johnnie Walker launching its super-premium Black, Blue or Gold versions without the iconic square bottle? Or a Mercedes S Class without the iconic Mercedes bonnet?).
- Level did not strongly mention Absolut on the label, nor in its advertising: it acted solo, thus benefiting neither from the Absolut aura nor from the Absolut brand equity.
- You do not sell a US$40 vodka without a very strong value proposition. Grey Goose had one (the world's best-tasting vodka, the smoothest). Absolut was obsessed by its competitor and claimed a 'balanced taste', forgetting that the higher you go up the price ladder the more identity is crucial, not positioning versus the competition (Kapferer and Bastien, 2009).

Beware of the elusive halo effect

Will the Crest toothpaste Pro line boost the brand equity of Crest and thus help the sales of the regular Crest line? It seems that the million dollars invested there, and borrowed from the regular Crest budget, did not help much. The same holds true for Olay: its range now extends from US$4.99 to $60 for the super-premium regimen pack.

All companies pursue the secret hope that introducing an upper line will create a halo effect on the other lines of the brand at the bottom, thus defending them better against private labels and price competition. This is why they invest advertising money on these upper lines, to a greater extent than would be justified if advertising had to pay off only for this specific upper line. As a consequence, they reduce or even stop advertising on the bottom lines, as a rule those with highest volume.

Halo effect is a classic in the luxury business, but does not work well in FMCG: why?

Chanel advertises considerably on its exclusive jewellery, far beyond what rationality would recommend from a mere return-on-sales standpoint. High-priced jewellery (above €50,000) does not need advertising, but it reinforces the brand credentials and helps boost the glamour of the name, to sell more accessories at accessible prices.

This is also a typical strategy in the wine business. Mouton Cadet is a Bordeaux best-seller. It is in fact one of the first 'brands of wine' ever created. Its success is mainly due to a mythical story linking it to one of the world's icons of luxury wines: Mouton Rothschild. The legend says that Baron Rothschild, once disappointed by the produce of his vineyards, decided not to sell it under that prestigious name but invented another name, Mouton Cadet (*cadet* in French means 'smallest son of'). Since then, the mass brand Mouton Cadet has always had a touch of class. This is a clear halo effect.

In FMCG markets, such vertical halo effects are often disappointing.

This is what happened to Olay in the United States. This mass brand created new lines with stronger and more expensive ingredients, delivering real effects. These lines were supported by heavy advertising to help create the halo effect: raising the Olay brand equity, in order to defend the lower lines present in supermarkets, Boots, etc. The advertising budget was focused on this new line, and reduced the allocation aimed at lower ranges, but the lines at the bottom lost market share, and money had to be quickly refuelled in advertising and promotion, thus taken from the promotion of the upper line.

Now why is the halo effect not taking place as expected? When is it likely to appear?

In FMCG markets, consumers buy a product from a brand, a mix of tangible utility and intangible values. In fashion and luxury they mostly buy a badge, an intangible.

Take Olay's best-selling product ($4.99, sold in all supermarkets): women know what it is made of, what it can do or not do for their skin. Why should these women forget their experience of a product they have known and used for years, just because they hear that Olay is launching something totally different and more expensive elsewhere? Why would the high line with its scientific rare ingredients help sell the basic product sold on supermarket shelves?

A brand image is not based on the latest advertising seen: it is the sum of all previous contacts with the brand – hence its inertia.

The same holds true for wine: wine is a product whose desirability is certainly influenced by the brand, but there is also an objective perception on the basis of such quality cues as the varietal, the vintage, the country, the region, what the *Wine Spectator* magazine says, what Robert Parker writes on his blog, etc.

Jacob's Creek is the number one imported wine brand in the UK, Australia's top drop. It started by selling two bottles of red and white wine at £1.99 some 25 years ago. Since then it has never stopped launching special series, upper lines, even a sparkling wine at around £10. This helps it receive grades from the *Wine Spectator*, etc, thus fuelling the buzz. The first goal is keep the early buyers who now want to try something better: they will go to the competition unless Jacob's Creek itself extends its line vertically upwards. The second goal is to offset the effect of volume on the brand image. Being perceived as wine market leader in volume does not trigger quality associations in people's minds. The role of communication is to make salient more positive evocations.

The Jacob's Creek example is quite different from the Olay one. In wine, consumers themselves want to trade up. Once they go into wine, they like to try a better one and pay a bit more for it. Extending the range is not to defend the basics, but to accompany consumers. The same held true for Nivea extensions. Do people buying Nivea Visage still buy the basic Nivea all-purpose cream? No.

To our knowledge, halo effects appear most on invisible dimensions of value, a fortiori on intangibles. Thus a fashionable brand will extend this intangible equity (being fashionable) to its whole range. Volkswagen's famed reliability exerts a halo effect on the whole range too. Reliability cannot be assessed at purchase: it is a belief.

However, Range Rover never really helped Rover: physically the two lines were too different. They were even perceived as two separate brands. Mouton Cadet benefited from the glamour of the name Mouton, but no one among the buyers of Mouton Cadet has ever tasted a real Mouton Rothschild.

Unlocking the secrets of super-premium brands

In most corporate headquarters, revenue management has become a priority. The pressure on prices and margins endangers revenues and profits. This is the consequence of the recession and of the constant rise of low-cost producers, hard discounters, private labels, and mass retailers with attractive prices (Zara, H&M, C&A, Ikea, etc).

Strategic revenue management entails auditing the brand and product portfolio, pricing policies, channel differentiation, rate of promotion, division of margin between the company and the trade, etc.

One of the key challenges is how to lower price sensitivity. The key answer is premiumization, also called trading up. Premiumization means moving the whole range from mainstream products and prices towards higher quality, image and prices. The end goal is to reach a higher profitability. As shown in Table 10.4, many FMCG companies have a portfolio balanced over three segments. Notice how the super-premium segment, representing only 11 per cent of the total volume, delivers a third of this typical company contribution margin.

Premiumization is visible everywhere: Johnnie Walker does not advertise Johnnie Walker Red, once the world icon, but now exclusively Johnnie Walker Black. Formula 1 racing cars bear the marque of this upper version. Visa moves its clientele from the basic card to the Premier, following Amex. The Volkswagen Phaeton aims at threatening the Mercedes E Class. Club Med abandoned its huts and cool villages, and substituted luxury villas and resorts.

In FMCG markets, the market leader is most often a premium product. Take Pampers, for instance: despite this, it is confronted by store brands and

TABLE 10.4 The financial equation of premiumization

	Mainstream	Premium	Super-premium	(Luxury)
Contribution margin	21%	43%	36%	17%
Net sales	27%	39%	34%	15%
Volume	46%	43%	11%	4%

Transformed and adapted from FMCG companies

low-cost generics. Raising its price would be too risky: the existing price gap is hard to defend.

Why not then directly launch new super-premium brands in the future?

All major companies are now benchmarking the latest successful super-premium brand launches to unlock their secrets. Everyone looks at Nespresso, Red Bull and Innocent with envy. Red Bull's sales at retail are $6 billion: this is two-thirds of the total world sales of Pampers!

From our own research, six lessons can be learned from the recent launches of super-premium brands:

1 Super-premium brands do not grow fast at the beginning, unlike mass brands that receive very high penetration goals in the first year, in order to reassure the mass retailers as to the viability of the new brand, and reach break-even faster. Super-premium brands follow an organic growth strategy. By taking time, these companies are sensitive to details: they can correct their early mistakes, improve their marketing mix, and develop a corporate culture obsessed with product quality and detail.

2 Super-premium brands use social media and not mass media when they start, because they are launched by small or medium companies without huge marketing budgets. They make use of their authenticity, for the person who talks on Facebook or answers the phone may be the founder, the person with an obsession who started a company.

They do not enter mass retailers, but rather qualitative distribution, speciality stores,

FIGURE 10.5 Typical launch pattern of mass versus super premium brands

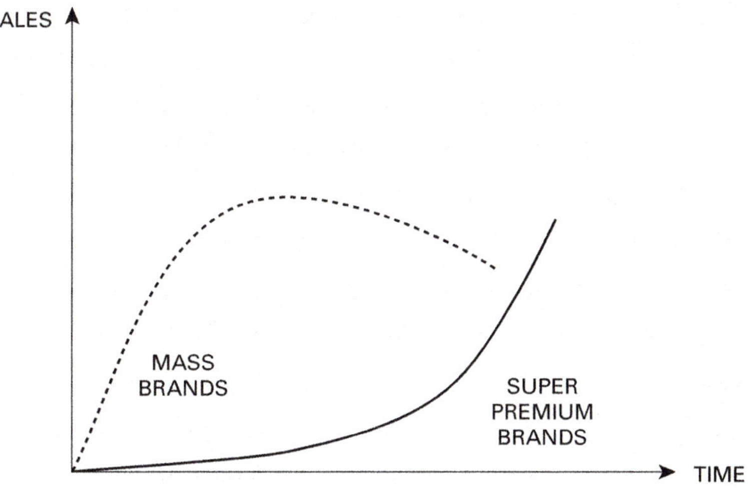

and channels of 'alterconsumption' (an alternative to mass consumption). These channels are points of equity and/or experience advice. Consumers can see, touch, feel and discuss rather than simply hear and read advertisements. Royal Canin sells through vets.

3 These channels are those of opinion leaders, innovators and quality-conscious consumers who will be the proselytes of the new brand as much because of its own story as because of the product itself. Founders of super-premium brands offer the substitution of quality of life for quantity of goods. They promote an alterconsumption model: this is their crusade.

4 The super-premium brands are able to create a community quite fast, because they tell authentic stories about why and how they were created: the founder's obsession. There was an appealing true story about Ben & Jerry's, or Innocent smoothies, or Starbucks. This helped create the buzz and raise immediate sympathy.

5 The super-premium brands are more than brands. They seem to be good companies to work for and with. They attract sympathy, especially if they develop excellent human relationships and become known for their work atmosphere.

Will FMCG groups be able to reproduce these factors? You cannot mix mass and super-premium cultures. IBM some 40 years ago decided to create a dedicated site in Boca Raton to let the developers of the first PC think un-IBM-ly. Nestlé Corporation acted the same way for Nespresso, or Toyota for Lexus, or BMW for MINI: they put them physically apart to let them develop their own culture and story.

Another plan for big groups is to wait and buy these start-ups later and then develop them worldwide. But will the spirit remain? Dove has lost its authenticity. The same holds true for Ben & Jerry's: consumers understand they are now managed by marketing techniques. Is the Body Shop still the same within the L'Oréal Group? Before it was Anita Roddick's fight of her life. Now it is a pawn among others within L'Oréal's portfolio in an area called market segmentation.

There are exceptions: when Gillette bought Braun, it kept it apart. Since Gillette became part of P&G, Braun's headquarters have moved to Geneva. The brand, which used to be like Apple, now risks losing its uniqueness and authenticity.

Brand equity versus customer equity: one needs the other

There is a debate about what is most important: customer equity or brand equity. This is a rather vain dispute. Loyalty bought through loyalty cards, rebates and gifts is a cost. Certainly it creates returns, but brands also need to nurture true love. On the other hand, CRM does help brands to demonstrate that they love customers and want to help them to get the products they need efficiently. Both aspects interact.

Even luxury brands have created customer databases so that the travelling shopper is recognized in any shop of any city. CRM also lets companies make sales propositions by e-mail, in a way that is very customized and matches the customer's personal profile.

The financial value of a brand is a function of the amount of its future expected return and of the degree of risk on these returns. A brand can only be strong if it has a strong supply of loyal customers. This established fact led to a revolution in the practice of marketing, under way since the beginning of the 1980s: the major concern is loyalty and its related factor, client satisfaction. Leaving behind an approach which implicitly concentrated on conquering clients away from the competition, firms now do all they can to keep their own clients. This is to be expected at a time when, as a result of the abundance of offers, buyers tend to jump from one brand to the next, from one manufacturer to the next. Rather than zero defaults, the aim is zero defections.

A lifetime client at British Airways brings on average £48,000 to the company in revenues. Thus under no circumstance should one customer be lost. It is the same for Carrefour where a loyal client brings £3,550 in annual sales. Besides, loyal clients are more profitable. According to a study from the Bain company, a household spends €330 per month in the supermarket to which it goes most often,

85 in the second most frequent and 22 for the one where it only goes occasionally. And not only do loyal clients spend more, but their expenditure grows with time, they become less sensitive to price and they are the source of positive word-of-mouth reports concerning their favoured supermarket or brand. Moreover, they are five times less costly to contact than non-clients. That is why, also according to Bain, by lowering the defection rate of clients by 5 per cent, benefits go up 25 to 85 per cent.

All strong brands are currently establishing loyalty programmes. Nevertheless, a cautionary remark is necessary: no programme of this kind will make up for a service that is not adapted or sufficient. The actions required to keep loyal customers have two aims: the first is defensive, to give the customer no reason for leaving the brand or the company; the other is offensive, to create a personalized relationship with the client, the basis of a more intimate and therefore more involving bond, what Americans call 'Customer bonding' (Cross and Smith, 1994).

The essential part of the defensive side is the identification of the causes of disloyalty and dissatisfied clients. Thus, dissatisfaction linked to the food provided induces, because of disloyalty, a loss in revenue amounting to £5 million pounds at British Airways. The dissatisfaction linked to bad seating costs close to £20 million! Paradoxically enough, the company seeks to get as many voiced dissatisfactions as possible. Indeed, the worst thing is a silent dissatisfied client who, saying nothing to the company representatives, spreads negative rumours among his relatives, colleagues and friends. And there are statistics to prove that a dissatisfied client who is well treated becomes a real proselyte, and even more loyal into the bargain. When asked if they will fly with British Airways again, the rate is 64 per cent 'yes' among those that have never contacted the complaints office. It is, however, 84 per cent among those who have. The treatment of complaints with diligence, care and respect becomes a key lever in customer loyalty.

Seeking client satisfaction implies adding a touch of management spirit where spirit of conquest reigns exclusively. This is why l'Oréal Coiffure is nowadays a company with a conquering as well as an innovative and entrepreneurial spirit. It launches new products one after the other. Hairdressers like the l'Oréal products and l'Oréal knows their product needs well. Unfortunately, this led the firm to somewhat overlook the management spirit: some deliveries were wrong, stockouts occurred, discounts were unevenly granted, etc. The firm responded well to sophisticated needs but somewhat forgot some of the more down-to-earth needs. The hairdresser who put in an order on Tuesday for a tube of light golden brown colouring for a client coming on Friday could not be sure it would be there on time. He could not always count on the company. That is why even when its product launchings were successful, and even if customers were attracted, the sales of l'Oréal Coiffure stagnated for a while. When focusing on client satisfaction, the product alone is not sufficient if the basic service is deficient.

When going over to the offensive, a brand must become a landmark of personal attention. More emphatically, Rapp and Collins (1994) talk of becoming a 'loving company', interested not in the client but in the person. This marks the end of anonymous marketing: attention has to be customized if it is to be efficient. But it has to be acknowledged that even if the terminology of market studies distinguishes between big, medium and small customers, up until recently few companies had developed programmes designed specifically for big customers, who as a rule are also the most loyal. But the loyal client wants to be recognized. He or she therefore has to be identified, a direct bond has to be established and he or she should be the focus of special attention. This is why what is commonly called relationship marketing (McKenna, 1991; Marconi, 1994) uses databases, customers' clubs and collective events, which unite the best customers of the brand. Moreover, realizing that a brand that does not have direct contact with customers becomes further and further out of reach – literally as well as figuratively – many brands have stepped out of mere television advertising and off the shelves to establish a direct relationship with customers. Nestlé offers to its customers a dietician, reachable by phone. Six days a week, Nintendo helps out 10,000 children who are stuck in a video game. The internet provides extended sources of services from the brands, even to non-clients.

In their efforts to increase brand loyalty, brand companies have realized that they have to care about their customer equity or market share. In other words, these companies should focus not only on augmenting brand preference as a mental attitude, but also on increasing brand usage, especially among the best customer prospects: the heavy buyers. Recent findings, for example, recognize that mass market brand profits come not from the mass market, but from the top third of category buyers. Furthermore, a brand's greatest potential for additional profit rests on its ability to increase share in this high-profit, heavy-buyer category (Hallberg, 1995).

Unfortunately, advertising misses the mark with these prime prospects. Instead, it reaches mostly non-buyers or small-quantity buyers. On the other hand, promotions *do* touch the high-profit segment. That is, frequent buyers are more likely to encounter price promotions, coupons, rebates, etc. However, promotions over-sensitize consumers to price and tend to decrease brand loyalty in the high-potential, high-profit segment.

As a consequence, most mega-brands are now experimenting with database marketing on a grand scale. The database marketing concept is two-fold:

- All marketing actions should target the prime segment more effectively. The goal is to increase this segment's rate of brand use.
- Effective targeting requires companies to identify each of these customers or households, almost nominally. As a consequence, a by-product of all promotional activities should be a database, ultimately comprising 100 per cent of the high-profit customers.

At this time Procter & Gamble's database in the USA holds more than 48 million names. Danone's database in France holds 2 million names. Nestlé is building its own in each major country, as is Unilever. And this ignores all the broker-created databases for rental to smaller companies.

The function of these selective databases is to deliver customized offers to specific targets, to bring the store shelf to the home (thus decreasing impulse buying and distributors' power), and to promote a 'private image' among loyal and heavy-user customers. Generally, these customers are more involved in the brand, so they deserve recognition and special treatment. They also merit specific information to nourish brand image and equity. These activities constitute the nurturing of a 'private image', as opposed to a broader, general public image.

Many consumers hold very favourable attitudes *vis-à-vis* particular brands. Nevertheless, their loyalty is insufficient to inhibit switching within a repertoire of brands. These customers are potential loyals only if a tailor-made programme is devised to increase the rate of purchase of a particular brand. On the other hand, some repeat buyers are actually pseudo-loyals: they do not hold strong attitudes regarding the brand. Perhaps, for instance, they buy the brand because of its price or availability. To increase their brand preference, these buyers require a reinforcement of their choice and an increased perception of the brand's superiority. Finally, active and committed loyals should be induced to try more and more new products, whether line or brand extensions. Figure 10.6 illustrates Sony's situation, where committed loyals comprise 19 per cent of Sony's entire customer franchise. The potential loyals represent 4 per cent, and the pseudo-loyals 35 per cent. Each group deserves a specific marketing proposition.

The customer demand for dialogue

Although most brands claim to put customers' needs first, this does not extend to creating a dialogue with them. Advertising does not count as dialogue. Neither does a relationship with a seller with clear marketing intentions, and neither do satisfaction questionnaires: they may be very useful in obtaining feedback on perceived quality, but a series of questions does not constitute a dialogue. Do consumer magazines provide a dialogue? Once again, no. And the same is true of direct marketing mailshots from sellers inviting consumers to see or try out a new product, and the like.

Why do we say 'customer demand'? Because customers want to be valued, listened to and heard, and not merely as an averaged-out statistic in a market segment, but for themselves as individuals. Furthermore, the new internet firms, with their ability to amass 'intelligent' information (which learns from the most recent call, person by person) and use this information in future contacts, have made them accustomed to a responsive reaction and a listening ear. The internet is often the best way to create this dialogue today. Brands now use Facebook and Twitter to become still more accessible.

From product to attentions: from client to VIP

Segmentation leads rapidly to the realization that not all customers carry the same sales potential. It is also true that not all customers have the same interest in an involvement with the brand and becoming

FIGURE 10.6 Brand capital and customer capital

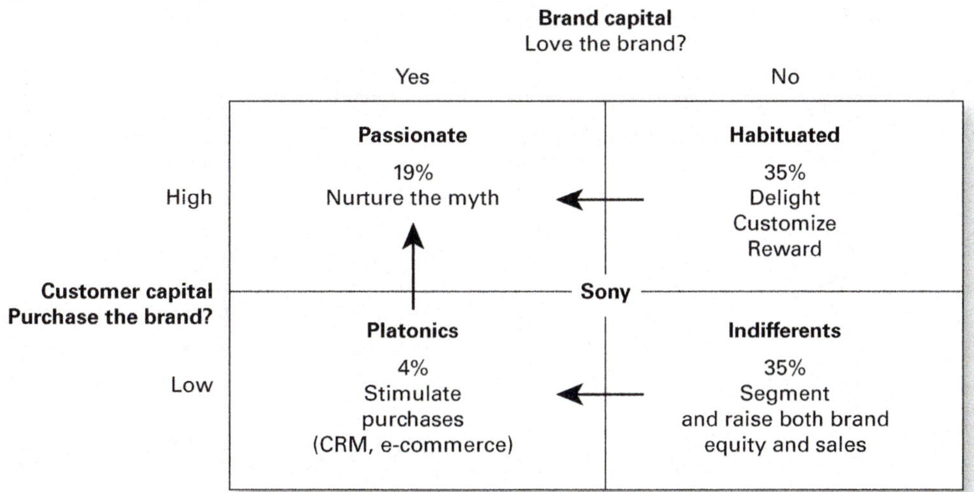

SOURCE Sofres, Megabrand system

its ambassadors. A brand cannot survive without loyal followers and ambassadors, especially if it has premium positioning in its segment: there are women who will spurn all washing powders other than the top-dollar Tide or Ariel brands. This is even more true in high-involvement markets such as automobiles and cosmetics.

Such markets have traditionally been driven by a product-oriented approach: this is why l'Oréal, the world leader, relies totally on research. The goal of its 1,000 PhD-holding researchers is to invent new products which will inspire dreams of beauty and youth among women of all ages and all countries. The l'Oréal Group's flagship brand, l'Oréal Paris, only discovered relational marketing fairly recently. The same is true of the luxury brand Lancôme, which took its first steps in this direction in South America at a time when a brutal economic recession had had a colossal impact on purchasing power. It was essential to retain existing customers and thus enable the business to survive. Clearly, it was not enough merely to expound the virtues of the products themselves: this was necessary, but insufficient under such circumstances. This is why Lancôme's local teams reacted by innovating – not with new products, but with the attention it paid its customers. This example is even more pertinent in that it involved retailers, and thus also created a trade relationship tool which generated business.

Lancôme instructed its authorized retailers to distribute a small smart card – the Lancôme beauty card – and to use equipment that would store the client's last few transactions when the card was presented. This was a revolutionary approach, since the retailers believed that a client record was their own property. In order to 'earn' the card, the client had to make an initial purchase of US$100. All subsequent purchases – regardless of the store, as long as it was a participant in the scheme and had an electronic recorder – would earn points. These points could be exchanged for Lancôme products, lingerie, jewellery and famous-name bags. Cards were also given to journalists and top fashion models. Once a database had been created, it became possible to create campaigns targeting VIPs, who are generally also big spenders, making repeated visits to their local sales point.

The company's first act was to produce and mail to these clients a woman's beauty magazine, paid for by advertising (from airline, jewellery, lingerie and similar companies). 'Sneak preview' announcements were also made of new products, and specific samples were provided, along with access to a dedicated, interactive MyLancôme.Vip website. The VIP card was accepted in selected restaurants and shops. Lastly, selective invitations to public relations events and fashion shows, offering meetings with leading figures, were issued regularly.

The database also becomes a tool for building a relationship between the brand and the sales outlets, for coordinating the promotion of new products, or performing a 'diary' function (reminding store clients of key dates – such as birthdays – appearing in the database, and prompting post-purchase calls). The aim of this is not only to make customers visit sales outlets, but also to enable them to be recognized as special and unique – receiving personalized attention to increase the pleasure of their visit. A VIP wants to be recognized as such.

Sustaining proximity with trendsetters

Today, mass targets have disappeared. Statistics should not create an illusion. What might appear to be mass targets are in fact made up of an aggregation of smaller ones, of micro targets. Even if mass advertising campaigns are still used, what is needed for a brand is a shared image, a collective bonding tool within societies. To develop the brand over time entails improving the brand's relationship with each of the strategic micro targets. These strategic targets are made of more involved customers, or those who are currently non-customers but have the potential to become involved. Once involved they can act as influencers. They can re-energize a brand image that is weakened by the deleterious effects of time.

This is critical for sustaining the equity of mature brands, facing new entrants. Such brands run the risk of losing contact with the trend-setting groups in a society. The risk is that they will be perceived as yesterday's brand. Recreating contact with trend-setting 'tribes' or micro-groups is of paramount importance even for brands that are not involved with fashion in any direct sense. Otherwise they run the risk of becoming just another supermarket brand.

Ricard provides a good example of best practice in its long-term engagement in recreating lost ties with critical groups. It is a historical leader in the aniseed-based alcoholic drinks sector, which comprises the fifth largest spirits sector in the world. It has introduced relational programmes aimed at three groups: women, those of high socio-economic status (SES), and young people. Ricard faces competition both from spirits such as whisky, vodka, gin, rum and tequila, and thus from world-famous brands such as Johnnie Walker, J&B, Absolut, Bacardi and Cacique, and from fashionable modern brands of beer. Finally, it is 40 per cent more expensive than the distributors' brands and other low-cost brands of aniseed drinks. Part of its resistance to these massive attacks has been to remain close to its core clients and to invest in reconquering proximity with the trend-setting groups, those most attracted and seduced by international competition.

Women may like the taste of Ricard but they did not like its image. They perceived it as a male, popular brand, not a sign of good manners. As a response, Ricard runs very specific adverts in trendy women's magazines, and sponsors events involving women. The brand sponsors literary events where new female writers are promoted. It is a major organizer of St Catherine's Day, a promotional event for national design schools. It continues to try out specific relational operations such as a cooperation with Mod's Hair, a youth-oriented hairdressing franchise. Typically, this involves the hairdresser's customers being offered a Ricard to drink while waiting in the salon in the summer. The new format RTD – ready to drink – is very useful for this purpose.

High-SES people of all sexes and ages are addressed through Espace Ricard, an art gallery, open to the latest forms of painting, thus creating a proximity with the most advanced artists and art lovers. In addition, advanced designers are regularly asked to redesign the basic 'tools' that accompany a drink of Ricard, a carafe and an ashtray. The world-famous designers Garouste and Bonetti did the latest versions.

To gain proximity to young people interested in music and sport, Ricard has developed three long-term actions supported by a specific budget allowance. One is creation of the Paul Ricard car racing circuit, compatible with F1 international racing standards, and now the most modern and safe circuit in France. It hosted most of the major international car races, until a law was introduced preventing sports sponsorship by alcoholic drink brands. It was then sold but the name has been retained.

The second innovation is the Ricard Live Music Tour, providing the largest free music events in Europe, featuring famous rock stars. It has attracted more than 1 million people each year, and its name has become synonymous with quality music and concerts. The company has gained unique know-how in organizing open concerts in the middle of major cities and synchronizing sales events around them to maximize synergy. Each concert attracts a great deal of free publicity.

The third youth-oriented initiative is the organization of 1,000 integration parties (for students just going up to university) and graduation parties each year. The targets for these are the top business and engineering schools, since their students will be the elite of tomorrow.

Of course, it is not possible to remain a popular brand without also maintaining a proximity to core consumers, existing heavy buyers and the engaged segment (see the segmentation scheme Figure 9.1). Locally, at the micro level, pétanque contests are still sponsored by the brand in Provence (the birthplace of the brand) and elsewhere. In summer, a squadron of Ricard 'fire girls' runs onto major beaches and offers sunbathers free drinks. For image management purposes, each brand needs to decide which of its many PR activities should receive publicity.

Nine lessons can be learnt from this example:

- Because change is permanent, and new competition is always coming in and can be very seductive, the brand's profile is always threatened over time. It must be nurtured and proximity eventually reconquered.
- No brand can stay apart from trend-setting tribes in its sector.
- Proximity and strong ties can only be built at points of direct contact.
- Strong ties need to be continuous: this is not a 'coup' policy, but a continuous decision.
- This activity must be supported by a strong investment.
- It must be done by courageous people. Trend-setting groups are not waiting to be approached by a currently unfashionable brand, and sometimes they will look down on its promoters.
- Again, targeting is key.
- Again, creativity and disruption are of paramount importance, to surprise and create a buzz.
- Finally, this is the occasion for creating selective publicity, deciding which of these ties should be most squarely in the spotlight.

Should brands follow their customers?

Regularly, the same question arises: should the brand aim at its existing customers or at its future buyers? Should it try to maximize its present customers' satisfaction or should it think of the new generation?

For sure, the global mantra of management today is to focus on existing customers. They are the most profitable source of cashflow. This is why all companies and brands invest in building up large customer databases, CRM software, and undertake in-depth surveys on customer satisfaction with the product or service. This leads to necessary improvements, and in theory it increases customer loyalty. We write 'in theory', for all automobile surveys show that 60 per cent of the consumers who did not buy the same brand on their next purchase were very satisfied with their former brand. Why then did they change? Because consumption is situational. New situations create new expectations: this is called 'value migration'. New generations too develop a new set of values and expectations.

Existing customers are essential for short and medium-term growth and profitability, but listening too much to existing customers is the main reason companies do not innovate enough. Professor Christensen has shown that the main reason companies disappear is that disruptive innovations transform the market and rapidly make their products or services obsolete. What prevents these companies, which are often adjudged to be excellent, from innovating? Arguably they are too well managed (Christensen, 1997). Well-managed companies select the innovations that please their clients and that provide good profitability forecasts with a high degree of certainty. Disruptive innovations are just the contrary: they are not well perceived by current customers, and nothing can be said with certainty about their profitability. But disrupting the market is how the minicomputer made mainframe companies obsolete, then the PC did the same for the minicomputer and so on.

Collins and Porras (1994) have reminded us of the power of the 'and'. Most of us keep on asking questions about alternatives: should the brand do this or do that? It is a mistake. We must do both. Brands must think of their present clients as the immediate source of growth, but they must also look to the future generation.

At present Smirnoff has 60 per cent of the UK vodka market. For most managers, this would be a good reason to be satisfied. Instead, the management of Smirnoff innovated to react to new entrants such as Absolut and Finlandia. Most importantly, it invented a vodka for the new generation, who were not interested in drinking vodka as their parents did, but could be persuaded to drink it outside pubs, not from a glass but straight from the bottle, like a beer. This is called dual management: already thinking of the emerging trends, new behaviours and customers, those who will be dominant tomorrow. Brands have targets: when their customers do not fit the target any more, they should be transferred to another brand. If not the brand will be expanded but also diluted.

11
Brand and products: identity and change

The only way a brand can grow is through movement. You cannot expect growth and lack of change. The brand is continually looking to create new markets, new segments in which it can become the reference and above all the market leader.

Mercedes could have repeated its famous sedans indefinitely, while always improving them, since they were the global image of what a luxury car should look like, to the point at which the Japanese Lexus copied their contours exactly. Meanwhile customers had changed. Those at the edge of leading opinion, who influence the opinion of 90 per cent of the rest, had changed their lifestyle and their points of reference. They were no longer wedded to sedans, but were looking for niche designs of car to suit them. The brand's hopes went into the Class A, the 'little Mercedes', and then the Class M, a luxury 4 × 4: a break with what had been the brand's contract with its customers. It represented a disruption, but not an incoherence or a contradiction. Mercedes could not afford to confine itself to a conception of a car that was becoming a minority taste. Its mission of offering the most reliable cars in the world needed to adapt itself to the requirements of the world.

Only radical change is visible. Otherwise, according to the psychological principle of 'perceptual assimilation', what we see is based on our preconceptions. Accordingly, brands should not hesitate to push their boundaries far from their original prototype. The frontiers of the brand's territory are made always to be pushed back, in the directions of products, geography and meaning. If, in order to manage the brand in the medium term (three to five years) there is a need for tools that fix its limits (such as the prism of identity), it is necessary to review them regularly, to adapt to changing circumstances, and indeed to prompt change. Equilibrium for a brand in a world in perpetual movement does not consist of staying static, but of introducing movement, of fighting a continual battle.

The US fragrance brands surprise us, because they have an air of incoherence. Calvin Klein went from the provocation of Obsession to the idealism of Eternity. Ralph Lauren jumped from the Boston WASP image of Polo to the Safari ambience of 'Out of Africa'. In reality one product does not follow on neatly from the previous one, in the sense of a repetitive coherence that continues the same concepts to infinity, leading the brand inevitably down a path of decline. These products are signs of a brand in movement. Calvin Klein is not either Obsession or Eternity. It is both, a brand both more complex and more open than others had imagined. Renault comprises both the Mégane and the Espace. The future belongs to brands that are able to handle this type of 'and', and to abandon the dichotomous choice of the 'or'.

This is also the message that Collins and Porras conveyed in their *Built to Last* (1994). Chanel surprised us in launching Coco and associating it with Vanessa Paradis. There was an incoherence, a break with the image it had conveyed through its previous figurehead, Carole Bouquet. But this kind of radical move does more to ensure the long-term survival of the brand in an era when it is faced with competition from American and Italian designers who know how to seduce the young.

The paradox is that at the same time, the brand only develops on the basis of a certain permanence, or perhaps a duration. The key concept of the brand's identity carries within itself the necessary continuity of 'identification': the meanings and expressions of the brand. We should not forget that the brand is a point of reference: it indicates a proposition, certain values. That is its first function. To create and build up a point of reference, the brand needs to have a clear sense of itself, a direction. A certain amount of continuity is also essential to the construction and development over time of the brand.

The parallel pursuit of these two requirements (identity and change) leads us to view the brand from two angles: the timeless angle of its basic meaning and identity, and the offensive, disruptive angle of its new developments. This is the theme of this chapter.

TABLE 11.1 From risk to desire: the dilemma of modern branding

Brand = capital	Brand = impulse
Capitalize	Surprise
Repeat	Diversify
Sameness	Variety
Identity	Lead the change

Bigger or better brands?

What are the main characteristics of Western markets? For us the most important thing is that most needs are satisfied. This has considerable consequences.

First, growth will be found in the BRIC countries. Second economic growth will rest on sustained consumption only if consumption itself can be stimulated. This means that brands will have to stimulate desire. This has great implications for brand management. Brands should now deliver experiences, and one of the first is to surprise their consumers.

Another key factor of mature markets is the wish to consume better. Globalization is now a reality for consumers. They are aware that first-world companies have their products made in China or Brazil, that underdeveloped countries will only be able to develop if trade is more equitable, that some companies are more ecology-conscious than others. These considerations have no impact on consumers when their main problem is to fulfil their basic needs. Maslow reminded us that higher-level needs become important when lower-level ones are satisfied. This means that modern consumers do not want bigger brands, but better brands. Sustainable development is here to stay. It is no fad. Perhaps many companies now mention sustainable development in their corporate annual reports purely because their competitors do so, or because they feel forced to do it. Meanwhile their competitors have realized that sustainable development and fair trade are sources of competitive edge. Today intelligence is moral intelligence.

From reassurance to stimulation of desire

Certainly the key concept of brand management is identity: we have been stressing it since 1990, when the first edition of this book was published. 'Identity' means that the brand should respect its key values and defining attributes. However, there is a point where too much repetition of the same creates boredom. Too much predictability is a drawback in modern markets. (Table 11.1.)

This is why the role of modern brands is to stimulate the consumer to have new experiences. The role of the brand in providing reassurance and generating trust is not dead, far from it: but it needs to be used to encourage the consumer to take more risks, explore new behaviours, try new unexpected products. In order to do so, disruptive innovations become very important. To grow through time while keeping its identity, the brand should continue differently.

To this end there is a need for new research tools. Why are all companies now listening to forecasting consultants, trend spotters? Because they need to think now about what consumers are not thinking about today, but will think about tomorrow. Classical marketing research analyses sources of satisfaction and dissatisfaction with the product or service or brand. The outcomes can be used to prompt immediate and continuous improvements. But can disruption come from this type of marketing research? Satisfaction is always linked to customers' existing values and goals. Research is needed also to spot how these values and goals will change, leading to new insights.

Kernel versus peripheral facets

Brand management needs a set of boundaries. This is called brand identity, which covers how the brand defines itself, its values, its mission, its know-how, its personality and so on. A clear sense of identity is necessary, for the brand meaning to be reinforced by repetition. On the other hand market fragmentation, competitive dynamism and the need for surprises call not for reinforcement but for diversification. As ever, brand management will act as a pendulum, going from an excess of sameness to an excess of diversity. There is nothing wrong with this. The same holds true of the local/global dilemma, or the ethics versus business dilemma.

Another consequence is the need to know the identity of the brand. What is its kernel (the attributes that are necessary for the brand to remain itself) and what are the traits that can show some flexibility (the peripheral facets)? If all the attributes of the brand belong to its kernel, that is to say, they are all necessary to its identity, its ability to change will be hampered. How can a brand surprise customers, evolve, adapt to new uses, situations and markets, if it is too rigidly defined? Peripheral attributes can change, or be present in some products but not in others. Eventually, innovations introduce new peripheral attributes, which may become incorporated into the kernel at some point in time. This is how brands evolve through time, how innovations have an impact on their identity. Peripheral traits act as the key long-term change agents within brands (Abric, 1994; Michel, 2000). The tools to identify the traits held by consumers as kernel traits of a brand are presented below but their use is not sufficiently widespread.

FIGURE 11.1 The identity versus diversity dilemma

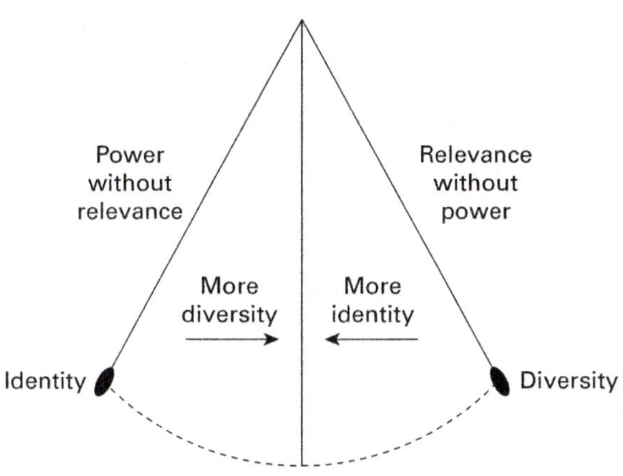

The brands that ultimately last are those that are able to surprise their customers, and the customers of tomorrow in particular. This sums up the challenge facing modern brand management in a nutshell. Far from seeking to capitalize on its past – and thus to repeat itself – the brand should surprise, and promote change. This is what should be termed the 'exploratory function', which plays an epistemic role for the brand (Heilbrunn, 2003). But how can you know what will surprise the customers of tomorrow?

Market studies provide a good understanding of today's customers; or at least, of the expectations they express. So much needs to be done to improve customer satisfaction. How long ago did readers receive a satisfaction questionnaire from their bank? Their car dealers? Their telephone company?

To surprise customers, you need to take a long-term view – hence the growing use of trends in brand management. Trends are hypotheses relating to change that occurs within small groups in our societies, but could potentially create a tidal wave among the general public. These trends are established on the basis of combined information regarding the demographic, technological, social and cultural future of our societies.

We thus need to define three levels of vision: long, medium and short term. Car concepts in the automobile sector, for example, are governed by long-term considerations. Decisions regarding models that are already part of the seven-year production plan are considered as medium term.

Consistency is not mere repetition

Brand messages and slogans are bound to evolve. Evian was, initially, the water of babies, then of the Alps, then the water of balance, later the water of balanced strength, and now a source of youth. These changes in positioning occurred over a long time period: they demonstrate the evolution of the consumer's attitude towards water, the maturation of the market and the evolution of competitive position. The functions and representations of water are not fixed: they depend on external factors linked to urbanization, industrialization, rediscovering nature, discovering pollution, new representations of the body, health and food hygiene. Positioning is the act of relating one brand facet to a set of consumer expectations, needs and desires. As these needs change through time, the brand is obliged to follow suit. However, Evian's identity remained consistent throughout these repositionings.

But within a brand's lifetime these changes in positioning should not happen too often, about every four or five years. However, the brand's means of expression can move faster to integrate with the evolution of fashion: new speech modes, new signs of modernity and new looks. It is essential that the brand is perceived as up to date although such necessary adjustments and changes make the brand run the risk of a loss of identity.

To retain their identity while changing, brands often stick to their communication codes, that is their fixed visual and audio symbols. This is undeniably a factor that contributes to a brand and what it represents being recognized. Even when not named, Coke commercials can be picked out: their music and their style are unique. But the style itself is subject to obsolescence. Continuing with it could prove fatal to the brand.

Unfortunately, it has to be acknowledged that brands have a hard time parting with their communication codes, even when they feel it is necessary. This is to be expected: they are afraid of losing their identity. But this reluctance is largely due to the fact that brand management concepts are essentially static. Time is not taken into account when it is a key parameter in markets. In that sense, the concept of 'communication territory' is a vision that clings to the ground: it has to do with all the visible signals that the brand uses to communicate its definition and what it represents. However, an identity that defines itself only through signs is subject to an alteration of their meaning. The brand is indeed recognized, but no longer in control of its meaning.

Brand and products: integration and differentiation

How, specifically, does a brand function? How are the relationships expressed between the brand and the products or services it sells? What are the consequences? What is brand coherence?

To borrow an expression from G. Mischel (2000), the brand is fundamentally a system that integrates and differentiates. The brand is first of all a tool of *integration*: it is a tool of coherence, by bringing together under its name a range of products and services, each of which must carry the central brand values. A product or service that is not representative of the brand must not carry the brand name. The brand is an explicit normative system: the brand's central values must be known internally and by everyone who has to set the brand in process. They are incumbent on them: we should therefore expect to find them in the products, services and communications. Admittedly, a Toyota at the bottom of the range does not have all the qualities of a top of the range model, but it should embody all the central values of Toyota (for example, exemplary reliability and an excellent quality–price ratio). This is why there cannot be too many central brand values.

The brand is also a tool of *differentiation*: its name sets all its products apart, through their common tangible and intangible values. Because it carries the logo of Danone, whose central value is active good health, Danette, although it is sugary and rich, appears much healthier than a Mars or Lion bar, typically associated with obesity, or a creamy dessert, or ice creams (Figure 11.2).

Like any well-managed brand, Virgin has explicitly stated its brand values: this is what is known as a brand platform. Virgin has six central values, those that belong to its identity kernel. They are 'fun, good quality/price ratio, quality, innovation, challenge, and brilliant client service'. This is its brand contract: as such it is non-negotiable. In fact, in everything that Virgin does, we can find these six ingredients. Hence the brand inspires respect, even if many of its attempts fail. These values are necessary because they help internally to decide whether a decision, action, product or service is 'Virgin enough' to be put on the market to face the competition. Naturally, depending on the products within a range, not everything will represent the brand values with the same relative intensity. A Virgin soft drink will have a lot of 'fun', but even Virgin Atlantic Business Class needs to have a little 'fun' about it, because otherwise it would not be Virgin, and because this is what differentiates it from the business classes of competing airlines.

These brand values are not invented: they are present from the first product that the brand produces.

This is the founding product or service that carries the meaning of a word previously unknown on the market (the brand name). Its commercial success confirms the relevance of these values, and this is strengthened by the extension of the range, which then constitutes the 'core business'. Later, the brand will extend into other businesses, segments and markets, but always under the name of the same values, integrating the whole and differentiating it from the competitors in each market or segment. Andros, an SME from the Lot region of France, based in Biars, began by developing a mass-distribution jam business. That became its core business. Then its competence in fruit and the trust attached to its name led it to penetrate other segments: compotes (against the Materne brand) and now fruit juices (against Tropicana, Joker and other brands).

Brand values and segment expectations

The brand's products must therefore all embody in their way all the central values of the brand, hence the necessity of restricting these in number to avoid creating paralysis. The brand is built through the coherence it imposes on everything it does, and which will be therefore lived experientially by the client.

If there are too many central brand values to maintain, the brand cannot evolve.

It is therefore necessary to differentiate between so-called 'kernel' values, that is, those values that are non-negotiable, and those known as 'peripheral' values, which may be present here but not there, in one market segment but not in another (see page 41). In fact, the brand's products, since they are each in competition in their particular segment with different competitors, should have specific 'pluses' that do not emanate from the brand's central values. Thus Nivea sun cream must be hypo-allergenic, which is highly coherent with Nivea's central value (taking care of oneself), but also add scientific reassurance (not a central value for Nivea), since it is in competition with sun creams from the giants in active cosmetics (the l'Oréal and Estée Lauder groups), which have established science as the dominant code of this market of protecting the skin from sun damage.

At the operational level, in order to manage a brand, the first thing to do is to specify clearly what is part of the brand's kernel (its central values and traits) and what could be variable, since it is peripheral, specific to each segment. This sorting must be explicit (written in a brand platform and diffused via an intranet), and should deal not only with the fundamental values, but also the personality traits of the brand and its tangible aspects. It is notable

FIGURE 11.2 The double role of brands: integration and differentiation

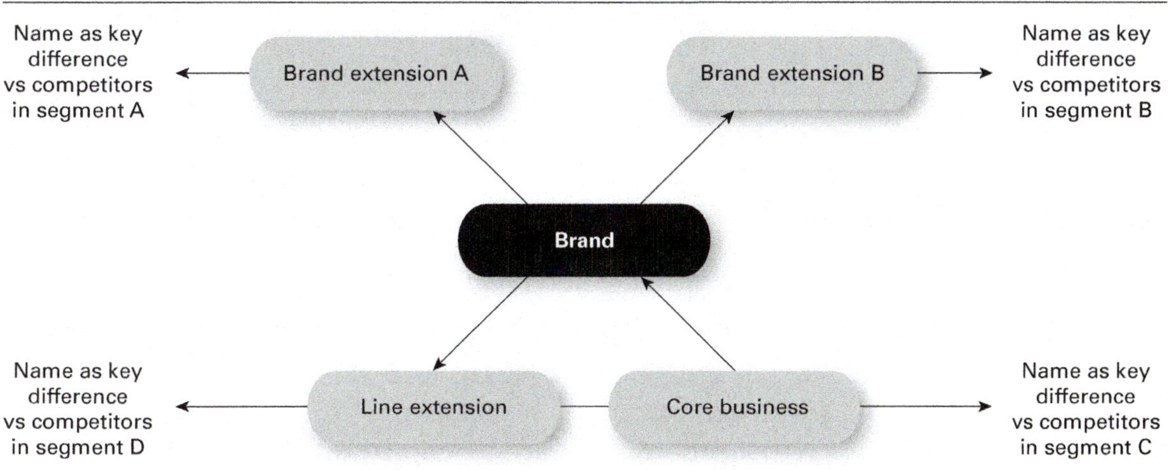

SOURCE Michel, 2000

that Virgin included its 'fun' side (a personality trait) in the central facets of the brand identity.

The exercise of sorting out what is negotiable or even variable, adaptable, must equally involve the physical aspects of the client experience. For the Novotel hotel brand, for example, it is necessary to specify whether its blue colour is negotiable or not, and also the appearance of the reception area in each hotel, the arrangement of the rooms, their furnishings and the level of service. Within a single country, even a region, the client experience cannot fluctuate: this is the effort that must be undertaken in order for the brand to become a benchmark of the quality it wishes to symbolize in an exemplary manner, and on which its reputation will be built. The answer is much less obvious from one continent to another. In fact, the Novotel on Broadway is in competition with other hotels with American standards, in the same way that the one in Bangkok on the banks of the Chao Praya is in competition with the mythical Hotel Oriental: it must be brought up to Asian standards, the highest in the world. Nevertheless, within the portfolio of Accor Group hotels, the hierarchy is always respected: the Bangkok Novotel does not offer the same level of services as the Bangkok Sofitel.

For service brands, rendering the client experience invariable is a challenge: Air France, with its 15,000 employees, has more difficulty homogenizing its in-flight services than, for example, Lufthansa or Singapore Airlines. From one flight to the next, the service delivered is variable, since the company's young stewards and stewardesses show a degree of heterogeneity.

Figure 11.3 provides a reminder that there must also be a physical brand signature, experiential and perceptible. It cannot be reduced to an intangible. Concretely, what must be the physical signature of all Martell cognacs, in comparison with all Hennessy cognacs? What is the physical signature of Lancôme compared with that of Estée Lauder products? It is up to the R&D researchers at Lancôme or the cellar masters in the case of Martell to answer: customers do not have this acuity of judgement.

Specialist brands and generalist brands

Is the Renault brand managed the same way as the BMW brand? Is the Galeries Lafayette brand

FIGURE 11.3 Differentiate what is variable from what is non-negotiable in the brand identity

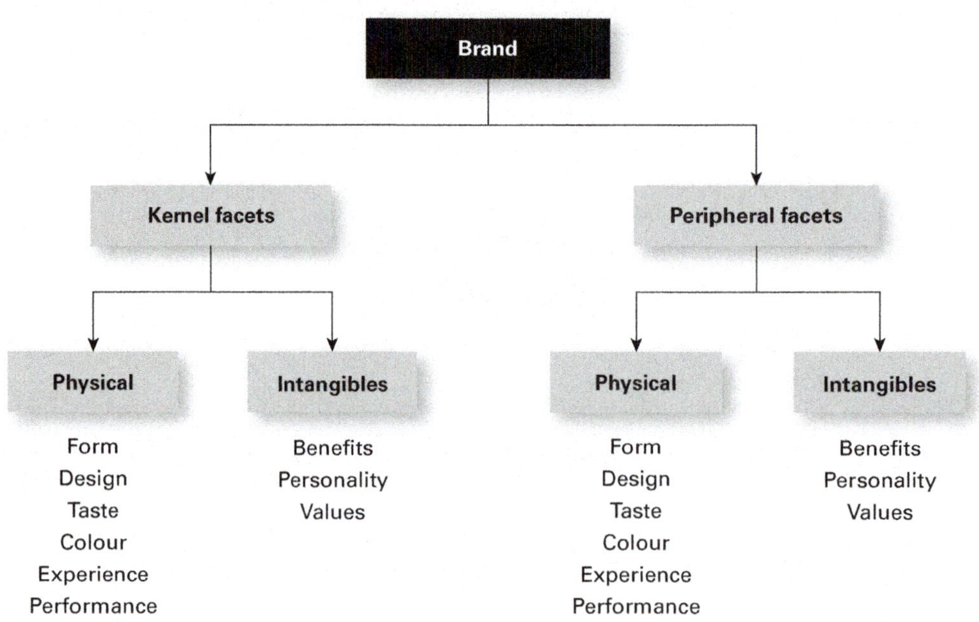

managed in the same way as Ikea? Is the Samsung brand managed in the same way as Apple? The generalist brand offers a broad range under its one name, aimed at covering the needs of all segments of its market sector. It is ecumenical and open. Its business model is that of capitalizing on customers' durable values: by attracting young people via Clio or Scenic, Renault hopes to win their loyalty and therefore later on to sell them a larger model corresponding to the evolution of their life cycle and the needs that follow from it.

The specialist brand is excluding. It sets itself a particular target market segment, of which people either are or are not part, and builds its range according to that single target. For example, BMW targets people looking to buy a car for more than €20,000.

But a brand is a brand: to manage the brand is to undertake a 360° approach to coherence, to create the perception of a differentiated offer, carrying added values, tangible and intangible. The brand is built, in fact, through the coherence of everything it undertakes. The foundation of this coherence is the 'brand kernel identity', that is, the necessary facets of the brand, those that define its singularity over the long term. Building a brand is first of all a matter of defining very clearly, explicitly and publicly what about the brand is non-negotiable, and what must therefore be transparent in everything it does. This preliminary work, called the brand platform, is necessary to help weigh up the daily decisions within the company and know how to say no. Among these questions we find, for example:

- When is a car no longer a Renault?
- When are client relationships no longer managed sufficiently in the Renault way?
- What should the welcome at a Renault dealership be like?
- When does a loyalty programme not carry enough of the values and personality of the Renault brand?
- Given the Renault values, but also its still poor recognition and reputation worldwide, should Renault continue to invest in Formula 1? We know that Michelin answered no to this question from 2007: in fact, the governing body of Formula 1 wished to have only one tyre manufacturer for all the cars, so that the attention would be placed more on the competition between the different motors than between the different tyres. Nothing is further from Michelin's deepest values than a competition without competitors.

At this point, a difficulty arises: the generalist business model is based on the widest range, aimed at all market and customer segments. The specialist model is the reverse: it chooses its segments and therefore its customers. The generalist brand is open and adaptive; the specialist brand is exclusive. The generalist brand must therefore adapt to the rules of each of its market segments in order to succeed there. But how can you introduce brand coherence if you must also adapt to the segments?

The temptation, for the generalist brand, is to define such general and bland brand values that they thereby cease to define a singular offer in each segment. The generalist brand then becomes simply a recognized name, a label of quality and no more, but with no aspirational power. In the stores, the salespeople take note: clients are in a hurry to discuss the size of the discount. They do not nurture any strong intrinsic desire to finally possess 'a Renault' or 'an Opel'. In short, the generalist brand becomes, to use an analogy, a belt from which the models are hung, rather than a pole of attraction expressed by the models. This is why the generalist promotes sub-brands ('the Golf', 'the Qashqai'), whereas the specialist promotes itself ('a BMW'). The generalist turns its models into brands themselves, each with its own personality: not so the specialist. Every BMW is a BMW.

Confronting the risk of the markets becoming humdrum, and therefore of the price-only reasoning that threatens them on the front line, the generalist brand must be boosted with an intrinsic value that is more than the sum of its models. Contrary to the natural catch-all tendency of the generalist, there is a need to give it an exclusive meta-value, a positioning: that is, the power to say no. Being selective means losing short-term turnover, but increasing long-term desirability.

The generalist brand must of course occupy all segments, always assuming that it can exercise its own personal brand imprint there. Will it be able to imprint its strong, aspirational central values there? If not, then it should not go there. Figure 11.4 shows clearly that, even if the base of the pyramid representing the generalist brand is larger by definition, all of

FIGURE 11.4 Generalist and specialist brands

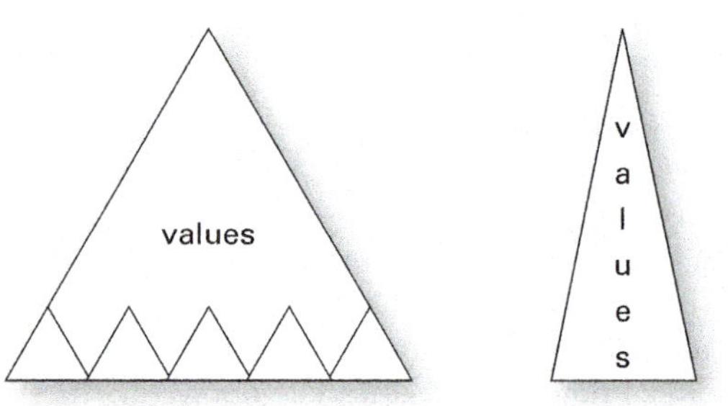

the models must be ruled by a strong common vision and conception. Of course the models must have personality, in order to be intrinsically boosted by added values, but there must be a *leitmotif* between them that cannot only be purely formal.

Peugeot is a model of a generalist brand that has understood how much thinking like a brand means imprinting its difference, and therefore its values, on all its models, all its acts and client relationships. From the little 107 to the splendid 508, all have the feline design that has become so characteristic of the brand: but let no one be deceived, the Peugeot brand is not Swatch, where the differentiation essentially comes down to design. The feline design merely expresses with personality the values found in the brand: audacity, dynamism, aesthetics and reliability. Citroën has also understood how the generalist brand is managed: not like a rake that catches everything, but as a precise, differentiating, aspirational automobile project. Then in each segment the models must each embody each of the three values of the brand's identity kernel. This is non-negotiable. The brand must also respect, in each segment, the price deciles that correspond to its positioning.

The relationship between brand and products also differs between the two cases. The specialist is by its nature highly typified, identifiable and exclusive. The reverse is true of the generalist. In this way we recognize a BMW immediately from its design, but also from a unique driving experience. BMW expresses the virtues of German engineering. Conversely, a Volkswagen is harder to recognize at first glance. This is not to say that its models do not have common traits: they must do, or they could not all carry the same brand. However, there are many more differences between the models in the Volkswagen range than the BMW range.

Volkswagen, like any generalist brand, sees itself as ecumenical: the car that will attract people looking for a small city car (the Lupo) is not the car that must steal market share from the Mercedes C-Class (the Phaeton). At BMW, between the 1 series and the 7 series, there are differences of degree only. They are almost all 100 per cent BMW. Each model reproduces and embodies the essential facets of what we mean by BMW, therefore what we expect from a BMW!

As a specialist brand, BMW is consequently intransigent regarding the conditions that decide whether a model may be called a BMW or not: there are a series of *sine qua non* characteristics. The generalist brand is more flexible: the Renault range went from Twingo and even Dacia Logan to Latitude (the replica of Samsung SM5 in Korea). The Renault brand also has its criteria for inclusion and exclusion, but they are designed to enable greater openness towards different types of car buyer: there are sporty Renaults and softer Renaults, estates and minivans, and so on. Volvo is also a specialist brand. Of course it wishes to grow but remain the model, the referent of cars where security, comfort and reliability come first. This also applies to trucks, cranes, public works equipment and so on. By doing this, Volvo cuts itself off from all those customers who do not have safety as a priority. To brand is to choose and learn to say no.

Building the brand through coherence

All brands grow through multiplication. The brand begins by introducing variants of the initial new product or service that founded its success. This policy of product differentiation makes it possible to increase the brand's relevance, enlarge its presence and therefore its visibility, whether online, among distributors, or on the shelf, if applicable. This also increases sales.

Growth also comes from enlarging the initial target market, and the regular concomitant adaptation of the brand's products. The adoption of new distribution channels often introduces a variation in the offer in order to avoid conflicts between channels, despite the thorny problem of price disparities. Finally, the conquest of the international market, for example via commercial agents, importers or even subsidiaries, may lead to a loss of control, and therefore to a local reinterpretation of the brand, not to mention the many demands for new products that will inevitably arise under the cover of better meeting the demands of consumers in the country in question.

Growth therefore introduces diversity. Hence the challenge: how to manage this enlivening diversity without losing identity? How to introduce variety without losing the brand's specificity, without diluting it? This is the problem of the necessary coherence of the brand. What is, for example, the coherence between Chanel No 5, and all the brand's recent perfumes such as Chance or Egoïste? What coherence is there between Calvin Klein's 'wicked' perfumes Obsession and CK One, aimed at adolescents, and Eternity, a hymn to the family, and Truth?

Since the brand only exists via its products or services, only overall coherence makes it possible to communicate what they have in common: that is, the brand identity. Curiously, the brand coherence criterion is rarely taken into account when evaluating new product projects. These are selected on the basis of their potential sales and profitability, their chances of success in the channel or country in question. The resources available for launching them are also taken into account. The link with the parent brand is a secondary criterion, not perceived to be strategic. The short term is therefore favoured over the long term.

Why brand coherence?

Why worry about coherence? After all, if products are selling well, the company will grow, as will its profits and the brand recognition. However, this is to forget that the company is pursuing another task: increasing its own financial and share valuation, which is affected by the strength of its brands. It is also necessary nowadays to build defences against the cheaper copies that will inevitably emerge on the market. So how does one build a strong brand? Through the total coherence of everything it does, which enables it to emerge from the group of competitors.

For managers, the brand is constructed in stages, from top to bottom: first of all the brand platform is written (the identity of the brand to be created), then the products, services and in-store experiences that best embody them are created. For consumers or customers, it is the other way around: the experience precedes the essence. Their perception of the brand is built through the coherence of their repeated experiences over time. This is why the first contacts with the brands are determining factors in the formation of a long-term image: in which products/services will the brand be embodied? In what channels? By which retailers, department stores or distributors? In which price quartile? Through which marketing communications? Managers must know in advance what perception they wish to create, and must hold fast to it over time, eliminate any action or product/service that does not conform. There is no brand without strong internal policing and without a strong external coherence as well.

Building the brand involves constructing the perception of the specificity of that brand, its exclusive and motivating added value. In perception, as in teaching, repetition and coherence over time are indispensable. Consumers must be exposed to messages and products that, through their diversity, tell perceptibly the same story, each in its own way. After all, if the products have the same brand name, it is necessarily because they have something in common. Admittedly Renault Trucks operates on the worldwide truck market and belongs to the Volvo Group, but it carries the Renault brand and therefore cannot have a clashing discourse.

It is clear therefore that to build a brand, the brand must have coherence, and paradoxically, it is the source of its own coherence. This is why good brand management requires a brand platform: that is, a very short document specifying what makes the brand unique (see Chapter 7). This base is integrative and normative: it must be upheld in order to introduce a necessary coherence if the market is to have a clear, readable perception of the brand.

Of course, repetition should not mean uniformity. Repeating oneself too much is boring: there is not enough innovation, and there are no surprises. Variety, diversity and surprise are ingredients of the modern brand that should permanently stir up interest in it. Too much diversity, however, leads to inefficiency, dispersal and a fuzzy perception of the brand (see Figure 11.1).

The challenge of coherence essentially relates to generalist brands, since their business model is precisely that of encompassing and integrating the ranges of various specialists. They increase in size by doing so, but may lose the perception of uniqueness, both internally (the managers no longer know) and externally (among clients).

No brand without family resemblance

To understand the notion of brand coherence, it is useful to proceed with an anthropomorphic analogy: that of a family. Two things characterize strong, large families: a strong common ethos (shared values or personality traits) and a certain physical resemblance. We recognize a member of the Kennedy clan at a glance. Admittedly, each member is also different from all the others in terms of personality, but they have a common ethos, and physical elements that identify them.

The same must be true of brands. Growth is normal, as long as the identity is maintained: the basis, and the identifying elements. The family membership must be seen and not merely read (the name common to all): in the end, it must be possible to recognize that a member belongs to the family without reading the name.

A brand name is a point of reference: a sign of added value. The fact of putting a product under this name, to categorize it as such, itself confirms that it is a full member of this family, of this brand. It is therefore necessary to visualize it: hence the importance of packaging, labels, design, and everything that is seen on office fronts, factories and distributors. This makes it possible to install the common visual elements that will point to a family relationship. This would seem to be self-evident, but often the first efforts of many managers when extending a range are to introduce a high degree of differentiation between its members, reducing their common elements as much as possible.

Family resemblance cannot be reduced to appearances. As the proverb has it, it is not the cowl that makes the monk, but his religion. It is therefore necessary to ensure that all the brand's products do indeed have the same religion, share the same values, even live them, and express them in their own way.

The objective of family resemblance is not only to create internal coherence and order; it is also a key factor in differentiating a brand from the competition. Of course each product has its own characteristics, but in carrying a name it inherits the promises of this name, which thereby constitute its genuine differentiation amongst its competitors. The main difference between Renault Trucks and DAF or Iveco or MAN is Renault. The same is true for Mercedes trucks.

Take Danone as an example: the central value of the Danone chilled products brand is 'active good health'. Danone likes the active lifestyle and contributes to it. This is not a hospital or a diet brand (like Weight Watchers). The extremely broad Danone range from Activia and Actimel, through to the double-cream gourmet dessert Danette. It could be considered that this constitutes brand incoherence. The gourmet product Danette does not spontaneously evoke 'active good health'. On the contrary, it is rather the halo attached to the Danone name that differentiates Danette (derived from milk) from its competitors (Cadbury's, Mont Blanc cream desserts, Mars bars and so on). This halo of active good health, carried by the parent brand, is the lever of difference.

Coherence is not uniformity. In mature markets, an excess of uniformity kills desire. The growth of the brand via an extension of its product range nevertheless occurs by upholding the brand's central values, or it will run the risk of diluting its specificity. At the same time, too great a resemblance between the models and versions of the brand damages the impression of renewal, and makes it impossible to indicate a clear differentiation within the range. This double requirement is almost contradictory: this is the challenge of brands today.

What cognitive psychology tells us: there are degrees of coherence

How, then, can we manage both resemblance and diversity? How can we include coherence without creating uniformity? In order to move forward on the operational level, a detour through theory will be useful. The questions above are precisely the subject of what is known as cognitive psychology, the study of how people think and form categories. The notion of coherence is not binary: there are degrees of coherence. To return to the brand, this means that not all the products represent the brand in the same way and to the same degree, in the same way that the members of a family do not all have the family resemblance to the same degree.

One of the central subjects of cognitive psychology is understanding the way in which we categorize real objects (Lakoff, 1987). In fact, the human mind is constantly sorting, classing objects together in order to reduce diversity and render reality simpler and more comprehensible. This task is known as categorization. We invent categories.

The modern, polymorphous brand, spread over several markets in different guises, cannot be considered simply as an example of a single category. Danone is not a kind of yoghurt. It is yoghurts, of course, but it is also bottled water, and dried biscuits in Asia. Nestlé gives its name to coffee, and to orange juice in Brazil, to chocolate, baby products, ice creams, iced tea and so on. The modern brand is itself in reality an abstract category, and thus a concept, which is manifested through products. The question of the inclusion/exclusion of these products under the umbrella of the 'brand' supposes an understanding of the laws of categorization. This analysis will be based on the major works of psychologists such as Lakoff (1987) and Boush (1993) in order to fuel the practice of brand management with their key contributions.

Mention is often made of the 'brand concept'. It is necessary to take this declaration literally: the brand is, and indeed works in the same way as, a concept. It is a concept in the same way that 'bird' is a concept, or 'game'. A concept is an abstraction that determines what goes together, and what could possibly be brought together under the same denomination. A concept is therefore a fantastic tool for inclusion and differentiation. We can begin to see the link with the brand here.

Let us take the concept of 'bird', which makes it possible to consider that things as different as a hummingbird and a parrot or a hen belong in fact to the same category (bird), whereas a butterfly (which also flies) cannot. However, an ostrich – which does not fly – is also a bird. The concept is therefore a classification mechanism, for bringing things together that may be very different in appearance.

In order to classify and bring together or exclude objects, the concept must have a content and a rule for admissibility/exclusion:

- Certain concepts class things according to the presence or absence of characteristics: for example, a bird is an animal that lays eggs and has feathers, and which can usually (but not always) fly. We see therefore that certain characteristics are essential (egg-laying, feathers), but others are not necessary for inclusion (flight). Either it is, or it is not, a bird. The frontier of the 'bird' concept is relatively clear-cut. A butterfly has no feathers and is therefore not a bird.
- Certain concepts bring things together on the basis of a group of factors, linked less to the object than to the effect of the object. Take 'game' as an example. What is a game? Thinking about it, the definition is a tricky one: what relationship is there between poker and hopscotch? Between chess (called a game of chess) and a game of hide and seek? Probably the answer lies in the motivations and gratifications that cause us to spend time on these activities, rather than the innate characteristics of the different occupations called 'games'.
- Finally, certain concepts bring things together in a symbolic manner: what is 'good'? Under the umbrella of 'good', we must be able to include some very disparate examples, provided that they symbolize 'goodness'.

This detour via cognitive psychology does not deviate from the question of brands.

- The first type of concept is typically that of specialized brands, with a highly typified product. A Saab, for example, is recognized through its design, its sounds and the driving experience. Porsche is too, but not Toyota.
- The second type of concept would involve a brand such as Volvo. Volvo is summed up in a word: safety, an advantage for users. Volvo is synonymous with security, even in very different markets: public works, cranes, trucks, cars and so on.
- The third type of concept is called 'metaphorical'. Take Nivea: when asked, the managers of this brand repeat *ad infinitum* that the Nivea concept is summed up by 'Love and care'. Its expression in cosmetic products is of a metaphorical kind as regards 'love'. The notion of care can be taken at both a physical level (skin care) and a psychological level (self-care).

Comparing these three types of concept, R van der Vorst (2004) has rightly emphasized that their capacity for integrating variety differs widely. Concepts of the first type (known as taxonomic) are highly specific about their inclusion criteria. As such, they allow very little product variety. The frontiers of the brand are precise.

At the other extreme, certain concepts are relatively vague on the nature of their members. Saying, as France Telecom does, that it is 'the brand of relationships' was fairly non-specific, but consequently rendered the brand open to variety. Its frontiers, however, were not clear.

At this point, a return to cognitive psychology is necessary. It teaches that a category may be defined either by its frontiers, or by its members. In fact, if we take the concept of 'game', it has no frontiers. At its furthest limit, anything could be a game as long as one took pleasure from it. You might think this is overly confusing, and taking it too far.

Cognitive psychology teaches that these categories are however ordered: not all members have the same status, the same representativeness. Some are very good examples of the category, others are less good examples. For example, each person spontaneously thinks of a particular game on hearing the word 'game'. For children it may be hopscotch; for adults, card games. All games can be classed in this way according to their perceived degree of representativeness of the concept 'game'. The most typical game, the best example, is called the 'prototype' (McGarty, 1999). The concept may not have clear frontiers, but its core, on the other hand, is precise, typified by the best example (the prototype).

To return to brands, the psychology of prototypes proves enlightening. What are the frontiers of the Nestlé brand? The brand regularly pushes them back by putting its name to more and more different products. Consumers, however, have no difficulty in classing the products marked Nestlé in order of representativeness, from the most typical to the least typical. Everything works as though they compared each product to the prototype of good Nestlé baby milk. The prototype is not necessarily a product: it can be a person. Richard Branson is the prototype of the Virgin brand: daring, fun and very friendly. This was also the case for Steve Jobs. He embodied 'Apple know-how', and the dwindling brand found a second wind when he returned to take charge. He is also symbolic of Apple values: simplicity, conviviality and creativity.

Relationships between concepts and examples, brand and products

As it is with concepts, so it is with brands. Two levels must be distinguished. The abstract level specifies the meaning of the concept (the brand meaning, the essence of its identity). The second level is that of the brand's embodiments, its products or services.

At the conceptual (brand) level, it is also necessary to distinguish between those facets of its identity that are essential ('kernel'), and those that are not necessary, which can be called 'peripheral'. This distinction is based on the contributions of social and representational psychology. Working on social stereotypes, researchers such as Asch (1946) and more recently in France Abric (1994), and in marketing Mischel (2000), have emphasized the need to sort those facets of identity without which the brand is no longer itself from the other, more peripheral facets. The first group are 'core facets'. For Apple, these were summarized as creativity, simplicity and conviviality. Design for Apple would be a more peripheral trait, specific to the iPod or iMac.

The product level is that of the embodiment of the brand identity. Placing the same name on several products is to tell or promise consumers that there is a certain equivalence between these products. Nevertheless, not all products represent the brand to the same degree. R van der Vorst (2004) recalls that products are constantly in competition. From this point of view, it is important to distinguish those facets of a product that are distinctive and differentiate from their competitors in that segment, and those that are not. Thus colour was highly differentiating for the iMac, not its memory capacity.

It is therefore possible to identify four types of relationship between brand and products, between the distinctive facets of the products and the essence of the brand (the facets of its core identity). (See Figure 11.5.)

- The 'typical example' relationship. In this case, the facets of the core identity of the brand are also the distinctive facets of the product, and vice versa.
- The 'similarity' relationship. In this case, the distinctive facets of the product are the same as those of the core identity, with one or two additional facets specific to the product (colour, for the iMac).

FIGURE 11.5 The different relationships between the brand and its products

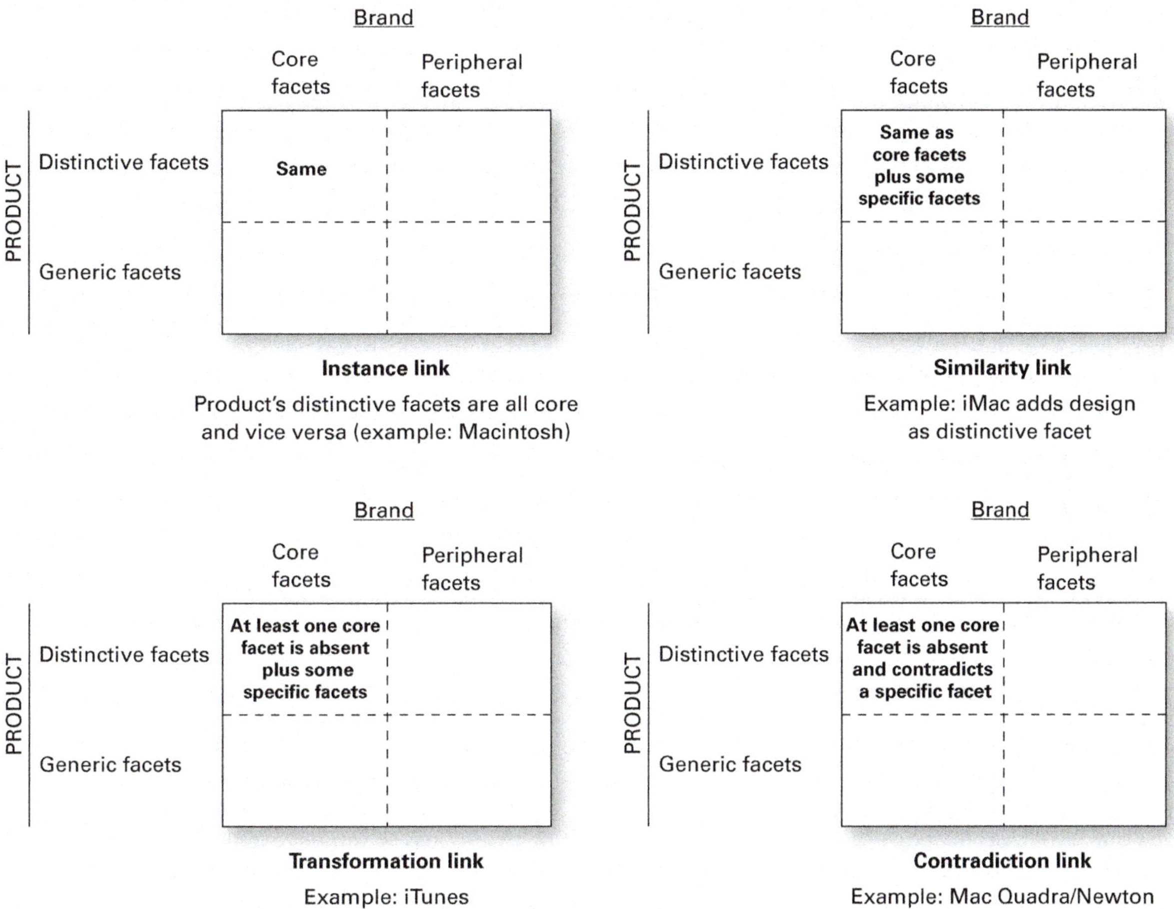

SOURCE adapted from R van der Vorst (2004)

- The 'transformation' relationship. In this case, one of the facets of the core is not found in the product's distinctive facets. This is the case with iTunes for Apple.
- The 'contradiction' relationship. In this case, not only is one of the identifying values not embodied in the product, but it is contradicted by a specific facet of the product in question. The Mac Quadra, a computer created by Apple and intended for company executives, might be thought to be such a case.

Throughout the development of a brand, it is expressed through examples. The primary best-seller becomes the brand's 'prototype', that which shapes the identity of which it is the living and recognized symbol. The small blue tub of Nivea is the 'prototype' of Nivea. In fact, Nivea breaks into all countries through this universal product, which sums up the essence of the brand (love and care) and its associated values (accessibility, universality, simplicity, closeness). This is the first contact for most families throughout the world: everyone uses Nivea moisturizing cream with its pleasant smell. Then the brand develops other self-care product lines, or other examples of the brand that are very similar to the prototype, aimed at a specific target or a particular use: for hands, against sun damage, for children and so on. Of course each one of these must have a specific element, in order to take into account competition in the segment. Their fatal weapon of differentiation, however, derives essentially from the respect for the brand's values and the status that the fact of carrying this brand name confers.

Then Nivea enlarges the circle of its product lines by introducing lines that are transformations of the brand (a key facet may be absent from the product's differentiating elements): deodorant lines, alcohol-based products for men, not to mention Nivea Beauty, where care is absent since it is a wide range of beauty products, of pure seduction (mascara, lipstick, eye shadow and so on). It might be asked whether Nivea Beauty was not in fact a contradiction from this point of view: not only was the care value missing from the distinctive facets of these products, arguably their sales arguments (seduction, artificiality) were contradictory to the brand's essence.

Growth, diversity and managing coherence

Brand coherence is rarely instilled from the beginning. The need for it is only felt when sales stabilize, when margins are reducing and price competition intensifies. Then it becomes necessary to close ranks and hunt down any inefficiencies in order to rededicate financial resources to innovation and communication. The multiplication of products without coherence leads to enormous waste of energy and money. Instead of building a strong, distinctive, unique brand, products are scattered widely under a single name. The first step is therefore to begin again from the name.

Defining the core identity of the brand

At Mars, a fundamental debate divided the company. What were the key facets of the Mars brand? For some, the answer is purely the taste and the sensory experience. For others, the uniqueness of the brand relates to the taste and the energy provided (physical and emotional). This discussion is not a matter of splitting hairs. Depending on Masterfoods' choice of one or other of the two visions of the essence of its Mars brand, certain product lines may or may not be in contradiction with the brand, and therefore incoherent.

Thus, from the first perspective (taste and sensory experience), Mars with almonds is a mistake. Yes, it sells. But nothing is more contradictory to the famous Mars sensory experience than the dry, crunchy aspect of an almond. In fact, many consumers like Mars less once they have tasted a Mars with almonds. The same is true for Mars drinks and the Mars chocolate egg.

From the second perspective, based on taste and energy, Mars with almonds is not contradictory, nor is a Mars drink, but the Mars egg remains so (it was created to counter the Kinder egg, so strong on the notion of the parental gift). Note that the two visions of Mars do not offer the same prospects in terms of variety, and therefore of the inclusion of new products and new consumers (van der Vorst, 2004).

Defining Mars as a 'taste and sensory experience' is to define inclusion according to the product's character. This is a concept with clear borders, linked to the characteristics of the product. On the other hand, it leaves open the consumer benefit and the targets. Nothing in this schema prohibits the creation of new products, coherent with Mars of course, but also with the added benefits of energy here, of indulgence there, of a gift there, of sharing there. Moreover, this brand perspective makes it possible to aim at very different targets: men with a chocolate bar, women with Mars Delight, children with Mars Mini and so on. This brand essence categorizes the products, but less so the clients (van der Vorst, 2004).

Defining Mars as 'taste and energy' opens up a multitude of organoleptic formats (bar, drink, biscuits, ice creams and so on) but is much more restrictive in terms of consumer benefits and clients. Here a choice has been made: to address those clients and situations where energy is a key expectation. This brand essence categorizes the clients, but less so the products.

How is the brand's core identity identified? Recall the central precept: the truth of a brand lies in the brand itself. By studying the heritage, roots and history of the brand (its DNA), potential facets of its core can be identified.

However, the evaluation of the clients themselves must be sought on this, in order to avoid a gap between an exhumed past identity, and the present reality (the market opinion): identity is not a point of view. For example, 'radical progress' is certainly in Citroen's DNA, but is it still attributed to the brand today? It is therefore also necessary to integrate the perception of consumers or industrial clients themselves. In addition to the image study that identifies the traits associated with the brand, another study must be carried out, to identify which of these traits are critical to the brand, the others being peripheral.

FIGURE 11.6 How to identify kernel and peripheral traits through research

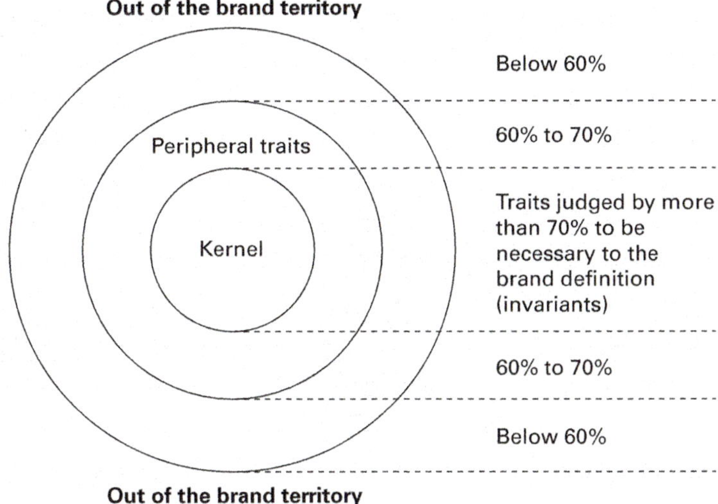

G Michel (2000) has contributed to this by transposing the methodology of social psychology to marketing.

To find the answer, it is enough to ask interviewees whether a new product that does not have one or other of the brand's image traits could nevertheless carry the name of said brand. If the majority say no, it is a non-negotiable trait: it belongs to the core identity. The peripheral traits may be present or not, according to the segments and the products of the range that correspond to them (Figure 11.6).

However, if the core identity is subjected too much to the judgement of consumers who are constantly evolving, a deviation could be created. For the directors of BMW, a BMW will always have rear-wheel drive, since this is the necessary physical signature of the unique driving experience of the cars of this brand. This would be true even if certain potential customers expressed the opinion that, for them, a front-wheel drive would not change their love of the brand. Managing is not about following, but about having a vision.

Confirming the presence of brand core facets in each product

There is no brand: there are only expressions thereof. These expressions shape the representation. For the brand to be strong and distinctive, every expression must carry the brand's identity facets, and these must be clearly visible. Therefore each of the products or each of the daughter brands will be analysed – their packaging, their physical product, their communication, their price, their merchandizing and so on – in order to identify whether the key facets, those of the core identity, are all well represented and active in these products and daughter brands. Figure 11.7 illustrates how the different Lacoste lines activate the three facets of the core identity (elegance, comfort and naturalness) and provide specific touches here or there (more technique, more fun, more luxury, more fashion). If this were not the case, the product would have to be brought into line with the brand, or dropped.

Identifying the role of each product line in the construction of the brand

At this stage it is necessary to understand the link that each product line and daughter brand has with the parent brand. Is it a prototype? Should it become tomorrow's prototype? Is it a typical example? Is it similar? Is it a transformation? Is it contradictory?

According to the link that each line must have, a greater or lesser degree of distance in the expression of the line itself will be accepted. First of all, signs of strong cohesion are expected: the distances can only

FIGURE 11.7 Each product line embodies most of the core facets and adds its own facets

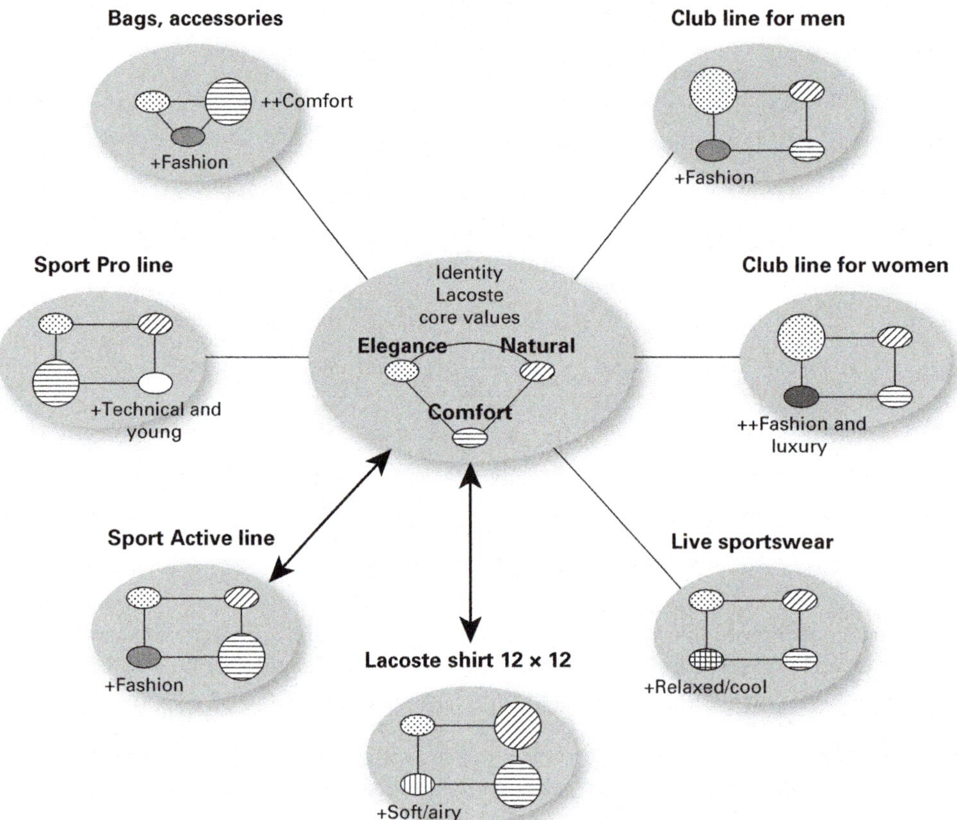

be a function of the link identified above. This also has an impact on the decision to give the product line its own name (giving it the status of a daughter brand) or not. Finally, this will determine the parent brand's posture towards its products: this will be examined further on through what are known as the umbrella, source, endorsement and maker's mark architectures (see Chapter 13).

The marketing function of each product line or daughter brand will also be specified: of course it must absolutely observe and activate the central values, but also bring a new contribution. This might be, for example:

- modernizing the brand by becoming its new prototype (Activia is the new Danone prototype, and has replaced its old prototype of natural yoghurt);
- rejuvenating the brand by opening it up to younger clienteles;
- bringing a new facet to the brand, such as technical expertise or a pleasure dimension;
- strengthening certain identity pillars of the brand: for example, the tennis lines strengthen the identity of Lacoste, the eponymous brand of the famous Musketeer René Lacoste, at the moment when its global competitor Ralph Lauren invented a tennis legitimacy for itself by sponsoring the 2006 Wimbledon tournament and launching a line of Wimbledon clothing.

Mapping the product line

The brand must therefore be thought of as a concept, whose meaning unifies the products and distinguishes

FIGURE 11.8 Organization of Mars masterbrand and products

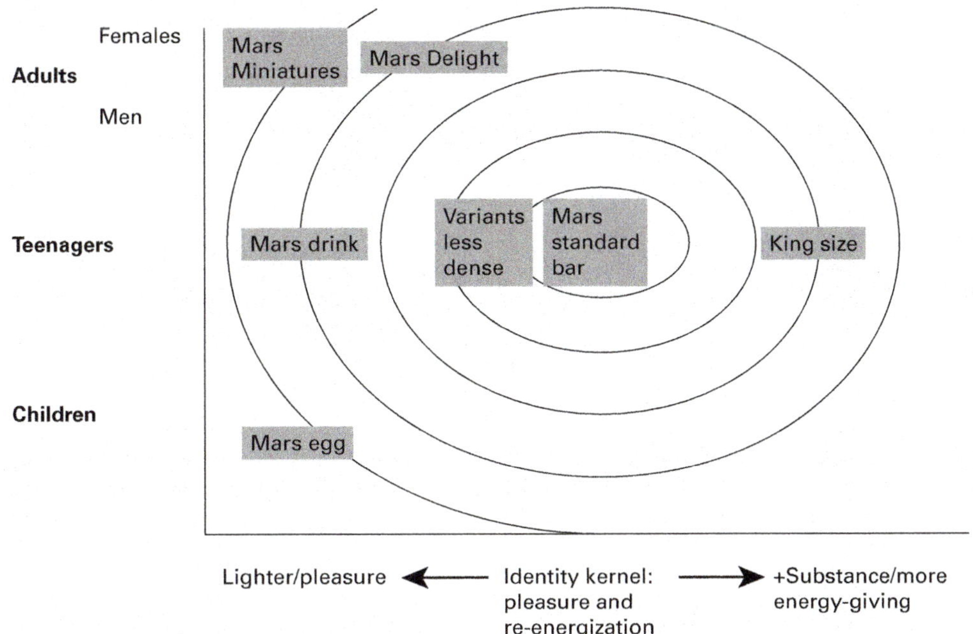

SOURCE R van der Vorst, 2004

them from the competition. It is only expressed through its products, communications and activities in stores and other aspects. It is important to understand the overall system set-up, by mapping all the products seen as expressions of the brand, placed according to their distance from the central values of the brand. In Figure 11.8, we have mapped out the current Mars system. This exercise is necessary to avoid a common pitfall: a system that is empty at its centre.

It is possible, in fact, for everyone to be conscious of the values of the parent brand (also known as the masterbrand) but for no product of the range to assume these values 100 per cent and become the prototype. What is often found is a situation where the brand has three distinctive facets A, B and C; certain products carry value A, others B, and the third group facet C. This situation, however, does nothing to build the brand up with values A, B and C.

The brand is not an average, the sum of disparate discourses. It is built up in image and sales through successive products. These must be bearers of all the core values. Admittedly it is possible to place a stronger emphasis on this or that facet, but all the facets must be well and truly present. Thus the premium line 'Club de Lacoste' does indeed emphasize elegance, but also activates the two other central brand values, comfort and naturalness.

Checking the coherence worldwide

The exercise described above should be carried out by geographic region. Here it may then appear that the same product does not have the same link to the parent brand on different continents, or the same role, or the same positioning. These situations lead to inefficiencies and should be corrected if necessary. It is nevertheless possible for local specificities to require adaptation. For example, in Germany, a country whose car-making pride is well known, the 'prototypes' of the Peugeot brand are the CC models of the 207 and 307. In fact, these represent a type of car that German car makers were not offering at the time: a convertible coupe. They represent more than 35 per cent of Peugeot sales in Germany, and carry the central image of the brand (dynamism, aesthetics and value), with emphasis on the first two facets.

Brand globalization therefore requires a double coherence: as discussed above, of the products in

FIGURE 11.9 How the brand is carried by its products, each with its own emphasis

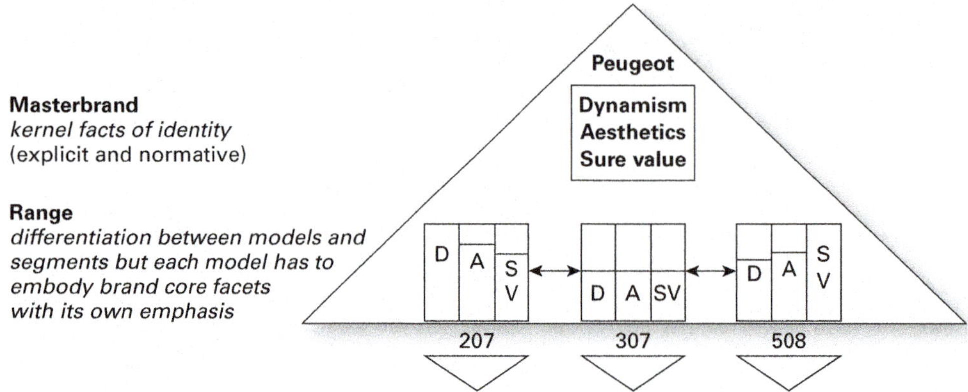

relation to the central facets of the masterbrand (masterbrand central or core facets), but also of each region of the world in relation to the identity of each product itself. (This point is developed further in the chapter on globalization.) Figure 11.9 summarizes our statement.

The three layers of a brand: kernel, codes and promises

The evolution of a brand needs a direction. Considering the brand as a vision about its product category, it is important to know in which direction it is looking. The brand being a genetic memory to help us manage the future, we must know what drives it, what is its prime reason for existing.

All these concepts (source of inspiration, statement, codes and communication themes) work together in a three-tier pyramid that is useful in managing the balance of change and identity.

- At the top of the pyramid is the kernel of the brand, the source of its identity. It must be known because it imparts coherence and consistency.
- The base of the pyramid are the themes: it is the tier of communication concepts and the product's positioning, of the promises linked to the latter.
- The middle level relates to the stylistic code, how the brand talks and which images it uses. It is through his or her style that an author (the brand) writes the theme and describes him- or herself as a brand. It is the style that leaves a mark.

Of course, there is a close relationship between the facets of the identity prism of a brand and the three tiers of its pyramid. An examination of advertising themes reveals that they refer to the physical nature of products or to customer attitudes or finally to the relationship between the two (particularly in service brands). They are the outward facets of identity, those that are visible and that lead to something tangible. The style, as with one's handwriting, reveals the brand's interior facets, its personality, its culture, the self concept it offers. Finally, the genetic code, the roots of a brand, inspires its whole structure and nurtures its culture. It is the driving mechanism. There is, therefore, a strong relationship between stylistic codes and identity. In Volkswagen's case, its sense of humour is the consequence of solidarity because it demonstrates the rejection of car idolization, the cult which leads to a hierarchical ranking of drivers and therefore to their animosity towards each other.

This idea of levels or tiers within the brand provides a tool which allows freedom for the brand in the sense that the brand no longer has to define itself by repeating the same themes. The choice of the theme has to integrate the needs of the times. It is founded on the reality of products and services. It corresponds to a concern or a desire of a particular market segment. Alongside these criteria, one must respect the brand's identity.

FIGURE 11.10 Identity and pyramid models

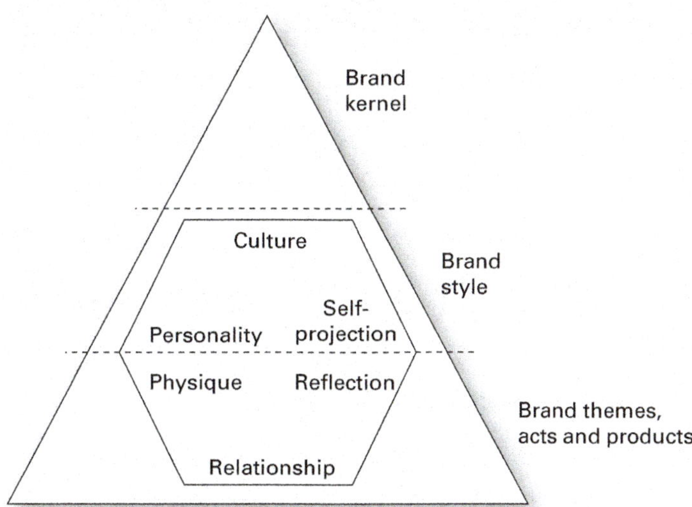

Brand communication can thus vary in its facets. Over time it seems first to start with the physique, goes through the reflected image and ends with the cultural facet. Benetton first launched its colourful sweaters, then modernized to appear more dyamic, before identifying with a set of universal values (friendship, racial tolerance, the world village). This evolution is normal: the brand goes from tangibles to intangibles. It starts as the name of a new product, an innovation and later acquires other meanings and autonomy. Benetton is now a cultural brand and addresses a range of moral issues. Nike moved from product communications to behavioural values (just do it!).

The pyramid model leads to a differentiated management of change. The brand's themes (its positionings) must evolve if they no longer motivate: it is obvious that Evian had to move from balance to youth. All themes tend to wear off and competitors do not stand still. The stylistic code, the expression of the personality and culture of the brand, has to be more stable: it enables the brand to gently pass without disruption from one theme to another. Finally, the genetic code is fixed. Changing it means building another brand, a homonym of the first, but different. This is how, even if the positioning of Evian has changed with time, from being the water of babies, to that of the Alps and that of the strength of balance, there is a strong sense that the basic identity has been preserved. Evian never was a water against something, but a water for something, natural and loving, a source of life. It is not for nothing that its label has always been pink: this colour is linked to the brand's kernel, its essential identity, those traits that are necessary to the brand. Without them, it would be another brand.

Finally, the idea of different tiers within the brand gives particular flexibility to those brands which embrace many products. In managing these products one must respect their individual position in their own markets. They may carry different promises for each product, provided they appear to emanate from a common source of inspiration. In this respect, brands work as a superstructure.

How each product builds the masterbrand

There are no brands without products. Clients buy branded products; they do not buy brands only, even if the brand name may weigh heavily on their choice. As a result, products must both be in line with the brand and offer better value compared to their competitors. In other words, a Mars ice cream must be far better than a Magnum, and a Mars drink must be more attractive than another cold chocolate drink. To ensure this, the product manager of Mars ice cream will look for product insights: what makes people love ice creams today, what are they looking

TABLE 11.2 Nivea: specifying how each sub-brand builds the masterbrand

Sub-brand	Role definition	Key personality
Nivea Cream	'Prototype' of Nivea	Uncomplicated
Nivea Soft	Rejuvenation of 'prototype'	Modern
Nivea Body	Adds harmony between body and soul	Vitality
Nivea Sun	Adds high protection expertise	Harmonious family
Nivea Visage	Builds up the brand credentials in cosmetics through innovations	Feminine
Nivea Vital	Nurtures the brand's skin and face care expertise for a new segment: the seniors	Honest
Nivea Baby	Adds competence in ultimate mildness	Warm
Nivea Deo	Adds dimensions of efficacy to that of mildness	Honest
Nivea Bath Care	Adds dimensions of pleasure	Individual
Nivea Hair Care	Adds dimensions of health and beauty	Active, dynamic
Nivea for Men	Innovative, adds universality	Non-macho, confident

for, and what for them are the signs of a desirable ice cream? The same applies to the Mars drink.

The consequence is that each product must add specific benefits or attributes and in the meantime sell the brand. We have analysed this point on page 177.

Products can be either variants or sub-brands. Variants reproduce the brand value with high loyalty. All Apple products express the kernel values of Apple in the same way, although in different categories. That is why they are named in a similar way: iPod, iPhone and iPad embody Apple's creativity, user orientation, aesthetics, ergonomics, delight, etc. Sub-brands all have a touch of value difference. They are not simply variants. Their role is to bring their difference to the masterbrand in order to make it more attractive.

Table 11.2, representing the Nivea system, shows how each sub-brand adds specific values to the core brand: for instance, Nivea Sun is the only one that needs strong scientific credentials. People fear the effects of the sun. A product signed Nivea must give security. Nivea's kernel (unlike that of L'Oréal Paris) does not include science. However, Nivea Sun does and adds this as a peripheral facet.

In addition, each sub-brand, competing in a specific segment, needs to have the ideal personality to compete in this segment.

FIGURE 11.11 Olympic brand architecture: the rings and the games

The Olympic symbol is the core 'brand' of the London 2012 Games, driven by the Olympic vision (one can build a better world through sport) and by the three Olympic core values (excellence, friendship and respect). The five colours are the five continents

London 2012 embodies all three Olympic core values and adds its own distinctive facets distinguishing it from former summer Olympic Games. Its unique positioning is 'open Olympics', meaning that everyone should participate, not only by viewing but by doing. Beyond sport it is also about culture, education and the environment.

Sochi 2014 will promote its own distinctive facets and reinforce the three Olympic core values.

Rio de Janeiro 2016 will be the first Olympic games held in the Southern hemisphere. Brazil will endow them with specific values.

12 Growth through brand extensions

Brand extension is now a classic of brand management. When they wish to enter product categories from which they have been absent, companies use the name of an existing brand, born in another category, rather than a new brand name created for that purpose. Yet brand extension is not a recent phenomenon (Gamble, 1967). It is inherent in the luxury goods sector: the luxury brands originating in haute couture have extended to accessories, fancy leather goods, jewellery, watch-making, even tableware and cosmetics.

In the same way, the first distributors' brands (Migros in Switzerland, St Michael in Great Britain) covered several differentiated categories of products. Industrial brands themselves were extended beyond their initial product type to cover a range of diversified activities under the same name: Siemens, Philips and Mitsubishi have been using brand extension for a long time. Indeed, brand extension is even used systematically by Japanese conglomerates: Mitsubishi includes shipyards, nuclear plants, cars, high-fidelity systems, banks and even food under the three-diamond brand (the visual symbol of Mitsubishi).

Brand extension has become common practice. What was reserved for luxury goods is becoming a general managerial procedure: Mars is no longer only the famous bar but an ice cream, a chocolate drink and a slab of chocolate; Virgin covers everything from airlines to soft drinks; McCain covers French fries, pizzas, buns and iced tea; Evian now endorses cosmetics. For all those executives brought up on sacrosanct Procterian dogma according to which a brand must correspond to one, and only one, product, the present situation leads to thorough rethinking; even Mars, for so long the typical example of a product brand, has become an umbrella brand covering very different segments and products. Such development is the direct consequence of the recognition that brands are the real capital of a company and a source of competitive advantage if they fight in-growth markets.

Brand extensions are one of the hottest topics in brand management. They have spawned a rich and intense body of research. Some experts keep claiming that brand extension should be avoided (Trout and Ries, 1981, 2000). However, today, most companies, even those that were culturally the least prone to engage in brand extensions, have extended their brands. In fact, as we shall demonstrate, brand extension is a necessary strategic move at some point in the life of a brand. It is an essential way to sustain the brand's growth, once other approaches have been explored. Let us remember that growth should be built:

- First, by increasing the volume of purchase per capita of present customers of the present product (see Chapter 9).
- Then by new product development and line extension to increase the brand's relevance and address the needs of more specific targets or situations. Line extensions are, in fact, proliferating in modern supermarkets (page 199).
- By the globalization of business in countries offering high growth opportunities (see Chapter 17).
- By innovating to modify the competitive situation, create new advantages or open new markets, thus benefiting from the pioneer advantage (page 201).

TABLE 12.1 Relating extensions to strategy

	Products	
Markets	**Present**	**New**
Present	Intensive growth	Market development
New	Market extensions	Diversification

At this time the question of naming the innovation becomes acute. Should one extend the brand portfolio by adding a new brand (as when the Coca-Cola Company added Tab to its portfolio) or call it instead by the name of an already existing brand (Diet Coke, for instance)?

When an innovation is not in the core market of the brand, it means that the brand will extend out of this core, a process also called brand stretching. This is why brand extension is such an important topic: it is about the redefinition of the brand meaning. It is not possible to grow the business indefinitely without changing some facets of the brand. Hence the question, is the essence of the brand intact? Does the extension preserve the kernel? Also, what does the extension bring to the brand equity, to the brand image, beyond growing the business? These are indeed strategic questions.

Beyond branding itself, extensions are often diversifications, entries into unknown markets, with a different product from previously (see Table 12.1). As such they are a strategic move.

What is new about brand extensions?

Why has brand extension become such an important topic? In fact, most companies have discovered the virtues of brand extensions only recently. Certainly most luxury brands have thrived through extensions, and so have Japanese brands, and indeed Nestlé, but in North America most marketers have been trained in a 'Procterian' vision of marketing. At Procter & Gamble, since its foundation, a brand has been a single product with a benefit. As a consequence, the rule has been that new products should form a new brand. P&G's Ariel (known as Tide in the United States) is a specific low-suds detergent. Other detergents have other brand names such as Dash and Vizir. This practice is thoroughly product-based. It worked in the United States because the domestic market was large enough. It does not work as well in smaller countries. That is why in Europe and Japan marketers have not adopted it.

The brand extension perspective introduces two radical modifications. First, it maintains that a brand is a single and long-lasting promise, but this promise can or should be expressed and embodied in different products, and eventually in different categories. 'Palmolive' represents softness, and from this perspective it makes sense to have Palmolive hand soap, dishwashing liquid, shaving cream, shampoo and so on.

Second, it asks us eventually to redefine the historical brand benefit by nesting it in a higher order value. Brand extension exemplifies the move from tangible to intangible values, from a single product-based promise to a larger brand benefit, thus making the brand able to cover a wider range of products. Is Gillette simply the best shaving product, or 'The best a man can get' as it says in its advertising baseline? This latter brand definition easily backs up the Gillette Mach 3 or Fusion, aimed at continually increasing the quality of a man's shave. It allows also the brand to grow by leveraging its reputation and trust to introduce a line of male toiletries, a profitable, growing market.

Brand extensions are an emotional topic because they are the first occasion on which the identity of a brand is redefined, when all the unwritten assumptions that may have been held for decades about the brand within the company are questioned. In addition, unlike mere line extensions, brand extensions are associated with diversification, so there is a sizeable impact on the company as a whole. Diversification is a strategic concept, which has implications for the whole company. Will it be able to learn all the new competences required to meet competition in the new market? At what price? With what delays? At what cost? Is it worth it? Is it sustainable? The brand and business perspective promoted by this book calls for a reinsertion of brand extension issues into the context of corporate strategy.

Finally, it is an involving topic because it is generally tied to a new product launch, which as for all new products commands time, energy, allocation of resources, and creates a situation of risk. This risk is increased by the fact that unlike line extensions, brand extensions lead the brand into new and unknown markets, which may be dominated by entrenched competitors. There is not only a straightforward financial risk should the extension fail, there is also potential damage to the image of the brand, in the distribution channels, among the trade, and among end users. A good example is the problems encountered by Mercedes when it launched its new Class A, a radical downward extension, after it decided to go where the market was and compete against Volkswagen. The car could not pass the 'elan test', thus destroying the sacrosanct image of Mercedes as one of the most secure cars in the world. The whole conception of a Mercedes car had to be redefined. One does not move easily from a high historical competence in manufacturing large sedan cars with rear wheel drive to making small compact cars with front wheel drive. Also for the first time, one could buy a new Mercedes for around €20,000.

This example illustrates the fact that brand extension decisions should not be looked at only through consumer research. However, consumers are quite conservative. They do not have a full picture of the Mercedes situation, and finally they do not have a long-term view. Very few people knew, for instance, that the average age of purchasers of the Class C, at that time the entry-level Mercedes, was 51. Also, very few people knew that unless the company was able to produce more than a million cars rapidly, its production costs would be too high to sustain modern competition even in the premium segments. Higher production costs provide no value to consumers.

Brand or line extensions?

When should one speak of line or of brand extension? We developed the case for line extensions in Chapter 9. This is a necessary step in growing the brand through:

- An extension of the line to enrich the basic promise through diversity (like providing new tastes, new flavours for a jam brand or a crush brand such as Minute Maid).
- A finer segmentation of a need (like the many variants of each shampoo brand according to the type of hair, age of customer, or kind of scalp problem).
- Providing complementary products. As mentioned in the discussion on line brand architecture (Chapter 13), a brand might provide all the products involved in solving a specific consumer problem. A brand fighting hair loss would not limit itself to its first product, a shampoo for instance, but also provide a gel, a hair dye and so on.

What is noticeable is that through these line extensions, the brand aims at intensive growth. It deepens its problem-solving ability more or less to the same customers, for the same need and consumption situation. This is not viewed as a diversification (which involves different clients and different products).

At the other extreme no one would quarrel with describing as brand extensions, rather than line extensions, Virgin Airlines, Hewlett-Packard's entry into the digital photo business, the Mercedes Class A, the Porsche Cayenne (its entry into the 4 × 4 market), Yamaha bikes (from a company originally known for its musical instruments), the Caterpillar fashion line, Salomon new surfboards (for the Hawaiian and Australian beaches), Ralph Lauren domestic paint, Evian cosmetics, Apple moving from computers to iTunes music store, or GE extending from electricity to capital investment. Typically in such brand extensions, the brand moves to another remote category, in which it is open to question whether it has the ability to deliver the same benefit, and therefore to stay the same. The buyers may be different, or the same: the first to buy the Porsche Cayenne were existing Porsche owners who now have two Porsche cars. In fact most of the early research on brand extension has focused on remote extensions, far from the prototypical product. Some of these brand extensions are more than simply brand extensions: they are real diversifications. The company wants to develop itself in new categories that may become dominant in its future sales. Certainly this is not the case for Caterpillar, but it could be the case for HP, stuck between Dell and IBM in its core activity. Few people recall that Findus, the name for frozen food, comes from 'Fruit Industry', the core original business of that Scandinavian company.

Where does line extension end, and where does brand extension start? Perrier is a case in point. To grow its sales the brand has launched three new products in three years:

- In 2001 it launched its first 'Pet' bottle, nicknamed 'rocket' because of its specific shape. It was the first time since the brand creation (in 1847) that a non-glass bottle had been created. It was aimed at mobile consumers and out-of-home consumption situations (such as stadiums and offices).
- In 2002 Perrier Fluo was created: it is an aromatized water in a plastic fluorescent-coloured small bottle. It is aimed at the young and competes in the soft drink market.
- In 2003, Eau de Perrier was launched to try to achieve better penetration in the table water market. The famous Perrier bubbles, which are the essence of the brand, prevent the brand from appealing to those who like to drink less bubbly water with meals. This extension had finer bubbles (like San Pellegrino) and a finer and more elegant bottle.

How should these extensions have been described? At Nestlé Water, the owner of Perrier, they are called line extensions for the sake of simplicity. However, despite the fact that all these new products are basically water, the soft drink entry qualifies as brand extension more than the others. It aims at a market dominated by other competitors, which is subject to other success factors, and is aimed at different consumers.

The ability of any product given the Perrier name to meet the demands of the soft drink market is surely a long-odds bet. Here promotion and place are essentials. Also, the brand evokes less fun than any other soft drink brand. This is why the decision was taken to have Perrier only endorse the product, the big name on the bottle being 'Fluo'. This refers both to the very odd colours of the bottle and to the fact that it is fluorescent in the darkness, a typical situation in discotheques and late-night bars. However the main question will be the ability of Nestlé Water to cater to these new circuits of distribution and consumption.

For Aaker and Keller (1990), brand extension refers to the use of the name of a brand on a different product category. This was the case when Bic went worldwide from ballpoint pens to disposable lighters, disposable razors, and even stockings and hosiery in central Europe. One should then speak of line extensions when the brand launches new products in the same category. Therefore Diet Coke should be called a line extension. Interestingly, at the Coca-Cola Company, Diet Coke is called the second 'brand' of the company, which says it has two worldwide leading brands: Coke and Diet Coke (called Coke Light in Europe). These differences in perception are not an academic problem. They hint at the fact that, although the product may be the same, the market, the 'category' may be different. Since the emergence of 'category management' we know that category does not mean product (Nielsen, 1992). Therefore, Perrier Fluo would be considered as a line extension by those who focus on the physical resemblance with the core product of the parent brand: basically it is the same water. For us, it qualifies as a real brand extension, for it aims at a different category of need, and of usage situation, and of users, and of competition. The same would hold true *a fortiori* for Evian spray, which vaporizes water onto the face. The product, created in 1968, holds the same water as any Evian bottle, but the need and usage are very different as the channel of distribution.

As for all concepts, the best tactic is also to realize that they are relative, and that they cannot obey simple yes/no cut-off points. One should acknowledge that there are both highly continuous extensions, which apparently capitalize on the real or perceived know-how of the brand (as with HP's entry in the digital market), and highly discontinuous extensions, which do not capitalize on this know-how but on a mission, a set of values driving all the behaviours of the brand whatever the market it decides to compete in. We analyse the Virgin case below.

This scale of discontinuity has a lot of implications. It is a measure of the risk taken by the corporation itself. The current brand literature focuses heavily on the intangible facets of brands, probably because they are treated as intangible assets in accounting terms. But this is a semantic confusion: a performance-based brand is also an intangible asset. Overlooking the performance source of brands leads us to underestimate the weight of corporate abilities. Some companies just do not have the know-how or resources necessitated by the extension of the brand into specific categories. Certainly they can use licensing as a way of circumventing the problem: for example Evian Affinity (a cosmetic line) is managed by Johnson & Johnson. The other possibility is to outsource. It is a classic way of moving more quickly and benefiting from low import prices. However, this often means reducing the perceived difference between brands, if most of them outsource to common OEM suppliers.

Another implication concerns the branding strategy itself. Should one give a brand name of its own to the extension, thus moving to a double-level branding architecture (that is, an endorsing or source brand architecture)? It is noticeable that Perrier is very discreet about Fluo, as all endorsing brands tend to be. Experimental literature shows that giving the product a different name prevents dilution of the parent brand image, especially in the case of downward extensions (where the product goes from a premium price to a mainstream price) (Kirmani, Sood and Bridges, 1999). One should therefore distinguish 'direct extensions' (without a specific name) and 'indirect extensions' (with a specific brand name in addition to the parent brand) (Farquhar *et al*, 1992).

The limits of the classical conception of a brand

Most brand limitations are self-imposed. This is why brand extension took so long to emerge as a normal practice of brand management. This is also why some authors still hold it in disrepute. These prejudices are based on a classic conception of brands, which reigned over marketers and all business schools for almost a century. However, it cannot resist the conditions of modern markets.

The classic conception of branding rests on the following equation:

1 brand = 1 product = 1 promise

For instance, in the Procter & Gamble tradition, every new product receives a specific name, which is totally independent from the other brands. Ariel corresponds to a certain promise, Dash to another, Vizir to a third. Let us compare this policy with that of Colgate-Palmolive: Palmolive is a toothpaste, a soap, a shaving cream and a dishwashing liquid; Ajax is a scrubbing powder, a household detergent and a window cleaning liquid.

The classic conception of branding leads to an increasing number of brands. If a brand corresponds to a single physical product, to a single promise, it cannot be used for other products. Under this conception it is a rigid designator, the name of a product, a proper noun, just as Aristotle is the name of the famous Greek philosopher (Cabat, 1989). It names a specific reality, as a commercial name is linked to a specific company.

Under this conception of the brand, few extensions are possible. The brand is in fact the name of a recipe. All that can be done is range extension, that is a variation around the central recipe either by:

- ameliorating the quality of its performances. The brand then gets a series number: for example Dash 1, then Dash 2 and Dash 3;
- increasing the number of sizes in order to adapt to the changing practices of the consumer (packet, tub, mini-tub);
- increasing the number of varieties (Woolite for wool and Woolite for synthetics).

According to this classic conception, brand extension barely goes beyond very similar products. The key concept is product or usage similarity.

The new conception of branding leads to extensions out of the initial category. The brand is different from the original product. It is a way of dealing with products, of transforming them, of giving them a common set of added values, both tangible and intangible: this way, a Swatch car is possible. An alliance with a company which has the technical know-how (Mercedes for example) suffices. This alliance, eventually made explicit through co-distribution, will give reassurance as to the car's quality and free consumers' desires.

The case of Lacoste helps to compare the operational consequences of each of the two conceptions of branding. Lacoste gained its reputation in 1933 through its tennis shirt made out of knitwear (called the 12 × 12), so a logical extension of Lacoste could be made not only toward other knitwear products, but also to other polo-shirts, sportswear and textiles in general. Under this conception, shoes and leather items are excluded (apart from tennis shoes), since they do not use the same know-how as textiles and knitwear. Under Lacoste's broader brand conception, the crocodile signals a typical attitude: with Lacoste, one is casual when smartly dressed, and smart even when dressed casually. Lacoste is beyond fashion: it is a classic. From this perspective, Lacoste can brand shoes or leather goods as long as they preserve the brand's originality; it must not brand products that have already been seen. The other condition is to brand only products which embody the values of the brand: flexibility, casualness, extreme finish, durability, distance from fashion, unisex use, etc. What enables Lacoste to brand a product is not the physical fit, but whether the product belongs to the Lacoste culture and high standards (see page 163).

This new perspective opens new sources of growth for brands. Instead of looking at themselves as product brands, they become concept brands, defined by a set of values and not by a single instance (Rijkenberg, 2001).

Why are brand extensions necessary?

Brand extensions are necessary. They are a direct consequence of competition in mature markets and of the fragmentation of media. The only justification for brand extension is growth and profitability.

Brand extension is not new: it is the core of the business model of luxury brands (see page 66). It can increase the power of the brand and its profitability. Typical margins in the ready-to-wear premium market are 53 per cent, but the average is 71 per cent for bags and 80 per cent for watches. This is why fashion brands extend so quickly to these categories. As to perfumes, sold under licence by l'Oréal, Procter & Gamble or Unilever, they provide royalties, and a considerable boost in international visibility to the extended brand. This is why extensions are strategic in the fashion and luxury sector. No name can survive without them. The first thing a capital investment fund does after having bought a name is to extend the brand. What would Armani, Ralph Lauren or Calvin Klein be without their licences and extensions?

Often, perfumes become the most visible part of the fashion brand, because of the high advertising budgets involved. In addition the perfume increases the brand awareness and dream value, a prerequisite before other extensions. In fact, without a perfume, can a designer brand succeed and be profitable? Success in modern competition means the ability to access a critical size and visibility. Although not always successful, launching a perfume under one's name is a classic, if not the only, way to build the brand and business. Interestingly, this is the argument used by an as yet little-known designer brand that sued P&G for damages when the latter decided to stop its plans of launching a perfume under its brand name. Without this expected boost, would the brand meet its growth and profitability objectives?

As long as growth and profitability can be achieved through the present customers and products, or through minor variations in these products and their benefits (also called line extensions) there is no need to extend. Globalization in search of the new areas of consumption in the world is also a natural route, but this does not solve the problem of growth in domestic markets, which are often saturated. Brand extensions allow brands to compete in less saturated markets, with a perspective of growth and profitability, as long as the brand's assets are assets in these markets. That is to say, the brand image must be able to act as a driver of purchase in the other market.

Brand extension relies on the ability to create a competitive advantage by leveraging the reputation attached to the brand name in a growth category, different from the brand's present categories. This bold move, which often surprises the competition in the category of extension, makes five crucial assumptions:

- The brand has strong equities (strong assets): it is strongly associated with a number of customer benefits (tangible or intangible) and it inspires a high level of trust.
- These assets are 'transferable' to the new and attractive destination category, that of the

extension. Its buyers will still believe and acknowledge that the new products (that is, the extension) are endowed with the benefits associated with the brand.

- These benefits and brand values are very relevant to that new category (extension). In fact, they should segment it in a previously unforeseen way, and leave the competition unable to react rapidly.
- The products and services (extension) named by the parent brand will deliver a real perceived advantage over the competition, both consumers and the trade.
- The brand and company behind it will be able to sustain competition in this new category over the long run. This refers to the question of resources needed to acquire leadership in the market in order to remain in it profitably.

As a consequence the most important part in the brand extension process is the selection of the destination category. This requires the company to assess various strategic parameters: the intrinsic attractiveness of the new category, the company's ability to acquire leadership in this category, and its ability to segment it profitably. These factors are to be found in the brand image, but also in the company's more general abilities and resources.

A second set of reasons that has pushed corporations to extend their brands is more defensive, or tied to efficiency and productivity factors:

- Facing higher media costs, most companies that started with a product brand architecture have realized the impossibility of sustaining growing advertising allowances behind each product or brand. They have transferred some of these formerly independent products or lines to a single mega-brand, which acts either as an endorser (Kraft or Nestlé) or like a source brand (l'Oréal Paris), as a quasi-branded house. This is why brand transfers have become so frequent.
- Some brands are in declining product categories. To avoid disappearing with their product they must move to another category. Why did Porsche enter the 4 × 4 market in 2003? As we shall see later, there is a danger in resting always on the same product, even if it is continually face-lifted, revamped and renewed. All over the world, data show that the share of the coupé in the overall car market is decreasing. If Porsche stayed in that niche without reacting to this trend, it would be competing in a shrinking market.

  Another example is that consumption of brown tobacco is strongly declining, a sure threat for Gauloises, the prototype of dark cigarettes. After decades of uncompromising battle against blond tobacco, the company had to make a hard choice. Should it let its banner brand die? It decided to extend it into the blond category, creating Gauloises Blondes, which now represent the largest part of its sales.
- In the business-to-business market, the logic of continually increasing customer value leads in itself to brand extension. Take a service provider, say a company providing cleaning services for hospitals. How can it increase its sales to its core clients? Rooms cannot be cleaned two times or three times a day. There is no other avenue than to propose extended services, for instance supplying flowers for hospital rooms, lobbies and offices. This is another competence, an extension.

  British Gas faced the same problem after the deregulation. How could it defend its business against all the new gas providers? It realized that its strength was its customer proximity: its engineers actually visited millions of households. It was time to leverage that competence and competitive advantage, and provide an extended set of home services including insurance and financial services to the customer base. This naturally entailed a change in name to facilitate consumer acceptance.
- Labeyrie is a brand that originated in the 'foie gras' sector. This is a very cyclical market, where most sales are made in three months of the year. To be able to advertise and gain a competitive advantage, Labeyrie decided to enlarge its scope and extend to other luxury foods such as smoked salmon and caviar. The resulting increase in its sales

volume made television advertising a realistic investment.

- Many companies make a brand extension because they do not have the resources to sustain two brands nationally and internationally. This is why in Spain Don Simon sells wine, gazpacho and orange juice under the same name. This small company invests all its resources in productivity and quality. It fights head on against Tropicana in the juice sector, and has now extended its market throughout Europe. We shall see later that although they are governed by necessity, such decisions may prove later to be a real blessing.
- Some sectors are under growing advertising constraints: cigarettes, spirits, beers and wine are all limited by law in their types of advertisement and sponsorship. They have to create brand extensions to circumvent these limitations. Such extensions actually act as surrogate brands. The most known and successful is Marlboro Classics, an offshoot of the cigarette brand, which has become a real outerwear fashion brand worldwide. It has a very specific design, and exclusive stores and concessions. This is a typical case of a successful licensing approach.

  In all countries, pharmaceutical laboratories have to make a choice: whether to produce freely available over-the-counter (OTC) products, or products that are only available on a doctor's prescription. OTC products are allowed to be advertised, but they are generally not prescribed and they tend to be expensive. In France, the market leader for paracetamol is called Doliprane. This is a prescription drug, so consumers can be reimbursed for its cost, but in addition it can be bought freely without a prescription. As a prescription drug, however, Doliprane is not allowed to advertise. To circumvent the regulations it launched two extensions, Doli'rhume and Doli'tabs ('rhume' means catching a cold in French). These two variants could be advertised, because they are only sold in the OTC market. The heavy advertising campaigns not only boosted the sales of the two new products, but had a positive spillover effect on the core product.

What should one think about the Caterpillar line of shoes and clothes aimed at the youth market? Was it necessary for the tractor brand to extend itself in this way? Of course not. What then was the rationale? When asked that question, the CEO answered that it was intended to increase the share value by giving more visibility to the brand name, beyond the trade circles in which it had previously been known. Many small investors now buy shares, and familiar corporate names act as symbols of value to the lay investor. In addition, Caterpillar clothes and shoes were able to express the exact values for which the Caterpillar was known: tough work, reliability, security and so on.

Similarly, why did Michelin extend its brand from tyres to guidebooks, over a century ago? The first Red Guide was produced to tell readers where to find a garage in the event of a breakdown. Soon it came to be aimed at inducing car owners to travel more, with tips about hotels and good restaurants. It was a great example of relational marketing before the word was ever invented.

Recently, Michelin, working with a partner, The Licensing Company, has created a dedicated company, Michelin Life Style Limited, based in London. It is marketing snow chains for cars, a product with obvious marketing synergy with tyres. There are plans to extend the brand into sport equipment such as ski shoes and running shoes, areas in which the use of rubber can increase comfort and security. These are the two key benefits of Michelin tyres.

In a slightly different way, My First Sony and My First Bosch are tactical extensions, designed to create early familiarity with the brand among soon-to-be clients.

Building the brand through systematic extensions: Nivea

In 2003, the three giants Procter & Gamble, Henkel and l'Oréal bid against each other to acquire Nivea, putting in very high offers – a sign of their extraordinary confidence in the growth potential of the company and its brand. What an astonishing outcome for a German company founded in 1912 in Hamburg on a single product: a little round, blue metallic box containing skin moisturising cream, which was treated almost like a medicine.

However, the company and its brand were split up after the war, and like other German brands (such as Persil), its assets were given to other companies across the world as war damages. This is why the brand had to be rebuilt with great patience, with the assets being bought back whenever and wherever possible, such as in the United States in 1974. In 2003 Nivea was the world's leading skincare brand, with a turnover of €2.5 billion and an average growth of 15 per cent per year. The brand's growth has been achieved entirely through progressive, carefully planned extensions repeated in country after country. As we saw, each extension constructs a specific facet of the brand while penetrating new markets or new needs, all the while remaining faithful to the brand's heritage and key values (page 260).

Nivea provides a good example of well-managed systematic extensions. The lifespan and growth of this world-leading skincare brand can be explained through two key factors: the modernization of the prototype product, Nivea cream, in its round blue box, and systematic brand extension via daughter brands (which Nivea calls 'sub-brands').

The little round box is the prototype of Nivea, and carries the brand's values. In every country it is introduced first, and made available at all sales points, explaining its penetration into all social environments. Next come the extensions, in a pre-established order, to build the brand: first care products, followed by hygiene, then hair products, and lastly make-up. The daughter brands expand these categories, with their specialization based on age (Nivea Baby), purpose (Nivea Sun), gender (Nivea for Men), and so on.

However, if it is to maintain itself, the brand must work tirelessly to recapture its relevance, and this is why it must innovate. Each advertisement for a Nivea daughter-brand now places the emphasis on innovation. But even the prototype has needed an update: this has been the role of Nivea Soft, with its white box, as modern generations look for a cream which is less greasy and penetrates the skin more quickly. Nivea Soft is bringing the brand's foundation up to date.

Extensions very soon came to form a part of Nivea's business model. An analysis of its brand launches in all countries – from the United States to Russia and China – reveals a fixed, well-planned pattern of development. The brand is launched in each country using its cornerstone (founding, prototype) product, portraying itself as a healthcare

FIGURE 12.1 The Nivea extensions galaxy

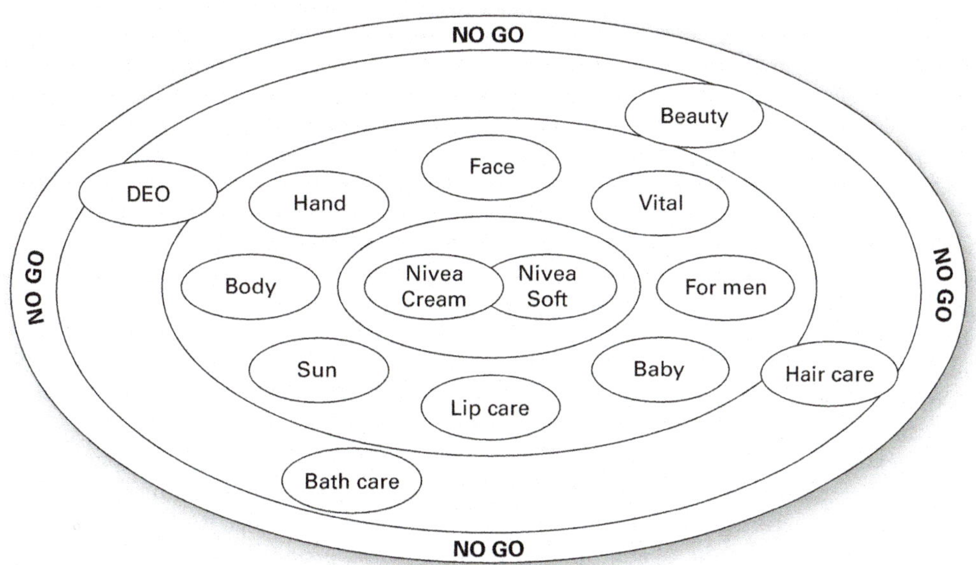

brand. Next follows Nivea Visage, a sub-brand which is key to its long-term business development. Nivea Visage is the perfect symbol of care: we entrust our faces to it.

After that follow the daughter brands judged to be most relevant for each different country, deepening this role and mission: Nivea Hand, Nivea Body, Nivea Sun, Nivea Lip Care, and three brands that are segmented by customer type: Nivea for Men, Nivea Vital (for the older market) and Nivea Baby (formerly known as Babyvea). The next to arrive are hygiene products, via the Nivea Deo and Nivea Bath Care daughter brands. Finally, these are followed by Nivea Hair Care and Nivea Beauty.

Thus, the order of entry in each new country is always carefully planned: care products first, followed by hygiene, then hair products and lastly make-up. Similarly, women's care products come before men's: Nivea Visage is always launched before Nivea for Men. Nivea's philosophy is that each country organization is free to choose to launch a daughter brand, depending on the available potential in that market. However, Nivea Visage is of key importance. For example, although the care products market in Brazil is small in comparison to hygiene products, the brand construction order is still maintained. After all, Nivea is not Dove. The latter (Unilever) brand is based on hygiene (with as its core product a soap containing 25 per cent moisturizing cream), but is now successfully expanding into the entire hygiene and beauty market worldwide.

The brand architecture is an umbrella, in the sense that each daughter brand is named descriptively, and thus represents a statement of the brand's values as they pertain to that category. However, note that the logos of each daughter brand are not uniform. This tiny difference makes the brand open, living and non-monolithic. Furthermore, each logo reflects a personality and values specific to the daughter brand. In this respect, the Nivea brand is also a sort of branded house (source brand) with two clear brand levels, even though the mother level is dominant in this case.

Indeed, each daughter brand has its own personality, and this is a deliberate decision. Furthermore, the aim of each extension is to provide not only a deepening of the core competence (loving care for the skin) and greater penetration of the category, but also specific components of the overall image. For example, Nivea Sun is where the family and protection aspect is communicated, and so advertising for Nivea Sun shows mothers and children, and fathers and children, together.

Likewise, the final extension – the one farthest from the core of the brand – is Nivea Beauty. By now we have come a long way from long-lasting products, simplicity and harmony. In this category, the key words are accelerated range renewal (four per year), the game, fun, seduction and so on. However, in highly developed, sophisticated countries this extension is necessary. It brings young girls to Nivea who would not otherwise have come, and who will subsequently try out other products from the range. It also adds a necessary touch to the brand image: more modernity and 'fashion'.

We can therefore see that under this system, daughter brands are not extensions in the iterative sense, as they would be for a hypothetical brand X asking itself what else it could do. In reality, they are the means through which the brand's 'big plan' takes shape. Extension presupposes the existence of a long-term vision. Before sinking the pillars for a bridge across a river, one must first have picked a clear destination point on the other side. These extensions are not extensions in the traditional sense, but rather components of a pre-planned whole which accumulates its meaning, coherency and scale through them.

As with any new product launch, the key question is that of perceived distinctiveness from the existing competition. Of course, the brand brings its own intangibles and image equities, but they are not enough on their own: a physical basis for differentiation is needed. This is, therefore, where innovation comes in:

- Nivea Visage launched Patch in Europe (the fruit of an alliance with the Japanese firm Kiaoré).
- Nivea for Men provides more care during shaving.
- Nivea Vital is developing the concept of mature skin.

Lastly, as with any system, there are certain no-go areas – such as, for example, anti-cellulite products. This is not because no market exists: it does exist, and it is a thriving one. Rather, it is because none of the existing products work well. To enter this area with another product that did not really deliver its promise would therefore be to break the link of consumer confidence in Nivea – and more than any other brand in its sector, Nivea wants to be the brand of confidence.

Identifying potential extensions

It goes without saying that before making any brand extension it is imperative to know the brand well. What are its attributes? What is its personality? What identity does it convey to its buyers and users? What are its latent associations or traits? The answers to these questions are based on both quantitative studies (to discover the popularity and the image of the brand) and qualitative interviews of the target public. A simple listing of the image characteristics does not give a full picture of the brand. Defining the prism of identity requires qualitative investigation.

Armed with this information, the second step of the investigation procedure involves the extrapolation of the brand's distinctive features in order to assess their consequences. If Dove is personified by gentleness, then what other products need to be gentle? If Christofle is a brand for knives, forks and spoons, could it, by metonymy, be extended to glasses, plates or other tableware in general? Since Rossignol is active in one area of sport (skiing), could it not also extend into tennis rackets and golf clubs?

Luxury product brands often find the reason and the inspiration for their extensions from within their own history. Thus René Lalique, founder of Lalique, made jewels, scarves and shawls. The extension of Baccarat into small items of furniture, jewellery, perfumes and lamps is also symbolic of the reconquest of unexploited areas.

Whatever the source, a long list emerges from this process of introspection and investigation into brand identity and extrapolations based on it. It is then subject to internal feasibility filters. Brand extension is a strategic choice that is also accompanied by other changes: in production, know-how, distribution channels, communication, corporate culture. These have to be financed either internally or by forming alliances. Thus, Boucheron sold 22 per cent of its shares, not those of its core business (high-fashion jewellery), but those of the company that managed the so-called 'first circle' extensions (jewellery, watches, spectacle frames, pens and perfumes) in order to increase its resources.

This shortlist is then tested with the target public. Opinion surveys are often used to achieve this. For every extension proposition consumers evaluate the product on a scale of interest to them such as 'very interesting, so-so, not interesting'. This leads to a popularity rating of the possible extensions.

This method is advantageous in that it is simple and that the grading is done by numbers. Its one drawback is that it is conservative. When a series of questions about a multitude of products are thrown at them, interviewees tend to comment only on the basis of the most striking features of the brand. Therefore, this technique is biased and conservative. Thus, when Bic was only making ballpoint pens, this strategy would have ended up by exhausting all the possibilities in stationery and completely rejecting the idea that Bic should sell razors.

Davidson (1987) distinguishes a number of concentric zones around an inner core: the outer core, the extension zones, and finally the no-go areas (see Figure 12.2). Close-ended questions in surveys provide information on the immediate vicinity of the brand (the outer core). In-depth qualitative phrases explore the remote extension zones.

Once again, it is necessary to proceed with a qualitative investigation to bring out the latent potential of a brand and to see how it can or cannot adopt each of these extensions. Through this same investigation we can also tell whether the resulting refusals were due to a conservative attitude linked to the actual situation, a lack of imagination on the part of the interviewee, or due to incompatibility with the brand.

The qualitative phase is a constructive one. Bearing in mind that a brand has to bring some added value to the product category, one would also like to know under what conditions the envisaged product would be legitimate for the brand. What attributes – objective and subjective – would be necessary for it to be able to bear the brand name? How is the product superior to the present market offer?

Thus, it is not enough to say that Lacoste could make jackets. One also has to describe what the characteristics of a Lacoste jacket would be

FIGURE 12.2 Perimeters of brand extension

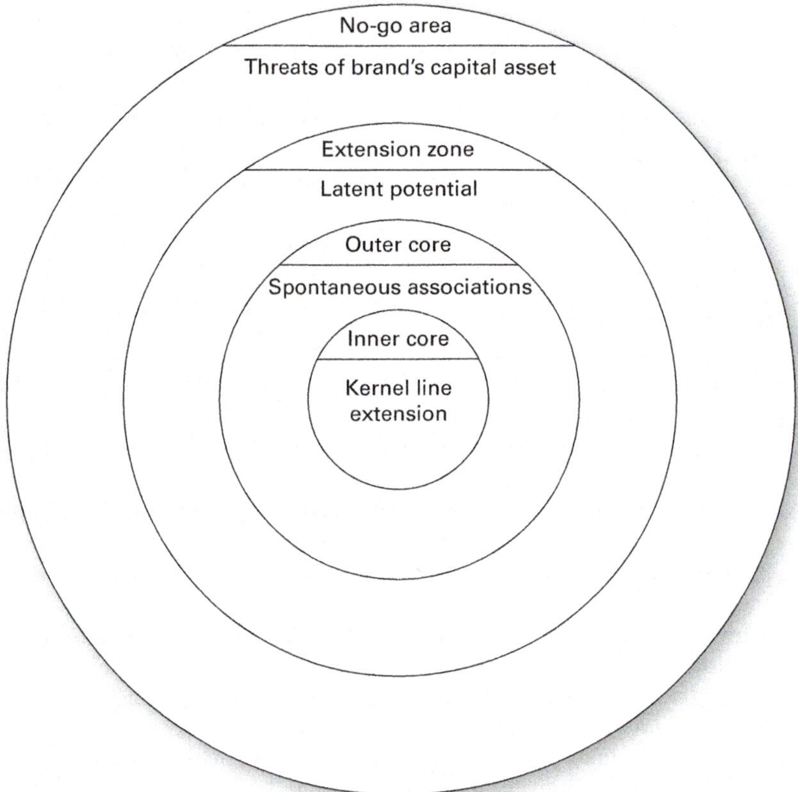

and those of a 'non-Lacoste' jacket. The Lacoste identity prism encompasses the following characteristics: knit, finish, durability, discretion, harmony, social aptness, conformity and adaptability. The reputation of the original Lacoste product is that of a second skin: it induces a distancing effect which constitutes the central value of the brand. It nurtures an image of supple transition between the personal and social – personal ease and social ease. The aerated knit is analogous to the skin and its pores. This identity prism defines the territories which are not Lacoste and which should be avoided for fear of losing the very meaning of the brand:

- since it conforms to a sporting ideal, Lacoste is transversal and cuts across all barriers of age and sex, thus it should not put its name to products which are exclusively feminine (in fact, the Lacoste aerobic line was a big failure), or hyper-masculine (eg hunting);
- Lacoste does not sell either garish colours or short-lived 'in' products;
- being a 'second skin', Lacoste does not make either heavy knitwear or shiny leather clothes.

One understands why there are no Lacoste leather jackets. They are very masculine, virile and fashionable, and they do not last. Only the suede jacket is capable of possessing Lacoste characteristics.

The qualitative stage also permits an understanding of the functions of the brand for its users. Is the brand a sign for itself or for others? Where would consumers like to see the brand signed? This information is essential for branding. On the pocket of a Lacoste blazer should the signature be Lacoste, the crocodile or Lacoste Club?

Fundamentally, the testing phase should not only find out whether the success factors of the extension category are coherent with the brand, but also whether the product is superior to its competitors when deprived of its brand. In spite of the many explications about image failure, many extensions fail simply because they are inferior to existing products and are more expensive. Above all, an extension is an innovation and its added-value should be considered. Finally, these projection techniques allow the tricky question of the boomerang effects on the brand capital to be dealt with.

The economics of brand extension

By capitalizing on the brand awareness, the esteem and the qualities attached to an existing brand, the practice of brand extension can help to increase the chances of success of a new product and lower its launch costs. These two alleged consequences have been verified.

As shown in Figure 12.3, only 30 per cent of new brands survive longer than four years, whereas the rate is over 50 per cent for brand extensions.

How does extension increase chances of survival? First, distributors themselves will allocate more space to an already well-known brand than to a newcomer. But brand extension also has an impact on the consumer (see Figure 12.4):

- in the trial rate, inducing a higher rate (123 vs 100);
- in the conversion rate (17 per cent vs 13 per cent);
- in the loyalty rate (index of 161 vs 100 for new brands).

Thus, for an equal facing and an equal unweighted distribution/weighted distribution ratio, consumers have a higher probability of trial, conversion and loyalty when the product bears an existing brand name, as this second OC&C analysis shows.

As far back as 1969, Claycamp and Liddy had measured the impact of a 'family name' (extension) on

FIGURE 12.3 Rate of success of new brands vs brand extensions

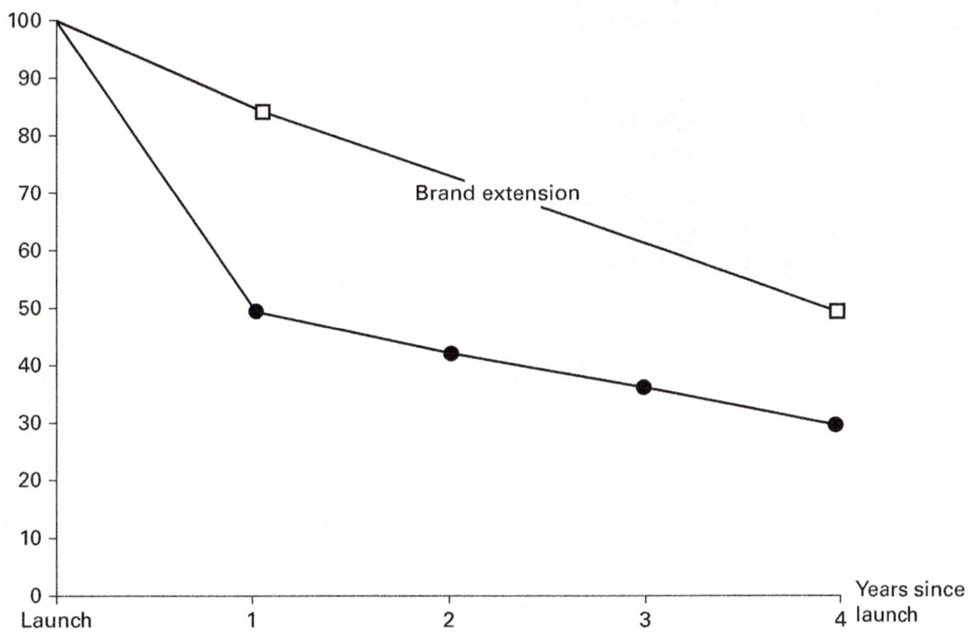

FIGURE 12.4 The impact of brand extension on the consumer adoption process (OC&C)

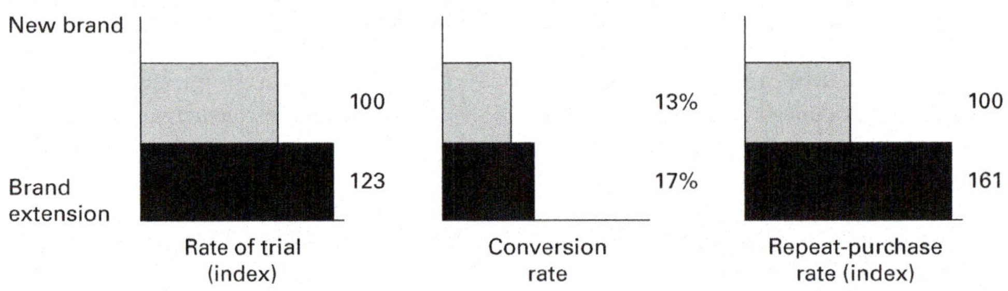

FIGURE 12.5 Ayer model: how a family name impacts the sales of a new product

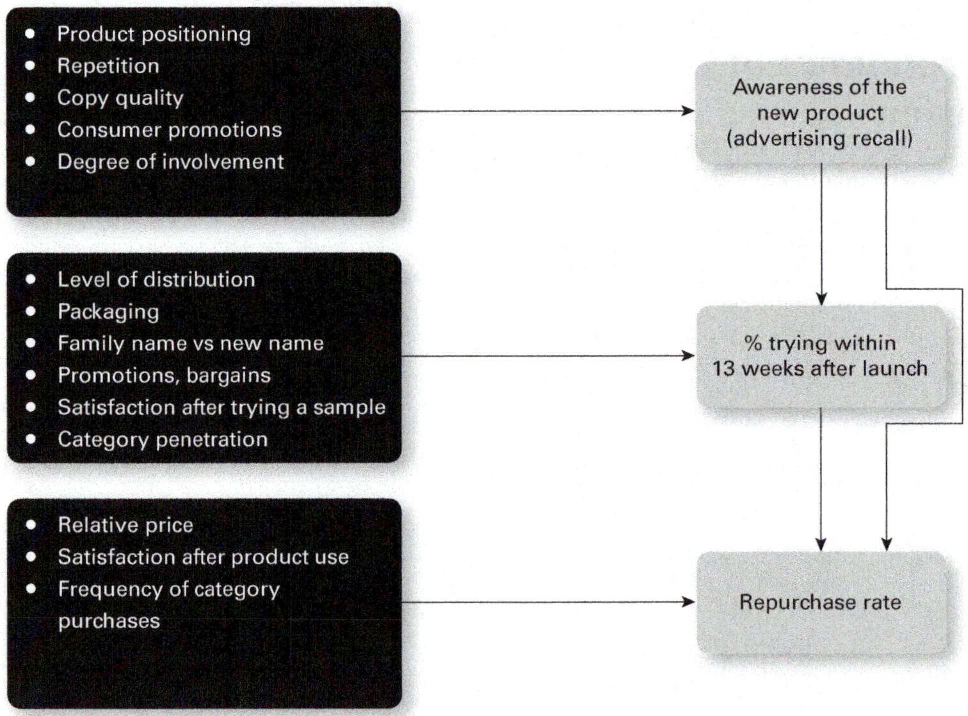

the trial rate of the new product. Their forecasting model, known as Ayer's model, rested on a database of 60 launches in 32 categories, half of these being in the food sector. The basic structure of the model is presented in Figure 12.5.

The estimate of the parameters of the model (through double regression) resulted in a very positive weight for the 'brand extension' variable. A previously known name directly and strongly induces the consumer to try the product. Moreover, Liddy and Claycamp noted that this variable was not correlated to advertising recall or even to weighted distribution. This last point is surprising: perhaps American distributors do not act as barriers to entry as much as their European colleagues.

What conclusions can be drawn from these studies? It would be wrong to think now that all new products must be launched under a known

TABLE 12.2 Brand extension impact on launching costs

	New brand	Brand extension	%
Launching budget:			
– pull	100	78	–22
– push	30	24	–20
Total	130	102	–21
Trial rate	100	123	+23
Cost/trial	1.3	0.83	–36

SOURCE OC&C

brand. This would mean forgetting the usefulness of multi-brand portfolios in the maximization of market coverage. Moreover, as will be discussed later, some brand extensions can hinder the success of a new product, or be detrimental to the brand capital itself. Thus Hermès refused to lease its name, in exchange for royalties, to the Wagons-Lits Group, which wanted to launch a top-of-range service of individual or package holidays. The service risks of hotels in exotic and far away countries were too high for Hermès to be willing to associate its name with that venture.

These figures also reveal that the consumers' view of the product is generally far less conservative than that of management itself. Quite often the latter is too blinkered by the origin of the brand and considers the manufacturing history of the brand as its definition. For management, Mars could not mean anything else but the chocolate bar. And yet the Mars ice-cream bar has been a success and the Mars biscuit launched in 2003 was also a hit. This proves that consumers distinguish rather well the brand from the product, or at least that they do not associate them irreversibly.

The second economic argument put forward to justify brand extension has to do with cost: launching a new brand would cost more than launching a new product under a well-known brand. Indeed, for consumer goods one estimate is that, as a result of lower expenses in 'push' and in 'pull', in promotion (to consumers and above all to distributors) as well as in media advertising, the savings due to the choice of brand extension amount to 21 per cent. Since the trial ratio is higher, the strategy of brand extension proves economical as far as cost per trial is concerned (see Table 12.2).

However, another study from Nielsen based on 115 launches gives apparently contradictory results: the new products launched under new names get market shares twice as high as those of the products launched under known brands (except for health and beauty products, for which the results are identical: 2.7 per cent vs 2.6 per cent) (see Figure 12.6). The reason for this difference can be seen in the second column. The extension strategy would not in fact be less efficient: the lower market shares are due to the fact that management uses smaller communication budgets in cases of brand extension, which lowers the share of advertising presence.

For an equal percentage of advertising presence, brand extension results in equivalent or even greater market shares in the field of health and beauty where, the risk perceived by the consumers being higher, there is a preference for known brands.

What can be deduced from these two studies? Are they contradictory? The first one concludes that extension is more efficient even with a lower budget. The contradiction could be solved by considering the fact that many managers, confident in the productivity of brand extension, reduce the advertising budget dedicated to the extension launch (thus the results of the first column of Figure 12.6). For

FIGURE 12.6 Comparative sales performance during first two years (Nielsen)

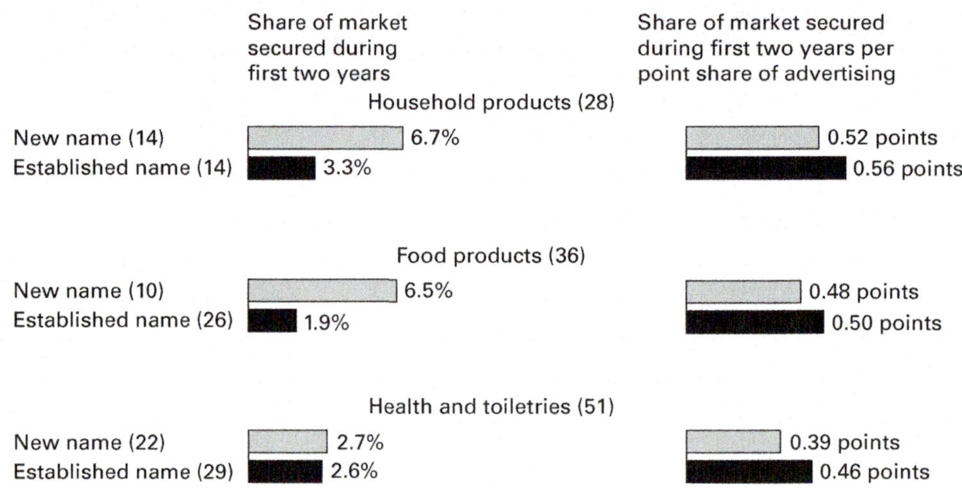

equal budgets, the extension strategy has a slight advantage which is not significant in the cleaning products and food sectors but significant in the health and beauty sector (0.46 vs 0.39). In addition, the fact that OC&C analyses efficiency in terms of trial rate (very tightly linked to the familiarity of the brand name) whereas Nielsen's is based on market share over 24 months, which reflects the marketing mix and product quality as a whole, may have some bearing. Finally, this low launch budget of the extension may be linked to a desire to keep the bulk of advertising on the core product of the brand to preserve its sales (a mistake since it underestimates the reciprocal spillover effects of advertising a new product on the sales of the core product) (Balachander and Ghose, 2003).

A hidden factor in each of these two studies is the moment of entry on the market. A risky, new market cannot be approached in the same way as the same market at a more mature stage. Sullivan's (1991) analysis of 96 launches in 11 categories of products gives interesting descriptive results (see Table 12.3).

First, this analysis noted that companies preferred to penetrate new markets with new brands. Of the 48 launches studied that had taken place on emerging markets, only 13 were brand extensions. However, in mature markets, 40 out of the 48 launches analysed were brand extensions. Sullivan also noted that the brands which used their own names in order to penetrate a young market were rather weak brands. For example, in the United States, Royal Crown Cola was the first brand to penetrate the diet cola segment under its own name. It was followed by Pepsi-Cola with Diet Pepsi. Coca-Cola had preferred to launch Tab and not to put its brand capital at risk. It introduced Diet Coke last. The survey shows that the brands which have become leaders in these markets were almost always new brands (Diet Coke is an exception).

Why do strong brands hesitate to penetrate young markets? Of course, they would benefit from the fact that there is no competition yet. But creating a market entails more risks for the creator (Schnaars, 1995) and a negative effect on the brand and its capital. In a young, badly defined market, a brand must be flexible in order to find the best positioning. Brand extension does not permit such flexibility. The attributes of the brand must be respected. Furthermore, launching a brand which is specific to a new market enables the brand to become the reference on that market, by benefiting from what is called the pioneer advantage (Carpenter and Nakamoto, 1990). Finally, many new markets are created in reaction to old ones. For example, the snow surfing market is a counterculture against alpine skiing and its competition-oriented values; its proponents have their own brands and have refused the surfboards of Rossignol, the established brand.

Apart from the case of weak brands trying to dominate a new market, it can be attractive to be

TABLE 12.3 Success rate of two alternative branding policies

	Market development	
	Growth	Maturity
Launches of new brands	57%	43%
Launches of brand extensions	46%	68%

SOURCE Sullivan (1991)

the only known and reassuring reference on a market where neither the offer nor distribution is structured, and where the consumer perceives a high risk. The consumer will appreciate the presence of a famous brand, even if it is far from its original market. Only its fame and serious reputation count. That is why Tefal penetrated the fledgling market of domestic appliances under its own name.

Finally, the analysis of success rates of the two launch strategies, depending on the degree of maturity of the markets, reveals a slight advantage for the new brand strategy in the market creation phase. But with time, the brand extension strategy seems more successful (see Table 12.3).

What is new on brand extension?

What research tells us about brand extensions

Since 1990, extension has attracted the attention of all marketing researchers and academics. This barren ground was seducing, and in addition the stakes were high. This research, mostly experimental and quantitative, has focused on identifying the determinants of consumers' attitudes to an extension. Would they find the concept attractive or not? It has also looked for the conditions where the brand equity could be diluted by an extension, which is generally true when an extension fails to bear the 'brand contract'. What is the impact on the parent brand image or on the sales of its core product?

This research has thus focused on only a small part of the brand extension process, which involves eight key steps:

1. Assessment of the brand equities (its image, or emotional assets, its key competencies among various segments of the population).
2. Assessment of the intrinsic attractiveness of likely extension categories.
3. Assessment of the transferability of the brand assets in the chosen extension category.
4. Assessment of the relevance of these assets: are these assets real benefits in this category?
5. Assessment of the ability of the company to deliver the expected benefits subsumed by the brand name.
6. Assessment of the perceived superiority of the extension to existing competition.
7. Assessment of the ability of the company to sustain competition in the extension category and to acquire leadership through time.
8. Assessment of the feedback effects on the parent brand and on the sales of the core product. What does the extension bring to the brand (new clients, new image traits, new sales)?

Academic research mostly addresses issues 1, 3 and 8. It aims at answering such questions as: When is brand equity transferable? What causes positive consumer reactions to extension proposals? When

FIGURE 12.7 The brand extension process

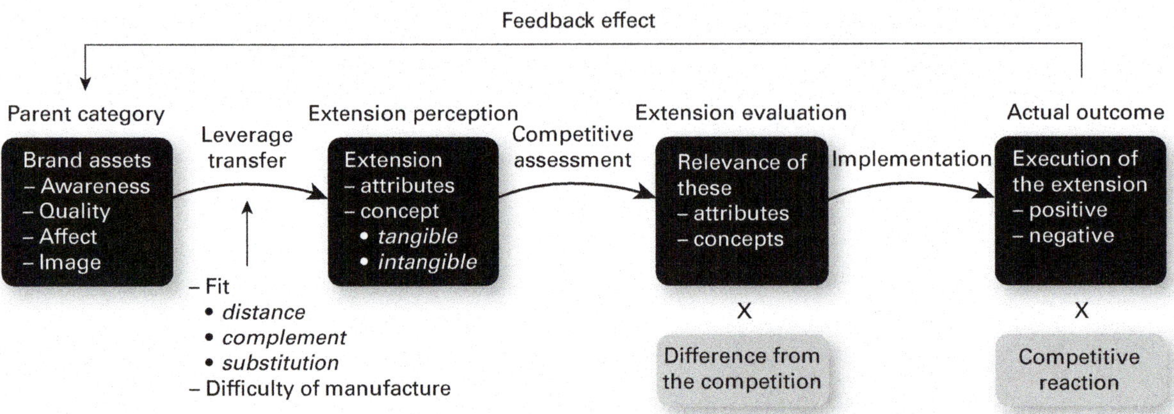

can brand equity be damaged by an unsatisfying extension? Its dominant paradigm is experimental research, using consumer evaluations (I like it, I do not like it) as the variable to be explained. Only recently have researchers analysed back data, and the historical sequence of market entries, to focus on sales and segment leadership and try to understand the determinants of success and failure. (See Figure 12.7.)

Early experimental studies on brand extension

The first study was presented in 1987 during a symposium on brand extension at the University of Minnesota. The attitude towards a fictitious brand of calculators (Tarco) was manipulated through the presentation of the results of tests evaluating six Tarco calculators. These tests concluded, according to the experimental group, that none of the six calculators were of poor quality, or one out of six, two out of six... up to six out of six. Naturally, the general attitude towards Tarco was much influenced by this manipulation. Then a list of new products to be launched by Tarco was presented: these ranged from a new calculator and 'close' extensions (microcomputers, digital watches, cash registers, etc) to 'distant' extensions (bicycles, pens, office chairs). The interviewees in each group were asked to state their feelings about each of these new Tarco products before having even seen them. The correlation between the attitude towards Tarco and the attitude towards these extension products of Tarco was measured. The correlation was stronger when the extension was close. In short, the transfer of attitude is facilitated by the perceived similarity between the category of brand origin and the category of the product extension.

Naturally, the bases of 'perceived similarity' vary with the individuals. As another study has shown, experts and non-experts use different indexes to evaluate the degree of similarity between two products. For example, the two following types of extension were shown to two groups of individuals, non-experts and experts:

- one was a superficial extension, using superficial similarity and relatedness (from tennis shoes to tennis rackets);
- the other was a 'deeper' extension, using the same know-how (that of carbon fibre, enabling a brand of golf clubs to introduce tennis rackets).

When asked about their perception of similarity between the starting category and the final category (tennis rackets), non-experts found the superficial extension very similar, but the experts not as much. On the other hand, an explanation of the process and material used convinced the experts more easily of the fact that tennis rackets and golf clubs are close products, while for non-experts they remain quite dissimilar. Thus, identical composition is not a factor of perceived similarity for non-experts: they base their opinions on more superficial signs. They are sensitive to extensions based on relationships of complementarity or substitutability between products, where this creates a sense of 'fit':

- Uncle Ben's sauce is complementary to Uncle Ben's rice;
- Nesquik cereals are substitutes for Nesquik milk chocolate.

Experts are not satisfied with these peripheral cues. They need a stronger rationale, such as that of Look's extension. This brand, famous for its ski bindings, was extended to the upper-range mountain-bike market, for it could apply here its mastery of the automatic grip pedals and of new composite materials.

In the first study, the fact that Tarco was a fictitious brand was intentional. This way, the brand had no capital – no particular trust and emotion were associated to the brand. This explains the importance of the criterion of similarity of products to facilitate the transfer of attitudes. In a normal situation, if the brand is a strong one, the relevance of its key values in the product class it wishes to enter is what determines the attractiveness of the extension even if the categories of products are very different (Broniarczyk and Alba, 1994). The success of Bic in pens, razors and lighters illustrates this fact.

The first sign of awareness of a mechanism independent from the product and stemming from the brand itself appeared in 1991, among Park and his colleagues. Two lists of products were given to the persons interviewed: functional products and expressive products:

Functional products	Expressive products
TV	perfume
compact disc	shoe
cassette-player	wallet
radio	shirt
videotape	bag
VCR	pen
walkman	ring
car radio	watch
video camera	belt
record-player	crystal
headphones	tie

Two questions were asked:

1. the traditional question about the degree of similarity between the products within each column;
2. a question about whether the products of each column 'fit' together.

The researchers asked these two questions in two ways:

- blindly, as above;
- using a brand, here Sony for the first list and Gucci for the second.

What were the results?

- For the expressive products, the fact that the brand was mentioned or not did not modify the judgements of low perceived similarity between the products. However, the presence of the Gucci brand name created a considerable fit between products which did not seem to fit much without the brand (3.68), but suddenly fitted together (4.74) under the brand.
- For functional products, the presence or not of the brand did not modify the judgements of perceived similarity and of 'fit'.

In short, the authors hinted at two processes by which consumers build an opinion on an extension:

- If the brand is mainly functional, the extension is evaluated from the bottom up, according to inherent links between the category of the original product and that of the extended product. The consumers' evaluations rest on the degree of perceived similarity between product categories.
- If the brand is symbolic, the concept of the brand creates a link between products which otherwise would not have one. In this case, the judgements on extension are independent of the physical characteristics of the products. Each extension is evaluated according to its belonging to the brand concept and to its coherence with the value system of this brand. This is a top-down process.

Some extensions bear the risk of dilution of the brand. Like an elastic band that has been pulled too much, the brand can become weak. Many factors explain the weakening of a brand by excessive extension. Evaluating this risk is no mean task: what would be the impact on Tuborg if a sparkling mineral water were introduced under this brand (such an extension does exist in Greece)?

A study demonstrated the existence of this risk. It focused on a well-known health and beauty brand, Neutrogena. Two extensions were presented to the consumers, one very unusual for Neutrogena, the other very typical of Neutrogena. The experiment consisted of informing the consumers that both extensions did very poorly in the two dimensions that make Neutrogena famous, softness and quality. What would be the impact of such a statement on the image of Neutrogena itself (Loken and Roedder John, 1993)? Would the image of softness and quality of typical Neutrogena products be affected, too? The study considered product A1, the brand prototype associated with Neutrogena by 83 per cent of consumers; product A2, associated by 61 per cent; product A3, by 55 per cent; product A4, by 39 per cent; and product A5, by 5 per cent. Here are the conclusions:

- Although of poor quality, the remote extension did not stain the image of the brand, nor the image of its other products. This phenomenon is well known to researchers on stereotypes: the exception does not harm the rule. The extension is atypical, therefore without influence on the heart of the brand.
- The situation is different for the more typical extension of Neutrogena. Its poor quality had a negative influence on both the image of the brand in its key attributes, and that of products typically and spontaneously associated to the brand. (A1, A2 and A3 had a statistically significant poorer softness image after exposure to the extension.) There has, indeed, been a negative impact on the brand and on its most significant products, but only in the case where the extension is typical of the brand. The danger concerns line extensions much more than brand extensions.

How attitudes about extensions are formed

Much research has been carried out into brand extension. In these studies, consumers were asked to evaluate ideas for extensions (a good idea/not a good idea; good/bad). The aim was to gain an understanding of the determining factors behind these evaluations from among a series of suggested values, such as the parent brand's reputation for quality, the perceived fit between the extension and the category of origin, and the perceived difficulty of constructing the extension, along with a number of other variables, without considering the interactions between variables. The perceived fit is the main variable to emerge from this pioneering research. It measures the psychological – and thus subjective – gap between the extension and the brand's typical product (its prototype). Traditionally, the fit is measured in three dimensions: the degree of perceived synergy between the extension and the prototype, the degree of perceived substitutability, and the perceived transferability of know-how.

Echambady *et al* (2006) reanalysed the initial study and seven repeat studies produced clear conclusions based on all of them:

- Consumers' evaluations of an extension are in the first place influenced by the perceived quality of the parent brand only if there is a high perceived fit. The dimensions of fit are 'synergy', 'transferability of know-how' and 'substitutability'.
- These evaluations are also influenced by the perceived difficulty in carrying out this extension.
- There is a direct influence produced by the perceived difficulty of manufacturing the extension: when this rises, the evaluation rises. Consumers do not like brands that are happy to put their names to excessively trivial products. It is true that the success of brand licences among children casts doubt on the extent to which they are influenced by this variable: the Harry Potter name has appeared on some of the most banal products (exercise books, erasers, pencils, pens, clothing and so on). However, perhaps the effect does apply to parents, helplessly watching the tidal wave of demand for licensed products bear down on them. It may also apply to technical brands, which would explain their reluctance to move down-range by manufacturing oversimplified products.

FIGURE 12.8 The consequences of product and concept fit and misfit

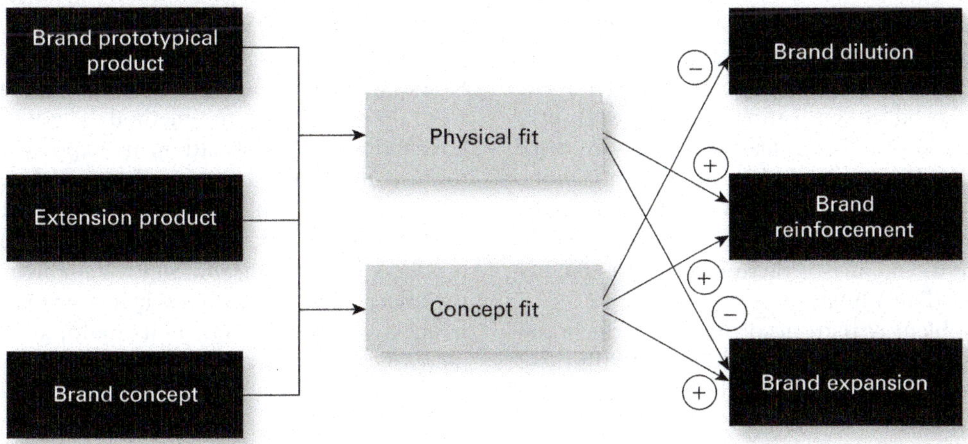

SOURCE Michel, 2000

The Aaker–Keller paradigm has provided an initial step in brand understanding. However, as can easily be seen, it has its roots in a traditional, cognitive view of the brand defined by its competence, objective attributes and know-how. To evaluate an extension, consumers are thus supposed to analyse the proximity of the extension product to the product that in their eyes most accurately represents the brand (its prototype). This is a bottom-up approach: the consumer's starting point is the similarities between products as a means of evaluating the brand extension. This applies well to so-called 'functional' brands.

But how much proximity is there between fries and pizza? Or between fries and buns, or fries and iced tea? There is little in a physical sense, and yet these products constitute the McCain range. In fact, the common factor behind the unity of this brand and the fit between its products is not the products themselves, but the brand concept, American food. In the future, McCain could start to sell brownies or ice cream. We may thus suppose that there is another way of evaluating fit other than just the three dimensions examined above: the evaluation of the fit with the intangible concept of the brand itself. In this case, consumers would use a top-down approach. Starting with the concept, they would ask themselves whether the product extension conforms to the concept.

Furthermore, extension serves to move a brand from being product-based ('McCain makes excellent frozen fries') to being concept-based ('McCain makes delicious American food products'). Becoming a concept brand enables preparation for future expansion via other new product introductions, thus increasing the brand's market power, turnover, profile and visibility: it becomes a mega-brand.

In acquiring an intangible dimension on which its identity is founded, the brand thus gains access to expansion. For as long as it stays a product brand, it remains confined to a product segment: if what you sell is Bic biros, how much further can you go than, say, erasers, marker pens and pencils? But when perceived as 'the brand of cool, simple, practical and plastic products', Bic can put its name to ballpoint pens and disposable razors and become a world leader in both these markets, as well as in the disposable lighter market.

The research can thus be summarized as in Figure 12.8: extension is based on physical fit and concept fit.

The limits of early research on extension

Who knows Genichi Kawakami? He was the CEO of Yamaha for 52 years, and died in 2002. When he succeeded his father as CEO in 1950, Yamaha was a harmonium and piano company. In 1954 the company made a radical diversification into motorbikes. In parallel, it also created synthethisers and acoustic and electric guitars. Then it extended its activity to skis, tennis rackets and carbon-based golf clubs. Later it was to enter the hi-fi market, positioned as a premium product, followed by extensions in the video market and now multimedia. At the heart of all these strategic moves lay the belief that product innovations are the only way to enter markets and to remain profitably in these markets. They were also underwritten by a genuine vision of this CEO, that of the leisure society. Of course, it never came to the mind of Genichi Kawakami to call any of these innovations by any name other than Yamaha.

The problem is that, according to early brand extension research (Aaker and Keller, 1990), these extensions should have all failed. This casts doubts on the theory.

The prime factor for consumer acceptance of an extension, stemming out from this research, is 'the fit', the feeling of perceived similarity between the core product and the extension if perceived quality is high. This result has been amply confirmed by subsequent research (Leif Heim Egil, 2002; Bottomley and Holden, 2001). What fit or resemblance is there between a piano and a motorbike? None. However, Yamaha is the world's leading brand for musical instruments and the world number two manufacturer of motorbikes. What fit is there between a ballpoint pen and a lighter, or a lighter and a disposable razor? None. However, Bic is the world leading brand in these three markets. It successfully managed its very dissimilar extensions under the same name. According to its CEO, having the same name was precisely one of the factors of their success. Certainly, consultants told him not to launch the lighter in 1973 under the same name as the ballpoint pen (launched in 1950) or the disposable razor, launched in 1975. But the management had another vision. These three products now make 53 per cent of their sales in North and Central America.

Why are the findings of this early research so far from this reality? In fact, this pioneering work (Aaker and Keller, 1990) rested entirely on laboratory research. In this special context, consumers were presented with ideas about extensions and had to make an immediate evaluation. In the real world, the extensions are launched as all-new products, with information about the intrinsic value of the extension and trust relayed by publicity and word of mouth. In the laboratory research setting, the interviewees had none of these, and this is why they relied on perceived fit, a measure of 'global sameness', or similarity between the extension and the brand. In brief, the conclusions of that research present the consumer as very conservative. Recently, Klink and Smith (2001) confirmed that the results were determined by the method. The interviewees have too limited information, are exposed only once to the concept (in contrast to the multiple exposures of a real advertising launch campaign), and typically are not the risk-taking innovators who try new products first. Klink and Smith demonstrated that the effect of fit diminishes when consumer innovativeness increases, and that multiple exposures increase the perceived fit between an extension and the brand.

After 20 years of academic research it was time to make a meta-analysis of all the articles or studies focusing on the overt discrepancies between generally held beliefs stemming from research and the reality of brand and business. It now appears that laboratory research produced conservative statements about brand extension. In the real world consumers are more informed and can better evaluate the extensions.

The new perspective of typicality

Above, we have spoken of typical and atypical extensions. This raises the question of how to judge whether the product resulting from an extension is at the heart, at the limit or outside the territory of a brand. This question is one more application of a more general question at the heart of research on cognitive psychology: according to what criteria is an object considered part of a category?

Indeed, the psychological study of classification by categories aims at identifying the processes by which we form categories, and assigns certain objects to one category rather than to another. The brand is, in that sense, a category.

For decades, the dominating, or 'classical', theory answered this question in the following way: a product or an object belongs to a category if it has the necessary and sufficient features of this category. This leads one to question 'the' definition of the concept (or the category), ie about the nature of these features determining the belonging or non-belonging. This model works well for certain categories (for example the category of 'even numbers'), but it seems less reliable for others. Specialist or niche car makers such as BMW or Saab have definite image and physical traits, which can qualify a new car as belonging or not to the brand. This is not the case for the generalist brands such as Ford, Opel, Vauxhall and Nissan. The same holds true for Braun vs Philips.

Indeed, in this classic model, all examples of the category are equivalent since they all have these necessary and sufficient traits: two is an even number as much as 18 or 40! All BMWs are BMW.

Experience proves that the situation is different for many categories: for example, some birds are more 'birdlike' than others, and even a butterfly is more 'birdlike' than an ostrich. Belonging to a category does not seem to be a clear-cut binary function (yes/no) but a probabilistic one. The frontier between the 'bird' and 'insect' categories is unclear. This does not nullify these two categories: indeed, we all have in mind the prototype of a bird and that of an insect, and these two prototypes cannot be mistaken one for the other! However, the frontiers of each category are not that separate. (See also Chapter 11.)

Thus the new tendency of research on categorization, led by Rosch (1978) and Lakoff (1987), admits that categories can also be groups with unclear boundaries which are not defined by a series of necessary and sufficient features but by a prototype, the best exemplar.

Basically, an extension is considered acceptable if it 'fits' the idea that consumers have of the parent brand. This feeling is based either on a high perceived similarity to the most typical product of the brand (also called the prototype), or on the coherence between the extension and the brand contract (also called its concept or identity).

When the extension is distant from the mother brand, which attributes of the latter are transferred to the extension product, and which are not? As the notion of distance is linked to a comparison with the prototypical product – or products – of the brand, the objective characteristics of the brand are the ones which will be transferred the least to remote extensions. On the contrary, the intangible, more symbolic characteristics ignore distance and have an influence on all extensions. The doctoral thesis of Gali (1993) under supervision of the author, demonstrates this. Consumers were asked to evaluate the Miele brand according to various image dimensions, then to evaluate according to the same dimensions the most typical product of Miele (the washing-machine) and two extensions, one slightly atypical (a television) and one very atypical (a microcomputer).

What did this research reveal?

- First, the very atypical extension receives very little of the Miele functional values.
- Generally speaking, objective qualities are not transferred as well as symbolic qualities. Thus, typical physical features of Miele – quality, innovation, reliability – are weakly transferred to the image of the two extensions. On the contrary, the extensions receive the following features: for the young, to show off, for innovators. For that reason, in a different context, luxury brands have little difficulty in practising extension even into dissimilar categories. Their primarily symbolic qualities ignore the distance between concrete objects. They can be transferred more easily.

How extensions impact the brand: a typology of effects

Beyond the growth of sales and profits, brand extensions influence the brand and its capital in six different ways:

1. Some extensions exploit the brand capital: the new product sells thanks to its name. This is what happens when the product receiving the brand is no different from the existing competitors on the market: the brand has not entirely played its transformation role, but it enables the product to benefit from its image. By using this practice too frequently – through a loose licensing policy for example – the brand capital wears out as the brand becomes associated with these now commonplace products, and with their unjustified price premium. Industrial

brands often fill up the gaps in their lines by buying the missing items from their competitors. This is typical of the photocopier market.

2. Other extensions destroy the brand capital, for instance when the extension is downwards. Porsche has cancelled its 924 range, cars which only justified their considerable price difference against their competitors (the Golf GTi) by the prestigious name. None of the objective or subjective values of Porsche could be found in the 924 model: neither masculinity, nor technology. This model seemed to announce the end of the Porsche myth. Since at that time the brand no longer took part in Formula 1 racing and was losing in the Le Mans 24-hour endurance race, the only communication element of the brand was advertising, of which a large part was dedicated to the 924. To return to its source, the brand ceased to manufacture the 924 and reinvested in the 911.
3. Some extensions have a neutral effect on the brand capital. The product is not out of place but is in tune with what is expected from the brand. Significantly, in the field of home appliances, some brands are thought to offer many more types of products than are actually produced, but if they decided to actually penetrate these markets, their image would not suffer. This shows that consumers have a perception of the brand which is different from that of those who manufacture it. They attribute to the brand areas of competence which are larger than and not limited to just the existing products.
4. Some extensions influence the meaning of the brand: when Rossignol added branded tennis rackets, the status of the brand changed. It is now less specialized and is characterized by a wider range of interests. Yet the two sports covered by Rossignol were not chosen randomly: the brand is still offering the equipment which extends the individual's body to help gain access to pleasure and performance. Nestlé increased its modernity by competing upfront under its own name with Danone on the ultra-fresh market (ie yoghurt).
5. Some extensions are regenerating. They revive the brand and its core, and re-express its base values in a new, stronger manner. Thus, the classic green blazer is a regenerating product for Lacoste. It represents a rare symbiosis between the features building the Lacoste brand: conformity, discretion, sociability but also a certain distance on fashion. As for the green colour, it is more casual than the blue blazer (too uniform for Lacoste) and refers to the green grass of the original tennis courts at Wimbledon. The green blazer brings Lacoste up to date and at the same time expresses its roots. The 'Marlboro Classics' line allows the brand to recommunicate its history, its roots and founding values.
6. Finally, some extensions, although not desired by the brand, are necessary to defend the brand capital: their purpose is, above all, to prevent the use of the brand name by another company in another category of products. Thus, Cartier may not want to develop along those lines, but they have to in order to prevent another company from registering the brand name Cartier on an international scale in the textiles category.

Avoiding the risk of dilution

In our many brand extension consulting missions, the recurring question concerns the risk of diluting the image capital. Could the business extension harm the brand's assets: its reputation, and the traits that comprise its value in the eyes of the market? For example, what will be the long-term effect on Danone's image if it starts selling Danone water too? What will be the long-term effect on Mercedes' image when it produces its A-Class range? What will be the long-term effect of Chanel's decision to start selling glasses at Afflelou, a discount franchise chain of opticians? What will be the long-term effect on the image of a brand that has sold only to professionals, but now starts selling to the general public too? What will be the long-term effect of an extension towards lower prices? What will be the long-term effect of selling not only pens but also cigarette lighters and razors under the Bic brand?

As these typical questions show, the problem lies in estimating the long-term effects. No study can predict the future. Second, the answer will depend to a large extent on the ability to perform the extension successfully and well. After all, an extension is more than just a brand extension: more importantly, it is a departure from the brand's tried and tested sphere of competence. Some learning will be necessary, and this may take time. For example, the little A-Class car revealed that Mercedes had not sufficiently mastered the engines and stability issues for this chassis type, thus reneging on the brand's traditional basic contract and its three essential attributes: reliability, safety and standing.

Extensions also entail taking risks other than just image-related ones. A brand extension generally brings about changes in target markets, distributors (and perhaps even buyers, from a mass retail perspective), prices, manufacturing and logistics. These changes may be a source of annoyance to the brand's historical distribution channel, opinion leaders or existing customers. There is thus a genuine business risk – and this may affect sales of the current flagship product which constitutes the main sales platform.

An example of brand dilution: Vichy

Vichy is an example of a brand whose changes over its history have led to a loss of identity and value. It started out as a cosmetics brand that promoted itself as the dermatologists' brand. However, in an attempt to increase sales, it dropped this label and began developing products with a strong cosmetics base. Freed of its dermatology tag, the brand was able to advertise on television and develop products which, in accordance with women's wishes, had a much more cosmetics-based slant – as well as bigger margins. The brand was able to launch more new products every year, as the whole clinical tests process was no longer necessary. In just a few years, it became just another run-of-the-mill pharmacy product.

Vichy's sales increased very rapidly, as did its margins. However, at the same time its image was being eroded. This policy, although a winner in the short term, had caused a loss of identity in the eyes of consumers who could no longer perceive the brand's distinctiveness or added value. It was no longer what chemists wanted either, at a time when the pharmacies channel as a whole was attempting to re-establish its legitimacy against new distribution channels also seeking the right to sell so-called 'parapharmacy' products.

It was back to the drawing board for Vichy's business model and brand mission. Vichy, the dedicated chemist's brand, needed to bolster its distribution channel. The brand was repositioned around the theme of health, and thus the brand slogan became *La santé passe aussi par la peau* ('Health is vital. Start with your skin'). Most importantly, all items and products that did not fit this philosophy were axed.

Such losses of identity are common: large groups often seek to make a profit out of their acquisitions and force small brands with a strong identity to move quickly into other distribution channels and categories. Neutrogena, for example, is facing this threat: it is expanding its presence in the worldwide food channel, but at the risk of losing the key values that make the brand truly distinctive.

Is the consumer bookkeeping or subtyping?

Academic research furnishes important information on the risk of image dilution. Unfortunately, however, it focuses exclusively on the misfit with the brand image: it does not consider risks arising from the fact that an extension is usually also accompanied by strategic changes in distribution and targets.

The foremost paradigm in research on dilution is a failure to honour the basic contract. What happens when the expectations created by the brand's name are dashed by the brand extension? Apart from this failure in itself, is there not a risk to the brand's image, or even to the sales of existing products? Basic research (Loken and Roedder John, 1993) has shown that any failure to honour the basic contract has a negative impact on the brand and its image for each image aspect that is ignored. A brand is constructed out of the sum of all of the impressions accumulated in consumers' memories. The only exception to this is if customers find themselves asking the question, is the unsatisfactory extension typical or atypical of the brand? If the extension is perceived as being atypical, the brand's image is safe. However, extensions that are fairly typical of the brand are the ones that dilute its image the most if they disappoint with regard to the brand contract. The problem is that there is no guarantee consumers will ask themselves whether the extension is typical or not. In the aforementioned study, researchers put the question to half the sampled group. The question did not spontaneously occur to the other half. It would therefore seem that consumers adopt a 'bookkeeping' approach in which the brand is responsible for everything it does, whether good or bad.

A second, more recent piece of research considered the question of the effect of breaking the brand contract during an extension on sales of the current flagship product (Roedder John, Loken, Joiner, 1998). Disappointment with the performance of a Johnson & Johnson brand extension did indeed impair the brand image with regard to the attribute that constituted its differentiating value: gentleness. However the sales of the prototype, or flagship product, was not affected. This suggests an 'experience effect'. Consumers who have already used the product are confident about qualities. They might view a brand extension negatively but this will not alter this confidence about the flagship product. However, J&J's flagship product (baby shampoo) *was* affected when the disappointment stemmed from a line extension (a simple modification to the basic product). Such very closely linked extensions are the ones that cause the most collateral damage to sales of the flagship product.

The risk of downward stretch

It is a well-known fact that price is an indication of quality, and can on its own create the image of a product with a high standing. In their extensions, some top-of-the-range prestige brands have been prompted to sell cheaper products in the search for a client base that is more numerous but less willing to pay a high price. This is the approach taken by brands such as Mercedes with its A-Class and Cartier with its Must de Cartier range. What effects do such acts have on the brand's existing clients?

Given that an expensive brand derives its value in part from the fact that it indicates the buyer has the financial means to afford expensive products (consumers' reflected image), it is hardly surprising that there is a negative reaction: their status has to be spread more thinly, and thus reduced. This has been confirmed by a study on 'The ownership effect in consumer response to brand stretches (Kirmani, Sood and Bridges, 1999). People who do not buy the prestige brand (BMW in this study) are pleased by its more accessible price extension; existing buyers are much less impressed. Current buyers, however, appreciate price-increasing 'upward-stretch' extensions far more than non-buyers do. With brands that are not of high standing (for example, Accura cars), there is no effect of this kind. This study also confirms that the act of using a sub-brand protects the top-of-the-range brand from image dilution in the event of a price-lowering 'downward-stretch' extension. This is what Cartier did with Must de Cartier, selling pens, cigarette lighters and leather goods in large retail stores to reach a wider clientele and increase its recognition, which until then had been restricted to a well-off elite.

Another interesting piece of research (Buchanan, Simmons and Bickart, 1999) analysed the risk of devaluation if a prestige brand adopts a less selective channel when entering a non-prestige market. For example, the luxury hairdresser J Dessange granted a licence to l'Oréal to use its name on a shampoo to be sold in supermarkets. The findings of this study were that it all depends on merchandising, and – in this case – on three factors. What is the brand's relative visibility, price gap and distance from one or more lesser known or lower prestige brands? If its relative visibility, distance from the competition and price gap tally with the consumer's impression of the brand's standing, the risk is reduced. If they do not, the consumer mentally lowers the brand's standing. For example, it is crucially important for a brand of standing to have a clearly separated display which is distinct from competitors'. If it does not, and the display is mixed, the consumer interprets this as a signal from the (supposedly expert) retailer that the brand of lower standing placed alongside the brand of high standing is just as good.

What can we draw from this research on the risk of dilution? First, we can conclude that customers of prestige brands are happy where they are: they form a conservative lobby. In so doing, they demonstrate a lack of awareness of the economic conundrum faced by the brand or company. As Jürgen Schremp, the CEO of Daimler-Benz, observed in 1998, Mercedes could either stay where it was and – like Rolls-Royce – go bankrupt; or it could change, and sell over a million cars. Conscious of the risk of losing the attachment of its existing customers, the brand has to take precautions:

- Even in its lower cost extensions, the brand contract must be honoured – and the first consideration is quality.
- The brand should manage its downward extension while at the same time continuing to nourish the legend that ensures its high standing. After the A-Class, Mercedes relaunched the S-Class – voted by experts as the best car in the world – and announced Maytag, an even more luxurious model.
- The brand can use a sub-brand for its downward stretch.
- It can also split its distribution into segments. Chanel boutiques concentrate on products with a minimum price of €1,000, while Chanel sunglasses and cosmetics are intended for wider channels.
- Current buyers benefit from a greater level of attention and distinctive signs of recognition, following the model established by credit cards. There is a basic card for everyone, but also far more exclusive Gold and Platinum cards which provide a way of re-establishing the differentiation from other cardholders.

The brand is extended to grow through changing its scope of influence. It is not possible to grow while at the same time keeping everything intact and unchanged.

With regard to non-prestige brands, the risk of dilution can often be exaggerated internally. For example, all spirit brands have asked themselves what the impact would be if they were to enter the ready-to-drink (RTD) pre-mix/alcopop market. Would this not have an effect on their image among the buyers of their basic products – Smirnoff, Ricard, Johnnie Walker, Bacardi and so on? In fact, company studies reveal that this is far from the case. Buyers of established but somewhat elderly brands are delighted to see that the brands are consumed even by today's young people, albeit in a very different way, a fact that is flattering to their parents. This is not to suggest that such extensions are entirely without risk, but the risks are business-related. The first of these is that the new product launch will fail. The second is that older buyers with a high volume potential will be replaced by younger buyers who – at least initially – will consume less. The trick will be to encourage them to migrate at a later date from an RTD-type product to the far more profitable 'real' product. Even if Bacardi Breezer is a genuine worldwide success – like Smirnoff Mule or Ice before it – and even if the products are high-margin on account of their low actual alcohol content (5 per cent), it is still a fact that Bacardi-Martini is a spirits group that expects the high profits commensurate with the spirits sector, not the lower profits of the RTD sector. The challenge is therefore to migrate current RTD customers in future to the proper Smirnoff and Bacardi products. We should add that the real risk would have been to do nothing and watch as young people deserted the brand as a result of its failure to adapt its products, consumption methods, sales and consumption locations and prices to new consumers. Extension is a necessity.

Balancing identity and adaptation to the extension market segments

Brand extension capitalizes on the brand's 'assets'. It hopes that there will be a transfer of these 'assets' between the parent category and the extension category, given the perceived subjective proximity between the two categories. It is therefore a question of capitalizing on identity: the intended result is an identity-based brand.

However, the success of an extension depends on its ability to deliver value to the client. In what way are these assets relevant? What makes them superior to the competition? This presents the problem of the extension's ability to exploit a genuine opportunity or real consumer insight in its market.

There is therefore always a balance to be struck between these two (equally legitimate) requirements. Since a name is a promise, the brand cannot make different promises with different products; but at the same time, unsuitability for the target market is the number one reason that new products fail: each market has its own 'drivers' and customer preference levers.

An extension category may be chosen for its contribution towards building the future brand. Nivea, for example, owns a raft of daughter brands, each positioned on extensions that have a highly specific role in building the Nivea brand over time (see page 260). The hygiene and beauty market – as the name suggests – consists of hygiene and care on one side, and make-up on the other. Why would a brand such as Nivea, positioned on skincare and having successfully offered all possible skincare permutations worldwide, use Nivea Beauty to enter the world of seduction, play and appearance against such well-established giants as Maybelline, Max Factor and Bourjois?

As always, the answer has to be growth, image and profitability. After all, the make-up market is a rich seam of double-figure growth. Furthermore, it attracts new young customers. This fashion aspect lends the brand image a very modern appearance. And lastly, it is a profitable category.

However, Nivea still had to acquire legitimacy in this unexpected area. The first advertising campaign of Nivea Beauty was a failure; during extension, brands are often (naturally enough, perhaps) more preoccupied with their brand identity than with the customers in the target market. Nivea relied on bad insights. The sub-brand's positioning was 'All the colours of care' – but to a young target audience in the mass retail channel, this is not a relevant promise. At a chemist's it would have been a different story, hence the existence of La Roche Posay and Roc cosmetics. The brand repositioned its beauty line on the market expectations and the long-term weaknesses of the competition. The new promise was, 'The most beautiful me'.

As we can see, this promise is no longer a straightforward translation of the essence of the brand (loving care for the skin), but neither is it inconsistent with the brand's equities. Nivea Beauty's promise is that it preserves a woman's natural beauty. This capitalizes on Nivea's fundamental intangible values: respect, humanity, love, naturalness, simplicity. The promise derives from a consumer insight as a reaction against the totalitarian line taken by many make-up, cosmetics and beauty products brands, urging women to look like top models and stars. This time around, the relaunch was a success. In terms of extension, the challenge lies in the balance between market appropriateness and faithfulness to the brand's identity: it is created through successive adjustments.

The McCain example provides another illustration of the difficulty inherent in brand extension. McCain is a Canadian company, operating worldwide, with three branches: frozen fries (it supplies McDonald's throughout the world), frozen pizzas, and soft drinks. In 1998, noting the rising popularity of tea-based drinks in the soft drinks market, it decided to launch an ice tea, Colorado by McCain. The firm justified its choice of an endorsing brand architecture by the over-prominence of the 'raw' product's image (in light of the previous launch of McCain fries and pizzas in the relevant countries). Consumers were therefore intended to ask for the Colorado tea drink, with its intangible youthful Tex-Mex connotations, thus fitting it into the overall American brand identity.

The marketing team was not limiting itself to image. Mindful of the competitive nature of the market, it also created a highly differentiated product embodying an essential McCain identity trait: generosity. As a result, the can of tea contained 33 cl instead of the competitors' usual 25 cl. This decision was based on sound logic: it differentiated the extension in terms of the brand's equities, both intangible and tangible. Sadly, this was also one of the causes of the extension's failure. In reality, this differentiation, embodying the brand's spirit of generosity (and thus larger portions, as befits the stereotypical American), proved to be a problem. The can, being taller than other standard cans in the category:

- was unsatisfactory to retailers, who like to keep storage issues as simple as possible;
- was rarely drunk in full by customers, who thought it contained too much;
- appeared more expensive in terms of its retail price, even though the per litre price was the same.

Paradoxically, then, this differentiation generated long-term dissatisfaction – a fundamental error in the cut-throat environment of this double-figure growth market.

The most serious problem faced by this extension was probably the fact that it was up against Lipton, the world's number one in tea products, aggressively pushing its two mega-brands (Lipton Ice Tea and Liptonic), with their associated promotional expenditure, to capture this market. Not even Nestea could compete, despite a strategic alliance with the Coca-Cola Company which ensured the distribution of its drink in all Coca-Cola vending machines. In the hypermarket – and thus the home consumption market – Nestea was powerless against Lipton.

At this point we should take another look at why strategic analysis is a higher priority than marketing analysis for the extension.

Preparing the brand for remote extensions

Not all brands lend themselves to extension. Some brands are defined only through their prototypical product or know-how. This is the case with cosmetic brands such as Clarins, Roc and Vichy. Their field of extension has to be limited within appropriate boundaries which combine both science and beauty.

Other brands are almost like sects and have quasi-religious principles: St Michael, the brand owned by Marks & Spencer, covers everything from food to clothes, from toys to para-pharmaceutical products and furnishing. Through its signature it imparts legitimacy to all that is in conformity with the Marks & Spencer ideology. Like a patron saint (etymologically, patron means pattern, ie model to be followed), the brand transforms and elevates all the products that it sanctifies.

If the brand is to remain intact in the eyes of the consumer and not be fragmented into disconnected units, the prerequisites of a remote extension must be taken into consideration. For the extension of one brand into various remote categories to look coherent, one has to draw upon the deeper meaning of the brand. This supposes that the brand either has such meaning or has the potential to acquire it. The Swiss brand, Caran d'Ache, built its reputation through upmarket pencils and writing tools. Its extension into scarves, wallets and leather items failed. The brand was missing the necessary deep meaning.

Figure 12.9 demonstrates the demands arising out of brand extension. Every degree of product dissimilarity changes the meaning and the status of the brand. Close extensions (B) are compatible with product or know-how brands: Heinz can market not only ketchup, but also mustard sauce. Extension one degree further (C) corresponds to brand benefits: Palmolive softens all that it embraces and Bic simplifies everything from pens to razors to lighters, making them disposable and cheap. A further ex-

FIGURE 12.9 Type of brand and ability to extend further

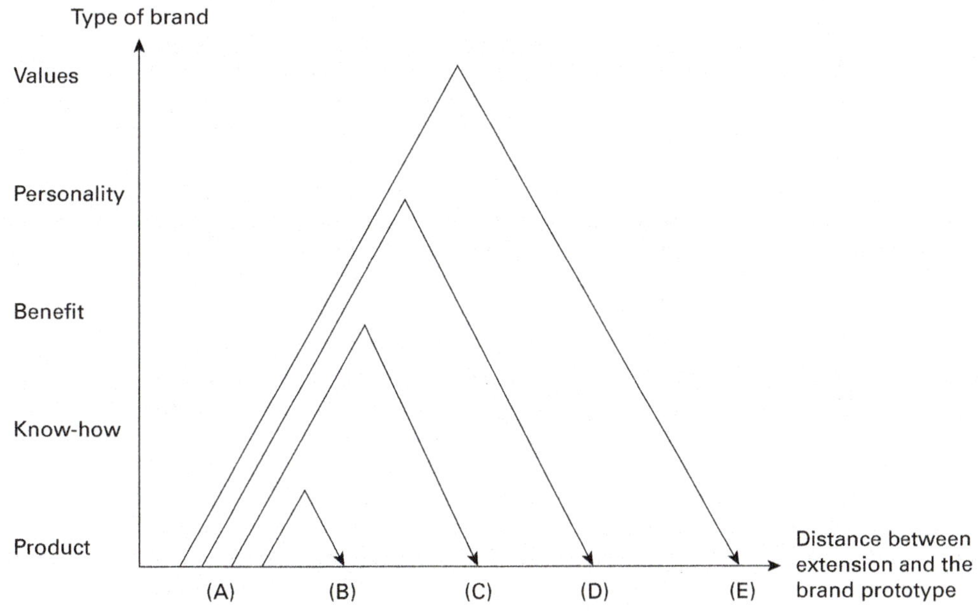

tension (D), in order to be coherent with the initial product (A), assumes a brand defined by its personality. In the beginning, Sony was a brand exclusively for hi-fi systems. But in a few years it has acquired fame in the field of television sets and videos and has therefore modified its image and its significance, but its core values still remain technology, precision and innovation with a specific elegant and refined personality. The last extension (E) assumes a brand that is defined by deep values. Virgin is a good example.

Thus, the only way for a brand to give a single meaning to a collection of extensions is to regard them from a higher viewpoint. To make distant extensions fit, the brand has to distance itself physically and serve more as a source of inspiration and a value system that can embed itself in different products. This is the case with Nestlé, a brand with a very large spectrum of offers. The distance helps to maintain the angle between the brand and its capacity to lend itself to different products. The steeper the angle, the greater force it exerts on the products (from A to E). The flatter this angle, the less is the force available to the brand to unify the products. Like an overstretched rubber band, the brand becomes weak, loses its grip and finally breaks.

More concretely, brands having only a physical facet (a product, a recipe) and no intangible identity do not lend themselves to remote extensions. They become diluted and are no more than numbers. This is the case with Mitsubishi. It no longer operates as a unifying brand but is only a corporate name and a factory trademark. It carries no signification other than the generic characteristics of Japanese technology and the image of industrial power that is associated with the group. Mitsubishi cars do not seem to embody any particular ideal and neither do Mitsubishi televisions or tools. This was also the case with Philips to a certain extent.

At the other end of the spectrum are the underexploited brands. These cover a very narrow product field but have an inner meaning which makes them legitimate over a large range of products. The brand Dole was a typical example of underexploitation. This brand underestimated its growth potential for a long time. Management considered the brand as a product and confined it to pineapple juice. But for consumers, Dole signified much more. Beyond its attributes (good taste, freshness and naturalness), lay a deeper core: sunshine. Dole was actually the sunshine brand and in this capacity could cover not only other fruit juices, but other products, eg ice creams. Very well known for a long time as a shoe brand, Salvatore Ferragamo has now successfully diversified into ladies' handbags, cardigans and ties.

As shown in Figure 12.9, the further a brand wants to move from its origins, the more it needs to have acquired a strong intangible meaning.

Research does, indeed, demonstrate that the order in which intermediate extensions are made affects consumer reaction to the final extension. Thus, in an experiment, consumers were presented with a sequence of five extensions for a number of brands. These extensions were chosen to represent five degrees of perceived distance or fit with the brand. In one case, consumers viewed an ordered sequence of extensions (from the closest to the farthest); in the second case they saw an unordered sequence of extensions (Dawar and Anderson, 1992). Two results emerged from this laboratory experiment.

As expected, there is a decrease in perceived coherence due to the distance between the extension and the brand's present product. However, the decrease in perceived coherence due to the distance is less steep when consumers saw the remote extension after a series of prior extensions presented in order of increasing distance. Each one may have acted as a stepping stone and prompted a category (brand) extension mechanism known as 'chaining' (Lakoff, 1987). The same result held true for the purchase likelihood for extensions.

Interestingly, it took less time to evaluate the farthest extension's coherence with the brand when that extension was seen at the end of the ordered sequence (4 seconds vs 4.34). Actually, the ordered sequence had itself modified the meaning of the brand, making it clear that it was not a product brand but a larger brand with a wider territory.

Again, a real-world illustration of this process is that of McCain. This brand entered the market with its frozen fries. After two years, it moved to large American pizzas, then to buns and recently to the fast-growing iced tea market. The meaning of McCain is now clear: American food, simple products, generous portions, fun to eat and innovative in their category. This brand territory will determine McCain's future extensions.

A second experiment demonstrated another basic rule of brand extension: only the coherence between extensions can create a brand territory. Two extensions may be equally remote from the core of the brand but not in the same direction. When a remote extension is presented to consumers after an intermediate extension in the same direction, this sequence increases the perceived coherence of that remote extension and its purchase likelihood (compared to the case where the intermediate extension is not in the same direction) (Dawar and Anderson, 1992).

Practical framework for evaluating extensions

In practice, how should marketers evaluate possible extensions? We have already analysed above how they could identify extension possibilities (see page 273), but what are the questions they should ask to make a relevant SWOT, prior to a go/no-go decision, or to evaluate the level of risk (Figure 12.10)?

It is important to avoid two types of risks: one is to accept an extension that would bring no real benefits to the brand (instead of trying to upgrade the core product). The other is to be overly fearful and to disregard a promising opportunity. The case of Apericube is exemplary of the second risk.

The extension that should never have existed: Apericube

Apericube is one of the oldest brand extensions of the Bel Group, a cheese manufacturing company acting worldwide and mostly known for its global brand the Laughing Cow. Although this famous cheese spread with its iconic brand character aims at the whole family, with a special focus on children, Apericube was aimed at the appetizer market (as its name, derived from 'aperitif', suggests). This is a small cube of soft cheese (the same cheese as the Laughing Cow) that goes with a beer or other alcohol in social situations, competing against peanuts, crisps, olives and the many new snacks that people eat while drinking in a social setting.

Why select this brand extension as a significant case? Because it is still a most successful one, created almost by chance some 50 years ago and now sold globally. However, if it were to be launched today, the idea would immediately be stopped or not even considered in the first place by management. How could a family and children's brand ever think

FIGURE 12.10 The managerial process of extension evaluation

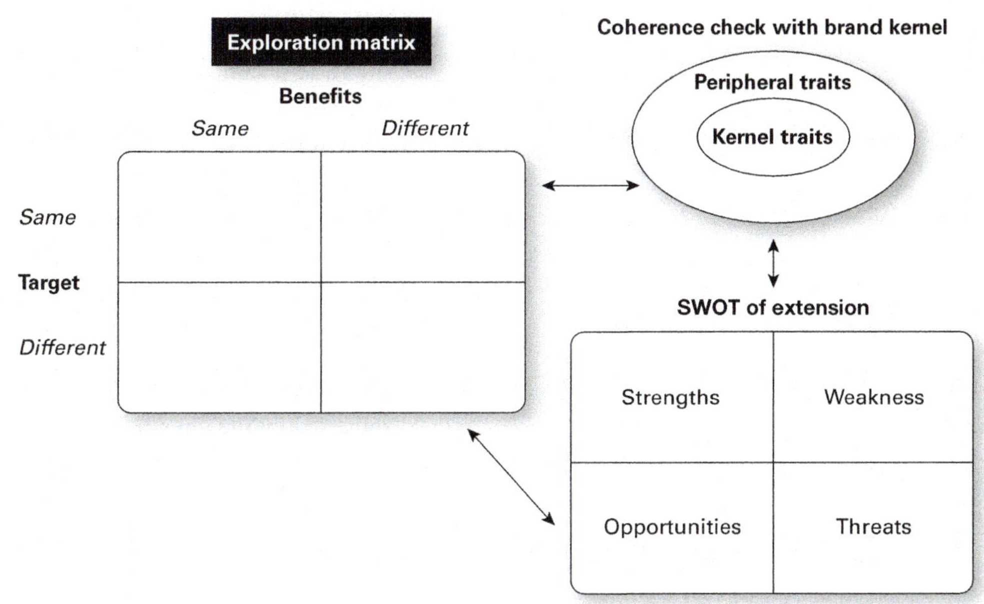

of a brand extension in an alcohol-consuming situation? There is clearly a contradiction between the brand's core values and the extension. According to academic theory, Apericube should be a failure. It is a long-term profitable success.

Today the main issue in risk-averse organizations or multinational companies is how not to discard what in fact would have been a very promising source of growth.

Much of brand extension theorizing is conservative: it would have recommended that Bic stick to the stationery business and as close as possible to ball pens. However, brands are dynamic and living forces, energized by intangible values. The choice of product classes to make these values become tangible consumer benefits is called strategy. Apple would not be the Apple brand of today without the decision to move out of the personal computer business. Brands evolve by drawing peripheral values from new product categories, which later become part of their kernel values (see page 41).

Let us return to Apericube. It is important to remind ourselves that manufacturing cheese cubes wrapped in aluminium foil, with an opening device that prevents fingers from touching the cheese itself, necessitates a quite sophisticated production process. This miniaturization process has not yet been copied by any competitor.

Six questions to evaluate extensions

The Apericube extension was launched haphazardly, without any strategic thinking as to its long-term future. It is however interesting to analyse it retroactively against the typical criteria of a brand extension selection grid. This will show how promising the extension was:

1. What is the attractiveness of the new category? The market for snacks that accompany alcohol consumption is growing. Moreover, it is not price sensitive. Consumers focus on the price of alcohol, not that of peanuts and crisps.
2. What advantage does this product bring compared to existing snack products?
   - Freshness (if the product is kept in the refrigerator).
   - It is not greasy, but very clean (unlike peanuts, olives and crisps).
3. How can this product advantage be made durable?
   - By convincing retailers to put it on a refrigerated shelf.
   - By the unique miniaturization know-how of the Bel Group.
4. What would be the level of defence or retaliation by the competition?
   - Weak. There are many products, but no strong brands or much advertising.
5. How are we legitimate here?
   - The brand icon (the Laughing Cow) is smiling and brings its good humour to the situation.
   - This is a well-known brand, trusted by all.
   - The Laughing Cow cheese taste is widely liked.
   - This is a family product for everyone: children and parents.
   - There seems to be a blatant contradiction between the brand equities (family oriented, safe, healthy, consensual, protective) of the Laughing Cow and the situation of adult, largely male alcohol consumption at home or in bars. Isn't it too regressive a brand, driving you back to your childhood, for a risk-taking adult situation (alcoholic drinking)? Most managers would stop the project because of this.
6. What would it bring to the parent brand itself (feedback effect)?
   - Isn't there a risk of brand dilution or of a reduction of its trust and family character? Certainly, if the extension received the majority of the advertising investment. However, that will not be the case, and using Apericube as a sub-brand, endorsed by the Laughing Cow figure, would limit the risk.
   - On the other hand, all brands aiming at children run the risk of becoming childish at a time when children themselves do not want to be seen too

long as children. As a result, today's childish brands have a shortened life cycle. This Apericube extension would counterbalance the risk and make the Laughing Cow brand less childish. After all, Coca-Cola is the most common beverage mixed with alcohol, from Cuba Libre (rum and Coke) to whisky and Coke. This has never hurt Coke's image, but the Coca-Cola Company remains purposively discreet on this huge part of their business, that of the night.

What lessons should we draw from this case? Academic extension research focuses too much on congruence of image and of targets: it is highly conservative in attitude. Business is about seizing opportunities that will pitch the brand ahead. Brand extensions must somehow surprise if they are to leave a mark. They should be both unexpected and quite consistent (see also page 190).

Think of Apple: each new extension surprised the market: how can it enter the music business (iPod, iTunes) and then the mobile phone one? What's next? The same holds true for Bic or Yamaha. Once the extension category has been decided, the main question becomes that of exploiting the brand equities to make best use of the product's advantages but also to defend its problems or added benefits against the competition's reaction.

Keys to successful brand extensions

Are brand values giving added value to the extension?

'Extension' is a brand-centric word. Consumers do not talk about brand extension. They say there is something new on the market and just evaluate it as for any innovation. Some innovation ideas are good, but the brand used to bring them to the market may not be the right one.

This is why brand extension managerial evaluation entails two phases: evaluation of the intrinsic appeal of the idea and the ability of the brand to sell it.

Why is the brand legitimate here? Classical words to describe this are 'congruence', 'coherence' and 'relevance'. They estimate if the equities attached to the brand (its kernel values) will add value to the innovation.

Another dimension of consumer evaluation is unexpectedness. It is certainly unexpected to see a Chanel surfboard, but it makes sense (fit). Fit and unexpectedness add value to an innovation.

Bic is one of the most innovating companies. Still a family-owned company, it has kept this entrepreneurial spirit. Starting as a ball pen company, it has regularly created new markets through value

FIGURE 12.11 Framework for evaluating extensions

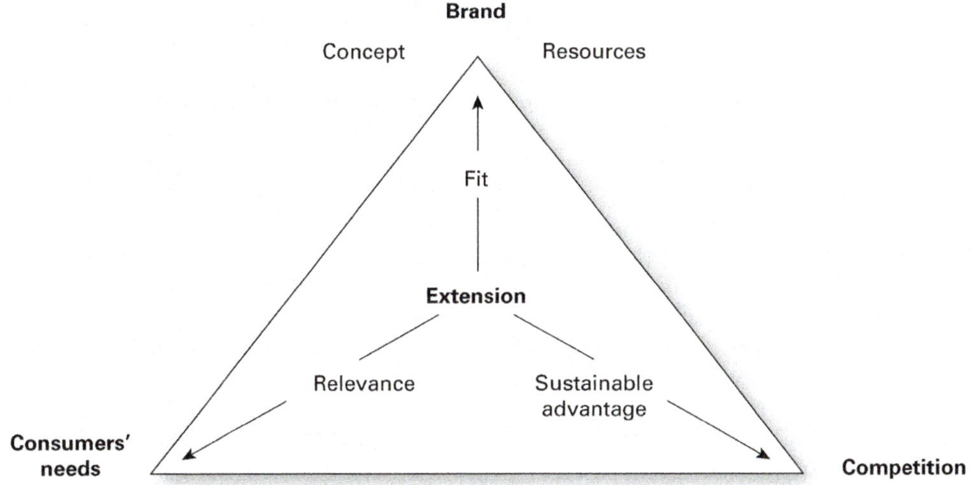

innovations, now also called blue ocean innovations or disruptive innovations (Dru, 1996). Bic invented the disposable razor market. Then it turned to the no-frills fragrance and the no-frills mobile phone. Both were unsuccessful, thus showing that blue ocean is not a guarantee of success (see also page 207).

The Bic phone was a clever idea: all mobile phone operators are upgrading their products with ever more features, more capacities, the internet, cameras, etc. Bic aimed at just the opposite: the many forgotten people who simply want the phone that is the least costly to purchase, elderly people desiring the easiest to use (the Bic phone allows only calls and SMS), tourists wanting a temporary local phone, and people over 35 with little money. Bic chose to enter this segment through a licence given to Orange (see also page 206). It was a failure.

The Bic brand certainly helped on one hand, but not on the other. Bic sells only disposable items: this equity met the characteristic of this mobile phone, which was for temporary use only. However, 'disposable' also means low quality in people's minds. This negative brand association created uncertainty: could one buy a product evoking the risk of unreliability because of its brand?

This risk could have been offset by a salesperson in-store, but because of the low cost Orange – the licensee – sold it in blister packs through self-service, so there was no one in-store to make a case for it.

Think of the full marketing mix of the extension

An extension is not simply a new product or service, it entails a full new marketing mix. It requires in fact that the organization think more about the consumer than the brand. When Nike launched its Nike Women extension, its management was so infatuated with the brand itself that it forgot consumers. This is why it was a failure: the products (shoes and clothes) had the same design as their male counterparts, and only the sizes were adapted to women. Nike Women was not really a line for women at all. Soon it was discovered that to succeed in this extension, it was first necessary to create relevant products. Female designers were hired to rethink the product offerings and stores.

Extension should meet trade expectations too

In its desire to maintain its dominant share of market in the UK, Smirnoff has shown the way by following a dual strategy. One part is aimed at adults, its present target market, with the introduction of Smirnoff Blue, Smirnoff Lemon and Smirnoff Black for instance, to compete with Absolut and Finlandia. The other is aimed at the youth market through Smirnoff Mule and later Smirnoff Ice, two ready-mixed drinks which gained high success and were soon imitated. The success of Smirnoff Mule demonstrates that all good innovations must provide value to the distributor *and* to the consumer.

The strategic goal was to establish these new products among young people for on-premise consumption. On Friday or Saturday nights, many pubs are literally full up and people gather outside them. Smirnoff Mule brings bartenders a faster way to serve clients than a draught beer, with a better margin: they just have to hand the bottle over to customers, without the need for a glass. Meanwhile, the bottle with its highly visible branding acts as a badge, an identifier for customers, unlike a glass of beer which generally does not carry a brand name. This is a very important motivation for 18–24-year-olds who are insecure about their image. In addition, advertising reinforced the modern status of the new drink. More than £4.5 million was spent on Smirnoff Ice to launch it among young males (Mule having been mostly chosen by females).

The question of resources

The main source of failure of extensions is a lack of resources for the launch. Companies should remember that if an extension is aimed at a different market, its launch should be treated as a new product launch. Unfortunately many companies extend their brand, thinking that it is a way to save money compared with launching a new brand, and that a simple mention at the end of the regular 30-second television ad will suffice. It might do for a simple line extension, a variant, but not for a brand extension.

Companies also hesitate to divert investment from core products to finance an extension. They feel that by doing so they will put their core product at risk from competition. As a consequence, they decide at the last moment not to support the extension with the required budget. This reasoning underestimates the reciprocal spillover effect. Communicating the benefits of a new product has an effect on the sales of the core product (see Chapter 9). This is one of the virtues of mega-brands covering multiple products: they get re-energized through communication about their new products.

Does the brand extension need a sub-brand?

Why is Chanel's entry in the cosmetics market called Precision, and why does Biotherm call its entry in the male market Biotherm Homme? Obviously the question of the name cannot be separated from that of the chosen brand architecture (see Chapter 13).

The naming decision must satisfy two demands. First, it should help the extension succeed. By a name one can underline specific traits or benefits of the extension, or counterbalance possible negative thoughts. Second, it should not dilute the parent brand equity.

Fashion and perfume brands are not that legitimate in the highly scientific cosmetic market, where women are looking for innovative ingredients, not just dreams or fashion. Chanel's choice of Precision helped bypass the negative prejudice against this type of extension for perfume and couturier brands.

To extend its brand into the female market, Gillette (a male brand) has chosen a sub-brand: Venus by Gillette.

Checking what the extension brings to the brand, its feedback effect

An extension uses brand capital. This is not surprising, since it was created to do so: the brand is a business development tool. It is therefore logical that we should seek to exploit this capital by putting it to productive use in new growth categories. However, we must also ensure a win–win outcome. After all, what does a brand extension really deliver? Sales alone are not enough. The benefits to be derived by the brand from this extension must be clearly specified.

Each extension from Kinder confectionery is aimed at a particular target, age segment or situation of use. Each also gives the brand widened relevance and less of a narrow image. This must be specified clearly in advance, and then measured afterwards.

Of course, we must be all the more careful to avoid any risk of dilution, as can happen when the values associated with the extension category contradict those of the brand, or when it is known that implementing the extension will be risky. After all, the implementation is the part customers see.

Make-or-buy decision: the Fedex case

Fedex is the leader of the intercontinental express market. It invented the hub model to guarantee a before-noon delivery anywhere in the world. It is number two in the intra-European air flight express market. Now a rational extension would be to expand in the intra-European local domestic market. Most companies have one single supplier for their express mail. Within companies the person in charge of choosing a supplier does not differentiate by destination. That is why, to boost its position in the very profitable intercontinental segment and in the intra-European one, Fedex thought of entering another market of frequent demand from companies, that of European ground deferred mail. This is a market where brand awareness and brand familiarity are built (through the person who is the representative of the brand, the one who picks the parcel up or delivers it: a key moment of truth and brand equity building). On the other hand, this meant an obligation to build a new factory and to adopt totally new processes, as it is a truck-based service. Here the hub system does not work; one goes from point to point by truck. Certainly trucks build brand awareness too, but Fedex would have the choice of either making or buying such services from a third party. What is the cost of learning the new know-how from scratch? What are the risks of delegating Fedex's reputation to a third party? Is there a reliable partner covering the whole of Europe?

Succeeding at vertical brand stretching

Vertical brand extension signals the desire of the brand to enter a higher- or lower-price segment where it has not competed so far.

In upward extension the goal is to access a segment with higher product margins, adding more costs to harvest more value. Another goal is to benefit from an alleged halo effect: building the buzz on expensive super-premium products should help increase the brand equity and as a consequence help sell the lower-priced lines, more easily justifying their price premium against the upcoming low-cost alternatives (we have analysed why this halo effect does not always happen, page 231).

Downward vertical extension signals a desire to make the brand more accessible. Prestige brands, focusing on a price premium as the measure of their brand equity, do not overlook the profitability goals: they make use of their reputation in inexpensive price zones in order to sell larger volumes.

There are risks in these two strategies.

Upward brand extensions

Upward extension's main risk is that of credibility. For buyers of the targeted high-priced segment, the brand comes from 'below'. Price bands are like private clubs, quite selective as to letting newcomers in, especially if their pedigree is not strong. That is why the Volkswagen group relaunched Audi to make a brand above Volkswagen. This strategy was imitated by Toyota, which created Lexus. Car brands are symbolic signs of where you stand on the ladder of material and professional success. Phaeton, Volkswagen's top of the range, is certainly an excellent premium car: it can be compared to the Mercedes C Class except that it is not called Mercedes. What VW Phaeton says is that the driver cannot buy a Mercedes. As a rule only previous VW fans are willing to stay with the brand and buy its top of the range; the same holds true for the remarkable and creative Citroën C6. That is why the Phaeton was not a success.

The second risk with upward trading is that of forgetting one's DNA: the brand is so obsessed by respecting the codes of this upward segment that it loses its uniqueness. It also sometimes enters this upward segment because it wants to match the competitor that created the segment. In both cases imitation forces dominate managerial thinking, leading to a disaster.

This is exactly what happened to Absolut vodka when in 2004 it tried to enter the US super-premium vodka segment created by newcomers such as Belvedere, Grey Goose, etc. Remember that Absolut vodka itself had created the premium vodka segment 20 years earlier by positioning its price 20 per cent above that of the world leader, Smirnoff. The new brand Grey Goose just repeated the manoeuvre, at the expense of Absolut. To fight back, Absolut launched Level for the US market, the world's number one super-premium vodka market. However, all that had made Absolut a world iconic product was absent from Level: no creativity at all, and a bottle clearly influenced by those of Grey Goose and Belvedere (abandoning the famous shape of Absolut). Level was a banal proposition, not tied to Absolut, without any clear value proposition. Finally, by sub-branding it without a clear reference to Absolut (calling it Level), the company prevented any halo effect from appearing.

Upward stretching by Diesel

In 2007 Diesel launched a new apparel line, called Diesel Black Gold (DBG), in order to enter a more premium market segment and compete with fashion brands' secondary lines (D&G, Marc by Marc Jacobs, etc). The goal was also to upgrade the overall perception of the brand, in order to justify its premium positioning. After two years of underperformance, a new manager was appointed in 2010 to turn around the business (see also page 229).

DBG is a radically new line: it differs from Diesel in design, material, communication and trade distribution:

- For design, a different designer was hired, who came from prêt-a-porter. The collection look is much more refined, adult and subtle than the main brand, even if the DNA remains the same.
- For material, all DBG denims are made in Italy, with high-quality Italian and Japanese fabric. Diesel also uses Italian fabrics, some in exclusivity, for its garments.
- For communication, DBG holds a catwalk show in New York during fashion week and also an event during Milan's male fashion week. Diesel also changed the labelling and other product 'packaging' in order to support the more premium and refined positioning.

- For trade distribution, even when targeting the same department stores, DBG is on a different floor, with different adjacent brands. DBG is also targeting opinion leader trade stores (L'Eclaireur in Paris, Barney's in New York, etc) in order clearly to segment the two labels. On the other hand, it is still distributed in 40 of the largest Diesel stores worldwide (15 per cent of the network) where it is feasible physically to create a dedicated space within the store.

Why did Diesel encounter difficulties, when Ralph Lauren seemed to succeed with its Black Label and Purple Label? There is a big difference between Ralph Lauren and Diesel from the standpoint of the problem of vertical extension.

Ralph Lauren proposes a lifestyle dream: the idealized and fantasized life of the Bostonian WASP bourgeoisie, *à la* Great Gatsby. There is no more elitist sport than polo. Even when they wear casual clothes, typical Ralph Lauren models in the ads remain quite formal, as expected in the codes of the bourgeoisie. This meant that Ralph Lauren's upper range was not a disruption of the brand cultural vision, the brand kernel (see page 163).

When one thinks of Diesel, one recalls the disruption of dominant cultural codes. Can Diesel, the icon of a counterculture, now propose a line that is within the codes of the culture it wanted to stigmatize earlier? Formal dress is in contradiction to the brand DNA. One need only ask: how does the founder of Diesel, Renzo Rosso, dress up when he goes to the Hollywood Oscars ceremony, for instance? Formalwear is definitely out of the brand's scope. Rosso had to involve himself and participate in the design and product sessions.

Downward brand stretches

Going downward creates another risk: that of brand dilution. Research has demonstrated what is called an ownership effect (Kirmani, Sood and Bridges, 1999). Owners of the upper versions in the range of status brands hate these downward moves and disparage them, for they destroy one of the key values of the status brand: a feeling of exclusivity. By making itself more accessible, the brand grows at the expense of the pride of its former clients. The status brand destroys value to increase volume. Jaguar, the car marque, knows it. It has now been sold by the Ford Prestige Division to the Indian Tata Motors. Jaguar forgot that the price of a luxury brand should always go up (Kapferer and Bastien, 2009): one can create accessible products only if new, extremely high-priced products are also created at the other end, just like the Mercedes S Class. The Mercedes A Class is an astute urban car full of plastic. Its price premium (compared to the price it should have on the basis of its product characteristics) is the measure of the pride of driving 'a Mercedes' at €20,000. Now this works because S Class or E Class cars are very visible during the Cannes Movie Festival or at Hollywood Oscars Night, and the ultra-rich of the world hide behind the black windows of these cars.

Now when an FMCG brand such as Danone launches a low-cost yoghurt, nothing of the kind happens. The brand is welcome to do so, as far as consumers are concerned. Only the trade is against it, for this low-cost Danone is entering the trade's own territory and competing against the private labels: that is why it failed. Low-cost Danone would have been bought by consumers, but they could not find it: multiple retailers did not list it.

Is the market really attractive?

The first thing to evaluate in a brand extension is not the extension, it is the attractiveness of the category. The key question in evaluating a brand extension is the intrinsic value of the market. Later, we examine this from the point of view of the business and the brand. This presupposes that we are considering not only the present but also the future of the category. An extension is not an overnight affair, it marks the beginning of a desire to invest in a new market. The extension itself is no more than a bridgehead. A realistic analysis of existing strengths, threats and opportunities is therefore required. Clearly, this corresponds to the traditional SWOT model (Figure 12.10).

Opportunities derive from the relationship between the factors for success in the category and the organization's key competences, both tangible and intangible. They also derive from the brand's ability to segment the category according to its own values, or in other words to create genuinely relevant differentiation. Strategic analysis also analyses the future of competition and the organization's relative strengths. Will its entry into the market trigger a competitive reaction, and if so, how big? To answer this question, it is necessary to evaluate the importance of the category to competitors.

To repeat, the fact that a brand *can* be extended does not mean it *should* be extended. One must take into account future competition and the costs of remaining a significant player in the category (the rate of innovation, rate of launches, marketing and sales investment and so on). Extension is not an inside feat: it must deliver a sustainable advantage. For instance, many food companies have thought of launching a frozen pizza, but what would they do next to capture shelf space from Buitoni or McCain, or to defend their own shelf share? In the middle term, who is in the best position to innovate most often? Table 12.4 presents a multi-criteria strategic evaluation grid.

TABLE 12.4 Extension strategic evaluation grid

	Extension 1	Extension 2	Extension 3
Is it a growing market?			
Are its success factors close to our strengths?			
Are the brand assets transferable?			
Are the brand assets still assets in this market?			
Will it impact positively the brand equity?			
How entrenched are competitors?			
How fast can they copy?			
Does the product have a clear differentiation?			
Is it a motivating difference?			
Can the company produce it?			
Can it produce at a normal cost?			
Will distribution accept it?			
Is it consistent with brand or company identity?			
Does it capitalize on the brand or company's present customers?			
Is it consistent with the brand or company's positioning?			
Does it capitalize on the company's expertise in:			
– production?			
– advertising?			
– logistics?			
– sales forces?			
– retail location?			
– pricing/promotion?			
Does is meet the company's profitability objectives?			
Can the company sustain competition (does it have the financial resources needed to compete)?			

Should we implement it alone? Partnerships and licences

It is difficult for a company to master the many new competences needed for an extension at the same time, which is why so many companies prefer alliances:

- Nestlé won the battle in Europe against Kellogg's once it decided to find a technical partnership with the American General Mills.
- Weight Watchers' expansion in the pre-cooked meals category was made possible through a co-branding agreement with Fleury Michon, a leader in this field.
- Evian asked Coca-Cola to distribute it in the United States, where its core brand urgently needed to be made more available. It also asked Johnson & Johnson to develop and market Evian Affinity (its cosmetics line) worldwide.

How should one manage licences?

Licensing to extend the brand

Strolling through the streets of Seoul or Shanghai, one finds Land Rover or Lamborghini stores, exclusively selling casual clothing. In Europe, the B2B brand Caterpillar is also a safety shoes line sold in urban stores aimed at youth. *Elle*, the women's magazine, has 250 licences throughout the world, either as local national *Elle* magazines or as products and accessories (children's apparel, casual wear, eyewear, home decoration, even restaurants, etc). This represents €400 million sales with annual royalties of €20 million. These brand extensions out of the core business would be impossible without a licensing agreement.

Licensing is the delegation of the creation, production and distribution of a brand in one of many product classes and in one or many countries. Licensing is not outsourcing. The licensor authorizes a third party (the licensee) to use the brand name, under strict controls, on its own creation, production and distribution. This authorization is tied to contractual engagements by the licensee concerning sales objectives. In exchange the licensor receives payment from the licensee, called royalties, as a rule a percentage of sales, with in any case a minimum guaranteed. Incidentally, royalties are the purest method of brand valuation, to estimate the financial value of a name: they indicate what percentage of the net sales are due to the brand name alone (see also Chapter 18).

For the licensor, licensing is most useful for rapid brand extensions into categories or markets where the company has no competence or know-how. It consists in lending the brand name to an operator specialized in this sector. Licensing concerns production and distribution. For the consumer, there is full brand consistency: the licensee is invisible. The front office is managed in full coherence with the brand identity norms.

Without licensing, Marlboro would never have extended its cigarette brand to the clothing business. The same applies to Caterpillar. Many young fashion brands are eager to find a fragrance licensee: their brand awareness will grow thanks to the huge media investments in the fragrance business. Licensing is also helpful in entering new parts of the world: in 1990 the Japanese licence was actually the only profitable part of the Burberry business (called Purple Label). It financed the Burberry brand turnaround successfully undertaken by Rose Marie Bravo (see page 397).

For the licensee, licences are either a full strategy or an escape from the profit crunch imposed by modern distribution. Some companies specialize in licences: Luxottica or Charmant for eyewear, Swatch for watches, Pentland for shoes, Mobilabs for mobile phones, L'Oréal, P&G Prestige Division, or Coty for fashion designers' fragrances.

Other companies, like those selling commodities to hypermarkets, try to compensate for their very small margins by high-margin licensed products. For instance, the Olympia company is market leader for socks sold in mass channels in France. The situation was getting difficult, since most of the market in volume was held by private labels. Olympia was obliged to manufacture private labels to occupy its factory full time. The negative slope of profitability has encouraged the management to search for licences (Burlington, Adidas, Airwell, etc). The same holds true for Esselte, a Swedish company specializing in stationery and office products: it now produces licensed binders (Diesel, etc) for pupils and students.

Licensing to overcome a credibility problem

Licensing is often a solution when the brand image does not allow its extension in a new category or segment, more attractive or profitable. Bic is market leader in the disposable razor segment, a segment it created. However, since then Gillette has created a me-too product to put the pressure on Bic. In the razor market, the blades themselves are a gold mine, just as printer heads are the source of HP's profitability. Bic might wish to enter this market. It has the know-how to produce remarkable blades too. However, because disposable razors are associated with teenage or female usage, the Bic brand lacks the equities to enter the blade market, mostly aimed at male consumption. How could Bic compete against the highly symbolic Gillette brand, 'the best a [real] man can get'? This is mission impossible. A solution is to attack not under the Bic name, but under licence: hypothetically some male celebrities might fit, or a fashion brand like Boss, or even Playboy.

Oddly enough, Carrefour is the number one client for the licensing of Disney cartoon characters. Carrefour is the world's number two retailer. Its policy is based on promoting its own store brand, which represents more than 40 per cent of the food and drug sales of Carrefour in Europe, but how does it compete against Pampers or Huggies, the two market leaders? By means of Disney licences, as the characters immediately attract the attention of children and mothers. Since the store brand cannot compete against the technology of Procter & Gamble, the strategy has been to use emotional branding.

Corporate attitudes vis-à-vis licensing

Brands have different attitudes vis-à-vis licences. Some use exclusively licences. They are Pierre Cardin, Daniel Hechter, Lacoste, etc. Others use a mix of licences and their own creation, production and distribution (Burberry). Finally, true luxury brands forbid licences: the business model of a true luxury strategy is vertical integration for fuller control.

Lacoste is a very unique company and brand. Created some 75 years ago by world tennis champion René Lacoste, the company has one business philosophy: never to have a factory or store. It is a 100 per cent pure licensor. Since its start, it has sold the famous polo shirt through a partner company, Devanlay, its worldwide licensee for clothes, in both production and distribution. Each product category is managed by a different licensee. The task of Lacoste itself is to manage the brand image and communication and to instil coherence among all licensees, which sell through different distribution channels and outlets.

The risk of licences is too great for prestige brands: licensees do not have a stake in building brand equity. They need to sell in order to make a profit while paying high royalties to the licensor. Even though, in theory, control is exerted from tip to toe, from production to retail selection and merchandizing, the natural sales orientation of licensees creates high risks of brand dilution. This is why prestige brands such as Ralph Lauren have purchased their licences. By doing so, not only did they regain control of the consumer experience, but also they could reduce the number of stores and integrate the distribution margin. This is also why real luxury brands never use licensing. Louis Vuitton manufactures all the products sold in its stores. It would not use licences, for no product can be sold outside the Louis Vuitton stores. This is why there is no Louis Vuitton fragrance: fragrances need to be sold in speciality shops, Sephora or Douglas, to reach high volumes. This would be a breach in the luxury strategy (Kapferer and Bastien, 2009).

Unintended consequences of licensing

Licences have been in disrepute for many years. The search for easy financial profits without a strong hold on the licensees, especially overseas, is a cause of frustration if not brand equity dilution.

The first disillusion comes from distribution. The brand finds its products in sales points well below its own standards. These standards may not be very well understood by the licensee in Indonesia or Thailand. The notion of quality, selectivity and prestige is quite variable from one country to another. Calvin Klein sued its main US licensee once it found that Calvin Klein jeans were sold in warehouse stores.

Another surprise arises when licensors discover that a local master licensee has launched extensions without prior agreement. *Elle* magazine found there were licensed toilet seat covers in Japan, representing 20 per cent of all sales of the local licensee.

The second problem is that of power relationships with the licensee. Licensees have a portfolio of licences, with a pecking order based on the volume of business and profitability, and the prestige of the brand.

Finally, the quality of the licensors' managers will play a role. As a result the licensor may not get the attention it deserves or expected. Decisions may be taken by the licensee without securing the necessary agreements or without really taking them into account.

It is advisable contractually to plan financial audits to secure the payment of all royalties due. This is not suspicion of fraud, but because the intricacies of global trade, with tax differences, etc, may cause some 'losses'.

Licensing may also backfire: most people in the world think of Dunhill as a cigarette brand. In fact cigarettes were a licence of the famous clothing, leather and fragrance brand Alfred Dunhill of London. This is a problem in Korea, where the brand has only recently opened its own stores. Korean consumers think it is a brand extension of the cigarette, into fashion, just as Marlboro did some 30 years ago, or Wills, the number one premium brand in India.

An extension-based business model: Virgin

Most brands conjure up an image of a product or service: shoes for Nike, yoghurt for Danone, ballpoint pens for Bic, a holiday village for Club Med, and so on. This is not surprising: before they became brands, they started out as a simple product or service, driven by marketing and sales. Virgin is an exception: who associates that brand with only one product or service? Indeed, Virgin now comprises 200 companies and 25,000 people working for the brand worldwide. It has a turnover in excess of €7 billion, and has become one of the world's top 50 brands. Even in countries in which it does not operate, it is still a famous brand.

It all started in 1969, when Richard Branson decided to launch a direct record-selling operation, enabling many groups without distribution by the 'majors' to gain access to the general public. The brand's DNA is already apparent in this founding act: Branson seeks out opportunities in markets choked by 'false' competition. He asks himself how he can operate differently from the leaders – who have usually frozen the market to their advantage. The Virgin name was chosen because it was friendly and modern, and could be applied to sectors other than just music. This last consideration alone presaged the business model that would follow.

Virgin's originality lies in the fact that it is held together by one entirely intangible 'glue', its brand. This is why the brand architecture is umbrella branding. Every year, Virgin launches itself into new businesses and pulls out of others. In under 20 years, Richard Branson has extended the brand to the following sectors (and subsequently pulled out of some of them):

- First business: mail order (1969).
- Records: Virgin Records (label created in 1973 and sold to EMI in 1992).
- Radio: Virgin Radio.
- Video games: Virgin Games (1983).
- Distribution: Virgin Vision (1983), Virgin Megastores (1988) and Virgin Bride (1996) for brides-to-be.
- Cosmetics: Virgin Vie.
- Drinks: Virgin Cola, Virgin Vodka (1994).
- Computers: PCs manufactured by ICL Fujitsu (1996), Internet terminals manufactured by Internet Appliance Network (2000).
- Air transport: Virgin Atlantic Airways (1984), Virgin Cargo (1984), Virgin Express (1996).
- Rail transport: Virgin Railways (1997).
- Tourism: Virgin Holidays (1895), tour operator, Virgin Sun.
- Hotels and pensions: Virgin Hotels, Virgin Pensions (for senior citizens).

FIGURE 12.12 The Virgin extension model

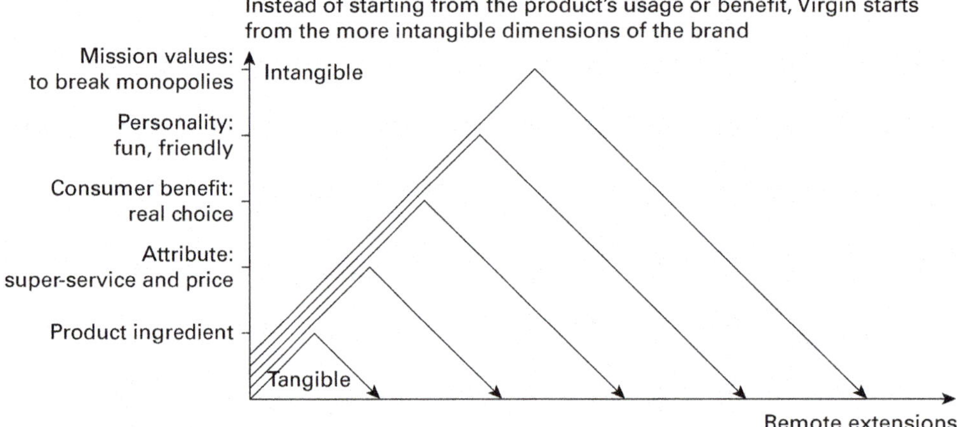

- Financial services: Virgin Direct Financial Services (by telephone, 1995), Virgin Bank.
- Internet: Virgin Net (1996).
- Utilities: Virgin Power House (2000): water, gas and electricity.

In a sense, Virgin is like the Japanese *keiretsus*, horizontally structured conglomerates consisting of independent companies that share one name and one set of values. How can a brand spread itself in so many directions without specific competencies and with minimal investment? Of course, the more widely the brand spreads itself into apparently dissimilar extensions, the greater the need for an intangible link (see Figure 12.12) – and this link consists of the Virgin brand's values. Its extensions actually form a family of independent companies that share the values of the Virgin brand.

To finance his expansion, Branson usually seeks support from appropriate partners in order to minimize his own investment, even if this means not being the majority shareholder. The partner thus provides the sector know-how, the money, and its own energy as an entrepreneur. For example, Virgin Megastores in the UK are 75 per cent owned by the W H Smith group. Similarly, Virgin Vodka was manufactured and distributed by William Grant in a 50/50 partnership with Branson.

Virgin allows start-ups to begin with a world brand as their 'birth gift', significantly reducing their necessary advertising expenditure – particularly as Branson is well aware of the financial benefits of repeated public relations exercises such as his balloon trip around the world, or riding down Fifth Avenue in a Patton tank to celebrate the launch of Virgin Cola. Branson also resells his businesses, but only after having added what makes them valuable in the eyes of the public – his brand. For example, the French Megastores were sold to Lagardère, and Virgin Atlantic Airways went to Singapore Airlines. Of course, the Virgin brand remains the property of Virgin Enterprises, a company of which he is the sole owner.

Virgin's extensions are remarkable in that they are truly based on a strategic analysis of the sector. But in addition, like any healthy extension, they deliver far more than just a name to customers: they represent true innovation which remains consistent with the brand's values. As its name so prophetically suggests, Virgin aims to take a brand new, 'virgin' approach to markets and operate in a different way from the 'majors'. Virgin has a rebellious, extraverted personality. Its ambition is to 'unblock' markets and liberate consumers from meaningless choices between dominant market leaders. Its commercial proposition is innovation, quality and fun. The result is a product range totally different from those of its competitors, targeting a younger audience and better value for money, all under the aegis of an aspirational brand.

After all, in order to succeed, innovation is required at every stage, even if it means being copied: Virgin Atlantic Airways was the first company to offer a Volvo-chauffeured collection service for its business class clients from their offices, and a bathroom at the arrival airport. On board, Virgin innovated with the first personal video screens, followed by relaxing massages and the like. Another example is Virgin Cola, which innovated by offering an excellent taste, produced by the Canadian firm Cotts (bought out by Virgin in 1998), at a price nominally 10–15 per cent lower than that of Coke, with widespread distribution.

However, the system has its limits: extensions do not always work (a fact that applies to Virgin just as it does to any other firm, of course). The further you get from the British zone of influence, the weaker and less emotive the Virgin brand becomes. This makes the high visibility associated with the Megastores' music and entertainment brand a prime tool for generating recognition and empathy among young people from all countries.

Paradoxically, Virgin's failures do not seem to have damaged its business model. In situations where many brands would have packed up and gone home, Virgin simply continues to expand elsewhere. After all, should we criticize David if he loses to the Goliaths every now and then? At least he tried. But can this brand and business model last forever? Not if the extensions fail too frequently. An analysis of the failures readily shows when an extension has been inappropriate:

- When it adds nothing other than just competition. This was what happened with Virgin Clothing, abandoned in 2000. London already buzzes with creators, rebels and anti-conformists. In a fragmented market with extremely wide price variations, what could Virgin add?

  The same is true of Virgin Cola. In Europe, Pepsi already plays the role of the fly in Coca-Cola's ointment. Furthermore, the multiples' purchasing centres chose not to stock the brand, thus starving it of access to the public. A question mark also hangs over Virgin Express: despite the fact that Virgin Atlantic Airways and its battle against British Airways assumed emblematic status, the act of starting yet another low-cost airline to compete with Ryanair failed to connect with the brand's mission. There are no dominant leaders in this sector, and customers do not feel trapped.
- When the scale of investment required pushes the fulfilment of the promise back into the long-term future. This is what has happened to Virgin Rail. In the UK, the brand's entry into commuter railways has not made any real difference to commuters' daily life: it has not been able to deliver a better experience. True, the dilapidated state of the rolling stock and infrastructure, handed over to the firm 'as is' under privatization, ensured there could be no miracle: a network cannot be changed that quickly. Similarly, profitability issues concerning the MGM cinemas taken over by Virgin in 1995 prevented any real price reductions – one of the terms of the brand contract.

Without Richard Branson himself, could the Virgin group succeed? Given its founder's aura, and his ability to attract the attention of the media and to concentrate energy and investors around him, it must be concluded that Virgin is Branson himself. This is the brand's strength, but also its weakness. As with luxury brands, we should remember that a brand only truly begins with the loss of its founder.

How execution kills a good idea: easyCar

EasyJet's success is well known; the failure of its brand extensions is less so. We examine here how an ostensibly good extension idea (easyRent car hire) led to major financial losses.

EasyJet and RyanAir are the two best-known 'low-cost' companies in Europe. They have both picked up the clever idea of Herb Kelleher, the founder of the world's first low-cost airline: Southwest Airlines, in the United States. The strategic idea is to aim at the market of all those people who have never flown before, rather than fight over those who take planes on a regular basis. The first market is enormous, and has never been seriously explored, whereas the second is a sea of blood as a result of intense competition and high operational costs. It was therefore possible to speak metaphorically of a 'blue ocean'. They needed to find a way to liberate this potential demand. The only brake was the price of an air ticket, and the opportunity existed provided that it could fall below a psychological threshold, the cost of the taxi that takes you to the airport.

To achieve this price, they had to invent a new business model, a new economic equation, in order to offer a brand value proposition of a type never seen before, a type that would revolutionize demand. This was achieved first by suppressing all costs, other than safety, that inflated the price. Therefore they removed or reduced:

- All selling costs, by making it obligatory to buy exclusively over the internet.
- All on-board service costs: there is very little available to eat or drink, and everything must be paid for. Consequently, customers consume very little on board, and use of the toilets is reduced. This makes it possible to remove one toilet and replace it with seats, which in turn bring in money and increase passenger numbers.
- The cost of cleaning the plane during stopovers: the crew do the cleaning.
- Parking costs during stopovers: every minute that a plane is on the ground costs money. This time was therefore reduced to a minimum by maximizing flying time and rotations per day. RyanAir was also able to exploit small, unknown, empty airports (such as Amiens, which is 142 km from Paris, as opposed to Roissy-Charles de Gaulle, which is only 30 km away). These smaller airports charge airlines much less, and there are grants available from local chambers of commerce for these low-cost airlines, which bring hundreds of tourists and create a regional economic boom.
- Plane maintenance costs, through a single-supplier policy. By buying only the same plane, and only from Boeing, all processes and costs can be simplified.
- Staff costs: these companies pay their staff much less than other airlines, and offer very few company benefits.
- Advertising costs: the founding directors were able to create regular media events through accusations against British Airways, for example, or fabulous offers (free flight for 10 people, etc). Anything became the pretext for staging an event.
- Costs linked to the lack of service: these companies try to avoid paying any compensation for (frequent) delays, or for lost luggage and the like, arguing that people cannot expect the lowest prices *and* compensation. After-flight service is defective, often non-existent.

Flushed with this success, Stelios Haji-Ioannou, the founder of easyJet, decided to extend the business model to many other activities, thereby imitating the approach of Richard Branson with his Virgin brand. He created the easy group, and launched products such as easyMoney, easyValue, easyInternet Café and easyCar.

It is true that the car rental market is an oligopoly, controlled worldwide by two giants, Hertz and Avis, whose margins and procedures showed that it should be easy to drastically reduce costs, and therefore prices. Furthermore, what could be more natural than to take advantage of travellers disembarking the easyJet plane by offering them a similar type of service to reduce the prices of car rental? Having paid just €30 for their plane ticket with easyJet, these travellers would choke at the notion of paying €100 for a day's car rental at Hertz or Avis. The idea was to offer managers travelling by plane an attractive car (Mercedes A-class) at €9 a day.

However, there are many differences between a plane and a car. On easyJet, the customer is required to have – non-negotiable – iron discipline from reservation to disembarkation. Moreover, the asset is not entrusted to the customer. The reverse is true for the car; customers refuse all constraints, and they are the ones entrusted with the asset (the car), the ones who manage it. Furthermore, customers arriving late (as they often do, since air travel is rarely punctual) find a queue at the easyCar counter, which is understaffed, thereby extending their wait: recriminations break out on all sides. On their return, they are in a hurry to return the car, and therefore mess up the formalities. This only multiplies the problems when the bill is received, since rental customers take less care of a hire car than they do of their own. EasyCar quickly crumpled under the complaints of customers, furious at finding themselves charged for repair costs.

In order to grow, easyCar opened agencies in town centres, which attracted a clientele particularly eager to get a bargain and try a Mercedes for €9. This led to an abnormally high number of damaged or dirty cars. It is difficult to immediately hire out a dirty or damaged car. The company could ask its flight crew to clean the cabin, but not its car rental clients. This therefore affected car rotation and created logistical complexities, leading to unforeseen costs that dragged the figures into the red, in addition to the ill will spread by aggravated customers. Finally, the Mercedes A-class was a brilliant choice of car, but an expensive one to maintain – and the buy-back price of the cars (in poor condition) was lower than anticipated.

13 Brand architecture

A brand has only one need: to grow, while maintaining its reputation and profits. Capitalizing on the success of its founding product or service, it does so by means of successive extensions, narrow to begin with (product line, range) or broader in scope (entry into new product categories).

When this extension of the perimeter of the brand's offer occurs, strategic questions arise: they concern the brand architecture. The answers to these will have a considerable effect on the value creation and the construction of brand capital. This is not a problem of aesthetics, but of efficiency.

The key questions of brand architecture

There are five types of question:

- What to call new products? Should they be given a descriptive name or a brand name? When Lafarge invented a revolutionary, fluid and therefore extremely smooth concrete, should it have called it simply fluid cement, or Agilia? In the latter case, how should the link be made between this so-called daughter brand, Agilia, and the so-called parent brand, Lafarge? Should one say Lafarge Agilia or Agilia by Lafarge? Does the same rule apply for all daughter brands? How should it be expressed on the packaging of cement sacks, on the products themselves, on distributors' shelves, or on the stands at trade shows?
- How many brand levels to adopt? Should there be only one brand name within the company? This is the choice for most Asian groups. This means naming the products in a descriptive manner in order to have one single brand. Thus, we talk about Samsung televisions, Samsung mobile phones and Samsung digital cameras. In the same way, there are Braun coffee machines, Braun razors, Braun electric toothbrushes and Braun hairdryers. Conversely, for decades Philips razors have been known by the name Philishave, and we talk of the Apple iMac and now the iPod.
- How much visibility to give to the corporate name, group name and the company name itself? Should everything be brought together under this one name, as Siemens and Axa have done, or should the name be given a role as a guarantee of daughter brands, as 3M and Danone have done? On all 3M products (such as Scotch and Post-It) we find a visible 3M signature. Conversely, you have to turn the Evian water bottle round to find the Danone Corp logo on the label at the back. As for Procter & Gamble's products and brands (Ariel, Tide, Dash, Always and so on), it takes a sharp eye to spot the name of the local subsidiary in the small print. Pharmaceutical laboratories answer these questions in different ways, depending on whether they operate in the prescribed products sector, or in over-the-counter (OTC) medication, or even manufacture generic medicines (Moss, 2007).

  Within groups, should the brand be situated at the corporate level (Accor), or at the divisional or business unit level, as with the Accor Casino or Accor Hotels brands, alongside the well-known product brands

(Formule 1, Motel 6, Red Roof, Etap, Mercure, Novotel, Sofitel, Suite Hotels and so on)?

- More generally, should there be a different name for the company and the commercial brand? Thus, France Telecom is still the name of the institution, and Orange is now the only commercial brand.
- Should the same architecture apply around the world? For example, in the country of origin, in Europe, in the United States and in Asia?

These are necessary, even crucial questions, which need to be answered in order to make the continually renewed product offer easy to read, while at the same time building the brand's reputation through this offer.

The term 'branding strategy' is used for decisions on:

- the number of brand levels to be implemented (one, two or even three?);
- the role of the corporate in the product value communication: should it be absent, strongly present, or hardly present?
- the relative weight of these brands, and the graphic arrangement of their coexistence on all the documents, packaging, and products, but also industrial sites, offices, and business cards of salespersons and managers;
- the degree of globalization of the architecture.

There are a few typical responses to these questions: these models are called *branding strategies*. They are discussed in detail below. First of all it is necessary to return to the key questions of brand architecture. Brand architecture is therefore a strategy: it may be ideal, or may lead to losses of efficiency, even to paralysis. In any case, what is expected is a coherent and well-founded response, even if it must change as competitive conditions evolve, rendering the previous choice of architecture null and void, or inefficient and too expensive. In fact, groups never cease to change their brand architecture, as the examples below illustrate.

In 1990, l'Oréal Paris, which had previously limited itself to endorsing its brand ranges worldwide (Elnett, Elsève, Studio Line, etc) by discreetly signing them, overturned this state of affairs, henceforth giving l'Oréal Paris a key role, under which all these so-called star brands had to fall into line, thereby displaying a community of values and communications style.

In the B2B sector, Henri Lachmann undertook the reverse change when he took over from Didier Pineau Valenciennes as managing director of the Schneider Electric Group. The latter was responsible for taking Schneider from a fragile status as ironmongers to that of a global high-tech company specializing in industrial electrical equipment, thanks to the acquisition of companies famous throughout the world (such as Merlin Gerin, Telemecanique, Yorkshire Switchgear, the Italian company Modicon and the American Square D). Pineau Valenciennes' goal was to achieve a unique corporate brand as quickly as possible, which would also play the part of a commercial brand: as its competitors Siemens, ABB, GE and Legrand and Hager do, Schneider Electric became the keystone of the whole offer. This involved the progressive disappearance of the specialized companies such as Telemécanique and Merlin Gerin, relegated to the rank of daughter brands, then to names of ranges. Taking over management of the company, Lachmann had a different vision. It was necessary to do the opposite, revitalizing the daughter brands to worldwide recognition, since they were the capital of the emerging company Schneider Electric. Today the process has ended with one brand only: Schneider Electric.

In 2005, all products manufactured anywhere in the world by Unilever, a leading group in mass-market products, had to carry the U logo in a highly visible and identifiable way. Until then the company had been hidden, or at least not identified on product packaging, except for the legally required mention of the legal name of the local subsidiary (such as 'Lever Industan Ltd' in India). This emergence of the corporate brand is a fundamental tendency, but Unilever's competitor, Procter & Gamble, still hides its identity on its packaging. It is true that the company has had to cope with a particularly persistent and unpleasant rumour (Kapferer, 1987).

In 2006, Veolia, the world leader in environmental services (water and waste treatment, energy, delegated public transport) decided to remove its three branch brands, through which it had communicated since their creation: Connex for transport, Dalkia for energy and Onyx for waste treatment, substituting them with the unifying name Veolia: so the brands became Veolia Transport, Veolia Energy and so on.

Clearly brand architecture is not a technical or tactical problem, but a strategic one. The choice of one leads to a commitment that lasts several years, and it may become a source of cost cutting or of expensive inefficiencies.

Type of brands

Let us look at a roll of adhesive tape. At the top and in large letters we find the name of the general public commercial brand name Scotch. Down and to the left we find 3M, or the company's corporate brand. Finally, under Scotch, comes the name of the product itself: Removable Magic™ Tape.

As we can see, there are three brand levels here, and a descriptor (or designator):

- the company's corporate brand 3M;
- the commercial brand Scotch, which acts as an umbrella brand for all the mass or general public products;
- the brand of the product line Magic™ Tape;
- the designator specifying what kind of Magic Tape it is: 'removable'.

3M is familiar with this three-level strategy.

The strategy of Nokia appears much simpler: here there is only one brand level. Everything is Nokia, followed by a serial number or code name that serves only to identify a reference, a code name that will be null and void in six months, given the speed at which the ranges in the field of telephony are rotated. Moreover, it is common to say, 'I'm going to buy "a Nokia"', without giving any other name. Then people specify which model they want to the salesperson by recalling the particular characteristics desired ('the one with this and that function and a very flat design' and so on).

As for Apple, the company has opted for two brand levels, Apple itself and iPod or iMac, named after the famous Macintosh. Apple's star products have all had their own name (sub-brand), except of course for the early ones that made the company's reputation. They were called Apples (1, then 2 then 3) and then a variant name. At l'Oréal also, the policy is not to mention the group name but to build the brands on star products (also called franchises) with their own names. For example, Garnier (the other global general public brand of the l'Oréal group) has built its reputation on the Fructis range, or the Recital line. Renault has built its reputation on brands that all have a name (Twingo, Clio, Laguna, Scenic, Latitude).

What explains the choice of architectures with one, two or even three brand levels? It is principally the market, its level of segmentation and the option of whether or not to lean on the corporate brand for support.

Products with very rapid rotation make it impossible to use anything other than a single brand name (Nokia, Samsung, Sony Ericsson, Sage and so on). It takes time to install a particular product brand.

In big industry, work is done by project: the name summarizes the company's competence, stature and power, the professionalism of its men and women, the underlying culture. This is why big industrial companies like to capitalize all their shares on a single name. Nevertheless, taking public works for example, as invitations to tender are done through trade bodies, the groups have a two-level brand policy. Vinci suggests the power of a leading group, Via is the reputed global brand in road construction.

In the mass market, where products are largely similar, it is necessary to help create perceptible differentiations. Brand names contribute to this. Pepito by Lu was aimed at children from 6 to 10 years, then Prince by Lu took them on to the age of 15. The first name also makes it possible to confer an intangible personality on the product, an added value in comparison to the distributor's copy.

Which role for which brands?

In the above example of the removable Scotch Magic™ Tape from the 3M company, it is easy to understand how each level plays a specific role. The manner in which the consumer talks about the product indicates which of these levels plays the leading role, that of seller (the motivator), the one in which the perceived value resides. The consumer rarely says 'I want a 3M.' On the other hand, the manager of a clinic or hospital, hospital attendants and doctors will find it easier to emphasize 3M. In their eyes, all the professionalism of a company that, through its innovations, has been able to create products so useful to surgeons at the most critical moments of surgery resides at this level.

When you buy a KitKat Chunky from Nestlé, you are buying first and foremost 'a KitKat' in its larger version (here called Chunky to increase the perception of volume and size), under the obvious auspices of the 'better living brand' Nestlé. If you turn over the product, you will see the corporate brand Nestlé itself (with its characteristic nest), which acts as a supreme guarantee, morally responsible for all the products made by its factories around the world, a kind of manufacturer's brand. Let us note that this manufacturing brand Nestlé is also present on the back of the regional European commercial processed meats brand Herta.

Through these examples may be distinguished the roles of:

- Motivator, the anchor point for value and driver of choice. From a certain point of view, this is the true brand: the one that most symbolizes the differentiation and creates the desire.
- Source of value for products. The commercial brand Nestlé applied as the aegis above all products indicates that these carry its values of taste, health and family.
- The producer's moral endorsement and responsibility, where the company supplies a telephone number that customers can call to report any deviation that they consider unacceptable, anywhere in the world. This is a manifestation of the demands of corporate social responsibility (CSR). Yesterday we said, 'Big is beautiful'; today we say, 'Big is responsible.'
- The designator of the specificity of the reference in question – when we say KitKat Chunky, to specify which one we wish to buy.
- An identifier of the origin: this is the role of the manufacturer's brand.

The accumulation of levels damages clarity, and appropriation by the client. It should therefore be combated, and only the indispensable levels should be kept. The debate on the presence or absence of the corporate brand on mass-market products cannot be decided only by questioning consumers. Of course, if they were asked whether they see any reason to keep the name 3M on the packaging, the majority would say no: they don't know 3M. Since the logo evokes nothing for them, they regard it as useless. However, the strategy cannot be based on this point of view alone. The legitimate ambition of enhancing the group's value on the stock exchange implies an awareness that cannot be built up through colossal advertising budgets, the money for which must necessarily be taken from the brands' operating budgets. It is therefore better to profit from the millions of stealth contacts offered by the products and the communication they make.

For this same reason, the Accor symbol appeared in the lobbies of all the group's hotels, regardless of brand. This made it clear that all of these hotels, previously presented as independent or even competitors, were in fact members of the same family. There was a loss in differentiation and probably in emotion, but Accor rapidly gained from it recognition as the leader in hotels and services in Europe.

The first alternative: branded house or house of brands?

The brand architecture is the coherent response given to the three questions examined above:

- How many brand levels should be used? One single level, or two? In other words, should brands be created to designate the activities or the professions or the products themselves?
- What linkage exists between these brand levels? This goes back to the question of the respective roles of the brands: where is the value located, who endorses whom, and so on?
- What visibility should the corporate brand have? And what role?

The answers to these questions are not independent. In reality they form six types of overall response, with precise impacts that go far beyond the descriptive (what name or symbol is in large font, or in small, at the top or the bottom) and concern the offer itself. They affect its content, its values: that is, the degree of variety that a brand can offer under its name. These overall responses or branding architecture types number six in total. From this point on we shall distinguish the following architectures:

FIGURE 13.1 Positioning alternative branding strategies

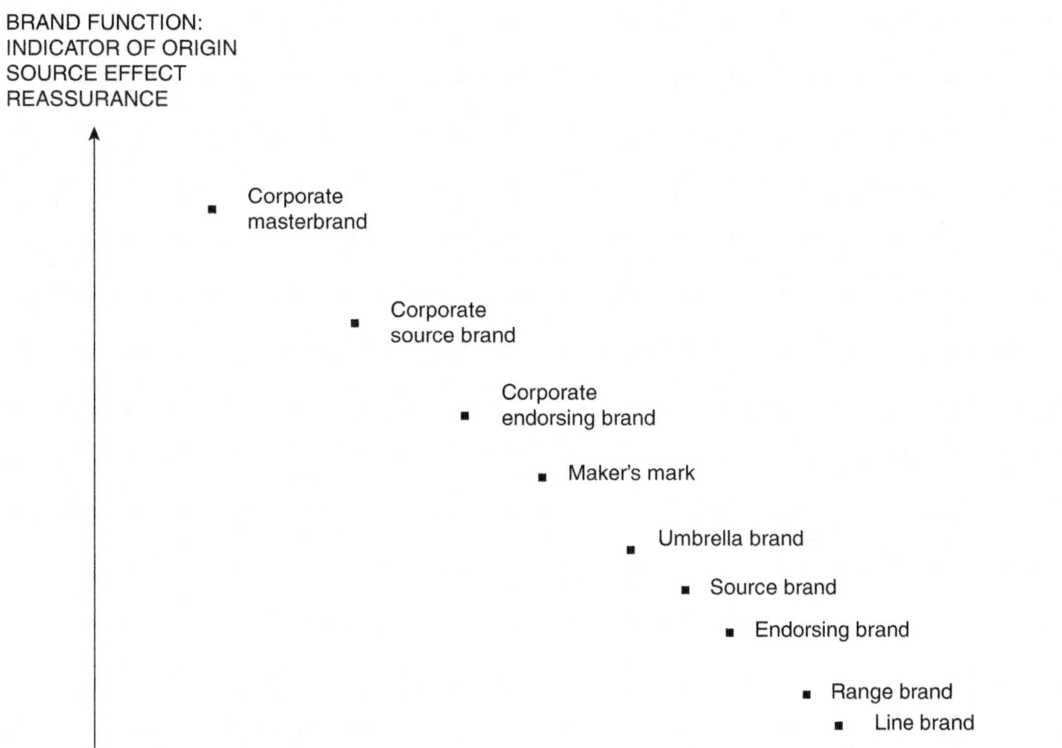

- the product-brand strategy and its variants, the line and range brands;
- the flexible umbrella strategy;
- the masterbrand strategy;
- the maker's mark strategy;
- the endorsing brand strategy;
- the source brand strategy.

These strategies are responses to the market. They may be structured along two axes (see Figure 13.1), according to whether the value sought by the brand relates more to power and stature on the one hand, or personalization, differentiation and identity on the other.

At one extreme, the strategy known as the *corporate masterbrand* is characterized by a single and unique brand level, often the corporate name, and that of the company itself. The whole of the company that adopts it must then fall into line with the brand's values, and be the carrier of these values. Either something is IBM, or it is not. Brands in the industrial and public worlds and the services sectors (banks, insurance, consultancies and so on) typically follow this strategy. Here, reputation is linked to reassuring size and power.

At the other extreme we find the *product-brand strategy*. In this strategy, the company is not identified at all. This is the case with brands of LVMH and Procter & Gamble, which does not strongly identify itself on each of its brands (Ariel, Tide, Pampers, Always, Dash, Swiffer and the rest). This makes it possible to function in the same market, for example washing powders, with a portfolio of apparently competing brands. The car manufacturer PSA also functions via a product-brand strategy: you can buy either a Peugeot or a Citroën, but not a PSA.

Architectures with two or more brand levels represent a compromise between the power requirements that push for a single dominant name (masterbrand) and the personalization requirements that push for segmented daughter brands, each having a clearly differentiated identity. In fact, generalized automobile brands attempt to capitalize on their name (Volkswagen, Toyota) but boost the attractiveness of the models themselves by means of a name that acts as a brand (Golf, Passat, Yaris, Prius).

It is also possible to classify these architectures according to the degree of constraint that they impose downstream, at the business, product and market levels. In this respect, the Americans distinguish between two basic alternatives: 'house of brands' or 'branded house' (that is, a basket of different brands or activities brought together under a single aegis) (see Table 13.1). These alternatives lead back in fact to the degree of constraint and coherence imposed on the products and markets. We will see that behind these basic alternatives can be found architectures that in practice are very different.

The first option (house of brands) relates to a situation of extreme freedom of management for the brands, subsidiaries, activities and divisions. This is typical of Japanese groups. For example, there is no coordination between the Mitsubishi Motors division and the Mitsubishi Electric division.

TABLE 13.1 'House of brands' or 'branded house'

House of brands	Branded house
Product-brand	Source brand
Line brand	
Range brand	
Maker's mark	
Endorsing brand	
Flexible umbrella brand	Masterbrand

It may be the same name, and the same company in legal terms, but each division, like a silo, acts as it sees fit. It carries out its own advertising, with its own arguments, its brand values and so on. The important things are commercial success, and the growth in recognition of the Mitsubishi name.

As we can see, 'house of brands' does not relate solely to the product-brand architecture, as David Aaker (1995) and Kevin Lane Keller (2007) write, but also applies to umbrella-type strategies (a single brand for the whole company) where in fact the decisions made downstream, in contact with the market, are very free, and seek only to reach the objectives linked to that specific market, without coherence as a whole at the image level. Michelin has acted in this way for decades. Michelin's Truck Division did not coordinate with Michelin Private Vehicles or with Michelin Aviation. There was no desire to create variations on a common, specific and normative brand platform in each of these markets.

The 'branded house' expresses the desire to give coherence to the whole under the auspices of a brand with central values that find embodiment at the market and product level. This path brings together the masterbrand and also dominant (source) brand strategies, giving a strongly normative structure to the daughter brands on the second level. This strategy is pursued by Nivea for example, l'Oréal Paris and Kinder. This second level must express the values of the parent brand. In this way the necessary coherence can be instilled, as dealt with in Chapter 11. The 'branded house' is a family with a high degree of internal unity.

This is why we can structure the strategies according to a matrix that classifies them. They are classified by the number of brand levels (one or two) and according to the degree of freedom allowed downstream, at market level, for decisions on product and service positioning. These will be examined here in turn.

Branding strategy and corporate valuation

Branding strategy should not be seen as a formal design problem but rather a matter of deciding on the value flows to be created between the different parts and products of a company. As such it affects the value of the company.

FIGURE 13.2 The six main brand architectures

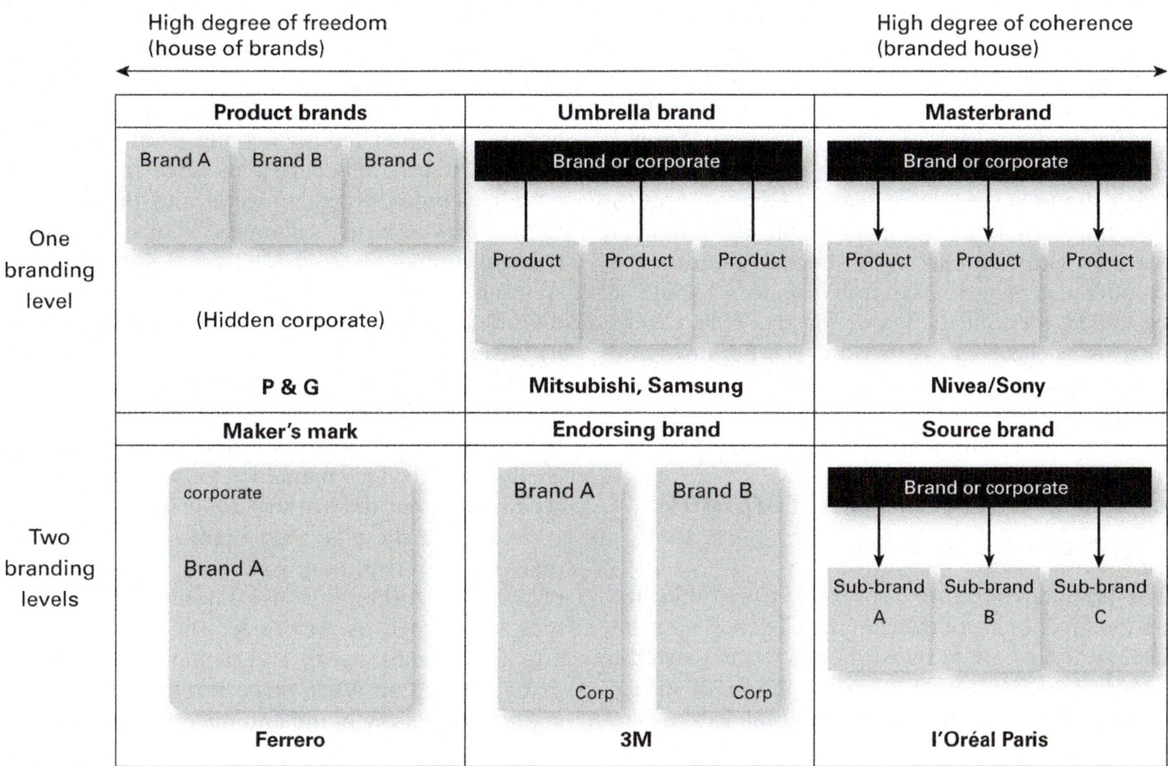

The business angels and investment funds have got it right. For example, in the cosmetics sector, there is more to be gained from the resale of a 'branded house' than a basket of mixed brands, however well known, grouped together within a 'house of brands'. For example, Garnier has become a 'branded house', a house with a house spirit and house values that in return influence the positioning of the brands under Garnier. In fact, Garnier is itself a brand with a specific identity. SCAD, on the other hand, is a 'house of brands' that groups together brands as diverse as Dop, Vivelle, Dessange and J L David. SCAD is merely a commercial and marketing organizational structure.

In the cosmetics sector, a 'house of brands' is valued at six times the profits, while a 'branded house' enjoys an overvaluation that brings the P/E (Price-Earnings) ratio to 7 or 8. Similarly, as soon as a company is quoted on a stock exchange, all internal separatist tendencies – such as sub-brand logos protected jealously from the corporate brand – must cease. What had previously been of little consequence becomes unacceptable.

Research by Rao, Agarwall and Dalhoff (2006) has examined how manifest branding strategies were related to the stock value of the corporation. The statistical results show that a one-brand strategy (branded house) is linked to a higher stock market value, followed by the mixed strategy. These results are not surprising, but they are misleading and likely to lead to wrong decisions.

Looking at the stars of Wall Street today, one finds the start-ups of the internet world (Google, Amazon and eBay) or of high technology (Cisco, Microsoft, Apple and Dell), or services (IBM, etc). These are recent companies focused on one single market, if not one activity. In itself eBay is a product brand name that has become a listed company. The same holds true for Amazon, etc. This means that it is normal that young companies, still focused on one need if not one service or product, in the fastest-growing part of the modern economy deliver high ROI and stock valuation multiples. Their branding strategy is only the correlate of the above-mentioned parameters and in no way a cause of the profits. Also, how useful is this type of result for say P&G, Lever or LVMH? These groups thrive by mastering a know-how (marketing here, luxury management there) and managing a portfolio of independent brands, each the leader in its own segment. Should P&G then abandon its branding strategy and use a single brand, just as the Korean or Japanese groups do? But then it would not be able to dominate markets with multiple entries (Ariel, Dash, etc in the laundry detergent market, for instance). Should it be called the Gillette Group or the Tide Group instead of P&G now that this corporate name has become the symbol of excellence in marketing FMCG goods?

Brand architecture and corporate internal organization

The brand architecture also has a strong influence on the functioning of the company. There is no masterbrand or source brand without a brand master, a guardian of the temple, someone who will ensure the necessary coherence, not only at the level of the logo or of the formal identity, across all countries and divisions. That would be to view this person as more than a guardian of policies – on character, on typographics, or on respect for graphic charts – (what is often referred to as a logo cop).

In reality, the more a company moves towards the 'branded house' type of architecture, the more it becomes necessary to install coordination and power structures. Hence at Schneider Electric, and also at the core of the Seb group, there exists a brand committee, made up not of communicators but of the managers of the business units and the divisions themselves. The profile of the participants in this brand committee is moreover symptomatic of how seriously or otherwise the company takes the notion of branding.

Japanese companies have recently become aware that their typical silo organization, although it certainly had advantages, was damaging to the emotional quality of the brand and its coherence. Each division pushes a functional characteristic of its product, and nobody takes responsibility for the brand values themselves. This is why, in 1999, Toshiba decided to name a 'Mr Brand' in the person of the previous worldwide director of research and development for the Toshiba group. It should also be noted that Korean groups such as Samsung, and in particular LG, did not take so long: they were quick to name brand guardians, with transverse and global authority.

If we examine the architectures in detail, the apparently banal fact of moving from two brand levels to one is in reality a message on the company's methods of organization and the distribution of power. In its beginnings, Veolia followed a house of brands strategy. Veolia was born from the splitting up of Vivendi Universal's public utilities division, but the value was located at the level of its business activities. In this way Connex brought together all the private trains, buses and subways throughout the world, Onyx was the global brand for waste management and Dalkia the brand for the energy branch. This marked a group where power coordinates, but the markets dominate.

Removing these division brands sends a strong message of integration, externally to clients and prospective clients, but also internally. The client may legitimately expect to see the organizational and IT silos disappear, and genuinely networked managers appear. When this is not the case, there is a gulf between the brand and the organization.

The main types of brand architecture

Let us now examine the individual characters of the principal brand architectures. We shall begin with those architectures that allow great freedom in terms of products and communication: the link between the company values and those of the divisions, activities and product is lax. They are brought together under the term 'house of brands'. Then we examine strategies that are more restrictive downstream, since the latter should reflect central values, of which the brand is the concrete expression (see Figure 13.2).

The product–brand strategy

It is widely known that a brand is at the same time a symbol, a word, an object and a concept: a symbol, since it has numerous facets and it incorporates figurative symbols such as logos, emblems,

FIGURE 13.3
The product–brand strategy

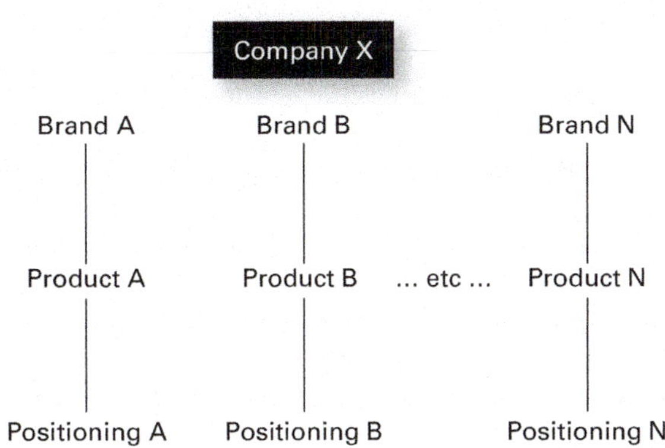

colours, forms, packaging and design; a word, because it is the brand name which serves as support for oral or written information on the product; an object, because the brand distinguishes each of the products from the other products or services; and finally, a concept in the sense that the brand, like any other symbol, imparts its own significance – in other words, its meaning.

The product–brand strategy involves the assignment of a particular name to one, and only one, product (or product line) as well as one exclusive positioning. The result of such a strategy is that each new product receives its own brand name that belongs only to it. Companies then have a brand portfolio that corresponds to their product portfolio as illustrated in Figure 13.3.

This brand strategy can be found in the hotel industry where the Accor Group has developed multiple brands for precise and exclusive positions: eg Sofitel, Novotel, Suit' Hotel, Ibis, Formule 1 and Motel 6. The company Procter & Gamble has made this strategy the symbol of its brand management philosophy. The company is represented in the European detergent market by the brands Ariel, Vizir, Dash and in the soaps market by Camay, Zest, etc. Each of these products has a precise, well-defined positioning and occupies a particular segment of the market: Camay is a seductive soap, Zest a soap for energy. Ariel positions itself as the best detergent in the market and Dash as the best value for money in the intermediate price range. Both have developed a product line including powder, liquid and tablets.

Innovative companies in the food sector create new speciality products which are then distinguished through individual names and therefore these companies have a large brand product portfolio. The cheese company Bongrain markets more than 10 brands, such as St Moret, Caprice des Dieux and Chaumes. The mineral water market is composed of only product brands: one asks for Vittel, Evian or Contrex, knowing very well that there will be no ambiguity and one will get the product asked for. Here, the brand, the name of a product, becomes a strict indication of identity.

In an extreme case, the product is so specific that there is no equivalent, and the product is not only a product, but an entire product category of which it is the sole representative. This phenomenon has been described by some through the neologism 'branduct' (Swiners, 1979), an abbreviation of brand product. These products are so unique, so specific that they have no other name than their brand name. We see this in 'Post-it', Bailey's Irish Cream, Malibu liqueur, Mars, Bounty, Nuts, etc.

How is the strict relationship between one name, one product and one positioning maintained over a period of time? First, the only way to achieve brand extension is by renewing the product. To keep the product at its height and original positioning, the Ariel formula has often been improved since it was launched in 1969. Ariel receives the best technological and chemical inputs from Procter & Gamble (like its competitor, Skip, from Lever) (Kapferer and Thoenig, 1989). Often, to emphasize an important improvement to the product, the company adds a number after the brand name (Dash 1, Dash 2, Dash 3). To keep up with changing consumer habits, the brand name is applied to various formats (for example, in packaging: packets, drums, in powder or liquid form).

What, then, are the advantages of the product brand strategy for companies? For firms focusing on one market, it is an offensive strategy designed to occupy the whole market. By indulging in the practice of multiple brand entries in the same market (Procter & Gamble has four detergent brands), the company occupies many segments with different needs and expectations and therefore has a greater consolidated share of the market: it becomes category leader. However, this remains inconspicuous, for the corporate name is kept discreet if not hidden.

Some companies do wish to remain at the back and focus the lights exclusively on their brands. The cases of Procter & Gamble, Unilever, Masterfoods and Bestfoods are well known, that of ITW is less so. ITW stands for Illinois Toolwork. It is a billion-US-dollar corporation, very acquisitive: it owns more than 500 companies throughout the world. Its brands aim at the construction professional: they are called Paslode, Duo-Fast for wood products, Spit and Buidex for steel and concrete. The goal is to provide very specialized tools to specialized workers: a policy of niche brands, addressing segmented needs, craftspeople and channels is a direct consequence of this goal. People working with wood want to be reinforced and differentiated from people working with other materials. ITW does not wish to hurt this desire, and AS resisted all temptations to grow the ITW brand itself, for instance as an endorser. ITW's success rests precisely on the exact contrary.

When the segments are closely related, choosing one name per product helps customers to perceive better the differences between the various brands. This may also be necessary when the products resemble each other externally. Thus, one sees that although all detergents are composed of the same basic ingredients, the proportion of these may vary according to the factor that is being optimized: stain removal properties, care for synthetic materials, colourfast control or suitability for hand washing. The association of a specific name for a type of need underlines the physical difference between the products.

The product brand strategy is one that is adapted to the needs of innovative companies who want to pre-empt a positioning. In fact, the first brand to appear in a new segment, if it proves to be effective, has the advantage of the first player in the market. It becomes the nominal reference for the thus innovative product and maybe even the absolute reference. The brand name patents the innovation. This is particularly important in markets where the success is likely to induce copying. In the pharmaceutical world where copies are a certainty, every new product is registered under two names: one for the product, the formula, and another for the brand. Even if they have the same formula, future copies appear different because the originality of the brand name (Zantac, Tagamet) provides an aura of exclusivity and of legal protection. On the other hand, where the law cannot provide protection, forgeries and copies attempt to exploit the potential of the brand name by imitating it as closely as possible. That is why large mass retailers often use product brands or, to be more precise, counter–product brands. Thus, Fortini copies Martini, Whip copies Skip, etc. Scared of having their other brands cast out of favour manufacturers have, until now, hesitated to legally challenge the distributors for forgery or illegal imitation. (See also page 215.)

Product brand policies allow firms to take risks in new markets. At a time when the future of the liquid detergent was still uncertain, Procter & Gamble preferred to launch a product brand: Vizir. Launching it under the name Ariel liquid would have threatened Ariel's brand image asset and launching it under the name Dash would have incurred the risk of associating a potentially powerful concept with a weak brand and thereby overshadowing it. Coca-Cola did just the same when it first launched Tab to test the diet market.

Product brand policy implies that the name of the company behind it remains unknown to the public and is therefore different from the brand names. This practice allows the firm considerable freedom to move whenever and wherever it wishes, especially into new markets. Procter & Gamble moved from the creation of the soap, Ivory, in 1882, to the culinary aid, Crisco, in 1911, Chipso in 1926 and the machine detergent, Dreft, in 1933, Tide in 1946, Joy, the dishwashing agent in 1950 and then Dash in 1955, the toothpaste, Crest, in 1955, the peanut-butter, Jif, in 1956, Pampers in 1961, the coffee, Folgers, in 1963, the antiseptic mouthwash, Scope, as well as household paper rolls, Bounce, in 1965, Pringle chips in 1968, sanitary napkins, Rely, in 1974, Always (Whisper) and Sunny Delight later on.

Since each brand is independent of the others, the failure of one of them has no risk of negative spillover on the others, or on the company name (in cases where the company name remains relatively unknown to the public and different from that of any of the brands).

Finally, the distribution parameter also favours this strategy heavily: the shelf space accorded by a retailer to a company depends on the number of (strong) brands that it has. When a brand covers many products, the retailer stocks certain products and not others. In the case of product brands, there is only one product per brand, or one product line per brand.

The drawbacks arising from product brands are essentially economic. Thus multi-brand strategy is not for the faint-hearted.

In fact, a new product launch is often a new brand launch. Considering today's media costs, this involves considerable investments in advertising and promotions. Furthermore, retailers, unwilling to take risks with new products whose future is uncertain, stock them only when reassured by heavy listing fees.

Multiplication of product brands in a market due to the increasingly narrow segmentation weighs heavily on the chances of a rapid return on investment. The volumes required to justify such investment (in R&D, equipment, and sales and marketing expenses) make the product brand strategy an ideal one for growing markets where a small market share could nevertheless mean high volumes. When the market is saturated, this possibility disappears. On the other hand, in a stable market it is sometimes more advantageous to nurture an existing brand with the innovation in question rather than attempt to give it product brand status by launching it under its own name.

The role of fire curtains between product brands is certainly important in times of crises, but in other times it prevents the brand from benefiting from the positive spillover effect created by other products under the same name. The success of brand A will not help other products because their names, B, C, D, etc are different and do not bear any relation to A. As we can see, in this strategy, the firm gives the brand a completely distinct and exclusive function and almost no hints about its origin. New products do not benefit from the renown of one of the already existing brands nor from the economies that one could derive from it. On the other hand, this advantage has no role among distributors who are well aware of the company name behind the brand and its reputation for success or failure.

The line brand strategy

Deglaude Laboratories launched a product brand, Foltene: a single product associated with a single benefit, the regrowth of hair. A strong TV advertising campaign made the market explode and Foltene became the leader with a single product and a 55 per cent market share. They should have remained thus, but consumer logic prevailed. Bald people were not looking for a single product. They wanted an all-encompassing service, a total care routine. They wrote asking that shampooing be combined with the Foltene treatment. In 1982 Deglaude launched a mild shampoo (which was later subdivided according to hair type) followed by a daily-use lotion. All this was by way of response to customer demands.

Christian Dior launched Capture, an anti-ageing liposome complex for the skin. Following its success, a first spin-off was soon launched: 'Capture, eye shaper', followed by lip shapers and then other products for the body. The Capture line was born.

Thus, to take up Botton and Cegarra's definition (1990), the line responds to the concern of offering one coherent response under a single name by proposing many complementary products. This goes from variations of the offer, as in the case of Capture or with the fragrances of an aftershave, to the inclusion of various products within one specific effect, as in the case of Foltene. This is also the case with Studio Line hair products from l'Oréal, which offers structuring gel, lacquer, a spray, etc. Calgon (a Benckiser brand) markets a dishwasher powder together with a rinsing agent and limescale inhibitor. That these products are completely different for the producer makes no difference to the consumer, who perceives them as related.

It should be clear that the line involves the exploitation of a successful concept by extending it but by staying very close to the initial product (eg Capture liposomes or the Foltene principle). In other cases, the line is launched as a complete ensemble, with many complementary products linked by a single central concept (for Studio it was allowing youngsters to do their own hair and give themselves a 'look'). The eventual extension of the line will involve only the marginal costs linked to retailers' discounts and to the packaging. It does not need advertising. It should be compared to the marginal number of consumers that could be won. As one can see, the line brand strategy offers multiple advantages:

- it reinforces the selling power of the brand and creates a strong brand image;
- it facilitates distribution for each line extension;
- it reduces launch costs.

The disadvantages of the line strategy lie in the tendency to forget that a line has limits. One should only include product innovations that are very closely linked to the existing ones. On the other hand, the inclusion of a powerful innovation could slow its development. Thus, even though Capture was the result of seven years' research in collaboration with the Pasteur Institute, received three patents and brought with it a revolutionary anti-ageing principle, Dior decided to attach it to a currently existing anti-ageing line. This did not prevent the success of Capture, but unnecessarily delayed it initially.

The range brand strategy

Campbell's Soup, Knorr, Birds Eye and Igloo all propose more than 100 frozen food products. But not all range brands are this extensive. The Tylenol range now covers a number of different products. Range brands bestow a single brand name and promote through a single promise a range of products belonging to the same area of competence. In range brand architecture, products guard their common name (fish à la provençale, mushroom pizza, pancakes with ham and cheese in the case of Birds Eye). In the Clarins cosmetic range, products are named 'purifying plant mask', extracts of 'fresh cells', multi-tensor toning solution, day or night soothing cream, etc.

Range brand structure is found in the food sector (Green Giant, Campbell, Heinz, Whiskas and so on), equipment (Moulinex, Seb, Rowenta, Samsonite) or in industry (Steelcase, Facom). These brands combine all their products through a unique principle, a brand concept, as is shown in Figure 13.4. The advantages and disadvantages of the structure are as follows:

- It avoids the random spread of external communications by focusing on a single name – the brand name – and thereby creating brand capital for itself which can even be shared by other products. Furthermore, in such a structure the brand communicates in a generic manner by developing its unique brand concept. Thus, the range brand of pet food, Fido, covers many products but in its advertisement it only has a taster dog who marks his approval on a product with a paw print. This commercial transfers the brand focalization and its pre-eminence to the animal. Another approach consists of communicating the brand concept by concentrating only on certain of the most representative products through which the brand can best express its meaning and convey consumer benefit. This can then be shared by other products of the range which are not directly mentioned.
- The brand can easily distribute new products that are consistent with its mission and fall within the same category. Furthermore, the cost of such new launches is very low.

FIGURE 13.4 Range brand formation

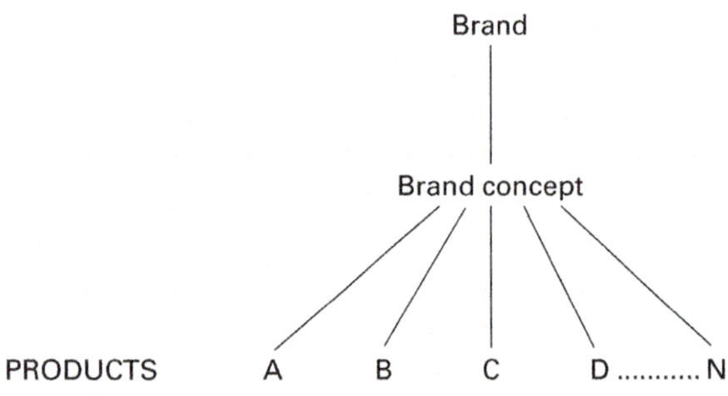

Among the problems that are most frequently encountered is one of brand opacity as it expands. The brand name Findus covers scores of savoury frozen products. It is a good brand – high quality, modern, a specialist in frozen products and a generalist as well because it makes all kinds of dishes. For years, product names were the names of the recipes. But these names are banal. Any brand can claim that it has the same recipe. To enrich the brand and to express its personality on one hand, and on the other hand to help the consumer choose from the mass of products that are on offer, an intermediate level of categorization must be created between the brand name and each actual product name. This is the role of specific lines such as:

- 'Lean cuisine' that regrouped 18 dishes all recognizable by their white packaging;
- 'Traditional' covering nine dishes with maroon outers;
- 'Seafoods' comprising nine kinds of dishes and assorted products (previously simply called hake cutlets, whiting fillets, etc) in blue packaging.

Such names for a line throw light on the products and also help to structure the range in the same way as retailers organize their shelves. The criteria for segmentation and for the creation of families of products depend on the brand. Thus, should we make the distinctions according to the content (poultry, beef, pork, etc, as in a butcher's shop) or according to consumer benefits (light, traditional, exotic, family orientated...)?

The line structures the offer, by putting together products which are undoubtedly heterogeneous, but all of which have the same function. Thus, in the Clarins cosmetic range brand, the offer is also made more clear and structured by way of lines. To assist the consumer in deciphering the scientific terms used on the products, the brand proposes lines as one would a prescription. For example:

- the 'soothing line' for sensitive skins includes a mild day cream and a mild night cream as well as a restructuring fluid in capsules;
- the 'slimming and firmness' line regroups an exfoliating scrub, a slimming bath, a 'bio-superactivated' reducing cream and an 'anti-water' oil.

The Clarins offer ceases to be a long list of creams, serums, lotions, balms and gels and now forms structured and coherent groups as seen in Figure 13.5.

The maker's mark strategy

For many years the Bel logo has been systematically marked on the packaging of cheeses produced by this company: Laughing Cow, Kiri, Mini Babybel, Leerdammer, Boursin and other brands. But what does Bel mean? Nothing else was done to explain the brand. It was the maker's mark, the maker's seal, a proto-brand in the sense that it did not seek to build itself a territory of meaning, of emotion. The Bel company added its seal to authenticate the product and guarantee its provenance. The function of this maker's seal was to create a recognition sign identifying the industrial group that made it. Consumers are not worried about this, but this sign is aimed essentially at distributors and department heads. It is also important internally, for all the international cheese-making companies acquired, who see in the application of this seal to their products, the sign of their full integration into the Bel family.

In formal terms, in relation to the previous architecture where the corporate brand is completely

FIGURE 13.5 Range brand structured in lines

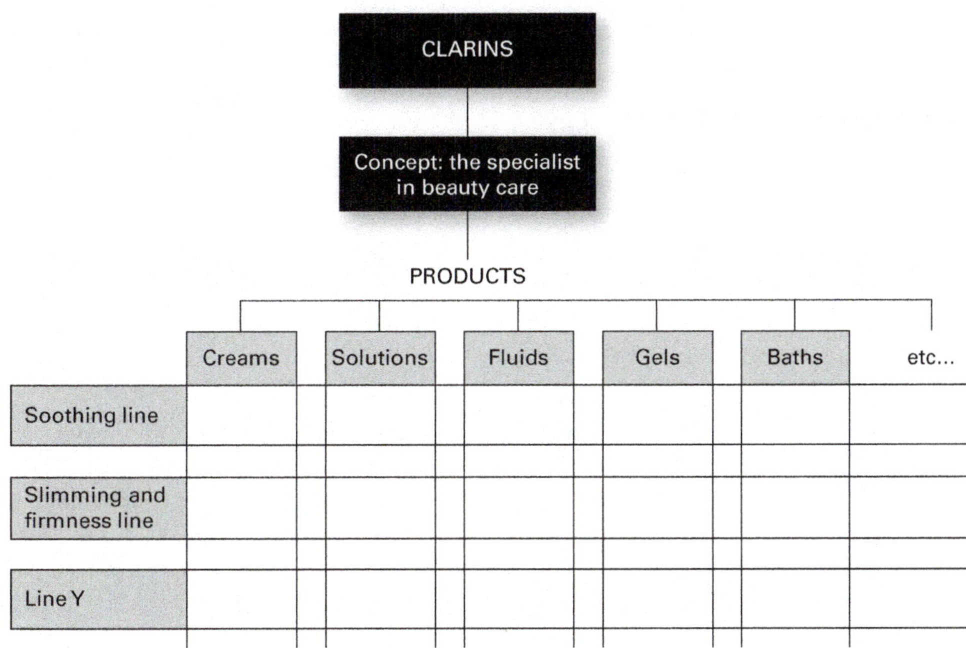

absent, this strategy is characterized by a discreet corporate logo, giving pre-eminence to the commercial brand. In a certain way, the presence of 3M on all its mass-market products must be a mystery in the eyes of its consumers, if they notice it at all. From this point of view, the architecture is close to that of the 'maker's mark'. In the United States, where 3M is better known, the application of the 3M logo plays more of an endorsing role.

Endorsing brand strategy

Everyone recognizes famous car brands such as Pontiac, Buick and Chevrolet in the United States or Opel in Europe. Next to their logos and to the signs of the dealers of these brands we always see the two letters: GM. It is obviously General Motors, the endorsing brand. Again, what is the link between the cleaner Pledge, Wizard Air Freshener and Toilet Duck? They are all Johnson products. The endorsing brand gives its approval to a wide diversity of products grouped under product brands, line brands or range brands. Johnson is the guarantor of their high quality and security. This having been said, each product is then free to manifest its originality: that is what gives rise to the different names seen in the range.

Figure 13.6 symbolizes endorsing brand strategy. As one can see, the endorsing brand is placed lower down because it acts as a base guarantor. Furthermore what the consumers buy is Pontiac or Opel: they drive choice. General Motors and Johnson are supports and assume a secondary position.

The brand endorsement can be indicated in a graphic manner by placing the emblem of the endorser next to the brand name or (when signed above, it acts as maker's mark) by simply signing the endorser's name.

The advantage of the endorsing brand is the greater freedom of movement that it allows. Unlike the source brand, the endorsing brand profits less from its products. Each particular product name evokes a forceful image and has a power of recall for the consumer. There is little image transfer to the endorser.

The endorsing brand strategy is one of the least expensive ways of giving substance to a company name and allowing it to achieve a minimal brand status. Thus, we can see the name Bayer on packets of garden products and Monsanto on Round Up. The high quality of these brands is guaranteed by the names of these major organizations. On the other hand, through their presence in everyday life these companies become more familiar and close to the people. Since the scientific and technical guarantees are assured by the endorsing brand, product brands can devote more time to expressing other facets of their personality.

Therefore, as one can see, there is a division of roles at each stage of the branding hierarchy. The endorsing brand becomes responsible for the

FIGURE 13.6 Endorsing brand strategy

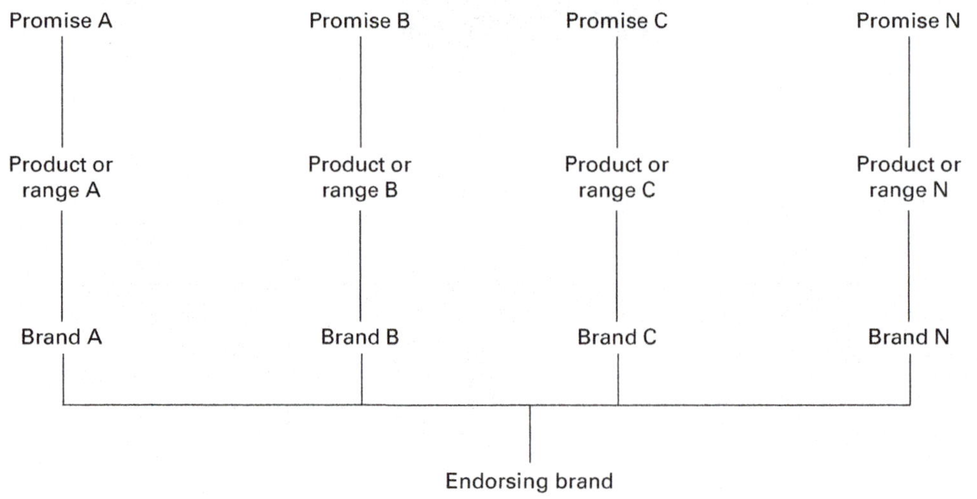

guarantee that is essential for all brands and, today, these guarantees not only cover areas such as quality and scientific expertise, but also civic responsibility, ethics and environmental concerns. The other brand functions are assumed by the specifically named brands: distinction, personalization and even pleasure (Kapferer and Laurent, 1992).

Umbrella brand strategies

Under the term 'umbrella brand', we find in fact two modes of implementation in companies, the first relatively liberal towards products and subsidiaries, the other exercising real control. We shall examine both in turn: the first is in reality a house of brands, the other a branded house.

The flexible umbrella brand

The umbrella brand strategy is characterized by a single brand level: the products are not given a daughter brand. They may possibly be given code names, but only with the aim of identifying them in catalogues or price lists. Philips televisions are known as 'televisions' (whereas Sony's is known as a 'Trinitron'), Philips razors are known as 'razors', and so on.

Unlike the product brand, where a brand relates to a single product and vice versa, the case of Philips underlines that here the umbrella brand covers several product categories, both figuratively and in reality. This is the principal advantage of this strategy, moreover: offering a common umbrella, a common name, to a highly diversified range.

It is important in these analyses to distinguish between two types of umbrella brand, according to the degree of freedom accorded to the products, divisions or branches. This flexible umbrella strategy is currently typical of Japanese, Korean and Chinese brands. Mitsubishi sells cars, electrical products, lifts and nuclear plants under its name, but also food products under the Three Diamonds brand (the Mitsubishi symbol is made up of three diamonds). Toshiba is only known in Europe for its laptop computers, but you only have to visit the Tokyo department stores to see Toshiba sewing machines and frying pans. There, Toshiba is rather like Philips in Europe.

In fact, the umbrella brand is typical of Asian organizations, where sales subsidiaries of Japanese, Korean or Chinese companies have a high degree of freedom. What is required of them is to establish themselves in the country, not to make waves, and to conquer the markets. Historically, the penetration of the United States and Europe by Japanese equipment products (radio, hi-fi, television, photography, reprographics, telephones, IT, games and so on) was carried out via the exportation of products made in Japan. The distribution subsidiaries were tasked only with selling them; they were managed by local people, since the Japanese did not like working abroad. Moreover, the emphasis placed locally on sales was convenient for subsidiaries essentially made up of in-country managers. Besides the sales objectives, and respect for corporate ethics, there were few constraints on the managers. There was a point on the brand map, if not the graphic map, but no value platforms. The Japanese global success was achieved on the basis of the advantages and the low prices of the products themselves, carried by quality commercial organizations, under the umbrella of a brand whose dispersion also contributed to building its recognition. The umbrella brand was a name, not a vision finding embodiment in services and products. This name was generally the corporate name, that of the industrial group.

This is why the subsidiaries had a high degree of freedom: their marketing communications were carried out by country. Within the same country, over several years, the advertising campaigns of Toshiba hi-fi, Toshiba lo-fi, Toshiba televisions, not to mention microcomputing, were not at all coordinated. Each had its own brand slogan and emphasized different values, and even worked with a different advertising agency.

It is known that brand strategies have organizational implications. The supple, flexible umbrella architecture gives the subsidiaries a great deal of

FIGURE 13.7 Umbrella brand strategy

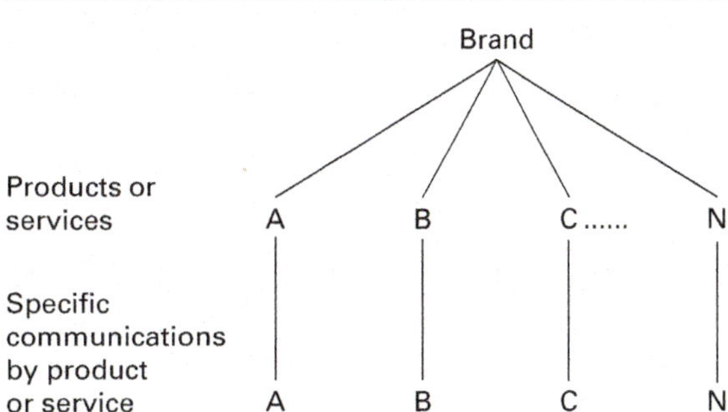

autonomy, which can motivate them and make it easier to recruit bosses with entrepreneurial profiles, which is very useful during the phase of conquering market shares. The international unity is through products, imported from Japan.

Another advantage: since the name is more a corporate name than a brand, there is no hesitation in placing it on products that are highly disparate from a Western point of view: sewing machines, saucepans and microcomputers. This is rather like the now-dead Thomson brand. In Asia, however, the more powerful a group, the more it is respected. From this point of view, manufacturing everything helps to increase power.

On the communications level, the emphasis is placed on the specific qualities and advantages of the products. Therefore there is little intangible added value, which would be very useful once the conquest phase is over. When the markets mature and the products become equivalent, it is then necessary to turn to other levers of attraction and attachment. On the other hand, it does build the country brand.

The disadvantages of this approach make themselves felt later in the brand's life. It is devoid of emotional content: it is not a source of aspiration, of tacit agreement, of affective attachment. Admittedly, it is perceived as a source of quality products, but it is also seen as cold and distant. As the global director of the Toshiba brand (a post newly created precisely to remedy this state of affairs) told us one evening, the brand could be compared to a highly technically skilled work colleague, whom you might ask for help, but whom you would not invite home for dinner.

In the West, the notion of a brand was forged on the notion of speciality. Procter & Gamble founded a school of thought that was taught for years in business schools the world over, where a brand does only one thing; a single product rigorously produced and varying according to its formats or forms (washing powder, washing liquid, tablets or pearls). We now know that this vision is restrictive. Of course a brand can only have one value system and make one central promise, but these may be applied to different products. The global success of Bic testifies to this, as does that of Nivea, l'Oréal Paris, Virgin and Amazon, not to mention distributor brands such as the Carrefour brand, which by its construction covers multiple product categories. The problem with the flexible umbrella brand is that the value system is not perceived; and it is through these values that the tacit agreement and the affective relationship are developed, beyond the satisfaction linked with the product or the excellence of the service. There is therefore a double rupture: no value link expressed between the corporate and the products, or between the products/categories themselves.

By signing its products without explaining why, the brand is diluted. Like an elastic band, it stretches and breaks. In the chapter on brand extension we saw that the brand may indeed bring together intrinsically different products, on condition that it gives them a common meaning. This is the case with luxury brands, but also Virgin, for example, or Apple. We know that the brand functions as a concept, and therefore has power to integrate objects that are different at first glance. Signing products from the ballpoint pen to the razor, to cigarette lighters, and to kayak canoes, with the name Bic is to say that there is Bic in each of them. Therefore, the common name presents a group of common values embodied in these different categories. The flexible umbrella structure offers none of this, other than generic propositions such as 'making quality products'. To achieve this, it is necessary to move to the encompassing umbrella, or masterbrand, strategy.

The aligning umbrella brand (masterbrand)

This is the second version of the umbrella brand. At first glance, in formal terms, nothing distinguishes it from the previous version: the company still accepts only a single brand for the whole, and consequently imposes descriptive names for the products and services or divisions and branches. Here we find sub-brands.

In practice, however, a gulf separates these two outworkings of the umbrella brand. Here the parent brand dominates: it provides not just a name, but a frame of reference behind which everything should align, in order eventually to become the embodiment of it, the living spokesperson. Here the brand is the surrounding framework. This is the clearest example of what we call a 'branded house'.

The masterbrand prototype is Nivea. A Nivea product or communication can be recognized at a glance. Nivea is active in a large number of categories: moisturizing creams, sunscreens, deodorants, shampoos, beauty products and make-up. Everywhere, in each of its categories, it faces specialist brands. It counters these with products embodying its two central values, 'love and care'. This embodiment begins with the composition of the products themselves, their harmlessness, their softness, and extends to the manner in which they are communicated. Everything is codified in a centralized manner. The masterbrand is strong because it brings together a broad offering of products under highly differentiating common values. At Nivea, the categories are each sold under a variant of the name Nivea and a descriptor of the function or target. In this way, we have Nivea Body, Nivea Sun, Nivea Hands, Nivea Visage and so on.

Other examples of this strategy are found in B2B, where there are strong brands such as Legrand and Hager for low-voltage electrical appliances.

The encompassing umbrella architecture is also known as masterbrand. The name 'masterbrand' implies a guardian of the temple: a person, judge or authority capable of policing, not dissident logos but projects, innovations and even advertisements that do not fully embody the brand's central values, since these are what dilutes its promise. The brand is only as strong as its weakest link.

The brand power conferred by this architecture, when properly implemented, is remarkable. It offers economies of scale linked to the variety of products and markets that the brand can cover while creating a brand identity (that is, a group of values that are highly differentiating and relevant in each of its markets).

Korean companies, which 20 years ago were content to imitate Japanese groups, even to their practice of the flexible umbrella brand, have acquired a strong global image by changing their brand architecture. LG has a clear brand platform that is imposed on all divisions and countries. The same is true for Samsung today.

In Europe, since 2004, Philips has been attempting to become a masterbrand, a strong surrounding framework. The new managing director has installed a new 'One brand' motto for all the divisions of this global group. It is difficult to imagine the cultural revolution created in this company by such an apparently simple declaration. Let us consider how it will differ from the situation before 2004, as I learnt in the Netherlands on a consultancy trip:

- Philips is active in many countries under another brand name. Thus, Philips razors are sold under Norelco in the United States. This is why Philips is unknown in the United States. It is therefore necessary to replace the best-known razor brand in the United States with an unknown name.
- Philips does admittedly act under its name alone in televisions and medical equipment and light bulbs, but everywhere in the world it goes by the name Philishave for razors. Therefore, Philishave must be abolished.
- Moreover, the division of small household appliances functions with first-name brands in order to differentiate its products from the competition and make them stars. It would therefore be necessary to cease this practice: and this division is the most profitable in the group.

However, one cannot build a mega-brand by balkanising it. It needs a platform (central values, core identity), and support at the highest levels of management. The products, divisions and branches must reposition themselves in order to present the central values of the brand at home and abroad. Hence a study was carried out to define the platform of the Philips brand and consider its consequences both at the level of the new products and services to be created, and at the communications level.

Source brand strategy

This is identical to the umbrella brand strategy except for one key point – the products have their own brand name. They are no longer called by one generic name such as eau de toilette or eau de parfum, but each has own name, eg Jazz, Poison, Opium, Nina, Loulou, etc. This two-tier brand structure, known as double-branding, is shown in Figure 13.8.

Since this strategy is often confused with the endorsing brand strategy, it is important to specify the differences at the beginning. When Nestlé puts its name on the chocolate Crunch and Galak, on the bars Yes, Nuts and KitKat and on Nescafé, Nesquik, etc, the corporate brand is endorsing the quality of the merchandise and acts as a maker's mark. The Nestlé name dispels the incertitude that

FIGURE 13.8 Source brand strategy

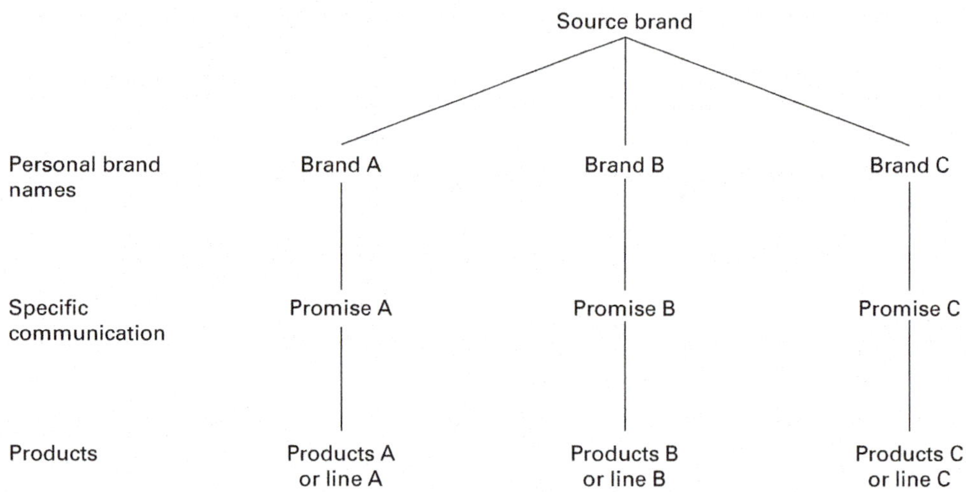

certain products can create. Nestlé takes a back seat position. The product itself is the driver of the consumers' choice; it is the hero to the extent that few customers of Crunch attribute it to Nestlé. On the contrary, when we see the Yves Saint Laurent name on a perfume such as Jazz, this name is more than a simple endorsement. Here, it is the brand name which holds sway and which accords Jazz the seal of approval and the distinction which it would not otherwise enjoy. Yves Saint Laurent is the driver of purchase, not Jazz. Jazz is another key to the door of the Yves Saint Laurent cultural universe. The problem with many brands is that they have converted from source brands to endorsing brands. Within the source brand concept, the family spirit dominates even if the offspring all have their own individual names. With the endorsing brand, however, the products are autonomous and have only the endorsing brand in common. Today, where do Nestlé, Kellogg's or Kraft stand? What about Du Pont or Bayer, Glaxo or Merck?

The benefit from the source brand strategy lies in its ability to provide a two-tiered sense of difference and depth. It is difficult to personalize an offer or a proposition to a client without any personalized vocabulary. The parent brand offers its significance and identity, modified and enriched by the daughter brand in order to attract a specific customer segment. Ranges having 'Christian names' allow a brand which needs to maintain its own brand image to win over newer consumer categories and new territory.

The limits of the source brand lie in the necessity to respect the core, the spirit and the identity of the parent brand. This defines the strict boundaries not to be infringed as far as brand extension and also product communication are concerned. Only the names that are related to the parent brand's field of activity should be associated with it. All product aids should share the same spirit. If greater freedom is sought, then the endorsing brand strategy is more suitable.

Garnier for example wanted to become a source brand and abandon its previous endorsing brand strategy. This is a delicate process for it means moving from patchwork to unity.

Becoming a source brand: from patchwork to alignment

Companies need to improve their efficiency on a regular basis. One way of doing this is to put an end to the natural dispersion of brands and identities, and reorganize supply under proper parent brands that fulfil more than an endorsing function. These parent brands would be a source of strong, differentiated and unique values shared by all products and sub-brands, which also have their own particular personality based on their target group, product territory and specific function. What the present work refers to as a 'source brand' partly corresponds to what some people have called a 'branded house' (as opposed to a 'patchwork' or 'house of brands'). It should be remembered that, unlike the umbrella brand, the source brand is a strategy with two layers of branding.

So how does a company convert a 'patchwork' into a real 'house'? The first thing it has to do is define the identity of the brand for the future. The real identity of a brand lies within the brand itself, while its future lies in its ability to adapt to the markets. It is therefore by analysing the roots and origins of the brand, its early products and performance that it is possible to isolate its core, its key values, the source of its influence and legitimacy. But this analysis must then be considered carefully within the context of the development of tomorrow's markets and consumers.

Garnier provides a good illustration of this process. Until 2002, this internationally renowned brand was known as Laboratoires Garnier. Its task was to become the other international brand of the mass-market network, alongside l'Oréal Paris, which was positioned as a more glamorous, more expensive product within the same shelf ranges. It was a question of finding values that were positive, aspirational, internally and externally motivating, and had popular appeal since the brand had been allotted a more accessible market position.

Historically speaking, the origins of Laboratoires Garnier date from 1904, when M. Garnier first invented a herbal hair tonic. This original product already had some of the key attributes of the brand – naturalness and beauty care. Some time later, after the Second World War, a hugely successful shampoo called Moëlle Garnier not only revitalized the 'genes' of the brand but also boosted business. Relaunched in 1986, the brand was extended by its sub-brands – Synergie (cosmetics), Ambre Solaire (sun care), Graphic (hair care), Ultra Doux (skin care) and Lumia (hair colour).

The brand achieved international renown and established a strong position on several European markets. However, its sub-brands declined in popularity and remained regional. All except one, that is, which had already been extremely successful outside Europe and appealed to the younger generation in countries throughout the world – Fructis, the first strengthening shampoo with active fruit concentrates. Fructis was a direct descendant of the Garnier line but with a more modern image. The real reinvention came with Fructis Style, a range of revolutionary styling products containing fruit wax and characterized by a complete range of strong, tactile sensations – the colours, consistency and aroma of fruit. With Fructis, a new generation of sensual products was born.

But to conquer the world market the brand needed a new identity that, while respecting its origins, would nevertheless make it an aspirational brand for modern young people worldwide. Fructis and especially Fructis Style would be the new prototype for the brand, while their casual and ironic tone would provide the basis for its reinvention.

What were the consequences for Garnier? In order to be attractive and accessible to young people in countries throughout the world, the brand had to change its name from Laboratoires Garnier and simply become known as Garnier. It was no longer a scientific or a French brand, it was accessible and international. Furthermore its brand contract, its values, were now written in English.

How does Garnier define its aims? 'Garnier believes in beauty through nature. Scientifically developed and enriched with selected natural ingredients, our products help you look healthy and feel good every day.' This contract is outlined in six core values:

- Natural high tech (which distinguishes it from Yves Rocher, which is not high tech, and l'Oréal Paris which does not focus on the natural element).
- Healthy beauty: Garnier is a healthy brand, which does not use top models, but unknown models who look and feel good (like the girl next door).
- Total experience: Garnier is not selling just a product but a complete experience that appeals to all five senses.
- Universal: it is multi-ethnic, multiracial, multigeneration.
- Accessible, as evidenced by price and distribution.
- Positive irreverence: this is a distinctive personality trait, found in all Garnier advertisements.

How was this new identity projected across all Garnier's daughter brands?

- The first stage was one of identification. Apart from modifying the name, a new logo was created in green, orange and red, the colours of fruit but also traffic lights.

- The next stage involved bringing the sub-brands portfolio into line with the source brand. Since Garnier is a source brand, the sub-brands must reflect its core values. So the Neutralia sub-brand (shower gel) was abandoned because its clinical purity no longer corresponded to the Garnier 'house' image, while the Ultra Doux brand was extended to replace Neutralia. Similarly, the Synergie sub-brand (cosmetics) became Skin Natural which was much more in line with Garnier's values.
- The third stage consisted of developing business by organizing an attack on growth markets, that is, deciding which sub-brands would target which countries and which segments. What would be the consequences in terms of range and adaptation to multiple niching (universality value)?
- The fourth stage involved defining how the advertising was to be handled. What distinguishes a Garnier advertisement? They all begin with a light-hearted statement of the problem, followed by the presentation of the solution, and involve a wide range of different people, all looking and feeling good and reflecting the cultural and racial diversity of the country in question. The slogan says 'Take care of yourself'.
- In the fifth stage, the promotional principles were established – an accessible brand that offers a full experience – and Garnier developed massive sampling and street marketing initiatives involving direct contact with consumers in all countries.

It is significant that the website is called GarnierBeautyBar.com. Visually, it is presented like a real 'house' where you can visit each room and discover and/or personally experiment with one of the Garnier sub-brands. The 'branded house' has constructed a 'virtual house' in which all the brands in the family are brought together with a view to offering an intense product experience. Garnier's (male and female) customers enter via the Garnier Hall from where they can go to the Beauty Lounge, Style Room, Tonic Area or Game Zone and try out their future looks, carry out personalized diagnostic tests or simply experiment and develop their customer loyalty.

From this it can be seen that the source brand is a structure that restructures all its parts. Many groups use this type of brand architecture to give greater impact to their diverse product ranges by making them converge on a common image. For example, all Danone products and brands now focus on health, the core value of the source brand, in the knowledge that there are seven types of health, and therefore seven different ways of presenting it. Danone has also changed its status from an 'endorsing brand' to a 'source brand'.

Mixed approaches within groups

The six branding strategies presented here are models, typical cases of branding. In reality, companies adopt mixed configurations where the same brand can be, according to the product, range, umbrella, parent or endorsing brand. For example, l'Oréal is a range brand of lipsticks. It is a source brand for Studio, Elsève or Plénitude. The hybrid character of the usage of the brand l'Oréal and the strategies adopted reflect its willingness to adapt to the decision-making processes of consumers in different sub-markets (hair care products, perfumes or cosmetics) or according to the distribution channels (ie self-service or specialist stores). In certain cases, l'Oréal guarantees reliability and technical capacity. In others, it wants to achieve recognition (ie in cosmetics) and therefore needs to place itself to the forefront. And finally, in still other cases, l'Oréal has to be invisible – either to avoid being associated with a low-price segment or to avoid hurting one of its prestige products. Nevertheless, many hybrid situations result out of the series of small decisions that are taken as and when a new product is launched. Due to the lack of an overall plan for a brand's relationship with its products, a number of non-coherent branding decisions often exist side by side.

3M provides an interesting example of the accumulation of separate branding policies, with as many as five denominational stages (quintuple branding). This is shown in Figure 13.9. 3M is a company focused on high-tech research into industrial and domestic applications of adhesives. This covers a vast area which includes glues, obviously, but also films, cassettes, medical plasters, transparencies and

FIGURE 13.9 A case of brand proliferation and dilution of identity

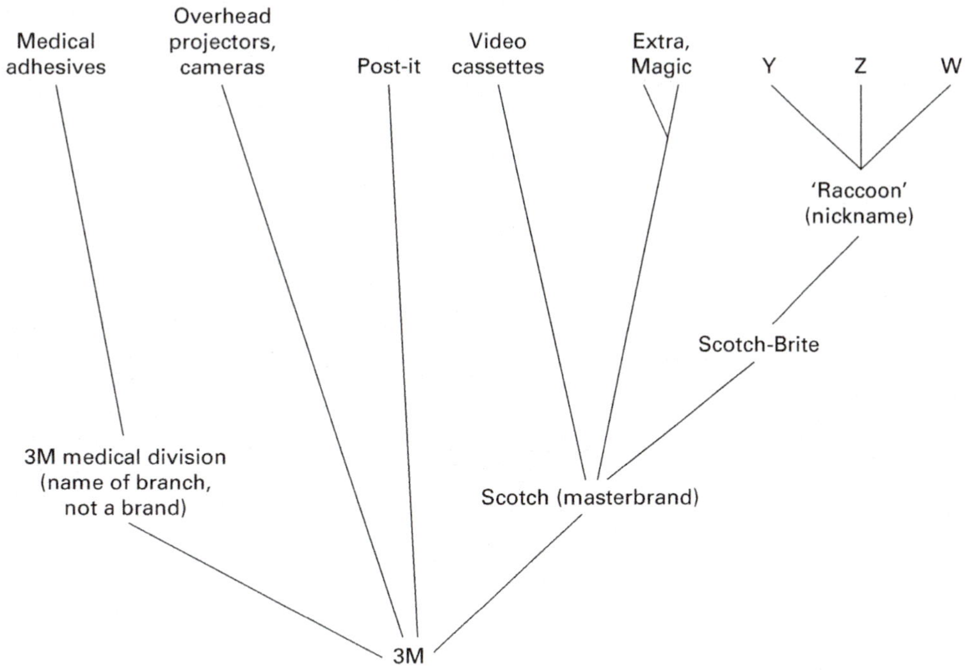

overhead projector products, etc. The 3M name is synonymous with seriousness, power and heavy R&D. But this also leaves an image of coldness. Thus, to humanize the contact with the general buyer, the umbrella brand Scotch was created. Video cassettes, glue sticks and sellotape are all branded Scotch directly. But for the scouring pads, on the other hand, a line brand called Scotch-Brite was created. To counter the challenge of a rival product from Spontex (who simply call them scouring pads) Scotch replaced the generic name by a particular name, the 'Raccoon' (just like the Volkswagen Beetle). This differentiated its product and explained its advantages in a unique manner and gave it a closer and more friendly image.

The 'Raccoon' itself has been expanded into many versions – green, blue, red – depending on its shape and use. For its general consumer products, such as sponges and glues, 3M was used as an endorsing brand with a signature in small print. Curiously enough, 3M is scarcely in evidence on Scotch cassettes. Is this to distinguish better from the video cassettes marked clearly and exclusively 3M and targeted at professional use? In fact, while 3M provides a guarantee of good performance and an endorsing brand for general consumer products, it serves as an umbrella brand for professional products: all the power and significance of the 3M name is reflected in products such as cameras, overhead projectors and dental cement (coming from the 3M health division). Post-it, the famous 'adhesive notes that serve as a memory tool or a message carrier', is also signed 3M. In order to patent this invention in a better way and to define it in a better manner than the long description used above, that it be given a proper name was to be expected.

Thus, depending on the level of professional end-use that a product has, or the need for an up-to-date image of excellence and performance, it is either signed 3M in a prominent manner or even perhaps exclusively. If not, 3M is present through the brand Scotch. Perhaps this is why the sellotape, Scotch Magic, used the name 3M only as a recall tool. On the other hand, aerosol glue for communication professionals bears the Scotch name in small print and 3M in large letters. There are also differentiated product advertisements for the 'Raccoon', general-use sellotape, Scotch cassettes and Post-it. Beyond the endorsing brand, there are no common codes of expression which appear independent in form and intent.

Choosing the appropriate branding strategy

Which is the best branding strategy? Procter & Gamble are firm supporters of product brands; are they right and l'Oréal, their more flexible competitor, wrong?

Each type of brand strategy has its own advantages and disadvantages, as has been described. However, a simple list of the pros and cons does not provide a procedure for making a choice in a given company in a given market. The choice of brand policy is not a stylistic exercise, but more a strategic decision aimed at promoting individual products and ranges as well as capitalizing the brand in the long term. It should be considered in the light of three factors: the product or service, consumer behaviour, and the firm's competitive position. Brand policy is a reflection of the strategy chosen by a particular company in a specific context.

What parameters should be taken into account when choosing a branding strategy?

1. **Tying in with corporate strategy.** Branding strategy is the symbol of corporate strategy. For example, in 2003, Schneider Electric, one of the leaders in the field of electrical distribution and industrial control, decided to revitalize its Merlin Gerin and Telemecanique brands, which were well known to research departments and electrical integrators and installers throughout the world. In so doing, Schneider ended an initiative launched some 10 years previously with a different aim in mind, namely to replace individual brands with a single, group brand. The company's new director, who had come from Steelcase, outlined the strategic positioning of Schneider Electric against GE, ABB and Siemens. Compared with these general electrical and electronic giants, Schneider Electric is not a small general electrical company but rather likes to see itself as a multi-specialist company. In fact, because it sells intermediate products, its customers are looking for a specialist company. On the other hand, when compared with its many single-specialist competitors, Schneider Electric is more of a general electrical company. So if it wants to position itself as a multi-specialist company, the specialities must be offered by specialist brands, united by a group brand, a single entity, which facilitates customer relations. This is why it was decided not to follow the single-brand path, but to bring the range of 50 product brands together under three integrated international brands – Merlin Gerin, Telemecanique and the US company Square D, in 130 countries. There is therefore a Schneider Electric front office and a Schneider Electric sales force organized by type of customer, and these customers are able to purchase products under different product brands.

   Another consequence is that distributors will once again become the official distributors of Merlin Gerin or Telemecanique without there being any obligation, as in the past, to automatically reference both brands.

   Similarly, Groupe SEB, world leader in small household appliances, decided to form itself into a multi-brand group, with four international brands – Moulinex, Tefal, Krups and Rowenta. Why not follow the tempting single-brand path, like Philips? Precisely because of Philips. The strategy lies in the art of being different. The single brand is an advantage if you are already a single brand like Philips, one of the few international brands whose reputation is based on the fact that it is distributed throughout the world – even, via its light bulbs, in the depths of the Amazon basin. It is basically too late to try to emulate Philips. In today's fragmented markets, with their aggressive distribution networks and consumer segments, it is far better to exploit the targeted reputation (in terms of product and values) of the brands that people have bought precisely because they were brands.

2. **Tying in with the business model.** In this respect it is interesting to compare companies within the same sector, since their brand

policy is often a reflection of their business model, the driving force of their competitive edge and their profitability. This can be illustrated by comparing three giants of the European cheese industry – Bel, Bongrain and Lactalis. Bel develops range brands around a central innovative product, thereby giving rise to an entire range of products with The Laughing Cow, Kiri or Mini Babybel signature. Bongrain develops product brands – Chaumes, Vieux Pané, Caprices des Dieux, Haut Ségur – while Lactalis uses a single brand (Président) as an umbrella for all its cheeses and butter, and even milk in Russia and Spain. So why the different brand policies?

In fact, the business models of these companies are not the same, hence the different brand strategies. Bel likes to see itself as the inventor of modernity, anti-traditionalism, accessibility and everyday values. It does not deal in those speciality cheeses bought as a weekend treat. As the inventor of modernity, it must therefore create brands, with their own particular shapes and characteristics, that can subsequently be offered in a variety of forms to capitalize on the investment in promotion. Bongrain decided to develop processed AOC (*appellations d'origine contrôlées*) cheeses to make them more accessible in terms of taste, price, preservability and usage. Vieux Pané is a processed version of the AOC cheese category called 'Pont l'Evêque' but, as such, does not have the right to use the name of the appellation. Bongrain therefore has to give each of the specialities it creates a new name – hence the product-brand policy. The disadvantage of this is that it has to promote each new brand, meanwhile supporting through advertising many small volume brands.

The business model of Lactalis is to segment generic categories in order to bring them up to date and into line with everyday life and the modern lifestyle. This model gives rise to an umbrella-brand policy – under a single brand (Président), there are descriptive names for each of the varieties, each of the various forms, with low-fat butter remaining a quality butter, Emmental a real Emmental, and Brie a real Brie.

3. **Cultural parameters.** The United States has developed the culture of the product brand – a brand that produces a single product. Ivory, the founder brand of Procter & Gamble, is and continues to remain a soap, which explains the company's reluctance to extend the brand and even the ideological opposition of such authors as Trout and Ries who have berated it in their work for the past 20 years. But the US domestic market favoured this product-brand policy. On the other hand, it also explains why Europe and Japan have been the main exponents of the umbrella-brand policy. Nivea and Nestlé are just two of the many European examples. In Japan, apart from the size of the domestic market, the concept of the company has also counted for a lot in the sense that, the more products and sectors a company covers, the greater its reputation. It would simply not occur to the director of a Japanese company not to use the corporate name to promote all kinds of brand extensions. Yamaha is a typical example, putting its name to such widely diverse products as motorcycles and pianos.
4. **Integrating the rhythm of innovations.** How do you develop product brands in a sector that updates its offer on an annual basis? In this instance, a single-brand policy covering the entire range is preferable, as in the case of Nokia, Sony-Ericsson, Alcatel, Samsung and even Whirlpool and GE.
5. **Added value.** This is the lever on which a product is based. This point is illustrated in Figure 13.1, giving the relative positioning of these different strategies. When the added value in a particular market is linked to reassurance, reputation and scale, a single-brand umbrella strategy is recommended (in the world of industry, this is often the corporate brand), although a source-branding strategy with two levels – a real 'branded house' like Garnier or l'Oréal Paris – can work equally well. However, the more segmented the market, with top-quality, personalized products, the more one has to favour either a portfolio of l'Oréal product

brands or an endorsing brand strategy that sanctions the sub-brands (the logic of Danone or Nestlé in dairy products).

6 **The question of resources.** In the absence of sufficient funding, a company should concentrate its efforts on a single brand, especially if it is international. The need to achieve a visibility threshold comes before all other considerations. However, in case of co-branding, it is impossible to do so: this is why Philips and Douwe Egberts (a leading coffee company) created a separate name (Senseo) to designate their joint innovation in coffee machines.

7 **The brand vision.** This affects the choice of architecture. In the cosmetic market there are thousands of products and many scientific terms, and innovations are essential. This is what leads to an opacity in the market. Brands serve as milestones and a question that is frequently asked is which naming strategy should be used? There is no single answer to such a general question: it depends a lot on the brand's conception of itself.

Lancôme prefers a mono-product policy with only a small range derived from the leading product (Progress for the face, eye-liner, anti-wrinkle cream, etc). Thus, recently the brand chose to launch mono-products for body care, each with its own brand instead of a line under one name. There was Cadence for the body (moisturizer), Exfoliance (scrub) and Sculptural (slimmer). Lancôme is not an endorsing brand. It wants to be a source brand and therefore the creator of a precise vision, that of French elegance. The brand wants to serve as a vehicle to express:

- the product's technological level and its performance;
- luxury as perceived in a French manner, that is to say natural sophistication; Lancôme makes laboratories appear charming.

Lancôme expresses itself through its products and the services that surround them (the dialogue and the advice of salespeople). They want a brand policy that is coherent and easily understandable on two levels: the consumer and the seller. But, consumers actually respond badly to brand policy in this sector: they do not usually memorize brand names and may simply ask for the 'moisturizing cream from Lancôme' when they enter the shop. The sales assistant then explains that there are two: Hydrix and Transhydrix. The two names help the assistant explain the existence of multiple products. Through these different product names, the customer understands the different products and the assistant can subsequently promote each one by stressing their individual functions, use and specific characteristics. Thus, at Lancôme, they try to give each product a different name to reflect a function (Nutrix nurtures the skin, Hydrix moisturizes it and Forte-Vital makes it firmer) or the main ingredient if it is something new or revolutionary (eg Niosome contains niosomes, Oligo-Majors has oligo elements). This naming policy makes the sales pitch clearer because it explains the differences between the products and other closely positioned products and therefore avoids the confusion that could have occurred had they been in the same line and under a single common name.

This would appear to close the argument clearly between product brands and line brands in favour of the former as far as cosmetics are concerned. But, at Clarins, as a general rule, there are no mono-products and their 70 products are all grouped into lines. Since Clarins is not Lancôme, it does not have the same image, the same identity or the same conception of itself. It projects itself as a Beauty Institute and the profession of beautician is very important to them. This concept implies the use of many products belonging to the same line, just as in a prescription. A mono-product cannot do everything and from this arises the preference for product lines that act in synergy. Clarins wants to create stable lines that can last for years and are in conformity with its identity, personality and brand culture. Finally, it prefers objective product promises rather than a plethora of slogans for mono-products that all play on one factor, presently 'victory over ageing'. From this arises the names for their products, which are always in the beauty sector. The names are always descriptive of the product's actions and do not play upon dreams and fantasies as did Christian Dior when he launched 'Capture'. At Clarins, names are constituted of two or three words, for example, 'Multi-Repair Restructuring Lotion'.

In the past, the creation of any new product was usually also accompanied by the creation of a new

FIGURE 13.10 3M branding options review

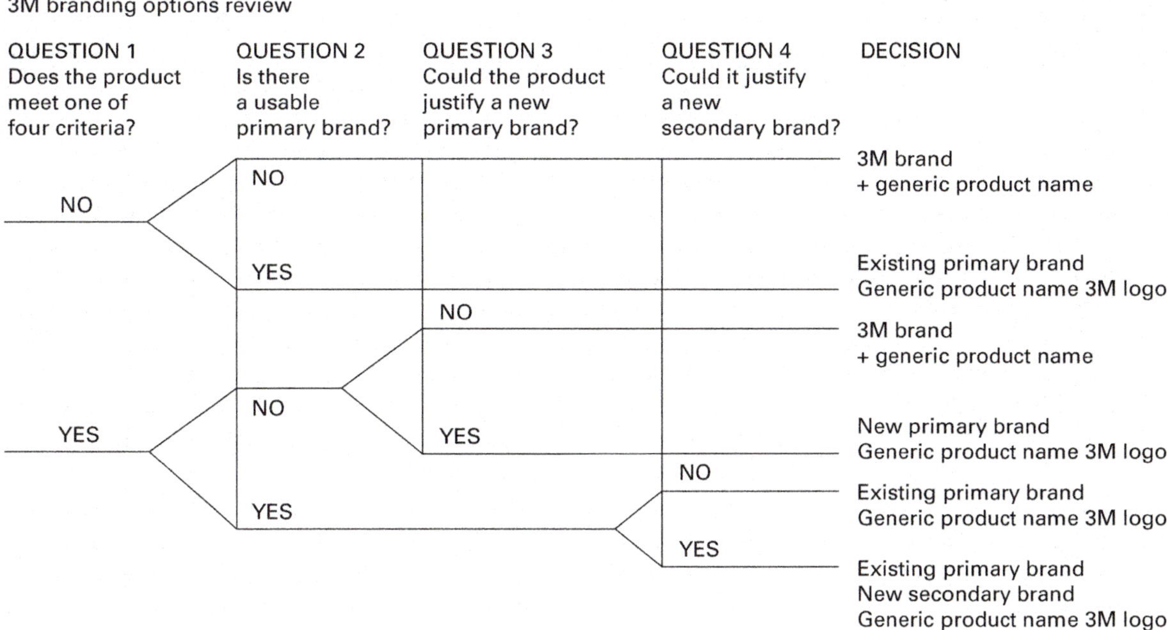

name. In christening the new product, the product manager gave it life. Without a name, the product had no real existence. Once branded, it had a life. In 1981, at 3M, 244 new brands were created and registered. In 1991, only four new brands were created. The same thing happened at Nestlé: in 1991, the company created 101 new products but only five new brands. The age of brand multiplication is over. What has led to this change in practice?

The realization that brands are the true capital of the company has led to this revolution. By capitalizing on fewer brands, companies had to sustain their equity by nurturing them through constant innovations and line or range extensions. Therefore, the question 'what name do we choose?' becomes 'which new product should we put under which already existing brand?'

Companies with decentralized management are particularly susceptible to brand proliferation. Thus, 3M, in spite of its high rank in the Fortune 500 companies and its 60,000 products, remained relatively unknown. One part of the explanation for this was the excessive number of trademarks with which it was burdened: over 1,500. In order to solve this problem, 3M decided to take the cat by the tail and created a branding committee at the highest level (Corporate Branding Policy Committee) whose mission was to establish a precise doctrine regarding brand policy. Its approval was necessary before the creation of any new brand. To make 3M become a real corporate brand, it was decided that from then on 3M would be used to sign or guarantee all products (except the cosmetic line). The second decision was the banning of the use of more than two names on one product (as was the case with Scotch Magic) in order to abolish brand pileups, as is shown in Figure 13.9. In order to facilitate the integration of the new brand policy that capitalized on a few mega-brands (also called primary or power brands), 3M distribute to all its subsidiaries a guide explaining the policy to be followed in case of branding when faced with a new product. The creation of this guide led to a drastic fall in the requests for new brand creation: be it parent brands (like Scotch) or daughter brand (like Magic).

The decision tree shown in Figure 13.10 puts each innovation through four questions which serve as filters to limit the creation of a new brand to certain very specific circumstances (like Post-it). The first filter question asks if the innovation satisfies one of the following four criteria: Is it a top priority innovation? Does it create a new kind of price/

quality relationship? Does it create a new product category that did not exist until then? Is it the outcome of an acquisition? The second filter question asks whether the brand could not be used to nurture an already existing parent brand in 3M's primary brands portfolio. The third filter question seeks to discover whether the new product can provide the occasion for the creation of a new parent brand. The last filter question evaluates the capacity of the new product to justify the creation of a new secondary brand (daughter brand). From the decision tree emerge six exhaustive branding possibilities that are based on measurable market parameters. They go from the extremely simple (slides for overhead projectors from 3M) to multiple level branding (Scotch Magic, the sellotape from 3M). As expected, the creation of a new brand (primary or secondary) became the exception rather than the rule. A number of restrictive conditions had to be fulfilled first: mainly, that the innovation creates new primary demand and that none of the existing primary brands are suited.

New trends in branding strategies

Companies do evolve in their branding strategies. An analysis of their international behaviour reveals significant trends.

Why the rise of branded houses?

An interesting classification of branding architectures is that of 'branded house' versus 'house of brands'. As its name indicates, the 'house of brands' refers to a company which operates through well-known brands but itself remains discreet if not hidden: this is the case of the ITW (Illinois Tool Works) operating with such brands as Paslode or Spit, and well known in professional circles. Procter & Gamble and Georgia Pacific also operate that way.

The branded house is the inverse case: the company itself is the one and single brand, acting as a banner and a federating force. For Aaker and Joachimstahler (2000), the models of such architecture are GE (GE Capital, GE Medical and so on) and Virgin. In fact, it is over-restrictive to assimilate the branded house to this type of case. The branded house is a strategy by which the corporation is the source of reputation and the federating force. This can be achieved by two branding architectures: the *corporate umbrella brand* (Sony, Philips, GE and Virgin are examples), and the *corporate source brand*, where there exist sub-brands or branded subsidiaries, but the leader is the parent company. This is typically the policy followed by HSBC, which puts its name or logotype before that of all subsidiaries, as long as these subsidiaries keep their name.

Two brand architectures correspond to the so-called 'house of brands': naturally what is called the *product brand* approach, and also the *endorsing brand* approach. When 3M puts its name at the bottom of all its products, is it really driving customers' perception of value? No. Although present, visibly it remains discreet: this is the sign of a 'house of brands'. The brands of the portfolio act very independently.

Paradoxically some corporate umbrellas are also very close to being quasi houses of brands. This may look as a contradiction with what has just been said. In fact, the whole issue is that of power and organization. Take Toshiba for instance. This conglomerate is organized in business units: computers, hi-fi, television, cookware (in Japan) and so on. Not only are the business unit directors totally independent, the country managers are also very independent. Their role is to sell the products coming from Japan. As a consequence, there is no desire at all to coordinate the communications between business units, and for a given business unit between countries. The result is that although they wear the same name, Toshiba hi-fi products do not have the same image as Toshiba computers, Toshiba television sets and so on. The Toshiba corporation up until now never thought of itself as a brand that needed to be managed globally as such. It is only recently that a VP was named with that objective, with worldwide responsibilities and authority. His or her first task will be to establish the Toshiba brand platform and to enforce it throughout all communications of any product in the world. Philips is itself now acting under the 'one Philips' internal motto.

Why do so many organizations move towards this branded house architecture to recreate identity where there is diversity, fragmentation, if not a patchwork? In modern developed markets, unlike the emerging ones, it is no longer sufficient to be known. One must also consistently evoke a set of values and stimulate emotional resonance. This supposes some discipline and less autonomy. Sales-oriented organizations, such as those of Korean and Japanese companies, assign high sales objectives to their country managers. In exchange they have a lot of freedom. This is why their communication is generally managed at the local level. Creating a branded house will meet resistance because one source of autonomy, and not least, advertising freedom, will be affected. However, a branded house does not automatically mean a global campaign: the spirit of the brand may emerge through different and even localized communications.

Loyalty needs more transverse brands

There is another reason for changing brand strategy – when the emphasis shifts from product logic to customer logic, from a desire to conquer new markets to developing customer loyalty. Accor Hotels, the European leader in the hotel industry, is a good example of a company that was able to react and modify certain fundamental principles of its brand policy. Accor owes its success to the creative brilliance of its two founders who invented the product brand in the hotel sector. Novotel, their first hotel chain, was based on the concept of total standardization – whichever hotel they stayed in, businessmen and women felt at home, down to the very layout and decoration of the rooms. Then they covered the different market segments with other product brands: Formule 1, Etap Hotels, Ibis, Mercure, Novotel, Sofitel and Suit'Hotel in Europe, and Motel 6 in the United States.

According to the original logic, Accor – the name of the holding company – was limited to that single function and was therefore invisible. Then, in view of the requirements of stock exchange valuation, it was decided to make the corporate brand more visible. It began to appear in small print on the hotel brochures, before being incorporated as the trade name – Accor Hotels – in the actual logo of each product brand.

The growth of the group's market share recently led to another reassessment: the decision to move from individual loyalty programmes for each brand to a corporate loyalty programme (Accor Hotels Favourite Guest).

It was this same need to develop loyalty that led l'Oréal Paris to break with its historic brand strategy. The decision was made in response to Nivea, whose simple strategy maximized brand loyalty within an increasingly broad portfolio of sub-brands that were in direct competition with the brands in the l'Oréal group. L'Oréal realized the limitations of a flagship-brand strategy in which l'Oréal Paris merely endorsed a large number of independent sub-brands – Elsève, Elnet, Plénitude and so on. Apart from the fact that the publicity budget was fragmented, there was no effective capitalization. The group therefore switched from a 'house of brands' logic (with l'Oréal Paris as the endorsing brand) to a 'branded house' logic, a source brand with a basic unity and a very distinctive form. This is when the so-called 'dream team' appeared on the international scene – a collection of internationally renowned top models and stars, each promoting a sub-brand from the l'Oréal Paris house, using the same creative platform and publicity signature ('because I am worth it'). At the same time, the l'Oréal Paris brand name became larger, more visible, and more prominent for such sub-brands as Elsève, on the packaging and in-store merchandizing. Finally, the denominative logic was applied to brand extension categories that were not yet sufficiently attributed to the brand (due to its historic associations with hair products). Plénitude, the brand then in competition with Nivea, was abandoned in favour of Dermo Expertise, Pure Zone and Solar Expertise, whose more descriptive names immediately suggest competence in the area concerned.

By doing this, l'Oréal Paris was also aiming to develop real customer loyalty across the different sections of the brand and thereby make up the time lost to Nivea in this respect.

Industry discovers the importance of branding

When branding policy is considered, the industrial sector does not immediately spring to mind. Paradoxically, since promotion in this sector is not done through costly publicity but through catalogues, the sales force and trade exhibitions, companies do not hesitate to register trademarks. Air Liquide, for example, has registered a total of 880 trademarks (effectively, brand names).

As well as representing a considerable cost, these trademarks also create confusion and opacity further down the line, at sales team and at catalogue level. The problem is that they are specialist names which it is hoped will be passed on by word of mouth and recommendation: 'I want some X.' But this is quite clearly impossible as there are far too many, which is why the industrial sector is beginning to incorporate the concept of the endorsing or source brand, and even the mega-brand, which creates an umbrella for a series of specialist products.

Internationalizing the architecture of the brand

Should companies globalize their branding architectures? Should they just duplicate them when entering new countries and continents? It is a fact that most branding architectures have been created slowly, through time in the domestic market. They benefited from low media costs, and a lower competition. This is why we so often find 'product brand' architectures. They resulted from the acquisition of a company by its main competitor: to avoid losing market share, the acquirer decided to keep the brands apart. Can the same portfolio architecture be applied when entering Russia or the United States?

In Russia, as in many former communist countries, there is a unique opportunity to rapidly take a dominant position by investing fast and heavily as long as Western competitors are not there, and media costs remain low. This is what Frito Lay did. This means capitalizing on one brand, used as source brand or endorsement, and rapidly pushing new products into new segments.

In the United States, the challenge is the media and distribution costs. The consequence is the obligation to nest products under an umbrella brand which remains to be created. As a result we see what can be called a 'vertical crunch' of brand architectures. There are in fact two types of 'vertical crunch'. The first is a bottom-up crunch, when a mere descriptor becomes a driver (the way consumers name what they buy). For instance in Europe, the whole shampoo line of l'Oréal Paris is sold under the brand Elsève: its many products have names such as Color Vive and Energance. In the United States, Elsève has not been launched. Instead of three levels, there are only two levels (l'Oréal Paris and a wide range made of names like Vita Vive, Nutri Vive, Hydra Vive, Curl Vive, Color Vive and Body Vive).

The other is a top-down crunch, when a mere endorsing brand becomes the driver. For instance in Europe the famous biscuit speciality Pim's is called Pim's by Lu. In the United States, it is Lu Pim's.

Companies also exploit local equities to carry international brands. For instance, all Unilever's global ice cream concepts (Magnum, Solero and so on) are endorsed by a local house brand, acting as reassurance by its long-established proximity and familiarity in the country.

Some classic dysfunctions

Brand architecture, like any plan, is one thing. Implementation is another. In practice, we find four classic branding dysfunctions.

The case of the parent brand swallowed up by a daughter brand

Sometimes, in fact, one of the daughter brands can prove remarkably successful, attracting to itself all the advertising investment. The result is that the parent brand has been taken over by the image created by this exclusive communication. It can no longer play its role as parent brand and create new daughter brands. This is the price of success: not only does the star product hide the others, but it drags the parent brand with it. For years the Nina Ricci brand was associated with a single perfume, its global success L'air du temps. This created a fundamental problem for licences: a luxury brand makes its profits through these. However, Nina Ricci no longer had its own identity, and potential licensees did not want to be licensees of L'air du temps, but of the parent brand. It was necessary to reconstitute the identity of the latter.

Volkswagen was swallowed up in image (and sales) by the Golf, a car which has known glory but which symbolizes the 1980s!

Company–product disconnection

Essilor is the worldwide number one company in corrective optical lenses. When a consumer goes to an optician in the United Kingdom with a prescription, this optician sends the prescription to Essilor UK, which manufactures the lenses during the night in its very automatized and modern factory in Portugal and has them sent back by Fedex to the optician the next day. What a gigantic service provided to the opticians: this is a B2B winning-business model.

One exception is Varilux, the worldwide name for Essilor's brand of progressive multi-focal lenses. It has been quite well advertised at the end-user level, so that people ask for Varilux lenses. What is changing is the distribution: huge multiple chains of dispensing opticians are developing, such as Grand Optical and Afflelou. Their innovation is to be able to produce directly in the store a large number of lens prescriptions, in one hour only. As a result Essilor is threatened. As a company it is not known by the end users. It is only known and respected by opticians: but some of them are grouping together and starting to limit Essilor's role to the difficult prescriptions that cannot immediately be made in the shop.

In the B2B sector Sage is an illustration of this problem. It is a giant in terms of market sector (number three in the world in management software) and a dwarf in terms of image, whereas everyone recognizes SAP, Microsoft, Oracle and Cegid. It is true that the company has a decentralized structure: communications are paid for by market, therefore by the products sold in each. This has two consequences: tomorrow's promising products are not communicated enough, and the communication places emphasis on the products, and not enough on the Sage brand. This may place a brake on organic growth. The Sage brand is well known to accountants (who buy its best-selling accounts software) but not people from other corporate functions, where tomorrow's growth segments are located.

Balkanization of the brand

If segmented, differentiated brands are created under its aegis, the parent brand is impoverished and becomes simply an endorsing brand. Diluted, it no longer imposes a framework, an individual vision, its identity or its values. It is a known name, with a story, but one that is now overtaken by the stories written in the media by its autonomous daughter brands.

For example, the segmentation of Dim products with daughter brands ended at one point by turning them into stars. Dim became a name on the packaging of tights and stockings, minor in comparison to that of the daughter brands (Macadam, Dim'up, Diam's and so on). Moreover, the coherence of a great brand was nowhere to be found. However, it is the parent brand, Dim, whose job it is to survive. In order to do so, it must remain intrinsically attractive, a source of desire. It does so, admittedly, through its daughter brands, who ensure its relevance today in growing market segments. Nevertheless, the daughter brands must be dissolved when they lose their relevance, and new ones must be created. It is therefore necessary to ensure the pre-eminence of the parent brand. To do this, it is necessary to:

- redefine the identity of the parent brand;
- redefine a true source brand strategy, ensuring the pre-eminence of the parent brand;
- align the daughter brands within the framework defined by the parent brand.

The parent brand, after all, is the surrounding framework. It is worth looking at this process in detail, since it should be implemented regularly in order to correct the effect of centrifugal forces.

What name for new products?

A company grows through its new products: they make it possible to gain a differential in products and services over the competition. They also make it possible to focus advertising on news that will interest the market. Finally, they provide the springboard for a revitalization of strategic image features of the brand. For every launch of a particular innovation, the same question arises from the parents of the project: what shall we call it?

The question of naming new products is important: it is not at all a euphonic problem (does the name sound nice?), but a fundamental one. In reality, the first question should be: do we need to call it anything?

Why, in fact, did 3M give the name 'Post-It' to something it could have called 'removable Scotch notes'? Scotch is 3M's well-known brand and the name indicates 'adhesive products'. Isn't Post-It an innovative variant of Scotch tape? Now a brand – in this case, Scotch – is only supported when it is nourished through innovation. Let us take another, B2B, example: an innovation by Lafarge. It is a revolutionary, ultra-fast, fine cement that makes it possible to obtain an extremely smooth surface. Should a new name be found for it, with the potential for turning it into a Lafarge product or range brand later, or should it simply be called 'the new Lafarge ultra-smooth cement', opting for a descriptive name, as it would be in a master-brand or umbrella strategy? The name therefore poses the underlying question of the brand strategy (the number of levels and the links between them, between the corporate and the products).

When should you create a sub-brand?

When a new product arrives, there is too great a tendency to opt for the creation of a specific brand. This is understandable; the inventor reacts like any parents who, proud of their child, seek to give it a first name. However, a first name is an identity, and a lasting commitment of a marketing budget in order to forge this identity and achieve recognition for the daughter brand. Moreover, in practice, by focusing on the so-called daughter brand, there is a tendency to let the parent brand take a step back, into the background, something that is quickly translated into the periodic monitoring studies of brand equity. The parent brand declines in spontaneous recognition and in image.

The reaction then is to change the status of the daughter brand, to turn it into a simple product. For example, the prepaid card from Bouygues Telecom was initially treated as a relatively autonomous daughter brand: Nomad! It later became the Bouygues Telecom Nomad card.

When, then, should one create a sub-brand?

- Chapter 11 on brand coherence presented the four figures of the relationship between product and brand: variant, similarity, transformation and contradiction. The closer one is to the variant, the more natural it becomes to give the product a purely descriptive name, or even to invent the descriptive name in question. Was a walkman a brand, or did it quickly become the generic word to describe this new piece of equipment created by Sony? People talk of the 'new Philips television'. Conversely, the further we move from the strict reproduction of the central values of the brand through the new product, the more a daughter brand is justified.
- A first name is necessary in order to create a category: iPhone! It could have been called the Apple smartphone. But there was a need in the mass communication to strongly signal the technological, sociological and cultural breakaway. Therefore, capitalizing on the pioneer's advantage, the category is structured around the pioneer, here iPhone. The new entrants position themselves in relation to the iPhone.

FIGURE 13.11 Which brand architecture is suitable for brand innovation?

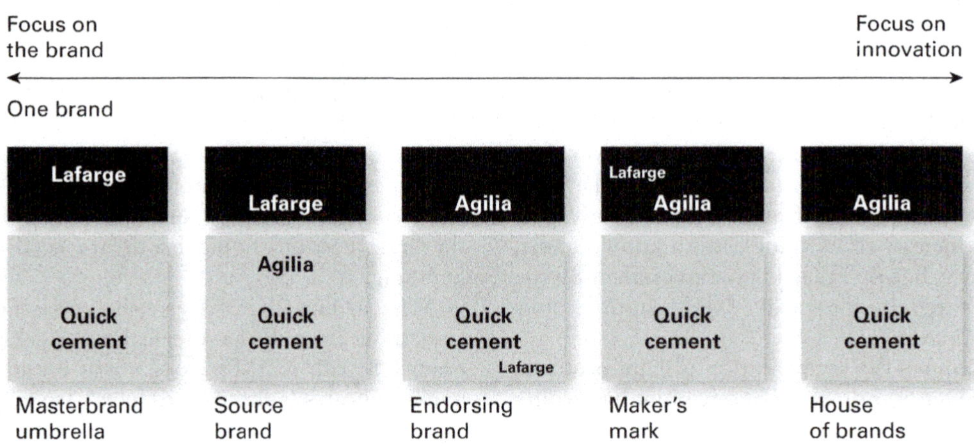

- A first name is necessary, albeit supported by a long-term investment in communication, when the protection of the innovation must be improved. When Candia, the milk brand, invented milk with a guaranteed vitamin content, it could have been called 'milk with guaranteed vitamin content' or 'vitamin milk'. After all, people say semi-skimmed milk or flavoured milk. However, it is necessary to account for the competitors' reaction. Carrefour, noting the success of the major brand's innovation, would not be slow in launching its copy under its own distributor's brand: Carrefour milk with guaranteed vitamin content. By launching its milk with guaranteed vitamin content under the name Viva, underpinned by long-term advertising campaigns, the Candia brand was able to create a halo of exclusivity, of differentiation. Viva not only created the segment: it is its referent. The consumers buy Viva with all its evocations of active good health. It is more than a product; it is a true (daughter) brand.
- A first name is necessary in order to correct the negative induced effects of an innovation. The sausage company Aoste (now acquired by Sara Lee) innovated by inventing the first industrial sausage: each of them had exactly the same weight and the same length. This was a complete break from the age-old practice of sausage-making, all slightly different in appearance, weight and length, but one that responded to the major expectation of large-scale distribution: economy of cost. In fact, there was no longer a need to weigh each product, hence there were savings in time, personnel and money. However, it was necessary to give it a name that would correct, even remove, the immediate evocations on seeing the product (it's an industrialized product, standardized to the maximum). It was launched under the name 'Shepherd's Stick' by Justin Bridou, in order to create a rural, rustic imaginary background for this industrial product. The 'Shepherd's Stick' became the leader of the segment it had created.
- With services, a first name is often necessary in order to give flesh to an innovation. In 2004, Gaz de France, a distribution company, wanted to provide a modular, global offer to its 10 million subscribers. It was a personalized diagnosis, a proposal according to the desired comfort level. Told in these terms, readers might ask themselves how this proposal was in any way revolutionary. After all, isn't all that part of the minimum client focus? The fact is that ordinary words make innovative proposals sound banal. This is why Gaz de France named their proposal 'Dolce Vita' and based all its advertising communication on this name, which became a daughter brand, with an emotional dimension. In Great Britain, British Gas created a daughter brand in services: Goldfish.
- When the parent brand does not (yet) have the image suitable for the targeted market, a relay or an intermediary is required. This is the goal of the first-name brand. Venus by Gillette made it possible for this very macho brand to target women. Peugeot motorcycles and scooters have used many first names: young people seeking emancipation need a badge. Buying 'a Peugeot' 15 years ago did not fulfil this function sufficiently, even if the product itself was remarkable; hence first names such as Booster.

  The maternal identity of Nestlé did not legitimate its presence in coffees. Nestlé is historically, and first of all in everyone's lives, baby milk. It was not possible to launch a 'Nestlé coffee'. Nescafé made it possible to say both 'instant, powdered', giving reassurance through the confidence linked with the name, while distancing the maternal image, and to say 'coffee'. The word café brought Nestlé an element that it had previously lacked. Conversely, the identity of Philips was already technological: it was enough to endorse the razor. Choosing to call the razors 'Philishave' rather than Philips razors brought nothing new: the activity descriptor 'shave' did not bring any added value and contributed to distancing the salience of Philips. In fact, Braun simply calls its razors – Braun razors.

Taking into account the tendency to think up a first name too quickly, several warnings should be heeded before launching into the choice of a daughter brand:

- No first names without a major, long-term advertising investment. Otherwise, the product will appear on shelves or in catalogues, with a mysterious name, and the customer will be unable to grasp what the new product has to offer. All too often there is a time lag between the decisions on the name, taken very early, and the fixing of the budget, which may change at the last moment.
- The second question concerns the future: will this daughter brand be able to provide an umbrella for other products? Will it be possible to put other future products under Agilia by Lafarge, for example, that will be coherent with this name? This criterion is essential and too rarely used: if it is not respected, the company plunges ahead into an economic impasse. In fact, it is difficult to support a single product in advertising and communication. Only the arrival of a genuine range, and other new products, will make it possible to acquire the critical mass that generates a sufficient size of marketing communications budget.
- Is the parent brand sufficiently well known to move on to the stage of having daughter brands? It is the parent brand that gives meaning to the daughter brand. How were the first Apple products known, for over 10 years? Apple 1, 2 and 3. Only later, in the place of the Apple 4, to clearly show the discontinuity, was the name Macintosh used. What did the low-cost telephone operator Free call its convergence offer? Free Box! Orange called its unique landline/mobile offer Orange Unix! The first Danone products were all called Danone or a variant thereof (Danette, Danessa, Danino, Dan'up and so on).

  In the industrial domain, Veolia Environment removed all its daughter brands, since the problem for Veolia is that it is an unknown group: it therefore has an urgent need to make itself known worldwide. Therefore, its global daughter branch brands, Connex, Dalkia and Onyx, were de-christened and renamed Veolia Transport, Veolia Energy and Veolia Waste.
- Before creating a daughter brand, would it not be better to launch the innovation under an existing daughter brand? For every daughter brand has to ward off its own obsolescence through innovation. Systematically placing innovations under new first-name brands handicaps the older ones. We will see below how 3M created a multi-criteria grid to manage this real risk.

A case in point: naming in the automobile industry

The car fascinates us. Innumerable reviews and magazines are dedicated to it. This sector only lives through innovation, giving us the desire to change cars. Different constructors have different policies regarding their new models. Renault gives them all proper names (Latitude, Laguna, Twingo, Clio and so on). Peugeot follows its three-digit logic with a zero in the middle (which forced the first Porsche known as 901 to become the 911 in order to avoid legal proceedings). Citroën opted at one point for proper brands (Citroën Xsara, Saxo, Xantia) before returning to the initials C1, C2, C3, C4 and so on. With BMW you buy a series number: series 1, 3, 5 or the top-of-the-range 7. What is the logic to these choices?

The first structuring factor of the decision concerns the maker's strategy: a generalist or a specialist? Generalists target all segments of the market, all consumers. Since they promote the car for everyone, their image is consequently not as strong as the specialists. As a result, their image is less in a position to dynamize new models, to bring them a strong emotional added value. These are reassuring brands, brands with guarantee and proximity through their network, not desire. The reverse is true for the specialists, who have segmented their market to a high degree and made their choice. The name alone of the specialist is the stuff of dreams: BMW, Saab, Volvo, Morgan, Mini and so on. According to their means, buyers take away a little or a lot of the dream: the 1 or 3 series, or later on the 5 or 7 series. As with Mercedes, one always buys 'class', A, B, C, M, E, S and so on.

There is no dreaming with generalists: it is therefore necessary to boost the model itself with imaginary added value, with emotion. Hence the need for a highly evocative individual name. Remember the Golf Gti! From whom? Volkswagen. In order to compete with Mercedes, Volkswagen concentrates on the Phaeton, since Volkswagen means 'people's car'.

Other parameters, however, come into play. Why, in fact, does Peugeot opt for numbers rather than model names, when it is a generalist? Before we answer this, let us recall that a number can play the part of a brand, like Chanel No 5, or 007, or number 23, the number of the football star David Beckham at Manchester United. Each of these numbers has an emotional potential. Likewise 205 or 911 in cars, through their association with a cult model, the first of which marked an era, the second of which marked several generations of men.

Peugeot's approach is explained by the specific positioning of the brand: it wants to be 'the most specialist of the generalists'. This is why the brand, although generalist, accentuates its differentiating traits and the radical design that makes it palpable.

As for Citroën's policy shift, it can be explained as a result of the costs incurred by a daughter brand policy. If a model lasts six years, it is therefore necessary to invest over this time period to give it recognition and an image before turning these into profits and losses. Moreover, Citroën's objective is to strengthen its image. The emphasis placed on first-name brands, in addition to being slow and costly, does not rebound strongly onto the parent brand. Hence the decision to group the portfolio of models around Citroën, a single brand. We then buy a variation on the theme according to segment: C1, C2, C3 and so on.

B2B mixes organization, subsidiary and brand

B2B creates specific problems for brand architecture decisions. B2B is about companies. Brand architecture models are easy to figure out and to implement when they concern objects or services (shampoos, yoghurts, computers, cars or hotels). Complexity and even confusion arise in B2B because three issues are interacting and mixed together:

FIGURE 13.12 How adding a designator to a name affects perceived value (psychological price) of a prestige or non-prestige brand

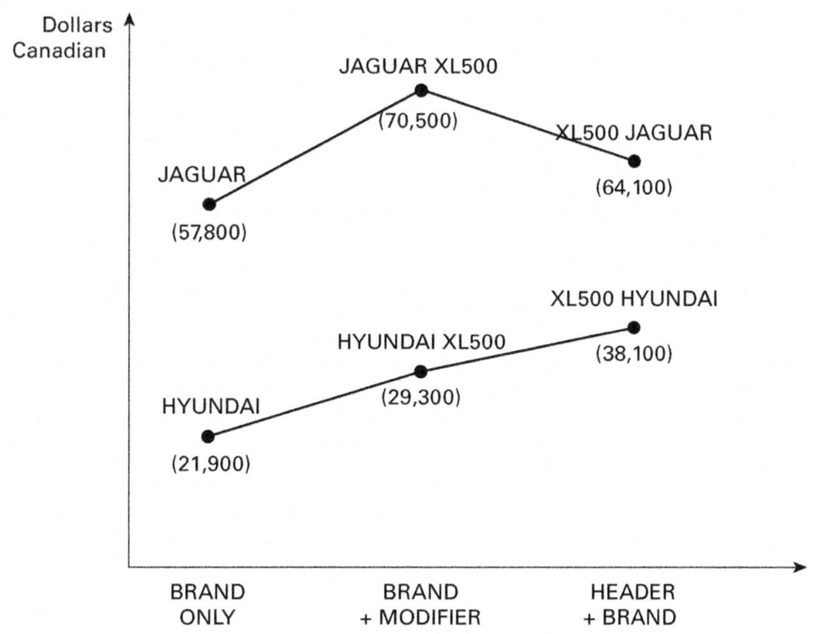

SOURCE Myung Su Jo, 2007

- the legal structure of the group;
- the organizational structure of the group;
- the brand architecture.

Decisions about the legal structure follow one's specific goals: tax optimization, preservation of ownership rights, power balance between shareholders, reduction of trade union power, control of social unrest risks, ability to have multiple compensation systems, motivation of staff at the decentralized level, and so on.

Decisions about the organization (whether to create a group or just a holding company, the number of divisions, branches and business units, the reporting structure, etc) aim to make the company as efficient as possible for the sake of the client.

The problem is that, within companies, most managers, even at the top, do not see how brand decisions are different. The legal and organizational perspectives tend to divide the whole into entities within a network of power and responsibility relationships, or ownership relationships. The brand perspective aims at influencing the markets by capitalizing on as few symbols of quality and fame as possible. The brand is by definition a symbol; it stands for something, for both inside and outside audiences.

An organizational perspective, for instance, would ask about the creation of a group, especially in companies that have grown by mergers and acquisitions. The relationship between people at group level and those within subsidiaries will have to be made clear. The brand perspective would ask if this group aims at becoming the primary purchase criterion of the market. If the answer is no, it can remain discreet and be called Group X or Y. If the answer is yes, one should abandon the word 'group'. Group is an organizational concept: this needs not concern the market. The market trusts L'Oréal, not Group L'Oréal.

The same holds true for divisions or branches. Samsung Electronics is not a brand. The brand is Samsung. Samsung Electronics is just the name of the organization in charge of developing the business of Samsung worldwide profitably, and driving the Samsung global brand equity up. A visit to the GE website is quite enlightening. GE is a conglomerate: it acts in a number of sectors (eg finance, energy and electronics). However, there is only one brand, GE, and one symbol. GE Capital is the name of a branch. It may itself have a legal name referring to the company enacting part of this activity in a given country. Sometimes branches may be brands. For instance, for many years Suez Group, a public utility group, did not want to act visibly and become both a corporate brand and a commercial brand. Suez Group acts through masterbrands worldwide, such as Sita for its waste management activity. This brand and logo are visible on the lorries picking up rubbish every day in major cities of the world. Sita entered Germany through an acquisition: Eric Böhm. On the letterhead one finds the logo and symbol for Sita, and far below, in very different type and quite separately, so that no confusion is possible, the legal name of the operating company: Eric Böhm GmbH.

People like to have their own brand, which is quite natural. When a new activity is created, with a manager at the top, the question of the brand soon arises because of the urgent need to make business cards. For instance, Veolia Transport decided to create a new cargo activity in Europe. The people involved would often think that the brand was Veolia Transport Cargo or, worse, Veolia Cargo. One should not confuse organizational identity and the brand. An activity is just one of the many arms of a single body whose flag is the brand. There can be only one flag.

Only when a company decides that a division should go public (trade on the stock exchange) can there be an exception. For instance, EDF is the number one electricity group in Europe and the world leader in nuclear energy. It sells civil nuclear plants and electrical diffusion networks to many countries in the world. EDF is a public company. It decided to create a subsidiary called EDF Energies Nouvelles, explicitly designed to develop this know-how and sell services linked to wind and solar energy to other countries. To separate both activities and allow a clear recognition on the stock exchange, the logo of EDF Energies Nouvelles is within a green capsule, unlike the logo of EDF itself.

As a rule it is useful to think of B2B brands as a flag. A single country cannot have two flags. Federal countries, however, have states, eg Germany has Länder. If they have their own flag, there is a clear subsidiarity. The two cannot be at the same level.

A final difficulty comes from the fact that, in mergers and acquisitions, groups buy personal companies whose name is that of a person, the creator of the company, still managing it some decades later.

Changing the name of that company is a sensitive issue: it is not just any name!

Our advice is simple: the merger and acquisition period is the best time to negotiate a change of name and to enact it fast. If that is not possible, one should at least impose the adoption of the group symbol. When the creator resigns or retires, then move to the group name immediately.

Corporate branding

Since 1990, there has been a basic tendency for corporate brands to be as visible as possible on the products themselves. For example, Pharmaceutical Laboratories now regard themselves as a brand in their own right and take much greater care to ensure that their brand name is clearly visible on the packaging of brands of medication. The back of all Nestlé products bears the Nestlé corporate brand name and the customer service phone number. It is the same for Danone, which has taken great care to create a logo for its Danone corporate brand, as distinct from the Danone commercial brand used for chilled products, and water and biscuits in Asia.

This tendency is part of a basic trend – the demand for responsibility and transparency. The company presents itself as the ultimate endorsement and no longer hides behind its brands. This also has the effect of increasing its visibility, and therefore its attractiveness to students, executives and the employment market in general. In Asia, television ads for Procter & Gamble and Unilever brands bear in the last seconds the signature of the companies themselves. This is not the case in the United States or in Europe, although – influenced by this Asian experience – Unilever is looking for some kind of higher public visibility to boost its corporate brand profile. In Asia, however, these two companies do not enjoy any reputation and this must therefore be established.

Finally, once a company is quoted on a stock exchange, it must try to influence the share price since, over and above the financial results published on a regular basis, market predictions are influenced by the company's name and reputation. So anything that makes people dream a little adds to its goodwill.

Companies regularly change their name and take the name of their flagship commercial brand. For example, the company formerly known as BSN changed its name to Danone Corp (it nearly became Evian Corp), while the Volkswagen group and l'Oréal group have both taken their name from their flagship brands. Mars, on the other hand, changed its name and became known as Masterfoods, as other companies are called Bestfoods (Unilever) or General Foods. So what are the reasons for these two diametrically opposed attitudes?

Capitalizing on a flagship brand by applying its name to the group makes it possible to take advantage of the halo effect, even if this involves two clearly distinct sources, since the image of the one influences the perception of the other. For example, the press regularly refers to Volkswagen as Europe's number one brand when it was not the brand but the multi-brand group that earned the title through the cumulative sales of each of its brands.

The l'Oréal group does not advertise a great deal. However, its brands use heavy advertising, along with research and development, as one of their main weapons. By sharing the name of its glamour ('l'Oréal Paris') brand, the l'Oréal group benefits from the impact of an international image that inspires confidence in shareholders and defines what they do.

It was for entirely opposite reasons that Mars took the less transparent name of Masterfoods. Apparently, it was difficult to sell brands of pet food such as Pedigree and Whiskas under the Mars corporate or group name, particularly since Mars conjures up the image of a single product, a legendary chocolate bar, which has growth limits in an extremely segmented market. There was also a risk of a negative halo effect on financial predictions. LVMH, the initials of Louis Vuitton Moet Hennessy, uses both strategies. On the one hand, the experts are familiar with the significance of the acronym, which refers to internationally renowned luxury brands. On the other, by retaining the acronym, the group demonstrates its intention to remain discreet by placing the emphasis at brand level rather than corporate level, and leaving the brands to develop through their own creativity, publicity and the quality of their distribution. From this, it can be seen that the position of the corporate brand in relation to its subsidiaries is in fact a reflection of the group's internal organization.

This essential part of group strategy is developed below.

Group and subsidiary relationships

In the industrial sector where external growth is the norm, the question of the status of corporate brands that have been acquired crops up again. Should they be left independent? Should they disappear? Should they be endorsed with a simple visual symbol of the parent company? Or joined to the name of the parent company? If they behave as mere holding companies such firms should not be surprised by their low public recognition. For instance, although it was founded in 1969 and was one of the largest chemical companies in the world, Akzo remained largely unknown. No wonder: all the companies acquired had kept their own company names and brand names (Warner Lambert, Stauffer, Montedison, Diamond Salt, etc). Akzo thus acquired a poor image in terms of technology because of its lack of visibility. It had become the biggest unknown company in the world.

General Electric has defined four brand policies and specifies the conditions for their application. These policies range from:

- The so-called monolithic approach where GE behaves like an umbrella brand and replaces the corporate brand which has been bought (either immediately or after a transitional period of double branding). The brands GE Silicons, GE Motors and GE Aircraft Engines have all emerged from this process.
- The endorsement approach where GE signs its name beside the name of the product or the company that has been acquired.
- The financial approach where GE behaves like a holding company and is only discreetly mentioned (X, member of the GE group).
- The autonomous approach where the acquired company or product makes no reference to GE.

To decide upon a policy, GE uses six selection criteria:

1. Does GE control the company?
2. Does GE have long-term commitments in this company?
3. Does the product category have an image value? Dynamic or not?
4. Is there a strong demand for GE quality in this industry?
5. Is the corporate brand which has been bought strong?
6. What could be the resultant impact on GE?

Group governance and branding strategy

At regular intervals, the major industrial groups ask themselves whether their branding strategy is as effective as it could be. There are three formal types of strategy that can be implemented within industrial groups. Although the terms 'subsidiaries', 'holding companies' and 'companies' tend to be used in this context, structurally speaking they represent the typical figures of branding strategy – source brand (A), endorsing brand (B) and umbrella brand (C). But beyond these terms, the impact on level-one subsidiaries (sub-brands) is self-evidently not the same. Above all, each branding architecture has organizational repercussions, with each playing a different role for the group in relation to its subsidiaries and subsubsidiaries:

- The strategy in which the group is a source brand can be likened to the role of an orchestra conductor or band leader.
- The strategy in which the group is an umbrella brand makes it a unifier.
- The strategy in which the group is an endorsing brand makes it a coordinator.

It is obviously not up to the branding decisions to determine the management style of a particular group – that would be a reversal of roles – but it should explain management choices and the criteria on which these choices are based.

Corporate brands and product brands

For years, companies have hidden behind their brands. Through prudence and fear of being affected in case of brand failure, company names have been separate from those of the brands. Thus Procter & Gamble remain unknown to the public while their brands are the stars (Ariel, Pampers). In fact, it is this that allowed the company to keep its turnover stable when the rumour of it being linked to a sect raged through the United States. The brands, autonomous from the company itself, suffered no setback. Nevertheless, such instances are rare and the tendency is more towards transparency due to communication obligations. Also, the public wants to know, in larger numbers than before, who are the actors behind the brands. Journalists want to disclose who is the 'brand behind the brand'. This also explains why so many companies have taken on the names of their most famous brands (eg Alcatel-Alsthom, Danone). They get more visibility and acknowledgement. This helps the stock exchange investor also, in cases where he is not an expert or very well-informed, to understand better what he is buying. It may also create a beneficial confusion for the brand itself. After it bought Audi, Seat and Skoda, Volkswagen Group is now co-leader in Europe on a cumulative basis. However, many people mistakenly speak of Volkswagen as a brand being the number one in Europe.

The trend towards greater visibility of corporate names also has other causes. Distribution is one of them. Distributors, multiple retailers and hypermarket chains are not very interested in brands. Their fundamental relationship is with corporations, not with brands. It is a business to business relationship. The name of the powerful corporation is therefore a potent reminder of that relationship.

Only corporate names can endow brands with stature, an extra dimension calling for respect. Would Audi have succeeded in its remarkable recovery had it not been known that Audi belonged to the Volkswagen Group? The same holds true for Seat and Skoda. Nissan's status will change because it is now part of the Renault group. As long as car makes are only brands and not part of a larger and more dynamic corporation, they arouse perceived risk among consumers and do not guarantee a long-term presence.

Many companies sell in industrial and commercial markets at the same time. Here, there is the problem of having to choose between the use of product brands or the use of the corporate reputation to support the products. This depends on the quality of the company's endorsement and the degree of visibility that it wants to acquire. In practice, the respective weight to be attributed to the product brand and the corporate brand depends on a case-by-case analysis of the returns brought by each of them on the many targets concerned. Table 13.2 presents the outline of such an analysis.

At ICI three kinds of brand policy were used (see Figure 13.13):

- The first policy is the classic umbrella brand where the products keep their generic names and are signed with the corporate name. Most often this concerns raw materials and undifferentiated products where the company guarantees a certain quality and the differentiation is essentially commercial (ie special conditions offered to the client on a case-by-case basis). An example would be ICI polyurethanes.
- The second policy is that of the endorsing brand. The company puts its name beside the product brand and this confers a status of high technology and reliability to the product. Thus, Dulux paints are accompanied by the ICI logo.
- The third policy makes exclusive use of the product brand. Tactel is one of the most widely sold fibres but it never mentioned ICI. The product was sold to the textile industry and to the fashion world, and it was feared that the mention of the ICI name might alter the positive images linked to Tactel. Similarly the insecticide, Karate, which is sold throughout the world, also did not make any mention of ICI. Does this have anything to do with not wanting to step on ecological toes and avoid the possibility of blame regarding the harmful effects of pesticides on ground water? This situation is not only changing through time, but it also changes according to the company. Decis, the world leader in pesticides, made a reference to its corporation, Roussel Uclaf (Agrevo division), on its packaging. Similarly, to benefit from its innovations, Du Pont de Nemours, former owner of the brand, used to mention clearly 'Lycra by Du Pont' on all its communications for Lycra, the fabric that has revolutionized women's lingerie.

Product innovations generally provide an ideal occasion to ask fundamental questions about the branding policy.

TABLE 13.2 Shared roles of the corporate and product brand

Targets	Product brand	Corporate brand
Customers	+++++	+
Trade associations	++++	+
Employees	+++	++
Suppliers	+++	+++
Press	+++	+++
Issues groups	++	++++
Local community	++	++++
Academia	++	++++
Regulatory authorities	+	++++
Government commission	+	++++
Financial markets	+	+++++
Stockholders	+	+++++

FIGURE 13.13 Corporate and product branding at ICI

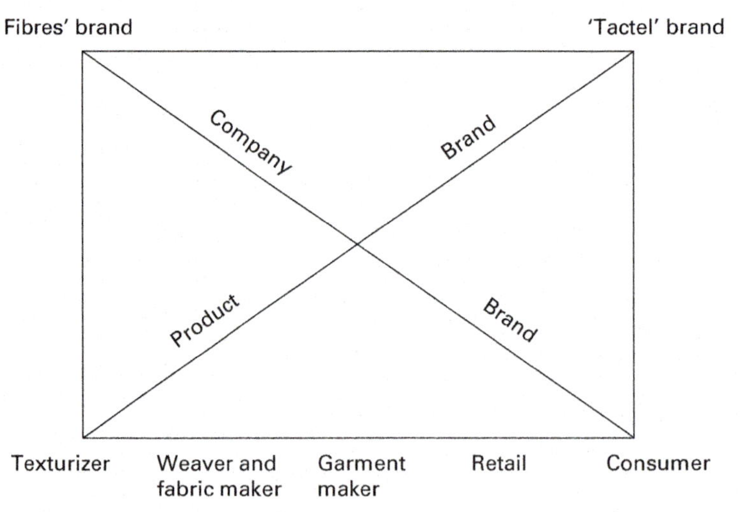

14 Multi-brand portfolios

There are limits to brand extension: a brand is not a catch-all. BMW values attract only 20 per cent of the premium car buyers worldwide. BMW refuses to dilute its brand and in order to grow it went international. It also bought the Mini and Rolls-Royce brands.

As an alternative to brand extension, the other way in which a company can grow is by creating new brands to meet the demand that existing brands cannot satisfy. But it takes courage to launch and position new brands.

It takes courage because, at a time when extensions are the order of the day, it is difficult to admit that even a mega-brand has its limits. Companies prefer to attribute failure to production problems so that they can try – and fail – again. Thus Mattel is facing the challenge of the 'tweens' (see Lindstrom, 2003) who are no longer really children but not quite teenagers or adolescents. There is a saying in the business that today's kids are getting older younger.

In concrete terms, this means that the company's business model for the 1970s, 1980s and 1990s is defunct. In the past, Mattel treated children in the 4–10 age group in exactly the same way, as a homogenous group. This had a major advantage in terms of cost (economies of scale) – they were all sold the same Barbie doll, which represented 40 per cent of the company's sales.

Mattel's first response to the tweens challenge was to segment the target group and create a special Barbie for 8–10-year-olds, the Barbie Generation Girl with the single Barbie signature. Then, to counter the success of MGA's Bratz dolls for 8–12-year-olds, Mattel relaunched My Scene Barbie, still with the Barbie signature but smaller. However,the company had to make up its mind to take the plunge and create a genuine new brand rather than a brand extension, and in 2003, the multinational launched Flavas to succeed Barbie. After all, there comes a time in every little girl's life when she no longer wishes to play with Barbie.

Levi's had already taken the plunge by launching Dockers after initially trying a simple brand extension – Levi's Tailored Classic. But the same brand cannot be simultaneously rebellious and classic. In the car sector, brands seem to represent progress up the social ladder. Thus, Honda created the Accura in the United States, just as Toyota created the Lexus and Nissan Infinity, since customers worldwide seem to equate changing the brand of their car with proof of financial success. This is why Renault really needed to buy Volvo to add some top-of-the-range brands to its portfolio.

This same rationale applies to the distribution networks. For example, Hanes – the largest apparel brand in the world – is sold in the big department stores but could not be sold in supermarkets, so Eggs was created for this network.

Basically, therefore, the purpose of multi-brand portfolios is to better meet the demands of segmented markets, and any reassessment of the portfolio raises the question of the segments to be retained.

Why rationalize portfolios?

The question of how many brands should be kept in each market has become a primary concern of all senior marketing managers. The fact is that, due to historical reasons, most firms have to manage a large portfolio of brands. The natural tendency during the growth of firms has been to add new brands each time they wanted to penetrate new market segments or new distribution channels. This was done so as not to create conflicts with former segments and channels which could have endangered their old brands. The vogue of company mergers and acquisitions brought additional brands that managers were reluctant to dispose of or merge with other brands. The size of brand portfolios, therefore, just grew and grew, with increased complexity and waste.

Times have changed though, and now the trend is to reduce the size of portfolios as quickly as possible. There are several reasons for this reverse in trends:

- Although it is easy to maintain several brands simultaneously in industrial markets where different brands are sometimes used for the same product to ease relations with distributors, in the retail market it is nearly impossible. The direct consequence is that only a few brands in a portfolio will be promoted, to gain a significant market share. The others will be abandoned, deleted.
- The concentration of the distribution trade has reduced the number of retailers and has even almost suppressed certain retail channels and small businesses. Brands that were previously uniquely handled by specific distribution channels and sold only in certain stores may now be found in a single wholesaler or purchasing group. This tends to lead to the reduction in their numbers. The trade has also pursued a policy of creating distributors' own brands. This, coupled with the fact that supermarket shelf space is limited, leads to the reduction of space allocated to the other brands, another factor causing a reduction in the number of references or brands themselves.
- Industrial production has also become concentrated. International competition has put the emphasis on high productivity and low costs and has led to the regrouping of production units and research and development activities. There is less justification for large brand portfolios when the products, however varied, come from the same factories, and even the same production line.
- Consumers, however, still have the last say and despite the fact that the objective of a brand is to clarify the market, their most frequent complaint is that they are confused by the growing number of brands. A company is fooling the consumer if it sells two identical products under two different brand names. Manufacturers respond by rationalizing their brands, deleting many of them.

How many brands, therefore, should be retained in a portfolio? It is obvious at this stage that there does not exist any magic formula or number. The question of the number of brands to retain is closely linked to the strategic role and status of the brands. In keeping only a single brand, we are assuming that an umbrella brand policy is possible and indeed pertinent in the market being considered. For decades, the Philips brand included both brown and white products, yet they parted with the latter markets, selling them to the American company Whirlpool. The decision regarding the number of brands to be retained should therefore be closely linked to an analysis of the brand's function in its respective market. Every market can be segmented, by product, customer expectation or type of clientele. This does not mean, though, that a market divided into six segments, for example, should necessarily call for six brands. This depends on their function (do we need endorsing, umbrella, range or product brands?). It also depends upon the long-term corporate objectives, the degree of competition and the resources of the company. The appropriate number of brands results from a multi-stage, multi-criteria decision process whereby various scenarios are presented and evaluated. A good example of this approach is Michelin.

From single to multiple brands: Michelin

Companies' attitudes to brands are changing – should they adopt a single-brand policy or penetrate markets from several different angles (multiple entries)? Some have decided to concentrate on a small number of international brands, which does not prevent them from promoting strong, local brands in their countries of origin. Some have concentrated on a single brand (Philips), while others have changed from a single-brand policy to a real portfolio – as in the case of Michelin, the world's leading tyre manufacturer. This last case is extremely interesting.

Initially, Michelin found it difficult to accept the need for a brand portfolio. The company's success was based on the fact that it focused on research in the interests of quality, under a single name – the name of the family that had created a set of values and the means to achieve a valid long-term policy.

Culturally speaking, everything at Michelin revolved around the Michelin name. Of course other brands existed, but they were often found in the basket of factories bought locally to penetrate the market – there are 80 Michelin factories worldwide. These factories did not receive any form of innovation or marketing support – they were purely tactical brands.

The problem with this is that the market is segmented. In the US automobile market, for example, there are certainly customers who want the best quality in the world, but there are also customers who want a major brand that offers good value for money, and those who only have US $100 to buy a set of tyres. There are also the 4 × 4 and pick-up drivers who are conscious of changing fashions and want customized tyres. For these drivers, the Michelin brand is too staid. A single brand cannot meet such a diverse demand, whereas a group can. This is why BF Goodrich is positioned as a sports brand in a flourishing market that pays little attention to price, namely the 4 × 4 market.

In the United States, Uniroyal targets the cost-conscious customer and is referenced by General Motors. This market segment is serviced by the Kleber brand in Europe where, following a series of mergers and the restructuring of groups, Uniroyal is still managed by Continental, Michelin's German competitor. In China, the role is fulfilled by the local brand Warrior, which has the largest market share. Distributor requirements also have to be taken into account since distributors are now demanding a quality tyre with their own brand name. Michelin has two policies in this respect. The first is to supply a tyre with the distributor's brand name, according to the latter's specifications. Thus, Michelin manufactures tyres for the Liberator brand, sold exclusively by Wal-Mart in the United States, and for Norauto in Europe. The second is to supply the distributor with a brand that belongs to Michelin. Thus Warrior, positioned as a middle-range brand in China, is used as the name for low-cost tyres in the United States and Europe. The same applies to the Japanese brand Riken, the Hungarian brand Taurus and the Czech brand Kormoran.

Michelin's global strategy aims to encourage customers to move from mass-produced products to middle- and then top-of-the-range products, with the different brands making it easier to emphasize perceived difference. Second, it involves adapting to the market. For example, the Chinese market was for a long time small and elitist because of the high proportion of top-of-the-range vehicles. Michelin's major share in this market was aided by the ill will created by accidents in Formula 1 racing that were linked to quality defects in the tyres produced by the Japanese group Bridgestone-Firestone. As the Chinese car market becomes increasingly democratic, there is a need to offer new buyers quality tyres, since those produced locally are dangerous at the speeds that can now be reached on the new Chinese motorways. The Michelin group must therefore provide a response to the middle range and the economical segments (if not it will be marginalized), but without endangering the reputation of Michelin as the world's number one brand for quality. The acquisition of the leading local brand Warrior has enabled it to complete its brand portfolio in this segment. In Japan and Korea, there is also a segment of clients demanding products 'made in the United States'. This demand has been satisfied by the acquisition of the US company BF Goodrich.

The last aspect of Michelin's global strategy, required to complete the picture, is that, because tyres are relatively inexpensive to transport, the tyre market is truly global (unlike the car market). Today, the group's Chinese factories manufacture tyres for distributors' brands (private labels) in the United States, and will soon be producing Uniroyal and BF Goodrich tyres for Michelin North America. One day, they will also be making Michelin tyres. Furthermore, the globalization of production makes it possible to circumvent customs barriers. For example, Japanese car manufacturers cannot export cars to the United States unless they include a minimum percentage of parts made in the United States, which is why these manufacturers fit their cars with Michelin tyres made in US factories. This has enabled Michelin to penetrate the reputedly nationalistic and closed Japanese market through this, as yet, fairly low-key distribution.

This example illustrates the flexibility and adaptation made possible by a brand portfolio – from local brands through middle-range brands to lifestyle and top-of-the-range brands, not forgetting the connection with the distribution networks via distributors' brands. All this adds up to global segmentation and the logic of globalized product platforms. Even so, as has been seen for the Michelin group, the branches are totally independent and the positioning of the brands is completely different in aviation, agriculture, the truck division and the car industry.

The benefits of multiple entries in a market

At the beginning of this chapter, we looked at the practical reasons why the number of brands had to be reduced, sometimes even to a single brand. They all correspond to a strategy of domination and competitive advantage via low cost. While recognizing the market segmentation, it has been decided not to take it into account at brand level, but only in terms of products.

The multi-brand approach, on the contrary, is the logical consequence of a differentiation strategy and as such cannot coexist with a low-cost policy, in view of reduced economies of scale, technical specialization, specific sales networks and necessary advertising investments. Nevertheless, with the exception of exclusive luxury brands, pressure remains. In order to take advantage of productivity gains, there is a tendency to fragment the production chain in the cause of differentiation at the last possible moment, thus exploiting the benefits of the learning curve. This is the case in the domestic appliances industry, making industrial regrouping a necessity, as well as in the food processing or automobile industries. The policy of having general car brands makes the most of all possible production and corporate communication synergism, and breeds the loyalty of the customer who progresses from one model to another within the same make.

With all the advantages of a mono-brand policy, what makes it necessary to have several brands on the market at the same time?

To start with, market growth. No single brand can develop a market on its own. Even if it forms the sole presence at the outset, once the brand has created the market, its development requires a multiplication of players, each investing to promote their respective differences. The collective presence of a number of contributors helps to promote a market. Beyond their differences, their combined advertising accentuates the common advantages of the product category. A multiple presence is necessary to support the market as a whole. It would not be in Philips' interest to see its competitors in the electric razor market disappear. This would only decrease the number of messages praising the merits of electric razors, which could only benefit Gillette and Wilkinson Sword. Philips should acquire a brand and maintain it as an active brand in the market. In the pharmaceutical industry, a laboratory discovering a new formula could certainly profit from 'co-marketing' it with other laboratories in order to accelerate its impact. An example of this is found in the case of aspartame.

Multiple brands allow for best market coverage. No single brand can cover a market on its own. As a market matures there is a need for differentiation and it becomes necessary to offer a wider range; the market is becoming segmented. A brand cannot be targeted at several different qualities at the same time without running the risk of losing its identity. In any case, consumers and retailers themselves will object to further brand ascendancy. This dual process is illustrated by the case of Rossignol. The company Rossignol followed a dual brand policy:

- a mono-brand multi-product policy: the hallmark Rossignol covers its skis, ski suits and ski boots (those coming from its acquisition of the Le Trappeur Brand, since then de-baptized);
- a multi-brand mono-product policy, with the Dynastar brand on skis, Kerma brand on sticks and Lange brand on boots.

With 20 per cent of the world ski market, Rossignol is the leading manufacturer. Its share in the upmarket ski sector is thought to be even greater, of the order of 40 per cent or more. This is an area where the company should not offend people's susceptibilities by expecting them to dress from head to toe in Rossignol products. If the world leader wants to grow even bigger, it should be the one increasing the choice, rather than its competitors. In this market, the distribution is still handled by a large number of small independent retailers, who fear the control of a single supplier. This is why each company brand has its own sales force. In the United States the Rossignol company presence is assured by two separate companies, Dynastar Inc. and Rossignol Inc. In the industrial sector, Facom and Legrand, two dominant leaders, successfully increased their hold on their market by creating apparently separate and autonomous brands. This enabled them to find new distributors, who were only too happy to have at their disposal a near exclusive brand, different from those of other retailers in that zone.

Multiple brands offer a tactical flexibility which also enables one to limit a competitor's field of extension. In this way Delsey, the leading European luggage manufacturer, cornered Samsonite. They created a new brand, Visa, positioned to undercut Samsonite prices, while at the same time Delsey restrained them from moving into the top-of-the-range market.

A multi-brand policy can stop any new competitors entering a market. A strong entry barrier to a market can be created by offering a complete range to retailers, with a brand name for each sector of the market. This is why in on-premises in the European market, soft drink companies create barriers to entry by providing the full range of products needed (Coke, Fanta, Sprite and so on).

A multi-brand policy is necessary to protect the main brand image. This partly explains why the Disney Corporation uses a number of brands in film production, for example Buena Vista and Touchstone. This enables them to produce films of every type without endangering the revered Disney name. Similarly, when the success of an innovation is not certain, it would be foolish to risk associating it with a successful brand. This is why Procter & Gamble launched their first liquid detergent under the brand name Vizir and not under the name of the leading market brand, Ariel. The inverse policy was adopted by the Cadbury Schweppes group when it decided to launch its new fizzy drinks not under the brand Wipps but as Dry de Schweppes. This was not only because Schweppes' name helped the sales but because it was thought that the new brand Wipps would reinforce the slightly old and stuck-up image of Schweppes, and would have, in the long term, threatened the value of the brand. In order to avoid having to lower the prices of its leading products, 3M created the sub-brand Tartan which only covers the products where 3M is the dominant leader. This minimizes the risk of unwanted cannibalization. Where 3M is not dominant but a challenger, retailers might be tempted to move directly to the lowest priced alternative from 3M.

Linking the brand portfolio to market segmentation

The brand portfolio is indicative of a company's desire to better meet the demands of the market, not only through differentiated products but also through different brands and therefore different identities. The organization of the brand portfolio reflects the type of market segmentation chosen by the company. Ferrero (Kinder) bases its market segmentation on narrow age groups and user status, l'Oréal bases it on distribution channels, Legrand on types of consumer motivators, Procter & Gamble and Volkswagen on price brackets, SEB on consumer populations and value systems, Evian on the benefits sought from the water, Guinness on occasions, and so on.

The following sections illustrate how the brand portfolio and segmentation are linked.

Socio-demographic segmentation

Although certain people regard socio-demographic segmentation as an outmoded concept, it is still a useful tool when it comes to understanding consumer behaviour and, as such, can be used to establish a brand portfolio. Ferrero (Kinder) is Europe's leading confectionery company. Unlike the Mars bar, Kinder has developed a portfolio that adheres rigorously to segmentation by age – from Kinder eggs for the very young to Kinder chocolate, Kinder Delice, Kinder Pingui, Kinder Country and Kinder Bueno for young adults. All magazine editors produce different titles based on age and gender. Their magazines target extremely narrow age groups and reflect progress at school or rather the child's cognitive development according to Piaget. Lego also has a brand portfolio based on different age groups, from the very young to pre-adolescence.

Psychographic segmentation

To whom should Pernod-Ricard sell Ballantines in China? And to whom should it sell Chivas? Both are some of the best products of Scotland. Clearly socio-demographics do not help. But the general lifestyle values, the attitudes about heritage vs modernity of the new rich in Shanghai, are not all the same.

Benefit segmentation

A key criterion for segmentation is the main benefit looked for by consumers. Companies can organize their brand portfolio by positioning each brand on one single motivation/benefit, as long as of course it is a profitable business. This is the basis of Danone Waters brand portfolio in Europe. Recent marketing research revealed the following motivations to purchase: status, good life (13 per cent); health

(57 per cent); and price (30 per cent). The macro motivation for health needs to be sub-segmented: for 16 per cent it refers to an aesthetic vision of health, for 15 per cent it means vitality and for 26 per cent this refers to specific problems. Danone Waters reorganized its brand portfolio of non-carbonated waters as follows:

- Evian targets 29 per cent of the consumers (those seeking status and aesthetic health).
- Volvic is positioned on vitality (15 per cent of the market), against Nestlé's Vittel.
- New brands were created on physiological needs: Taillefine against Contrex (Nestlé), both on remaining slim, and Talians, another new brand.
- A host of source waters to fulfil distribution expectations of a low-cost brand.

In this portfolio, Evian's role is to be the referent of the market, and to valorize water as much as possible (in addition, this is consistent with the fact that Evian's supply is not unlimited: it takes time for the Alps to create this water). As a consequence, some brand extensions are forbidden, such as the growing area of aromatized waters. The second brand of the group, Volvic, priced 10 per cent below Evian, has the ability to stimulate the market through such extensions. Taillefine (known as Vitalinea in other countries) is actually an extension in the field of water of a dairy brand positioned on 0 per cent fat. To compete in the weight-conscious segment, against Contrex (segment leader, from Nestlé), instead of launching from scratch a new brand, it was decided to extend this global franchise to water.

Attitude segmentation

Unlike most automobile manufacturers, which organize their portfolio along a vertical price line, PSA has chosen to develop two parallel generalist brands, Peugeot and Citroën. In 2010 PSA was the second largest European car manufacturer. What is the basis then of the segmentation? Peugeot has in its roots, its identity, a number of core values (reliability/quality but also dynamism and aesthetics) which address primarily the consumers who like to drive, to master their car, deriving pleasure out of it. Citroën, although its cars share 60 per cent of their hidden parts with the Peugeot models, delivers a totally different driving and living experience. Once a brand with character, ingenuity, innovativeness, it went bankrupt twice before being bought by Peugeot. Reinventing Citroën, PSA has made it a car brand for people expecting their car to foresee the evolution of lifestyles (Folz, 2003).

There are strong gains in having two parallel brands, beyond sharing the same platform for manufacturing. Aiming at the same price segment, when one model of a brand starts declining in its life cycle, the other brand launches its own model. As a result, the rate of innovation of the group within each price segment is exceptionally high compared with competitors, a key success factor in modern markets. Also, with only two brands, one avoids the problems of Volkswagen with its four brands largely overlapping, a factor that negatively affects the profitability of the global portfolio. Salespeople trade consumers down by suggesting they consider Skoda or Seat cars, entry brands, which are essentially the same as Volkswagen cars. In addition, these two entry brands now face growth problems: where should Skoda and Seat go? To capitalize on their recently built brand loyalty, they wish to trade their own consumers up with higher-priced models, but run the risk of increased cannibalization, and of a still larger lack of differentiation from Volkswagen's lower lines.

Channel segmentation

This is a growing mode of segmentation and organization of brands. The rationale is that channels are fighting against each other. An allocation of different brands to each channel avoids conflicts, price harmonization problems, and maximizes the adaptation of the brand to the motives of channel patrons. In addition, taking the small appliance business for instance, being sold exclusively at Wal-Mart prevents brands from having a presence in the selective distribution channels, which still represent more than 55 per cent of the market in the United States. This is why a portfolio is very helpful in allocating brands to channels.

The paradigm of this approach is l'Oréal: all its brands have to be sold in one and one only channel:

- There are brands for selective premium distribution and department stores: Lancôme, Helena Rubinstein, Biotherm, Kiehl's and Shu Uemura.
- There are brands for mass channels: l'Oréal Paris, Garnier and Maybelline.

- There are brands for pharmacies: La Roche Posay and Vichy.
- There is a brand for direct sales by mail order: CCB (Club des Créateurs de Beauté) although this name is really a handicap for the globalization of the brand.
- There are brands for the professional hairdresser channel: l'Oréal Paris Professionnel, Redken, Matrix, Kerastase and Inné.
- There are brands with their own stores: Kiehl's and Body Shop.

When a channel is not already present in a country, it is reconstructed thanks to the presence of two or more brands so that costs can be shared. For instance, if pharmacies in Canada do not sell cosmetics, a specific counter can be developed in department stores, with a pharmacist to assist consumers, selling both La Roche Posay and Vichy.

Of course there is another segmentation criterion: price. In each channel, there is a premium brand and a mainstream brand. Finally each brand epitomizes one universal model of beauty. In the mass channels, everywhere in the world, l'Oréal Paris symbolizes Paris, and Maybelline the American style of beauty.

L'Oréal's profitability rests largely on this systematic channel-based brand portfolio organization. It gives this group the ability to price the same product very differently from one channel to another, capitalizing on the fact that consumers' price sensitivity is not at all the same across channels and purchase situations. For instance, a hair fixing gel sold to consumers at a hairdressing salon for €9 under the brand Tecni Art (l'Oréal Paris Professional) is bought by the hairdresser for half this price, that is to say for more or less the price at which a consumer would find the product under Fructis (Garnier) or Studio Line (l'Oréal Paris) in mass distribution. Kerastase shampoos are sold at €8 to the consumer in a hair salon, but the same product is sold at €2.5 under the Elsève brand at a multiple retailer.

The same holds true for an industrial group like Saint Gobain. This group has created a portfolio of stores aiming at building and construction:

- from Platforme du Bâtiment, a cash and carry for small general contractors;
- to the mass multiple retailer Point P aimed at craftspeople;
- to Lapeyre aimed at the DIY expert, able to buy a window and install it without professional help;
- and K par K (literally, case by case), a chain of mini-stores selling tailor-made new windows, fully installed at your home.

Of course, the last option is the most expensive (€1,000 for a replacement window, with everything included), but in most of the cases, the windows that need replacing are standard in size and design. It is therefore a standard window that is bought (not a customized one), essentially the same product as could be found at Lapeyre for instance at a fraction of the price, but without any service. The same reasoning applies to the other brands in the portfolio.

Occasion segmentation

An increasing number of companies have become aware of the importance of occasion segmentation (see also Chapter 9). All products are in fact purchased or consumed on a particular occasion. The real issue is therefore to influence the occasions affecting consumption rather than the consumers themselves. In fact, the same person can consume a product in different ways during the course of the same day if he or she has encountered several clearly differentiated occasions. Each occasion gives rise to clearly differentiated expectations, and therefore to a specific type of competition for the brand since, on each occasion, the brand does not encounter the same set of circumstances.

In the case of Guinness, the occasion not only forms the basis of the brand portfolio but also structures the organization of sales and marketing. Today, there are occasion managers, just as there used to be brand managers. Thus Guinness is positioned on the so-called 'affiliation' occasion typical of the pub environment, while Carlsberg corresponds to the 'release' occasion in nightclubs and Budweiser targets the 'relaxing at home' occasion.

When dealing with occasion segmentation, the first thing a company should do before developing several new brands is to consider whether line extensions could enable a particular brand to expand by gaining a foothold in situations or places that have so far been inaccessible. However, there are limits to this extension, which is where the brand portfolio comes in.

Price segmentation

This is a most classic organization of the portfolio. The whole Group Volkswagen brand portfolio is based on it, with entries ranging from the low-end Skoda or Seat to Volkswagen itself, Audi and luxury brands like Bentley. Accor, Europe's leading hotel group, has achieved its success by launching a set of product brands, all positioned at a specific price. The Chanel-Bourjois company has two entries, the luxury brand Chanel, and Bourjois for the mass market.

In the construction market, Velux is one of the most global brands: it stands for roof windows in 40 countries all around the world. It has just introduced Roof Light as a low-cost alternative, targeting the price-sensitive market segment. The price gap with Velux is 30 per cent, less expensive than Velux's main competitors (Roto and Fakro), which are sold with a 20 per cent price gap. It is also sold as a private label of large multiple retailers in the DIY market.

In fact, very few brands have successfully managed to cover substantially different price ranges. It is true that generalist car manufacturers like Renault build a wide range of cars, from the Twingo to the Latitude. But they cannot really enter the top-of-the-range market. This was also one of the aims of their association with Volvo, a brand more easily associated with top of the range cars. Toyota took the approach of creating a separate brand, Lexus. A brand portfolio makes it possible to cover the different price sectors without affecting the reputation of each brand. The Sanford group, having taken over Parker, Waterman and Paper Mate, can specialize its brands in terms of price and style. By reputation, Parker represents the top of the range in each product segment, from the ballpoint pen to the ink pen. Waterman represents the middle of the range. The Whirlpool group allocates to each of its brands a price bracket. The average price of the Whirlpool brand itself must be that of the middle of the market. The average price of the Laden brand corresponds to the lower quartile of the market price range and that of Bauknecht the higher quartile (see Figure 14.1).

A multi-brand portfolio only makes sense if, in the long term, each brand has its own territory. This is not always the case – companies hang on to brands whose images are not different enough to justify the economies of the multi-brand policy.

Linking brand portfolio to prescription segmentation

In the business-to-business sector, the type of key influencer targeted constitutes a strategic criterion for segmentation. The market can in fact be segmented according to the decision-making process. Along the value distribution chain several participants play a key role, and brands have different ideas of what they consider to be a key role.

For example, in the aluminium systems market for the residential and service sectors, the leading European company HBS (Hydro Building Systems) has three brands – Wicona from Germany, Domal from Italy and Technal from France – all represented to varying degrees in Europe, depending on the level of maturity and development of the markets. In reality, each brand targets a different operator-prescriber:

- Wicona targets architects, research departments and engineering companies.

FIGURE 14.1 Segmenting the brand portfolio by price spectrum

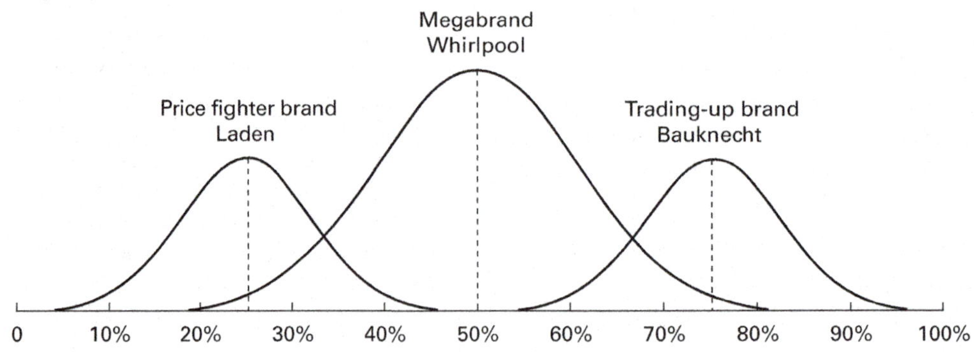

- Domal targets installation companies, general companies that win tenders associated with building sites. It supplies flexible and inexpensive extruded aluminium systems manufactured in its small plants.
- Technal aims directly at the end-users via television and a network of well-known registered installers who also co-finance the advertising.

Legrand, Europe's leading electrical appliance company, uses the same type of organization. Legrand's expansionist policy is based on external growth. In the electrical equipment sector, standards vary significantly from country to county in order to prevent access to national markets. There is also a great deal of intense lobbying by operators who want to perpetuate a situation that creates a network of local markets. The only way to penetrate these markets is to buy the leading local company, which is why Legrand acquired the Italian company Bticino. It then specialized the brands, allocating Bticino to the prescribers, engineering bureaux and research departments, while Legrand became the installers' brand, offering them a broad and totally integrated range of products in which ease of installation is the cardinal virtue.

Another example of this type of brand portfolio organization was provided by the UK company Arjo Wiggins, formerly a leading manufacturer of top-quality paper for companies and professionals. This company reorganized its basket of brands to create mega-brands, whose size is critical, bringing together what were previously small product brands under the umbrella of each one. The new organization is structured as follows:

- AW Curious Collection targets creators and designers in advertising and design agencies, since they are the key influencers for projects and creations in which innovation and creativity count for a great deal. For example, the Curious Collection ranges include aluminium and steel paper.
- AW Impressions targets the printers who are the key prescribers for a great many of the jobs they are asked to do by companies – for instance, letterheads.
- Conqueror targets the general public, the end-users who want a quality paper to reflect their company or their personal image.

Global portfolio strategy

For the last few years big groups have been carrying out a policy of stuffing their portfolios with additional brands, either through acquisition or partnerships, at the same time as extending the product range of some of their brands. Nestlé has become the world's number one food processing company thanks to its acquisition of Carnation and Stouffer in the USA, Rowntree in the UK, Buitoni-Perugina in Italy and Perrier in France.

This trend towards company size growth is partly motivated by the gains that can result from joining forces in research and development, logistics, manufacturing, distribution and sales. Another reason is due to the levels of financial and human resources that are now necessary to compete on the world market. A third reason is the desire to buy a dominant position and be able to restrict the market to a duopoly or an oligopoly. A final reason is to be able to resist the pressure exerted by the concentration of distributors.

It is worth remembering that besides this quantitative aspect, the idea of a portfolio implies a global vision of the competition in a market or category. A portfolio also forces the relationships between one brand and the others in the portfolio to be considered, the idea being that a brand's value can be enhanced by belonging to a larger portfolio. There are several decision grids, the most famous being the Boston Consulting Group's. Hence at Pernod-Ricard one speaks of growth products, contributors and the famous cash cows. To these can be added the concept of a 'strategic brand': Pacific, a non-alcoholic aniseed drink, may not be financially interesting but is vital for the long-term prospects as it accustoms future customers to the aniseed taste. Masterfoods (Mars) control half the cat food market thanks to a portfolio that is made up from the following brands: Ronron, Kit-e-Kat, Whiskas and Sheba. These can be classified into strategic, value and tactical brands. Whiskas is strategically aimed at being the invincible brand in the market, with the biggest range, large profits, central consumer benefit (best nutrition) and the most expensive advertising campaign. Sheba is a value brand: its market share in money is three times as much as its market share in volume. Sheba, a high-quality product, is targeted at the most dedicated owners. Ronron is a buffer brand, low in price and hardly given any advertising support; it is there to counter-attack the distributor own brands. Strategic, niche and tactical brands can also be distinguished in the Heineken Breweries.

The case of industrial brand portfolios

In the industrial world, since brands do not need television advertising, multi-brand strategies have very few constraints, and they can easily carry too many brands.

The case is illustrated by the chemical industry in the agricultural market. As each herbicide brand is associated with one unique active principle, a single company often stocks 500 trademarks or even more!

When a brand is strategic and the portfolio corresponds to the segmentation of the final market, the brand must mean more than a mere difference in name or logo on the product. In this way BASF used to sell paint to coach builders worldwide under two brands, Glasurit and RM. They are, in fact, the same product. In the car world there is a difficulty with the idea of two different qualities – no one would buy the inferior one. The two brands are thus supplementary and not complementary.

Glasurit is aimed at the technically minded coach builder. As its international slogan points out, Glasurit is the 'Preferred Technology Partner'. As its slogan indicates, RM is the thoughtful coach builder partner, 'The key to your success'. It is aimed at the other segment of coach builder who expect service to increase their activity. They see themselves rather as company directors than as painters.

To maximize their chances of success, BASF gave each brand the necessary means to defend itself. Dictating who did what would only weaken both brands and give the advantage to their competitor Akzo. Instead BASF decided to:

- create two separate management teams (as opposed to a common marketing department, which was for a long time the case), based in two different countries;
- have two separate sales forces in charge of the distribution, so as to minimize cannibalization from the inside;
- avoid all references to the parent company BASF, in order to increase the perceived difference between the two brands;
- develop services in line with the positioning of each brand;
- have different advertising campaigns on a worldwide scale.

This is how BASF maximized its cover of the market. It adapted itself to the two distinct segments of the car refinish market and to the psychology of the constructors. Mercedes, for instance, would not like the idea that its paint supplier also supplied the Russian brand Lada!

The constraints associated with multi-brands are often underestimated in the industrial world, where a brand is considered just a name or a reference in a catalogue. When a brand corresponds to a strategic segmentation this underestimation can undermine or even break the strategy. In the industrial electrical equipment market, the manufacturers have to decide whom to favour, the installing company, the wholesaler/distributor or the end-user. It is impossible to favour all three at the same time. Merlin-Gerin, who concentrated on the distributors, were losing touch with the fitters. For the latter, the Sarel company was created. This increased the proportion of the market that could be reached, provided that all links with Merlin-Gerin were hidden. In practice, in the various countries they operated in, because of the different turnovers of Merlin-Gerin and Sarel the constraints of their multi-brand strategy were soon forgotten for the sake of saving costs.

- Sarel could sometimes be found in the same office block as Merlin-Gerin's local headquarters.
- The published organization charts did nothing to hide the Sarel–Merlin-Gerin link. Sound management on the organizational front could instead dictate that, despite its small size, Sarel be directly linked with Schneider's, their common parent company, and not Merlin-Gerin's local manager.
- On occasions, in order to save money, both Sarel and Merlin-Gerin shared the same trade exhibition stands.

The organization of brands in the business-to-business sector poses specific problems that need to be addressed as such. For example, industrial groups whose growth typically involves the acquisition of companies soon begin to wonder whether or not to keep the brand name of the newly acquired company, and how much independence it should have in relation to the purchasing group.

Furthermore, the engineering culture might make the product central to the group or company identity, while the brand is little more than an appendage and is often the name of a reference. This explains the increasing number of references, registered throughout the world, that preoccupy companies' legal departments and give rise to regular complaints about the excessive number of brands. However, although there may be a brand name in legal terms, there is every reason to believe that these names are not in fact real brands with real market power.

It is therefore a question of reducing the number of brand names in the portfolio, and reorganizing them around a few valid mega-brands that serve as an umbrella, a central point of reference. From this it can be seen that the task of rationalizing the brand portfolio is in fact indicative of the need to reorganize the business. How do you manage multi-product mega-brands within a structure of business units, knowing that the mega-brand may well cover several business units? Do you need to create a brand committee, from across the business units, that meets on a regular basis with a view to making decisions about problems of coherence in the development of the brand – coherence in terms of products and services, price positioning on the various markets, advertising and catalogues? At this stage, large-scale industry begins to consider how other more 'lowly' sectors – the mass-consumer market and FMCG market – have resolved this type of problem.

The role of the sales force in designing the portfolio organization

In business-to-business contexts, it is essential to include sales in any consideration of brands since it is ultimately the sales force, the technical and commercial engineers, and the front office who represent the brand. It is therefore important to distinguish four types of brand:

1. The *integrating brand* is usually the corporate brand when it is used to sell a global service to a single client. It is client-centred. To this end, it brings together the skills and synergies of the different business units. The front office and sales force represent the name of the group. Typical examples of this are Vinci, Schneider Electric in its promotion of global services, and Suez Industrial Solutions.

   The integrating brand (usually the group) also ensures the transversality of the product brands at the level of the catalogue, invoicing and shared vision (for example, when the brand/group issues a communication on 'security').
2. The *integrated brand* is usually the name of an acquired company, internationally renowned for a particular application, a particular need or a particular area of expertise. However, the front office and sales force operates under the name of the group.
3. The *endorsed brand* only uses the name of the group as an endorsement (as with a company that is a member of XXXX) and has its own name and front office. This is typically the case when the brand uses a business model that is different from the group's area of expertise.
4. The *independent brand* is presented as completely independent, with no links to the group, which in theory implies separate offices in the different countries concerned. It therefore has its own name and front office and there is no visible relationship with the group. This type of brand makes it possible to overcome the problem of expanding market coverage when a brand is already dominant. Thus, when a brand in the group already covers more than 50 per cent of a particular market, it is logical to launch an independent brand for all those who do not want to work with the first. Furthermore, the independent brand is often used to advocate a policy that contradicts the official policy of the group, in order to increase market coverage without placing the group in a precarious position.

Linking the brand portfolio to the corporate strategy

So how many brands does a company put on the market? Does it adopt the single-brand or the brand-portfolio model? These are the type of questions asked by modern company and group managers. And this is how group policies evolve, based on the lessons learnt from the development of their market shares and from the diagnosis of the causes of a possible upper limit on profits.

As has already been seen, Michelin is a typical example of a group whose global market share reached an upper limit in spite of the widely acclaimed excellence, not to say superiority, of Michelin tyres, including Formula 1 versions. After years of using a virtually single-brand model, the Michelin group decided to change its policy. Michelin certainly remained the flagship, but it was no longer the only brand to be the focus of innovative ideas and new advertising. In the private car market, Michelin realized the advantages of double segmentation – the first linked to price, the second to the fashion for status tyres. There are customers throughout the world who want value for money but, while recognizing the superiority of the Michelin brand, are not committed enough to want to buy Michelin tyres. But should they simply be left, as in the past, to turn to the competition in the form of Bridgestone? The demands of this segment of smart buyers needed to be met, and this was done via Kleber in Europe – an old brand in the portfolio that has been revitalized through innovation, such as the non-puncturing tyre – and Uniroyal in the United States.

But there is also a segment of drivers, usually drivers of pick-ups and 4 × 4s in the United States and Europe, for whom tyres are a kind of status symbol. They want their tyres to be flashy and ostentatious and are not attracted by Michelin because, in their eyes, a brand that focuses on safety, performance and long-term development is too staid, not fashionable enough, not different enough. It is to these drivers that the group dedicated its US brand Goodrich, with a policy of offering a regularly updated range of large, custom-made tyres. However, while Kleber is cheaper than Michelin, Goodrich is positioned in the same price bracket.

SEB, world leader in small household appliances, decided to concentrate on four major brands (Moulinex, Tefal, Rowenta, Krups) to compete with Philips on the international market, while for the moment retaining certain local and regional brands such as Calor, SEB and Arno. However, there was a strong temptation to emulate Philips and its single-brand policy on the domestic market. But this would have been a mistake since there is no point in imitating a market leader on a smaller – and therefore less visible and less successful – scale.

The growth of Legrand, the market leader in small electrical appliances for the residential and service sector, was achieved through the acquisition of specialist brands. Then Legrand picked up 80 per cent of its catalogue and 'Legrandized' it, making it simple, ergonomic, user-friendly for installers and electricians, and above all compatible with the rest of the catalogue (based on the Lego model). Legrand became the reference catalogue for the sector – a business model that is repeated worldwide. So what does Legrand do with the brands it buys? It keeps them to create a protective barrier, using them in a preventative capacity to ensure its domination of the market. The electrical installation market is no different from other markets and Legrand, like other market leaders, creates the desire to be different among certain customers, making sure they do not want to have the same brand as their colleagues and competitors. So, rather than leaving them to turn to its competitors, Legrand keeps their custom by offering – albeit much reduced – specialist brands. As already stated, these brands also create a protective barrier for Legrand so that a newcomer trying to penetrate the market could not replace Legrand in the eyes of wholesalers. It would be offered the place of a small specialist brand.

There are also parameters linked to the distribution strategy that explain why the Volvo truck division that bought Renault Trucks has maintained the Renault brand name. But this can only be understood by taking account of the general strategy of manufacturers in response to the liberalization of the European car and truck market. Agents are now no longer obliged to deal exclusively with a single brand so, if they want to prevent another manufacturer from filling the breach, it is better to offer two fairly well differentiated brands, but which belong to the same group. And this is exactly what Volvo did. To prevent the risk of any drift towards the lower-priced models (as is happening in the Volkswagen group), the price of Renault Trucks was re-evaluated, which helped to greatly increase the profitability of the division.

The l'Oréal group continues to buy new brands and thereby extend its portfolio. In fact, it is moving out of Europe, is currently targeting the United States and has plans for Asia where it is still a modest player.

To accompany this expansionist strategy, the group buys strong local brands either because they are the leaders in their market segment or because they anticipate the trends of the future. This is why it bought the US mainstream brand of make-up, Maybelline, as well as Softsheen Carson, which specializes in haircare for African-Americans. It has also bought the US brands Redken, a very fashionable haircare brand for professionals, and Kiehl's, a 'long-term development' and 'niche' brand of cosmetics. In Japan, it has bought the Sue Uemura brand. One interesting fact that will be examined in the chapter on globalization is that l'Oréal subsequently globalized these local brands.

Key rules to manage a multi-brand portfolio

There are a few principles to be followed to optimize the results of multi-brand entries in a competitive market. Although simple to express, they pose implementation problems to organizations built and organized on other principles than brand logic.

Portfolios need strong coordination

Brand portfolios do not manage themselves, they need some form of coordination and even a coordinator above brand level. Experience has shown that companies are 'porous', with ideas passing between departments, across corridors and even between buildings. This gives rise to an – albeit involuntary – tendency to duplicate brands within the same portfolio. The allocation of innovations also gives rise to difficulties, with each brand wanting the innovation before the others. This is why companies have either a brand coordinator or a brand committee responsible for addressing these problems.

Allocate innovations according to each brand's positioning

It is a well-known fact that innovations are the lifeblood of a brand, since they renew its relevance and differentiation. This is why it is essential to have clear and precise platforms (a charter of identity) for each brand – a tool for clarifying the main lines of development and innovation of the brand. This makes it possible to allocate innovation according to brand values and not under pressure from the sales force, which wants each brand to enjoy the same advantages. In fact, it should be quite the opposite – it is through innovation that the brand reveals its identity. It is therefore important to distinguish between exclusive innovations (such as coupés for Peugeot) and innovations that will be introduced over a period of time (phased innovations), and also to establish the order in which these innovations will be allocated to the brands.

Apart from brand values, positioning and market share also influence the allocation of innovations. For example, there is no point in allocating a specialized innovation (targeting a small number of households) to a mass-market brand. It is far better to reserve an exclusive innovation for a top-of-the-range brand which, by definition, targets a more limited clientele. This is how Fagor Brandt manages the allocation of innovations between its mass-market brand Brandt and its top-of-the-range brand De Dietrich.

However, the rule for allocating innovations as a function of brand identity comes up against another type of logic, the logic of cost reduction. For example, the logic of platforms where an increasing number of parts are shared between different brand models totally contradicts the principle of allocating innovations according to brand value. Nothing could be more a function of identity than Citroën's hydropneumatic suspension, which reflects the identity and very essence of the brand – overcoming technical constraints to increase passenger comfort. This suspension – the historic attribute dating from the famous DS models – is only found at the very top of the Citroën range. But if it had to be invented today, what industrial group governed by the logic of production platforms would agree to create and develop such an innovation for a single brand, let alone a single model?

Conversely, to increase the relevance of the Peugeot 607, it was necessary to adopt the rear-wheel drive option typical of the German top-of-the-range models that set the international standards. The 607 was constructed on the top-of-the-range Citroën platform which, as everyone knows, is a front-wheel drive. Given the design issues and costs of a production line for a rear-wheel drive, it is easy to understand why an industrial group might hesitate to commit itself to this option for the only top-of-the-range model of a single brand. The future lies in partnerships with other manufacturers.

Do not 'rob Peter to pay Paul'

Since the aim is to create a portfolio of strong brands, you must avoid making this mistake. Although it is standard practice to position brands clearly in relation to one another in order to maximize their appropriateness for the segments targeted, a brand should not be prevented from becoming strong. Thus innovation is an integral part of the key values of PSA's two general brands Peugeot and Citroën. Limiting this value (innovativeness) to one brand would destroy the other. There is simply no future for non-innovative brands in the car market.

A brand portfolio is not an accumulation of independent brands but the reflection of a global strategy of market domination

This makes the procedures and intervention of the US Federal Authorities and the European Commission rather paradoxical since, for these bodies, the fact of maintaining a sufficient level of competition is essential to accept or refuse a proposed merger or an acquisition. But there is no point in hiding the naked truth. Corporate mergers and brand acquisitions are largely determined by a single objective – market domination – over and above the synergies and cost reductions achieved by pooling resources. Why did Coca-Cola want to buy Orangina and pay US $1 billion for this predominately local brand? Quite simply because it would have enabled the group to force Pepsi-Cola out of the market. Since it did not have a fizzy orange drink in its portfolio to offset Coca-Cola's Fanta, Pepsico had in fact signed a strategic distribution agreement with Orangina.

A portfolio is therefore a global approach on the chessboard of competition, with a precise role allocated to each brand. Brand managers should therefore receive a set of instructions so that they understand their role and do not deviate from the global plan by carrying out a series of independent initiatives over a period of time.

A portfolio is not a simple collection of brands that just happen to be there as a result of the vagaries of history, but a well-structured and coherent group in which each brand has a place and clearly defined role:

- For example, this may be a financial role, in which the brand contributes to the financing of another brand. This is typically the case of local brands which are leaders in their own market. These brands are and must remain important contributors to enable the portfolio under construction to develop as a whole.
- The role of a brand may also be to defend the brand leader. For example, Colgate Palmolive, thinking that a price war was about to be declared on its leading fabric softener Soupline, was prepared to lower the price of its 'flanker' brand Doulinge to avoid lowering the price of its brand leader. Legrand successfully covered the market and rendered its general brand impervious to attacks from competitors by a precise allocation of roles between the Legrand general brand and the specialist brands it had bought and maintained (Arnoult, Planet Watthom and so on). These brands formed an outer barrier at wholesaler level in the event of foreign competitors trying to enter the market. If the wholesalers were disloyal to Legrand and referenced a newcomer, at least they only affected the escort ships and not the flagship.
- A brand can also fulfil the role of group banner brand, especially if the brand has the same name as the group.
- It is worthy of note that this rationale is equally valid for daughter brands and their role in the construction, reinforcement and defence of the parent brand. It has already been seen that, apart from their specific positioning relating to a particular need or clientele, the 14 sub-brands of Nivea all had a specific role to play and made their contribution to the Nivea 'house' in terms of a specialized area of competence as well as an input of innovation, sensuality and fashion. There is no doubt that they are all very much Nivea brands but nonetheless each adds a personal touch, which is why, in spite of a very strong 'Nivea-ness' and very precise guidelines on how the brand should be presented, it does not come across as monolithic.
- The consequence of the portfolio logic is that it is dangerous to acquire a brand leader without the smaller brands that go with it.

If Schneider had succeeded in merging with Legrand, it would have been crucial to preserve the network of more modest, more specialized brands maintained precisely because they created an effective barrier that protected the star brand, Legrand. All too often, company rescuers, especially if they are investment funds, do not have this long-term vision. They resell the small brands without taking account of their collective role.

Within all large companies, there is an inevitable tendency to replicate

Take the Seb group, managing four global brands of small appliances: Krups, Rowenta, Moulinex and Tefal. How do we prevent ideas and designs from being known by another and adopted, hence diluting brand identity?

This must be combated since it destroys the competitiveness and imagination of the brands concerned. It is partly because there is always an underlying competition based on prices, since the basic function of groups is to reduce costs by pooling as many resources as possible. The main danger of groups is that, in the interests of making economies (which is quite natural), they tend to erode the identity of their brand in their portfolio by giving the common areas too much prominence when they should be concealing them, or by publicizing too much information on the fact that the different brand models come from the same platform. It is crucial to ensure that all the visible parts of these brands are different. Now 'visible' does not only refer to design: companies that buy trucks look at the engine and some key hidden technical parts of the truck, especially for long-haul models. It will be a challenge for Volvo AG to keep enough differentiating competencies between long-haul Volvo Trucks, Mack Trucks and Renault Trucks. The brand positionings should be the guiding force.

Focus each brand of the portfolio on a different competitor

This is one way of preventing the brands in a portfolio from replicating each other, apart from permanent surveillance by the brand committee or brand coordinator. This reminds managers that the best way to cover the market is via the logic of multi-brand portfolios and not by 'narrowing the focus'. Choosing a target competitor for each brand increases the chances of achieving this objective. It also indicates who is to be defeated.

A classic risk of brand portfolios is their complexity

This is true since exaggerated fragmentation does not allow each brand to achieve its critical size. This is what business-to-business companies look out for since, for them, a brand – even registered – is merely a name and not a long-term publicity and promotional medium. This is why their legal departments are gradually collapsing under the cost of registering and monitoring trademarks (brand names), and it is what led Air Liquide to reassess its entire portfolio of more than 700 'brands' in 2003. Distributors are also susceptible to the same risk when they rethink their portfolio of distributors' brands (private labels). Decathlon managed to avoid this pitfall; when it changed from the single Decathlon brand to the so-called 'passion brands' portfolio, as many as 13 brands were envisaged before some were merged and the company decided on 7.

The Volkswagen group is currently subject to this risk. Although Seat and Skoda should, in theory, have been separated geographically, the four brands Seat, Skoda, Volkswagen and Audi are still found in several countries, each with its own network of agents. Sustaining an independent commercial network requires a large product range and the ability to create customer loyalty. This means that Seat and Skoda have to move upmarket, but where do they stop and how are they to be differentiated from the very similar newcomers from Volkswagen and Audi? Price is one solution, but the publicity based on the fact that these four brands come from the same factories and even the same platforms has created the ideal conditions for internal cannibalization. The agents selling Seat and Skoda use it as a sales argument.

The growing role of design in portfolio management

Design plays a crucial role in the battle for differentiation. It is design that structures customer expectations, design that evokes brand values, creates visible differences and develops new favourites on mature markets. This is why it has to observe several key principles:

- The principle of radicalization. Design cannot be vague – since the strategy is to attack the market with a small number of brands, they must be clearly defined, with a specific design, all the more so since organizations have a natural tendency to soften the hard edges, which leads to a resemblance on the shelves that has a dramatic effect on perceived differentiation. Radical design must also compensate for the increasing lack of differentiation due to the industrial logic of platforms. There is no place on today's mature markets for half-hearted designs. If there is a brand identity, it must be clearly visible.
- The principle of externalization. If the company is responsible for defining the story to be told by each brand, that is, creating its identity, it is important to seek outside help for the design itself by appointing a designer for each brand who is totally committed to that brand. Thomson did the opposite and entrusted the design of its four brands, Thomson, Saba, Telefunken and Brandt, to the same designer, Philippe Starck, who was a brand in his own right. This is why, within an organization, design must be positioned at brand level, not corporate level, even if this requires robust coordination to avoid replication between brands, a tendency that is all too frequent. But this risk is avoided if the company appoints an external designer, for each brand, who is inspired by its strategic platform.
- The principle of business. The function of design is to promote and develop business, not art. Design should not become self-absorbed. For example, the aim of designing a coffee pot is not to enable consumers to invite their friends round to admire their coffee pot, but to offer them a good cup of coffee. In short, the purpose of design is to enable the brand not just to look good but to function efficiently.
- The principle of courage. The key question in design is whether a design can be properly tested. Certainly, the ergonomics and functionality of a product must always be tested at user-status level. But apart from that, what is the relevance of a few individuals' (interviewees') opinions of a design when it is, by definition, the opinion leaders (the press) who decide whether or not a product is in good taste when it is launched in a few months' or years' time? Design is a risk. In the car sector, for example, how can you predict which design will be perceived as avant-garde in another four years, in the event that the brand could be said to be a trend setter? Renault took the risk with its audacious (some will say over-audacious) design. But four years ahead of its time, it is difficult to forecast perceptions with any degree of accuracy.

Does the corporate organization match the brand portfolio?

A brand is only successful if the factors governing its production work together in a coordinated and motivated manner. The success of a group logic and a brand portfolio cannot be assessed without analysing the conditions of its development and, above all, the type of organization. Since this is not widely publicized, or may even be deliberately played down, it tends to be overlooked as a key factor in the success of a brand portfolio policy.

The main risk of a brand portfolio is the gradual de-energizing of the brands, reduced to the state of increasingly undifferentiated 'outer casings' that are little more than publicity devices. This is exacerbated by the fact that the economic press only talks in terms of groups and therefore publicizes the fact that brands that were once different are now produced by the same group. Its readers, often opinion leaders, are within their rights to ask certain questions, behind the bodywork, what remains of the brand identity? Do Jaguars still have a Jaguar engine or do they have a Ford engine? Will the specificity of Saab disappear with its integration within the GM group?

The essence of a brand is differentiation. Anything that detracts from this is a threat – within the context of a favourable economic equation, of course.

To a certain extent, over-centralization is responsible for the loss of differentiation. At Fiat, the different brands are managed within the same department, with Alfa Romeo alongside Lancia and Fiat, a type of organization that leads one to wonder whether the company still believes in its brands. Conversely, PSA – Europe's second largest car manufacturer, almost on a par with Volkswagen – may use the same factories but Peugeot and Citroën remain separate organizations with their own product plan, marketing, design, publicity, sponsorship and, of course, distribution network (Folz, 2003). Volkswagen has abolished the VAG (Volkswagen Audi) network and given each brand its own distribution network. It has to be said that the sales force in the VAG network had a strong tendency to push the Volkswagen models rather than the very similar Audi models, which were 10 per cent more expensive.

Part of Seagram's problems could be explained by the over-centralized organization of its international brands. The development of international campaigns at all price levels is a classic tendency among all centralized organizations. It is significant that the first thing the buyer of Seagram did was to decentralize the organization of the brand portfolio. Thus the management of Martell, the flagship of cognac worldwide, was relocated in Cognac where famous brandy is produced, while Chivas was returned to London.

LVMH, world leader in the luxury market with such famous brands as Christian Dior, Christian Lacroix, Vuitton, Moet, Hennessy and Tag Heuer, has an interesting business model. The group manages 60 international luxury brands. When asked about the upper limit on the number of brands in such a portfolio, the group's CEO, B Arnault, replied that there wasn't one. In fact, success in the luxury sector depends on there being three types of people able to work together – in design, management and marketing – but this is impossible to achieve at a centralized level. At LVMH, however, each brand is a 'house', a mini-company, and this makes it possible to create the optimum conditions under which extremely talented people from these three areas of competence are able to work together. As heads of their 'brand-company', they are more motivated and their remuneration is directly proportional to their financial results and the international reputation of the brand.

Although it is not as widely known, l'Oréal functions in the same way. It is significant that within the l'Oréal group, reference is made to the Garnier 'house', the Lancôme 'house' and so on. These 'houses' are autonomous operational units that manage their business with an international approach.

In the field of distributor brands, changing from the single brand – usually a store brand – to private labels also affects the organization. The recent transformation of Decathlon (the world's fifth largest retailer of sports clothing and equipment), from the Decathlon brand to the so-called 'passion brands' portfolio, had far-reaching repercussions for the organization – is it in fact possible to develop 'passion brands' within a centralizing structure? The first people who have to be inspired by this passion are those within the organization, the managers and the teams, then the co-designers, the fans and the opinion leaders. There is a need to recreate a formal autonomy.

Auditing the portfolio strategically

Companies regularly reassess the relevance of their brand portfolio. Numerous matrices have been devised to help them do this – all derived from matrices used for the evaluation of the activity portfolios created by consultants such as the Boston Consulting Group, McKinsey and Mercier. These matrices incorporate profitability, the competitive situation and the potential for growth. But can matrices for the analysis of an activity portfolio be simply converted into matrices for the evaluation of a brand portfolio?

There are two possible levels of analysis. The first is the intra-brand level which evaluates the portfolio of brand products (sub-brands or daughter brands) according to the criteria mentioned above – are they in declining or non-cash generating segments, what are the growth vectors for the future? The second level asks the same questions at multi-brand level, on the global chessboard of actual and predictable competition. The lines and columns of the matrix are growth and profitability. The markets are then shown as circles whose size reflects the actual size of the market. Brands are represented as portions of these circles (markets) where the portions reflect their market share.

The most classic way of structuring a portfolio is to divide the brands into groups according to attractiveness and function. This makes it possible to identify:

- Global brands, which should theoretically be the largest source of growth in the brand contribution, and as such should receive the lion's share of investment in advertising and promotion.
- Local or regional growth brands, which have the potential to one day become global brands.
- Local or regional brands that can be qualified as 'fortress' brands and which are often the historic market leaders, 'entrenched', and therefore very profitable. There is therefore a strategic interest in maintaining these 'fortress' brands since they in fact finance the development of global brands in their own country. They are often brands in mainstream segments.
- Local or regional 'cash-cow' brands, which have a low growth rate but a strong contribution margin.

Another form of audit consists of regularly evaluating the ability of the current portfolio to ensure the profitable coverage of future markets. Is the current portfolio the right response to market developments and competitive logic?

Thus, in the insurance sector, everyone is familiar with the growth of new distribution methods, like the telephone and the internet. An insurance company cannot afford not to be represented in this way. However, since the conditions offered are so very different from those offered by the network of general agents and brokers, they need to be represented by a specialist brand. This is how UK insurer Aviva structured its brand portfolio. Eurofil was created to cover the growing segment of low-cost car insurance without creating conflict with Aviva's other insurance distribution networks.

The segmentation of a market by user status (linking volumes, expectations and competitors to the use made of the product) also makes it possible to identify unexploited pockets of growth in the current portfolio. The first question to be asked is whether a range extension would offer an opportunity to gain a foothold in these areas. In this respect, all Nivea's sub-brands reflect this determination to exploit all the potential sources of growth on the beauty-care market by capitalizing on the single Nivea brand.

When this cannot be done, a company must have the courage to launch a new brand. For instance, in 2003, after trying everything under the global Barbie brand, Mattel decided to launch the new Flavas brand.

Auditing the portfolio can also reveal if it does constitute enough of a barrier to prevent competitors entering the market, or even an incitement for them to leave. For example, it is impossible to find Orangina on the French TGV (high-speed train) network or in many airports and stations, even though it is the second largest soft-drinks brand in the country. The logic of the operators of the café-hotel-restaurant network is to choose one soft-drinks distributor offering a complete portfolio – from cola to lime and fruit juice. So clients of the Coca-Cola Company receive Fanta (a fizzy orange drink) and Minute Maid (fresh orange juice) but not Orangina. This therefore creates a local monopoly and prevents free choice among end consumers.

Portfolio management: allocating investments according to brand potential

Portfolio management entails permanent trade-offs: the company cannot invest in all its brands at the same time. One should invest only in those brands most able to deliver a high ROI in the future. Diageo has isolated eight world brands that would receive the majority of the Group's marketing investments. L'Oréal concentrates on ten brands with a marketing–sales ratio of 30 per cent.

The competitiveness of the brand and its ability to command long-term profits will be made up of two factors: its present status in the market and its ability to resist incoming attacks. The first factor taps such KPIs as relative market share (ratio of the brand's market share to market share of other brands), the size of the market and its likely future growth. Resistance is derived from the brand equity itself (how strong consumers' emotional ties to the brand are, and their beliefs vis-à-vis the brand).

Momentum also stems from the perceived innovativeness of the brand and its capacity to shape the market's evolution. Finally, for all those that depend

FIGURE 14.2 Six criteria to assess brand long-term potential

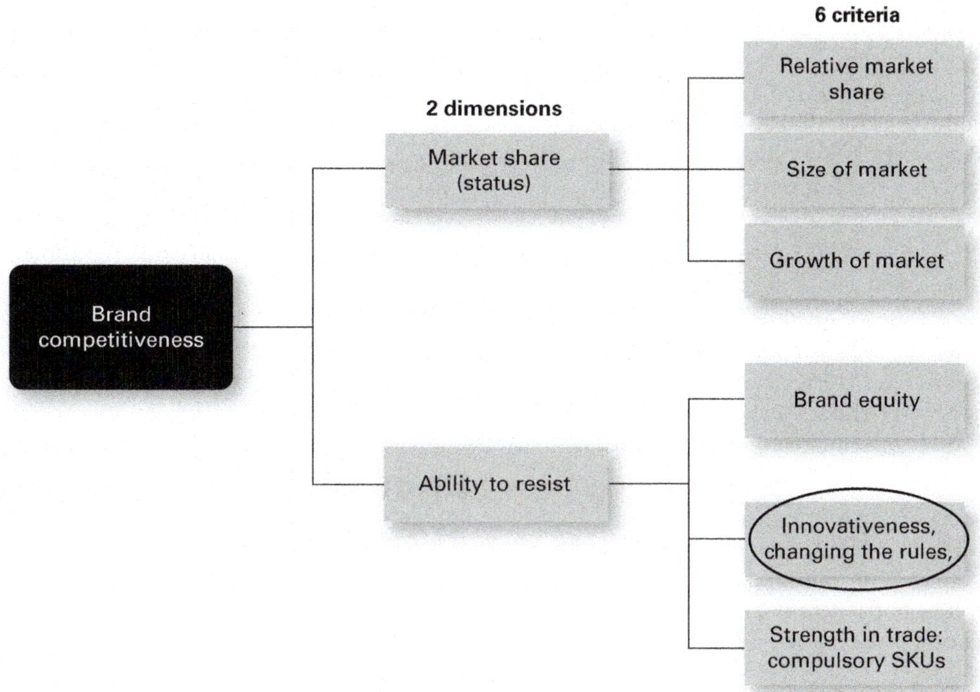

upon mass retailers, the future is brighter for those brands that have SKUs the retailer needs to create a credible shelf. These SKUs should receive a lot of attention (through incremental innovations) in order to sustain their intrinsic desirability and relevance (see Figure 14.2).

A local and global portfolio – Nestlé

How do the multinationals organize their brand portfolio to improve the efficiency of their brands simultaneously? Nestlé is an interesting example of this.

The Nestlé portfolio of 8,500 brands is organized by geographical status and role. Together they create a 'hierarchy of brands' in which each product is associated with at least two brands, at different levels in the hierarchy (not to mention brands of ingredients). The geographical criterion allows three groups of brands to be distinguished – international, regional and local brands.

These brands fulfil different functions and roles, depending on the customers, and represent the principal families of brand architecture. There are 'family brands' (or source brands), range brands, product brands and endorsing brands. Eighty per cent of the Nestlé Group's activity is brought together under six strategic corporate brands – Nestlé, Nescafé, Nestea, Maggi, Buitoni and Purina. Seventy strategic international brands, designating either ranges or products, come under – or even outside – the umbrella of these six corporate brands. They include Nesquik (an extensive range of chocolate milk products), but also product brands such as KitKat, Lion, Friskies and the mineral waters Perrier, San Pellegrino, Vittel and Nestlé Pure Life.

A third category of brands groups together 83 brands known as 'strategic regional brands', which are regional rather than international, such as mineral waters like Aquarel and Contrex, the Nuts bar, and Herta cold meats. Finally, there is a fourth category of local brands sold only in their country of origin.

Thus the Nestlé brand refers to several levels and roles:

- It is a corporate brand and as such acts as an endorsement for all the products and brands in the group. This endorsement function means that the corporate brand usually appears on the side of the packaging or on the labelling on the back.
- The Nestlé brand is also one of the six strategic corporate brands, with the status of a family brand or source brand. It covers categories as diverse as baby products, products for children, chocolates, ice cream, chocolate bars and fresh dairy products.
- The Nestlé brand is sometimes simply a product or range brand, as for example Nestlé chocolate or Nestlé condensed milk. These are the basic products, the symbolic products that lie – both literally and figuratively – at the heart of the Nestlé galaxy.

To help identify the different extensions of Nestlé the commercial brand, according to category, the categories have a different symbol. This means that, beyond the unity, there is recognition of the fact that what customers expect from a yoghurt is not the same as what they expect from baby food. Similarly, there is also a logo and symbol for Nestlé the company, that is, the corporate brand.

It is worth pointing out that 20 per cent of Nestlé's turnover is not produced under the six famous 'strategic corporate brands'. This is the case with mineral waters, for example. Perrier, which is classified as a recreational drink for adults, is indeed managed within the Nestlé Water division. But this division does not have a brand – its identification is a matter of internal organization. For clients the world over, Perrier is simply Perrier.

Brand deletion, business preservation

When a brand is no longer profitable, it should be deleted. But in order to keep its customers, its own products should be transfered to another brand of the portfolio. We now analyse this process of brand transfer.

15
Handling name changes and brand transfers

One of the most spectacular aspects of brand management, but also one of the most risky, is the changing of brand names. Some cases immediately spring to mind: Philips–Whirlpool, Raider–Twix, Andersen–Accenture, Pal–Pedigree, Datsun–Nissan. The industrial world is now used to external growth by company acquisitions and to the creation of large groups such as Novartis, AstraZeneca, Veolia and Schneider by the fusion of identities which were previously separate and independent.

This growth in brand transfers is normal: it is the consequence of capitalization, the key to modern brand management. The reorganization of multi-brand portfolios and the reduction in the number of brands has meant that the products under brands due to disappear will have to be transferred to one of the remaining brands. The same applies for companies themselves. This approach is risky: the deletion of a brand means that the market is going to lose one of its benchmarks, one of its choices or even one of the loyal customers' favourite choices. The risk of losing part of your market share is high. This is why the transfer of a brand is a strategic decision that is not to be taken lightly. To this day, empirical studies on the question are either scarce (Riezebos and Snellen, 1993), or private and confidential (Greig and Poynter, 1994). It is possible though, thanks to the accumulated experience of ten or so cases, to define the conditions for successful name changes on a local level or multinational plane.

Brand transfers are more than a name change

Brand transfers are too often thought of simply as name changes, though admittedly this is the most risky facet of the change. In the customers' minds a well-known name is linked with mental associations, empathy and personal preferences. However, a brand is made up of many components, which cannot be reduced to just one, the name. In fact, when you examine the numerous examples that have occured both in Europe and the United States, the situation is far from simple. Many of them involve other changes in the marketing mix.

Some brand changes are also product changes. What disturbed Treets fans, apart from the loss of a name they loved, was that M&Ms included two different products: peanuts covered in chocolate and a sweet similar to Smarties. It was therefore a transition from a simple and familiar situation to a confusing one. When Shell changed the name of its oil from Puissance to Helix it also modified the characteristics of the product. However, the fact that these characteristics are 'hidden', hardly perceptible by the customers, meant that this was not a risky move for Shell. The change of the oil formula could be used as an alibi for the introduction of the new name.

As regards name changes, the risks associated vary immensely depending on whether we are dealing with product brands, umbrella brands, endorsing brands or source brands. Examples of the first two cases are Raider/Twix and Philips/Whirlpool respectively. The change only affects the one and only nominal indicator of the product or products. Conversely, Puissance has become Helix but still remains under the mother brand Shell. Changing a name when the product is defined by a hierarchy of brand names is far less problematic.

With self-service, visual identity has become crucial as an aid to customers to quickly pick out their brand. Distributors' own-brands capitalize on this: their imitations, which aim at confusing the customer, rely less and less on similar names (for example Sablito against Pépito) and more and more on near identical copies of colour codes of the national brands that are targeted on the shelves (Kapferer and Thoenig, 1992). In this way, in the UK, a fierce conflict arose between Coca-Cola and the retailer Sainsbury, whose colas totally imitated the Coca-Cola colours: red for classic cola, white for sugar-free cola and gold for sugar- and caffeine-free cola. Conversely, some brand changes are accompanied by profound modifications of the colour codes. Thus, the brown Shell Puissance 5 oilcan became the yellow Shell Helix Standard oilcan. The long and gradual change from Pal to Pedigree was accompanied by the adoption worldwide of a new colour, bright yellow, striking and eye-catching, to reinforce the impact on the shelves. Since colour is the first thing that consumers notice in a self-service situation, how risky such modifications can be is all the more evident.

The shape of packaging is the second most important visual recognition factor. This is why, despite the savings that could have been achieved by adopting a unique European oilcan, Shell immediately refused to abandon its easily recognizable and very practical 'spout' can. Part of Shell oil's added value comes from this can. Finally, brand transitions can be accompanied by changes to the logo or trade mark as well as to visual symbols. As regards this last point, the impact of the disappearance of visual brand symbols shouldn't be underestimated. Replacing Nesquik's gentle giant Groquick by a rabbit in some countries for reasons of international coordination is playing with the relationship children have with Nesquik. The same applies to people associated with a brand. The disappearance of emblematic figures can have drastic consequences for a brand.

Finally, with written and musical slogans now under copyright, it has to be realized how important they are, as they are what people will remember. When Raider was changed to Twix, Mars hesitated but decided not to keep the same brand music. Music is one of the vehicles of a brand's personality. A slogan is also, in the long run, an integral part of a brand and can now be put under copyright. The famous slogan 'Melts in your mouth not in your hand' was lost when Treets became M&Ms.

Reasons for brand transfers

What are the aims behind the numerous brand changes that we are witnessing? The reasons are numerous:

- Many local brands are bought with the intention of transferring their activities to the buyer's international own brand. In this way, the latter becomes truly global. This is what Electrolux is currently doing, worldwide.
- The creation of worldwide companies leads to the same results. Ciba-Geigy and Sandoz merged under the new name Novartis.
- Firms decide to transfer brands when they decide to stop some of their activities. So when General Electric wanted to withdraw from the small domestic appliances market, Black & Decker took over with the agreement that they could only use the GE name for a limited period. No brand would want part of its image to be controlled by another company. It was the same for Philips and Whirlpool: the takeover of the former's 'white goods' activities by the latter included the agreement that the Philips name could only be used for a limited period. Looking to concentrate only on its 'brown' products and small domestic appliances, Philips only conceded its name to Whirlpool temporarily. Whirlpool bought the white activities for the European market share it immediately gave them, as well as the chance to be the world's number one domestic appliances manufacturer.
- The search for the critical size also provides an explanation for brand transfers. The Mars group abandoned its European brands Treets and Bonitos to merge them into the global brand M&Ms. To compete against McDonald's, the European Quick bought Free Time and changed its trade name.

- Brand transition is a common tactic used when trying to access a foreign market. It is basically the same ploy as the 'Trojan Horse'. The local industries in a country are often highly protected using all kinds of domestic regulations to prevent foreign product invasions. Foreign companies buy a local hero with the objective of changing its name in the future, to that of a global brand.
- With time, the name attached to a brand can become a burden to the brand's development, for example when wanting to access new activities, international markets or simply when wanting to rejuvenate a brand. Corporate names that attract bad will have to change: Philip Morris became Altria Group, Vivendi became Veolia. BSN became Danone in order to instantly gain international recognition, which would have been lengthy if not impossible with an acronym.
- Brand transfers can also be the result of lost court cases. For example, Yves Saint Laurent had to abandon the name of its brand of perfume Champagne in several countries, turning it into Yvresse. The New Zealand wine brand Montana had to change its name, because it evoked the United States. Danone Bio had to become Danone Activia because of EU rules on the right to be called 'bio'.

Moving local names to a single one, such as a US name, allows the organization to delocalize plants easily under this foreign name. This also has fiscal reasons. The foreign name can receive royalties from the subsidiaries, reducing local tax liabilities.

Financial spin-offs and divestments

Zodiac started a century ago as an aviation equipment company, which included the fabric for airships and balloons. From this stemmed its world-famous diversification: Zodiac lifeboats. However, this affected the perception of the stock market in the long run, which is why Zodiac sold its marine operations along with the name Zodiac to a hedge fund. After the sale, the remainder of the company changed its name to Zodiac Aerospace, to make it clear that Zodiac was an aerospace-only company.

Similarly, the 3M stock market evaluation was hampered by products that would suffer from the digital revolution (overhead projectors, floppy disks, etc). 3M created the Imation Company, a spin-off, and remained an adhesive and medical company. This helped the 3M stock market evaluation reappraisal.

The challenge of brand transfers

Brand transfers are everywhere. This is hardly surprising since this is the age of mergers and acquisitions, which always give rise to the rationalization of ranges, products and brand portfolios. Companies have to choose between brands that have hitherto been competitive with parallel ranges. On mature, low-growth markets, the need to make economies, create synergies and increase efficiency has the same result. Finally, globalization brings its share of brand transfers to the advantage of the global brand. For all the above reasons, reducing the number of brands is the order of the day.

This explains the wealth of publicity announcing – if you know how to read between the lines – an imminent brand transfer. For example, the Swedish company Electrolux, the world's leading manufacturer of household appliances, prepared the worldwide transfer of its local brands – the historic leaders of their market, acquired country by country. It acted as the endorsement for these local brands – Zanussi Electrolux in the UK, Arthur Martin Electrolux in France, Rex Electrolux in Italy, and so on – and appeared as such in the promotional publicity. It has to be said that, in 2003, only 15 per cent of sales were made under the brand name of this international group. The aim was to increase this figure to between 60 and 70 per cent by 2010, so that 55 per cent of consumers would include Electrolux among the 'three brands they have in mind when entering an electrical appliance store' – what is known as an 'evoked set' or 'consideration set'. In 2001, this could be said of only 21 per cent of consumers. In 2007 the local names had to change to Electrolux.

Berated by financial analysts the world over for not having enough global brands with a turnover of more than US $1 billion, the Unilever Group made the decision to reduce drastically the number of these brands in a process known as the 'path to growth'.

The group's Elida-Fabergé division played a pioneering role – by reducing the number of brands from 13 to 8, growth increased from less than 2 per cent to 11 per cent.

But this objective of reducing the size of brand portfolios also creates challenging problems in certain product categories. This happens when the brands to be merged are well established and do not have the same positioning on the market. For example, the famous detergents category is not particularly profitable compared with other categories since distribution costs are extremely high and the market is fragmented. Many of the smaller brands no longer justify the promotional support. Throughout Europe, Lever has organized its portfolio in three price-related segments – the premium segment with Skip (in competition with Procter & Gamble's Ariel), the smart buyer segment with Omo for example, and the economy (or low-price) segment with Persil (except in the UK where, for historical reasons, Persil replaced Skip). The question therefore arises, given the market shares and Lever's declared intention of concentrating its business around strong brands, how to unite the brand in the smart buyer segment with the brand in the economy segment. The difficulty becomes all the more apparent since in many countries, these are well-established brands that, over time, have forged a very specific bond with a section of the public. The issue should involve the distributors who, throughout Europe, are wondering about the future of the low-price segment, positioned just above their distributors' brands. Should this segment in fact be allowed to survive?

When the risks are too great, it is better to avoid them and choose another strategy.

When one should not switch

The internationalization of companies raises the question of the globalization of brand portfolios. This involves changing the name of the products or services of a well-known and very popular local brand to that of a less well-known and less familiar international brand. However, before considering how a company goes about making such changes in order to effect a brand transfer, the following caveat should be borne in mind. There are occasions when this transfer should not be made, if it presents too great a risk for the business and the brand capital. Thus, when BP bought the German Aral service stations in 2003, it decided not to change the brand name as it had done in California when it bought Arco. In the same year, Shell bought the other major German service-station group, DEA, but decided to bring it under the Shell banner. So who was right – BP or Shell?

In fact, they were both right. Aral is a very strong local brand, almost a national symbol, rather like the Continental tyres fitted on all Mercedes manufactured in Europe. So why would BP run the risk of severing this extremely rare bond that generates customer loyalty, in a sector already threatened by 'commoditization'? Conversely, although DEA has a good customer service record, it does not inspire the same emotional attachment and its transfer would therefore be less risky. Customer service relations are created by the people who work for the company. So, if these people remain in situ, the continuity of satisfaction is maintained and customer loyalty guaranteed.

There are other instances when a brand transfer should not be made to the advantage of a new, global brand and when it is better to retain the local name, for example when the meaning of the name to be internationalized proves problematic in the other country. Procter & Gamble's German competitor Henkel could not extend its product brand 'Somat' – designed to make glassware shine – in the UK since the word 'matt' is the opposite of shiny.

There is no shortage of examples where, to an outsider, the local brand seemed little more than a legacy from the past but was regarded locally as an icon. This happened in the case of many leading Eastern European brands, which the multinationals decided had to be replaced by the global – European or US – brand. But they had not taken account of the consumers who are often extremely emotionally attached to the local brands that are part of their everyday life and past memories. The Danone Group had to reverse such a decision in the Czech Republic. After abandoning the Opavia brand in favour of the global Danone brand, it had to reintroduce Opavia – famous for its biscuits and the country's favourite food brand – because it was a national symbol.

In this respect, the Bel group was well advised not to pursue a potential brand transfer which involved replacing the German brand Adler, famous for its processed cheese portions, with the international mega-brand, The Laughing Cow, whose prototype is also processed cheese portions. However, the symbol of the Adler brand, familiar to all Germans, has long been the imperial eagle. It is hard to imagine the juxtaposition of two more paradoxical animal logos.

L'Oréal is pragmatic when it comes to brand transfers. In line with its expressed intention of developing mainly via its 17 global brands, the group bought Maybelline, a brand of make-up sold on the US mass market. In the space of a few years, it launched the brand in 80 countries but to do so had to effect a transfer with the local brand in the principal countries concerned. The problem was that the local brand was often a strong brand that was popular with both distributors and customers – Jade in Germany, Colorama in Brazil, Missiland in Argentina, Gemey in France – while Maybelline means nothing in these countries. The group has carried out a deliberate policy of double branding for five years, introducing an increasing number of US concepts and innovations but, even so, there is still no question of setting an exact date for phasing out the local brand. Yet, as far as the financial analysts and major multinational distribution groups are concerned, l'Oréal has achieved the desired effect – by increasing the sales of co-branded products in each country, the group can say that Maybelline is the leading international brand of make-up in the mass-market sector.

When brand transfer fails

Companies that are overconfident in themselves often underestimate the emotional attachment created by local brands, long since written off by the advocates of globalization. In so doing, they do not realize to what extent brand transfers can destroy value and, above all, the value of the market share. This is illustrated by the example of Fairy in Germany. In 2000, the buzzword at Procter & Gamble was 'globalization' at all costs. In Europe, the group introduced global segmentation and all the brands that did not fit within the framework were eliminated (Kapferer, 2001, p 52). Furthermore, local brand names were to be replaced by the global brand name corresponding to each segment.

In Germany, Procter & Gamble had been successfully marketing a washing-up liquid under the name Fairy for years, with the brand reaching 12 per cent of the market share in terms of value. In the middle of 2000, the Fairy brand became known as Dawn, the name of Procter & Gamble's international brand. Nothing had changed except the name, which is a good measure of the power of the brand. However, in spite of colossal investments to inform people that Fairy was now called Dawn, the market share plummeted and, in the last quarter of 2001, stood at just 4.7 per cent, whereas it was still at 11.9 per cent on the day before the name changed. It was estimated that, in 2001, Procter & Gamble sustained a loss in turnover in Germany of US $8 million (Schroiff and Arnold, 2003). The group made the same mistake in Austria when it tried to replace Bold with Dash. In view of the destruction of value caused by these two costly mistakes, it was decided to return to the previous brand names.

What was the reasoning behind these two brand transfers? Because Fairy used the same consumer benefit as Dawn, the ability to cut through grease, Procter & Gamble thought that the brand transfer would be easy. However, this transfer was not even attempted in the UK, possibly because Fairy was positioned according to a different consumer benefit from Dawn. But the brand can also be much more than a name – it can be the sign of a certain product guarantee. Local brands inspire customer loyalty through their origins, their being a part of everyday life, their proximity, their confidence (Schuiling and Kapferer, 2003). There is a real emotional dimension in the attachment to certain brands, as has been shown by Fournier (2001) (see Figure 15.1).

So what lessons can be learnt from this example? A transfer must first of all take account of consumer opinion. A transfer must offer some form of benefit and create value for consumers. This is the key to successful transfers. Second, in the process of convergence implemented within the multinationals, the principle source of productivity is the product platform. But people tend to focus on the visible part of the product, the actual change of name, whereas this is not in fact the real issue – far from it. In globalization, the homogenization of names should be the last problem to be solved. There are also a great many fringe benefits to be gained by unifying and reducing the number of different packages, non-standardized parts and product platforms. Furthermore, productivity is vastly improved by the convergence of brand platforms, which makes it possible to use a single agency and employ the best designers. It is not important if a product has to have a different name in different regions. To quote just three examples, a leading line of male toiletries is known as Axe in Europe and Lynx in the UK, a brand of washing powder as Skip in Europe and Persil in the UK, while the Opel brand in Europe is Vauxhall in the UK.

Analysing best practices

There is not much academic research on brand transfers. It is however possible to draw on some brand and business models to clarify the conditions of a successful transfer. We selected them because they illustrate very different market situations and brand role, from mere impulse to highly risky purchase decisions, from products to services.

From Raider to Twix

In the autumn of 1991, continental Europeans were informed by a massive advertising campaign that the chocolate bar Raider was to be henceforth called Twix, Twix being the name used everywhere else in the world from New York to Tokyo and London. The difference from the Mars group's previous brand transfer (from Treets to M&Ms) where everything had changed, including the product, was that this time, great care was taken not to disturb the customers. Nothing was changed apart from the name. It was a success.

Why was the brand change necessary? Philippe Villemus, the marketing director of Mars, explained (for more details see Villemus, 1996) that Mars was a worldwide group with six brands each worth more than a billion (US) dollars, and that it wanted only to have mega-brands which satisfy the five following conditions:

- is able to meet an important, durable and global need;
- represents the highest level of quality;
- is omnipresent all over the world, and within every one's reach both physically and financially;
- creates a high level of public confidence; and
- is the leader in their segment (when this is not the case the brand is simply removed, like Treets and Bonitos).

For legal reasons it can happen that a trademark cannot be registered in a particular country or region. This was the case with the Twix name in continental Europe. As soon as the legal aspect had been dealt with by the acquisition of legal rights in certain countries, the group did not hesitate to rename Raider and to give Europe the global name.

What were the objectives behind this change of brand? In the first instance, it was to gain more market share and increase sales, otherwise, according to Villemus, there would have been no point to the operation. It is important to remember that a brand transition is not an exercise in style, but a unique opportunity to increase the share of the market. It is a competitive move. A second objective was to have a global brand. A third objective was to reduce production, packaging and advertising costs.

FIGURE 15.1 When rebranding fails: from Fairy to Dawn (P&G)

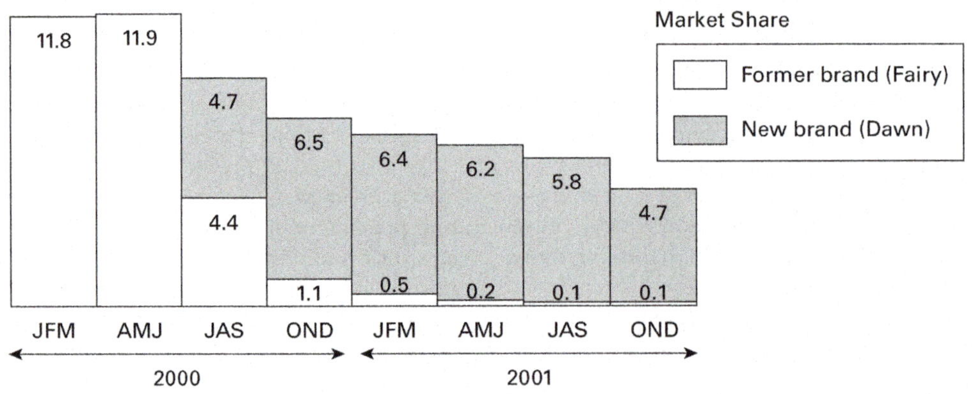

A fourth objective was to make its management easier. Finally, it was desirable to have one brand name so as to make the preparations easier for the intended brand extensions towards new sectors such as ice creams.

Raider had a strong brand equity in Europe so the transition was no small matter. It was the second most popular chocolate bar after Mars and it had an annual volume growth rate of 12 per cent. This was thanks to its specific concept and its slogan, which included a physical description of the product as well as its benefits for the customer. In France, for example, spontaneous recognition was 43 per cent, assisted recognition was 96 per cent and that of the slogan was 88 per cent. Eighty-five per cent of all adolescents had tried Raider and 44 per cent bought it on a regular basis. Knowing this, Twix was marketed as the ideal snack for adolescents and young people between the ages of 15 and 25.

Even though the customers thought that the transition was rapid, in truth it took over a year. From October 1990 to October 1991, the Raider's wrapping carried the words 'known globally as Twix' and for six months after the transition, 'Raider's new name'.

The communication objectives given to the campaign by the marketing director were:

- to communicate clearly and simply that only the name was changing;
- to transfer all Raider's values to Twix;
- to quickly obtain a high brand awareness within the target group of young people (30 per cent unaided, 80 per cent assisted);
- to make the change popular using the alibi that the new name was in tune with the rest of the world, and that Twix was a global brand for young people all over the world.

The key elements of the success of the operation were due to the flawless implementation of the strategy:

- it was very rapid: 15 days to change everything in one country (the whole transfer in Europe took three months);
- Mars made a big event of it, which maximized its visibility and the awareness created;
- promotional activities at sales outlets contributed to the impact and trial of Twix;
- finally, great care was taken to ensure good coordination with field activities. It was decided that, even if it meant buying back stock, on the day of the transfer no stocks of Raider should be left in any shops.

Looking more closely at the different means of communication that were used, we see that the packaging was the first medium. It was used for one year before the transfer to warn customers of, and to familiarize them with, the new name. It was used for six months after that to explain the transfer. In order to meet the communication objectives the advertising campaign was characterized by:

- a strong emphasis on the pack-shot to maximize the recognition;
- the interruption of all communication of the Raider brand six months before transfer day to hasten the drop in its awareness;
- a high-impact European commercial starring David Bowie;
- a strong concentration of means: in three weeks as much as the total advertisement budget for two years was spent on television advertisements alone (it is now easy to understand why it was absolutely vital that all Raider packets were removed from all sales outlets).

In shops, Twix was given prominence and was put on visible display. Twix was the focal point of all the sales force, and all other brands were sidelined in terms of priority. Supermarkets had, of course, been informed well in advance. The bar code was kept the same so that supermarkets did not take Twix to be listed as a new brand and hence claim a listing fee.

Six months after the operation, Twix's market share was the same as Raider's had been. But from then on there was only one brand name, one factory and far less complexity. Due to its young and international status, Twix's image was more modern than Raider's.

Looking back, all the decisions taken seem logical. All successful operations give the impression of being easy. But the decisions were not taken without debate. For example, some people recommended improving the recipe and announcing 'even better'. In the end it was decided, after reflection on the opposite approach of Treets/M&Ms, to change the product as little as possible. It might also have been a good idea not to change the Raider music in the change-over film to Twix. Was the modification necessary? It is said to have disturbed some customers, which goes to show just how much the brand's music is an integral part of its identity and personality.

From Philips to Whirlpool

On 1 January 1989, Philips and Whirlpool joined together to create the world's biggest household appliances group, Whirlpool International, owned 53 per cent by Whirlpool and 47 per cent by Philips. This partnership was formed with the intention of attaining a significant global size which would enable and ensure the development of a long-lasting manufacturing firm. Besides, Philips wanted to concentrate on its core activity. Finally, both companies were highly complementary, in their plant layout and industrial capacity, in innovation and in their geographic market coverage. Philips was the most important domestic appliances brand in Europe. Whirlpool, for its part, was the number one in the United States, Mexico and Brazil. With 11.1 per cent of all the goods manufactured, Philips Whirlpool overtook Electrolux (9.6 per cent) to become the world leader in the household appliances market. In 1990 the Philips Whirlpool brand was launched in Europe by a spectacular advertising campaign (US $50 million). In 1991, Whirlpool bought the remaining 47 per cent held by Philips. In January 1993, the Philips Whirlpool brand became Whirlpool in all communications, but the dual brand was kept on its products. In the last countries to make the switch, Philips was removed from all products in 1996. Via this brand transfer Whirlpool became the world number one domestic appliance brand. The importance of what was at stake and the risks involved during the brand transition become evident when one looks at the significance customers put on a brand when buying durable goods which are perceived as high-risk investments. According to a study carried out by Landor, in Europe Philips was the second-most powerful brand over all sectors. In France, another study showed that when customers were asked to mention names of brands from any sector off the top of their head, Philips was placed fifth after Renault, Peugeot, Adidas and Citroën (Kapferer, 1996). Nevertheless, it is worth noting that Philips' market share and its public brand recognition differed from country to country. This is why it was quickly apparent that it would be impossible to carry out the change in different European countries simultaneously. In the same way, the guarantee role of brands in the domestic appliances market rules out a sudden, quick transfer as was the case with Raider/Twix.

In January 1990, the assisted brand awareness of Whirlpool in Europe was non-existent. This was why a stage-by-stage progressive approach was decided upon. This included a Philips Whirlpool stage before Philips was abandoned. The case is different, therefore, from that of Black & Decker's takeover of General Electric's domestic appliances activities in the United States where both names already had a good reputation.

Another reason favoured the stage-by-stage approach. In order to ensure global coherence, Philips' products left in stores would have had to have been bought back, as Twix had been for the transfer to Raider. But this of course would have been impossible for both practical and financial reasons.

So what was Whirlpool's transfer strategy and why did they choose it? In the first instance early research had shown that customers perceived favourably the Philips Whirlpool partnership. Both companies had very different images. Whirlpool had potential, it evoked change, fluidity, movement and dynamism. It had the ideal qualities required to give the brand transfer a positive image. The fusion of both companies gave the Philips Whirlpool brand an ideal image, the dynamism of one was tempered by the solidarity of the other. Research showed that the Philips Whirlpool couple was perceived as 'sure and dynamic, solid and robust, classic and stylish, reliable and innovating'. In Europe, the arrival of Whirlpool was seen by consumers as bringing new impetus to Philips, a touch of high tech to a reliable classic brand, imagination to a brand characterized by experience.

The first thing that needed to be done was to decide upon the nature of the dual brand and its visual form. To start with, should it be called Whirlpool Philips or Philips Whirlpool? Tests revealed that the first option did not inspire confidence and that it evoked a confused perception. People associated it with jacuzzis and all 'water equipment'. On the other hand, Philips Whirlpool evoked a healthy equitable partnership or even a slight predominance of Philips. Only a minority thought that it referred to a Philips product range like that of the Philips Tracer razors. The second question regarded the graphic trademark. Should both names be written on the same line or one on top of the other? The first choice was adopted because it inspired an image of partnership and looked better.

With regard to the communication, what target should it be aimed at? Obviously the priority was the distributors. Only 20 per cent of domestic appliance customers visit a shop with a specific brand in mind, and only 10 per cent, ie half of them, actually buy that brand. This shows the importance of sales outlet staff in the sale of these products. Whirlpool started in 1990 a considerable communication effort aimed at retailers – this is a little known facet of brand transfers. This, of course, was addressed to the big European or national retail bosses, but it was also used by Whirlpool's sales force with customers, shop owners and sales staff whose opinions were so influential on consumers. Moreover, Whirlpool's image was that of an innovating leader, so merely confining oneself to innovations in products and services would have been limited. Whirlpool brought about a revolution in producer–distributor relations, a new approach that distributors weren't accustomed to, which not only touched on services but market information and more besides. As regards the consumers, the plan was to reassure them as quickly as possible by the rapid acquisition of brand awareness and a strong image of quality and innovation.

These communication objectives had several important operational consequences. On the one hand, wanting to associate with Whirlpool an image of quality and innovation implied that the brand transfer on the products themselves had to take place progressively, in line with the launch of new products and the rejuvenation of Philips' old ranges. If this had not been the case the project would have suffered from the Talbot-Chrysler syndrome, where the only thing that was changed on the vehicles was the name on the bonnet. The Whirlpool brand on its own was not to be found on an old product. Launching a new brand implies taking great care over the early impressions the brand would create among the European audiences. Giving Whirlpool a quality image involved prohibiting all promotional advertising of any sort in the media during the first years of establishing the brand in Europe. Finally, as it is impossible to pursue an image objective and an awareness objective at the same time, it was obvious that to the classic advertising a media action had to be added so as to quickly reach the required level of brand awareness before the final brand transfer, ie two-thirds of the assisted awareness of Philips. It is certainly true that, in the case of durable goods, the involvement of consumers is low when they are not actually engaged in the buying process – which is most of the time. When the consumer is not considering a purchase, the means of persuasion that should be adopted are very specific. When consumers' attention disperses, a multiple contact approach should be privileged, even if received incidentally. This calls for a high number of (gross rating point) *GRP*. Consumer resistance can become weak; in this case contact should be received in an agreeable ambience to benefit the effect of the affective transfer to the brand. Finally, when the consumer is not ready to make a cognitive effort one must repeat the consumer benefits of the brand rather than point out the difference between specific products.

This is why, in some countries, Whirlpool invested large amounts of money sponsoring prime-time TV programmes. This choice was no coincidence; they represent viewers' favourite moments on the most popular channels, and are often associated with a relaxed family atmosphere. Thanks to this strategy, the brand awareness made considerable progress. In all the countries where only traditional commercials were used, the awareness reached was less significant.

It was indeed important to separate the treatment of the Philips brand in the media and in sales outlets. In the media, it was necessary to stop mentioning the brand as quickly as possible, otherwise the brand would only have been reinforced when the objective was to see a decline in its spontaneous awareness. This is why, during the short period when the dual brand existed, Philips Whirlpool adverts finished with the dual brand but the signature tune only mentioned Whirlpool. This was to ensure that only this brand was associated with the innovations.

As early as January 1993, it was decided to remove Philips from all TV adverts. This put an end to any reinforcement of Philips' awareness. What is more, it sent the message to retailers that Whirlpool, the market leader, no longer needed the Philips guarantee and that the transfer programme was ahead of schedule.

On a European level, how was the multiplicity of countries to be dealt with? Taking into account the differences in the market shares and the brand equity that Philips had from country to country, all monolithic approaches were ruled out. Some countries wanted to pass to the single brand, Whirlpool, quickly. Others would have liked more time: where Philips' reputation was excellent, it could not be removed overnight if the objective was not only to maintain market share but also use the transfer to increase it. The order in which each country was to have the Whirlpool brand transfer was decided using a multi-criteria analysis, which took into account, for each country:

- Philips' market share;
- the presumed reaction of the distributors (based on an ad hoc survey);
- the strength of the brand in the eyes of consumers (brand recognition, evoked set, preference);
- the influence of retailers on the customers' decisions;
- the feeling that the management in the country was ready for the abandonment of the Philips brand.

Recent research on the transfer from the local brand Libertel to Vodafone seems to indicate that a dual branding phase does not in fact transfer values from the former to the latter. In fact brand values must be built, they are not simply transferred by this tactic of dual naming for a while. Attaching two names is creating a third one. In the Philips–Whirlpool case, the dual naming gave saliency (brand awareness) to Whirlpool, but did not transfer the values of Philips onto Whirlpool. Its first objective was to maintain the consumer or customer loyalty and the trade franchise, which would have deserted if the name Philips had not been maintained as an endorser of the totally unknown American newcomer.

Transferring a service brand

Services need to be analysed separately. On the one hand, unlike product brands, service brands have nothing to show: they are intangible. Their name is the proof of their existence. Brand awareness and saliency is of vital importance. On the other hand, their nature can make brand transfers easier, because they are often tied to a place (the specific geographical location of service delivery, of 'servuction'). In addition, the driver of loyalty is the direct relation with the salesperson, agent or staff. This is not to say that the brand is of no importance: when BP and Shell took over two German networks of petrol distribution, much care was taken in handling the situation. Not recognizing the name and visual identity of the gas station they have historically, if not ritually, used acts as a deterrent for many German consumers.

However, global brands are created by replacing local leaders by global names. This is how Axa built its global worldwide brand recognition, acquiring local leaders and instantaneously moving them to Axa, as a way of immediately indicating internally what the strategy was, namely to become the local arm of the first worldwide insurance brand. In the service business, hesitations and dual brandings may create some internal doubts about the future strategy, and lead people to defend their former identity instead of thinking of the new future. As a result, the internal phase comes first and foremost in service brand transfers. A lot of discussion groups must be created, for the sake of communication and release of tensions, whereby all parts of the company that has been taken over can express how they see the future and concretely build the pathways to become the quality arm of the new global brand. Two recent cases are interesting in that respect, Accenture and Orange.

The Accenture case

On 7 August 2000 the International Arbitrage Court, in the case between Andersen Consulting (AC) and Arthur Andersen and Andersen Worldwide, ruled that among others things, AC would not be allowed to use its existing name after 1 January 2001. It had less than 145 days to transfer its intellectual, technological and reputational capital to a new brand.

The first step in this process consisted of an internal wide-scale and in-depth interrogation on what was expected from the new brand:

- What new values should it foster?
- It should attract what types of new consultants?
- How could it contribute to the development of business?
- How could it reinforce differentiation?
- What changes could be suggested?

The process of name choice was also internally managed by means of a 'brandstorming' process. All employees were asked to participate. On 1 September 2000 various names were proposed by

Landor, a globally known design agency. On 21 September, 2,677 proposals were made internally, for such names as Future Creation Group, Global Already, Deep Thought, Mind Rocket and Global Curves. On 5 October, 68 names were screened for legal registrability, international semantic connotations, availability of the domain name and so on. On 12 October, 29 finalists were submitted to a vote at the firm's Miami Congress, and 10 of these were discussed by a brand steering committee on 23 October. Finally, on 25 October, Accenture was selected. This name had been proposed by the Norwegian senior manager, to convey putting the accent on the future. To help fulfil the mission (reinventing the business to win in the new economic context), the key words linked to this brand would be agile, visionary, well connected and passionate.

As a rule, communicating a new brand aims at creating an immediate boost of unaided awareness and suggesting the new values of the brand. To regain its status within the very closed club of the big five accountancy/consulting firms, a blitz communication strategy was chosen in this case. US $175 million was budgeted to reach these two objectives worldwide, and the goal was to reach 30 per cent awareness in three months.

Here again, the emphasis of service brands is on employees. For the sake of an efficient brand alignment, 50 work groups were created to manage the name change in 137 countries. This involved creating a new internet site, internal communication kits, communication with 20,000 managers in client companies, communication with thousands of potential candidates, and of course communication for introducing the name on stock exchanges. As the global campaign put it, the company was renamed, redefined, reborn.

Moving to Orange

On 30 May 2000 the UK's third largest mobile phone operator, Orange, was acquired by FT, the incumbent national French operator. As with all former monopolies, FT needed a commercial brand to carry its offer and eventually extend it to other services internationally. British Gas had created a precedent with the creation of a commercial brand to offer services to households, including its traditional utilities but also insurance and financial services. The goal of FT was to make Orange the second largest operator in Europe, after Vodafone. In 2005, the objective was to be present in 50 countries.

In each country, the strategy was to rename the local operating company as Orange, exploiting this opportunity to capture the high-consumption-rate young consumers segment. Up to then the former monopoly telecomms organizations had not looked very attractive to them. The success of Orange in the UK had been based on a disruptive approach to the mobile phone business, epitomized by the simplicity of its name. In fact, its six brand values were dynamism, modernity, simplicity, transparency, proximity and responsibility. These values contrasted strongly with those of the UK's former monopoly telecomms company, BT. Orange in the UK had been a challenger brand, proposing a true relationship with consumers, an innovation after decades of monopoly offerings.

In the countries in which Orange would now operate, the challenge became to make a local former monopoly, often still the market leader, acquire the brand and adopt its values. The goal of the brand transfer was first and foremost to get across the 'Orange attitude'. The difficulty was to align the company itself, the employees and the newly acquired brand values in each country. The process was divided into three steps: 'Let's build Orange' (defining the brand's values, and understanding them), 'Let's live Orange' (understanding how to put these values into action), and 'Let's launch Orange' (the communication launch itself).

The second phase involved an in-depth immersion of each employee in the new values, both individually and within his/her functional team. Scores of focus groups, internal meetings, and global sessions would slowly build up that understanding over a period of one year.

The director of human resources would naturally be part of the process of 'Let's live Orange'. For instance, an evaluation grid was created, to help measure how each participant stood in achieving the brand values. In addition, to foster group adhesion, this form was to be completed by all the members of the individual's team, as a measure of how others saw each person's performance. Two other regular features, 'all in store' and 'all on line' were intended to help employees understand in practice the challenges of selling the Orange way.

The 'Let's launch Orange' phase was designed to provide the opportunity to make a strong impression, accentuating the idea that a radical new offer was now present in the marketplace. The media were key in conveying this impression and helping to immediately capture new consumers. Employees were also involved, and each one was sent a cassette and CD-ROM outlining the full launch process. Finally, all existing clients were to be contacted individually to tell them about the name change and what it would mean for them.

How soon after an acquisition should the name change?

There are two paths to growth: organic, internal growth, or the acquisition of brands and products from elsewhere. Companies are increasingly coming to rely on external growth. In fact, we are used to hearing that one company has bought another: Google buys YouTube or MySpace. In industrial electrical equipment, Hager grows in Europe through buying out local leaders (such as Ashley and Klik in the United Kingdom) – leaders that have market share, reputation, a loyal client base and the respect of distributors. The question then arises of whether these brand names, with their reputations at the local or technical specialist level, should be retained.

Four factors explain the enthusiasm for external growth:

- It is a consequence of saturated markets: growth is achieved by buying the market share of another company, linked to a headline product, an innovation and a brand.
- We can also note a degree of dissatisfaction with internal innovation. Spotting external tendencies and snapping them up is the faster route.
- It is the end result of the tendency to fall back on the 'core business', on what the company is best at and where its competitive advantage is greatest. This is why groups sell their so-called peripheral businesses. Thus Bel (Laughing Cow, Kiri, and so on) sold its 'regional' cheese business (for example le Rouy) to Lactalis (Président and Société) in 2003. During these acquisitions, the question of names and architectures raises its head. For example, should le Rouy be called le Rouy by Président?
- Finally, these acquisitions are often part of a strategic plan consisting not only of buying market share, but also of developing a European or world brand.

The question of architecture immediately arises for innovations stemming from external growth. Can the acquiring company impose its name from the start, without losing customers – in both senses of the word 'lose'? For example, Philips bought the Sonicare company (no relation to Sony), a specialist in oral hygiene the world over. Sonicare sold an innovative product under its name, a revolutionary electric toothbrush, which had become the reference among dentists. What should this innovation be called once it had entered the Philips fold, and what brand(s) should it have? Sonicare has a good reputation in the United States and Japan, but less so in Europe. The reverse is true for Philips. Should it then follow the same architecture, in accordance with the dogma of globalization? Or should it adapt to the markets?

Fundamentally, three phases of the decision process can be identified:

- First is the question of coherence. Is this innovation coherent with the brand the organization hopes to build? Imagine that Philips wished to reinvent its brand worldwide around the values of sense and simplicity. Philips wants to be recognized – to a greater extent than current image studies show – as a leader in innovation with sense, innovation that is close to and simplifies daily life. This kernel identity of two values allows it to carry out an initial sorting of innovations that do or do not follow this direction, and of companies to buy and not to buy. Sonicare was in fact coherent with Philips' new desired identity. In contrast, when we worked with Citroën on its repositioning, the brand's executive director reminded us that since the products designed three or four years ago had not yet been launched on the market, it was impossible to enact a public repositioning. It would have been immediately contradicted by the models to be launched, themselves the fruit of a previous vision of what Citroën would become.

- The question of strategy: should the product be launched alone, or should it be part of a strategic alliance? In the case of an alliance, the daughter brand is almost obligatory, since with co-branding neither brand can innovate graphically.

  For example, Philips allied itself with the Dutch coffee giant Douwe Egberts to create Senseo, a coffee-maker that makes the best coffee at home, without having to pay the high prices for Nespresso. Note that in the latter case, Nestlé appears to have retained mastery over the project, since the daughter brand is a variation on the word Nestlé, combined with the generic word espresso, whereas the coffee maker is made by Krups, part of the Seb group.
- The third question is that of acceptability to the market. In short, there may be a difference between the brand's 10-year vision and its current situation among particular targets. One must not mistake desire for reality. In this case, the brand cannot act alone. It needs an ally, an intermediary: this is the role of the daughter brand. For example, in order to penetrate and dominate the feminine shaving market, Gillette uses a worldwide daughter brand, Venus. Furthermore, it follows the endorsement brand architecture. Venus is written in large type, with Gillette mentioned in small letters at the bottom of the packaging.

  In truth, Gillette is a masculine brand – some might even say macho. 'Masculine perfection' is the brand's international slogan. This image profile is hardly likely to generate value among the majority of women. They insist on maintaining their self-concept – even though there are genuine advantages to the product. Gillette remained pragmatic and discreet, and emphasized Venus, a reassuring hymn to femininity. This example shows clearly how the choice of a name arises from the choice of an architecture. The product is indeed Venus – by Gillette.

Depending on the gap that exists between the brand's current profile and the expectations of the target of the innovation in question, different architectures will be selected. The more the image is a handicap, the more likely it is that reduced visibility will be selected (maker's mark architecture). Otherwise, it is possible to go as far as dual branding architecture, or source branding.

- The fourth question is planned evolution. In fact, the architecture selected in the first phase is only provisional. Remember that one of the functions of the innovation is to provide the brand's identity kernel with traits that it had previously lacked. Once these traits have been acquired, and the gulf that existed between the brand and the target has been reduced, the architecture originally chosen no longer has any reason for existing. It needs to evolve. This is expressed in Figure 15.2, showing a decision-making model developed with the Dutch consultancy agency VODW.

  If everyone is in agreement with the final objective of a brand transfer, the timetable and the phases of the operation are crucial. As the schema shows, as the brand becomes more coherent with the market's expectations, under the effects of communication and time, the brand can take greater visibility on the product and move from a discreet endorsement or maker's mark to that of the unique source or masterbrand in the final phase.

The decision-making tree is based on the image diagnosis among the targeted clients – whether and how much the overall brand (later to become the only brand) is in step with the specific category expectations in the country in question. If it is already at 100 per cent, then a rapid brand change is desirable. If it is low, then the image of the generalist brand risks causing offence and damaging the product's sales, making the competing sales forces' job easier. This is typically the case during the takeover by a generalist of a highly specialized brand, fetishized by a particular segment. It is important to not forget the final objective (to finally arrive at a single name), but to proceed in stages.

We have sketched out the stages to indicate the different phases to be followed in the graphical relationship between the product-brand and the global brand. Through the different stages, an evolution of perception occurs, bringing the global brand's image closer to the expectations of the category's or

FIGURE 15.2 A stepwise approach to brand transfers (relating the speed of transfer to the image gap) (Kapferer/VODW)

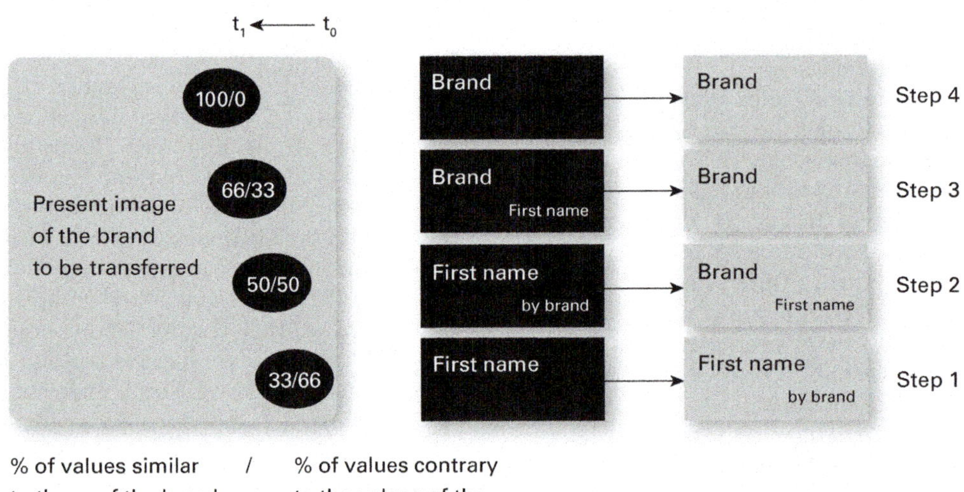

segment's customers in the country, or the segment in question. This makes it possible to move to the final stage, above. This process should be undertaken at a regional level: even for global brands, business is always local. Therefore, these progressive transfers should be implemented along a local timetable, determined according to the local image diagnostic.

Managing resistance to change

It is a fact that brand changes arouse hostility, which can be a real danger in terms of the effect on market share. The source of the opposition can be found with consumers, with distributors and also internally. From the clients' point of view a brand change is not a superficial act, but it affects the very identity of the product. There is therefore a perceived risk of altering the implied contract. This is especially the case in emerging countries. A change of design is interpreted as a sign of a counterfeit product. It is also the case in the service industry. When there is a lack of any tangible element the brand becomes the heart of all contractual relations. Besides, we have already seen that a brand can only be successfully extended to cover a new category of products if it is seen to be legitimate (Chapter 9). This was Black & Decker's principal challenge when it took over General Electric's domestic electrical appliance activities.

A successful brand transfer also has to deal with distributors. In the industrial world with long distribution channels, retailers tend to choose a few complementary brands that they stick with. Having promoted these brands, they have inevitably linked their reputation with them and their customer loyalty derives from them. To change a brand is therefore like questioning 10 or 15 years of good and loyal service. A retailer loyal to a brand expects something in return from the company. A simple presentation of the strategic reasons why a company should replace brand X by brand Y is not enough, even if the products remain identical. There must be some compensation. The situation is completely different when dealing with supermarkets who care far less about brands apart from their own. Here their analysis is much more down to earth: is this an opportunity to receive a listing allowance for the new brand or a contribution to the temporary hassle incurred by the transfer? Also, distributors will not hesitate to criticize any operations aimed at placing a weak brand under the umbrella of a strong one in order to improve its shelf prominence.

Finally, one must not forget the internal and human elements of resistance. Generally speaking, all brand changes have to pass through managers who will inevitably be attached to their own brand. When l'Oréal decided to give Ambre Solaire a modern technological dimension by placing it under the umbrella brand Garnier, the division came up against numerous pockets of resistance in Europe. In the UK, where Ambre Solaire had a good name and Garnier was unknown, the partisans against the change pushed forward the fact that the future signature brand Garnier had little recognition. The opposite was true in France: the Garnier management argued on the basis that Ambre Solaire suffered from a bad reputation, and that the change might devalue their brand. In the end the operation did take place and Ambre Solaire sales increased from €4 million to €20 million.

The precautions taken by the British group ICI when it made an apparently insignificant brand change, transferring the leading paint brand in the French market Valentine to 'ICI Dulux Valentine', illustrate the need to take into account these three stumbling blocks. The precautions aimed solely at the personnel showed just how much they were involved. The personnel at Valentine were attached to their brand so much that they saw themselves as its trustees and looked after it as if it were their own. This is why they took any brand modification to heart, and the dividing line between evolution and dispossession was very fine. The importance of internal communication during this brand change was therefore absolutely crucial if feelings of loss of identity were to be avoided and all thoughts of disappearance kept at bay.

As a result, one of the first things to be done was the setting up of a selective information policy. Only the people who worked closely on the project were informed of progress. The project itself was given a code name rather than a title which would have given the game away. Afterwards, when the deadline date was imminent, the personnel were told. The operation was presented as a step forward and not as the end of the Valentine company once bought by the ICI giant.

The sales force was gathered for a big presentation on the evolution of the European market, on ICI and on its Dulux brand. Particular attention was given to the worldwide importance of Dulux, to its long history (founded in 1930), to its sympathetic and relaxed communication strategy (projection of advertisements), to its content and to its corporate values. The change was presented not as a big event but rather a natural evolution which would bring real and important benefits to the customer.

This gathering was held six months before the brand change. A notable consequence of this date was that all internal rumours were avoided, at least on a large scale.

Some of the distributors were informed very early on of the name change. It is worth remembering that they were part of the cause of the decision to change, because they also favoured a European extension and therefore wanted a European brand. They could not therefore oppose the principle of a brand change. All that was needed was to show them that everything would be done to assure a smooth transition.

Some retailers were informed a whole year before the name change directly by Valentine managers, when internally only the people responsible for the project knew about it. On the other hand, shopkeepers were forewarned by Valentine sales representatives only three months beforehand. Finally, department or shelf managers were informed by mail, just before the change, that on 23 March 1992, ICI Valentine was to become ICI Dulux Valentine. The letter was accompanied by a free luxurious badge of the Valentine mascot, a panther. And when the Valentine sales force next came by they distributed an ICI Dulux Valentine watch (blue background, 12 yellow stars for the 12 hours of the clock and a black panther in the middle) which was such a great success that some people still wear it.

In fact, if this brand transfer was carried out without any hitches, it is because it was presented as an adaptation to meet the constraints of the retailers, and therefore more for their benefit than a revolutionary brand change. What is more the new packaging was intended to make the distributors' life easier and the product clearer and more comprehensible for the consumer, and it permitted a more homogeneous organization of the shelves.

It had already been established that it was more practical, from the clients' point of view, to organize shelves according to purpose (paint for floors, for ceilings, for wood, for steel, etc), rather than according to brands. Thanks to the new packaging, customers could easily find all the information they needed, paint for the kitchen, for the bedroom, etc.

What is more, Valentine made sure that the brand change would not upset the shelf layouts and that no extra work was needed by the distributors. They also decided that at no point should there be the two different brand names on the same shelf. This is why 180 people carried out the necessary relabelling when the transfer took place in each of the 620 shops concerned. What is more, a freephone number was made available to the retailers should any kind of problem occur.

Tests to measure consumer reactions were also carried out before the brand change. Tachytoscope tests (successive presentations of the old and new packaging) revealed that both versions of the packaging were equally well associated to the brand.

Another benefit for the customer was the opportunity to quickly reorganize the whole range of paint products into sectors according to the main kinds of uses. In normal circumstances this would have taken three years. This makes the customers' choice much easier when they do not know what kind of paint to use in the room or on the surface that they are repainting.

Factors of successful brand transfers

Although the cases looked at and their particular situations vary a lot, it is still possible to draw an overall lesson from the principal experiences in this domain. For fast-moving consumer goods a good summary is by Philippe Villemus, former marketing director of Mars, who remarks:

> Above all, this kind of operation requires a combined effort from all the company departments: production, logistics, sales force, marketing and general management. All will be concerned and any false note will be a source of problems.
>
> Second, it is vital that this event be considered an opportunity and not a constraint. The transfer must be an occasion for reappraisal, when the strengths and weakness of the brand can be rethought, and an occasion to gain new market shares by profiting from the extra attention that the new brand will have for a while. In this respect the transfer has to be seen positively by the personnel, the distributors and the consumers, so the benefits that the new brand will bring for each of them must be specified.
>
> A brand transfer cannot be improvised, it must be well prepared. The retailers, prescribers, opinion leaders and the personnel must all be warned well in advance.
>
> The time factor is crucial: one must wait until all the customers are aware of the change, and if the operation has to be carried out quickly, one must have, at one's disposal, the communications means necessary to be able to let them know.
>
> You cannot force a brand change on retailers. Not only should they be informed but everything possible should be done to facilitate their work. That means no double stock. The same product codes should be maintained. This approach not only reduces demands for listing allowances, it makes the rotation of the new brand easier. In the case where a new code is introduced, the chances are that the optical check-outs will not be able to read them because the new reference has not been registered at a central level nor in the shop's computer system.
>
> Even when the transfer is to take place in transitional phases, like a double brand phase before the actual inversion, one should still opt for the quickest time frame. It is true that the average purchase frequency should be taken into account; the frequency of paint purchases compared to that of ultra-fresh produce leads to very different minimal transitional periods. To linger too long only results in being bogged down and losing one's way. This was the case of the Pal to Pedigree transition which took several years. Retrospectively, the process would have benefited if it had been shorter, or even, as in the Raider/Twix case, instantaneous and accompanied by a strong advertising campaign.
>
> Nothing is more shocking to the customer than the strategy of 'fait accompli', imposed without warning, information or explanations. The loyalty to the brand is dented by this sudden disaffection and lack of consideration. Lessons have been drawn from the Treets/M&Ms mishap.
>
> (Villemus, 1996)

A typical 'fait accompli' is the sudden change from Coke to New Coke on 8 May 1985. That event was called the marketing blunder of the century. In fact the brand change nearly created a revolution in the United States that forced the return of the classic Coca-Cola to the shelves and the disappearance of New Coke. After having advertised during more than a century that Coke was the real thing, it was odd to force consumers to change without any warning. Consumers need to be respected: they want to understand how a change will create value for them.

A brand transfer is always an act of violence, unlike mere extensions which preserve the consumers' freedom of choice. A brand is much more than a name, it is an emotional link (Fournier, 2000). One does not lose a friend without harm and pain, even resentment.

Today, most brand transfers are explained to clients or consumers. They are forewarned and reassured. They learn how the new brand intends to provide more value to them. Also, in order to not lose consumers at the point of purchase, the former brand recognition signs are maintained for a while. Finally, a tag line can be added on the packages, after the shift, reminding that 'this is the new name of ...'.

Last, but not least, to achieve successful brand transfers it is important to know what characteristics the customer identifies with the brand and where its equity lies. The Shell Helix case is revealing in this respect. Having decided to replace all its local lubricant brands with one European brand, Shell left the coordination of the transition to its subsidiaries. France was a particular problem in view of the share of the automobile oils market enjoyed by the self-service supermarkets (more than 50 per cent). The strategy that was adopted consisted of the launch in September 1992 of a top-of-the-range oil called Shell Helix Ultra. It was added to the local Puissance range of products, keeping its characteristic can with a practical spout, but in a different colour, grey.

In reality, despite the brand awareness scores of the name Puissance, the strength of the brand was in fact associated not with its name but with its colour! The customers should have been informed of a transition from brown to yellow rather than solely a name change from Puissance to Helix.

In durable goods sectors and in service sectors, in fact in all sectors with high perceived risk, it is important to stress the role of internal communications. Brands are not abstractions, they are literally carried by people who identify with them. To change the brand is to change their identification. They need to adhere. This is of paramount importance for corporate brand changes.

A prerequisite: informing the fans

Odd as it may look, some marketers have still not realized that brands belong to their public as much as to their legal owner. Gap had forgotten it but learned it at its own expense in October 2010. The brand, shaken by an identity crisis, had decided to change its logo... without warning anyone. It showed its new logo, which was supposed to look more modern, on 8 October. This created such a backlash from fans in the social media that Gap had to revert to the old logo, which everyone liked as it was. Gap management apparently had not drawn lessons from New Coke. In an age of consumer empowerment, iconic brands must be very careful not to lose the support of their fans. This has been a key success factor for MINI: BMW took care. It informed and consulted the Mini fan clubs all around the world. Had these fan clubs sent negative warnings about the loss of the Mini spirit, MINI would not have achieved 250,000 cars after a year of sales.

Name changes create an opportunity to talk about the future, to consult and to ask for advice. Fans like to participate, to be consulted and to co-create. We market with them, not to them.

Changing the corporate brand

To the precautions to take when changing a brand name a few more can be added when dealing with company names. These are based on the fact that there is always a strong internal public and a multitude of external micro-publics.

The first problem that should be avoided is that of rumours, which will always portray a different picture of the change than the reality. The internal public is quick to interpret any change in terms of a crisis, serious problems or shareholder pressure, especially when new majority shareholders have arrived. A big effort is therefore needed to explain the situation. As regards the external public, they generally under-evaluate internal problems. The name change does not bring them any specific advantages so there is no reason for them to pay too much attention. But if they did understand they might go along with the decision, so the name change must be made relevant to them. Finally, each micro-public demands a specific action. In this way, with regard to the transfer of corporate names, the first problem that has to be resolved is that of the stock market traders. If the company is quoted in about 10 markets around the world, it has to be certain that right from day one all financiers will be looking for the right letter in the finance sections of their newspapers.

In July 1999 a small energy company, Total, took over the large Elf company, thus creating the fourth largest energy company in the world, and the only one that was not Anglo-Saxon in origin. Naturally, the success of such corporate mergers goes far beyond the topic of the present chapter. Reducing it to a name change would be looking through a tunnel. However, names do play a role in such mergers. In this case the names were not changed immediately to increase the chances of success of the whole operation.

According to the general management of TotalFinaElf, the merger was a success because of the following factors:

- It was well prepared by the company taking over. For instance, they had already analysed all the personnel of the target company. Just one month after the takeover, a new organization chart was issued, so all the employees in the former Elf company learned quickly where they would now stand.
- The company taking over had the courage of respecting a 50:50 equilibrium in all assignments, teams and staffs and did not act as a victor.
- Hundreds of committees were created to discuss all types of topics, so that yesterday's enemies became less hostile, learnt to know each other and eventually became friends.
- After the takeover the group took as its name TotalFinaElf and kept it for three years. This name was chosen for internal purposes. It indicated that no one was defeated. Keeping the name of the companies that had been taken over was a sign of respect. Externally it was a sign of power.
- Only in 2003 was the group name changed to Total, after an intense probe of the internal climate. However, the Total logo did change at this occasion. The new Total is not the same as the former Total: the new logo conveyed the new values of this leading European fuel company. A merger is a unique opportunity to create a leap forward. Why come back to a former name, and not start with a clean slate as Novartis (formerly Ciba Sandoz) or Aventis (formerly Hoechst Rhone Poulenc) have done? These laboratories have brands as assets, their medical and pharmaceutical product brands. The assets of an energy company are found in its petrol reserves. They depend heavily on the reputation the company has built up under its name in all oil-producing countries over 50 years of activity. Total was a key asset: it meant trust all around the world. In addition, the international financial community expect the Total financial management team to continue in place, and the continuity was intended as a way of reassuring them.

Do corporate name changes affect stock value?

Some corporate name changes are cosmetic, as when Alsthom decided to drop the h and become Alstom. Some others are non-events, as when Bank Paribas became Paribas or Group Schneider Electric became Schneider Electric. Other changes introduce news, as when TotalFinaElf became Total again (Total had bought the two other companies two years earlier). However, there are also important name changes associated with the birth of a new organization or company, as when Adia and Ecco merged and became Adecco or when Snecma and Sagem decided to reduce their dual name, too long and difficult to pronounce, and moved to Safran.

To change a corporate name is to send a strong message both internally and externally, to the financial markets. Symbolically it announces a new company, based on new projects. Does the official announcement of the name change lead to an increase in share value, or has the stock market already internalized the change prior to the announcement?

Research has indicated mixed results. For instance, Horsky and Swyngedow (1987) found that name changes do improve profit performance, although modestly. Naturally it is not the mere name that achieves this result, but the accompanying new organization. However, Bosch and Hirschey (1989) found a negative valuation effect in the post-announcement period, cancelling the benefits registered around the announcement date. Akhme and Kapferer (2006) analysed stock variations from 10 days before till

10 days after the official announcement date. This time dimension was chosen because it is the period in which rumours are flourishing in the financial markets (Kapferer, 1990). As a result, the markets may very well have anticipated the name change before its official announcement. Hence there may be a corrective negative effect once the announcement is made.

As can be seen from Figure 15.3, the name change does have an effect on the market valuation. This effect is stronger for radical name changes. Not all name changes create surprise or send an important message. It is noticeable that the effect starts before the official announcement. The authors demonstrated that this effect was strongest for service companies, followed by the financial sector and banks.

FIGURE 15.3 How strong corporate name changes produce excess returns on the stock exchange

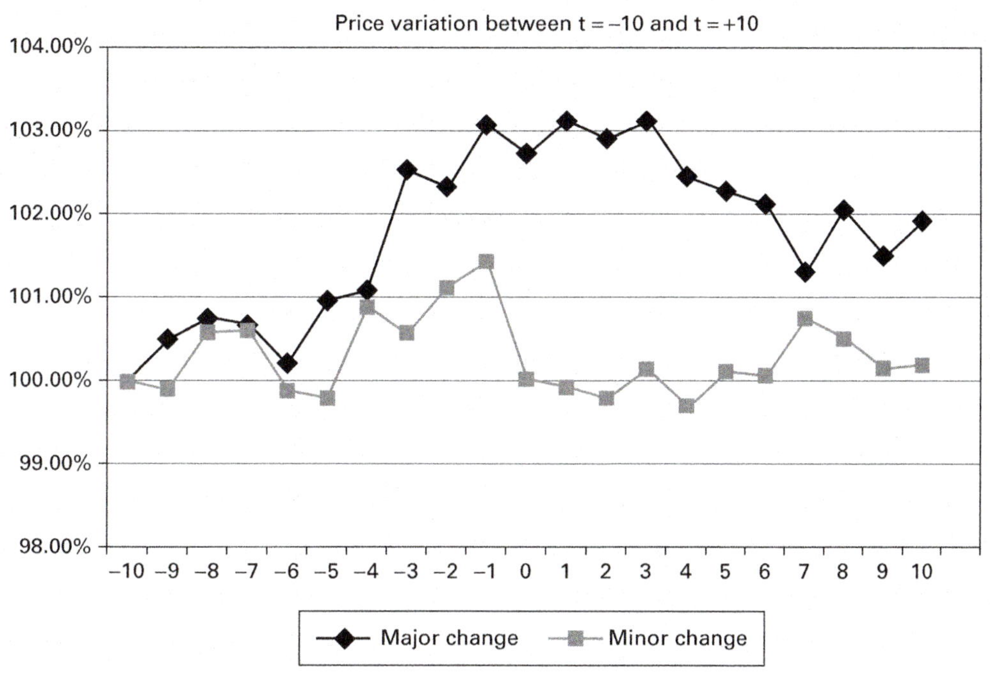

SOURCE Akhme and Kapferer (2006)

16 Brand turnaround and rejuvenation

Regularly brands that had disappeared make a comeback. New management or an investment fund may have decided to recapitalize on their name and make a new offer to modern targets. Investment funds and business angels are fond of sleeping beauties, brands whose name still evokes resonance in our memory. There are good reasons for that. As assets, these brands are still endowed with brand awareness, attributes, beliefs: it is less costly to start from these premises than to restart from scratch. This is why, for instance, in 2001 BMW relaunched the Mini, the iconic British car brand.

Second, old brands evoke nostalgia, a value enhancing emotion. Part of the youth of many consumers in our ageing societies, they evoke the ebb of life and good times past. Some of these consumers may want to recapture these emotions, as a symbolic way to stop the passage of time (Brown *et al*, 2003). Third, their values still have relevance for today's consumers.

It is necessary to differentiate clearly between a number of close and related concepts: a vintage product relaunch, a reinvention, an old product facelift and a brand revitalization:

- An old product relaunch consists in taking a product from the past and selling it as it was. In 2001, Wal-Mart listed a new and unknown brand, Lorina. This brand comes from a small company selling lemonade. For all distributors, lemonade is a commodity: the cheapest is the better. One litre of standard lemonade is sold at around a quarter-euro. Lorina sells it for €4. It has recreated the exact lemonade people used to drink in the 1950s, with a typical glass bottle, a very specific cap and a recipe from that time. Who are the buyers? People of 50 and older.
- An old product reinvention is the new VW Beetle. No one, except collectors, would be prepared now to drive an old Beetle: it is too insecure and uncomfortable by modern standards. This is why Volkswagen decided to reskin it a little while keeping its unique design, and to completely revise all its functionalities to match a modern consumer's bottom-line expectations. Who are the buyers? Old consumers and those younger people who are willing to adhere to the brand community.
- Brand revitalization or turnaround consists of recreating a consistent flow of sales, putting the brand back to life, on a growth slope again. This typically entails two actions in parallel: keeping the old typical product globally as it is (to keep its franchise) and reinventing it for new and younger consumers (that is to say asking the question, what would this product be today, if we had to invent it from scratch for the needs of modern consumers?). Burberry is the typical example.
- Brand facelifts (Lehu, 2006) refer to an upgrading of the performance and/or design of the brand to keep up with the competition. VW did it with the Golf 7.

Brand revitalization captures the attention of various parties:

- Young investors or venture capitalists who buy an ailing brand at low price, often an old brand, with the objective of reselling it in a few years at a profit, after revitalizing it. This was how Bernard Arnault became successful: buying Dior at a low price.

- Small businesses that will never have enough money to create their own brand, but are willing to buy the name of a formerly active brand for a reasonable price. For instance, 10 years after having stopped selling the European yogurt brand Chambourcy, Nestlé thought it could sell it. A small company bought it, but the fact that the name was still known did not guarantee the success of the revitalization, and it soon went out of business. A brand alone without a viable economic equation is of no use. (Nestlé had, of course, put a number of restrictions on the use of the brand, since it did not want to find it competing against itself.) In addition, the sales of a brand are the result not only of the attractiveness of that brand to consumers, but also of the muscles of the corporation operating it. Modern mass retailers also tend to value much more the capacity of a company to sustain competition, and to deliver products efficiently to their storage facilities, than its possession of a known but old brand.
- Large companies are also interested in revitalizing old brands, but only if these brands are not perceived as old, that is to say as brands with no relevance for today, associated exclusively with older consumers. This is how Ford bought Jaguar and had to invest as much again into putting it back to use as a marque for quality cars. Unfortunately, Ford used classical marketing to sell a luxury car. It failed.
- Global companies might buy a leading local brand in order to ease and finance the local development of their international stars. The local brand is a door opener with local distribution. However, it is often found that these so-called local leaders present the clear symptoms of ageing (no innovation, too few younger clients, little challenge of the past practices, no systematic upgrading of packages, designs and communication).

The decay of brand equity

Although they may have ceased their commercial activity, brands do not immediately lose their assets. Learnt through time, their brand image is not erased from consumers' long-term memories. Indeed, after many years a brand can still evoke a number of positive or negative associations. What is lost however is the key brand asset: brand salience, the capacity of the brand to be evoked spontaneously in consumers' minds as soon as the need to buy the product type appears. This is why belonging to the consumer 'evoked set' (or consideration set) is a key measure of brand equity, signifying both brand presence and its perceived unique relevance for that need.

Table 16.1 illustrates how brand equity decays over time. Brand X is a FMCG food brand in a very popular category (with almost 100 per cent penetration). Until recently, this brand was the number two

TABLE 16.1 How brand equity decays over time

Years after the end of the brand's commercial activity								
	1	2	3	4	5	6	7	8
Top of mind (saliency)	13	12	7	7	6	3	1	5
Total unaided awareness	26	28	20	29	15	14	11	16
Aided awareness	86	83	76	73	68	50	55	55
Bought last 12 months	27	29	17	19	12	15	10	13

FMCG food brand; sample size 450/year; all figures are percentages in its market. Then it was bought by market number three, which immediately sold all Brand X's factories so that the acquisition of the brand paid off immediately. Most important, it discontinued its activity and as a result became the market number two in volume and number one in value. Eight years after the end of any kind of commercial activity, the brand equity had not disappeared. Top-of-mind awareness had dropped from 13 per cent to 5 per cent and aided awareness from 86 per cent to 55 per cent. Interestingly, there are still 13 per cent of consumers who declare that they have bought it at least once over the preceding 12 months. This latter figure casts doubts on the validity of such indicators of brand equity in this FMCG category: it seems to be a mere reflection of spontaneous awareness.

How much would this brand be worth if its owner decided to sell it? Not far from zero. The owner would never take the risk of selling it so that it could be revived in its own market. Out of this market, it is just a name with faded remote credentials: there will be no buyer. Could the owner itself revitalize that brand? Probably in specific segments or niches. As far as the mainstream market is concerned, a return to the shelves would be impossible. They are now overcrowded, first by private labels, and second by the few remaining producers' brands, which have become mega-brands. Typically, a shift of channel would be possible. For instance, a drink brand might be sold via on-premise distribution (for consumption in canteens and business restaurants), if this were a channel where it could add value without meeting fierce competition. Channel and use changes are a classic form of revitalization for this very reason.

This example illustrates a fact too often overlooked: the value of a brand does not lie in its assets, but in the ability of a company to make a profitable business with these assets. After eight years of inactivity the whole commercial environment will have changed. Nature abhors a vacuum, and business does too. As soon as the brand disappears from the stores, the shelves are filled with other products from other brands, including the distributors' own brand. In order to sell the original again, they would need to be displaced. It costs a lot to induce the modern distribution to reallocate space for a comeback, with very little guarantee of success. A brand is not enough to stage a comeback, one needs an innovation.

It is clear why it is essential to prevent decline, and how a brand loses value after a period of inactivity. But what are the factors of decline?

Factors of decline and deletion

Following the analysis of the factors of a brand's longevity in Chapter 10, one could simply say that in contrast, brands decline when they are not respected. In fact, their decline always comes from mismanagement. When a company ceases to be interested in its brands (thus creating a lack of innovation, advertising or productivity), it can expect the consumer also to lose interest. And if the brand loses dynamism, energy, and shows fewer and fewer signs of vitality, how can one possibly hope that it will arouse passion and proselytism? Apart from these rules, which are so basic that it is astonishing that they can be forgotten, there are some factors that accelerate decline. These will now be studied.

When quality is forgotten

The first and surest road to decline is through the degradation of the quality of the products. The brand ceases to be a sign of quality. Low-cost competition obliges companies to cut corners with regard to quality, albeit in minor steps, and unfortunately, far too frequently. For instance, when l'Oréal bought out Lanvin, its leading perfume Arpège was a mere shadow of its former self. The fragrance had originally been made up of natural oils but by then included a fair amount of artificial ingredients. The bottle had even lost its round shape. Consumers around the world were conscious that they were no longer respected since Arpège had been so badly mistreated. L'Oréal's first step was to give back to this perfume the case, the bottle and the ingredients of the quality that it deserved. This task, which was not spectacular but was expensive, was absolutely necessary. It enabled contact to be re-established with the consumers who had been forsaken, and the rebuilding of acceptable foundations for the brand.

Beware of non-significant differences

The change in the level of quality of a product is rarely abrupt, but results from the insidious logic of statistical tests. Each change is tested against the product's previous version: if consumers have a lower opinion of the changed product but statistical analysis reveals that the difference is not significant, the company will not hesitate to carry out the change to provide a source of financial savings. The problem entirely rests with the expression 'no significant difference'. All the decisions are based on the so-called 'alpha risk threshold' (generally 5 per cent). As long as the difference observed in the sample, just due to chance, affects less than 5 per cent of the cases, it is declared non-significant. In sciences, the aim of this high-risk threshold is to avoid taking for real a phenomenon which would not exist in reality. The problem is that in marketing, it is the 'beta risk' that should be taken into account, the aim of which is to avoid considering as false a hypothesis that is in reality true. For, through modifying a product even by the smallest amount which each time has been declared 'non-significant', a considerable risk is taken. Consumers are not fooled. They avoid the product, then abandon it, even sometimes spreading by word of mouth a very negative opinion. From then on, any modification of the product must be approached with caution if it is rated below the standard product, even if the difference is said to be non-significant.

Missing the new trends

The third factor of decline is the refusal to follow immediately a durable change. Thus Taylor Made, for a long time the world reference for golf clubs, did not believe the gigantic head launched by the Callaway brand under the suggestive name of 'Big Bertha' would catch on. By clinging to a different conception that was more demanding for the average player, ie for the majority of the market, Taylor Made suddenly lost its leadership. In the same way, Sony seems to have missed the internet wave and the MP3 wave. Sony's name is attached to Walkman, Apple's to iPod.

In 2001, according to Zandl, a specialized US marketing research company, the jeans was still number one in the youth clothing preference. However, young people now quote 112 different brands as being their 'preferred brand for jeans'. The market has become fragmented, a challenge for Levi's, whose image and sales are very much associated with a mono-product, the 501.

Fragmentation led tribes, small groups to prefer new types of jeans, more adapted to new usages, and new brands. A lot of new competitors filled niches. Pepe and Diesel addressed the urban rebel, 'For us by us' and underground streetwear. Gap also became a major player. Levi's had expressed disbelief in streetwear and neglected the rappers and gliders, who are in fact the opinion leaders of the new youth. Tight 501s are totally unadapted to skateboarding and roller-skating. Skaters wish to wear an XXXXL rolled up their knees, and rappers like multi-pocket trousers. On the other end of the spectrum, girls desired Tommy Hilfiger and Polo jeans, not to speak of Armani and Versace jeans. It was clearly the end of the mass market. Levi's had not foreseen it, and worse, it had not reacted when the trends were there.

The mono-product syndrome

Still at the level of product policy, the brands associated with a single product are more vulnerable. They risk being carried away by the decline of that product. This again is part of what happened to Levi's, with its too-long association with the mythical 501. Wonderbra is another clear instance of a brand that fell into the mono-product trap.

Who has never heard about Wonderbra? Very few, either women or men. Although the product is in fact comparatively old (it was invented in Canada in 1953 by Canadelle Corp), its real launch in Europe was quite recent (1994). Sara Lee had bought the company and gave Playtex the responsibility of launching the Wonderbra in Europe. The fantastic advertising campaign ('Hello boys') and accompanying publicity made this innovation famous. The brand helped women who felt they had small breasts look more sexy and gain self-assurance as a result. It created a new segment. In 1995, 5 million units were sold in Europe, and 86 per cent of its consumers were less than 35 years old. Now where is Wonderbra? Still trying to find pathways for growth, if not prevent decline. Despite an aided awareness level of 70 per cent, its goodwill has come close to bad will in some countries, in the trade channels.

After the peak sales of 1995, sales started to decline. Competitors with known brands entered this segment too.

The problem was that Wonderbra became associated not with a brand but with one product, and its brand name became a generic name: people spoke of 'the wonderbra'. This highly technical product (it had 42 parts, and needed a specific manufacturing technology) was much adored inside the company. Everyone was very proud of it. Where to go next? If innovation is the key to market penetration, a brand has to become more than a name of a product. But Wonderbra did not innovate sufficiently, and consumers did not repurchase its products. Today, 61 per cent of Wonderbra consumers possess only one Wonderbra. They wear it for special occasions, and rarely on weekdays. Wonderbra might instead have capitalized on its sexy positioning but offered new products based on different reasons for purchase. The very same benefit could have been expressed using different materials or shapes. Instead it remained too narrow, preventing the consumer from moving freely within the brand.

Another difficulty was the global management of the brand. New models were designed essentially for the UK, its leading European market, because of an excess of centralization at Playtex (Sara Lee). The management did not recognize that the tastes and wishes of Italian, French and Spanish women were not those of English women. As a result European sales became one-country sales.

When the channel falters

The relationship with a distribution channel can be a factor of decline if the brand does not live up to the new expectations of it. Because companies such as l'Oréal developed particular brands for supermarket distribution, such as Plénitude for cosmetics, Vichy's status in the field of pharmaceuticals is under threat. Consumers who go to a chemist shop to buy such products expect from them a higher level of quality as befits the laboratory guarantee. But over time, Vichy had become a generalist brand more focused on lifestyle than scientific quality. It found itself, in 2000, carrying products which no longer corresponded with the products which consumers wanted to buy in a chemist shop. Vichy's survival was contingent upon a qualitative upgrade of all its products and its repositioning on the benefit of better health through the skin.

Other brands have collapsed because they have allowed themselves to become trapped in a declining distribution network. The recent rise of large liquor stores in Japan, at the expense of small convenience outlets, has caused the immediate decline of all the brands lacking a sufficient level of public awareness. In small outlets, they did not need it: the store owner pushed the brand, sold it to his clients. In modern distribution the brand has to sell itself, it needs market pull.

Preferring below-the-line investments

Finally, communication can accelerate the decline of brands. Threatened by private labels, many brands have cut advertising budgets to sell more volume on promotion. They will die soon. P&G television expenditures were redeveloped in 2011 for just that reason.

Excessive sub-branding can also kill a brand. If the sub-brands are too much in the spotlight, the mother brand can be adversely affected and give the impression that it is in decline. This happened with Dim, a hosiery brand. Although the brand was by far the main advertiser in its hosiery market, and even in the textile market in general, it seemed to be declining, less active. Such an imbalance between the actual share of voice and the feeling of loss of energy felt by the market worried the management of the Sara Lee group. In fact, the diagnosis was clear: the promotional tactics of the daughter brands had been carried so far that they had fragmented Dim's image. Indeed, it was appropriate to clarify Dim's wide range by attributing names to different products which did not propose the same customer benefits, hence the appearance of Sublim, Diam's and other lines. On the other hand, this measure produced a dispersion of the Dim image, even the disappearance of Dim to the benefit of the daughter brands.

The first symptom of this condition was the packaging. There was no longer any homogeneity between the different packagings, and the mother brand appeared in a minor endorsing role in variable places. Moreover, in the context of the organizational change, further divisions had been introduced (tights, lingerie, men's items). Unfortunately, there was no longer anybody in charge of coherence between the divisions and of the defence of the Dim mother brand's capital. Finally, since the Dim logotype only appeared clearly on bottom-end products and was concealed on advanced products, this increased the perception that its quality had declined. At the same time, the market was moving towards opaque tights, a more durable and more top-end product, which could easily make Dim the symbol, not of today's woman, but rather of a poor quality.

In order to correct these dangerous impressions, Dim undertook to increase the added value of all its products, including the basic product, to upgrade all its packagings, to return the status of source-brand by replacing the first-name brands under a visible umbrella, and to clearly advertise 'Dim presents the new Diam's' instead of 'This is the new Diam's by Dim'. (This example illustrates, in passing, a tendency which is fatal for a brand: its systematic distance from the best new products, thereby confining it to an offer which is static, obsolete or old-fashioned.)

How big groups weaken brands they have just purchased

The strength of big groups is their marketing acumen, their processes and their economies of scale. They look with envy at the many premium brands that enjoy a very high affective loyalty from their consumers, making them almost price insensitive. Not knowing how to launch premium brands (see also page 232), groups are tempted to buy these brands once they are successful. The problem is how to maintain the momentum of these brands once they have been integrated into the organization. How can L'Oréal maintain the authenticity and engagement that Anita Roddick put into the retail chain she created alone? How can the group preserve the uniqueness of Kiehl's, which is using counter-marketing rules? The danger is high: why?

- International groups have higher quality standards and impose them on these brands. This seems to be a good idea, but the brands had thrived precisely because they were different in their processes.
- International groups have bureaucratic decision processes that cut creativity. If four people have to agree on a decision, it cannot be creative. These brands developed with intuitive marketing and very short and reactive decision processes.
- International groups, to spare on overhead costs, tend to regroup all their brands under the same roof. Braun could have been the Apple of beauty accessories. To achieve this, a creative tandem should have been set up at the head of the company, with a lot of autonomy and at a distance from the group. Instead, P&G integrated Braun into its structure. When Martell was purchased by Seagram, its cognac decision centres were moved to the Seagram Building in New York. The first thing Pernod-Ricard did when it bought Martell from Seagram was to send Martell back to the place of its roots: the town of Cognac itself. The brand is now growing again as never before.

When a brand becomes generic

The highest degree of dilution of the brand's added value occurs when the brand becomes generic. The brand is considered a descriptive word, part of everyday vocabulary with no distinctive properties. The classic examples are well-known: Scotch, Kleenex, Xerox, Nylon, Velux. What causes a brand to be reduced to the point of becoming generic? The abandonment of any communication on the brand's specific nature and purpose can cause its decline. Thus, any dominant brand of a new product risks becoming a generic name. This can be prevented by taking certain precautions, for example:

- create a word to designate the product of the brand;
- never mention the brand's name alone, but together with the product's generic designation;
- never use the brand's name as a verb (in the United States, for instance, to xerox means to make a photocopy) or as a noun, but as an adjective;
- systematically protest whenever the brand's name is used as a common noun by third parties and the media; for instance, request that an erratum be published. Through not having reacted strongly enough, Du Pont de Nemours lost the ownership of Nylon and Teflon, which have since become generic terms;
- nurture the perceived difference between the brand and competitive products, either with

tangible attributes or with intangible values. In any event introduce new products.

Preventing the brand from ageing and deletion

It is frequently said that a brand is ageing, shows signs of ageing or seems aged. This impression may be felt by customers, non-customers, suppliers, distributors or employees themselves, who acknowledge a difference between them and their competitors. Ballantines, Martini, Black & White, Club Med, Yves Saint Laurent and Guy Laroche have all been described as ageing.

The concept of ageing has in fact two different meanings:

- The general meaning suggests a slow but systematic decline over a long period of time. The brand is not destined to end rapidly but seems likely to be inevitably phased out with time. Yesterday strong and active, it appears today much more mundane, as if it no longer had anything to say or to propose to the market and lived exclusively on its loyal clients. One symptom of this is the widening gap between the spontaneous awareness and the assisted awareness. The brand still rings a bell, but it is not one of the brands which has an impact on the market. It does not launch new products as often as the category actors. It does not surprise. It repeats itself. There is only a small difference between repetition and boredom.
- The second meaning refers to the reflected image of the customer. Everything points to the typical customer being older. And even in the case of a company whose marketing is deliberately targeted at older customers, it is never advisable for the image of a brand to be too closely associated with an older clientele. Although it is aiming at the flourishing older customer market (that is, customers over 50), Damart must make sure not to be associated with the clientele who are 60 or 70. Without going to that extreme, the Yves Saint Laurent label appears to young people to represent a clientele older than that of Dior's and Chanel.

What is it that produces these impressions of ageing? Most of the time these impressions are well founded: the brand no longer seems to belong to its time and has lost its inner energy.

Many brands allow themselves to be associated with the products of another age. With the acceleration of time, the notion of another era now refers to a close past. In all markets dominated by technology, obsolescence can occur very rapidly. Little can be done for brands linked to a dated technology, or those which seem not to have kept up to date with progress or with the internet.

A brand can be recent and threatened with ageing. The challenge for the eau de toilette Eau Jeune (ie Young Water), launched by l'Oréal for supermarket distribution, is to be still considered Eau Jeune by the next generation of 18- to 25-year-olds, but who are so different. If this brand had remained a single product, it would have disappeared. What symbolized youth in 1997 no longer symbolizes it in 2012.

The point of view expressed by the brand on its market can also sometimes seem to be suddenly behind the new dominant values. As long as decisions regarding Playtex in Europe were taken in the United States, the brand never seemed to take into consideration the role of femininity in women's choices. Even though the products were of high quality, they were purely functional, that is based on the tangible problem of breast support. What was relevant in the United States was totally opposite to the way European women related to their bodies. In its tone and inflexibility, Playtex seemed to be addressing the mothers, not the daughters.

Although it was still the world's leading brand for shoes and ski bindings, Salomon recently realized that it was in great danger of ageing within a few years. In fact, Salomon, in the same way as Rossignol does, has represented the values of alpine skiing for half a century: effort, order, competition, gaining one hundredth of a second, beating all others by a microsecond. The new generations no longer subscribe to these values: a counter-culture, originating in the surf, is dominant on the slopes, bringing with it new sports and new values. What has been called the 'glide generation' has not learnt alpine skiing and probably never will. They instinctively practise snowboarding on the slopes in winter and roller-skating or rollerblading in the streets. They put as paramount values friendship and emotion: they eschew competition and the brands associated with yesteryear. They have elected their own gods: Burton, Airwalk, Quiksilver, Oxbow. All these brands are new and symbolize another vision of sport.

The lack of evolution in a brand's outward signs indicates its present lack of interest in attracting new customers.

Certain brands also come to a standstill because they remain associated with the same celebrities. The fact that Yves Saint Laurent seems more dated than Dior or Chanel is connected with the omnipresence of the ageing creator himself and association with Catherine Deneuve. Lancôme was sensible enough to bring in younger and international stars.

As for the clientele, the loss of direct contact with young people is the surest symptom of ageing. This is what differentiates Johnnie Walker from Jack Daniel's or Martini from Bacardi.

Without necessarily having to appeal to young people between the ages of 20 and 25, the brand should always be attractive to tomorrow's consumers. The buyers who are today in their forties will modify their functional expectations when they reach their fifties. But they will also like to show that they have not changed by staying with their usual brands. They will refuse to support the ghetto brands which signal their entry into old age. Coke is the senior person's preferred soft drink, but does not appear so. Damart sells warm underwear to seniors, but to be attractive to this target its future depends on its image among 45- to 55-year-olds. They should not see the brand as a marker of old age. If they do, they will not buy it in 10 years' time. Damart has to work on the evolution of its image, not of its target clientele.

As has been noted, keeping in touch with young people implies a cultural revolution among management. The efforts to be made may seem huge to an older internal team who often do not appreciate the danger they are facing as their own reference points always seem secure. Finally, with consumers living longer, the effects of the clientele's ageing may pass unnoticed. The decline is slow and never spectacular. But unfortunately, as with a cancer, without an obvious sign of decline to react rapidly to, it may sometimes be too late.

To make the radical internal changes required to energize an organization which has aged with its own reference points, there should be no hesitation in rejuvenating the entire management with younger people. The revitalization of brands always starts with a major work of internal rejuvenation.

Brand turnaround: Audi

Can an average brand turn into a premium one? This is called a brand turnaround. Audi provides a typical success story. In 2010 in Europe, Audi was number two after Ferrari in the desirability rankings. It sells more than a million cars annually.

However, very few people remember what Audi was in 1980. At that time the brand was an average generalist German car maker, medium priced, without an image. Its story is that of three brands that merged into one (NSU Prinz, Auto Union and DKW).

Its future was set by Ferdinand Piech, Volkswagen Group CEO, and gave one goal to the brand: become the luxury brand of the group. Piech added time: the brand would have 20 years to succeed! This is the mark of great vision. The brand has kept this long-term perspective since. Most brands, when they talk to their dealers each year, focus on the two forthcoming years. Audi always talks about what will happen in the next 10 years. It is in its DNA.

Why 20 years? In the car business, you do not change people's perception overnight. In the fashion business, it took five years for Burberry (see later) to succeed in its turnaround and rejuvenation. In the automobile market, there was a lag effect for Audi. Between the idea and the first car coming out of the factory embodying this idea, it took six years. In addition, when the new car was launched, a lot of old Audi cars were still visible on the streets, thus re-stimulating the former images and mental associations of the brand.

Audi's brand platform (see page 172) was clear from the outset. Since Audi was a brand without a past, it could only have a future. The core value of Audi is avant-garde. Its core belief, or obsession, is that technology can bring progress and, in fact, that progress can come only from technology. The second value is quality: Audi would never save money on quality. Luxury is in the details: Audi would be in the details too.

Audi had to invent a new type of luxury: a luxury without a past – a bit like Apple. All its competitors – Mercedes Benz, BMW, Jaguar – made use of their history to nourish prestige and status. Luxury sells a compression of time. This was why Audi needed 20 years, which Piech understood.

At that time, Audi was a dwarf in the Volkswagen Group, losing money. To win a new crusade, you need crusaders. However, nobody really wanted to quit Volkswagen to work for Audi: there was no pride at that time, and the goal was too distant. As a result, only mavericks went there, or people before retirement and young ones without much experience. However, as for a start-up, this created a specific spirit and the energy to take one's revenge inside the group. This is why the average age at Audi was quite young.

To change an image one needs new prototypes. Cognitive theory teaches that people figure out abstract concepts only through examples. Some of them are the best examples: they are the prototype of the concept. The same holds for brands. Audi is a concept, which would remain fuzzy as long as there was no visible Audi.

The first prototype on the stairway to becoming the avant-garde of the car industry was the Audi Quattro. It was an expensive car, not because of luxury, but because of its sportiness. The dashboard was made of plastic, as was the wheel, but it was a four-wheel drive full of technology. It won many racing contests and became a hero.

In 1990 came the disruption: the Audi A4 as a substitute for the Audi 80. The A4 represented what Audi wanted to stand for: design, purity, technology, performance, discreetness. Audi was also associated with an aluminium engine, which was much lighter and more modern looking.

The A4 was also 25 per cent more expensive than the Audi 80 – on purpose. The brand lost all of its Audi 80 owners. They just could not follow: the price was too high. This is also how one builds a luxury brand: by exclusion of some in order to include others. This upward move had an unforeseen consequence: many Audi dealers wanted to quit the brand. At that price, their salespeople had to look for clients who were considering buying a Mercedes or a BMW, but Audi's brand equity was not at that time what it is now.

To justify the price increase, it was no longer possible to sell Audis with VWs. Luxury needs its own territory to create its own charisma.

Audi's next challenge was service. There is no luxury without service, but service is delivered by people. To deliver a premium service the Audi dealers would have to invest money in rebuilding their garages and showrooms, as the place where service is delivered strongly influences perception of the service. The problem was that Audi car dealers were not motivated to make the investment. The business model of any car dealer rests on three pillars: new sales, after-sales and second-hand sales. For Audi, since the brand was the new luxury dream, dealers were very profitable just by selling new cars. They needed to adopt a long-term vision and think about sustaining brand equity, not simply contribution margin made now. Further, people buying expensive Audis would not accept for long too great a discrepancy between the service they got and the VIP one they expected.

Revitalizing an old brand

How should one rejuvenate an old brand? How can a past brand revive? How do you recreate a durable growth for a brand that has for long been declining? Although there exist a wide variety of situations, the goal is the same: to bring a brand back to life. This leads to the core question, what life? Whose life? As a rule, it will rarely be the same as formerly.

There is a big difference between respecting one's roots and cultivating the past. Revitalizations, revivals are based on an updating of the overall offer of the brand while staying true to part of its identity. Revival means aiming at a new growth market. The brand must find a new relevance and differentiation. The term 'revival' of a brand is not quite accurate since it always implies a change in the product, or in the market, or in the target market. It is a relaunch but not necessarily among the same people as before, or in the same distribution channels, for the same uses, or whatever. With time the consumers, the markets and competition will have changed.

A successful revitalization: MINI

The relaunch of Mini as MINI by BMW is a success story highlighting the subtle balance to be achieved between respecting the former brand and product characteristics and modernization for the sake of more security, performance and comfort. Mini had been created in 1959 by a genius engineer and visionary, Alec Issigonis, in England. After the Suez Canal crisis, he saw the dangers of the oil shortage and created a very small car, with little oil consumption, yet allocating 80 per cent of the space to passengers (four adults) thanks to a transversal engine. This car was to be an urban car, very easy to drive, yet giving go-kart sensations, being very low and well motorized. The Mini Cooper S version won the famous Monte Carlo Rally in the Alps many times and created a halo effect for the brand image. Soon the Mini became another symbol of the swinging sixties and the cultural revolution led by the UK (pop music, street fashion, etc). To grow, the Mini developed a large range, with station wagon models and beach open models (the Mini Moke). Mini became a cult brand: its design is considered a hallmark of modern design. It was more than a car; it was a statement about oneself, and it expressed strong values linked to modern UK cultural leadership too. The brand has a world fan community, with internet sites, forums, Facebook pages, and car owners' meetings and races.

From 1959 till 2000, 5.5 million Mini cars were sold worldwide, yet Mini never made any profit. BMW wanted this niche brand and had to buy Rover to get it in the global deal. BMW sold Rover and kept MINI. It is to the credit of BMW that it understood the DNA of the brand and shielded it from over-Germanization, which would have killed the myth.

What was religiously maintained? The name Mini became MINI. The design was respected. The factory was left in the UK, although totally rebuilt and robotized to manufacture cars (with their many options) at the level of what is expected by modern buyers paying an average of €30,000. The whole concept of the car was meticulously respected. (See Table 16.2.)

Interestingly the average age of MINI buyers in the world is 40, but the communication conveys a younger customer self-image – on purpose.

Let us compare the former and the new positioning. Mini Austin brand positioning was 'the British non-conventional and cheeky small economical car with style and sportiness'. MINI's new positioning is 'the irresistible small car that will make you stand out from the automobile crowd'. In fact there are no two MINIs alike in the world: each buyer has to choose between 300 interior options and 370 exterior options. As a result the average purchasing price today is €30,000 (as against less than £600 when the Mini was introduced in 1959).

TABLE 16.2 Comparison of the Mini and MINI

	Mini	MINI
Length of car	3.05 m	3.699 m
Weight	635 kg	1,135 kg
Horsepower	34	90
Engine	843 cm^3	1,000 cm^3
Maximum speed	120 km/h	185 km/h
Comfort	Four adults	Four adults
Quality	Medium	Premium
Brand experience	Go-kart	Lively, very reactive, but safe
Brand personality	Fun	Exciting
Brand culture	Fashionable	Trendsetter, classy chic
Customer reflection	Female, blonde	Young at heart

MINI has now adopted a luxury strategy (see Kapferer and Bastien, 2009). What stepwise process does this MINI case exemplify?

Redefining the brand essence

Even forgotten brands have an internal meaning, a domain of legitimacy to be exploited. The first task in a brand revitalization is to understand which values of this brand still have a high relevance, and which have lost meaning. Burberry rediscovered its DNA: the ability to epitomize the classic eccentric dandy in English fashion. Old brands have disseminated bits of associations in people's memories, even among non-customers or newer generations. These weak memories act as a 'humus'. It is important to analyse this humus. What is left about the brand essence? What are the potentialities emerging from it? What market opportunities could be met? It is useful to analyse this as shown in Figure 16.1.

As a rule, declining brands have few positive salient evocations, or these evocations are generic and lack differentiation. The real potential usually lies in the latent associations. It will be the role of marketing to choose the right set from among these buried positive associations. Then the brand will have to embody them in new products or services and channels aimed at the new target.

FIGURE 16.1 Analysing and managing the potentialities of an old brand

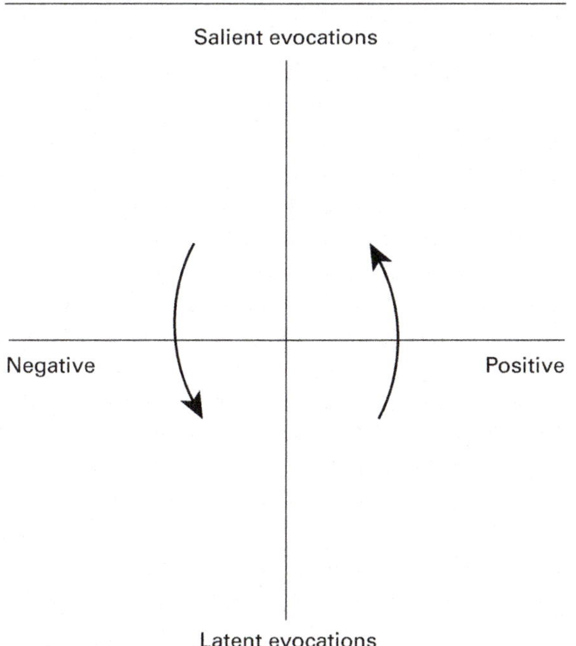

Revitalizing through new uses

The revitalization of a brand usually follows new paths that are very different from those that led to its initial success. If there has been a decline, it is because these paths did not lead to any new demand or pocket of growth.

Revitalization involves establishing new parameters for the brand. Since its original consumers are no longer able to ensure its success, it has to attract a new clientele, develop new user occasions, new distribution channels and new consumer networks.

Brandy is a classic example. It is typically associated with the 'after-dinner' and 'connoisseurs enjoying a brandy together' type of occasion, an image and occasion that have been responsible for a massive decline in the volume of brandy sales worldwide. After years of decline in the face of competition from white spirits, which are much easier to drink and much trendier (Bacardi, Absolut, Seagram's Gin and so on), brandy sales have recently soared in the United States. But with one major difference – 50 per cent of the volume of brandy currently consumed in the United States is consumed by the black community, which represents 12 per cent of the population. It has become the favourite cocktail drink of African-American males, within the context of a lively social situation, where status value is essential. They ask for Martell or Hennessy, as well as Thackeray (gin) and Crystal Roederer (champagne).

To target a new consumer group, a company must be ready to call its traditional marketing into question and define an optimum marketing mix for its new target group. The process begins with new customers, their lifestyle and new occasions on which the product is consumed or purchased. Innovation is therefore central to the revitalization of old brands.

Revitalizing through distribution change

In fact, it seems that a classic revitalization strategy is to use known brands in different distribution circuits. For instance, a supermarket food brand could be moved to a channel that rests on 'push' marketing rather than 'pull' marketing. This is why one sees many formerly famous brands in canteens, or office restaurants for instance. It creates value in the eyes of the clients (more than an unknown brand or a private label) and these brands are cheaper than well-known leading brands. The obverse is also true. One company has specialized in purchasing old pharmaceutical brands, with 100 per cent aided awareness, that are little prescribed these days. Some of them have become generic names. The strategy consists in selling them on the shelves of supermarkets, where their name triggers immediate recognition and trust.

Revitalizing through innovations

Barely 10 years ago, Mercedes was under threat. The brand had certainly gained international acclaim, but the signs were nevertheless worrying. In California, where new consumer trends are created, Mercedes was no longer an aspirational brand. It had been replaced by Lexus, the top-of-the-range brand from Toyota. And in Europe the average buyer of the smallest Mercedes of that period, the C-Class, was 51 years old.

Clearly Mercedes was becoming a brand for older people. The company's CEO made a harsh but accurate diagnosis: either the brand remain as it was and the company would go bankrupt (like Rolls-Royce) or it would have to evolve.

The first step was to re-establish the conditions that would create a favourable economic equation – the company would have to produce 1 million vehicles to lower production costs to an acceptable level. The second was to attract a younger clientele – they could not be left to the competition until they reached 51! To do this, the company had to break with the standard design of all Mercedes cars for the previous 60 years.

This is why the event that revitalized Mercedes was the launch of the A-Class. This little car, which was in direct competition with the Volkswagen Golf, was the brand's new 'prototype' in Europe. It departed from the traditional Mercedes image on two counts – it had front-wheel drive and a completely different design. However, it still had the interior space of the C-Class and the safety of the E-Class. In fact, it currently accounts for 30 per cent of Mercedes sales in Europe. Above all, it has attracted a younger clientele (with an average age of 37), more women and the style conscious.

In the United States, the new Mercedes prototype is the luxury 4 × 4 M-Class, which has re-established contact with the trendy set of California and elsewhere.

To target even younger consumers, the beautiful CLK Roadster was deliberately positioned at an attractive price. Its beauty, sensitivity and design are now part of the new Mercedes brand contract. Of course, any form of extension modifies the original brand, and Mercedes is no longer an exclusively luxury brand. The new Mercedes management is more segmented, more attuned to the needs of its consumers and their lifestyle. The brand regularly renews its status as the world's leading car manufacturer via its top of the range models, of which the S-Class is the symbol.

Revitalizing through segmentation

To revitalize Burberry, Rose Marie Bravo knew she had to segment the lines and sub-brand them. Burberry London is a modernized offering for the classic clients. Burberry Prorsum is very fashionable and modern. Thomas Burberry is aimed at teenagers. The first segment ensures cashflow and makes it possible to take a risk on cash-demanding fashion stores. Zegna created Zegna Sport.

Revitalizing by contact with new opinion leaders

Why did Hush Puppies become fashionable again in the United States in 1993 (Gladwell, 2000)? Because East Side Manhattan fashionistas found them cute and appropriate for their quest of permanent differentiation.

Ageing brands have generally lost contact with the trendsetters in their category, the tribes that prefigure change. Advertising and product innovation will be of no help without the active support of these trendsetting tribes. It is not easy to make friends again with people one has not called for years, during which time they have been seduced by the competition, including new entrants. In addition the ageing brand is held as an icon of the past, and may attract bad will, not goodwill.

The task of recreating proximity through direct contacts and shared emotional experiences will be difficult, but it is an essential part of any comeback.

Salomon, which had lost contact with the surfers who were its future market, had to create an internal cultural revolution, changing its management and hiring young people who were likely to be able to recreate the lost connection.

Ballantines, formerly at Allied Domecq, realized recently that it too had lost all contact with youth. Managers more concerned with their own fate in the midst of mergers and acquisitions in their sector concentrated on the brand's core clients, not the future clients. They forgot that sustaining brand equity means addressing current and future business alike. For instance, in 1995 brand equity monitoring showed that in some European countries, brand spontaneous awareness among 18–24-year-olds had dropped from 47 per cent to 13 per cent in seven years.

It is not possible to get out of this dramatic problem just by changing one's advertising. Sometimes creating a new product is needed, because in between, everything has changed: consumers, their habits, the competition, places of consumption and so on.

Regaining contact is a preliminary. A brand is not a product with a name, it is a relationship. After years of indifference, not to say neglect by Ballantines, the brand had to reconquer the lost relationship. It might still have been number one in some countries, but that was because of a core of frequent buyers, all ageing. Benchmarking the best practice of Pernod-Ricard, the brand decided to invest massively in Europe, and also in South America, to reconquer proximity by contact. Targeting is crucial: what key tribe? The management identified snowboarding as representing the core values of the new generation.

In cooperation with the International Snowboarding Federation, which was fighting against the International Ski Federation, it sponsored all alpine snowboard events, and created a night event in discos. However, to be effective today at regaining contact, sponsoring must go far beyond just stamping the event with the brand name everywhere. The brand must be at the centre, or a key ally of the event.

Step two entailed recognition that urban youth was the target. Ballantines decided to bring snowboarding to cities through the 'Ballantines Urban High' Tour. In the middle of capital cities from Berlin to Rio de Janeiro, or on their beaches, Ballantines had a huge ramp built, covered in artificial snow, to host three-day national contests to find the best freelance snowboarders. The contest was preceded by country-wide selection phases, thereby creating a mounting buzz through word of mouth. The event fuelled involvement. The first event of the series took place in October 1995 in Berlin, symbolically at the Brandenburg Gate (which used to be the only gate in the Berlin Wall where people from the former East Germany could come through to the free West). Because among young people everything goes together, during the contest there were an open air concert (with the group Prodigy), grunge fashion shows, and night-time promotions in all the city's discos around snowboarding themes. In addition for the cream of the cream, Ballantines created Ballantines orbit, a huge mobile tent, with restricted invitation to those perceived as style leaders to listen to live techno music. After Berlin the tour went on to Prague, Milan, Moscow, Rio de Janeiro – it still goes on.

The lessons that can be drawn from this case are that proximity today means bumping into the lives of the target group, not just being there as a passive sponsor. A multidimensional event was created, merging fashion, sport, music, dancing, entertainment and video games, showing a high level of investment, and a very good understanding of the target audience's desires. A special logo was created, Ballantines Urban High, which could eventually become a label for licensed products (a clothing line, T-shirts, music and so on), certainly a website, and why not a franchised store chain in the future?

The event was well prepared for through the selection phases and brand presence across the country. The budget commitment was high (about €600,000) for the Berlin event, which was attended by 100,000 young people (so it cost €5 per person for a contact that should create a long-lasting emotional memory and involvement with the brand).

Changing the business model

Once in a while daring entrepreneurs buy an old and ailing brand and decide to revitalize it. It also happens that big groups do so. What is often presented as a brand revitalization is actually a change in the business model. In Chapter 1 we emphasized that a brand that cannot provide benefits has no real value. By benefits is meant financial benefits, economic value added (EVA) once the cost of capital had been paid (see also Chapter 18). What makes an ailing brand more valuable is the new business model on which it will rely.

For decades l'Aigle, a former subsidiary of Hutchinson, was known for its rubber boots. Its name was also its symbol: it came directly from the American Eagle. It had become a cult brand among fishermen, hunters, nature lovers and country landowners. But Chinese imports and modern distribution created too many problems, the company went broke, and it was bought in an LBO. Now there are Aigle stores opening everywhere in the world. Has the brand changed? In name terms it has lost a letter, moving from l'Aigle to Aigle, gaining simplicity and internationality. Most important, it moved from a boots brand to a leisurewear brand, whose prototype (most symbolic product) has moved from the rubber boots to a parka, a solid product, as the main value of the brand commands. The vintage rubber boots are still there to nurture the myth, but business grew through the new prototype. There are a lot of benefits in this change of business model:

- Brands that rely too much on a mono-product are always in danger, as they cannot smooth out a drop in sales. Boots sell less when climate becomes dryer. Also, since the rubber boots were of excellent quality, they lasted a long time. Brand loyalty was high but the time between purchases was too long.
- Extending the line to leisurewear made it possible to free the brand from the grip of modern distribution and build its own selective distribution network. The extended line made it more than possible to fill each store.
- Leisure wear is fashion conscious: people buy new garments each year even if they already own similar ones. It is also a less price-sensitive sector.

This example is a reminder that too often the success of the revitalization is attributed to 'the brand' as a short cut, because there is a lack of information on the company itself, the strategy, the back office. Certainly the brand reputation was an invaluable asset, but that asset was worth nothing as long as it was not supported by a valid business model.

How the Olympic brand remains forever young

The Olympic symbol is one of the most powerful brands in the world. Known by 96 per cent of people, it is highly respected and even loved. Although it is a brand with no name on the symbol, it represents the Olympic Movement as it was revitalized by Baron Pierre de Coubertin in 1894. The vision of the Olympic Movement attached to the five rings (one per continent) is that one can promote peace and progress through sport. Its values are excellence, friendship and respect. The first mission of the International Olympic Committee is to organize the pinnacle event that unites the people of the world: the Olympic Games.

Since 1894 the Olympic symbol has never been so powerful: so known, respected and followed. What is the mystery explaining why this century-old brand remains so strong, resisting the effects of time?

The first one is that the Olympic Games take place every four years. For athletes it is the peak of their achievement. They think during the four years of the seconds that will give them either gold and glory or nothing. The Olympics communicate strongly, but only every four years. This avoids dilution and loss of interest: the silence between two sessions of the games re-creates desire and a permanently renewed freshness.

The second factor of this long-lasting freshness is that, like the phoenix, the games are reborn at each session. The choice of town to host the Olympic Games is based on two sets of criteria. First are technical criteria: the town must be able to run the games and accommodate a million tourists in full security. Second are cultural criteria: the town must symbolize values that are meaningful for the present and the future. In addition, its candidacy rests on the proposition of the specific values it wants to convey during the games. The Olympic values themselves are non-negotiable and eternal: they originate in Greek history and have been made explicit in the Olympic Charter. However, each town must make the games relevant to the present time. Therefore one can talk of the Olympic brand and its flagship product, the games themselves, always being regenerated by the organizing town, acting as a sub-brand.

What do the 2012 London Olympic Games stand for? While respecting the legacy, they have their own personality: they aim at being everyone's games, being the open Olympics (beyond elites), bringing not only sport but education, culture and environment, with not only the classical massive spectacle but also a lot of experiences around it, where the participation of all is encouraged (it is not simply for the elite, and it is not just watching but also doing). The brand slogan could be 'Everyone can be part of it.' It can be observed that the sub-brand name is composed of a date and a place. The Rio Olympics will take place in 2016 with other values, those of Brazil, the Southern hemisphere, ecology and nature (see page 261, Figure 11.11).

One understands how each Olympic town and year with its specific set of values acts as a facelift or rejuvenation treatment for the brand every four years.

Growing older but not ageing

Louis Vuitton is 150 years old! It is also the most fashionable luxury brand in Asia. One way of understanding revitalization is to consider brands that have not 'aged'. How have they done it? Typically, the brands that have defied the passage of time have adopted a dual logic, as illustrated by Nivea and Lacoste. To follow their example and stay young, a brand must implement three types of initiatives towards the product. These can also be used as a model for relaunching a brand.

Facelifting, reinventing and innovating

The management of a brand involves maintaining the present (what the brand is now) while at the same time working for the future. It is the present that constitutes the source of income and therefore allows the development of the growth products of the future. As shown in Figure 16.2, in order to stay young, a brand must implement three types of initiatives at the same time:

- It must continually modernize the 'prototype' in the same way that Nivea introduced Nivea Soft to modernize its basic in the famous metallic blue jar. Nivea Soft is lighter and less greasy, and is marketed in a white jar. Lacoste regularly improves its famous 12 × 12 polo shirt in terms of the quality of the wool, the colours, the sleeves and so on.
- It must also reinvent the 'prototype', just as Lacoste produced a tight-fitting shirt with Lycra since this is how the woman of 2005 liked to dress. It was an immediate hit. For example, imagine a brand of haircare products whose basic product is a lotion. It would certainly have to modernize it in terms of the packaging, and update the formulation. But it should above all consider how today's customers would want to apply the product. It is quite possible that rubbing a lotion into the scalp is something that is no longer done, even though the product itself is extremely relevant. In this case, another method of application would certainly be the best form of innovation. You only have to think of Nivea, which invented the first spray-on sun lotion.
- Finally, it must innovate by actively seeking out the trends and behaviour that currently

FIGURE 16.2 Sustaining brand equity long term: dual management in practice

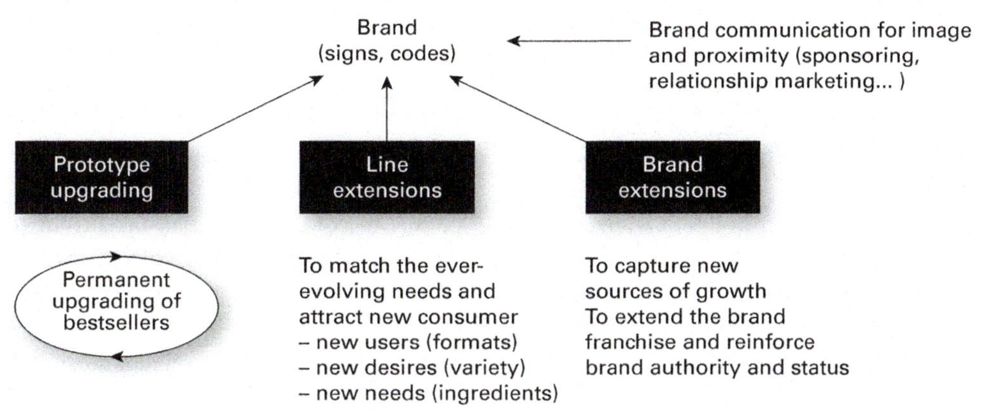

dominate the younger consumer segments, since these are the segments that will generate customer loyalty in the future. To return to the example of the hair-care brand, it simply cannot afford not to create new products – which are of course in line with its brand contract. Young people are mad about hair gels, styling products and hair colour. These markets certainly exist already, but the brand can create new segments within these markets that work in its favour.

Actively seeking out new types of behaviour means opening up to the idea of exploring new distribution channels, since new behaviour is often linked to new places and situations. These innovations also provide an opportunity to launch new and truly groundbreaking publicity campaigns, both in terms of their basic structure and especially their style. In this way, the brand sends out clear signals that it is reinventing itself. At the same time, these campaigns aim to launch the business of these innovations, just as they would for any new product.

Detecting the symptoms of ageing brands

Brands are built by the sum of all their behaviours creating value at contact points with customers. This is why brands should regularly monitor their behaviour. There are many sure symptoms of a brand dropping off, and they can be grouped into seven main types.

Insufficient preparation for the future

- Insufficient rate of new products in the yearly sales.
- Low rate of patent registration.
- Low rate of trademark registration (a sign of little need to name new products and services).
- Insufficient investment in R&D, in market sensing, in trend spotting.
- Insufficient knowledge about new uses and new emerging situations of use.
- Date of the last executive committee meeting to address these issues.

Insufficient dual management

- Insufficient knowledge about non-consumers, modern consumers, tomorrow's consumers.
- More and more sales to a reduced number of clients.
- Following the demands of existing clients, not foreseeing the changes in the market.
- Slow but regular increase of the average age of clients.

Insufficient capacity to capture growth pockets as they emerge

- Thinking the brand only through its historical product, without being ready to capture emerging new materials and demands.
- Excessive vision of what is called brand coherence, thus limiting the types of extensions to be made by the brand.

Insufficient meaningfulness

- Weakening of the present positioning and values.
- Weakening of the way values are materialized.
- Date of the last customer satisfaction questionnaire.
- Date of the last interview with lost customers.
- Increase in proportion of customers declaring they are 'moderately satisfied'.
- Date of the last blind test.
- Lowering rate of repeat purchase.
- Decrease in spontaneous awareness (saliency).
- Decrease in number of spontaneous press quotes and buzz on internet.

Insufficient vitality at contact

- Lack of regular updating of the quality of the logo and visual symbol of the brand.
- Date of last change or facelift for the packaging (design, ergonomics).
- Lack of regular facelifts for stores or concessions.
- Lack of organized merchandizing, lack of plans to regularly rethink it.

- Lack of service (call centres, websites and no presence in social media).
- Lack of brand proximity marketing.
- Lack of advertising.

Insufficient self-stimulation

- Lack of curiosity.
- Lack of desire to surprise.
- Lack of PR events.
- Lack of contacts with new opinion leaders, with the press.

Insufficient staffing

- Lack of young managers.
- Sex imbalance among executives (100 per cent male or 100 per cent female).

Back to the future

Often a brand's decline is tied to forgetting the brand's mission. Little by little small adjustments have been added to the strategy, and cumulatively they have led the brand astray. This is how heavy discounters become less heavy discounters, luxury brands become less luxurious, feminine brands become less feminine and so on. 'Back to the core' is a classic revitalizing strategy. It does not mean being obsessed with the past, but if the early vision and mission are still valid, trying to come back to it while acknowledging that the product itself may need to be updated.

Many groups act preventively by regularly checking the relevance of their identity and the fact that the operations are actually in line with this strategy. For instance, at Decathlon, as soon as operating margins get higher, the alarm bell rings. Decathlon's deep culture focuses on making people happy through sport and physical activities. This is achieved through a remarkable policy of providing own brands with the best performance/price ratio on the market. Higher margins seem to indicate that this ratio is becoming less exceptional than it should be.

This is also very typical of hotel management. Regularly at Accor Hotels, each brand holds a seminar called 'Back to the future'. The goal is to assess if the strategy is being followed or if in fact it has subtly changed. If it is the case, what services should be deleted or added in order to once more fulfil the brand's mission?

Financial strategies at the end of life

What strategy should be used to postpone the end of the brand? Financially speaking, companies tend to milk the brand then: they stop investing in it and harvest as much operating profit as they can. Another approach is to boost sales artificially in order to sell the brand while it stills looks as though it is endowed with a real brand capital (awareness, image, affect, etc). A third strategy is licensing. The owner of the brand stops developing its activity, but looks for licences in a number of markets, thereby moving to a financial strategy based on earning royalties.

A typical case is Agfa. This brand almost went bankrupt after its sales to the mass market considerably decreased in a short period of time. Digital cameras and smartphones signalled the end of the classic photo business. The brand is now held by a holding company, AgfaPhoto Holding GmbH in Germany, which has the responsibility to find licensors in relevant markets. Thus one now finds five licensors in Germany:

- Sagem for digital photo frames;
- Peach for compatible printer heads;
- CCM GmbH (Creative Chemical Manufacturing) for products to clean PCs and data processing machines;
- GBT GmbH (German Battery Trading) for batteries;
- Plawa GmbH for digital cameras.

The royalty rate is said to be 8 per cent.

Pierre Cardin is said to have more than 200 licences all around the world. The brand exists now only through its licences. The brand momentum is gone, but a wide variety of licensed products can be found in all countries, from clothes to kitchen equipment, furniture, decoration, bathroom linen and even toilet seats. The brand exploits the aura of prestige it still has in new countries. In developed ones, and especially its homeland, the brand acts as an accessible luxury aimed at the C+/B– social groups. In fact it is now one of the most profitable male apparel brands.

17 Managing global brands

Geographic extension is the necessary fate of brands. On it depend the brand's growth, and its ability to innovate and to sustain its competitive edge in terms of economies of scale and productivity. As such, marketing directors are no longer questioning the principle of international expansion, but are preoccupied with the means by which this can be accomplished. They ask themselves: Where should we go? What balance do we maintain between a global brand which shuns linguistic and national frontiers, and one which makes provision for local requirements and context? Which brands are destined to have global significance and which should remain on a national footing? Finally, how do we rationalize the portfolio of national brands into a small number of global brands? Any such transition must be carefully managed.

The debate between advocates of brand globalization and those of a sound adaptation to local markets was set in an academic fashion in the 1980s through the articles of Levitt (1983), and Quelch and Hoff (1986). One had to choose sides almost ideologically. Twenty-five years later, we are able to learn from past experience which was more or less successful. If on a global scale we cannot deny the existence of certain factors that bring together countries and cultures, we must not forget that the speed of this coming together is sometimes slower than reckoned. Moreover, if at a certain level of generality or social and cultural trends consumers in many countries declare the same motivations and expectations, a closer look reveals slight differences that must be taken into account. This chapter urges us to a pragmatic approach. The empires built by Marlboro or Coca-Cola will not be replicated, as they benefited from particular historical and time factors. The international expansion of Coca-Cola was fostered in great part by two world wars and the presence of GIs in Europe and Asia. It took Marlboro 35 years to conquer the world and McDonald's 22 years! A contemplation of these models, however agreeable it may be, is quite useless for Danone, for example, whose brand image varies from one country to the next because the products through which it penetrated these countries cannot be the same: creamy desserts in Germany, plain yoghurts in France, fruit yoghurts in Great Britain. How do you then create a uniform image around the concept of health if in concrete terms the brand does not have the same products in each market or country? This is the reality for most brands today. They are not much helped by the models of brands that have created a new category (Coke, Amazon, IBM, Chanel). They need other models, more relevant to the situation most companies and brands are facing, when they operate in already existing categories.

From global to post-global

In May–June 1983, an article entitled 'The globalization of markets', by Professor Theodore Levitt, was published in the *Harvard Business Review*. The direct and simple nature of its argument was to make it one of the most quoted and influential articles in the field of business management. According to Professor Levitt, national differences and preferences would no longer carry any weight in the face of the progress and reduced costs associated with international products and brands. With everyone in the world travelling either physically or, in most cases, via satellite television, the desire to buy products and brands sold in other countries would also greatly increase (Friedman, 2005).

In short, while recognizing that the world was indeed round, companies had a vested interest in regarding it as flat, and treating it like a single market. This was the strategy adopted by Coca-Cola, McDonald's and Microsoft, and by the many companies that followed in their wake. The main obstacle to the globalization of markets was decentralized organization and its symbol – national marketing directors who, by their very nature, could not help but promote the opposite argument, the one that justified their position.

Twenty years later, how far has this prediction of globalized markets been fulfilled? Anyone who travels knows that the same brands are found in countries throughout the world, whether it is Philips, Michelin, Sony, Hugo Boss, Nike, HSBC or Axa. However, beneath the surface, what do companies really think of globalized brands? Is it still what they want? Is it still their ideal?

It should first of all be pointed out that Professor Levitt's prediction was based essentially on factors associated with production and on the unmistakable competitive advantages of economies of scale. In fact, most globalization has taken place at production level, which is why it has been the target of some of the criticisms levelled by the anti-globalization lobby. In her very interesting book *No Logo* (1999), Naomi Klein berates the companies that do not have factories and, as a result, wash their hands of anything that goes on in the archaic factories of their Asian subcontractors. Nike is a good example of this. By contrast, when Jean Mantelet, the creator of Moulinex, tried to keep employment in Upper Normandy at all costs, it ultimately cost him his company (but not the brand). The movement towards globalization of the upstream (production) stage is therefore unavoidable. Successful companies have globalized their factories and supply chains to bring them closer to their markets and/or take advantage of lower costs. The car industry is a typical example.

It should, however, be recognized that this is a movement that has affected products more than services. While the circulation of the flow of money and information no longer encounters any barriers and is instantaneous, the movement towards the relocation of, for example, the processing of financial information, data files and bank databases is only just beginning. UK banks and insurance companies have taken the initiative by finding in Bangalore, the Indian equivalent of Silicon Valley, a well-qualified but much less expensive workforce. Call centres serving French customers are often based on the island of Mauritius.

There is one point on which the forecast of globalized markets can be challenged – the downstream stage of brands and products that are a long way from the predicted standardization. Of course, you find Porsche and Jaguar worldwide, but these are exported brands, like Chanel. They are the standard bearers of a particular country or culture, and appeal to an international clientele. The car industry provides a good illustration of why the concept of the global product is in fact a myth. Paradoxically, the most global product that ever existed in the car sector was Ford's famous Model T – it was totally standardized, with 20 million cars manufactured and sold worldwide. Even though the domestic market was by far its principal market, the Model T was a truly universal product. In 1981, the launch of the famous Ford Escort in the United States and Europe appeared to be a sign of globalization. In fact the US and European models only had one part in common – the radiator cap. Hardly a global product! More recently, the Ford Focus was launched in Europe (1990) and the United States (2000), and this time the models from these two world regions had 65 per cent of parts in common. But Ford does not think it can go much further – there are too many structural and long-term factors against it. So what are they exactly?

- The first is that energy is very cheap in the United States, which it will never be again in Europe. Low-energy innovations that have an enhanced value in Europe are regarded as irrelevant in the United States. This is why the engine type cannot be the same in both regions.
- The second is that vehicle standards and testing remain primarily national and in any event regional. Manufacturers therefore have to adapt their vehicles to suit the specifications and requirements of local test centres. Safety standards in the United States are less stringent than in Europe and Asia.
- The third factor concerns structural differences such as the type of roads,

climate, humidity and the resulting use of vehicles. This therefore involves very different drivers of preference on either side of the Atlantic.

- The last factor is the customers themselves. Everyone knows that the Germans like a certain type of comfort, the British and French another. Today, manufacturers are flocking to China which alone will shortly represent 25 per cent of the growth of the world car market. They are opening factories and establishing joint ventures like PSA Peugeot Citroën, but not with the aim of slavishly duplicating European models. It is impossible to appeal to a market of 300 million Chinese who now have the financial resources to access the market without taking account of the customers themselves.

The time has in fact come to recognize the *post-global brand* – the brand that no longer tries to adhere unreservedly to the model of total globalization, which is no longer perceived as ideal. Of course, globalization at the upstream or production stage remains a priority in many sectors. Like the car sector, which has reduced costs by sharing production platforms, companies can still save more money by creating a smaller number of product platforms that are able, if the need arises, to produce differentiated models. The service sector could also benefit from upstream globalization.

However, the further you go downstream and the closer you get to the customer, the more obvious it becomes that the global concept tends to be replaced by the regional or local concept in the case of a large country. There will therefore never be a car that is truly global, but a more American type for the United States, and other types that are characteristically European and Chinese. This has already happened on other mass-consumption markets. For example, the strategy of the US company Procter & Gamble is based on regionalization, with the US flagship brands Tide, Whisper and Clairol becoming Ariel, Allways and Wella in Europe. The company has a factory in Europe for all its detergents.

It is becoming more and more common for companies to develop products for specific geographical regions, in the way that Hennessy created Pure White for Europe. Dannon (USA) could not sell its drinkable, low-fat yoghurts in Europe since they neither correspond to local taste nor meet the current food standards requirements. It is however true that initiatives designed to open up regional markets, such as the EU, Mercosur and Alena, help to make the region, in the broader sense of the term, a relevant market segment. Furthermore, it is at regional level that the world's markets, and even its historical and cultural communities, are at their most permeable.

Finally, even when a brand appears to be global, when it is distributed and well known in countries throughout the world, closer examination reveals that the product is often far from standardized – it is more of a composite, hybrid or highly adapted product. For example, l'Oréal differentiates between the cosmetic products of its so-called global brands by basing them on the four types of climates in China, since they determine four skin types.

The idea of a global market and the standardization that it implies, has usefully served to start a basic movement in all companies. But over-globalization leads to loss of relevance, a lesson that companies have often learnt to their cost since 1983. This is why today's brands are post-global – they have assimilated the myth and distanced themselves from it without exactly renouncing it. Today, it is more appropriate to refer to selective globalization.

Why are American brands ideologically more global, and the European ones less so? We hypothesize that the American globalized brands were exports of successful brands that had taken many years to find their optimal functioning and positioning in the United States. The idea that this equation of success would simply apply elsewhere seemed to be taken for granted, for the United States themselves constitute a non-homogeneous market. As an example, it is noticeable that Wal-Mart's first store outside the United States, in Mexico, was created 30 years after the creation of Wal-Mart (Bell, Lal and Salmon, 2003). Its worldwide competitor Carrefour opened its first foreign hypermarket in 1969, only six years after it created its first store. Unsurprisingly Wal-Mart applied the rules that made its success in the United States, but in some countries, more remote from the United States than Mexico, such as Brazil, the golden rule of everyday low price does not seem to work. The average Brazilian consumer is instead eager to capitalize on special bargains. Carrefour, being unsure about its optimal formula, was more open to the specificities of the new countries.

The same holds true for Nestlé, number one food company in the world. How can Nestlé be sure that the situation is the same everywhere when it comes from a small country like Switzerland? In fact Nestlé internationalized to four countries its first-ever product, powdered milk, four months after it was launched in Switzerland.

We tend to favour extreme solutions (to be or not to be global?), for they are rhetorically more provocative. Real life is in the middle, but it is more complicated. People have to collaborate in the organization. Then the question becomes how to build a collaborative organization (Hansen and Nohria, 2003).

What is new then? Realism in globalization, the mark of the post-global brand.

The pendulum is swinging back to local

Brand globalization is a strategy. It aims at defeating local competition by providing three major benefits only global brands can create:

- a much lower price by means of economies of scale (the model is Ikea);
- a flow of innovations (the model is L'Oréal, Samsung, Google or Toyota);
- an international image, often more attractive among the mobile and young segments of society (the model is Ralph Lauren or Armani).

Corporations have radically adapted their organization to the demands of globalization.

The most important adaptation has been to create global, transverse structures and treat the world as one. The country of origin is now one country among others. The goal of the global corporations is to capitalize on economies of scale, synergies and cross-fertilization between countries in order to reduce costs and develop efficiency gains. This is why the ideal of such companies is the unified marketing mix. After all, Chanel No 5 is the same everywhere.

Strict globalization has been the dominant corporate religion since 1990. All demands for local exceptions were considered a sign of backward management. Hardly any articles developed the case for local brands (Schuilling *et al*, 1996). Brands had to act globally as much as possible: same products, same pricing, same channels and same communication.

Some signals indicate that the pendulum is swinging back. Knowing that the consumer is always local, there are growing demands for local adaptations and customization to local tastes. What was impossible yesterday is becoming feasible today.

Some examples are significant:

- In the luxury industry homogenization is the norm. This sector is supposed to be the paragon of globalization, a result of vertical integration and total control of operations to master all the details. However, in Saudi Arabia the Armani logo is translated into Arabic characters. The same goes for Clinique skin care. In 2010 Biotherm decided to use a Korean male model for all its advertising in Korea, thus ending 20 years of global advertising with Western male models. Sales went up by 15 per cent. Asians tend to trust an Asian model more when it is about the effect of a cream on their own skin. Lancôme decided to go on television in China to build its brand awareness and be perceived as the leader by the millions of people who are discovering it. The future number one luxury market in the world deserved it.
- Citroën has developed a special car for South America, and especially Brazil. This very unique market will be strategic for the brand: there is a Citroën plant there. Mercedes and BMW have launched elongated cars in China, to give more comfort in the back seat. Car owners in China also want to have a large boot, which is a sign of status.
- To penetrate the very exacting European market, Ralph Lauren launched two exclusive and high-priced special lines there: Black Label and Purple Label, both made in Italy and claiming it.

Interestingly, groups that used to swear they would promote only global brands are now looking to buy local ones. In Morocco, for instance, there are very refined essential oils brands that are quite accessible, with a high degree of elegance and quality. Groups such as L'Oréal might be interested in buying them. L'Oréal's current problem, like that of all groups, is that demand in Europe is flat, as is demand in mature countries in general. Where is growth to be found tomorrow? In the emerging countries with high population growth and the desire to consume, but only if the brand is accessible. Certainly the global brands are less accessible than the local ones. In time these local ones could be exported and become regional brands at least. And this is not to mention the bottom-of-the-pyramid brands.

Certainly this is not the end of global brands. Ikea's catalogue is the same all around the world. But there are signs that loyalty is created by empathy: adapting the McDonald's menu to the tastes of Chinese consumers in their home country is the best way to conquer their purse and their hearts.

Facing counterfeited products and logos

Brands work exactly like banknotes. They symbolize value. A one-dollar banknote is worth money, in the same way as a brand name on a polo shirt. The Lacoste crocodile is worth $85. It took 75 years to create this value.

Just as there is forgery all around the world (such as making false US dollars or euros), an industry to capture the value of your brands is now flourishing. Here are some examples:

- Multiple retailers copy the trade dress of the big brands for their own private labels (Kapferer, 1995; Zaichkowsky, 2006). They imitate their colour codes, designs and even names.
- They use the fame built over years around your brand in one sector and use it in another sector.
- They use the fame developed in one part of the world and use the same name and strategy in another part where the brand is not present. This what the Crocodile company did at a time when Lacoste was hardly present in Asia, many decades ago.
- The counterfeiting industry is now hitting the auto parts business, sports goods, pharmaceutical products, chemical products, cigarettes, hi-fi equipment and luxury goods. It is an organized global industry with links to the local mafias and often hidden support from local high political figures.
- Ambush marketing should also be mentioned here. At each Olympic Games, FMCG promotional campaigns flourish that use circles and rings in their design (a reference to the five Olympic rings that only the official sponsors and partners can use in co-branding).

Sustaining brand value entails a strong legal department and a willingness to be very sensitive to all attempts at stealing your brand equity.

Defending the brand name to prevent reputation dilution

In the defence of intellectual property rights, the principle of specialization prevails. One cannot register a brand name for all product and service categories. This would be a barrier to free trade. That is why a brand name, to be well registered, must specify a product class. As a result Benetton is the well-known clothing brand, but also a long-established small stationery brand. This principle seems simple, but the vogue of brand extensions creates legal problems. There used to be two Apple companies: the one in the United States was initially a computer company, and the other, a British-based company, was producing the music of the Beatles. Thirty years later, the US Apple company entered the music business with the iPod and iTunes, thus infringing the rights of the British Apple company in music. Only a truce agreement could solve that issue between these two companies.

To be fully valid, new brand names must actually be used. Brands gain value only through business operations. The same holds true for brand financial valuation (see Chapter 18): one needs a business plan to estimate the contribution of the name to future profits. The registering company can lose its rights if this new name is not used within five years: proofs of a real commercial activity must be visible. Otherwise companies would register thousands of names just to block competitors' entrance.

There is an exception to this principle of specialization: when the brand is so well known that its fame extends beyond its original speciality. Luxury brands such as Cartier or Louis Vuitton are very cautious about this: they check worldwide any type of usage of their name, whatever the product class. Even China has now accepted it should protect well-known foreign brands against local companies hijacking the fame of these brands. In October 2008, Michelin noticed that a Chinese company was selling hi-fi sound equipment under the name Miqolin, which was pronounced *mi-tcho-lin*. Now the defenders argued that no confusion was possible between tyres and hi-fi sound equipment. However, in a ruling in October 2010 the court in Canton stated that it was a case of counterfeit, even if no confusion was possible between the two product classes. The argument of the court was as follows:

- Michelin is a well-known brand (its brand awareness in China is beyond 60 per cent).
- Its fame is tied to a century of specialization in tyre manufacturing worldwide.
- The Chinese company tried to make a personal profit stemming from the halo of quality associated with the name without asking Michelin first or paying royalties.
- This abusive usage is likely to dilute the value of the Michelin brand, diminishing its distinctiveness (brand extensions do reduce the image of specialization of a brand in one single product class).

This last case is interesting, as it shows the slow evolution of China, a country where counterfeiting is a normal activity. Since China joined the World Trade Organization (WTO), it has had to start changing its attitude vis-à-vis intellectual property rights, not really recognized previously. In other countries, counterfeit activities are now linked to international mafias and criminal organizations, and are even backed by local political support. To fight entails acting in very differentiated ways on both the supply side of counterfeited products and the demand side. The fact that eBay, the world's number one auction website, feels unconcerned by the fact that sellers of luxury products on its site are selling counterfeited products (see also Chapter 18) shows how much the defence of intellectual property rights is far from accepted in practice even in the United States. However, eBay lost all its court cases against LVMH, the world's premier luxury group, which had sued the website for deriving profit from illegal trade of counterfeited products.

Patterns of brand globalization

Before we move forward, it is important to specify the meaning of global. For most managers a brand is global when it is sold everywhere in the world. Finding ads in all airports about Nokia, Dell, IBM or Alcatel seems to be a living sign of real globalization. However, this may be a superficial vision.

We know from Chapter 1 that a brand is a system relating three facets, a concept, a name, and a product or service. It can be pictured as a triangle. As a consequence, when one speaks of globalization, one should specify of what?

We saw that there are strong compelling economic reasons to globalize products or platforms. There are also good reasons to use the same name, for the sake of capitalizing on one single name and exploiting the extra value of global perception. Finally, some concepts are reflections of the existence of global segments. Actually, the combination of these three poles creates eight possible alternative strategies as far as the continuum from globalization to localization is concerned (see Table 17.1).

When people refer to globalization, it is generally in a loose sense, a feeling that the brand is known, visible and distributed everywhere. When we travel abroad some brands do seem global: we see them on billboards as soon as we land at an airport. It is this vision that creates negative attitudes about globalization, the feeling of an inescapable loss of country differences. All commercial centres sell now the same stuff, the same brands, throughout the world. Human richness and diversity now seem dangerously eroded by the law of economies of scale. Of course, those who do not travel are pleased by the possibility of accessing the brands and products they see on television while watching the world.

What are these eight structural types obtained by combining the two possible answers on each part of the brand system?

TABLE 17.1 From global to local: eight alternative patterns of globalization

(Yes = global, No = localized)								
Type	1	2	3	4	5	6	7	8
Name	Yes	Yes	Yes	Yes	No	No	No	No
Positioning	Yes	No	Yes	No	Yes	No	Yes	No
Product	Yes	Yes	No	No	Yes	Yes	No	No
Examples :	Coke Chanel Amex Sony	Mars Martell	Nescafé Garnier	Persil	Ariel/Tide Vauxhall/ Opel	Volkswagen (Group) Benckiser	Cycleurope (Group)	Pure local

- Type 1 is the fully global model. Here there are very few adaptations, except for details.
- Type 2 recognizes the need for different positioning strategy: Mars is a meal substitute in UK (have a Mars a day), but an energizer in Europe. Cars follow the same approach. What is a small car for the German market is seen as a family car in Portugal.
- Type 3 acknowledges the need for important product adaptations. Different countries have different tastes for coffee. The skin and hair of Brazilians are not the same as those of Argentinians. In China, according to the l'Oréal Group, because of the differences in climate, sun and humidity, there are four types of skin balance to be respected from north to south, east to west. Connex is a world ground transportation brand: it operates railways, buses and metro systems wherever municipalities want to create concessions for this public service. However, the same concept, 'security', means very different things in Stockholm, where Connex operated the metro, and in Rio de Janeiro. Thus, obedience to the same brand values cannot mean providing the same secure product everywhere. Local expectations are not as high in South America as they are in Scandinavia for instance, or the capacity to pay the price.
- Type 4 is the result of brands being split between companies. This is the case of Persil: this brand is operated by Unilever and by Henkel. The same holds true for Gervais, an ice cream brand at Nestlé, and a range brand of dairies at Danone.
- Type 5 results when the company cannot use the same name for legal reasons everywhere. For instance Vauxhall in the UK is Opel in Europe.
- Type 6 results when almost similar products are sold under two world brands with different price positionings. It is what is currently happening at the high end of the Volkswagen range, where the cars are very close even in design to the Audi entry models.
- Type 7 is the business model of Cycleurope, leader in the bicycle market. Cycleurope is a Swedish company, which has bought the market leading bike brands in other countries. These are typical local names, with high recognition and proximity. There are strong differences in the bike standards expected by the Dutch, Swedes, Germans, French and Italians: the size of the wheel, the gear, the height of the bike are different. Standardization can only concern the frames.
- Type eight is the fully local model.

Looking more specifically at two of these variables, the brand name and the product platform (is it

TABLE 17.2 Globalization matrix

	Different brands	Same brand everywhere
Same products or concepts	Different brands, identical platforms (Unilever, Danone) **(B)**	Global brands, no adaptation of product (Coca-Cola, Chanel, Sony) **(D)**
Different products or concepts	Sum of local tastes Franchises **(A)**	Nestlé (Nescafé) Yoplait President **(C)**

common or are there widely different products?), there are four strategies.

Danone for instance, like Unilever, is not obsessed with common names, but with the creation of products/concepts that reach an annual turnover worldwide of €1 billion. The CEO, Frank Riboud, states that 'our ambition is not to develop brands that are number one in the world, but brands that are number one locally with global world concepts/products'. For instance 'Taillefine' (literally, slim waist), whose name changes according to the country (Light'fit in the United States, Silhouette in Canada, Corpus in Brazil, Ser in Argentina, Vitalinea in Spain, Vitasnella in Italy, Vitaline in Greece), is a concept of adult tasty food aimed at those maintaining a low-fat diet. It is stretched over the three divisions of Danone group, dairies, water and biscuits. As such one finds the products of this concept either as purified water, or as biscuits under Lu source brand, or as dairies under Danone source brand. But in Argentina the group has kept the endorsing local brand Serenissima, with its 65 per cent market share, to reinforce its competitiveness. This local brand, number one in Argentina, now endorses the global concepts.

Another global concept is Actimel, a specific yoghurt designed to reinforce the body's natural defences. It is sold in 22 countries, with a sales turnover of half a billion euros, and a sales growth of 40 per cent in 2012. A final example of a world concept is the aromatized water sold as Danone Activ'Aro in the UK, Volvic Magic in France, and Bonafont Levite in Mexico. On the whole more than 60 per cent of the Danone group sales are made by concepts that are the market leader in most of the countries where they are sold.

Unilever has been criticized for having more than 1,400 brands, none of which reach the critical size (US $1 billion) to become a world mega-brand. It is now engaged in a fierce reduction of the number of brands. However, to take the ice-cream business, it is operated under the endorsement of the well-known names of the former local market leaders (Walls in the UK, Miko in France and so on), all presenting a common international logo. But their sales are made through power products that are sold globally and managed as real brands: Magnum, Solero and so on. In the margarine business, trust is very important. Local names have been maintained, but the whole company operates four typical product platforms for the whole European market.

The matrix in Table 17.2 reminds us that most companies started in quadrant A. They were international in sales before they thought they had an asset called a brand, and by default before they realized they had to globalize their business. Mostly operating in existing categories, and they do not consider Coke or McDonald's as a valid benchmark for them.

From A they can move either to B or C. B entails rationalizing the products: it is the main source of profits and synergies. C means creating brand transfers to reduce the number of brands. The output is less strong and the risks higher. However, for all disruptive new products such as Actimel, the quadrant D strategy should be adopted.

We have no intention of creating a single global brand!

Who has ever heard of Belron? It is the company holding such brands as Carglass in Europe and

Brazil, Safelite in the United States, Autoglass in the UK and Ireland, Smith & Smith in New Zealand and O'Brien in Australia. It is the leader in windscreen repairs, with 1,700 repair points in the world, 8,000 mobile repair cars and 10 million clients. Belron is the first buyer of car glass worldwide. Looking at this heterogeneous brand portfolio, most consultants would immediately recommend a global rebranding and the adoption of one single global brand.

This is exactly what Belron will not do. In this business, top-of-mind awareness is the prime criterion. When they have an accident and damage to their windscreens, consumers are anxious and expect fast and reliable treatment. Belron policy has been to acquire the local top-of-mind operator and accentuate its leadership with the adoption of the same methods that proved efficient worldwide (servicing, relationship with the car insurance companies, and heavy television and radio advertising campaigns). They follow policy B.

A rebranding would be a dramatic value destruction: the loss of top-of-mind local stars (typically above 65 per cent, the first competitor being at 10 per cent). Now of course if the company were starting today it would choose a global name (policy D).

Moving today to a global name would bring nothing in terms of business: motorists use Belron services mostly in their home country. Those who travel by car would do this in Europe, where the brand is the same across 20 countries. In addition, because of language differences, in spite of leaks from an adjacent country to another, most people watch the television programmes of their own country, so no one realizes that Carglass in France is Safelite in the United States.

However, to maximize the synergies between countries, the service has been unified across all countries. Belron intends to create a single brand personality through the adoption of a common advertising format. This will also facilitate the use of best practices from any country.

Why globalize?

An economic necessity

Very few people dispute the need to internationalize business. World commerce has existed since caravans brought spices from all over Asia to Europe. The great naval explorers of the 15th and 16th centuries were also motivated by the prospect of opening new routes to merchandize. Colonization had economic motives: access to raw materials, to gold, then wheat, then oil.

Production was the first business function to be delocalized. Finance is international. It is the time of marketing. Why then global brands? Why not simply international or multi-local brands?

In the competitive race, economies of scale provide a strategic lever in that they contribute to competitive pricing. A company designing a car with worldwide market potential in mind has a competitive advantage over the manufacturer who only sets his sights locally. Even though the latter may produce a car which better reflects the tastes of his own country, the difference in price from that of a Japanese or a Korean car designed from the start with a worldwide market in mind will naturally make even the most patriotic motorist hesitate. This is why Renault's Twingo, whose low price is a key element of positioning for the easy-to-live-with car, was designed from the start for a whole continent: the same product everywhere.

The local company – even if it is positioned in a niche – has no other way of overcoming the price handicap than to extend its outlets while innovating. Geographical extension is an essential condition in the race for survival.

If the brand is to remain competitive, its innovation must be offered immediately to all at the lowest possible price. The marginal cost of each progressive feature rises day by day. Hundreds of researchers are needed to even hope to innovate. Industrial investments and research costs must now be set against low unit margins. Using the awareness and public confidence which it has acquired, the brand provides the firm with access to outlets on an ever-widening scale. Without these, such investments could not be economically justified. The manufacturer's brand opens the way to progress and, at the same time, makes it available for all.

The global name: a source of advantages

In certain market areas, the global brand is a necessity, whereas in many other cases it is a means of exploiting and taking advantage of new opportunities in communication.

The single brand is a necessity whenever the clients themselves are already operating worldwide. Firms using IBM or Dell in London would see no sense in having the same equipment in their Bogota or Kuala Lumpur offices under a different brand name. The same applies to most technological industries. Caterpillar, Sumitomo, Schlumberger, Siemens and Alcatel are of necessity world brands – quite apart from the fact that they are global enterprises.

It is also necessary to retain a single brand when the brand itself corresponds to the signature or *griffe* of its individual creator. Take the luxury trade – Pierre Cardin is Pierre Cardin wherever his products are found, just as Ralph Lauren is Ralph Lauren. Their creations are bought around the world because their signature bears witness to the values of their creator. Whether or not the creator lives on in body or in spirit does not change the rule: from a single source comes a single name.

These cases apart, the single brand permits the exploitation of new international opportunities:

- As tourism develops, for instance, it is a disadvantage that certain products have different names in different countries. If this were not the case, tourists could find their brands. Seeing the queues of comforted tourists from all countries in front of McDonald's instead of Quick is enough to convince anyone. This argument applies, however, more to some sectors than to others: to food more than lingerie and to car oil more than cooking oil. But the main advantage is linked to the synergy: the exposure of an American executive to DHL in Europe will benefit the renown and the reputation of DHL in the United States. Brands acquire additional credibility when they prove to have international appeal. This is why in 1989 Ariel brought out the first advertising commercial featuring testimony from housewives from different European countries.
- The more international media develop, the greater the opportunities they provide for the single brand. This has long been the case with traditional media; it now concerns satellite, cable and the internet. Real opportunities for worldwide coverage are provided by such events as Grand Slam tennis tournaments, the Tour de France, the World Soccer Cup, the Olympic Games, Formula 1 motor racing, etc. Through its sponsorship of the Roland Garros tournament, the BNP Bank is known as far afield as California where they speak of the tournament as the 'BNP Tournament', just as there is a 'Volvo Grand Prix'. These programmes reach an international audience and therefore in practical terms exclude on-the-spot local brands, since the costs involved in appealing to only part of the audience would be prohibitive. Only global brands can be present in worldwide events such as the Olympic games or Formula 1 motor racing. Only the global brand can justify the cost of sponsoring such worldwide stars as Tiger Woods or Roger Federer.

The emergence of global segments

All sociocultural studies underscore the convergence of lifestyles. There are fewer differences between top executives in Japan and in Germany than between executives and employees within Germany. In addition identification models act on a worldwide basis: some Chinese women identify with American woman, others with the French, and a growing number now identify with Korea's style of beauty. The same may be true in Holland or in New York. This is why l'Oréal has developed a wide array of global brands: far from pushing towards uniformity, this group diffuses heterogeneity. This is why it takes much care in offering brands that symbolize not one single type of beauty but all of them, from Softsheen Carson for the black community worldwide, to Sue Uemura or Maybelline. The group takes much care in leaving each of its brand's headquarters in its home country to preserve its specificity. However, they must globalize their concept and products and communications. Global segments should each have a global brand corresponding to their needs.

Pricing issues

Finally, the price factor will be a key component of the homogenization of brand strategies in the future. Indeed everything points to reducing the price span within which the same brand can evolve from one country to another, from one area to another.

- The existence of a concentration of distributors on a regional or international level creates a major destabilizing threat to brands that optimize locally their price policy. There is nothing to prevent the distributors from demanding the lowest price to be seen in Europe, which may be in Portugal for instance, or in a country that has lowered its prices as a means of competition.
- The emergence of parallel markets needs to be avoided as these would destabilize the normal distribution channels of a country and therefore the relationship between a brand and its distributors.

There is indeed a close relationship between price positioning and market positioning. A brand cannot be the most expensive on the market in one place and in the mainstream in another. The price level situates the brand in terms of perceived quality, performance and prestige. In the market for special vintages of champagne, for example, to be the most expensive, on a par with or cheaper than Dom Perignon, does not position its challenger Veuve Clicquot in the same way. Reducing the international price variance of a brand is a factor which encourages uniform positioning and, by extension, affects the whole brand policy. Unless a policy is explicitly chosen that allows optimum prices locally and strong price differences from one country to another, identical products need to be sold under different brand names in each country. This is the strategy followed by Benckiser, which buys strong local brands. R&D are indeed by necessity European, using the principle of a 'lead country' for the development of new products and the definition of the marketing mix.

Fighting the grey market

A classical consequence of economic heterogeneity is the grey market. To reach public accessibility, brands must align their prices on the local economic level. However, when a gap exists among countries not too far apart in distance, a grey market grows, disturbing the sales and trade goodwill in the country invaded by parallel imports. Of course, in the case of luxury goods with selective distribution agreements, the first reaction is to install some form of trace, in order to identify those commercial agents that break these agreements, reselling outside their zone.

A second approach is to change the brand. Thus in Northern Europe Viakal, an anti-limescaling household product, became Antikal to stop the grey market of Italian Viakal products, which were sold there at a price 30 per cent lower. Without going to such extremes, Hennessy cognac decided to stop selling its VSOP product in Western Europe, and instead created a customized product called Fine de Cognac. Europe was in any case drinking less and less VSOP, but it had become a source of a grey market for Russia. In fact, throughout the world, global brands are developing more and more regional products for these commercial reasons.

A final approach of course is to create a price corridor across all countries of a region or continent. This cuts the risk of a grey market growing, but handicaps the sales where the brand is overpriced for the sake of respecting the international corridor.

The benefits of a global image

A great deal has been written on the subject of global brands, but what exactly do we know about them? In fact very little, until recently when the subject was further clarified by the three studies outlined below. Two of these studies focus on the benefits of having – that is, being perceived as having – a global image. But how does perceived brand globalness (PBG) create value? There are a number of reasons for creating a global brand – economies of scale, synergies between countries, the speed with which innovations created worldwide can be brought onto the market, the existence of exploitable global segments and finally, as has already been suggested, the benefits of having an international image. Today, in the age of cultural integration, modernity is expressed via internationalism. The perception of globalness would therefore increase perceived value. It is symptomatic that, in countries throughout the world, young people's favourite brands are usually international, whereas the reverse is true for adults.

One of the studies (Alden, Steenkamp and Batra, 1999) set out to validate this hypothesis. In a quantitative study carried out in the United States and South Korea, the authors demonstrated that perceived globalness (the fact of being perceived to be selling products worldwide) exerted a strong influence over purchase decisions. But contrary to expectation, this influence was not because perceived globalness enabled consumers to participate in a global culture. In fact, perceived globalness primarily influenced the perceived quality, and second the perceived prestige, of the brand. These effects were however not quite as strong for ethnocentric consumers, that is, those who were more focused on national values. These results needed to be extended to other countries and include other criteria for consumer segmentation, since the cultural connections between South Korea and the United States are well known.

This was done by Holt, Quelch and Taylor (2003) when they studied how global perceptions drive value, using a sample of 1,800 respondents in 12 countries. According to the study, perceived globalness influences brand preferences via five levers:

- As an indicator of quality (higher quality due to perceived globalness). This effect is in fact the most important, and explained 34 per cent of the variance in preferences observed by the study.
- The second effect is the increased status conferred on the brand by its perceived globalness. This explained 12 per cent of the variance and coincides with the results of the previous study.
- The third lever is linked to the images and special characteristics attributed to individual countries. Global brands are often associated with a country of origin and therefore a stereotype of competence, such as clocks and watches (Switzerland), TGV high speed trains (France). This accounted for 10 per cent of the variance.
- Increased responsibility, fostered by perceived brand globalness. Because they are represented worldwide, global brands have a higher profile and therefore have to be more environmentally and socially aware than other brands. Being big is equated with being more responsible. This effect only explained 8 per cent of the variance. However, it was extremely important for 22 per cent of respondents, and important for 41 per cent of this group.
- Finally, the American image, or the American dream, is associated with a number of global brands. This effect did not explain the variance in preferences between brands when consumers were taken as a whole. However, as soon as these international consumers were segmented, the American image was a dream for 39 per cent, which made it a factor of preference, while it was anathema for 29 per cent and therefore a negative factor and rejection.

To their credit, Holt *et al* segmented the consumers. In the seven segments that resulted – from 'pro-west' to 'anti-globalization' – the hierarchy of the five levers was completely different. How people understand and value global brands is very segmented. Countries are also heterogeneous. China, for instance, is both pro and anti American values: it has consumers belonging to both groups. Muslim countries such as Indonesia, Turkey and Egypt are very influenced by the perception of globalness. However, one should recall that the interviewees were not laypeople, but well off ones, probably with a Westernized lifestyle. People in India, Brazil and South Africa were not very much influenced by perceptions of globalness; is it because they have a strong local culture they are proud of? Finally, those least influenced by the perception of brand globalness are US consumers.

This should not be a surprise: the Americans do not consider that the choice of other countries is relevant. It is an ethnocentric country. Also, since many of the so-called global brands are American in origin, their status is ambiguous. They are selling everywhere in the world but they seem to be deep local brands.

Schuiling and Kapferer (2004) have compared the distinctive properties of local and international food brands, separating, however, international brands in their home country from the same brands in other countries. In fact, their data show that the best brand profile is that of the international brands in their home country. No wonder: countries export their best in class brands. The data also show how global brands really differ from local ones. Working

TABLE 17.3 How global and local brands differ (in percentages, after adjusting for brand awareness level)

	Local brand (B. Aw = 85%)	Global brand (B. Aw = 85%)	Global–local
High quality	25.29	27.07	+1.78
Trust	22.11	20.23	–1.88
Reliable	22.11	19.06	–3.05
Fashionable	14.04	15.50	+1.46
Original	13.57	14.64	+1.07
Distinct	12.56	13.70	+1.14
Sympathetic	11.74	13.19	+1.45
Funny	9.76	12.90	+3.14
Pleasing	7.08	12.90	+5.82
Healthy	15.56	12.27	–3.29
Innovating	6.08	11.50	+5.42
A leader	8.07	9.33	+1.26
Unique	4.40	7.61	+3.21

(Base 9,739 respondents , 507 brands)

SOURCE Schuiling and Kapferer (2004)

on a database of 507 brands in four countries, and 9,739 respondents, Schuiling and Kapferer have isolated the discriminant properties of each type of brand: local (that is, sold in one country, whatever its perception by the public) and international (sold in all countries, whatever the perception of the public). The authors first notice that on the whole local brands that have been present for a much longer time in the country are endowed with a higher brand awareness score than more recent international arrivals. Since brand awareness is correlated with image (see page 21), are the so-called differences of image only an outcome of this brand awareness gap? When the data are adjusted for awareness, there do remain differences in image, some negative, some positive, as evidenced by Table 17.3.

It is noticeable that, compared with local brands, global brands have a significant deficit on:

- health value (–3.29 per cent);
- reliability (–3.05 per cent);
- trust (–1.88 per cent).

On the other hand, they outperform local brands on the following levers:

- pleasing (+5.82 per cent);
- innovativeness (+5.42 per cent);
- uniqueness (+3.21 per cent);
- fun, thrill (+3.14 per cent);
- high quality (+1.78 per cent);
- fashionable (+1.46 per cent);
- sympathetic (+1.45 per cent).

Conditions favouring global brands

Certain situations make global communication and brand policy easier. They are linked to the product, to the markets, to the force of brand identity and also to the organization of companies.

Social and cultural changes provide a favourable platform for global brands. Under these circumstances, part of the market no longer identifies with long-established local values and seeks new models on which to build its identity. Turning its back on prevailing national values, it is open to outside influence from abroad. In drinking Coca-Cola, we are drinking the American myth – in other words the fresh, open, bubbling, young and dynamic all-American images. Youngsters form a target in search of identity and in need of their own reference points. In an effort to stand out from the rest, they draw their sources of identity from media-personified cultural models. Levi's are linked with a mythical image of breaking away down the long, lonely road – the rebel. Nike encourages them to strive to surpass themselves, turning its back on the national confines of race and culture. Women also constitute a clientele looking for new models; Estée Lauder could portray the free, independent and seductive woman, and use this image for its own globalization. Brands corresponding to new eating habits also have to impose forcefully their view of the world in order to rally consumers in search of change. In this way, the brand is seen as a new flag-waver.

New, unexplored sectors have not, by definition, inherited a system of values. Everything is there for the making, and it's up to the brand to do it. This is why there is nothing to prevent the global marketing of high-tech, computer, internet, photographic, electronic and telecommunications or service brands. Dell can, and must, spread its brand everywhere, because brands themselves are the only point of reference in these markets. Only the themes of the campaigns will change to take into account the country's level of economic development, hence its preoccupation. Globalization also applies to new services: Hertz, Avis and Europcar globalized their campaigns by portraying the stereotype of the hurried businessman – and in any event an Italian businessman wants to identify more with being a businessman than with being an Italian. The argument of novelty works also for McDonald's, Malibu or Corona!

The world has been standardized by the increasing and levelling power of technology – this is Levitt's point (1983). Its products no longer stem from local culture but belong to our times. They are the fruit of science and time. They therefore escape the local cultural contingencies that hinder global communication.

In general terms, globalization is possible – and indeed desirable – in markets which revolve around mobility. This applies to multimedia, the hotel industry, car rental, airlines, and also the transfer of pictures and sounds. When the brand is perceived as being international, its authority and expertise are automatically accepted. Again, brands have a clear opportunity to organize and structure those market sectors which symbolize the disappearance of time and space constraints. It is their role to deploy their system of values, which can only be unique faced with mobile clients.

Globalization is possible when the brand is totally built into a cultural stereotype. AEG, Bosch, Siemens, Mercedes and BMW rest secure in the 'Made in Germany' model, which opens up the global market, since the stereotype invoked is a collective symbol breaking national bounds. It conjures up a meaning of robust performance in any country. The Barilla name is another stereotype built on the classic Italian image of tomato sauce, pasta, a carefree way of life, songs and sun. Volvo, Ericson, ABB and Saab epitomize Sweden.

Finally, certain brands represent archetypes or 'universal truths', to paraphrase Zaltman (Wathieu, Zaltman and Liu, 2003). Snuggles fabric softener not only arouses the same notion in every country – that of gentleness (which is not in itself original) – but also the image of reliance, love and security as in one's childhood, as symbolized by the teddy bear. This is why, in order to express the notion of 'snuggling, caressing, cajoling', the brand name is translated as Cajoline in France, Kuchelweib in Germany, Yumos in Turkey, Mimosin in Spain and Cocolino in Italy. La Vache Qui Rit, which corresponds to the archetype of the generous mother, is likewise translated (Die Lächende Kuhe or The Laughing Cow). Marlboro embodies the archetype of the macho man – alone and untouched, authentic, yet modernized and popularized throughout the world in Western sagas of the conquest of America. Maybelline expresses American beauty. Lancôme expresses the French woman.

Several of the above factors explain why luxury brands and *griffes* have gained a worldwide appeal. In the first place, they bear a message – each creator is expressing his or her own personal values. They were not conceived as a result of any market study or consumer analysis from one country to the next. It is the creator's identity and his or her desire to express his or her own values that form the automatic basis of the brand's identity, in no matter what part of the world. Second, behind every luxury brand there is a guiding standard – sometimes even an archetype. Cacharel and Nina Ricci represent the dawning of femininity, a dawn tinted with shyness and modesty. Yves Saint Laurent stands for female independence, even rebellion. Finally, the 'Made in France' label and the myth of Paris imbue these brands with definitive cultural undertones. All these are reasons why such brands are able to impose their own vision of the world on national outlooks. Like any religion, brands that set out to convert must believe in their message and spread it unerringly among the multitudes.

On the whole, brands whose identity focuses on the product and its roots can more easily go global. Jack Daniel's whiskey builds the pivot of its brand identity from its distillery and its tradition, which leads to advertising which has been remarkably stable throughout time and similar in all countries. Even though it is working with different agencies, the articles and conditions are such that each one produces commercials or announcements that are typically Jack Daniel's.

Certain organizational factors also ease the shift to a global brand. One-person companies and brands that bear the name of their creator who is still alive are from the start more global. Countries have less ability to modulate locally the identity of Ralph Lauren since the head of the company is precisely Ralph Lauren. It is also true for Bic or Paloma Picasso.

American companies are more ready to globalize because marketing on their domestic market is in essence global, considering the social and cultural diversity of the American melting-pot. Organizational factors also point in the same direction. When expanding towards Europe, these companies created European headquarters from the beginning, based most often in Brussels or London. Individual countries therefore had to account for their results to these European centres. As seen from the US, there was very early on the need for a centre for 'European operations', for considering Europe as a single and homogeneous area.

Finally, a single centre for production in Europe or South America is also a strong factor for globalization, at least for products. The fact that one factory centralizes the production of detergents for Procter & Gamble in the whole of Europe leads to a standard product offer throughout and to the spread of technical innovations to all countries at the same time. In markets where the product advantage is key in the positioning of the brand, this centralization of production and of R&D leaves little room for differentiation on a local basis.

Disruption versus optimizing products

Apart from factors linked to the market or to the organizations themselves, the same company may have to follow two different policies according to the status of its products. One analysis that explains the differences in observed behaviour is linked to the type of marketing. Certain products are the optimization of an existing offer. Others are complete breaks from what is on offer, innovations even to the extent of creating a new segment that did not exist before. This distinction has an impact on the chosen international policy. Optimization marketing leads to more flexibility when there is a need to adapt to local conditions. Strong innovation, however, that which conveys new vision, tends to impose itself on all countries and hardly needs any adapting. This is the case for the iPhone.

Generally speaking, a strong new concept is capable of breaking the rules and borders. For example, alcoholic beverages are generally promoted using local strategies. What is more cultural than alcohol? Moreover, it is drunk by adults and as we get older our tastes and preferences solidify (unlike

TABLE 17.4 What differences between countries would compel you to adapt the marketing mix of the brand?

Type of difference	Necessary adaptation (%)
Legal differences	55
Competition	47
Consumption habits	41
Distribution structure	39
Brand awareness	38
Brand distribution level	37
Media audience	37
Marketing programme success	34
Consumers' needs	33
Media availability	32
Brand images	30.5
Norms for products manufacturing	27.5
Brand history	25.2
Lifestyle differences	25
Cultural differences	25
Subsidiary sales	23
Consumers' buying power	22
Consumers' age differences	12

SOURCE Kapferer/Eurocom pan-European survey

with soft-drinks for teenagers). However, very new concepts in this field are able to have a worldwide impact: Corona, Absolut, Bailey's, Malibu. It is the same for cheese: La Vache Qui Rit is a global concept.

Barriers to globalization

What are the strongest barriers to globalization? What are the parameters that, according to managers themselves, make difficult, even impossible, brand globalization? Table 17.4 is particularly revealing in this regard.

The first and only factor that justifies for most people interviewed (55.2 per cent) the non-application of a global strategy is legal differences. It is true, for example, that laws which deal with the definition of products, the right to sell, the authorization and manner of advertising of alcohol and the use of children in advertising vary considerably. However, because of the Single European Act, Mercosur in South America or the GATT, these differences in legislation will have to be evened out, thus suppressing the major obstacle to globalization. The second factor is linked to the local competitive situation (number and strength of competitors, levels of brand awareness, type and level of distribution, stage in the product life cycle). Taking the example of Orangina once more, it is not possible to approach the market where Orangina is a close second to Coca-Cola in the same way as the English market, where it occupies a niche in the premium segment of carbonated orange soft drinks and competes with Fanta, Sunkist and Tango, the local dominant brand. This has a deep impact on market strategy and positioning, but the Orangina identity is nevertheless the same. Moreover, since they are known in advance, these very different market situations can be integrated when filming commercials. Some commercials destined for countries where Orangina is not known will need longer sequences on the product and on shaking the pulp. At the other end of the scale these sequences can be reduced in other countries. The significance of this factor concerning the local competitive situation explains in some measure global success of brands such as Mars, Gillette, McDonald's, Coke, Bailey's, Dell, eBay, Ryanair, Somfy and so on. They didn't really have any competitors in the market, and they were new products, creating new segments or revealing the start of a latent transnational demand. They were driven by the feeling that they had an excellent product and extended their programme to all countries. The third factor hindering globalization is the differences in consumer habits: these are, as we have seen, fatal for products such as Ricard that are deeply rooted in a particular culture. Moreover, to become truly global, a brand must play down its ethnic component. As long as Bailey's was an 'Irish Cream' its potential was limited. An 'exotic' beverage coming from afar, its 'strangeness' relegated it to small sales volumes, to fans of Ireland who would sip it in the evening by the fireplace. But how many people know Ireland throughout the world? Who will still drink alcohol as a liqueur? The globalization of Bailey's consisted of breaking away from the association with the liqueur set ('The Bailey's moment is whenever') and the promotion of Ireland as a tourist destination, and promoting instead 'Baileys on ice' (see page 000).

Table 17.5 presents the facets that are most easily globalized for pan-European brands.

As we can see, the percentage varies from 10 per cent to 93 per cent. Such a variance is linked to the fact that the phrase 'brand globalization' refers both to identity and to action (the marketing mix).

TABLE 17.5 Which facets of the brand mix are most often globalized? (Kapferer/Eurocom)

	%
Logotype, trademark	93
Brand name	81
Product features	67
Packaging	53
After-sales service	48
Distribution channels	46
Sponsoring (arts)	32
Sponsoring (sports)	29
Advertising positioning	29
Advertising execution	25
Relative pricing	24
Direct marketing	18
Sales promotion	10

It is the fixed image of the brand (its fixed logo) that is the most globalized, a sign that image precedes sound. What counts is that the exclusive typography and the red colour of Coca-Cola can be found throughout the world, even if it isn't written 'Coca-Cola'. Unilever does not use its Motta brand of ice cream everywhere, but its local equivalents use the same colour and signal codes. The brand name comes in second. It is true that most companies have inherited some odd situations where what is called Dash in Italy is called Ariel in Europe and so on. When brands are local strengths it is not a good idea to risk standardizing too fast. The operational facets of the marketing mix are naturally adapted to local markets, all the more so as we approach below-the-line activities or local financial optimisation regarding the price. In the era of television and multi-media, image wins over word. All the more so in Third World countries where illiteracy is common. Colour codes and graphics must be global: Coke is red, Heineken is green. However, even the strongest brands hesitate when the question arises of what to call them in the enormous Chinese market (see below).

Let us analyse in depth how these barriers impact the internationalization of brands.

Coping with local service

How do global brands integrate the true diversity of the world, economic, legislative and cultural? How do they build a global brand in such heterogeneous conditions? Can the brand be in fact truly global?

Global brands, but local service

Globalization is a simplification process for the sake of profitability. Now there is a point where simplification becomes oversimplification and hurts the results. For instance, in Saudi Arabia a famous Western skin care brand has adapted its packaging, which is now fully written in Arabic and makes reference to local uses to position its products ('an alternative to essential oils'). Sales grew immediately.

Everywhere global brands have to make these choices. What is the point of globalizing 100 per cent of the consumer experience if it does not create value locally and position accordingly? For instance, can Lacoste be managed the same way in the United States, where it must trade up from a fun alligator brand to a sophisticated lifestyle brand, and in China, where there is no tennis or golf culture and where people see no difference between the Crocodile brand, a local official me-too, and the dozens of counterfeiting brands (Cartelo, etc)? In Europe Louis Vuitton means creativity and is attached to the name of Marc Jacobs. In China, now the land of vertical mobility, Louis Vuitton means conformism and success.

Another source of difference is the level of service to be delivered by a brand and its globalization:

- Gift wrapping is essential in Japan and Korea, but far less in the United States, whose culture is dominated by functionality and value for a dollar. In addition, in mature Western countries save-the-planet groups criticize brands that use excessive paper.
- Queuing acceptability: the Chinese accept 15 minutes and the Americans 21 minutes when queuing in theme parks.
- Delivery: in India a luxury product will commonly be delivered to your hotel in a banal plastic bag. Unless one asks for it, this is not done in Western shops.
- At-home product trial may be the preferred mode of service in the Middle East, where women do not feel comfortable trying on clothes in a store. It is not needed in Europe at all.

Economic heterogeneity: bottom of the pyramid

Economies where people earn less than a dollar a day create a formidable challenge to multinational companies. Most of their brands are simply not accessible here, and by this we do not mean only that they are far too expensive. Take Danone brands in the dairies market: Danone's products need a whole supply chain with a fully controlled temperature, something that cannot be assured in Bangladesh, for instance. Here the roads and the distribution system make the 'last kilometre' prohibitive. The poor just cannot be accessed. It is important to think of completely different business, manufacturing and distribution systems: for instance, with hundreds of individuals carrying small quantities each day on their bikes, which they would have bought thanks to a micro-credit structure like the Grameen Bank of Nobel Prize winner Muhammad Yunus. Danone has been experimenting with different scenarios and models to find a way of feeding the world at a profit. Unless this is found, millions of people will rely on human solidarity funding to survive. This innovation is called Indovation or Chinovation.

Naming problems

The ultimate symbol of successful globalization is the ability to use the same name worldwide. However, a brand name often poses problems for globalization. The main ones are outlined below:

- First of all, there is the problem of prior registration by a local company. For example, the name Eurostar had already been registered by a service company and had to be bought from that company, a solution that is not always possible. Less straightforward was the problem of the Crocodile brand, registered by a Chinese company and rapidly reinforced by a vast network of stores known as The Crocodile Shop, just as the global brand Lacoste accessed the Asian market. Lacoste's logo is a crocodile.
- Second, the name can be a problem in terms of its meaning in a specific language. There is no shortage of anecdotes about brand names that have sexual connotations in other countries.
- A less common problem is the translation of descriptive names. Traditionally, the Americans do not translate their descriptive brand names – Pampers are Pampers the world over, as is Head & Shoulders. But for an international brand of cheese such as La Vache Qui Rit (The Laughing Cow), the name is important because it conveys a message and permits the correct interpretation of the brand symbol (a cow's head). Without it, the cow could appear stupid, smiling or mad. In this case, there is a link between the brand name and brand symbol. The question therefore arises as to whether or not to translate this descriptive brand name for each country, and if so, whether to keep a reference to the brand name in French. If this is done, should this reference be above or below the local translation? Finally, should the answers to these questions be different for each region, since the answers depend on the added value desired?

  In certain areas, there is a real problem of counterfeited goods and therefore a need to reassure consumers that the product is in fact the real thing. In some areas (such as Saudi Arabia, the Middle East and Germany), the added value comes from the reference to France.
- Finally China poses a specific problem because of its very different regional dialects.

Naming in China

Naming in China often forces managers to face a choice: should they name semantically or phonetically (Schmitt and Zhang, 2001)? The dilemma is as follows: should one respect the sound of the name even if it has no local meaning and is therefore difficult to pronounce and to memorize, or should one respect the concept even if it means parting from the international sound of the brand name? Ideally of course, one would say both. The Chinese sound should resemble the international pronunciation, but the meaning should also be appropriate. Microsoft's semantic name would be Wei Jua, which means micro flexible and soft. In addition it is a pleasant sound to a Chinese ear. Coca-Cola and Carrefour found both a semantic and phonetic appropriate translation: Keu Ko Keu Leu means 'good to drink and makes happy', Tia-leu-Fu means something close to 'the house of happiness'. The leading worldwide brand of insecticide, Decis from Aventis, is pronounced Di-Cha-Seu which luckily means 'at them until death'.

Others are less lucky. Peugeot is said as 'Piao Je', but in Cantonese, it evokes a prostitute. Orangina starts with an O: in Chinese there are no nice words starting with an O.

There is a danger however in localizing the name too much in China. Foreign brands are now valued much more than local brands. All signs which accentuate the perception of being a local brand may erode brand equity in the long term. The size of this market requires that all due precautions be taken.

Achieving the delicate local–global balance

Each company has to find its own balance between localization (the adaptation of its products to local markets) and the deep-rooted *raison d'être* of globalization, the pursuit of a competitive advantage through reduced costs. It is therefore possible to say that there is a contradiction between the need to create value – via the adaptation of products and symbols to suit a particular country, market segment and even ethnic groups, communities or individuals on a one-to-one basis – and the economic requirement of reducing costs. As with any dilemma, every company knows there is no single solution, just progressive adaptations and even policy reviews when they have placed too much emphasis on localization or standardization.

Cosmetic groups (such as Estée Lauder, Shiseido and l'Oréal) and car manufacturers are in the throes of this dilemma since they are both 'high-tech' and 'high-touch'. It is a well-known fact that globalization was born of technology, and aids the diffusion of research via the ever-decreasing costs of that technology. However, because cosmetic brands target the beauty of individual women, they must be ultra-sensitive and therefore 'high-touch' and, as such, adapt as far as possible to specific physiological characteristics, as well as to the basic and cultural characteristics of women in countries throughout the world. There is no longer an overall concept of beauty, but an acceptance of the diversity of different types of beauty within the same country and between generations. The dilemma is equally acute for the car industry when a car is not simply positioned as a low-priced vehicle. A car has a special significance for individual consumers, and since each consumer is different, there is not only an expectation of diversity at brand level, but also in respect of models, line extensions and even the personalization of the relationship with the brand.

Everyone to their own balance?

To take one category, cosmetics for example, it is significant that the brands positioned as 'mass market' have to develop their proximity much more than the so-called elitist brands. As such, they not only make greater use of direct-contact marketing but also tend to adapt products and publicity much more within the well-defined framework of the brand identity, on the one hand, and the brand's economic equation, on the other. Thus Garnier and Maybelline adapt much more than Lancôme, and in the case of Garnier, this adaptation is automatic and built in from the outset. For example, Garnier offers the most extensive range of cosmetics to meet the demands of all skin and hair types in Europe and the United States. Depending on the country, its subsidiaries select the products best suited to their requirements, since each country develops its own market. The same applies to the format of the packaging and labelling. The differentiation is situated at national level and not at the level of the region or zone, since the women of – albeit geographically close – countries such as Korea, Taiwan and Japan in fact have very different expectations. The Lancôme customer, on the other hand, is widely travelled and expects to be able to buy the same products in Tokyo or Paris – by being over-adapted, these products would lose their status. Naturally, Lancôme develops specific skin-whitening products to meet the very strong demand among Asian women in these countries.

So how do companies reconcile this fine-tuned adaptation and the economic equation? By making the economic equation the criterion for the acceptance of the adaptation. Thus for l'Oréal, innovation assumes the status of a religion, with over 500 patents registered each year. This innovation can come from one of three sources:

- one of four basic research laboratories – two in the United States, one in Europe and one in Japan;
- from brand marketing teams throughout the world;
- from any of the various national retail distribution subsidiaries.

Sometimes there is a strong local demand in a particular country. For example, in 1997, Brazil expressed a desire for a specific haircare product since Brazilian hair – the result of the country's ethnic melting pot – is characteristically dry and unmanageable and needs a moisturizing conditioner. Brazilian women are proud of their hair, which they regard, even more than their faces, as the symbol of their sensuality. They therefore want it to be long and flowing, to move with their body, what the Brazilians call *cacheado*, or curling and wavy. So the European laboratory developed a unique formula and then l'Oréal considered the economic equation. Could enough of this new product be sold in Brazil and, of course, elsewhere in the world? It was called Elsève Hydramax and soon became the most popular haircare product in Brazil before being extended to other countries.

Globalizing local demands

Maybelline provides another example. Although it is a US brand and its teams are based in New York, the Japanese laboratory discovered an innovative active ingredient that was able to meet the very specific demands of very trendy and 'hip' young Japanese women, typical of Tokyo's Shibuya district, for a particular type of lipstick. These are young women with small mouths, and in Japan mother-of-pearl is very popular. This molecule created the effect of water, giving the lipstick a 'wet look'. After careful economic analysis, the product was developed in Japan under the name Maybelline Watershine Diamonds. In the space of a year, it made Maybelline the best-selling mass-market make-up brand in Japan, and was subsequently extended to the United States and Europe where it enjoyed a similar meteoric success.

In both these cases, the local innovations were only accepted when they were considered 'globalizable' with the potential for global successes. This is a far cry from the 'think global, act local' business model. It is more a case of 'think local, act global'.

Competitive advantage through adaptation

Globalization at all price has a cost: failure. On the other hand, some examples, not much publicized, show how market adaptation helps in developing a profitable business and slowly gaining market leadership.

Year after year, Nestlé has tried to compete against Kellogg's in the cereals market. This is normal: cereals are close to the core product of Nestlé, milk. They address the same target too (children), and the same benefit: growth.

As long as Nestlé copied Kellogg's it was unsuccessful. In addition, Nestlé had no know-how in cereals. It needed an alliance. General Mills in the United States was itself looking for a way to enter Europe, after Kellogg's, Quaker Oats, and the private labels of strong or even dominant multiple retailers. To compete against a leader one needs an innovation. Because of Nestlé's decentralized culture, local subsidiaries have some autonomy. The French subsidiary identified a need so far untapped by Kellogg's: children love chocolate. They wish to have chocolate for breakfast. Why didn't Kellogg's identify this need? First, it was a local need, and centralized global companies are not fitted to adapt to local needs. Second, it did not fit with the ideology of cereals for growth and health. Finally, leaders tend to defend their acquired position instead of looking for new markets (Christensen, 1997). Also, as a chocolate brand, Nestlé had more insight into this market. The result was the launch of a local new product, thanks to the know-how of General Mills, marketed and distributed by Nestlé: Chocapic, the first cereals in chocolate. Soon this product became the market leader with a share of 11 per cent: all multiple retailers had to distribute it. This is how Nestlé fought back successfully. It innovated in a high-volume market, then Chocapic was rapidly extended to other European and world countries.

Everyone has heard about Malibu, a white rum and coconut light drink. What about Soho or Ditta, which recently passed Malibu in volume and value sales? Soho and Ditta are the two names of the same product, a mixer based on lychees. Why are there two names? Because it is not possible to sell a lychee mixer drink the same way in Japan (where it is now the number one brand) and in Europe. In Japan, Ditta is aimed at young women who typically go to bars to chat together, a classic of Japanese social behaviour. The communication target was the bar staff who promoted imaginative new cocktails. In Europe, the brand called Soho is mostly sold off-premises, in multiple retailers, thanks to in-store wet trial campaigns. The target market is women as a basis for cocktails (with grapefruit for instance). Here again, leadership came from adaptation.

Adaptation: a necessity for growth through time

A final example is Barilla, a mainstream popular pasta brand that is number one in Italy. It decided to extend geographically in Europe, by means of a positioning very different from its own domestic positioning: it created the premium pasta market in Europe. Barilla was introduced almost as a luxury brand (see Table 17.6). This was implemented through cartons with a specific design and the launch of a collection of forms of pasta unknown in most countries. Naturally the price was 25 per cent higher than the local leader, which itself often had an Italian name but did not play on this image dimension, having lost all links with Italy a long time ago.

Barilla's goal is not to remain a niche player in all foreign countries, but to become the number two if not the number one. This necessitates addressing the local habits of average consumers, not elitist ones. As a consequence, the brand has to widen its range and lower its prices on new lines adapted to children and family consumption, even if this means producing products that are hardly typically Italian but represent a large part of local consumption (like noodles). This also entails packaging these lines in a far less premium style (no more cartons). Finally, the advertising itself should bring the brand closer to the markets: it has to stop being perceived as the brand of Italians. Positioning a brand on export markets as the one preferred by consumers in its domestic market contributes to reinforcing an alien image. Some consumers may like to imitate the choices of foreigners, but becoming a local leader means addressing the needs of this market, the first one being to be relevant for that market.

Integration factors

How does a company speed up perceived integration and acquire the desired level of assimilation in a country? This is an issue that even involves high-tech companies if they do not want to be perceived as cold, distant and indifferent to public concerns, simply content to sell and therefore a symbol of the predatory multinationals. The first thing is to tune into local needs and then implement a local marketing campaign – on the streets, in sports stadia, as part of local life. Media advertising should be balanced by direct contact and involvement in a country's everyday life. It was not by chance that Garnier launched its new Fructis Style product on, among other things, more than 100 buses in each country – buses that would travel back and forth across towns and cities, in direct contact with the general public.

Last but not least, and bearing in mind that the brand and company are one and the same thing in the eyes of the general public, it is a distinct advantage to have factories and produce the product in the countries in question. This not only helps the brand to put down roots but also increases its status, since it provides employment. If the company also has a well-developed social policy, people will talk about it and it will gain respect and confidence. Far from behaving like a colonizer or a predator, the brand will be seen as seeking to share its success. The local publicity given to the social initiatives of Danone (the company) in Mexico greatly helped to speed up the brand's assimilation in this key country. As can be seen, in the age of the responsible and ethical brand, companies no longer hide behind their brands (quite the opposite, in fact) in their penetration of foreign markets.

Local brands can strike back

Who knows Bean Pole? It is the main competitor of Ralph Lauren in Korea, stronger than Tommy Hilfiger, Lacoste and Fred Perry together. Yet Bean Pole is a local brand that looks more American than Ralph Lauren itself. It is worth considering how many leading brands are in fact not local. The leading brands on a number of markets – fruit juices, beer, cooking oil, butter, cheese – are all local brands. It could be argued that these are traditional products, but it is significant that in Korea and Japan, the number one hamburger is not McDonald's or Burger King, but Lotteria (an offshoot of the Lotte department stores). The same is true in Belgium where Quick is still the market leader, more than 10 years after the US giant penetrated the Belgian market. The paradox is explained by the 'first mover advantage'. In these countries, it was the local brands that established the hamburger restaurants and the market for which they became the referents. There is no difference in the structures of these competitors, but the key factor of the success of any restaurant is its position – when McDonald's arrived in Korea and Belgium, the best sites were already taken.

Today, many global brands affirm that they try not to appear global. This is certainly true in the case of Danone, which is in fact legally the local brand in four different countries. The Danone brand, the result of an innovation, was created in Spain in 1919 by Isaac Carasso, who named it after his son (Danon is the Catalan diminutive for Daniel). Danone was registered in France in 1929, while Dannon Milk Products, Inc. was created in New York in 1942 by Daniel Carasso, who had emigrated to the United States. The brand was subsequently extended to Mexico. In each of these four countries, Danone or Dannon is regarded as a local brand. Strangely enough, according to its directors, the German brand Nivea also aspires to be perceived as a local brand even though it is one of the most widely distributed brands in the world. The same applies to the Danish brand Velux, the number one roof window manufacturer, Bic, Garnier and others.

In 1998, the trend was for globalization at all costs, and having bought the Czech company Opavia, the Danone group decided to replace this local brand with its own global brand. However, Danone had seriously underestimated the strength of the local brand and had to back-pedal. Opavia had more than 70 per cent of the market share in the Czech Republic. During the communist era, the only 'treat' available to the Czechs was biscuits, and Opavia had become their friend and ally. Last but not least, Opavia was also the name of a Czech town, which made it a patriotic brand. All these factors were difficult to appreciate when legislating from a distance. Each country has its own icon brands and globalization simply cannot afford to ignore the consumer.

The international study referred to earlier (Schuiling and Kapferer, 2004; see page 417) identified the levers specific to local brands – confidence and proximity. These are key factors of success if the local brand also knows how to market its products effectively.

Developing local brands

Since many brands are and will continue to remain local, how can they be developed in the face of international competition? Because their processes and business models are specific, they are much more accessible to the mass market and can represent a welcome source of unlimited future growth in emerging economies. The strength of local brands has already been demonstrated (Schuiling and Kapferer, 2004) and their strong points compared with global brands. But confidence and proximity will not provide indefinite protection – they have to be maintained, and the strategies that maintain them are therefore particularly important. But it is equally important to address the weaknesses of local brands – a lack of innovation, fun and fashion, according to the new, younger generation of consumers. Local brands also suffer from a number of weaknesses and limitations at management level, and these are outlined below:

- The first is often inertia – too used to simply being there, because of their history rather than their ambition, local brands often lack energy because they lack ambition. The brand therefore needs to be revitalized from within, and its aims, mission statements and advantages clearly redefined.
- Local brands are often too widely dispersed. It is therefore crucial to refocus resources on certain markets or market segments in which they can hope to dominate or at least be joint market leaders. They also have to accept the need to part with some of their business in order to concentrate on the segments with the potential to dominate the market. Alternatively they can target niches, small but profitable markets, in a way that the multinationals are unable to do.
- Local brands often lack innovation – they rely too heavily on loyalty as a driver of preference and have therefore lost their relevance because their products are no longer modern enough or sufficiently well adapted to meet present-day demands. It cannot be said often enough that innovations are the lifeblood of a brand. There are several types of innovation. Some demand huge investments in R&D and are beyond the scope of local brands, while

others are more closely identified with the user values of the products and are therefore more accessible. A third type is related not so much to basic research (new active ingredients) as to the search for new concepts that are linked to a consumer insight.

- Local brands tend to have an established form of management. There is a need to bring in new managers who relate to and therefore understand the new markets and segments, who can identify consumer insights and convert them into ideas.
- Local brands are too self-restricting. In an age that glorifies globalization, there is little in the way of advice or articles to support local brands (Kapferer, 2001). They therefore run the risk of being too self-restricting, as in the case of the Norwegian company DBS, a local market leader in the bicycle sector. DBS did not think it would be able to sell modern mountain bikes under its own name, in the face of competition from Giant or the US company Cannondale. In fact, it was a huge success – consumers were delighted to be able to buy quality products throughout Norway (due to the extended distribution of the brand), under the national brand name. Of course, there are always people who will only buy international brands, but it is important to take account of the less obsessive majority.
- There is another form of geographical self-restriction. There is no reason why a local brand should not seek opportunities for growth in neighbouring countries, which are often familiar with the brand or have cultural similarities that favour its assimilation. Thus, it is quite natural for local Estonian brands to be sold in Lithuania and Latvia, or for Polish brands to be sold in Hungary and the Czech Republic. But the geographical area can extend further afield. One of the key factors of the success of small and medium-sized enterprises is their assimilation at international level very early on in their development (Simon, 2000). It is significant that in the case of Wal-Mart, the world's leading distributor, a development team travels the world in search of innovative products that will differentiate the store's ranges from those of its competitors and add an element of surprise for customers. This was how the micro-company Lorina, which had relaunched the 'orange crush' drinks popular in the past, was spotted at a trade exhibition for new products and then referenced in the United States a year after its creation. This referencing with a mega-distributor is often tied to an exclusivity agreement that guarantees a certain continuity for a brand's international development.
- Finally, local brands must not appear local. Except in the case of ethnic or traditional craft products linked to a particular region, modernity is expressed via cultural integration. Who knows whether or not Hollywood chewing gum is a local brand? Or Gemey, Dop, Tango or Wall's ice cream? The top three brands in the world's largest market in terms of volume (France) for Scotch whisky are all local brands. Certainly these whiskies come from Scotland, where whisky is produced to excess, but these brands were created by wines and spirits merchants – two low-price brands, based essentially on trade marketing (William Peel, Label 5), and a mainstream brand (Clan Campbell). It was these brands, less expensive than the big international brands, that enabled the French market to double in size in the space of 15 years.

A good example of management of local brands against increasing international competition is Amore Pacific, Korea's dynamic and leading cosmetics company, and strong market leader thanks to a wide brand portfolio. How did Amore Pacific strengthen its brand proactively?

- First, the brands are allocated by distribution route: one brand, one channel. This includes the very dominant direct sales channel (door to door or through customer-led parties), a channel imported brand cannot penetrate for it requires a know-how and resources it will not possess.
- Second, small brands have been merged into larger ones, to create mega-brands and reach

a higher critical size, a condition of higher marketing investments.

- Third, brands are permanently nurtured by innovations.
- Fourth, local brands do not look at all local. La Neige for instance aims at the youth market, with a French-looking name and capitalizes on its proximity to French customers. Hera (the name of a Greek goddess) is a direct competitor of Lancôme and Estée Lauder: as such it is strongly visible in all premium department stores as in the duty free zone of Korean Airports.
- Finally, Amore Pacific has extended its best brands to other countries. La Neige has been successfully launched in Hong Kong and Shanghai, as Hera. There is a growing demand in Asia for Asian brands that understand Asian women better than Western imported ones.

The process of brand globalization

Key stages in the process of brand globalization are:

- defining brand identity;
- choosing regions and countries;
- accessing the markets;
- choosing the brand architecture;
- choosing products adapted to the markets;
- constructing global campaigns.

Defining global brand identity

Brand globalization presupposes the definition of the brand to be globalized. That is, the brand must have an identity that will serve as a medium for its globalization, in both tangible and intangible terms. The company must therefore start by defining and writing the parameters of the brand's identity. This is essential for coherence, all the more so since globalization will greatly increase the brand's centrifugal tendencies, with everyone wanting to interpret it in their own particular way. To limit these tendencies, there must be a clear and concise platform with salient points and flesh.

It should be remembered that the modern brand is no longer a simple 'product plus' (a mere definition of a product with a plus value, like 'the best toothpaste for helping prevent tooth decay'). It is a source that has to be defined. To avoid problems of understanding and translation, globalization very often involves the choice of all-purpose words that have the advantage of creating consensus the world over, such as 'high quality', 'client focused', 'dynamic' and 'competent'. But it is important to be wary of international consensus since it usually reflects a certain weakness in the brand definition and therefore the brand identity.

Brands are based on differentiation. They have to have character, salient and original points. But would Marlboro dare to launch its brand today using the symbol of a solitary, macho, craggy, outdoor figure?

Global brands are universal stereotypes

As a rule each brand should be based on a consumer or customer insight. An insight is literally an insight into the consumer or customer, a short sentence encapsulating the state of mind or expectation or attitude the brand is responding to.

As a consequence, global brands tend to address universal truths, global insights. Taking the spirit market, what are the universal truths of alcohols? Here consumption is conspicuous: by drinking, men try to enhance their male status. By its symbolic character, and the values it promotes ('keep walking', that is to say persevere) Johnnie Walker represents the adult male achievement. It is about effort and masculinity, about being a real male throughout the world. J&B is about social success. Chivas encourages joy and conspicuous consumption. Bacardi is an escape to paradise.

Give sharpness to your identity

There are several ways of preventing the salient points of the brand identity becoming lost in the globalization process:

- by accompanying the facets of the brand identity with a comparison, saying what the brand is and what it is not;

- by accompanying the words with images (brand concept board);
- by reinforcing the facets through training initiatives and creating local brand relays (keepers of the flame);
- by not delegating strategic implementation (such as advertising and the web) to the local level.

Separate the domestic and the international positioning

When it leaves its country of origin, a brand is transformed, and changes its nature. For example, Barilla in Italy is a popular 'mainstream' pasta brand that offers good value for money and inspires confidence. As shown by Table 17.6, in other countries it is positioned as the ultimate Italian 'must have', top quality, traditional and fashionable, but loses its 'value for money' and 'confidence' – it takes time to build up confidence.

Generally speaking, exported brands must be positioned at the top of the range since they have to support transport costs and customs duties. Furthermore, it is an opportunity to take advantage of the spillover effects of perceived brand globalness (PBG). In this way, the Swedish vodka Absolut created the top-of-the-range (premium) segment in the United States, where it is sold for 20 per cent more than the local market leader (Smirnoff), which has factories scattered throughout the region.

Selecting regions and countries

An examination of the so-called global brands reveals that they are far from being as widely distributed throughout the world as we are led to believe. Of course, this could be because conquering world markets is a gradual process and a company must first of all establish itself as the leader in its domestic market. For example, the first Wal-Mart was not established outside the United States until 1991, 30 years after the creation of the first store in this famous US chain, while McDonald's accessed other markets gradually, one by one.

However, there is another explanation – not all countries are potential customers for the brand in question. For example, dairy products are not part of Asian culture, which is a handicap for Danone. Similarly, yoghurt is not a part of US culture and this is a handicap for Dannon USA which, although created in 1942, has not managed to impose itself as a major brand. The Japanese do not like their perfume to impinge on others, which is a handicap for all brands of strong perfume. This is why brands such as Paloma Picasso, with its characteristically Spanish values and strong essences, sell better in Texas, California and of course southern Europe, but also in countries (such as Germany) whose tourists visit southern Europe.

At this stage a strategic analysis should be carried out to assess the potentials of each country and the barriers to accessing their markets. This analysis should incorporate:

TABLE 17.6 Barilla's international and domestic image

Percentage perceiving the brand to be:	Italy	France	Germany
High quality	34.9	56.9	40.6
Trustworthy	56.6	44.8	17.4
Good quality/price	33.8	26.8	17.2
Fashionable	11.0	19.6	26.1
Authentic	8.9	16.0	13.7

SOURCE Schuiling and Kapferer (2004)

- the size of the existing market;
- indicators of growth and/or the latent potentials of this market, and its 'segmentability' – sociocultural developments and the growth of purchasing power;
- consumer insights on their prospects for rapid development;
- the nature of any competition and its ability to react – does the brand in question have the potential for strong differentiation, or a 'plus value'?
- the existence of a rudimentary brand equity in the country or region (via tourism or the international media which transmit brand images into homes throughout the world);
- the existence of adequate distribution channels likely to promote the brand concept;
- the existence of a media network;
- the existence of adequate commercial partners at local level;
- the non-existence of barriers to market access – customs, formal and informal regulations;
- the potential for registering or buying the brand name (a check that it is not already owned locally).

The presence of trade barriers was why countries like India, fearing a sort of neocolonialism through the intermediary of companies, for a long time remained closed to imports. It would have been theoretically possible, for example, to manufacture a major brand of car in that country, but this would require all the subcontractors who are a necessary part of the production process to do the same thing. In the absence of subcontractors and adequate partners, there is a risk of departing from the brand contract in that particular country – its cars will sell but will be of inferior quality. This was also a problem in Brazil for a long time.

The result of the strategic analysis of the countries in question sometimes explains the distribution of sales of international brands. Thus, the three key countries for The Laughing Cow brand are of course its country of origin but also Germany and Saudi Arabia, where temperatures are so high that processed cheese is the only way to provide the daily milk intake for both adults and children. The creation of factories in Morocco and Egypt has also reduced the problem of customs barriers.

Within the context of globalization, the order in which countries, regions and continents are 'conquered' is also a strategic issue. For example, Amore Pacific is the international flagship brand of the Korean company of the same name – it embodies its know-how, values and ethics. It is also a modern brand that seeks to ally itself with the concept of Western beauty without rejecting its Asiatic origins. In 2003 the question arose as to which it should penetrate first, the US or European market. Apart from the issues addressed above, the company was concerned whether it was in its best interest to advertise success in Europe then the United States, or vice versa. Given that perceived brand globalness is not a driver of preference in the United States, or at least less so than in Europe (Holt, Quelch and Taylor, 2003), it was decided to penetrate the US market first. In addition, the United States seem geographically, socially and culturally much closer to Korea than Europe, which is not only distant and fragmented, but also has strong well-established brands.

It will come as no surprise that, today, all Western brands are looking towards the East:

Entering the selected markets

Globally speaking, there are two major strategies for accessing national markets, by creating a new category or segmenting an existing category.

Creating a new category

Garnier is a typical example of this. The parent brand establishes itself by launching a daughter brand that becomes the reference, the pioneer of a new category which has the benefit of the 'first mover advantage', little or no competition and easier negotiations with distributors who are eager for creative innovations and value rather than a mere change of brands between competitors. The downside of this strategy is that it requires a greater investment in marketing and advertising. Its success also establishes the meaning of the parent brand, which enables it to launch its other daughter brands at a later date.

Nivea uses the same strategy even though it has an 'umbrella brand' architecture. It launches Nivea Cream before the lines that establish its competence in the facial and body care sector, the keys to creating a long-term bond of confidence.

Segmenting an existing category

The alternative strategy involves the immediate creation of a significant volume of business by launching a differentiated product, based on the brand values, but in a large-volume local category. For example, in Lebanon Yoplait began by launching two traditional local dairy products, Laban and Labneh. The aim was to quickly become the referent for traditional fresh dairy products by giving the country what a large industrial company can give – superior and consistent quality, more hygienic products, a more subtle taste, products with a longer shelf life, and more practical packaging.

Lactalis, an international giant of the cheese industry, globalized its umbrella brand Président in the same way. The Président business model is the segmentation of generic categories. Created in 1968, it became the leading brand of France's leading cheese (Camembert) and then the leading brand of butter, before extending to other products such as Brie and Emmental. By segmenting the generic category, Président introduces modern quality, practicality, adaptability to new uses and so on. The mistake would be to try to globalize Président by exporting Camembert – for example, why would the Spanish, Russians or Kazakhs want to eat Camembert? At best it would appeal to a tiny minority (a niche). This is not how a leading brand is recreated – and this is the key issue.

It is the business model of the brand that has to be globalized. For Président, this involves recreating – in Russia, Kazakhstan, Spain or any other country – the initiative used to successfully create the original brand, by segmenting a large-volume traditional local category.

It is worth noting that Danone, unable to create a new category of dairy products in Asia, decided to establish itself by segmenting an existing category to embody its key value, health. Throughout the world, Danone is famous for its yoghurts and mineral water. In Asia it puts its name to biscuits – that promise health (growth and vitamins) to parents and children – via global daughter brands such as Prince and Pepito, or by endorsing an ultra-popular, leading local brand such as Jacob's in Indonesia, Thailand and Singapore, and Tiger in China.

Adapting the brand architecture

Should the brand architecture be the same in all countries? Maybe it 'should' but can it in fact be the same? The gradual globalization of a brand with two levels of branding (including a source brand or endorsing brand) automatically raises this type of question. Also, adaptation is governed by practical considerations – it is impossible to recreate what was achieved without the pressures of time and profitability in other markets, including the country of origin. Depending on the country, the type of brand architecture used will be the 'horizontal crunch' and/or the 'vertical crunch'.

The 'horizontal crunch' involves reducing the horizontal range of brands and 'nicheing' certain brands below others. Thus, in the United States, it is possible to find a Mini Babybel cheese with a taste of Bonbel, the whole being endorsed by The Laughing Cow, whereas in France and Germany these three names correspond to three different brands. But when a company moves into the United States, the problem is not so much ensuring greater market coverage with a portfolio containing a range of speciality products as surviving by capitalizing. What was an independent brand becomes a daughter brand or an additional item under the same brand name (line extension).

The 'vertical crunch' has the reverse effect – vertical brand architectures with three levels of branding are reduced to two levels for reasons of efficiency and practicality. This type of crunch is subdivided into the 'top-down crunch' and the 'bottom-up crunch'.

The 'bottom-up crunch' helps to reduce the number of levels by suppressing the one in the middle and raising the one at the bottom. In Europe, l'Oréal Paris is represented in the shampoo market by the Elsève brand, whose products have names (such as Color Vive) that describe the function of the product. They are therefore referred to as Elsève Color Vive by l'Oréal. The driver (what the consumer actually buys) is Elsève, while l'Oréal Paris acts as an endorsement.

In the United States, it was decided to do away with Elsève but to give all the products in the range the suffix 'Vive': Nutri Vive, Vita Vive, Color Vive,

Curl Vive, Hydra Vive, Body Vive. This makes the relationship between l'Oréal and its products much stronger and more direct, which in turn promotes a reciprocal regeneration. The brand now has a co-driver since US consumers are not buying l'Oréal shampoo or Color Vive, but a combination of the two – l'Oréal Color Vive. This also avoids the fragmentation of publicity in a country where media costs are extremely high.

The 'top-down crunch' occurs when an endorsing brand becomes a driver and relegates the daughter brand to the role of descriptor. It is significant that in Europe, the European brand of biscuits Lu is sold by speciality brands. According to the packaging, Lu comes under the aegis of its daughter brands Prince, Pim's and Mikado. Below the names, each specific product may even be described as an 'energy added' biscuit, for example.

In the countries to be 'conquered' by the brand (like the United States), Lu has been upgraded from an endorsing brand to a range brand, while the other names are less prominent on the packaging and become descriptors.

Creating products relevant to the markets

In India, Lux shampoo comes in individual sachets. In China, Tide is not a powder or a liquid detergent; it is a solid soap to wash the laundry. Managing the growth of business and the establishment of the brand simultaneously means constantly adapting the marketing – and therefore the product ranges – to the market, but within the framework of a well-defined and coherent international strategy. As has already been stated, the 'prototypes' must be chosen as a function of the image to be created. Gone are the days when importers decided which products would be allowed into a country on the basis of purely short-term requirements. These importers were merchants and intermediaries, not shareholders in the company, and therefore had no long-term objectives. This was why many brands were launched via different products in countries that were in fact quite close to the country of origin. Within the space of a few years, this led to discrepancies in the product image and therefore to significant discrepancies in the price premium.

Products must be a source of rapid growth and yet comply with the sphere of influence that the brand wants to establish over a period of time. Product campaigns, especially in the initial stages, can help to achieve this. The different ways in which products are adapted to suit different countries, areas and regions were examined earlier as part of the localization–globalization dilemma.

Constructing global campaigns

Not all brands want to globalize their communication. Japanese companies typically allow their subsidiaries, in all their branches, a great deal of freedom at local level. Of course, this creates an impression of disunity since the images projected by the various branches within the same country tend to be very different. But from a cultural point of view, large Japanese – and more recently Korean – groups seem to want to offset the extreme standardization of their global products (the source of economies of scale) by allowing this freedom at local level. These local subsidiaries are mainly sales subsidiaries whose purpose is to optimize the sales of global products in a particular country. Their local managers are judged on these results, not on the attendant creation of brand equity. Their marketing structures are essentially operational marketing structures, with the exception of Sony, which has developed its brand concept in other countries, and Toyota in the United States.

Another brand that favours a local approach is Bonduelle, a leading company on the European vegetable market, where it has to confront an amazing diversity of situations. In Spain, for example, the brand had to access the market via the frozen foods sector, in Russia via tinned sweetcorn. Peas, its flagship product, vary greatly from country to country. The Germans and Dutch like large, green peas, while the French prefer small, sweet, extra fine peas. In Italy, Germany and the Netherlands, peas are mainly used for decoration (as in a salad), which gave rise to the launch of Bonduelle's 'Crea Salad'. Faced with such diversity, the company has centred its globalization initiatives around internal values and company dialogue. Furthermore, the name, logo and packaging are the same for all products, although advertising remains very local.

An increasing number of brands want to control their global image. While it is important to start by creating a brand identity platform, this serves no purpose unless it is presented coherently throughout the world. So, if a brand has decided to conduct a voluntarist policy of globalization, it needs to develop its own procedures for constructing its global campaigns. The most typical are outlined below.

Globalizing communications: processes and problems

Today, brands want to globalize their advertising, although this may not be possible in certain situations for practical reasons. There is no shortage of questions on this score. How do brands construct global campaigns without damaging promotional creativity? How do they avoid demotivating the countries concerned? How do they inject a positive spiral into the company, throughout the countries concerned, to destroy the not-invented-here (NIH) syndrome? The great progress made in this field provides benchmarks from which lessons can be learnt. In the following analysis, it will be noted that, first and foremost, these campaigns identify what unites the brand, which is what it wants to globalize:

- the brand spirit, the parameters of brand identity;
- the brand's visual identity;
- the strategic product (prototype);
- the executional codes of the campaign.

These must be identified before moving any closer towards an identical copy strategy, a common creative concept or even a global campaign. Companies also vary depending on whether they impose a certain discipline or encourage the search for standardization.

Contrary to appearances, McDonald's is not particularly prescriptive when it comes to brand advertising. Of course the marketing is global, like the product. With a few exceptions and adaptations (which are the focus of media attention), the concept is strong because it is standardized the world over – even though McDonald's is organized according to national subsidiaries that are virtually independent. With regard to advertising, the company's corporate headquarters run the Ronald McDonald films and charity initiatives, and offer guidelines without seeking to impose any form of obligation or control. This is explained by the McDonald's business model – the form of the advertising cannot be imposed upon those who pay for it, the franchisees in each country who pay 4 per cent of their turnover for the franchise. Once a month, a vote is taken at the country's executive headquarters in respect of future campaigns.

Even so, an incredible impression of 'commonness' emerges from the television ads in all the franchise countries. But this is not the result of any form of constraint – at McDonald's, informality is the unifying principle. It is due to the high level of understanding and sharing, by the group's advertising managers worldwide, of the following elements:

- the state of mind of the brand, its concept (food, family and fun, simple human truths) and the essence of the brand (the child within us);
- the brand promise expressed according to a traditional 'laddering' (features, functions, rewards, values, personality);
- the golden rules of advertising (tenets of Great McDonald's Advertising), such as 'every McDonald's ad is a brand ad' or 'show human relationships', 'stay current: understand me, the client' or 'woven into the fabric of local, everyday life', or 'always put emotion into it'.

As a result, the baselines vary greatly depending on the country, but they all represent the same source, the same identity, whether it is 'Mac your day' (Australia), 'Every time a good time' (Germany), 'Smile' (South America), or 'You know our products from the cradle' (Poland).

To promote even greater standardization, without damaging the McDonald's business model, advertising films from all over the world are shown at the Creative Brand Seminars held on a regular basis. This encourages countries to use very creative films that, although produced in other countries, are still extremely relevant. The 'best practices' are posted on the intranet and discussed at McDonald's Hamburger University. Finally, incentives are offered for using other countries' films. Today, 50 per cent of McDonald's television advertising is based on the sharing and use of these 'best practices'.

The car manufacturing group Volkswagen is extremely centralized in respect of marketing, but when it comes to advertising, allows great freedom of expression within a strong brand framework. For example, each country can produce a different film (based on the same strategic and creative brief) for the market's most popular models, because creative advertising is not centralized. However, for less 'mainstream' products such as the 4 × 4 Touareg or the Phaeton, a single film is produced by the German group's corporate headquarters.

The Polo provides a good example of the creative process. It is based on the very strong Volkswagen brand platform. In the past, the brand concept was centred around reliability and the tone characterized by an implicit understanding (humour) with the consumer. Today, due to the presence of the Skoda and Seat brands, the brand concept has evolved – it is now based on the democratization of excellence. Then there is the platform of the daughter brand, the framework of the positioning of the model and the consideration of all the models in the 'Tone and Style of VW Advertising' framework. This framework is reminiscent of the principles used by the Tribal DDB advertising agency since 1960, which have created the exceptional distinctiveness of VW advertising and invested the brand with its unique personality. It includes such principles as: 'Do not exaggerate: call a spade a spade', ' Don't shout, he can hear you especially if you talk sense', 'Be authentic, honest, human, open, accessible', 'Make people think and smile', 'Be teasing, elliptic: one should understand only at the point of revelation' and finally and most importantly 'Be original'. In DDB ads, Volkswagen cars rarely move.

The positioning of the Polo that provided a worldwide framework was 'Polo inspires self confidence because you can feel it is the only car in its class that is built without compromise'. Then a creative brief was produced that summarized the advertising objectives, the advertising target and the consumer insight ('I feel I can take on the world'), the product range and the reason to believe. Using this brief, local DDB agencies set to work and came up with the creative idea that was finally used: 'Tough new Polo, careful it doesn't go to your head'. Then the films based on this creative concept were produced by the local teams in each country.

Philips was recently restructured as a centralized organization for a global brand, with its headquarters in the Netherlands. The new 'unique' brand concept was established – 'A unique experience' – valid for all three market segments (home entertainment, personal expression and professional business products). The company's senior management now decides on the choice of transnational products that will form the basis of the brand's publicity. It centralizes briefings and develops the advertising campaigns with local design teams. The pretest procedure is centralized, as is production, with additional items built in at the filming stage of the ad, to reduce the cost of line extensions.

Nivea uses a similar model, with very explicit guidelines on the brand identity, the personality of each sub-brand, and the strict provisos for handling the publicity that create the 'Niveaness' so typical of all the brand ads, in spite of their diversity. The director of Nivea's Worldwide Marketing, based in Hamburg, appoints three local marketing directors to work on a project, in partnership with the TBWA Hamburg advertising agency. They are chosen from countries throughout the world and their task is to define the creative platform. This is then sent to the local TBWA agencies of the three marketing directors which produce creative ideas and then campaigns. The campaign chosen is then imposed in all countries unless it has to be customized. This happened in the case of the campaign to relaunch Nivea Soft, for which the creative idea was 'soft as the morning rain'. But this had to be adapted for three countries – the UK, where it rains a lot, Saudi Arabia, where it hardly rains at all, and Indonesia, where rain is associated with the devastation caused by monsoons. The adapted ideas for each of these countries were:

- so light, soft sensation for beautiful skin (UK and Australia);
- it feels like under the trees (Indonesia);
- it feels like the summer rain (Saudi Arabia).

These case studies illustrate the typical processes of groups wanting to globalize their advertising. But it should be remembered that globalization must be pragmatic and take account of strong regional differences (different competitors, different consumer needs). It is therefore advisable to:

- Start by globalizing at regional level. For example, start in Asia and then incorporate the United States and Europe, or vice versa.
- Establish common brand platforms (identity) and share the spirit of the brand to create an implicit sense of affinity.

FIGURE 17.1 Managing the globalization process between headquarters and subsidiaries

Brand mix \ Function	Ignore	Inform	Persuade	Approve	Decide	Oblige
Product Concept Positioning Price Distribution CRM Web activity Activation Promotion Advertising – creative concept – executional guides – production						
	Decentralized			Centralized		

SOURCE TBWA

- Establish guidelines for the handling of advertising, which are either limited to using common symbols of recognition or go much further in order to bring out the personality of the brand.
- If necessary, admit that the angle of attack cannot be the same for all markets (positioning versus competitors, the unique compelling competitive advantage), depending on regions and/or continents.
- Remember that, while a single advertisement is of course economically justifiable in the pursuit of this objective, the objective of branding is not to save money but to boost business. Working at international level is expensive since it requires the creation of an international structure, the organization of lots of meetings, and so on.
- Possibly be more prescriptive with regard to common strategic products than local tactical products.

In conclusion, it is important to define the relationship to be established with the countries concerned – is it a logic of supplier and customer or one of authority, between decision maker and subordinate? Depending on the possibilities, there is a choice between decentralized or centralized management. There are six types of relationship or different managerial functions, as summarized in Figure 17.1, that can be applied to all elements of brand marketing. The globalization process of each company can be represented on this grid by marking (with a cross) the point of intersection between an element of the marketing mix and the type of relationship with the countries concerned, in respect of this particular element.

Making local brands converge

A classic strategy for globalization consists of unifying the local brands inherited during the growth of the groups. Big groups have, historically speaking, often chosen a strategy of external growth through the buying up of strong local brands. The industrial sector typically uses this strategy: Schneider has never stopped purchasing local leading brands of electronics, for instance. In buying these well-established reputations, these companies were able to smooth their way through local markets. This approach also involves fast-moving consumer goods. The former BSN took over the famous Belgian biscuit brand, Beukelaer, the local equivalent of Lu. The Swedish group Molnycke bought Nana in France, which then joined the Scandinavian brand of sanitary protection, Libresse.

Given this patchwork type of situation where there is not much standardization in the brand portfolio, companies proceed to regroup brands around the same positioning.

Two scenarios are then possible:

- The company changes the names of the local brands by substituting the name of its own brand.
- In the second scenario, the company decides to keep the local brand equities connected to the brand names. General Motor's branch in Europe is called Opel while in the UK it is known as Vauxhall. However, these brands do need to converge.

The harmonizing process of a brand portfolio is quite tricky and should always be conducted on a voluntary basis, since the initial situations of each separate brand name are never the same. A systematic programme of unification according to the style, but above all according to the product basis, must be implemented. The example of Mölnycke is interesting from this point of view. In the female hygiene market, the intimate relationship which has slowly been built up with the client is a key factor in the capital of the brand, of course, there is the product benefit, but there is also the climate of a relationship within the brand identity. This relationship must be maintained. Having judged it necessary to preserve the brand capital attached to Nana in Southern Europe and to Libresse in Northern Europe, at the same time as Procter & Gamble was entering the market with Always, the Mölnycke group progressed in three steps.

The first step consisted of determining together what the unique positioning of these two brands could be. The positioning revolved around the concept of what is 'natural'. Deeper examination revealed that this concept gave rise to different readings, according to the country under examination. In Scandinavian countries, the home territory for Libresse, nature in its strictest sense was evoked, whereas in the home countries of Nana nature connoted spontaneity. The second step consisted of bringing the brand image of Libresse and Nana closer together as they were quite different to start with. Libresse had to develop a more feminine image and more humour, going so far as to include a man in the advertisement for the first time. As for the Nana woman, she had to evolve in her commercials, become more natural with less frivolity, more pared down to the essential, more thoughtful.

This second step was brought about by specific communications, but then having achieved a single concept for the brand, the third step consisted of launching new products shared by both brands with the same commercial.

In conclusion, analysis of this internationalization strategy enables the definition of the typical pathway to follow in all countries with similar constraints. The process is made up of seven basic steps (see Table 17.7). A consensus of opinion about the kernel of the brand, the deep identity to which all subsidiaries must adhere, is the essential starting point of these seven steps. This adhesion is revealed through visible signs such as logos, codes, tone and style. The ultimate phase is the quest for commercials that resemble each other more and more, until a single commercial is possible for all.

The reader will have understood by now that whether or not to have common advertising is not the important issue. One cannot reduce the question of globalization to knowing whether it is possible to produce a standard commercial.

Of much greater importance are the existence of one common invisible kernel and competitive positioning and economies of scale at the production level.

TABLE 17.7 How to make local brands converge

Step 1	Is internationalization necessary? Pertinence of globalization for the brand or brands?
Step 2	Which brand facets should be internationalized? Which ones should not?
Step 3	Agreed-upon description for the network of the common kernel, brand platform, identity prism and positioning
Step 4	Definition of the common visible facets, of the graphic charters, packaging charters, charters of advertising expression
Step 5	Definition of the common copy strategy
Step 6	Definition of the common advertising execution
Step 7	Global launching of common products

SOURCE Adapted from F Bonnal/DDB

PART FOUR
Brand valuation

18 Financial valuation and accounting for brands

Financial evaluation and accounting procedures for brands have become subjects of considerable interest and debate, as can be seen by the numerous articles that have been published on the subject. This intense interest in the subject has several technical, economic and fiscal aspects, but especially reflects the discovery of the importance of intangible investments in modern companies, and of the growth that a brand can generate in certain cases. The debates are international, as they concern the IAS new norms of accounting as they affect large multinational corporations that they acquired and hence need to value fairly, and revalue regularly.

The reason for the sudden interest in this subject – it was hardly mentioned before 1985 – is the large increase in the number of takeover bids for companies with brands. The financial and tax implications of the new problems posed by goodwill were considerable.

Each year Interbrand, an international brand design agency, and Millward Brown, a marketing research company, publish their own estimates of the financial value of the top 100 global brands. These skyrocketing and often discrepant figures (see Table 1.5 and Table 18.2) create a lot of buzz and publicity, which is their primary objective. These figures are also reassuring for marketing departments and bring optimism to compensate for the demise of so many well-known brands facing low-cost or technological new competition. Financial evaluation of brands can be made only by those with access to all the data of the brands and companies, ie by insiders. The purpose of this chapter is to explain how. It is not a technical chapter. Brand valuation gets at the heart of how brands create value.

When one company is bought by another, there is often a huge difference between the book value of the company assets and the price paid, especially if there are strong brands and positive forecasts of growth. This difference is called goodwill: it is actually a measure of the financial markets' positive attitude to the future of the company. For accounting purposes, the payment by the acquiring company must lead to the inclusion in its balance sheet of what has effectively been bought (assets minus debts) so as to get a perfect match between these elements and the price paid (see Figure 18.1).

In all modern accounting systems and norms, goodwill must be allocated to the specific items that have created it. Brands are one of these, as well as patents, know-how and databases. Hence, it can be said that the question of brand valuation has stemmed from the necessity to account for sometimes huge goodwill payments when major corporations were sold. There are other situations where brands need to be evaluated. For instance, when a brand is purchased, the value of this asset must be made explicit.

Accounting is governed by the principle of prudence. Its evaluations must be shown to be valid, coherent and reproduceable. This is why, paradoxically, only the brands that have been bought individually, or that were included in the price paid for a company, can be posted in the balance sheet of the acquiring company. The overall price paid gives an upper limit to their value. So far, all over the world,

FIGURE 18.1 The issue of fair valuation of brands

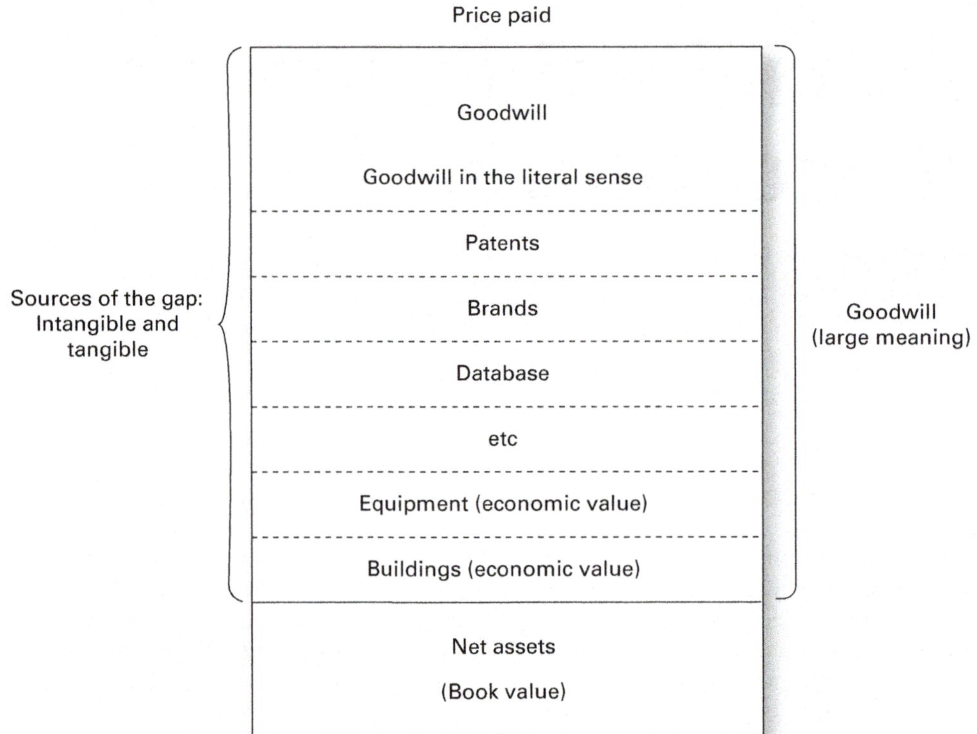

the principle of prudence has led national and international accounting norms and standards to forbid the posting in the balance sheet of internally grown brands. It is of course possible to propose brand valuations, but as long as the brands have not been bought and sold, there is too much doubt about the validity of these estimates. Brands acquire value through the market.

Accounting for brands: the debate

The debate on the inclusion of all of the brands, whether they be purchased or created, raises basic questions about the very essence of accounting. Why do balance sheets and company accounts exist? Is it to give an estimation of the true financial value of the company (which of course is very subjective) or, following the accounting prudence principle, to include only objective data and to assess only past and recorded transactions? Until now the second idea has been chosen in all countries: therefore only transactions involving external brands are recorded. If the internal brands were to be noted, the principle of reality would be respected at the expense of reliability and of the consistency of accounting. In fact, what would we think of a balance sheet which was based on non-uniform and sometimes subjective methods of evaluation? The inclusion of an acquired brand does not violate the principle of bookkeeping at historical costs, which is a fundamental accounting principle. How then can internal brands be valued? As we will see later on, the valuation methods, which are based on historical costs or replacement costs, are not good enough. The best methods are those based on projections of future income, which are highly subjective. A certain amount of uncertainty and heterogeneity, which are against the rules of caution, would be created if these were included in the balance sheet.

But one may contend that the function of accounting is to present a framework to identify and deal with a company's commercial expenses which are accumulated in the form of intangible assets that are developed internally. For the moment, these outlays are treated as expenses and are deducted from the company's income for the year in question; this in turn reduces the amount of tax that the company has to pay. However, some tax authorities are beginning to clamp down on the payment of back taxes. For example, they now consider that the money spent to produce advertising commercials can no longer be classified as expenses but are rather investments and thus are no longer exempt from tax.

Accountancy, just like taxation, is interested in the recording of costs (as expenses or as investments). Financial analysis estimates the discounted value of certain assets as a function of the probability of the future income that they are supposed to generate. Thus, there will not be only one value of the brand because valuation methods depend on the goals of the valuation. The accounting principles already exist and can integrate with some reservations the costs accrued during the creation of a brand. It is for the finance people to estimate the market value of these assets according to their own methods. This reasoning already exists for buildings and thus can also be applied to brands.

Here, a first conclusion is taking shape concerning the monetary value of brands: ideally for a valuation method to be acceptable it should be possible to apply it equally well to brands which are to be bought and to brands that already exist within the company, with a financial aim as well as an accounting aim. However, this is not possible.

The notion of value is highly dependent on your position. Rowntree was worth £1 billion for its shareholders and £2.4 billion for Nestlé! For Midland Bank, Lanvin was worth £400 million; for Henri Racamier and l'Oréal it was worth £500 million. On top of this, accountancy is controlled by a principle of prudence, objectivity and coherence through time. By definition, in its own evaluation, a raider thinks and acts differently. He does not want to be prudent and is rather subjective. The valuation of brands in the context of mergers and acquisitions is a one-off operation: it aims to fix a price at the start given the intentions and synergies that can be expected by the potential buyer. Accounting for brands should obey different norms since their value derives from a different point of view. When there is no transaction involved, the internal brand is valued either as a function of accrued costs or as a function of its everyday usage (and not what another party could do with it). Therefore, there will definitely be a gap between the value of the brand which is bought and of the brand which is created. Moreover, the need to constantly revalue brand values either up or down, in a subjective manner, if they are legitimately noted in the balance sheet introduces fluctuations which undermine the reliability of company accounts. We can reply that the value of the inventory which, in Europe, is indicated annually in the notes to the accounts does not have this effect. It is understandable why the accounting experts at the London Business School who were studying the case for the inclusion of all brands on the balance sheet gave an unfavourable opinion (Barwise, 1989) concerning home-grown brands.

It is a paradox that those who support the most the argument of posting brand values are the marketing people. Perhaps they are hoping to find a method accepted by accountants and financiers of valuing the long-term effects of marketing decisions. However, even though everybody agrees orally that, for example, advertising has both short- and long-term effects, controllers analyse brand performance within a short span of time. Product or brand managers have to produce positive annual operating accounts, positive profit and loss accounts. Thus, evaluation and control are done on an annual basis. This type of behaviour encourages all decisions which are profitable in the short-term. Marketing people would like to have a way to counterbalance this short-term bias, which has the effect of ballooning annual earnings but of eventually undermining brand equity through rapid promotions and brand extensions which are too far from the core activity. On the other hand, looking for gains in awareness at any price may not always add to the marginal increase in brand equity and thus should be halted, with the money put to better use.

More generally, the value of a brand can be measured if the sources of this value can be located, in other words to measure is to understand. Therefore the resulting figure does not interest marketing as much as the process by which it is acquired, that is, the understanding of how a brand works, of its growth, of its increase or loss in value. This understanding is a learning experience and introduces logical and analytical elements to areas where magical beliefs dominated. It also supplies the means for a real communication between people working in marketing, accounting, finance, tax and law. Finally, even if, for reasons linked to tax or respect for the principle of objectivity and accounting coherence, the inclusion of internal brands on the balance sheet is still not recommended and should not be practised by the company, brand valuation remains a worthy exercise to be carried out internally, for all the above mentioned reasons. Mergers and acquisitions are in the end exceptional events even though they do catch the media's attention. The valuation of brands should not be restricted simply to mergers and acquisitions, it is also needed for the benefits that can be obtained from the point of view of management: for help in the decision-making process, for management control, for information systems, for marketing training and for education of product and brand managers. At this time when much is being said about the decline of brands, it is healthy to wonder what the real value of their awareness, image and public esteem is. Brand equity is based on psychological indicators, which are measured from the consumers' point of view, and is only worth something if it results in extra profits. The demands which arise from the presentation of company accounts and from shareholder and investor information are one thing, those arising from a management control system are another. The two should not be mixed up because they do not have the same objectives nor are they faced with the same constraints. There is no single value.

The notion of value is ambiguous and a source of several misunderstandings. It is important to understand that there is no single value for a brand; in fact, there are several because the valuation will be different depending on its aims:

- the value of liquidity in the case of a forced sale;
- the book value for company accounts;
- the value needed in order to encourage banks to lend the company money;
- the value of losses or damage to the worth of the brand should an adverse event occur;
- the value in order to estimate the price of licences;
- the value for management control, which depends on the behaviour encouraged by managers;
- the value for the partial sale of assets;
- the value in case of a takeover or of a merger and acquisition.

For the last case the buyer only asks one question: by how much will actual income rise due to the acquisition of a company with a strong brand? In order to reply to this question the company will evaluate any possible synergies that may exist between the two companies, any resulting cost savings (due to production, logistics, distribution, marketing), any extra capacity to impose one's decisions on distributors or the possibility of brand extensions or internationalization. The proposed price for buying the company will be shaped by these questions. However, none of these questions will have any influence on the book value of the company's brands.

What conclusions should be drawn at this stage? Financial valuation of brands allows for the multidisciplinary meeting of all the company's departments: marketing, audit, finance, production, tax, etc. A capitalistic perspective is introduced in the long run, counterbalancing the logic of annual valuation perspectives. It acts as a reminder of the fact that a company's wealth no longer comes solely from the land, plant and equipment but also from its intangible assets (know-how, patents, brands, etc).

The debate on the value of brands and the way to account for them as assets is essentially an accounting one. This is not the essential benefit, but rather the integration of brand value in evaluating marketing and advertising decisions, which have been up to now subject to one single criterion: the preservation of the annual operating statement of the brand. Before we start to talk about the different valuation techniques, it is important to remember that the real objective of a valuation (for an acquisition or for the presentation of company accounts or for management) modifies the criteria of valuation for these methods. Depending on this objective we will have to choose between these demands which are, unfortunately, not very compatible: more validity or more reliability? more subjectivity or more objectivity? more present value or more historical costs?

What is financial brand equity?

The 1990s witnessed the flourishing of the concept of brand equity (Aaker, 1990; Kapferer, 1990). The act of combining a financial concept (equity) with a manifestly marketing-based notion (the brand) is

FIGURE 18.2 What is 'brand equity'?

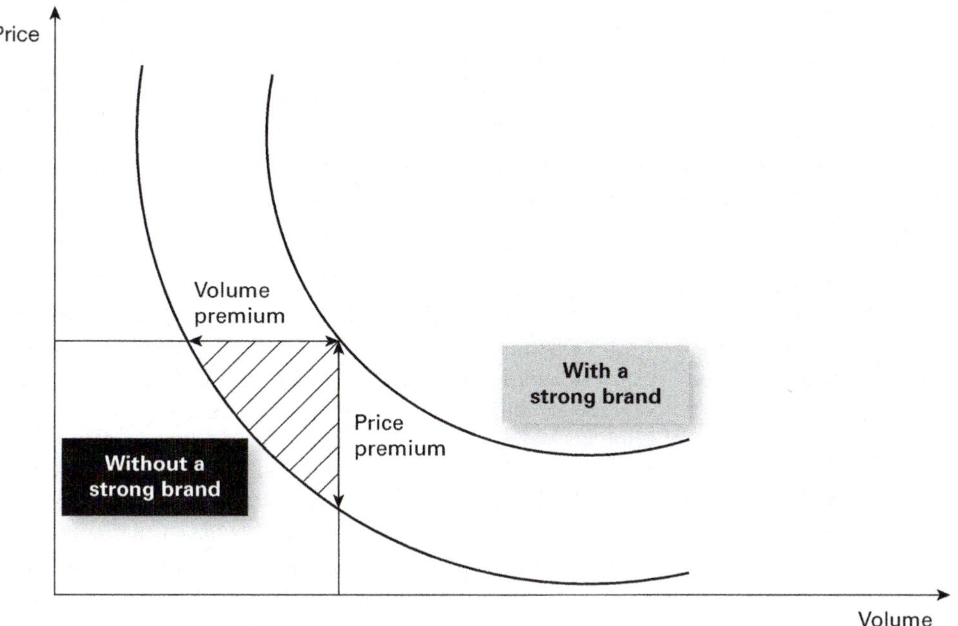

symptomatic of a growing awareness of the financial value of brands, which has emerged from the exclusive world of advertising and marketing to become a very serious factor which – given the importance of equity – has a major impact on overall management (Figure 18.2).

It is worth mentioning again what is meant by 'equity' in financial terms, and thus what connotations emerge from the combination of the terms 'brand' and 'equity'. Literally, equity is 'the owner's claim on the business'. It represents an ownership interest in an enterprise. This equity (called equity securities) is opposed to debt securities, although both are sources of funds, hence liabilities in the balance sheet. The use of the term 'equity' when attached to a brand refers in fact not to a liability but to an asset, built over time thanks to the investment of the business in it. For the sake of precision one should speak in fact of brand assets, not of brand equity.

Curiously enough, although the term 'brand equity' represents an invitation to combine the marketing perspective with the economic and financial perspective, subsequent events have revealed a disagreement within the community of experts. When it came to measuring this brand equity and discussing what makes a strong brand, there was a split between what some called 'consumer-based brand equity' and others referred to as 'financial brand equity'.

The former school of thought (consumer-based brand equity) approaches the question of brand value by taking the customer's point of view. This in turn leads to several different theories. Some believe that brand value exists wherever the preferences expressed for a brand are greater than a simple assessment of the utility of the product or service's attributes would have suggested. We can see that this approach considers the brand as a surplus, a preference that cannot be accounted for by the product alone. It is measured as a residual:

BE = Declared preference – preference predicted by product utilities

As we can see, this theory sees the brand as the degree of influence that exists over and above the product itself: the brand is thus restricted entirely to an intangible, emotional dimension. However, BMW – one of the world's strongest brands – owes its strength and attraction as much to a product with special, unique performance as it does to the image of its owners that the brand conveys.

Others (Aaker, 1990) maintain that brand value incorporates all of the following variables: recognition, perceived quality, imagery, loyalty and patent quality. Note that according to this definition – and in contrast to the previous definition – the product is included in brand equity because of the patents that make it different or even superior.

Still others, taking a purely cognitive approach (Keller, 1998), see the brand as a collection of memory associations that generate a different reaction to the brand. Keller, for example, speaks of positive customer-based brand equity if identification of the brand produces a more favourable reaction than if the brand is not identified. However, he also defines negative customer-based brand equity as a situation in which such identification leads to a less favourable reaction. Note that in the financial context which produced the notion of equity, there is no such thing as negative equity. The latter school of thought is populated by financial analysts whose role it is to evaluate assets (which can sometimes include intangible assets, and thus brands). From their economic perspective, brand equity is the value today of profits imputable to the brand in the future.

An economic analysis of brand equity requires us to look more closely at the word 'imputable'. The question is, imputable by whom? In contrast to the consumer-based approaches, the economic analysis prompts a simple yet fundamental observation: the brand is a conditional asset (Nussenbaum, 2003). After all, without a product (or service) there is no brand. In order to produce a profit or EVA (economic value added), there must already be sales, and thus a tangible base for the brand and its distribution. Here, 'already' means in advance: spending and paying come before receiving. This gives us the basic equation:

$$\text{Value} = -I + R$$

This equation is exactly the same as the following, more fully developed, version giving the value of any asset. Since an asset is a factor with inherent future values, its value appreciates by the present sum of its future expected profits once the initial investment has been deducted.

$$V = I + \sum_{t=1}^{n} \frac{(R_i - D_i)}{(1+r)^i}$$

Imputation of added value to the conditional asset that is the brand presupposes the following:

1 That a value already exists to be shared.
2 That the tangible and intangible factors required for its production have been factored in.
3 That a residual or excess profit remains after paying for these advance assets, which make production and distribution possible.

We believe it is time to bring the two approaches to the concept of brand equity together. After all, the brand is a tool for increasing business: its value is linked to, and dependent on, this objective.

Economic analysis tells us that, irrespective of a brand's reputation, image, preference factors and loyalty, the brand has no value if the company does not produce an excess profit capable of paying off the existing assets (tangible and intangible). Reputation and image do not constitute value in themselves if they do not translate into a profitable product or service.

Seen in this way, it is an illusion to believe that a brand has value simply because it has 'magic'. Many entrepreneurs have bought brands on this basis, but have never been able to convert this value into a hard profit. A brand is only worth anything if a profitable economic formula can be built around it; which is something of a paradox, given that this is an entirely consumer-based concept. However, the economic realities are clear: even if a name has an attraction for consumers, it does not guarantee future profits.

This can be illustrated by an example. The now-defunct Ribourel (property development) brand was the subject of a debate on the exact theme of this chapter. How much was it worth? It was shown that it was worth nothing: the brand's image was associated with value for money, but there was no way of turning this into a profit margin. The Ribourel concept was founded on an idea that was strong and attractive, but economically unachievable. The brand had no economic value under such circumstances.

The reader may remember the terse, shocking statement issued by Daewoo in offering to buy Thomson for the symbolic price of €1. The point being made was that the brand had no value. One might retort that quite the reverse was shown to be true under the management of CEO Thierry Breton;

but in fact, what Thierry Breton did was to bring about a change in the business model in order to return the company to added value.

Using the same logic, if a brand can induce the consumer to pay a price differential but the cost of creating the brand is greater than the price increase, the brand has no value.

We should therefore put forward a unifying definition of a brand that has value (strong brand equity): *a strong brand is a name that influences buyers through the value it offers and is backed by a profitable business model.*

In this definition, several points should be noted:

- Modern competition revolves around concepts and ideas. A name is associated with an attractive, unique value that provides the source of its purchasing influence.
- Strength can also refer to the number of people who associate the brand with this idea. A brand is a strong shared idea; for example, everyone says that BMWs are the best cars.
- This must be turned into an economically profitable reality.

We can clearly see both the connection and the ambiguity between the purely consumer-based and purely economic approaches. It all hangs on the use of one common word 'value', which takes on two different meanings. From the point of view of the marketer, taking his cue from the work of the psychologist M Rokeach, a value is an ideal to be attained, mobilizing our energies and directing our choices. For the economist, however, it is a balance: V = –I + R.

A strong brand thus focuses its efforts on attaining a value through the consumption of a product or service which is given its meaning by marketing and advertising. However, this same brand has no economic value if this approach does not result in EVA: it is useless.

An economic formula for the brand does exist: this is one of the two keys to its value.

From economic value added to the brand

Over the last 10 years, intense accounting debates have raged in the United States, mainland Europe and Great Britain over the evaluation of brands. These debates centre around questions with significant repercussions for companies and their profit-and-loss accounts:

- When can a brand be activated and recorded on the balance sheet? Does it have to have been bought? If so, this excludes home-grown brands.
- Should brands be depreciated? If so, over what period?
- How do you reliably assess the value of a brand?

These issues should not be perceived as being of academic interest only: in fact, they ask important questions as to the very nature of brands and their impact on the added value created by the company over the lifespan of the brand. This last point thus prompts the following question: do brands have a life cycle? We know that in retrospect, we can reconstruct the life cycle of a product, with its typical launch, growth, maturity and decline phases. We say 'in retrospect' because during the life of a product, it is always possible to maintain that the situation we know as the mature stage simply points to insufficient effort (too few line extensions, too little international expansion, and so on).

Now, by feeding on new products that replace the old, the brand 'surfs' product life cycles and acquires from them an apparently indefinite lifespan. Nevertheless, the debate on the depreciation of brands leads to very different conclusions depending on whether one believes that brands have a life cycle (and should thus be depreciated), or that they do not. If a brand's lifespan cannot be determined in advance, there is no justification for depreciation.

However, we should start at the beginning, with the question of the nature of brands. Remember that a brand cannot exist without a product (or service): a product or service is needed before the brand can perform its economic role, which is to add value through the differentiation it creates and the added values it promises. In this respect, a brand is a true conditional asset. Its value can take a tangible form only if the company has already made a capital investment in producing and deploying the brand platform – its products or services. The consequences of this point are crucial: the brand is an added value, and thus if we are to take financial advantage of it, we must have profits, but only once we have allowed (at a given rate, t) for the capital required for its production (Nussenbaum, 2003). The company must therefore already have produced EVA. Remember the EVA equation:

$$\text{EVA} = \text{nett EBIT after tax} - t\,(\text{Tangible Assets} + \text{Working Capital Requirement})$$

Still following the basic theory which dictates that the brand is a conditional asset, we should also factor in the cost of other intangible assets that have contributed to the business; for example, patents (which are crucial in the high-tech or medical marketing industries). Once these directly evaluable assets have been factored in, the residual thus derived will create the envelope within which we find the economic value of the brand and of other intangibles that cannot easily be evaluated directly.

This once again raises the question of identifying these other sources of added value. It stems from an assumption which forms the basis of economic and accounting practice worldwide – that a brand has no value unless it is able to produce excess profit even after taking into account the factors that enable the production and distribution of the products and services, regardless of whether these factors are physical and tangible or non-physical and intangible.

This theory of conditional assets accounts for the progressive, steady process of evaluating brands by means of allocating successive residual balances: EBIT, nett EBIT (after the imposition of company tax), EVA, and EVA after the direct identification of certain intangible assets.

Theoretically speaking, then, the brand evaluation process is simple (it consists of a series of successive residual balance allocations). However, for reasons related not so much to methodology as to the company's information system, it is tricky to implement in practice. To put a value on a brand, we have to be able to identify its profits – yet a brand can span many markets governed by a variety of different economic mechanisms, or markets in which factors such as the relative value of the brand in comparison to other assets might not be the same. For example, the relative importance of the brand in sales of a hair products brand is not the same in all distribution channels: it is important in the modern channel (supermarkets and hypermarkets), but very weak when the same product is sold directly by hairdressers, on account of the strong influence of the hairdresser's recommendation to the customer. To develop this idea further: for any given brand in any given channel, the degree to which this brand influences the customer's purchasing decision will vary depending on whether the product is a shampoo or a hair colouring product. Analyses must therefore be conducted individually at the relevant level, not collectively at the overall level. The question thus becomes: do we have the appropriate reporting data that such an analysis requires?

The brand: an identifiable asset?

We know that according to standard accounting practices, an asset can only be entered in the accounts if it can be identified and clear future economic benefits can be attributed to it. Inter-country debate currently rages on the criteria for such identifiability.

Some countries implement a difficult criterion: transferability. It is a tough condition because before an asset can be transferable, legal rights for this asset must be held; not only this, but a market must also exist. An alternative criterion has a more economic basis: it is sufficient to be able to trace specific revenue back to this asset. How is this viewed in worldwide terms?

Under current international accounting standards (IAS), an asset is deemed to be identifiable if we hold rights over it: in other words, if these rights can be protected. Logically, therefore, according to this concept, the company can exercise no legal rights over market share or a client base. From the IAS standpoint, an intangible asset can be recorded if:

- the recorder controls, holds the aforementioned legal rights;
- it is transferable (separable);
- it is the source of specific future revenue extending beyond the yearly accounting period.

In other countries such as France, market share can be activated and posted in the balance sheet.

The US position is a pragmatic one: what conditions must be met here before an intangible asset can be entered separately into the consolidated accounts once a company has been absorbed or bought out? They are two-fold: separability (it can be transferred independently of the rest of the company) and the unambiguous allocation of specific revenues.

Pragmatically, to avoid ambiguity, the US standard supplies a list of intangible assets. In the Statement of Financial Accounting Standards no 141, (FASB), this list specifies exactly what can be allocated: no reference is made to market share. Nor is know-how included, as this is an abstract concept (except in the form of computer software). However, it does include the valuation of a customer database. The US position thus concerns itself less with legal property, instead taking a more economic approach.

The new draft IAS, which will become prevalent in stock-exchange-listed companies throughout the world, is similar in design to the US model.

However, a case does exist where the brand is, and remains, unrecordable: when it is an 'internal' brand, that is, one created by the company itself and thus not bought, or one found in a company that has been bought by or merged with the company. Accounting is subject to the principle of prudence: what is a brand worth? The price paid by a party buying the company already offers an indication in the form of an upper threshold, once all other assets within the company have been deducted at their economic value. When there is a market transaction, then, the value acquires a physical form. Until that time, it is merely a virtual, potential value. In all countries, recording unreliable information in the accounts is perceived as a much greater evil than that of failing to take an economic value (the brand) into consideration.

Value depends on the evaluation goals

Incongruous though it may seem, the brand contains not one value but many: everything depends on the evaluation goals. Thus, if the goal is to assess a contribution containing an intangible asset, to be checked by an auditor, a prudent approach should be taken.

Similarly, it is a universal truth that value is in the eye of the beholder. For example, only Coca-Cola could offer US $1 billion to buy the little round Orangina bottle. With its network of bottlers in all countries worldwide, it would instantly be able to multiply sales of the product – which was based on the same business model as Coke (selling syrup to bottlers) – ten-fold. Pepsi-Cola offered less, as did Schweppes: hardly surprisingly, since their brand development plan was simply not on the same scale as Coca-Cola's.

Lastly, we are bound to get different figures when evaluating for estimation purposes than when evaluating for balance sheet recording purposes. In producing an estimate, it is permissible to include future plans, new production factories and shops that may be opened, or brand extensions into other categories. This makes the brand's future potential look even brighter. However, when it comes to recording for accounting purposes, prudence is required. It is not possible to make use of such predictions, since the projected factories, stores and extensions do not actually exist, and therefore cannot be included. Under European accounting law, no allowance can be made for that which does not exist. However, under IAS such possibilities could be taken into account, taking their cue from the more flexible US standards.

In the Coca-Cola/Orangina case, we therefore find ourselves in an odd situation: the value of the brand appears to differ depending on which company perspective we consider the question from. In the consolidated accounts of Coca-Cola in the United States, the value recorded for the Orangina brand would have taken into consideration the expansion potential from its new distribution. In the accounts of Pernod-Ricard, the company originally holding the Orangina brand, it would have had a different value as part of a transfer operation.

The financial value of Absolut vodka

In 2009, Pernod-Ricard, the world's number two wine and spirits group, bought Absolut vodka for €3.9 billion. Interestingly Interbrand, a brand design agency that receives a lot of publicity each year when it publishes its own brand valuation, does not put Absolut vodka even in its top 100 most valuable global brands, meaning it evaluates Absolut below US$3 billion (€2.2 billion). Which should one believe: Interbrand, whose estimates are based on external data, or Pernod-Ricard itself, which bought Absolut after having evaluated all the sources of additional profits it could derive from this acquisition? Pernod-Ricard paid €3.9 billion because it estimated that Absolut was not worth €4 billion.

How can one know Absolut vodka is worth €3.9 billion? As one knows, value is always in the eye of the beholder. There is no real value outside a business plan. The lists of brand values regularly published by *Businessweek* and the like stimulate buzz and create publicity (this is their goal) but have little relationship with the price a company will pay. Google's 2010 brand valuation by Millward Brown was $114 billion; it was $43 billion by Interbrand! In reality brand valuation is an internal methodical exercise whereby a company estimates the incremental profit the brand will bring in the future to its own operations:

- through direct sales (unlike the previous owner, which was very volume oriented, Pernod-Ricard follows a premiumization strategy, which led it to increase by 40 per cent Absolut's price in China, its growth market of the future);
- through synergies (offering Absolut, the world's number four spirit, in the portfolio helps sell the other brands of the portfolio);
- through economies of scale (media discounts, human resources).

One understands why brand valuation estimates provided by external agencies are all so different and have little connection with the figure a company will determine taking into account real information.

Assessment of brand value is not a purely financial exercise. It makes people from marketing and finance work together. In fact, as soon as there were rumours about a probable sale of Absolut vodka by the Swedish government, Pernod-Ricard created a task force with financiers, marketers, and distribution and sales executives. Important market studies were carried out in the United States and China to assess the potentialities of this brand in these two opposite countries: one where Absolut had been launched in 1979 and levelled off, the other being its next Eldorado. The profitability of the purchase of Absolut by Pernod-Ricard would rest on the answers given to such strategic questions as:

- Is the brand already global, or does it still have to become global?
- What is its growth profile? Can the company premiumize the brand, increasing its average price?
- What is its intrinsic profitability now?
- Can the company integrate the distributor margin?
- Can Absolut still bring about a major crusade as it did in the 1980s?

Pernod-Ricard paid Absolut 17 times its yearly contribution. It knew the maximum price it would pay for Absolut. Bacardi-Martini had paid Grey Goose, the fastest-growing super-premium vodka in the United States, 23 times its contribution.

Now how does one know if the acquisition of Absolut will be good for Pernod-Ricard? Only if it creates value for shareholders. This may come from two sources: 1) if the company pays a price that is inferior to its real expectations of gain (estimated by the discounted cashflow method); 2) if the company can 'beat the WACC' (weighted average cost of capital), that is to say make the return on its investment greater than the average expectations of its shareholders (8 per cent).

Evaluating brand valuation methods

A number of methods have been proposed to define the value posted in the balance sheet when a brand is part of the assets of an acquired company, or any other instance when this valuation is needed. They can be positioned on a two-dimensional mapping. The horizontal axis refers to time (but do we base the analysis on the past, the present or the future?). This axis discriminates between valuations based on historical costs (those that helped build the

FIGURE 18.3 Positioning brand valuation methods

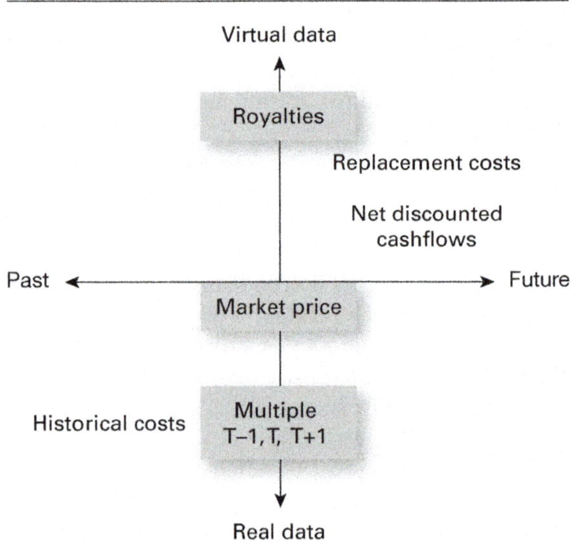

brand), valuations based on present earnings, on market price, and those which rely on a business plan: that is to say, a forecast. The vertical axis is a real/virtual dimension. Some analysts rely on hard facts (historical accounts are facts, as well as present earnings). However, some methods rely more on estimates about the present (the replacement method), or about the future (the discounted cashflow method). We now analyse these methods in turn.

Valuation by historical costs

The brand is an asset whose value comes from investments over a period of time (even though accountants do not strictly regard this as a true form of investment). The logical approach would therefore be to add together all the costs associated with a particular period: development costs, marketing costs, advertising and communication costs, etc. These costs can be determined objectively, and will have been in past income statements.

As we can see, this approach allows us to overcome the tricky problem of separability, by isolating the direct costs associated with the brand and also by attributing to it the indirect costs such as the sales force and general expenses. Even though this method is simple and logical, it nevertheless raises the following practical difficulties, which reintroduce a certain subjectivity:

- Over what period should costs be accounted for? Numerous brands are very old as we have seen: Coca-Cola dates back to 1887, Danone to 1919, Lacoste to 1933, Yves Saint Laurent to 1958, Dim to 1965. Should we include costs right from their beginnings? Everyone knows of old brands that no longer exist. Companies must go back in time and ask themselves if past advertising still has an effect today.
- Which costs should be taken into account? Investment in advertising has a dual marketing role: one part generates extra sales, which can be measured immediately, while the other part builds brand awareness and image which facilitates future sales. The practical difficulty is in estimating year by year the weight that should be attributed to each part. Also, how far ahead are we looking when talking about future sales? On top of this we have to look at the advertising wear-out curves over a given time period. If, as has been shown in studies on the persistence of attitude changes, such effects decrease in a linear manner over, for example, five years, it may be that expenses arising over this period, including only 20 per cent of those for year $n - 5$, can be posted.
- It is not simply a question of adding up the costs, you also have to take into account an appropriate discount rate which has to be calculated.

On top of the subjective nature of the answers to the above questions, valuation by costs causes several basic problems which are linked directly to a partial understanding of the brand:

- When creating a brand, a large part of the long-term investment does not involve a cash outlay, and therefore cannot be posted to the accounts. These include stringent quality controls, accumulated know-how, specific expertise, involvement of personnel, etc. All of these are essential for encouraging repurchase, for the brand's long-term reputation and for word-of-mouth. There would be no trace in the accounts of brands like Rolls-Royce because there were no advertisements for it.
- One of the major strategies to create a strong brand consists of choosing a competitive launch price, which may be the same as that of competitors' even though the product is upgraded. Swatch is an ideal example of this. They could have opted for a slight price differential, or a price premium, to cover the costs of innovation and of upgrading the product. They decided, however, to set an aggressive price that was equal to that of their competitors, thus maximizing the brand's price/quality ratio and enhancing its attractiveness. This is one of its key success factors. Unfortunately, this non-cash investment would not appear in a system where only cash expenditures are registered.
- The method therefore favours brands whose value only comes from advertising and marketing and which have a significant price premium. It would not apply to brands such as Rolls-Royce or St Michael (Marks & Spencer's brand) which advertise very little. It could also be said that past expenditure is not a guarantee

of present value. There are several brands that are heavily advertised but of little value and are coming to the end of their life.

- This method is favourable to recent brands and *a fortiori* to internal brands that are in the process of being created, as we have already seen.

Valuation by replacement costs

To overcome the difficulties arising from the historical costs approach, it might be better to place oneself in the present and to confront the problem by resorting to the classic alternative – as we cannot buy this brand, how much would it cost to recreate it? By taking its various characteristics into account (awareness, percentage of trial purchases and repurchases, absolute and relative market share, distribution network, image, leadership, quality of the legal deposition and presence in how many countries), how much would we have to spend, and over what period, in order to create an equivalent brand?

Is it possible to remake Coca-Cola, Schweppes, Mars, Buitoni or Martell? Probably not. How about Benetton, Bang & Olufsen, Saab or Epson? More than likely. For a certain number of brands, the question no longer arises since it is impossible to recreate them. The context has changed too much:

- They were created in an era when advertising expenditure was negligible and the brand was nurtured over time by word-of-mouth. Today, it costs so much for a 1 per cent share of voice that it has become impossible to create a leading brand through unaided awareness. In any case unaided awareness is a restricted area and to gain access a competing brand must leave. This is because of memory blocks. There is no reason why today's well-known brands should allow themselves to be thrown out.
- It is difficult to imitate the performance level of brand leaders. Backed by research and development and an intangible but very real know-how, they enjoy a long-lasting competitive advantage and a resulting image of stability. Any challenger is taking a risk. Unless they have access to the necessary technology, their chances of encouraging repurchasing and loyalty are virtually zero.
- Major retailers have now become exacting gatekeepers. They give pride of place to their own brands, only selling one or two national brands that tomorrow will be international.
- Finally, considering the high failure rate of new product launches, it is easy to understand the uncertainty of the return on the large amount of money that has to be invested in the long term. If you are going to pay a lot you might as well buy certainty. Hence, the clutter of takeover bids, raids, mergers and acquisitions of firms with strong brands that are already market leaders.

On the other hand, when these factors which hinder market entry are no longer present, the market is more accessible. The possibility of creating tomorrow's brand leaders from scratch ceases to be theoretical, even though uncertainty and the necessary time element may still exist. Therefore, future Benettons will probably be created. Franchising allows wider market penetration without admitting defeat at the hands of major retailers. What is more, the fashion industry is open to new ideas. In this domain, style is more important than technology. Computer services and the high-tech world in general are also open to innovation. Generally speaking, the future will see the emergence of new international brands, each positioned in its own particular niche. They will thus no longer seek global awareness but will aspire to be leaders in particular market segments.

Brand valuation by replacement costs nevertheless remains very subjective. It requires the combined opinions of experts and ambiguous procedures. On top of this it should be remembered that the aim of the valuation process is not, in itself, to arrive at a value but to get an idea of the economic value of the asset in question – in this case the brand. Cost methods focus on the inputs, whereas the economic value is based on the outputs – what the brand produces and not what it consumes. Profit is not generated through investments but through market domination and leadership.

Valuation by market price

When valuing a brand why not start with the value of similar brands on the market? This is how property or second-hand cars are valued. Each apartment or car is inspected and given a price that is above, equal to or below the average market price of similar goods.

Even though this method is very appealing, it raises two major problems when applied to brands. First, the market doesn't exist. Although such transactions are often cited in the financial pages, acquisitions and brand sales are relatively few. Brands are not bought to be sold again. In spite of this, we can get an idea of the multiples applicable to each sector of activity (from 25 to 30) thanks to the number of transactions that have taken place since 1983. Thus, such an approach could tempt some wishing to value a brand.

However, there is a major difference between the real estate market and the market for brands, which is relatively small. On the real estate market the buyer is a price-taker, that is, the price is fixed by the market. Irrespective of the use that he or she will make of the property, the price remains the same. For brands, the buyer is a price-setter, that is, he or she sets the price of the brand. Each buyer bases his/her valuation on his/her own views, on potential synergies and on his/her future strategy. Why did Unilever pay €100 million for Boursin, the well-known brand of cheese? It can be explained by the pressing need of this group to acquire shelf space in major supermarkets in which it had previously been absent. Having at its disposal a compulsory brand, they saw a way of opening the door to other speciality products. In April 1990 Jean-Louis Sherrer was bought for three times less than the price that Mr Chevalier paid for Balmain two months earlier. For Mr Chevalier, Balmain was a means of entry – or rather re-entry – into the luxury market. Hermès, which was already present on this market, didn't need to pay this price (Melin, 1990).

In abstract terms the purchase price is not the price paid for the brand but is the interaction between brand and purchaser. To use the price paid for a similar brand as a reference, without knowing the specific reasons behind that brand's purchase, ignores the fact that an essential part of the price probably included the synergies and the specific objectives of the buyer in question. Each buyer has his/her own intentions and ideas. The value cannot be determined by proxy.

This is what distinguishes fundamentally the market for brands from that for real estate, or for example for advertising agencies. In the case of the latter, norms and standards exist that are not dependent on the buyers' intentions (50 to 70 per cent of the gross margin on top of the net assets). Despite this, valuations in the luxury market frequently take into account recent transactions and use a multiple of the sales (1.5 for Yves Saint Laurent, 2 for Lanvin and for Balmain, 2.9 for Martell, 2 for Bénédictine).

Considering the difficulties which are inherent in the cost-based methods or in the referential methods on a hypothetical market, prospective buyers tend rather to look at the expected profits from brand ownership. Since the third type of approach relies on two major philosophies, we are devoting a special section to it.

Valuation by royalties

What annual royalties could the company hope to receive if it licensed the rights to use the brand? The answer to this question would form a means of directly measuring the brand's financial contribution and would also solve the problem of separability. The figure obtained could subsequently be used to calculate the discounted cashflows over several years. The difficulty is that this is not a very common practice in most markets. They are found in the luxury and textile markets.

From a conceptual point of view, it is not certain that this method properly separates just the value of the brand (Barwise, 1989). In fact, companies often use licences to reach countries where their brand is not present. However, the royalty fee does not include solely the use of the brand. The brand owner also undertakes to supply a package of basic materials, know-how and services, which allow the licensee to maintain the brand's appropriate quality level.

Valuation by future earnings

Since the brand aspires to become an asset, it is best to begin by a reminder of what an asset is. It is an element which will generate future profits with reasonable certainty. Valuation methods have been developed on the basis of expected returns of brand ownership. Naturally, these tie in fully with the purchaser's intentions. If he/she wishes to internationalize the brand, it will be of more value to him/her than to a buyer wishing to keep it as a local brand. The value measured by expected profits cannot be separated from the characteristics of the future buyer

FIGURE 18.4 A multi-step approach to brand valuation

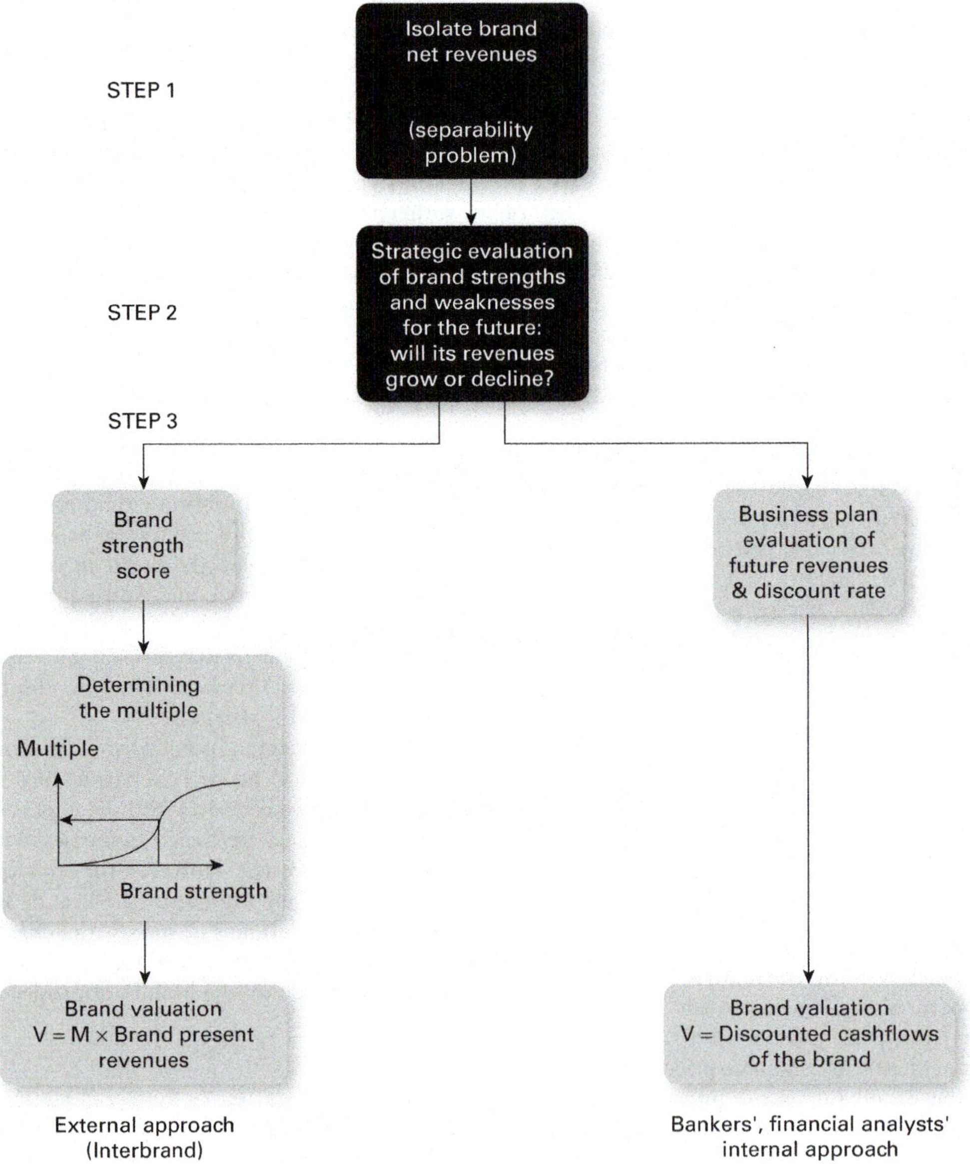

and from his/her strategies for the brand. This explains why the stock market value compared to a predator's value of a branded company will always be structurally lower. The former valuation is related to the existing business, taking into account current facts and figures provided by the firm. The latter comes from the overvaluation created by the prospect of synergies, complementary marketing processes and the attainment of strategic market positions.

The process of valuing the expected profits of the brand can be divided into three independent stages (see Figure 18.4):

1. The first step involves separating and isolating the net income associated with the brand (and not with the company for example).
2. The second step is to estimate the future cashflows. This requires a strategic

analysis of the brand in its market or markets.

3 The third step involves choosing, by using a classic financial method, a discount rate and period.

This is the classic method of valuing all investments, whether tangible or intangible. The analyst calculates the anticipated annual income attributable to the brand over a 5- or 10-year period. The discount rate used is the weighted average cost of capital, which if necessary is increased to take account of the risks arising from a weak brand (that is to reduce the weight of future revenues in the calculation of the present value). Beyond this period, the residual value is calculated by assuming that the income is constant or growing at a constant rate for infinity (Nussenbaum, 1990). The following formula is used:

$$\text{Value of the brand} = \sum_{t=1}^{N} \frac{RB_t}{(1+r)^t} + \frac{\text{Residual value}}{(1+r)^N}$$

where:
RB_t = Anticipated revenue in year t, attributable to the brand
r = Discounting rate

$$\text{Residual value after year } N = \frac{RB_n}{r} \text{ or } \frac{RB_N}{r-g}$$

where:
g = rate of revenue growth

This is the classic model for valuation by the discounted cashflow method, even though analysts offer numerous variations of it (Mauguère, 1990; Melin, 1990). This method was used to value Cognac Hennessy at 6.9 billion francs, based on a capitalization of its net revenue over 25 years at a rate of 6.5 per cent (Blanc and Hoffstetter, 1990).

This method was also used to value the Candia milk brand as part of a restructuring programme. The final figure, which was around 1.8 billion francs (€300 million), was the result of a business plan within which two questions were discussed:

- Knowing that milk is a commodity, what percentage of Candia's future sales will be generated by products which are heavily marketed, differentiated and have a strong identity which justifies a price premium?
- At how much do we estimate the price premium that Candia can demand over more ordinary products? In such markets, even a tiny difference may amount to huge profits.

Sceptics of this method (Murphy, 1990; Ward, 1989) object to its three sources of uncertainty: the anticipation of cashflows, the choice of period and the discount rate:

- By definition any forecast is uncertain. This does not apply only to brands, but to any investment evaluation – tangible or intangible – which is calculated by the above method. For brands, cashflow forecasts could be ruined if a competitor launched a superior product which was not accounted for in the calculations. This argument overlooks the fact that these forecasts were made after an in-depth analysis of the brand's strengths and weaknesses (on the basis of the criteria presented earlier). It can be assumed that these were included when the anticipated cashflows were calculated. In any case the discounting rate takes into account the anticipated risk factor.
- A second criticism lies in the subjective nature of the choice of a discounting rate. However, on the one hand analysts test the sensitivity of their findings against variations in this rate, and on the other hand, this rate is fixed by taking into account stable company data, such as its average cost of capital. The only subjective factors are the risk premium and the future rate of inflation. Furthermore, very often the risk is zero from the purchaser's point of view as he or she feels that success is a certainty.
- Finally, there are those who criticize the choice of period for calculating cashflows. Why 10 years and not 15? What is the value of forecasts made so far ahead? On the one hand, the brand may disappear after only a few years and on the other, in certain volatile sectors three years is already a long time (eg laptop computers).

TABLE 18.1 A method of valuing brand strength

Factor of valuation	Maximum score	Brand A	Brand B	Brand C
Leadership	25	19	19	10
Stability	15	12	9	7
Market	10	7	6	8
Internationality	25	18	5	2
Trend	10	7	5	7
Support	10	8	7	8
Protection	5	5	3	4
Brand strength	100	76	54	46

SOURCE Penrose/Interbrand (1990)

This is where certain valuations come from: brand value should be based on that which is certain, ie the net income of the brand at the moment. This is the basis of the multiple method (see Table 1.4). Brand value is calculated by applying a multiple to the current profits of the brand, measured over three years ($t - 1$, $t + 1$). This approach does not need internal data.

Valuation by present earnings

Who can predict the future? How can one be sure that the forecasts of a business plan will be matched? In fact, one of the reasons so many internet brands have been heavily overvalued is that they made no profit whatsoever (eBay excepted). The brand valuation process relied exclusively on forecasts and business plans which were created just to attract new investors, so the founders could resell before the collapse of the illusion.

Interbrand, a major brand valuation company, has promoted a specific approach to circumvent this problem. No business, no brand. Interbrand valuations rely exclusively on three years: last year, this year and next year. After partitioning each year's revenue to pay for the invested capital which made the business possible and other direct intangible assets, one is left with a global residue, made of a weighted average of the residues of each of these three years. This residue should be then multiplied by a figure called 'the multiple', hence the name of the Interbrand proprietary method: the multiple method. Although Interbrand seems to have moved now to the most orthodox method (discounted cashflow), we analyse this former approach on which many brand valuations have been based.

In the financial valuation of companies, it is typical to examine what is known as the price/earnings ratio (P/E). This ratio links the market capitalization of a firm to its net profits. A high ratio is a signal of high investor confidence and optimism in the growth of future profits. Even though the brand is not the company, the same reasoning can be applied:

$$\text{Firm : P/E} = \frac{\text{Market value of equity}}{\text{Known profits}}$$

$$\text{Brand : Multiple} = \frac{\text{Value to be calculated}}{\text{Net profits of brand}}$$

The only difference lies in the fact that for a brand there are no data on its market capitalization because it doesn't exist, therefore it is this that we are trying

FIGURE 18.5 The Interbrand S-curve – relation between brand strength and multiple

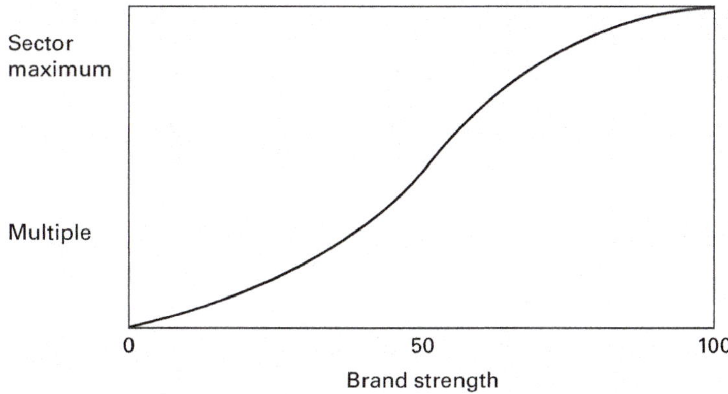

to calculate. This notional market value of equity is the price to be paid for the brand (before the effect of overbidding). In order to calculate this, it is necessary to determine M, the multiple which is equivalent to the P/E ratio specific to the brand.

There are four stages to this method:

1 **Calculating the applicable net profit.** Interbrand used the profits for the last three years ($t - 2$, $t - 1$, t), thus avoiding a possibly atypical evaluation based upon a single year. These profits were discounted to take account of inflation. A weighted average of these three figures was calculated in accordance with what we consider to be the most and least important years. This weighted average after-tax net profit which is attributable to the brand forms the basis of all calculations.

2 **Assessing the brand's strength.** This method uses a set of marketing and strategic criteria to give the brand an overall mark. Interbrand uses only seven of these factors and takes a weighted sum of the individual marks for each factor in order to calculate the overall mark, as can be seen in Table 18.1 (Penrose, 1989).

3 **Estimating the multiple.** A relationship necessarily exists between the multiple (an indicator of confidence about the future) and this score for brand strength. If this relationship was known precisely, the multiple would then be predicted by the brand strength score. For this, Interbrand developed a model known as the 'S-curve' which plots the multiple against brand strength.

The model is based on Interbrand's examination of the multiples involved in numerous brand negotiations over recent periods – in sectors close to the one being studied. The P/E of the companies with the closest comparable brands are used. Interbrand then reconstructed the company's profile and brand strength. Plotting the multiples (P/E) against the reconstructed scores results in an S-shaped curve (see Figure 18.5).

4 **Calculating brand value.** This is calculated by multiplying the applicable net brand profit by the relevant multiple.

We can illustrate this method by an actual case. In 1988 Reckitt & Colman valued its brands in this way. They valued household and hygienic goods where they were market leaders, as well as food products (condiments) where they were also a leader, and finally pharmaceutical goods where they had an average position.

The specific situation enjoyed by those brands in the first group is as follows:

- world leadership;
- growing markets, with few new entrants except for distributors' own-brands;
- unaided brand awareness (eg Airwick) high in the UK and in Anglo-Saxon countries but less so in France;
- customers' brand loyalty;
- strong brand image and assurance of quality;
- for each of its brands, little possibility for diversification.

Reckitt & Colman estimated that 5 per cent of profits on these brands came from sales under distributors' own-brands. Interbrand considered that the remaining 95 per cent was the brand's gross profit. The income generated by the brand can be calculated by subtracting the expected return on investment from net assets. The net revenue was weighted according to the importance of each brand and discounted for the previous three years. The following results were obtained for each category:

- household and hygienic products: £53.8 million;
- food products: £24.7 million;
- pharmaceutical goods: £17.1 million.

What multiple should be applied? For the first group, the multiple used by Reckitt & Colman in 1985 when buying Airwick was applied. A multiple of 17 was used for food products and was based on recent transactions in the sector during the last few years, for example the BSN–Nabisco takeover bid. Finally, a multiple of 20 was used for the pharmaceutical group. In fact, recent transactions in the pharmaceutical industry had been using multiples which were closer to 30. A lower multiple was chosen in this case because of Reckitt & Colman's relatively weak position in the sector. By applying these figures to the net revenue in each category, the following brand values were estimated:

- household and hygienic products: 53.8 × 20 = £1,076 million;
- food products: 24.7 × 17 = £420 million;
- pharmaceutical goods: 17.1 × 20 = £342 million.

Comparison of the cashflow and multiple method

The multiple method, which was developed in the UK, is becoming a classic. It was, in fact, used by such companies as Rank Hovis McDougall and Grand Metropolitan whose decisions to post brand values to their balance sheets caused a controversy which is still not settled. It is also the method which communicates the most through books, articles and seminars. The simplicity of the method used is such that it is uncharacteristic of the stringent world of financial analysis. All this said, is it valid?

First, the multiple method is not all that different from the classic method of discounted cashflow. It is a particular example of it.

When a constant and infinite annual cashflow is expected, the present value of the brand is defined thus:

$$\text{Brand value} = \frac{RB}{(1+r)} + \frac{RB}{(1+r)^2} + \frac{RB}{(1+r)^3} + \ldots + \frac{RB}{(1+r)^\infty} = \frac{RB}{r}$$

As we can see, the multiple is none other than the inverse of the cost of capital adjusted for risk ($1/r$). If a constant growth rate (g) of annual income is expected, the multiple is:

$$B = \frac{1}{r-g}$$

Equations aside, the point to remember is that we cannot reproach the method of discounted cashflows for making certain hypotheses, since the multiple approach is itself a particular hypothesis, which is equally as questionable but not explicit. It draws its apparent validity from the fact that all its calculations are based upon:

- net known profits attributable to the brand over the previous three years;
- marketing data and the subjective opinions of managers regarding brand strength;
- multiples based on recent transactions by similar companies;
- an S-curve, using information from a database to plot these multiples (or P/E ratios) against brand strength scores.

However, face validity (or appearance) does not mean validity *per se*. In its present form, Interbrand's method poses various problems:

1. Market multiples, which were used as parameters for the S-curve, are not valid indicators of the strength of the brands even though they were the mainstay of these transactions. In fact the final transaction price includes both the estimated value of

the brand and a certain amount which is due to overbidding. For example, in the fight between Jacob Suchard and Nestlé, the initial bid was 630 pence and the final bid was, 1,075 pence! Market prices include the effect of this overbidding and thus overvalue the brand. It is therefore rather curious that we are trying to link market multiples to a value for brand strength as this value ignores the effect of overbidding. For this reason a certain doubt arises about the applicability of this method to value and post to the balance sheet unacquired, internally created brands. The value attributed to the asset will be greater than the value of the brand as it will include an unspecified amount which is a result of overbidding! The fact that companies may nevertheless have used this method to represent their brands as assets in no way validates this approach.

2 Even in a market where there is no overbidding, the stated multiple measures the value of the brand from the point of view of the potential buyer. It expresses his vision, his strategies and any synergies that he may expect. The fact that in 1985 BSN did not buy Buitoni despite it being reasonably priced does not mean that Buitoni was worth less but means that it was worth less in the eyes of BSN. In 1988 Nestlé valued it at several billion Swiss francs. It again seems strange to try to relate market multiples, which are closely linked to the buyer, to the scores for brand strength, which are calculated by an outsider and do not include the synergistic benefits. This poses a problem when internally created brands are posted to the balance sheet. They are valued in the context of a 'going concern' according to their current benefit to the companies who own them. On the other hand, multiples supplied by the market are calculated with the idea of using them for a totally different reason.

3 For the moment, no illustrations of the S-curve showing the variance around the curve have been published. This variance is a measure of the quality of the empirical relationship between the two variables. As it is, the curve would have us believe that there is zero variance, which is impossible. A single brand strength score probably corresponds to several multiples or at least to a range of values (within which the S-curve is found). Such uncertainty causes problems as in reality the financial value of a brand is very sensitive to even a slight change in the multiple. Going back to the Reckitt & Colman's household and hygiene brands, we see that a one point variation in the multiple results in either a £53.8 million increase or decrease in the value of the brand. This is a far cry from the principles of prudence, reliability and rational certainty which govern accounting practice and information.

4 The very validity of the S-curve is questionable. Interbrand uses the following argument: a new brand grows slowly during its early stages. Then, once it moves from being a national brand to being an international one, its growth is exponential. Finally, as it moves from the international to the worldwide arena, its growth slows once more. For example, the difference between Buitoni's purchase and resale price signalled the transition of a national brand to a European wide one.

Experience shows that brands are susceptible to large threshold effects. Their strength with customers and retailers is developed in stages. Thus, today, a moderately known brand may be worth virtually the same as a little known one. However, beyond a certain threshold, it grows in value. Research on brand awareness has shown that, in markets with intensive communication, it is only once a brand has reached a certain level of aided awareness that its unaided awareness will start to increase. This is due to a memory block. Likewise, major retailers are replacing middle-of-the-range brands with their own products. These brands rely more on supply than on demand and they would cease to be sold if the retailers replaced them with their own brands. Thus their future is very unstable. This would lead us to believe that the relationship between brand strength and the multiple – provided that both are assessed by the same potential buyer – is

FIGURE 18.6 Stepped graph showing relationship between brand strength and multiple

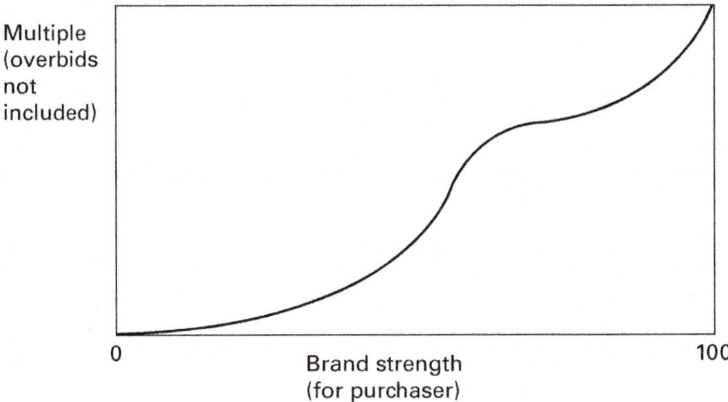

better illustrated by a stepped graph (see Figure 18.6).

In conclusion, the widespread use of the multiple method is not proof of validity, as we have just seen, but testifies to its simplicity and handiness for non-specialists, and therefore its internal educational value. A small variation in the chosen multiple leads to important differences in the value of the brand. The present method of choosing the multiple is unsatisfactory from the point of view of reference multiples and of the brand strength scores. What can we make of a total score which is obtained after subjective weightings of factors which are sometimes redundant or in any case correlated? This wish for simplicity is to the detriment of the method's validity. Despite its claim to be accurate, the multiple method in its present form is just as subjective as that of discounted cashflows. To use a hundred or so criteria instead of seven would change nothing. By doing this, we introduce a certain amount of redundancy between the criteria, which results in more weight being given to some factors. As long as the method is subjective, it should remain transparent. The multi-criteria method gains nothing from being summarized in a single score since there are many implicit hypotheses in the weightings. The brand profile should be used instead to make a realistic, valid business plan, materializing in discounted cashflows.

Last but not least, the multiple method is too sensitive to small variations of the multiple itself. Multiplying 800 million by seven or eight makes a lot of a difference. Such sensitivity is at odds with the principle of prudence. Brand valuation is not an exact science. It is not acceptable to obtain outputs that can vary by millions of pounds just by changing the multiple by 1 unit. This is probably why recently Interbrand moved unobtrusively towards the classic financial methodology, the discounted cashflow approach (Table 18.2).

Brand valuation in practice

How do we evaluate the brand in practice using the discounted cashflow method? During a company acquisition, as soon as the target company has been taken over by its buyer, it becomes necessary to record its assets *at their true value* in the consolidated accounts of the buyer company or group. These assets include tangible and intangible assets; the brand falls into the latter category.

Given that the purchase price for the company is generally well above its nett accounting value, the difference (or gap) is known as the first consolidation difference, or goodwill in the wider sense of the term. It must be allocated to its various components, the company assets, evaluated at their 'fair value'. The non-allocated residual balance will be referred to as goodwill in the strict sense. How then do we determine the value of each asset and, in particular, the value of a brand? This takes the form of a nine-stage procedure:

1. The first key stage is to segment the brand into strategic units. In order to be able to isolate the share of added value imputable to

TABLE 18.2 Another estimate of the financial value of brands (2010)

Rank	Brand	Value (US$ billion)
1	Coca-Cola	70,452
2	IBM	64,727
3	Microsoft	60,895
4	Google	43,557
5	GE	42,808
6	McDonald's	33,578
7	Intel	32,015
8	Nokia	29,495
9	Disney	28,731
10	HP	26,867
11	Toyota	26,192
12	Mercedes Benz	25,179
13	Gillette	23,298
14	Cisco	23,219
15	BMW	22,322
16	Louis Vuitton	21,860
17	Apple	21,143
18	Marlboro	19,961
19	Samsung	19,491
20	Honda	18,506

SOURCE *Businessweek*/Interbrand, 6 August 2010

the brand, we need to work from the bottom up, starting with the factors that produce the sales and profits: the 'cash-generating units' and 'reporting units'. We must identify the excess profit of each of these strategic units, which then allows us to establish what share of this excess profit is imputable to the brand, remembering that this share can vary from one unit to another. Furthermore, the individual profitability structures and growth potential for each unit may be very different.

Thus, for a hygiene and beauty brand, the relevant unit would operate at product level for each distribution channel. Each product has its own individual profitability structure; and furthermore, the relative weight of the brand in the consumer's decision-making process varies from product to product. Lastly, sales and growth potential also vary from product to product and from channel to channel.

2 The second stage will be to build the forecasted profit accounts using the business plan. Like any asset, the brand has no value apart from the potential for future profit derived from its use. What will this use be? What sales do we expect? At what price? With what sales and marketing expenditure?

This second stage aims to define the overall share imputable to intangible assets in the financial results forecasted for each of these units, and is known as the EVA (economic value added). This is obtained by taking the product or business's trading profit and subtracting company tax (which gives nett EBIT), then allowing for permanent invested capital and working capital requirement (which gives the EVA). Invested capital is entered at a 'normal' rate (t), the average cost of the capital. This produces the following sequence of residual balances:

$$\text{EBIT} - \text{Taxes} = t\,(\text{Tangible Assets} + \text{WCR}) + t'\,(\text{Intangible Assets})$$

$$\text{Nett EBIT} - t\,(\text{Tangible Assets} + \text{WCR}) = \text{EVA} = t'\,(\text{Intangible Assets})$$

Remember that these calculations are based on a business plan: they are forecasts for future profits under a specific growth hypothesis.

3 The third stage is where we deduct from this EVA the contributions of other intangible assets once they become directly evaluable: for example, assigning a value to patents based on the usual rates applied in this area, or the virtual allowance made for a portfolio of customers or subscribers, a function of market practices. We should add that if the brand operated exclusively through licences (as is the case with certain luxury brands), its contribution could then be evaluated directly. This deduction, made in order to account for other intangible assets required for business, reminds us that the brand is indeed a conditional asset.

4 So is this residual balance the share of the profit attributable to the brand? Not necessarily: this is where the allocations to the brand and to other potential candidates stage comes in. Here, we should ask ourselves what weight the brand carries in the customer's purchasing decision for each analysis unit (that is, each product in its distribution channel). This is a question for an expert jury to answer. Other methods exist. The customers themselves could be interviewed. A typical study consists first of identifying all the product choice criteria, then measuring the influence each one has in the customer's decision, and lastly evaluating the brand's share in the perception associated with each criterion. For example, we know that the brand has a strong influence on the perception of taste: in blind testings, consumers preferred Pepsi to Coca-Cola, but as soon as the brand is identified, they claim to have preferred the glass of Coca-Cola. Conversely, recognition of the brand has no influence on the perception of its presence in stores. By adding together the respective influence of each of these criteria and balancing these against the role played by the brand in evaluating each of them, we obtain an overall percentage which measures the brand's total influence in the purchase. A typical service station brand will score a 30 per cent rating, whereas a soft drink brand will be of the order of 70 per cent.

5 Once armed with this percentage, we can then calculate year by year, in the business plan, the share of excess profit attributable to the brand for each cash-generating unit or reporting unit.

6 Given that the ultimate goal is to produce a discounted sum of these revenues specifically attributable to the brand, we must first fix on the discount rate to be used. It will depend on our understanding of risks: in other words, are the brand's levers of added value durable in the long term? How is the market growing? Is it open to competition? Is it becoming commoditized? Is it becoming sensitive to price, and thus to distributor's brands? What is its state of innovation? What is its R&D potential, and so on?

7 The purpose of this seventh stage is to conduct a strategic audit of the brand and a 'risks and opportunities' audit, by examining (see Table 18.3):

- the risks associated with the market;
- the risks associated with the brand and the long-term status of its differentiating features;
- the risks associated with the product itself;
- the risks associated with the company, its staff and its finances for developing the brand;
- the opportunities for geographical expansion;
- the opportunities for brand extension into other product categories.

This strategic analysis produces a risk evaluation, and thus a discounting rate for future use.

8 This stage is that of the discounted sum of profits attributable to the brand, based on the discount rate identified above, after the strategic audit of the brand. It produces the brand's value, which will in theory be taken as a deduction from goodwill and recorded on the balance sheet as such. It is a good idea at this stage to check whether the value obtained is especially sensitive to the discount rate used.

9 Finally, an evaluation should not be confined to one single method. The goal of reliable

TABLE 18.3 Assessing brand strength: strategic diagnosis

Risks associated with the future market	Growth of the market Profitability of the market Importance of competitor and retailer brands Expected technological innovations Changes in customer expectations Strength of barriers to entry
Risks associated with the sources of brand value	Quality of past advertising support Image and reputation Quality of trademarks and their registration Customer loyalty Distributor attitudes and loyalty Attitudes of opinion leaders Relative position in the market
Risks associated with the product	Life of patents Existence of 'me-too' brands and product copiability R&D perspectives
Risks associated with the business	Financial support Strategic coherence
Potential	Potential for geographical extension Licensing potential Potential for extension into other product categories

accounts and fair value evaluation demands cross-checking against other evaluation sources. It is true that only the discounted cashflow method is economically valid and accepted by official accounting and auditing bodies. But it is also true that other methods exist; these may not be accepted to the same degree, but they can be used for cross-checking results. Fair value has to be obtained through a narrowing-down process; it cannot be calculated directly.

For this reason, it is common to cross-check results obtained from the discounted sum of revenues imputable to the brand with an evaluation based on the royalties method. To do this, we calculate which royalty rate would, when applied to forecasted turnover, give the same overall current royalty value after discounting. It is reassuring if this rate matches standard figures for the sector. For example, in the haircare products sector, l'Oréal would pay Jacques Dessange 3 per cent of its turnover for products sold under its licence name.

If the gap between the results produced by these two approaches is too wide, a complete rethink is necessary in order to identify the sources of the discrepancy and, if appropriate, to correct them. For example, in an evaluation, the value of non-directly-calculated intangibles works out at a royalty rate of nearly 30 per cent. This is impossible. After analysis, it is decided to impute one-third of the value to the brand and two-thirds to the market share (an asset that can be recorded on the balance sheet in some countries).

An alternative version of the above procedure exists. It consists of taking (during Stage 4) the discounted sum of the combined value of all intangible assets; that is to say, the EVA taken as a whole – after having used the strategic audit matrix to establish the discount rate to be used, of course. This overall intangible asset value is thus distributed between each of them afterwards. As we can see, this variation assumes that the basis for distribution remains more or less the same regardless of which cash-generating units and products are involved.

The evaluation of complex cases

The above method works well for most brands, and is the standard approach. However, there are cases where, in order to evaluate certain brands – or brands in unusual market situations – we have to use one of the other methods examined above.

The case of loss-making brands

The above procedure is based on the theory that the brand is a conditional asset, and hence its value is obtained after the deduction of an allowance for the capital invested in production. This poses the problem of how to value brands owned by loss-making companies.

According to the above approach – which assumes a profitable balance – if there are no profits then the brand has no economic value in its current sphere of activity. It acquires value only if a new business plan, with very different cost structures, can demonstrate not only that the company can generate a profit, but also that there will be excess profits even after an allowance has been made for the tangible and intangible assets required for the production and distribution of the product or service.

Financial valuation thus dispels any mirages surrounding the brand: regardless of its reputation and image, a brand acquires value only if it is backed by a profit-making business plan. The term 'mirage' is an apposite one, as many buyers allow themselves to be seduced by brand awareness and image statistics. The economic approach reminds us that reputation and image are worth nothing unless they produce profit – with the help of other assets, which have to be factored in.

The case of dead brands to be revitalized

Companies regularly kill off brands; in order for mega-brands to be created, business operations have to be contracted to just a handful of brands, and many must thus be disposed of. For example, Nestlé abandoned Chambourcy, and PSA abandoned Talbot. Nevertheless, brands can be sold on after several years of inactivity. How can we use the multi-stage approach shown above if there has been no economic activity, and therefore no profit or loss figures? How, for example, can we estimate the value of a brand which has lain dormant for years, such as Talbot, Simca, Studebaker or Plymouth? According to the successive residuals approach, we should assess it as part of the new business plan incorporating this revitalized brand; or in any event, this is what the buyer should do before buying.

Another evaluation method consists of measuring the additional price and margin that the use of the hitherto defunct brand would enable its new user to command.

We have to consider this in terms of the differential margin: although the brand might make it possible to charge a higher public price at the retail level, the retailer might well keep the majority of this increase and hand over only a modest proportion to the end-purchaser. In fact, this is often what actually happens: when the brand is weak, and returns to the marketplace after a long absence, retailers take advantage of the fact to increase the size of their cut.

It is in the interests of the seller to use a different valuation method. A good candidate is the replacement cost method (the amount that has to be spent now to rebuild the brand and its residual reputation, along with all of its copyright registrations worldwide, for example). As a last resort, there is always sale by auction.

How can weak brands be evaluated?

Some brands remain brands only in the legal sense: they have become mere names, and no longer influence buyers. How are these to be evaluated? This is a common scenario. Given that money was paid for these brands, the replacement cost method is advisable. For example, how much would need to be spent today to:

- create a brand in this sector: name research, name tests and so on;
- trademark it in all relevant countries;
- devise a graphic theme for a new logo and so on?

How can young brands be evaluated?

This case is similar to the previous one. Once a young brand has proven that it can be profitable (for example, in the fashion market), the commodity being sold is in fact the time and money saved in establishing the legal and image foundations of the brand (its name and visual identity). Going beyond this means indulging in the same sort of risks taken by all investors in the dot.com brands, often to their cost. Unlike our fashion example, these brands had provided no proof that they could one day make money. Without a business, and in any case without profits, they could not be evaluated in any reliable way. This was the cause of the internet boom: five-year business plans produced estimated revenues which, when multiplied by a factor of between three and seven, resulted in exorbitant valuations.

How can parent brands be evaluated?

Today, brand theory dictates a two-level architecture with a parent brand and daughter brands. For example, Garnier is a parent brand, while Fructis, Ambre Solaire, Feria and Graphic are daughter brands. So how can we calculate the value of parent brands such as Garnier and l'Oréal Paris?

Remember that the first essential stage in the process is segmentation into strategic units: cash reporting units.

It is this requirement that the analysis be conducted at the level of reporting units and cash generating units that provides an explanation of how to evaluate parent brands that contain several daughter brands. Typical examples are Chanel and Dior. For example, there is no such thing as a Chanel perfume; rather, there are products with brands such as Chanel No 5, and Chanel No 18. These are daughter brands. The same is true with Dior Parfum: the reason it has created a Fahrenheit unit, producing profit and loss accounts, is that value is being created at this point. By adding up our evaluations of individual daughter brands, we arrive at an overall cumulative value for them. The value of Dior itself, separated from its daughter brands, is thus a residual one.

What about the brand values published annually in the press?

Given the rigour and hard work required in an evaluation of intangible assets conducted by the company itself, which has full access to all relevant information, what should we make of the annual 'hit parade' charts which appear in the economics press, giving new values for the top worldwide brands (see Table 18.2)? Why such big differences between valuations?

The Interbrand design company, which was the first to produce such data, has used two methods over time. Historically, it has attempted to derive values for brand EVA from public information in the annual reports of stock-exchange-listed companies and a variety of other public sources. Not being able to work with a business plan, given the confidentiality of company plans, Interbrand instead analysed data from the last two years. So how does it make the leap from EVA to brand value? It used an estimation of the share of EVA attributable to the brand, multiplied by a figure (the 'multiple'), itself derived from a statistical model based on the analysis of the price/earnings ratio (p/e) for stock-exchange-listed companies such as Gillette. The price/earnings ratio is actually a multiple itself. It compares the stock value with the profits associated with that stock: this will indicate, say, that a stock is worth 10 times its dividend price.

Interbrand configured its statistical model using stock-exchange-listed companies. Knowing the multiple (p/e) for each company, it performed a strategic analysis of its brands, following a method similar to the one we have described for our strategic audit of the brand. The end result of Interbrand's strategic evaluation of the brand is an overall score for the brand, measuring the strength of the brand (the 'brand strength index'). This is the sum of the partial scores obtained from each of the individual audit criteria (see Table 18.1). The criteria are leadership, stability and so on. It is then easy to identify the statistical relationship between the recalculated strength of the brands and the virtual multiple approximated by the price/earnings ratio (p/e) on the stock exchange. This statistical relationship has never been published, but has been represented as shown in Figure 18.5.

Having produced an external estimate of the EVA for each brand, it was then easy for Interbrand to calculate the brand strength index which, when factored into the statistical model, identifies the virtual multiple. All that remained at this point was to measure this virtual multiple as the share of estimated EVA allocated to the brand.

Several remarks can be made about this external procedure, which is used to produce the published 'league tables' of global brand value.

The tables are based on this logic, except that they are not in possession of all of the relevant information (as opposed to, say, an auditor appointed by the company to value its brands). They are thus obliged to obtain an external estimation based on the accounts published by stock-exchange-listed companies, and the figures are subject to a wide margin of error. Furthermore, these league tables cannot measure the value of brands belonging to family-run companies such as Mars, Levi's and Lacoste, which do not release public figures. Nor can they include brands belonging to companies producing consolidated accounts that are not broken down by brand. Lastly, they exclude cases in which sales may be attributable to factors other than pure demand. Consider air transport, for example, where the policy of alliances means that it is possible to end up flying with Delta Airlines after having bought an Air France ticket. Also, a significant part of demand is influenced by exit barriers such as frequent flyer cards: this is not pure demand driven by customer preference.

Other critical remarks may be made about this approach, as we have already seen, including sensitivity to variations in the multiple, and the validity of the graph.

Recently, Interbrand has changed its method of producing its 'global brand value' league tables, moving towards a more conventional financial and economic approach. Although its methodology has not been explicitly published, reference has been made to 'net present value of future brand earnings', which would be more in line with our recommended nine-step process. However, questions must be asked as to the validity of estimating these future brand earnings, without internal access to the company in question, by 'experts' with no knowledge of the actual business plan or the real financial data. Yet it is on such fragile estimates that the annual brand table published by *Businessweek* – and faithfully reproduced by the world's economic press – is based. The other source of brand valuation, Brandz, from Millward Brown, a market research company, still relies on multiples.

Unintended impact of the IFRS norms on brand valuations

IFRS norms have been enacted since 2005. Paradoxically the IFRS norms, which were supposed to bring order and coherence to the brand valuation procedures, have had an unintended consequence, that of reducing the importance of the amounts posted in the balance sheet. This is the consequence of the fact that brands are not amortized. However, auditors and accounting companies feel better when they can attribute intangibles to amortizable items (such as patents, databases, etc). Accountants discovered the brand in 1990 when it was a hot topic. At that time brands exerted a hegemony. Huge amounts of non-amortizable goodwill were then posted in the balance sheet, as a reflection of the power of brands, newly highlighted by experts.

Accountants and auditors realized that they sometimes had to depreciate these amounts, especially during economic crises. Then the company concerned was doubly penalized: it had to announce not only financial losses, but also a loss of value. According to the IFRS norms a yearly impairment test had to be made to check whether the brand had lost part of its value. This impairment test is asymmetrical:

brand value can be re-evaluated downward, but not upward.

To avoid this yearly drama, accountants and auditors prefer to cut the goodwill into slices and allocate them to amortizable intangible assets. The brand value itself has been considerably reduced. As European brand valuation authority M Nussenbaum puts it: 'Underlying this vision, the brand has now become the mere attraction of the name, separate from the means to achieve it' (Nussenbaum and Jacquot, 2011).

On the other hand the IFRS norms have also favoured a price inflation in the market for brands. Looking for local brands that have an international potential, global companies do not hesitate to propose huge amounts: since the amounts will not be amortized, they will not be included in the costs.

Financially evaluating the cost of an image prejudice

It is well known that it takes years and even decades to build a reputation but only weeks or months to lose it. Toyota's many product recalls in the United States, from December 2009 to June 2010, led to a value destruction estimated as 14 per cent on the New York Stock Exchange and 11 per cent on the Nikkei (Chevillard and Turpin, 2010).

On 3 September 2010, a French court of appeal ruled that the online auction site eBay should pay LVMH (the world's number one luxury group) €5.7 million for allowing its sellers to trade fake LVMH goods such as handbags. The court also fined eBay for selling authentic LVMH products that the luxury retailer preferred to sell in its exclusive outlets, a key facet of a pure luxury strategy. The estimation of damages was based on the fact that eBay not only received commissions from the sales of counterfeited products, but also received money from the adverts posted by the sellers of these counterfeited products. No one is supposed to profit from hosting illegal trade actions, be it on the web or elsewhere. The court also estimated that, by contributing to the diffusion of fake handbags, eBay had destroyed part of the exclusivity value attached to Louis Vuitton, a condition of the group's high prices, slowly built year after year by an obsession with quality and huge communication investments. Clearly there was an image prejudice to be repaired.

The eBay case is just one of many instances where counterfeited products not only steal sales from an original product and brand, but induce loss of brand equity by the lower quality of the counterfeited products sold under the famous name, as well as by the breach in the feelings of privilege attached to the name (Nussenbaum, 2010). To repair this dilution of brand reputation, companies have to invest money and communicate: this must also be taken into account when counterfeiters are sued and ordered to repair the prejudice.

Counterfeits are becoming widespread, far beyond the luxury sector: pharmaceuticals, car accessories, cigarettes, etc. In some countries, they are a whole sector of industry, with support at a high political level and popular back-up. Brands are like banknotes: the money value written on a banknote has no relationship with the value of the paper of the banknote. It is a measure of trust in the state. This is why so many people try to make counterfeit money: they are attracted by the gap between the cost of paper and the value of the banknote.

Brands must exert a strong legal pressure on all counterfeiters. When a company is identified as a counterfeiter, it is generally fined for three kinds of damages:

1. The loss of sales by the original brand due to the sales of counterfeits. To evaluate this loss the original brand must prove that clients bought the counterfeits because they believed they were the real product or the real brand. This is not always the case: a buyer of a fake Rolex at a very low price knows that it is not a genuine Rolex. In addition, Rolex would never sell at such a low price. In such a case, the courts hold that, although no loss of sales was incurred by the original brand, nonetheless it is a private property infringement.
2. Unpaid royalties. Brands, logos, models and patents are all intellectual property. As property it must be defended: no one can use your property without paying some kind of rental or royalty fee. Counterfeiters should have paid the original brand a royalty for using its name and signs, but at what rate of royalty? This should not be the usual royalty

rate of the sector, but double or much more. Why? Because the original brand would certainly have refused to let the counterfeiter use its name, so the royalty rate to be used is a rate that would have deterred the counterfeiter from making counterfeits, as it would have left almost no profit.

3 Brand equity dilution. The brand loses its distinctiveness and/or the price premium attached to feelings of privilege. This loss is hardly measurable. However, the cost of repair should be estimated. What is the budget of a communication investment that would offset the negative image thus created? Because negative information flows more easily and faster than positive information, and because the use of advertising in the media is today very costly, much more than mere word of mouth, in the eBay/LVMH case the court used a multiple of four (Nussenbaum, 2010). It estimated that the costs of repairing the damage to the luxury brand image were four times as great as the total amount of money spent on eBay by counterfeited luxury product resellers.

BIBLIOGRAPHY

Aaker, D (1990) Brand extensions: the good, the bad and the ugly, *Sloan Management Review*, Summer, pp 47–56

Aaker, D (1991) *Managing Brand Equity*, Free Press, New York

Aaker, D (1995) *Building Strong Brands*, Free Press, New York

Aaker, D (1996) *Building Strong Brands*, Free Press, New York

Aaker, D (2011) *Brand Relevance: Making competitors irrelevant*, Jossey-Bass, San Francisco, CA

Aaker, D and Biel, A (1993) *Brand Equity and Advertising*, Lawrence Erlbaum, Hillsdale, New Jersey

Aaker, D and Joachimstahler, E (2000) *Brand Leadership*, Free Press, New York

Aaker, D and Keller, K L (1990) Consumer evaluations of brand extensions, *Journal of Marketing*, Jan, **54** (1), pp 27–41

Aaker, J (1995) Conceptualizing and measuring brand personality, Working Paper no 255, Anderson Graduate School of Management, UCLA

Aaker, J (1997) Dimensions of brand personality, *Journal of Marketing Research*, **24**, Aug, pp 347–56

Abric, J-C (1994) Pratiques sociales et représentations, Presses Universitaires de France, Paris

Advertising Research Foundation (1995) *Exploring Brand Equity*, Advertising Research Foundation, New York

Agefi (1990) Le goodwill, objet de controversé en Europe, *Agefi*, 1 Feb

AhluWalia, R (2000) Examination of psychological processes underlying resistance to persuasion, *Journal of Consumer Research*, **27** (2), Sep, pp 217–32

Ahonen, T T and Moore, A (2005) *Communities Dominate Brands*, Future Text, London

Ailawadi, K and Harlam, B (2004) The determinants of retail margins: the role of store brand share, *Journal of Marketing*, **68** (1), Jan, pp 147–65

Ailawadi, K, Lehmann, D and Neslin, S (2003) Revenue premium as an outcome measure of brand equity, *Journal of Marketing*, **67** (4), Oct, pp 1–17

Akhme, D and Kapferer, J-N (2006) *An empirical analysis of the effects of a corporate name change preannouncement on stock value*, HEC Paris, Master's thesis

Alba, J W and Chattopadhyay, A (1986) Salience effects in brand recall, *Journal of Marketing Research*, **23**, p 369

Alden, D, Steenkamp, and Batra, R (1999) Brand positioning through advertising in a global consumer culture, *Journal of Marketing*, 63

Alden, D, Steenkamp, J-B and Smith, R E (1999) Brand positioning in Asia, North America and Europe, *Journal of Marketing*, **63** (1), pp 75–87

Alpert, J (2012) *The Mobile Marketing Revolution*, McGraw Hill, London

Ambler, T and Styles, C (1996) Brand development versus new product development, *Marketing Intelligence and Planning*, **14** (7), pp 10–19

Anholt, S and Hildreth, J (2005) *Brand America*, Cyan Communications, London

Arnault, B (2000) *La Passion Creative*, Plon: Pocket, Paris

Arnold, T (1989) Accounting for the value of brands, *Accountant's Magazine*, Feb, p 12

Asch, S (1946) Forming impressions of personality, *Journal of Abnormal and Social Psychology*, **41**, pp 25–90

Azoulay, A and Kapferer, J-N (2003) Do brand personality scales really measure brand personality?, *Journal of Brand Management*, **11** (2), Nov, pp 143–55

Baillot, J (1990) La marque et 1'automobile, *Humanisme et Entreprise*, **181**, June, pp 5–8

Balachander, S and Ghose, S (2003) Reciprocal spillover effects: a strategic benefit of brand extensions, *Journal of Marketing*, **67** (1), Jan, pp 4–14

Baldinger, A (1992) What CEOs are saying about brand equity, *Journal of Advertising Research*, Jul/Aug, **32** (4), pp 6–12

Barwise, P (1989) *Accounting for Brands*, London Business School

Barwise, P (1993) Brand equity: snark or boojum, *International Journal of Research in Marketing*, **10** (2), pp 93–104

Bastien, V, Dubourdeau, P-L, Leclère, M (2011) *Marque France*, Presses des Mines, Paris

Batra, R (2002) How brand reputation affects the relationship of advertising and brand equity outcomes, *Journal of Advertising Research*

Bedbury, S (2002) *A New Brand World*, Viking, New York

Bell, D, Lal, R and Salmon, W (2003) Globalization of retailing, Globalization of Markets Colloquium, Harvard Business School, May

Berard, C (1990) La marque: élément du patrimoine de l'entreprise, *Revue de l'ENA*, 202, May, pp 24–25

Berry, N C (1988) Revitalizing brands, *Journal of Consumer Marketing*, **5** (Summer), pp 15–20

Birkigt, K and Stadler, M M (1980) *Corporate Identity: Grundlagen, Funktionen, Fallbeispiele*, Verlag Moderne Industrie, Munich

Birol, J and Kapferer, J-N (1991) Les campagnes collectives, Internal document, Agence Sicquier-Courcelles/HEC

Blackett, T (1985) The role of brand valuation in marketing strategy, *Marketing and Research Today*, Nov, pp 245–47

Blackston, M (1992) Building brand equity by managing the brand's relationships, *Journal of Advertising Research*, May/Jun, **32** (3), pp 79–83

Blanc, C and Hoffstetter, P (1990) L'évaluation des marques, HEC Research paper, under the direction of J-N Kapferer, June, Jouy-en-Josas

Blattberg, R (2001) *Customer Equity*, Harvard Business School Press, Cambridge, MA

Blattberg, R C, Briesch, R and Fox, E J (1995) How promotions work, *Marketing Science*, Vol. 14, N°3, part 2 of 2, pp 124–32

Boddewyn, J, Soehl, R and Picard, J (1986) Standardization in international marketing: is Ted Levitt in fact right?, *Business Horizons*, pp 69–75

Bon, J, Michon, C and Ollivier, A (1981) Etude empirique de la demographie des marques: le rôle de la publicité, Fondation Jours de France pour la recherche en publicité, Paris

Bonnal, F (2008) *Realliance: The post individualistic society*, Payot edn, Paris

Bontemps, A and Lehu, J-M (2002) *Lifting de marque*, Editions d'Organisation, Paris

Bosch, J and Hirschey, M (1989) The valuation effects of corporate name changes, *Financial Management* 18, 64–73

Bottomley, P P and Holden, S (2001) Do we really know how consumers evaluate brand extensions?, *Journal of Marketing Research*, **38**, Nov, pp 494–501

Botton, M and Cegarra, J J (1990) *Le Nom de Marque*, McGraw-Hill, Paris

Boush, D (1993) Brands as categories, in *Brand Equity and Advertising*, ed D Aaker and A Biel, Lawrence Erlbaum, Hillsdale, NJ, pp 299–312

Brandenburger, A and Nalebuff, B (1996) *Coopetition*, Doubleday, New York

Broadbent, S (1983) *Advertising Works 2*, Holt, Rinehart and Winston, London

Brodbeck, D and Mongibeaux, J F (1990) *Chic et Toc: le vrai livre des contrefaçons*, Balland, Paris

Broniarczyk, S and Alba, J (1994) The importance of the brand in brand extension, *Journal of Marketing Research*, **31**, May, pp 214–28

Brown, S, Kozinets, R and Sherry, J F (2003) Teaching old brands new tricks, *Journal of Marketing*, **67** (3), Jul, pp 19–33

Brown, T and Dacin, P (1997) The company and the product: corporate associations and consumer product responses, *Journal of Marketing*, **61** (1), Jan, pp 68–84

Buchan, E and Brown, A (1989) Mergers and acquisitions, in *Brand Valuation*, ed J Murphy, Hutchinson Business Books, London, pp 81–94

Buchanan, W, Simmons, R and Bickart, S (1999) Brand equity dilution: retailer display and context brand effects, *Journal of Marketing Research*, Aug, **36**, pp 345–55

Buck, S (1997) The continuing grocery revolution, *Journal of Brand Management*, **4** (4), pp 227–38

Burgaud, D and Mourier, P (1989) Europe: développement d'une marque, *MOCI*, **889**, pp 125–28

Burmann, C and Arnhold, U (2008) *User generated branding*, LIT-verlag.de

Buzzell, R D (1968) Can you standardize multinational marketing?, *Harvard Business Review*, Nov–Dec

Buzzell, R D and Gale, B T (1987) *The PIMS Principles*, Free Press, New York

Buzzell, R D and Quelch, J A (1988) *Multinational Marketing Management*, Addison Wesley, New York

Buzzell, R D and Quelch, J A (1990) *The Marketing Challenge of 1992*, Addison Wesley, New York

Buzzell, R D, Gale, B T and Sultan, R G (1975) Market share – a key to profitability, *Harvard Business Review*, Jan–Feb, pp 97–106

Cabat, O (1989) Archéologie de la marque moderne, in *La marque*, ed J-N Kapferer and J C Thoenig, McGraw-Hill, Paris

Carpenter, G and Nakamoto, K (1990) Competitive strategies for late entry into market with a dominant brand, *Management Science*, **36** (10), pp 1268–78

Carratu, V (1987) Commercial counterfeiting, in *Branding: A key marketing tool*, ed J Murphy, McGraw-Hill, London

Carroll, J M (1985) *What's in a Name?* Freeman, New York

Cauzard, D, Perret, J and Ronin, Y (1989) *Image de marque et marque d'image*, Ramsay, Paris

Chadha, R and Husband, P (2006) *The Cult of the Luxury Brand*, Nicholas Brealey, London

Chan, K W and Mauborne, R (2000) Value innovation, *Harvard Business Review*

Channon, C (1987) *Advertising Works 4*, Cassell, London

Chanterac, V (1989) La marque a travers le droit, in *La marque*, ed J-N Kapferer and J C Thoenig, McGraw-Hill, Paris

Charbonnier, C and Lombard, E (1998) Can multi-product brands support various personalities? Esomar Annual Conference Proceedings, Vienna

Chateau, J (1972) *Les sources de l'imaginaire*, Editions Universitaires, Paris

Chaudhuri, A (2002) How brand reputation affects the advertising brand equity link, *Journal of Advertising Research*, May-June

Chevalier, M (2003) *Pro Logo*, Editions d'Organisation, Paris

Chevillard, N and Turpin, M (2010) *An Application of the event discontinuity method for the évaluation of the impact of a crisis: the Toyota case*, Finance Masters' Thesis N°225 – Paris Dauphine University

Chinardet, C (1994) *Trade-Marketing*, Editions d'Organisation, Paris

Chip, H, Bell, C and Sternberg, E (2001) Emotional selection in memes: the case of urban legends, *Journal of Personality and Social Psychology*, **81**, Dec, pp 1028–41

Christensen, C (1997) *The Innovator's Dilemma*, Harvard Business School Press, Cambridge, MA

Clarke, D G (1976) Econometric measurement of the duration of advertising effect on sales, *Journal of Marketing Research*, **13**, Nov, pp 345–50

Claycamp, H and Liddy, L (1969) Prediction of new product performance, *Journal of Marketing Research*, **6** (3), Nov, pp 414–20

Cohen, J M and Serog, P (2006) *Savoir Manger: Le guide des aliments (Knowing how to eat: a guide to food)*, Flammarion, Paris

Cohen, M, Eliashberg, J and Ho, T (1997) An anatomy of a decision support system for developing and launching line extensions, *Journal of Marketing Research*, **34** (1), Feb, pp 117–29

Collins, J and Porras, J (1994) *Built to Last*, Harper Business, London

Conseil National de la Comptabilité (1989) La formation du capital commercial dans 1'entreprise, 27.A.89.16, Sep

Cooper, M (1989a) The basis of brand evaluation, *Accountancy*, Mar, p 32

Cooper, M (1989b) Brand valuation in the balance, *Accountancy*, Jul, p 28

Corstjens, J and Corstjens, M (1995) *Store Wars: The battle for mindspace and shelfspace*, Wiley, London

Corstjens, M (1999) *Store Wars*, Wiley, Chichester

Corstjens, M and Lal, R (2000) Building store loyalty through store brands, *Journal of Marketing Research*, **37** (3)

Coumau, J B, Gagne, J-F and Josserand, E (2005) *Manager par la marque (Brand management)*, Editions d'Organisation, Paris

Cova, B, Kozinets, R and Shankar, A (2007) *Consumer Tribes*, Butterworth-Heinemann, Oxford

Crimmins, J (1992) Better measurement and management of brand value, *Journal of Advertising Research*, Jul/Aug, **32** (4), pp 11–19

Cross, R and Smith, J (1994) *Customer Bonding*, NTC Business Books

Crozier, M (1989) *L'Entreprise à l'Ecoute: apprendre le management post-industriel*, InterEditions, Paris

Dacin, P and Smith, D (1994) The effect of brand portfolio characteristics on consumer evaluations of brand extensions, *Journal of Marketing Research*, **31**, May, pp 229–42

Danziger, P (2004) *Why People Buy Things They Do Not Need*, Kaplan, New York

Darby, M and Kami, E (1973) Free competition and the optimal amount of fraud, *Journal of Law and Economics*, **16** (1), pp 67–88

Davidson, J H (1987) *Offensive Marketing*, Gower Press, London

Davis, S (2000) *Brand Asset Management*, Jossey-Bass, San Francisco, CA

Dawar, N (2002) How brand reputation affects the relationship of advertising and brand equity outcomes, *Journal of Advertising Research*

Dawar, N and Anderson, P (1992) Determining the order and direction of multiple brand extensions, Working Paper no 92/36/MKT, INSEAD

De Bono, E (2009) *Lateral Thinking*, Penguin Books, London

De Chernatony, L (1996) Integrated brand building using brand taxonomies, *Marketing Intelligence and Planning*, **14** (7), pp 40–45

De Chernatony, L and McDonald, M (1994) *Creating Powerful Brands*, Butterworth-Heinemann, Oxford

Defever, P (1989) L'utilisation de la communication électronique sur les lieux de vente, *Revue francaise du marketing*, **123** (3), pp 5–15

Degon, R (1994) La marque et le prix, *Journée IREP La Marque*, Sep, pp 28–38

DeJean, J (2006) *The Essence of Style*, Free Press, New York

Denier S, Kapferer, J-N (2011) *Can a sport celebrity become a brand? A Framework for decision?* HEC Paris. Masters' thesis. Marketing Dept.

Derek, R D and Galinsky, A D (2009) Conspicuous Consumption versus Utilitarian Ideals: How different levels of power shape consumer consumption, *Journal of Experimental Social Psychology*, **45**: 549–55

Dhalla, N K (1978) Assessing the long term value of advertising, *Business Review*, **56**, Jan–Feb, pp 87–95

Diamond, J (2006) *Collapse: How societies choose to fail or survive*, Penguin, London

Diefenbach, J (1987) The corporate identity as the brand, in *Branding: A key marketing tool*, ed J Murphy, McGraw-Hill, London

Dinnie, K (2011) *City Branding*, Palgrave Macmillan, Basingstoke

Donaton, S (2004) *Madison and Vine*, Crain Communication, Chicago, IL

Dru, J-M (1996) *Disruption*, Wiley, New York

Dru, J-M (2002) *Beyond Disruption*, Wiley, New York

Dru, J-M (2007) *How disruption brought order*, Palgrave McMillan, Basingstoke

Dubois, B and Paternault, C (1995) Understanding the world of international luxury brands, *Journal of Advertising Research*, **35** (4), Jul–Aug, pp 69–76

Durand, G (1964) *L'imagination symbolique*, PUP, Paris

Durand, G (1969) *Les Structures Anthropologiques de l'Imaginaire*, Bordas, Paris

Duvillier, J P (1987) L'absence d'enregistrement à l'actif du fonds de commerce, *Revue française de comptabilité*, October, **183**, p 36

Dyson, P, Farr, A and Hollis, N (1996) Understanding, measuring and using brand equity, *Journal of Advertising Research*, **36** (6), Nov–Dec, pp 9–21

East, R and Hammund, K (1996) The erosion of repeat-purchase loyalty, *Marketing Letters*, **7** (2), pp 163–71

Echambadi, R, Inigo, A, Reinartz, W and Junsoo Lee (2006) Empirical generalizations from brand extension research: How sure are we? *International Journal of Research in Marketing*, Volume 23, Issue 3, September 2006, pp 253–61

Edwards, H and Day, D (2005) *Creating Passion Brands*, Kogan Page, London

Ehrenberg, A (1972) *Repeat Buying*, Edward Arnold, London

Ehrenberg, A, Barnard, N, Kennedy, R and Bloom, H (2002) Brand advertising as creative publicity, *Journal of Advertising Research*, **42** (4), Jul/Aug, pp 7–18

Eiglier, P and Langeard, E (1990) *Servuction*, Editions d'Organisation, Paris

Eliade, M (1952) *Images et Symboles*, Gallimard, Paris

Erdem, T, Zhao, Y and Valenzuela, A (2004) Performance of store brands: a cross country analysis of consumer store brand preferences, perceptions and risk, *Journal of Marketing Research*, **41**, pp 86–100

Etchegoyen, A (2004) *La Force de la Fidelité (Power and fidelity)*, Anne Carriere, Paris

Farquhar, P H (1989) Managing brand equity, *Marketing Research*, Sep, **1** (3), pp 24–33

Farquhar, P H (1994) Strategic challenges for branding, *Marketing Management*, **3** (2), pp 9–15

Farquhar, P H, Han, J, Herr, P and Ijiri, Y (1992) Strategies for leveraging master brands, *Marketing Research*, Sep, pp 32–39

Feldwick, P (1996) What is brand equity anyway and how do you measure it?, *Journal of the Market Research Society*, **38**, pp 85–104

Feldwick, P and Bonnal, F (1995) Reports of the death of brands have been greatly exaggerated, *Marketing and Research Today*, **23** (2), May, pp 86–95

Feral, F (1989) Les signes de qualité en France à la veille du grand marché communautaire et à la lumière d'autres systèmes, *CERVAC*, Université d'Aix Marseille 3, October

Fetscherin, M, Fournier, S, Breazale, M and Melewar, T C (2012) *Consumer-Brand Relationships: Insights for theory and practice*, Routledge, London

Financial Times (1993) *Accounting for Brands*, London, FTBI Report

Firat, F and Dholakia, N (1998) *Consuming People*, Routledge, London

Flament, C (1993) Structure, dynamique et transformation des représentations sociales. In J C Abric (Ed) *Pratiques et Représentations Sociales*, PUF, Paris

Folz, J-M (2003) Managing two brands for success: Peugeot and Citroën, in *Marken Management in der Automobilindustrie*, ed R Kalmbach and B Gottschalk, Auto Business Verlag, pp 341–62

Fombrun, C (2001) Corporate reputation, *Thexis*, **4**, pp 23–27

Fombrun, C, Gardberg, J and Sever, J (2000) The reputation quotient, a multi stakeholder measure of corporate reputation, *Journal of Brand Management* (7), pp 241–55

Fombrun, C and Van Riel, C B M (2008) *Fame and Fortune: How successful companies build winning reputations*, FT Press

Fourcade, A and Cabat, O (1981) *Anthropologie de la publicité*, Fondation Jours de France pour la recherche en publicité

Fournier, S (1998) Consumers and their brands, *Journal of Consumer Research*, **24** (4), Mar, pp 343–73

Frey, J B (1989) Measuring corporate reputation and its value, Marketing Science Conference, Duke University, NC, USA, 17 March

Friedman, T L (2000) *The Lexus and the Olive Tree*, Anchor Books, New York

Friedman, T L (2005) *The World is Flat*, Farrar, Straus and Giroux eds

Fry, J N (1967) Family branding and consumer brand choice, *Journal of Marketing Research*, **4**, Aug, pp 237–47

Fry, J N, Shaw, D, Haehling, C and Dipchand, C (1973) Customer loyalty to banks: a longitudinal study, *Journal of Business*, **46**, pp 517–25

Fukuyama, F (2006) *The End of History and the Last Man*, Free Press, New York

Gali, J (1993) Does consumer involvement impact evaluations of brand extensions?, unpublished doctoral dissertation, HEC Graduate School of Management

Gamble, T (1967) Brand extension, in *Plotting Marketing Strategy*, ed L Adler, Interpublic Press Books, New York

Garbett, T (1981) *Corporate Advertising*, McGraw-Hill, New York

Geary, M (1990) Fusions et acquisitions: le problème de goodwill, in *Seminaire: Le traitement du goodwill*, 1 February, PF Publications Conferences, Paris

Gelle, T (1990) La comptabilisation des marques, HEC research paper, under the direction of L Collins, May, Jouy-en-Josas

Gladwell, M (2000) *The Tipping Point*, Schuster, London

Glemer, F and Mira, R (1993) The brand leader's dilemma, *McKinsey Quarterly*, **2**, pp 34–44

Godin, S (1999) *Permission Marketing*, Simon Schuster, New York

Greener, M (1989) The bomb in the balance sheet, *Accountancy*, August, p 30

Greig, I and Poynter, R (1994) Brand transfer: building the Whirlpool brand in Europe, *Esomar Conference Proceedings, 26–29 October, Building Successful Brands*, pp 65–78

Guest, L (1964) Brand loyalty revisited: a twenty years report, *Journal of Applied Psychology*, **48** (2), pp 93–97

Guevel, M and Bô, D (2009) *Brand Content*, Dunod edn, Paris

Gürhan-Canli and Maheswaran (1998) The effects of extensions on brand name dilution enhancement, *Journal of Consumer Research*, **35**, Nov, pp 464–73

Hague, P and Jackson, P (1994) *The Power of Industrial Brands*, McGraw-Hill, London

Hallberg, G (1995) *All Consumers are not Created Equal*, Wiley, New York

Hambleton, R (1990) *The Branding of America*, Country Roads, USA

Hamel, G and Prahalad, C (1985) Do you really have a global strategy?, *Harvard Business Review*, Jul–Aug

Hamel, G and Prahalad, C K (1994) *Competing for the Future*, Harvard Business School Press, Boston, MA

Heather, E (1958) What's in a brand name, *Management Review*, Jun, pp 33–35

Heilbrunn, B (2003) The drivers of brand attachment, Working paper, EM Lyon

Heller, R (1986) On the awareness effects of mere distribution, *Marketing Science*, **5**, Summer, p 273

Hem, L (2003) Context effects in brand extensions: implications for evaluations, *Annual EMAC Conference Proceedings*

Henderson, P and Cote, J (1998) Guidelines for selecting or modifying logos, *Journal of Marketing*, **62** (2), Apr, pp 14–30

Hill, S and Lederer, C (2001) *The Infinite Asset*, Harvard Business School Press, Boston, MA

Hirschmann, E and Holbrook, M (1982) Hedonic consumption, *Journal of Marketing*, **46** (2), pp 92–101

Hite, R and Fraser, C (1988) International advertising strategies of multinational corporations, *Journal of Advertising Research*, Aug/Sep, **28** (4), pp 9–17

Hoch, S (1996) How should national brands think about private labels?, *Sloan Management Review*, **37**, Winter, pp 89–102

Hoch, S and Banerji, S (1993) When do private labels succeed?, *Sloan Management Review*, Summer, pp 57–67

Holbrook, M and Hirschmann, E (1982) The experiential aspects of consumption, *Journal of Consumer Research*, **9**, 2, Sep, pp 132–40

Holt, D B (2004) *How Brands Become Icons*, Harvard Business School Press, Cambridge, MA

Holt, D and Cameron, D (2010) *Cultural Strategy: Using innovative ideologies to build breakthrough brands*, Oxford University Press, Oxford

Holt, D, Quelch, J and Taylor, E (2003) Managing the transnational brand: how global perceptions drive value, Globalization of Markets Colloquium, Harvard Business School

Horsky, D and Swyngedouw, P (1987) Does it pay to change your company's name? A stock market perspective, *Marketing Science* **6**, pp 320–35.

Hout, T, Porter, M and Rudder, E (1982) How global companies win out, *Harvard Business Review*, Sep–Oct

Hussey, R and Ong, A (1997) Accounting for goodwill and intangible assets, *Journal of Brand Management*, **4** (4), pp 239–47

Ind, N (2001) *Living the Brand*, Kogan Page, London

Ind, N (2005) *Beyond Branding*, Kogan Page, London

Ind, N, Fuller, C and Trevail, C (2012) *Brand Together: How co-creation generates innovation*, Kogan Page, London

Interbrand (1997) *Brand Valuation*, Premier Books, London

Interbrand (1998) *Brands: The new wealth creators*, Macmillan Business, Basingstoke

IREP (1994) *La Marque*, Seminar on Branding, September, Institut de Recherches et d'Etudes Publicitaires, Paris

Jacobson, R and Aaker, D (1985) Is market share all that it's cracked up to be?, *Journal of Marketing*, **45** (4), Fall, pp 11–22

Jacoby, J and Chestnut, R (1978) *Brand Loyalty and Measurement*, Wiley, New York

Jaubert, M J (1985) *Slogan, mon Amour*, Bernard Barrault Editeur, Paris

Jensen, R (1999) *The Dream Society*, McGraw Hill, New York

Joachimsthaler, E and Aaker, D (1997) Building brands without mass media, *Harvard Business Review*, **75** (1), Jan–Feb, pp 39–52

Jones, J P (1986) *What's in a Name: Advertising and the concept of brands*, Lexington Books, Lexington, KY

Kapferer, J-N (1986) Beyond positioning, retailer's identity, *Esomar Seminar Proceedings, Brussels, 4–6 June*, pp 167–76

Kapferer, J-N (1987) *Rumeurs: Le plus vieux media du monde (Rumours: the oldest medium in the world)*, Le Seuil, Paris

Kapferer, J-N (1990) *Rumors: Image uses and management*, Transaction Books, New Brunswick

Kapferer, J-N (1991) *Rumors: Uses, interpretations and images*, Transactions, New Brunswick

Kapferer, J-N (1995a) Stealing brand equity: measuring perceptual confusion between national brands and copycat own-label products, *Marketing and Research Today*, **23** (2), May, pp 96–103

Kapferer, J-N (1995b) Brand confusion: empirical study of a legal concept, *Psychology and Marketing*, **12** (6), pp 551–68

Kapferer, J-N (1996) Alternative methods for measuring brand confusion created by retailers imitation, HEC Research Report

Kapferer, J-N (1998) The role of branding in medical prescription, HEC Graduate School of Management, Research Paper Series

Kapferer, J-N (2000) Why are we seduced by luxury brands? *Journal of Brand Management*, Nov/Dec

Kapferer, J-N (2001) *Reinventing the Brand*, Kogan Page, London

Kapferer, J-N (2003) Corporate and brand identity, in *Corporate and Organizational Identities*, ed B Moingeon, Routledge, London

Kapferer, J-N (2004) Building brands by rumors, in *Rumours as Medium: Facetten der medienkultur* (Vol 5), ed M Bruhn, V Kaufmann, W Wunderlich and A Haupt, Springer, Berlin

Kapferer, J-N and Bastien, V (2009) *The Luxury Strategy*, Kogan Page, London

Kapferer, J-N and Laurent, G (1988) Consumers' brand sensitivity: a new concept for brand management, in *Defining, Measuring and Managing Brand Equity, Marketing Science Institute: A conference summary*, Report pp 88–104, MSI, Cambridge, MA

Kapferer, J-N and Laurent, G (1995) *La Sensibilité aux Marques*, Editions d'Organisation, Paris

Kapferer, J-N and Laurent, G (1996) How consumers build their perception of mega-brands, unpublished working paper, HEC Graduate School of Management

Kapferer, J-N and Laurent, G (2002) *Identifying Brand Prototypes*, HEC Research Report

Kapferer, J-N and Thoenig, J C (1989) *La Marque*, McGraw-Hill, Paris

Kapferer, J-N and Thoenig, J C (1992) *La Confusion des Marques*, Prodimarques, Paris

Kapferer, J-N, Thoenig, J C *et al* (1991) Une analyse empirique des effets de l'imitation des marques par les contremarques: mesure des taux de confusion au tachystoscope, *Revue française du marketing*, Jan, 136, pp 53–68

Kapferer, P and Gaston Breton, T (2002) Lacoste: the legend, chen Church Ridir, Paris

Kapferer, P and Gaston Breton, T (2004) *Carte Bleue, la petite carte qui a changé notre vie*, Cherche Midi, France

Kapferer, P and Gaston Breton, T (2005) *Renault Trucks, une autre idée du camion (Renault Trucks, another concept of a lorry)*, Cherche Midi, France

Kapferer, P and Gaston Breton, T (2006) *Rungis: Le plus grand marché du monde (Rungis: the largest market in the world)*, Cherche Midi, France

Kapferer, P and Gaston Breton, T (2007) *HEC: Excellence Européenne, rayonnement mondial (HEC: European excellence, global reach)*, Cherche Midi, France

Keller, K L (1992) Conceptualising, measuring and managing customer based brand equity, *Journal of Marketing*, Jan, pp 1–22

Keller, K L (1998) *Strategic Brand Management*, Prentice Hall

Keller, K (2003) Brand synthesis: the multidimensionality of brand knowledge, *Journal of Consumer Research*, 29 (4), pp 595–600

Keller, Kevin Lane (2007) *Strategic Brand Management*, Prentice Hall, New York

Keller, K L and Aaker, D (1992) The effects of sequential introduction of brand extensions, *Journal of Marketing Research*, **29** (1), Feb, pp 35–50

Keller, K, Heckler, S and Houston, M (1998) The effects of brand name suggestiveness on advertising recall, *Journal of Marketing*, **62** (1), pp 48–58

Kim, C and Mauborgne, R (2005) *Blue Ocean Strategy*, Harvard Business School Press, Cambridge, MA

King, S (1973) *Developing New Brands*, Wiley, New York

Kirmani, A, Sood, S and Bridges, S (1999) The ownership effect in consumer responses to brand line stretches, *Journal of Marketing*, **63** (1), pp 88–101

Kleiber, G (1990) *La Semantique du Prototype*, Presses Universitaires de France, Paris

Klein, N (1999) *No Logo*, Picador, New York

Klink, R and Smith, D (2001) Threats to the external validity of extension research, *Journal of Marketing Research*, **38**, Aug, pp 326–35

Knox, S (1996) The death of brand deference, *Marketing Intelligence and Planning*, **14** (7), pp 35–39

Kotler, P (1997) *The Marketing of Nations*, McGraw Hill, New York

Kotler, P (2002) *Kotler on Marketing*, Village Mondial, Paris

Kotler, P and Dubois, B (1991) *Marketing Management*, Publi-Union, Paris

Kotler, P and Gertner, D (2002) Country as a brand, product and beyond, *Journal of Brand Management*, **9** (4–5), Apr, pp 249–61

Kotler, P, Pfoertsch, W and Michi, I (2007) *B2B Branding*, Springer, Berlin

Kozinets, R (2002) Tribalized marketing: the strategic implications of virtual communities of consumption, *European Management Journal*, **17**, June, pp 252–64

Krief, Y (1986) L'entreprise, l'institution, la marque, *Revue française du marketing*, **109**, pp 77–96

Krief, Y and Barjansky, M (1981) La marque: nature et fonction, *Stratégies*, 261 and 262, pp 37–41, 32–36

Kripke, S (1980) *Naming and Necessity*, Harvard University Press, Cambridge, MA

Kumar, N and Steenkamp, J-B (2007) *Private Label Strategy*, Harvard Business School Press, Cambridge, MA

Laforet, S and Saunders, J (1994) Managing brand portfolios: how the leaders do it, *Journal of Advertising Research*, **34** (5), pp 64–67

Lai, K and Zaichkowsky, J (1999) Brand imitation: do the Chinese have different views, *Asia Pacific Journal of Management*, **16** (2), pp 179–92

Lakoff, G (1987) *Women, Fire and Dangerous Things*, University of Chicago Press, IL

Lane, V and Jacobson, R (1995) Stock market reactions to brand extension announcements, *Journal of Marketing*, **59** (1), pp 63–77

Laurent, G and Kapferer, J-N (1985) Measuring consumer involvement profiles, *Journal of Marketing Research*, **22**, pp 41–53

Laurent, G, Kapferer, J-N and Roussel, F (1987) Thresholds in brand awareness, *40th Esomar Marketing Research Congress Proceedings*, Montreux, Sep 13–17, pp 677–99

Laurent, G, Kapferer, J-N and Roussel, F (1995) The underlying structure of brand awareness scores, *Marketing Science*, **14** (3), pp 170–79

Leclerc, F, Schmitt, B H and Dube-Rioux, L (1989) Brand name à la francaise? Oui, but for the right product!, *Advances in Consumer Research*, **16**, pp 253–57

Lehu, J M (2006) *Brand Rejuvenation*, Kogan Page, London

Leif Heim Egil (2002) Variables moderating consumers' reactions to brand extensions, Association for Consumer Research, European Conference Proceedings

Leuthesser, L (1988) Defining, measuring and managing brand equity, Marketing Science Institute, Report no 88–104, Cambridge, MA

Levitt, T (1967) Market stretching, in *Plotting Marketing Strategy*, ed L Adler, Interpublic Press Books, New York

Levitt, T (1969) The augmented product concept, in *The Marketing Mode: Pathways to corporate growth*, McGraw-Hill, New York

Levitt, T (1981) Marketing intangible products and product intangibles, *Harvard Business Review*, **59** (3), May/Jun, pp 94–102

Levitt, T (1983) The globalization of markets, *Harvard Business Review*, May/June

Levy, S (1999) *Brands, Consumers, Symbols and Research*, Sage, Thousand Oaks, CA

Lewi, C and Kapferer, J-N (1996) Consumers' preference for retailers' brands, *Esomar Conference Proceedings – The Big Brand Challenge*, Oct 9–11, pp 229–41

Lindsay, M (1990) Establish brand equity through advertising, *Marketing News*, 22 Jan, pp 16–17

Lindstrom, M (2003) *BRANDchild*, Kogan Page, London

Lindstrom, M (2005) *Brand Sense*, Free Press, New York

Lipowetsky, J and Roux, E (2004) *Le luxe (Luxury)*, Flammarion, Paris

Loden, D J (1992) *Mega Brands*, Irwin, IL

Loken, B and Roedder John, D (1993) Diluting brand beliefs: when do brand extensions have a negative impact?, *Journal of Marketing*, **57**, July, pp 71–84

MacInnis, D J and Nakamoto, P K (1990) Examining factors that influence the perceived goodness of brand extensions, Working Paper no 54, University of Arizona

Macrae, C (1991) *World Class Brands*, Addison-Wesley, England

Macrae, C (1996) *The Brand Chartering Handbook*, Addison-Wesley, Harlow, UK

Maffesoli, M (1996) *The Time of the Tribes: The decline of individualism in mass societies*, Sage, Thousand Oaks, CA

Maffesoli, M (2007) *Le Réenchantement (Reenchantment)*, La Table Ronde, Paris

Magrath, A J (1990) Brands can either grow old gracefully or become dinosaurs, *Marketing News*, 22 Jan, pp 16–17

Marconi, J (1994) *Beyond Branding*, Probus, Chicago, IL

Margolis, S E (1989) Monopolistic competition and multiproduct brand names, *Journal of Business*, **62** (2), pp 199–210

Marion, G (1989) *Les images de l'entreprise*, Les Editions d'Organisation, Paris

Marketing Mix (1987) Monter une gamme: un problème majeur, *Marketing Mix*, **17**, Nov, pp 40–6

Martin, D N (1989) *Romancing the Brand*, American Management Association, New York

Martin, Dick (2007) *Rebuilding Brand America*, Amacom, New York

Mauguère, H (1990) *L'évaluation des entreprises non cotées*, Dunod Entreprise, Paris

Maurice, A (1989) Enquête sur les contremarques: les apprentis sorciers, *References*, May, pp 16–20

Mazanec, J A and Schweiger, G C (1981) Improved marketing efficiency through multiproduct brand names? *European Research*, Jan, pp 32–44

McAlexander, J H, Schouten, J W and Koenig, H F (2002) Building brand community, *Journal of Marketing*, **66** (1), Jan, pp 38–54

McCartney, S (2005) *The Fake Factor*, Cyan, London

McGarty, Craig (1999) *Categorization in Social Psychology*, Sage, Thousand Oaks, IL

McKenna, R (1991) *Relationship Marketing*, Addison-Wesley, Reading, MA

McKinsey Corp (1990) *The Luxury Industry*, McKinsey, Paris

McWilliam, G (1989) Managing the brand manager, in *Brand Valuation*, ed J Murphy, Hutchinson Business Books, London, pp 154–65

Meffert, H and Bruhn, M (1984) *Marken Strategien in Wettbewerb Gabler*, Wiesbaden

Melin, B (1990) Comment evaluer les marques, Research paper, under the direction of J-N Kapferer, HEC, June, Jouy-en-Josas

Meyers-Levy, J (1989) Investigating dimensions of brand names that influence the perceived familiarity of brands, *Advances in Consumer Research*, **16**, pp 258–63

Michel, G (2000) *La Stratégie d'Extension de Marque (Brand extension strategy)*, Vuibert, Paris

Micheli, J A (2006) *The Starbucks Experience*, McGraw Hill, New York

Milligan, A (2004) *Brand it Like Beckham*, Cyan, London

Miniard, Sirdeshmukh and Innis (1992) Peripheral persuasion and brand choice, *Journal of Consumer Research*, **19**, Sep, pp 226–39

Moingeon, B and Soenen, G (2003) *Corporate and organizational identities*, Routledge, London

Moliner, P (1989) Validation experimentale de l'hypothèse du noyau central des représentations sociales, *Bulletin de Psychologie*, **42**, pp 749–62

Mongibeaux, J F (1990) Contrefaçons et contremarques, *Revue de l'ENA*, Sep–Oct

Monroe, Kent B (1973) Buyers' Subjective Perceptions of Price, *Journal of Marketing Research*, **10** (February), pp 70–80

Moore, E, Wilkie, W and Lutz, R (2002) Passing the torch: intergenerational influences as sources of brand equity, *Journal of Marketing*, **66** (2), Apr, pp 17–37

Moore, J (2006) *Tribal Knowledge*, Kaplan, Chicago, IL

Moorhouse, M (1989) Brand accounting, in *Brand Valuation*, ed J Murphy, Hutchinson Business Books, London, pp 143–53

Moss, G D (2007) *Pharmaceuticals: Where's the brand logic?*, Haworth, New York

Muller, M and Mainz, A (1989) Brands, bids and balance sheets: putting a price on protected products, *Acquisitions Monthly*, Apr, **24**, pp 26–27

Muniz, A and O'Guinn, T (2001) Brand community, *Journal of Consumer Research*, **27** (4), March, pp 412–32

Murphy, J (1989) *Brand Valuation*, Hutchinson Business Books, London

Murphy, J (1990) *Brand Strategy*, Director Books, London

Myung Soo Jo (2007) Should a quality sub-brand be located before or after the parent brand? An application of composite concept theory, *Journal of the Academy of Marketing Science* Volume 35, Number 2, pp 184–96

Nedungadi, P and Hutchinson, J W (1985) The prototypicality of brands, in *Advances in Consumer Research*, 12, ed E Hirschmann and M Holbrook, Association for Consumer Research, pp 498–503

Nelson, P (1970) Information and consumer behavior, *Journal of Political Economy*, **78** (2), pp 311–329

Neuhaus, C F and Taylor, J R (1972) Variables affecting sales of family-branded products, *Journal of Marketing Research*, **14**, Nov, pp 419–22

Neyrinck, J (2000) *Les paradoxes du marketing*, Editions d'Organisation, Paris

Nidumolu, R, Prahalad, C K and Rangaswami, M R (2009) Why Sustainability Is Now the Key Driver of Innovation, *Harvard Business Review*, September

Nielsen, (1992) *Category Management*, NTC Business Books

Nohria, N and Hansen, M (2003) Organising multinational companies, Harvard Business School Globalization Conference Proceedings

Norman, D A (2004) *Emotional Design*, Basic Books, London

Nussenbaum, M (1990) Comment évaluer les marques, *Option Finance*, 7 May, **113**, pp 20–2

Nussenbaum, M (2003) Juste valeur et actifs incorporels, *Revue d'Economie Financière*, **71**, pp 71–86

Nussenbaum, M (2010) Financial methods for evaluating of an image prejudice. Sorgem Reports, Paris

Nussenbaum, M and Jacquot, G (2003), « La marque, actif à géométrie variable », *Prodimarques, la revue des marques*, n°41, January, pp 20–23.

Nussenbaum, M and Jacquot, G (2011) « Unintended impact of the new IFRS norms on brand valuation », Paris Dauphine University Research reports, Finance Department

Olins, W (1978) *The Corporate Personality*, Mayflower, New York

Olins, W (1989) *Corporate Identity*, Thames and Hudson, London

Oliver, T (1987) The wide world of branding, in *Branding: A key marketing tool*, ed J Murphy, McGraw-Hill, London

Parameswaran, M G (2001) *Brand Building Advertising*, Tata McGraw-Hill, New Delhi

Pariente, S (1989) *La concurrence dans les relations industrie–commerce*, Institut du commerce et de la consommation, Paris

Park, C W, Javorskey, B J and MacInnis, D J (1986) Strategic brand concept–image management, *Journal of Marketing*, **50** (Oct) pp 135–45

Park, C W, Milberg, S and Lawson, R (1991) Evaluation of brand extensions, *Journal of Consumer Research*, **18**, Sep, pp 185–93

Pastoureau, M (1992) *Dictionnaire des couleurs de notre temps*, Editions Bonneton

Pauwels, K and Srinivasan, S (2002) Who benefits from store brand entry, Working Paper, UCLA

Pearson, S (1996) *Building Brands Directly*, Macmillan, Basingstoke

Peckham, J O (1981) *The Wheel of Marketing*, Nielsen, Chicago, IL

Pendergrast, M (1993) *For God, Country and Coca-Cola*, Maxwell MacMillan, New York

Penrose, N (1989) Valuation of brand names and trade marks, in *Brand Valuation*, ed J Murphy, Hutchinson Business Books, London, pp 32–45

Peppers, D and Rogers, M (1993) *The One to One Future*, Piatkus, London

Perrier, R (1989) Valuation and licensing, in *Brand Valuation*, ed J Murphy, Hutchinson Business Books, London, pp 104–12

Pettis, C (1995) *Technobrands*, Amacom, New York

Porter, M (1980) Choix stratégiques et concurrence, *Economica*, Paris

Pourquery, D (1987) Mais ou est donc passé Béatrice Foods? *Le monde affaires*, 7 November, pp 10–12

Prahalad, C K (2004) *Fortune at the Bottom of the Pyramid*, Wharton School Publishing

Publicis (1988) Advertising in Europe, *Publicis*, September, 1

Quelch, J and Harding, D (1996) Brands versus private labels, fighting to win, *Harvard Business Review*, Jan–Feb, **74** (1), pp 99–111

Quelch, J and Hoff, E (1986) Customizing global marketing, *Harvard Business Review*, May/Jun

Quelch, J and Kenny, D (1994) Extend profits, not product lines, *Harvard Business Review*, Sep–Oct, **72** (4), pp 153–64

Ramsay, W (1992) The decline and fall of manufacturer branding, *Esomar Conference Proceedings – The Challenge of Branding*, 28–30 October, pp 233–52

Rangaswamy, A, Burke, R and Oliva, T (1993) Brand equity and the extendibility of brand names, *International Journal of Research in Marketing*, **10** (1), pp 61–75

Rao, V R, Agarwal, M K, Dalhoff, D (2004) How Is Manifest Branding Strategy Related to the Intangible Value of a Corporation?, *Journal of Marketing*, 68, 4, pp 126–41

Rao, V R, Mahajan, V and Varaiya, N (1990) A balance model for evaluating firms for acquisition, Working Paper, Graduate School of Management, Cornell University, NY, Jan

Rapp, S and Collins, L (1994) *Beyond Maxi-Marketing*, McGraw-Hill

Rastoin, N (1981) Sortez vos griffes, *Coopération – distribution – consommation*, **5**, pp 26–35

Reddy, S, Holak, S and Bhat, S (1994) To extend or not to extend, *Journal of Marketing Research*, **31**, May, pp 243–62

Rege, P (1959) *A vos marques*, Favre, Lausanne

Regouby, C (1988) *La Communication globale*, Les Editions d'Organisation, Paris

Reichheld, F (1996) *The Loyalty Effect*, Harvard Business School Press, Boston, MA

Reichheld, F (2006) *The Ultimate Question*, Harvard Business School Press, Cambridge, MA

Resnik, A, Turney, P and Mason, J (1979) Marketers turn to counter segmentation, *Harvard Business Review*, **57** (3), pp 115–29

Revue Française de Comptabilité (1989) Le débat sur les marques en Grande-Bretagne, *Revue Française de Comptabilité*, Oct, **205**, p 19

Revue Française de Comptabilité (1990) Incorporels identifiables: le projet australien, *Revue Française de Comptabilité*, Jan, **208**, p 11

Ridderstrale, J and Nordstrom, K (2000) *Funky Business*, FT Publishing, London

Ries, A (2000) *Advertising is Dead*, McGraw-Hill

Ries, A and Ries, L (2004) *The Origin of Brands*, Harper Business, New York

Ries, A and Trout, J (1987) *Positioning*, McGraw-Hill, Paris

Ries, A and Trout, J (1990) *Bottom Up Marketing*, PLUME books

Riezebos, H (1994) *Brand-Added Value*, Eburon, Delft, Netherlands

Riezebos, H and Snellen, M (1993) *Brand Names Changes*, Erasmus, Management Report Series, no 149

Riezebos, R (2003) *Brand Management*, Prentice Hall, New York

Rijkenberg, J (2001) *Concepting*, Warc, New York

RISC (1991) *Brand Value and Management in the Luxury Industry*, Sep, International Research Institute on Social Charge, Paris

Roberts, K (2005) *Lovemarks*, Power House Books, London

Roeder-John, D, Loken, B and Joiner, C (1995) The negative impact of brand extensions: can you dilute flagship products, Research paper, University of Minnesota

Romaniuk, J and Ehrenberg, A (2003) Do brands lack personality?, Marketing Science Centre Research Report no 14, May, University of South Australia

Rosch, E (1978) Principles of categorization, in *Cognition and Categorization*, ed E Rosch and B Lloyd, Lawrence Erlbaum, Hillsdale, NJ, pp 27–48

Rosch, E and Lloyd, B (1978) *Cognition and Categorization*, Lawrence Erlbaum, Hillsdale, NJ

Rubinson, J (1992) Marketers need new research tools to manage the complex brand portfolios of the 90s, *Marketing Research*, **5** (3), pp 7–11

Russell, A (2002) Investigating the effectiveness of product placements in television shows: the role of modality and plot connection congruence on brand memory and attitude, *Journal of Consumer Research*, Dec, pp 306–18

Rutteman, P (1989) Mergers, acquisitions, brand and goodwill, *Accountancy*, September, p 27

Rutteman, P (1990) Boosting the profits of the brands industry, *Accountancy*, January, pp 26–27

Samways, A and Whittome, K (1994) UK brand strategies: facing the competitive challenge, a Financial Times Management Report, Financial Times, London

Santi, M (1996) The determinants of profitability among suppliers of distributors' own brands, unpublished working paper, HEC Graduate School of Management

Sapolsky, H M (1986) *Consuming Fears: The politics of product risks*, Basic Books, New York

Saporito, B (1986) Has been brands go back to work, *Fortune*, 28 Apr, pp 123–24

Sappington, D and Wernerfelt, B (1985) To brand or not to brand? *Journal of Business*, **58**, Jul, pp 279–93

Sattler, H (1994) *Der Wert von Marken*, Research Paper no 341, Institut für Betriebswirtschaftslehre, Kiel University

Saunders, J and Guoqun, F (1996) Dual branding: how corporate names add value, *Marketing Intelligence and Planning*, **14** (7), pp 29–34

Saunders, J and Watters, R (1993) Branding financial services, *International Journal of Bank Marketing*, **11** (6), pp 32–38

Schechter, A (1993) Names changes increase, *Marketing News*, American Marketing Association, 1 March, p 1

Schlossberg, H (1990) Brand value can be worth more than physical assets, *Marketing News*, 5 Mar, p 6

Schmitt, B (1999) *Experiential Marketing*, Free Press, New York

Schmitt, B (2003) *Customer Experience Management*, Wiley, New York

Schmitt, B and Zhang, S (2001) Creating local brands in multi lingual international markets, *The Journal of Marketing Research*, **38** (3)

Schnaars, D (1995) *Imitation Strategies*, Free Press, New York

Schroeder, J E and Salzer-Mörling, M (2006) *Brand Culture*, Routledge, London

Schroiff, H-W and Arnold, D (2003) Managing the brand–product continuum in global markets, Globalization of Markets Colloquium, Harvard Business School, May

Schuiling, I and Kapferer, J-N (2004) How global brands really differ from local brands, paper under review, Université Catholique de Louvain, Belgium and HEC Paris, France

Schuiling, I and Kapferer, J N(2004) 'Real differences between local and international brands', *Journal of International Marketing*, vol 12, no 4, pp 97–123

Schultz, M, Antorini, Y M and Csaba, F F (2005) *Corporate Branding*, Copenhagen Business School Press

Schwebig, P (1985) *L'identité de l'entreprise*, McGraw Hill, Paris

Schwebig, P (1988) *Les communications de l'entreprise*, McGraw-Hill, Paris

Scoble, R and Israel, S (2006) *Naked Conversations*, Wiley, New York

Seguela, J (1982) *Hollywood Lave Plus Blanc*, Flammarion, Paris

Selame, E and Selame, J (1988) *The Company Image*, Wiley, New York

Selden, L and Colvin, G (2003) *Angel Customers and Demon Customers*, Portfolio, London and New York

Sicard, M C (2003) *Luxe, mensonge et marketing*, Village Mondial, Paris

Silverstein, M and Fiske, N (2003) *Trading Up*, Portfolio Penguin

Silverstein, R (2006) *Trading Up*, Portfolio, London and New York

Simmons, J (2008) Innocent: Building a brand from nothing but the fruit, Cyan Communications, London

Simon, C J and Sullivan, M W (1989) The measurement and determinants of brand equity: a financial approach, Working Paper, Oct, University of Chicago, IL

Simon, H (2000) *Hidden Champions*, Harvard Business School Press, Cambridge, MA

Simon, H, Bilstein, F and Luby, F (2006) *Manage for Profit not for Market Share*, Harvard Business School Press, Cambridge, MA

Smith, D and Park, C W (1992) The effects of brand extensions on market share and advertising efficiency, *Journal of Marketing Research*, **29**, Aug, pp 296–313

Steenkamp, J B, Batra, R and Alden, D (2002) How perceived globalness creates brand value, *Journal of International Business Studies*, **33**, pp 35–47

Stobart, P (1989) Brand valuation: a true and fair view, *Accountancy*, Oct, p 27

Stobart, P (1994) *Brand Power*, Macmillan, Basingstoke

Sudovar, B (1987) Branding in the pharmaceutical industry, in *Branding: A key marketing tool*, ed J Murphy, McGraw-Hill, London

Sullivan, M (1988) Measuring image spillovers in umbrella branded products, Working Paper, Graduate School of Business, University of Chicago, IL

Sullivan, M (1991) Brand extension and order of entry, Marketing Science Institute, Report no 91–105, Cambridge, MA

Sullivan, M (1992) Brand extensions: when to use them, *Management Science*, **38**, Jun, pp 793–806

Swaminathan, V, Fox, R and Reddy, S (2001) The impact of brand extension introduction on choice, *Journal of Marketing*, **65** (4), pp 1–15

Swiners, J L (1979) Bilan critique du rôle de la copy–stratégie dans la pratique publicitaire actuelle, *IREP*, Jun, 19

SymphonyIRI, (2011) « What future for Brands », ILEC Conference, Paris

Szymanowski, M and Gijsbrechts, E (2010) Copycat Private Labels: Friend or Foe? Quality Belief Spillovers and Choice Share Effects for Imitating Retailer and Imitated National Brands. *Under review*

Szymanowski, M and Gijsbrechts, E (2012) Consumption Based Cross-Brand Learning: Are Private Labels Really Private? *Journal of Marketing Research*. Forthcoming

Tafani, É, Michel, G and Rosa, E (2009) Vertical product line extension strategies: an evaluation of brand halo effect according to range level, *Recherche et Applications en Marketing*, **24** (2), pp 73–90

Tauber, E (1988) Brand leverage: strategy for growth in a cost-control world, *Journal of Advertising Research*, Aug–Sep, **28** (4), pp 26–30

Taylor, R (1987) The branding of services, *in Branding: A key marketing tool*, ed J Murphy, McGraw-Hill, London

Tchakhotine, S (1952) *La Propagande Politique*, Gallimard, Paris

Terrasse, C and Kapferer, J-N (2006) L'engagement: une facette clé de la valeur de la marque. Doctoral thesis, HEC

Thil, E and Baroux, C (1983) *Un Pave dans la Marque*, Flammarion, Paris

Thiolon, B (1990) La marque et la banque, *Humanisme et Entreprise*, **181**, June, pp 29–32

Thoenig, J C (1990) *Les performances économiques de l'industrie de produits de marque et de la distribution*, ILEC, Paris

Thoenig, J-C and Waldman, C (2005) *De l'Entreprise marchande à l'Entreprise Marquante (From market enterprise to brand enterprise)*, Editions d'Organisation, Paris

Thomassen, L, Lincoln, K and Aconis, A (2006) *Retailization*, Kogan Page, London

Touche Ross Europe (1989) *Accounting for Europe Success by A D 2000*, Internal Report, Touche Ross Europe, London

Trout, J and Ries, A (1981) *Positioning: The battle for your mind*, McGraw Hill

Trout, J and Rivkin, S (2000) *Differentiate or die*, Wiley

Turngate, M (2005) *Fashion Brands*, Kogan Page, London

Tuvee, L (1987) L'histoire du marketing global: bibliographic commentée, *Revue Française du Marketing*, **114** (4), pp 19–48

Twitchell, J B (2006) *Branded Nation*, Simon Schuster, New York

University of Minnesota Consumer Behavior Seminar (1987) Affect generalization to similar and dissimilar brand extensions, *Psychology and Marketing*, **4** (Fall), pp 225–37

Upshaw, L (1995) *Building Brand Identity*, Wiley, New York

Valette Florence, P (2004) La personnalite de la marque, *Recherches et Applications en Marketing*

Van der Vorst, R (2004) *Branding: A systems theoretic perspective*, Nijmegen University, Netherlands

Van Gelder, S (2003) *Global Brand Strategy*, Kogan Page, London

Van Riel, C (2001) Corporate branding management, *Thexis*, **4**, pp 5–12

Van Riel, C B M and Fombrun, C (2007) *Essentials of Corporate Communications*, Routledge, London

Veblen, T (1889) *The Theory of The Leisure Class*, Macmillan, New York

Verlegh, P and Steenkamp, JB (1999) A review and meta-analysis of country-of-origin research, *Journal of Economic Psychology*, **20**, pp 521–46

Viale, F (1994) Faut-il inscrire les marques an bilan? *Les Echos*, 11 Nov

Viale, F and Lafay, F (1990) Les marques: un nouvel enjeu pour les entreprises, *Revue Francaise de Comptabilité*, **216**, Oct, pp 92–99

Ville, G (1986) Maîtriser et optimiser 1'avenir d'une marque, *Esomar Congress Proceedings*, pp 527–41

Villemus, P (1996) *La Déroute des Marques*, Editions d'Organisation, Paris

Vincent, L (2002) *Legendary Brands*, Dearborn, Chicago, IL

Wansink, B and Ray, M (1996) Advertising strategies to increase usage frequency, *Journal of Marketing*, **60** (1), Jan, pp 31–47

Ward, K (1989) Can the cash flows of brands really be capitalized? in *Brand Valuation*, ed J Murphy, Hutchinson Business Books, London, pp 70–80

Warin, G and Tubiana, A (2003) *Marques sous licence*, Editions d'Organisation, Paris

Wathieu, L, Zaltman, G and Liu, Y (2003) Rooting marketing strategy in human universals, Globalization of Markets Colloquium, Harvard Business School

Watkins, T (1986) *The Economics of the Brands: A marketing analysis*, McGraw-Hill

Wentz, L (1989) How experts value brands, *Advertising Age*, 16 Jan, p 24

Wernerfelt, B (1988) Umbrella branding as a signal of new product quality, *Rand Journal of Economics*, **19** (Autumn), pp 458–66

Wernerfelt, B (1990) Advertising content when brand choice is a signal, *Journal of Business*, **63** (1), pp 91–98

Winram, S (1987) The opportunity for world brands, in *Branding: A key marketing tool*, ed J Murphy, McGraw-Hill, London

Wu, Y (2010) What's in a name? What leads a firm to change its name and what the new name foreshadows, *Journal of Banking & Finance* **34**, 1344–59

Yentis, A and Bond, J (1995) Andres comes out of the closet, *Marketing and Research Today*, **23** (2), May, pp 104–12

Yoshimori, M (1989) Concepts et stratégies de marque au Japon, in *La marque*, ed J-N Kapferer and J C Thoenig, McGraw-Hill, Paris

Young, R (1967) Multibrand entries, in *Plotting Marketing Strategy*, ed L Adler, Interpublic Press Books, New York

Young & Rubicam (1994) *Brand Asset Valuator*, Young & Rubicam, London

Yovovich, B G (1988) What is your brand really worth? *Adweek's Marketing Week*, 8 August, pp 18–24

Yovovich, B G (1995) *New Marketing Imperatives*, Prentice Hall, Englewood Cliffs, NJ

Zaichkowsky, J and Simpson, R (1996) The effect of experience with a brand imitator on the original brand, *Marketing Letters*, **7** (1), pp 31–39

Zaichkowsky, J L (1995) *Defending Your Brand Against Imitation: Consumer behavior, marketing strategies, and legal issues*, Quorum Books

Zaichkowsky, J L (2006) *The Psychology Behind Trademark Infringement and Counterfeiting*, LEA ed, June

Zareer, P (1987) De la valeur des marques de commerce, *CA Magazine*, Feb, p 72

Zhang, S and Schmitt, B (2001) Creating local brands in a multilingual international market, *Journal of Marketing Research*, **38**, Aug, pp 313–25

Zyman, S (1999) *The End of Marketing as We Know It*, Harper Business, New York

INDEX

NB: page numbers in *italic* indicate figures or tables

CPSIA information can be obtained at www.ICGtesting.com
Printed in the USA
BVOW09s1652060116

431988BV00011B/65/P